39 Forever

Second Edition

Volume 1: Radio, May 1932 – May 1942

By

Laura Leff

President, International Jack Benny Fan Club

© Copyright 2004, Laura Leff

ISBN 0-9651893-2-5

BookSurge, LLC • City & State: North Charleston, SC
Library of Congress Control Number: 2004107398

CONTENTS

CAN YOU TELL ME...?

A big part of being the President of the International Jack Benny Fan Club is answering questions about Jack and his work. These start with basic facts, like "When was Jack Benny born?" or "How long did Jack Benny's radio show last?" Then they either go into more subjective areas (e.g., "Did Jack Benny really play the violin badly?") or more minute detail on the facts (e.g., "Can you tell me the date of every show where they did the Si-Sy routine?"). Sometimes I'll get an E-mail that seems to be a random Benny pop quiz from an often-unidentified source, a list of disconnected questions on Jack's life and work. Hope I got an "A".

The majority of Jack's fans today focus on his radio programs. They are the most easily accessible of his work, and can be taken along on walks or in the car for enjoyment anywhere. I am still awaiting the day when I see someone shouldering a boom box blasting a Benny show. Listening to these shows leads to many different questions, such as confirming the date of a recording, tracking down running gags, trying to find the date of a show heard years ago, and examining the birth and growth of the characters and comedy bits that have become so familiar to millions of Benny fans all over the world.

Very few of the shows before 1934 are circulating in audio, and almost the entire year of 1935 is considered lost (save two shows). This makes it difficult to fully understand the genesis and development of the show in its earliest years, and understanding what brought it from a fledgling to a consistent top 5 rating.

39 FOREVER – SECOND EDITION

39 Forever was originally published in 1989 as "the ultimate log of Jack Benny radio and television shows, appearances and specials, plus movies, books, magazine articles, and discography". Radio and television shows had one-line descriptions and a guest index, and shows that were not in circulation were often not included. This volume is the first in a series that will comprise the Second Edition of 39 Forever, and provide the most comprehensive study, to date, of Jack Benny's work.

There are two basic goals for this volume:
- Provide complete information for each weekly (or semi-weekly) Jack Benny radio program between May 1932 and May 1942, along with indexes and cross-references to enable readers to locate shows based on actor names, skit titles, song titles, etc.
- Provide a document where readers can better understand the evolution and development of the Jack Benny radio programs, through detailed plot summaries, notable trivia, and cast lists

For example, how did Love in Bloom come to be Jack Benny's theme song? This occurred during the lost year of 1935, so special attention has been paid to tracking its recurrence in these shows. How did Phil Harris' character develop? In looking at shows from 1936 through 1939, you can see the progressive introduction of character traits: his woman-chasing, lack of education, drinking (initially through the Frank Carson character in the Buck Benny series), calling Jack "Jackson" (and why), and his catch phrase of "That's a lu-luuuu!". These things didn't happen overnight; they happened over years of experimentation and character development.

The end of the 1941-42 season was chosen as a volume break point because it was the end of the Jell-O series; and the 1932-42 time period includes 451 shows, roughly half of

Jack's complete body of regular radio programs. Volume 2 is planned to include 1942-1955.

This expansion of 39 Forever is a tremendous labor of love, requiring hundreds (and eventually thousands) of hours of tracking shows in detail, cross-referencing, fact-checking, script reading, and typing. My first thanks must go to my husband, Dan, for understanding when I spend hours in front of the computer working on shows, and being patient with my excitement over discovering some hidden nuance, like finding the character of Schlepper(man) showing up months before Sam Hearn joined the show. Also his withstanding having an occasional corny Harry Conn pun thrown at him, only retorting with an eye roll and displayed tongue. Dan lets me work, but he also lets me know when to stop, which is just as important.

Many thanks to Joan Benny, all her family, and the Benny estate for their continued support of the work of the International Jack Benny Fan Club. Thanks to the many helpful folks in UCLA Special Collections, who tolerated my occasional outbursts of laughter in their reading room as I perused the Benny scripts. Also thanks to the members of the IJBFC, for your many expressions of enthusiasm and support through the years. It is a pleasure and privilege to work with all of you.

GENERAL NOTES

- In 1932, the similarities between the character of George Olsen and that of the ultimate Jack Benny character are truly striking. Jack constantly jokes about Olsen's cheapness, Olsen drives a very old car (a Saxon), he gives a party at the Automat, etc. With the departure of Olsen, such gags started being written about Jack's character. Additionally, Ethel Shutta serves in a role that is roughly equivalent to Mary Livingstone's role through the 1930s, sans flirtation with Jack or other men (as she was married to Olsen).
- In the early and mid 1930s, the re-use of skits and gags is very high. For weeks on Canada Dry, Jack would announce some new contest, where listeners had to do silly things for ridiculous prizes. Script outlines (and often many specific gags) were also reused between series; such as "Ladies' Night" appearing on 6/1/32 and 3/24/33, and "Babies' Night" appearing on 6/29/32 and 4/14/33. Frequently reused skits included (under various names): Grind Hotel, Why Gals Leave Home (leaving for a sponsor's product, or leaving to make money and returning home at the last moment to pay the mortgage), School Days (schoolroom scenes), Grocery Store (or Drug Store, etc.), and The Hills of Old Kentucky (feud between two families). Some of these skits even had lives well beyond their original broadcast, such as the Jekyll and Hyde skit which was originally broadcast on April 7, 1933 (after the 1931 Fredric March movie version of the story) and redone on November 30, 1941 (around the release of the Spencer Tracy movie version).
- Some Jell-O scripts have different commercials for the East Coast vs. West Coast. For example, Jell-O might be promoted on one coast, and Jello Ice Cream Powder on the other. Or the commercials would be worded differently, including notations like "And remember, Jell-O is made right here in California." Don's line would also frequently include a place for a pause, where the local station could break away and do a separate Jell-O promotion. This distinctive pause can often be heard on the closing commercials of the mid- and late-30s, and a number of the circulating copies of the 1941-42 shows have inset commercials from KFI.

- The script is given ultimate authority on spelling and punctuation. Therefore, items like "What of it." (with a period, not a question mark) or "Travelling Thru China" ("thru" vs. "through") are included verbatim based on the script.

SHOW INFORMATION KEY

Date: Date of the show's broadcast. The format is Month/Day/Year (MM/DD/YYYY).

Sponsor: Show sponsor

City: City where the broadcast performance took place. A city in parentheses indicates that the exact city of origin is not known, but the city given is a safe guess based on surrounding evidence.

Recording source:
- **None:** There is no known recording of the given show
- **Unknown:** It is not possible, based on current information, to determine the exact source of a show's recording
- **Station call letters (e.g., WJZ, KFI):** When known, the station call letter ID from which the recording was taken is indicated. This is usually determined from the recording itself, based on the ID at the top or bottom of the hour. However, this may also be determined by other evidence such as a local announcements or consistency of a non-network announcer with other recordings with known IDs.
- **East Coast, West Coast:** If a show can be pinpointed as an East or West Coast broadcast, this is indicated. This is sometimes done by side comments in the show, such as "We'll get a better gag tonight" indicating that a gag hadn't gone as well as expected and would be punched up for the later West Coast show. Likewise, gags on the recording but crossed out in the script can indicate that the recording originates from the East Coast performance. A small number of shows from military bases were transcribed for rebroadcast, resulting in only an East Coast performance.
- **Both:** Both East and West Coast versions are in circulation. (Woo hoo!)

Problems: Issues with circulating recording of the show. These include:
- **Poor sound:** Audio is scratchy, distorted, or otherwise deteriorated through a majority of the show. Shows with rough patches for a few minutes but otherwise acceptable are not given this notation. Keeping in mind that these shows go back to the early 1930s, we are fortunate that very few shows are unlistenable.
- **Partial show:** A significant portion of the show is missing from the recording in circulation. This does not include openings or closings that are clipped, but shows where approximately 5 minutes or more are missing. The notes may include additional detail under "Recording".
- **Wrong speed:** The recording in circulation is at the wrong speed, either too fast or two slow. This is determined by ear and the overall time duration of the show recording.

- **Music clipped:** The musical numbers in the show are omitted from the recording. In the early-mid 30s, show transcribers sometimes omitted musical numbers in order to save a disc. Sadly, this has resulted in very few surviving songs by the popular tenor Frank Parker, as well as the omission of the first surviving performance by the Chicken Sisters. A few 1940s shows also did this, possibly for the same reason during wartime.
- **Ads clipped:** The commercials have been omitted in the circulating recording. This does not include instances where a local ad was inset over the network ad, as in some of the 1940s recordings. There are two recordings from 1936 that feature an ad for New York and New England listeners only, announcing the release of Jell-O Ice Cream Mix (which later morphed into the national Jell-O Freezing Mix). The problem of ads being clipped is more of a factor for Armed Forces Radio Service broadcasts (who were required to edit ads), of which there are none in the shows covered by this volume.
- **Other:** There is some other issue with the recording, which is detailed in the Notes section under "Recording".

First line: The text of the first comedy line of a program. This is included to facilitate quick dating of shows, as an improvement over analyzing dialogue to see if it matches a plot summary. The Jell-O shows usually started with a song announcement, performance/commercial, and song back announcement, so the first comedic line is usually after those announcements. Lines without speaker credit are done by Don Wilson; any other speaker is indicated by name. If the line is interrupted by another character (e.g., Jack saying "Yes, sir!"), then only the portion before the interruption is included, unless the excerpt is so brief that it cannot be distinguished from other shows. A few particularly long introductions have been included only in part, such as Jack's opening monologues from the early 1930s shows.

Summary: Plot summary of the show. This is written to give a feel of the flow of the show and indicate major sections or routines. Gags are occasionally included, but this section is not intended to be an exhaustive listing of gags (or this book would be twice the size and never finished). Items that are connected or flow directly between the gags are separated by a comma, and general portions are separated by "…" (with a nod of format credit to Herb Caen).

Common script devices is often represented by a brief summary only. For example, there are many shows featuring a schoolroom scene where Jack plays the teacher. The structure of all these skits is almost identical: students come in, the teacher calls roll (e.g., "Jean Harlow!" "She's not here." "Darn it, I wanted to keep her after school."), the teacher has the students do morning exercises, the teacher quizzes the class ("Where did the Boston Tea Party take place?" "I don't know, I drink coffee."), and something happens to end the skit. The majority of the skit is a series of interchangeable call-and-response gags with no consistent plot line connecting them. The same goes for grocery store scenes, hotel front desk scenes, and others. So the skit notation may be simply "teacher calls roll…teacher quizzes the class". For more information on these skits, I recommend that you listen to one of the existing shows that has such a skit. They're all the same, only the individual gags are different.

For shows which have no known script or recording, the summary is taken directly from the script index.

Cast:

Cast members in alphabetical order by last name, the roles played by them, and whether they appeared as a guest star.

The scripts usually indicate actor first or last names before lines, and occasionally list both on the first line of a supporting actor. When a first or last name is known but not its counterpart, a "?" is put in the unknown part (e.g., "George ?"). When there is evidence to suggest that a role may be played by a person but there is no conclusive proof, the portion in question is indicated with a "?" (e.g., "Dave W. Fess?" = Dave known, last name believed to be Fess; "A. Purvis? Pullen" = Pullen known, believed to be A. Purvis). If the part is listed only by the character name (e.g., "Boy", "Leonard"), no actor name is given.

A note of thanks to both Jack Benny and Harry Baldwin, as they had an occasional penchant for writing the full names of non-regular cast members on the cover of the script. Without those accompanying notes, many of these people would have remained unidentified.

Part names that are only minor variants of a person's real name (e.g., Don Wilson playing Deputy Wilson) are periodically omitted, as the actor-character connection is obvious.

Some additional comments on Mary Livingstone: in her initial performances, Mary's lines are prompted as "Sadye". Therefore, she is listed as Sadye Benny (since Jack was using that name publicly and privately) playing Mary Livingston. Eventually there is a "crossover " script, prompting her lines as "Sadye" in one part and "Mary" in another part. After that time, her lines are consistently prompted as "Mary", and Sadye is left to history (except for one passing mention as someone's girlfriend's name).

This also brings up the great long-standing debate over whether her name was "Mary Livingston" or "Mary Livingstone". Initially, the name had no ending "e". Later the scripts go back and forth between "Livingston" and "Livingstone", seemingly at the whim of the script typist. These variations are indicated in the cast list. By the time Mary is given opening introduction credit, the name had been standardized to "Livingstone". However, I have a 1941 rehearsal script where it is spelled "Livingston" (broadcast script spells it "Livingstone"), so it is truly a long-standing issue.

The part of Shlepperman played by Sam Hearn has the same challenge, with the spelling varying in the scripts between "Schlepperman" and "Shlepperman" for the duration of the shows in this volume. This variation is also indicated in the cast listing.

The research is occasionally at the mercy of typographical errors of the script typist. For example, Hilliard Marks (Mary's real-life brother) played a few minor roles on some shows in California. During the same period, there is a minor character prompted as "Hillard" in one script. Is it the same person? Mmm…could be. Being that there was no other actor on the show that had the name Hillard (unless he was in an otherwise uncredited role), it's a relatively safe bet that it was Hilliard Marks.

Guest stars are non-recurring performers who appeared as themselves. Therefore, Burns and Allen or Orson Welles would be considered guest stars. Andy Devine plays himself, but he's on often enough to be considered part of the main cast. Kenny Baker is listed as a guest star when he appears on the program after leaving the regular cast. Jesse Block and Eve Sully appeared on the 4/25/1937 show playing Sam Clunk and Thelma Snodgrass. While they were known performers from vaudeville, they are listed as supporting players because they were not performing as themselves. On their performance of 3/22/1936 as themselves, they are listed as guest stars.

In very early 1930s shows, the announcer is frequently not referred to by name or has lines prompted as simply "Announcer". This role is sometimes listed as "Announcer" rather than by the person's name.

For shows that have no known script or recording, only minimum cast regulars are listed.

Songs: The order of songs is the order of their performance on the show.

Title is the title of the song. In the case of medleys where the individual songs are identified, they are separated by a hyphen ("-"). On some occasions, the songs on the circulating recording and the songs listed in the script differ; sometimes because songs were flipped in performance order, or others where a completely different song is indicated. In these cases, the song or songs on the broadcast recording are indicated first and the song from the script is indicated second, separated by a slash ("/"). Sometimes the script is inconsistent about the title of a song between broadcasts (e.g., "That's How We Make Music" vs. "How We All Make Music"). I have attempted to make these titles consistent in the index, based on the most frequent spelling. When a title in a script varies from the title I have normally heard for a song, the script is given priority (except for 3/16/1941 where I have listed "In Dublin's Fair City" as a.k.a. "Cockles and Mussels"). If a song is neither identified on the show nor in the script, it is listed as "Unidentified".

Only major songs performed are listed. Music used as incidental or bridge music (e.g., "I'm an Old Cowhand" as the lead-in to Buck Benny skits) or brief music (e.g., Jack playing four bars of "Love in Bloom") is not included in this section.

For a period in the 1940s, the opening song titles are (or strongly seem to be) fictitious; e.g., "The Phil Harris Concerto #6 for Oboe and Drum", "Brown Eyes Why Are You So Close to My Nose", "Encino Madness". Titles suspected to be fictitious are indicated with an asterisk ("*"). In the scripts, these are sometimes prompted as "Phil Harris Tune #2" or "Harris Spec. #3". It is my belief that toward the end of 1940, Phil Harris and/or Mahlon Merrick wrote a folio of six untitled tunes that could be used for opening or closing numbers, since so little of the actual tunes are heard outside of the commercial voice-over. This would enable the band to reduce the number of new songs to be learned each week, and lower the royalties to be paid as well. After the start of the War, these songs are heard no more for the duration of shows in this volume, except for the opening song of 3/29/1942.

Performers are the artists that performed the given number. Songs with multiple performers are listed multiple times with each performer on a separate line, except for occasions where there is an unnamed chorus or a group such as the Sportsmen Quartet.

Vocal indicates whether the listed performer contributes a vocal accompaniment to the number. A song may have multiple performers, but not necessarily at the same time. For example, Phil Harris may sing a chorus, then Mary and Andy Devine duet on the second chorus, then Jack and Don sing a final chorus (probably with modified lyrics to promote Jell-O). Also, Phil and Mary performed a vocal duet on "How About You", but Jack provides a non-vocal violin accompaniment on the second chorus. And darn it, that's one of those few 1940s shows where the songs are partially edited. Ah well, what can you do...

Notes: The notes include various information on the show not covered in other sections.

Blooper: A misread line, a verbal stumble, a missed cue, or other error in conveying the content of the script. Not every slip is documented, but attention is paid to slips that get audience reaction or a comment from Jack. Attention is also paid to interesting or unusual slips, such as Don calling the product "Jell-O Freezing Milk" instead of "Jell-O Freezing Mix".

I find it particularly amazing that in spot-checking a few bloopers with the scripts, some of them were not bloopers but fully intentional and scripted slips. One time Jack says, "You haven't an ounce of sediment...er...sentiment." To my ears, it sounded like a real blooper. But in looking at the script, Jack had written "sediment" in pencil just above the line. It may have been a conscious edit for script improvement. Perhaps it was fluffed in rehearsal, and they decided to keep it in. It may have been fluffed in the East Coast show, and kept for the West Coast. It is impossible to know now. I have not cross-checked every blooper, but I wanted to acknowledge that some listed in this volume were intentional.

Notable: Anything that makes a program unique, or other miscellaneous comment not covered elsewhere. Examples are "First show for General Tire" or "First mention of Jack's violin playing". This also includes interesting or unusual occurrences, such as "Jack ad libs to Mary 'Gee, you're cute tonight'" or "Rochester breaks character for a moment on his blooper".

Recording: Additional detail on the circulating recording of a show, such as "Ending clipped in middle of Jack-Rochester dialogue" or "Only 12 minutes of show currently in circulation".

Running gag: A recurring gag or plot device, such as Mary reading a poem. See the "Running Gag Key" below for detailed information on various running gags. What is and isn't a running gag is a delicate question; I have not tracked every time Jack said "Oh, Rohhhhh-chester" or every time Jack makes Don do a middle commercial with a pun based on something he's just said. My selections are based on three criteria:

1) They must be gags, not catch phrases (like "Oh Roh-chester" or "That's a lu-luuuu!")
2) Gags that were used extensively in different situations (e.g., Hair hair) or used well beyond the radio show (e.g., But but but and Relay)
3) Gags that fans still talk about regularly (e.g., Mary's poems or the Baby talk Jell-O flavors)

Skit: The title of a skit performed in the show. The first title announced is listed, although many had an additional subtitle. For example, "Murder on the Gridiron, or He Had Ten Yards to Go When He Went" is listed as simply "Murder on the Gridiron". "She Done Him Wrong and we're going to do him right" is listed as "She Done Him Wrong".

RUNNING GAG KEY

Hair hair – Originates with "Who Killed Mr. Stooge" series, where Jack plays Sergeant O'Hare. Gag has Jack saying his name to someone and them not getting it, then saying "Hair! Hair! What's on your head?" and a variety of punch lines. The same structure was eventually used with multiple words in place of "hair".

Mary does Mae West – Mary did a fairly good impersonation of Mae West's purring delivery, and it was used on many occasions, both in skits and individual lines.

Mary's mother communication – Mary communicates with her mother. This may be in the form of a telegram or special delivery that interrupts the show, Mary's mother calling, Mary calling her mother, or Mary bringing a letter that she received from her mother.

Mary's poem – Mary reads a poem, sometimes in part or with some interruption. At times, she writes the poem during the course of the show. Her poems during wartime often ended with a plug for people to buy war bonds or other support of the troops.

Relay – Gag starts with someone saying something (e.g., "Quiet!"), then a chorus of other voices progressively joining in and shouting the same thing.

Relay question and answer – Gag starts with someone asking a question or making a statement, which then gets yelled from person to person. In certain instances, someone eventually answers the question or responds to the statement, and the answer gets yelled from person to person in reverse order. For example:

Jack:	I'm Jack Benny!
Mary:	Hey Sara, he's Jack Benny!
Sara:	Hey Blanche, he's Jack Benny!
Blanche:	Hey Mabel, he's Jack Benny!
Mabel:	Who's Jack Benny?
Blanche:	I don't know. Sara, who's Jack Benny?
Sara:	I don't know. Mary, who's Jack Benny?
Mary:	I don't know, ask him!

Baby talk Jell-O flavors – A cast member (often Don) will be playing a child and pronounces the Jell-O flavors as "stwawbewwy, chewwy, waspbewwy, owange, wemon and wime."

CORRECTIONS

Everyone purchasing this log is hereby deputized as a spotter for corrections. In managing the sheer volume of information in this book, I may have been inconsistent in the spelling of a character (e.g., "Livingstone" in the cast but "Livingston" in song listing for the same show), forgotten to indicate a guest star, listed a medley of songs with a "/" instead of "-", etc., etc., etc. You may also be able to identify one of the unidentified songs, or provide a first or last name for one of the supporting actors currently identified by one name only. I welcome any and all corrections which will help this to be an even more complete reference in the future.

However, I do ask that you base your corrections on some compelling evidence. Matters of consistency in spelling, punctuation, etc. should be readily apparent. However, corrections in cast identities are a stickier matter. For example, people have hotly debated whether the Blue Fairy was played by Mary Kelly or Blanche Stewart. The script prompts the Blue Fairy lines as "Kelly", so the part is listed here as being played by Mary Kelly. In cross-checking the script prompts and the recordings, I have found the scripts to seldom, if ever, be wrong. (The only occasion I have found thus far was a one-line part credited to Harry Baldwin, but the recording doesn't really sound like Baldwin. However with no other evidence, I have taken the script as authority.)

If you are providing the full name of a partially-identified actor, please provide a recording of their work that can be cross-referenced with the Benny show recording. If you feel that a particular running gag has not been tracked, then please provide all the dates of shows that include the gag in question. If you have a recording that does not have the problems indicated or contains conclusive proof of its source when it is listed here as "Unknown", then please include a copy of your recording for inclusion in (and improvement of) the IJBFC library.

Attached is a form for submitting corrections. You can use this format or an electronic one, but please include all the requested information. Many thanks to everyone for helping with the continuous improvement of this volume.

39 Forever Correction Form

Your name: _____

E-mail: _____

Phone number: _____

Date of show: _____

Information needing correction: _____

_____

_____

_____

Correct information: _____

_____

_____

_____

_____

Explanation of evidence supporting correction: _____

_____

_____

_____

_____

Reference material supporting correction (e.g., enclosed recordings, etc.):

_____

_____

_____

Please mail to: IJBFC – 39 Forever corrections, P.O. Box 11288, Piedmont, CA 94611

JACK BENNY SERIES SUMMARY

Dates: May 2, 1932 to October 26, 1932
Sponsor: Canada Dry
Air Times: Monday and Wednesday, 9:30 – 10:00 PM
Network: NBC Blue
Announcers: Alois Havrilla, George Hicks, Ed Thorgerson, Jimmy Wallington
Orchestra: George Olsen
Vocalists: Bobby Borger, Fran Frey, Dick Hotcha Gardner, Dave Marshall, Bob Rice, Ethel Shutta, Paul Small
Total shows: 52 shows

Dates: October 30, 1932 to January 26, 1933
Sponsor: Canada Dry
Air Times: Sunday at 10:00 – 10:30 PM, Thursday at 8:15 – 8:45 PM
Network: NBC Blue
Announcers: Paul Douglas, Bob Gregory, ? Smith,
Orchestra: Ted Weems
Vocalists: Parker Gibbs, Red Ingle, Andrea Marsh, Elmo Tanner (whistler), Country Washburn
Total shows: 26 shows

Dates: March 3, 1933 to June 23, 1933
Sponsor: Chevrolet
Air Times: Friday 10:00 - 10:30 PM
Network: NBC Red
Announcer: Howard Claney
Orchestra: Frank Black
Vocalist: Edith Evans, James Melton
Total shows: 17 shows

Dates: October 1, 1933 to April 1, 1934
Sponsor: Chevrolet
Air Times: Sunday 10:00 – 10:30 PM
Network: NBC Red
Announcer: Alois Havrilla
Orchestra: Frank Black
Vocalist: Frank Parker
Total shows: 26 shows

Dates: April 6, 1934 to September 28, 1934
Sponsor: General Tire
Air Times: Friday 10:30 – 11:00 PM
Network: NBC Red
Announcer: Don Wilson
Orchestra: Don Bestor
Vocalist: Frank Parker
Total shows: 26 shows

Dates: October 14, 1934 to May 31, 1942
Sponsor: Jell-O

Air Times:	Sunday 7:00-7:30 PM (Eastern), 6:00-6:30 PM (Central), 9:30-10:00 PM (Mountain), 8:30-9:00 PM (Pacific)
	(Note: Variations in observance of Daylight Saving Time altered some local broadcast times)

Networks:	NBC Blue, NBC
Announcer:	Don Wilson
Orchestras:	Don Bestor, Johnny Green, Jimmy Grier, Phil Harris
Vocalists:	Michael Bartlett, Dennis Day, Frank Parker
Total shows:	303 shows

JACK BENNY RATINGS SUMMARY[1]

Note: Only top five shows are listed for years when the Benny program was in the top five. 1933 lists shows sufficient to show the placement of the Benny program.

1932 - 1933
No Cooperative Analysis of Broadcasting (C.A.B.) rating

1933-1934

Ranking	Program	C.A.B. Rating
1	Eddie Cantor	50.2
2	Maxwell House Show Boat	45.9
3	Rudy Vallee Varieties	39.0
4	Joe Penner	35.2
5	Ed Wynn	31.6
6	Lowell Thomas	30.7
7	Amos n Andy	30.3
8	Burns and Allen	30.2
9	Paul Whiteman Revue	29.9
10	First Nighter	28.0
11	Phil Baker	27.1
12	Ben Bernie Orchestra	26.5
13	Jack Benny (Chevrolet)	25.3

1934 – 1935

Ranking	Program	C.A.B. Rating
1	Rudy Vallee Varieties	38.5
2	Maxwell House Show Boat	37.3
3	Jack Benny (Jell-O)	36.4
4	Fred Allen	32.0
5	Joe Penner	30.3

1935 – 1936

Ranking	Program	Hooper Rating
1	Major Bowes Amateur Hour	45.2
2	Rudy Vallee Varieties	28.2
3	Jack Benny	26.8

---

[1] Summers, Harrison B., A Thirty-Year History of Programs Carried on National Radio Networks in the United States 1926-1956, Ohio State University, 1958.

| 4 | March of Time | 23.5 |
| 5 | Burns and Allen | 23.0 |

1936 – 1937

Ranking	Program	Hooper Rating
1	Eddie Cantor	29.1
2	Jack Benny	28.6
3	Lux Radio Theatre	25.1
4	Burns and Allen	24.0
5	Major Bowes Amateur Hour	23.2

1937 – 1938

Ranking	Program	Hooper Rating
1	Charlie McCarthy	39.4
2	Jack Benny	34.0
3	Burns and Allen	27.5
4	Lux Radio Theatre	25.5
5	Al Jolson	23.5

1938 – 1939

Ranking	Program	Hooper Rating
1	Charlie McCarthy	35.1
2	Jack Benny	31.4
3	Lux Radio Theatre	27.0
4	Bing Crosby	24.5
5	Frank Morgan – Fannie Brice	20.2

1939 – 1940

Ranking	Program	Hooper Rating
1	Charlie McCarthy	34.6
2	Jack Benny	34.1
3	One Man's Family	28.7
4	Lux Radio Theatre	26.9
5	Bob Hope	25.0

1940 – 1941

Ranking	Program	Hooper Rating
1	Jack Benny	36.2
2	Charlie McCarthy	32.2
3	Bob Hope	28.2
4	Fibber McGee and Molly	27.4
5	Lux Radio Theatre	26.8

1941 – 1942

Ranking	Program	Hooper Rating
1	Charlie McCarthy	35.2
2	Fibber McGee and Molly	33.3
3	Walter Winchell	33.1
4	Bob Hope	31.7
5	Jack Benny	31.0

Date: 5/2/1932   **Sponsor:** Canada Dry   **City:** New York, NY

Recording Source: WJZ   **Problems:** None

First line:
Thorgerson: Tonight, Canada Dry, the champagne of ginger ales, presents a series of programs to advertise the new, made-to-order Canada Dry, which you can now buy by the glass at drug stores and soda fountains.

Summary:
Jack says it's the first time he's appearing professionally (the first time he's getting paid)...George Olson comes to work on roller skates...Jack says his car is a bicycle built for two...Ethel Shutta has a nervous soprano...Jack has a girl in Newark, NJ who poses for "Before" picture in beauty magazines...her father drank everything here, then went north to drink Canada dry...George's uncle needs fresh air but no heavy lifting, so became a garbage man in Scotland...Jack's relatives are listening, and he doesn't want them to know he's working

Cast:

Last name	First name	Roles	Guest star
Benny	Jack	Jack Benny	No
Borger	Bobby	Bobby Borger	No
Frey	Fran	Fran Frey	No
Olsen	George	George Olsen	No
Rice	Bob	Bob Rice	No
Shutta	Ethel	Ethel Shutta	No
Thorgerson	Ed	Ed Thorgerson	No

Songs:

Order	Title	Performers	Vocal
1	Train theme	George Olsen	No
2	I Beg Your Pardon Mademoiselle	George Olsen	Yes
3	I Found a Million Dollar Baby	Ethel Shutta	Yes
3	I Found a Million Dollar Baby	Fran Frey	Yes
4	I Love a Parade	Fran Frey	Yes
4	I Love a Parade	Bobby Borger	Yes
4	I Love a Parade	Bob Rice	Yes
5	Paradise	George Olsen	No
6	How We All Make Music	George Olsen	Yes
7	Come West Little Girl Come West	Ethel Shutta	Yes
8	Drums in My Heart	George Olsen	No

Notes:

Notable	First show on radio
Notable	First show for Canada Dry
Notable	First closing in the format of "That, ladies and gentlemen, was the last number on our first program on the second of May."

Date: 5/4/1932   **Sponsor:** Canada Dry   **City:** New York, NY

Recording Source: None   **Problems:** None

First line:

Jack: Greetings, old friends, and welcome to our program, new friends. This is Jack Benny, folks - Benny, B like in Broke, E like in Ego, N like in Pneumonia and the other n, like in Double Pneumonia and Y like in Yiolin.

Summary:

Olsen's band doesn't talk to each other...Jack interviews Olsen and Shutta...Canada Dry made-to-order is syrup and carbonated water...complaints about the cornet player...Jack has a screenplay

Cast:

Last name	First name	Roles	Guest star
Benny	Jack	Jack Benny	No
Frey	Fran	Fran Frey	No
Olsen	George	George Olsen	No
Shutta	Ethel	Ethel Shutta	No
Thorgerson	Ed	Ed Thorgerson	No

Songs:

Order	Title	Performers	Vocal
1	Jolly Good Company	George Olsen	No
2	Humming to Myself	Ethel Shutta	Yes
3	Sing a New Song	George Olsen	No
4	I'll Miss You in the Evening	George Olsen	No
5	I Know You're Lying	Ethel Shutta	Yes
5	I Know You're Lying	Fran Frey	Yes
6	Rose Room	George Olsen	No

Notes:

Notable	When Jack interviews Olsen and Shutta, Olsen says he's 42 and Shutta says he's 39

Date: 5/9/1932   **Sponsor:** Canada Dry   **City:** (New York, NY)

Summary:
Contest begins

Cast:

Last name	First name	Roles	Guest star
Benny	Jack	Jack Benny	No
Olsen	George	George Olsen	No
Shutta	Ethel	Ethel Shutta	No
Thorgerson	Ed	Ed Thorgerson	No

Notes:

Notable	No script or recording exists for this show

Date: 5/11/1932   **Sponsor:** Canada Dry   **City:** New York, NY

Recording Source: None   **Problems:** None

First line:
Jack: Hello somebody. This is Jack Benny talking. There will be a slight pause while you say "What of it."

Summary:
Jack to recite Canada Dry version of "The Shooting of Dan McGrew" next week...Olsen walks in his sleep...Shutta drinks Canada Dry to improve her voice...Jack reads fan mail...Jack and Olsen compliment each other...contest started Monday for people to write why they like Canada Dry in 20,000 words or fewer, then changes it to writing it on a straw...Jack explains the story of a French song from his vaudeville act

Cast:

Last name	First name	Roles	Guest star
Baker	Jerry	Jerry Baker	No
Benny	Jack	Jack Benny	No
Frey	Fran	Fran Frey	No
Olsen	George	George Olsen	No
Shutta	Ethel	Ethel Shutta	No
Thorgerson	Ed	Ed Thorgerson	No

Songs:

Order	Title	Performers	Vocal
1	Ooh, That Kiss	Fran Frey	Yes
2	There I Go Dreaming Again	Ethel Shutta	Yes
3	Crazy People	Fran Frey	Yes
4	When the Sun Kisses the World Goodbye	Ethel Shutta	Yes
5	I'm Pins and Needles in Love With You	Fran Frey	Yes
5	I'm Pins and Needles in Love With You	Ethel Shutta	Yes
6	When the Lights Are Soft and Low	Ethel Shutta	Yes
7	Got a Date With an Angel	Jerry Baker	Yes

Notes:

Notable	First show with theme song "Jolly Good Company"
Notable	First show with closing theme "Rockabye Moon"
Notable	First mention of Jack being from Waukegan
Notable	First mention of Jack's violin playing

Date: 5/16/1932   **Sponsor:** Canada Dry   **City:** New York, NY

Recording Source: None   **Problems:** None

First line:
Jack: Hello anybody. Remember me? I'm the fellow that's been annoying you every Monday and Wednesday.

Summary:
What the public wants…George Olsen works hard…Shutta wants to tell a joke (take-off on Nora Bayes stage routine)…reads fan letter from woman who lost 100 pounds drinking Canada Dry…contest is extended for another year, prize may be three-day vacation in Siam…gives progress of contest, has contestants write about Canada Dry on a shirt…Olsen gave Jack a tip on a horse

Cast:

Last name	First name	Roles	Guest star
Benny	Jack	Jack Benny	No
Borger	Bobby	Bobby Borger	No
Frey	Fran	Fran Frey	No
Olsen	George	George Olsen	No
Rice	Bob	Bob Rice	No
Shutta	Ethel	Ethel Shutta	No
Thorgerson	Ed	Ed Thorgerson	No

Songs:

Order	Title	Performers	Vocal
1	Who	Bob Rice	Yes
1	Who	Fran Frey	Yes
1	Who	Bobby Borger	Yes
2	My Mom	George Olsen	No
3	She Didn't Say Yes	Fran Frey	Yes
3	She Didn't Say Yes	Ethel Shutta	Yes
4	That's How We Make Music	George Olsen	Yes
5	When We're One	Ethel Shutta	Yes
6	Getting Along With Your Gal	Ethel Shutta	Yes
6	Getting Along With Your Gal	Fran Frey	Yes

Notes:

Date: 5/18/1932   **Sponsor:** Canada Dry   **City:** (New York, NY)

Recording Source: None   **Problems:** None

Summary:
"Stay Six Months" story…color routine…limerick contest

Cast:

Last name	First name	Roles	Guest star
Benny	Jack	Jack Benny	No
Olsen	George	George Olsen	No
Shutta	Ethel	Ethel Shutta	No
Thorgerson	Ed	Ed Thorgerson	No

Notes:

Notable	No script or recording exists for this show

Date: 5/23/1932   **Sponsor:** Canada Dry   **City:** New York, NY

Recording Source: None   **Problems:** None

First line:
Jack: Good evening, Easterners--good afternoon,Weseterners--and good morning, Siam! This is Jack Benny talking -- Jack Benny with new jokes, new contest rules, new shoes and a haircut.

Summary:
Jack is playing at the Paramount Theatre in New York and had trouble getting to the broadcast...listener writes that she tried to dry her dishes with Canada Dry and they're still wet...Jack and Shutta discuss her dress...Jack and Olsen played golf...fade to scene at soda founatin of Jack getting a Canada Dry...Ethel goes to Jack back to the studio...on previous show, asked contestants to send contest entries as limericks between two slices of bread...asks entries to be written in whipped cream on birthday cakes...contest prize is a hairless St. Bernard dog, second prize is a real German police dog, third prize is a Swiss echo

Cast:
Last name	First name	Roles	Guest star
Allen	?	Malted milk customer	No
Benny	Jack	Jack Benny	No
Frey	Fran	Fran Frey	No
Gardner	Dick Hotcha	Dick Hotcha Gardner	No
Olsen	George	George Olsen	No
Shutta	Ethel	Ethel Shutta	No
Small	Paul	Paul Small	No
Thorgerson	Ed	Ed Thorgerson	No

Songs:
Order	Title	Performers	Vocal
1	Blue Danube	George Olsen	No
2	Roaming for Romance	Ethel Shutta	Yes
3	Silent Love	Paul Small	Yes
4	I've Got the Potatoes	Paul Small	Yes
5	Tender Child	Ethel Shutta	Yes
5	Tender Child	Fran Frey	Yes
6	Yeah Man	Dick Hotcha Gardner	Yes

Notes:
Notable	First non-studio scenario at soda fountain

Date: 5/25/1932   **Sponsor:** Canada Dry   **City:** New York, NY

Recording Source: None   **Problems:** None

First line:
Jack: Hello anybody. This is Jack Benny telling…Are you asking, hmmm?

Summary:
Jack introduces the janitor…janitor scared Dracula…Olsen and Shutta going to see a James Cagney movie…Jack says he was assistant lover to Ramon Navarro in movies…Shutta says she saw "The Medicine Man" ("Oh, you're the one who saw it.")…Jack went around with Zazu Pitts' sister, Peach Pitts…Jack tells of a man who drank Canada Dry and became able to walk (with crutches)…Herbert Hoover reviews contest ("It is contests like yours that will bring back prosperity - to England.")…contest dropped 16 1/4 points and sheriff attached prizes…first prize won by George Olsen's brother, second prize to Robert Jennings (second violin in Olsen's band)…had 36,000 men test Canada Dry blindfolded, and only three said it was Russ Columbo

Cast:

Last name	First name	Roles	Guest star
Benny	Jack	Jack Benny	No
Frey	Fran	Fran Frey	No
Moore	Bobby	Janitor Philander Kvetch	No
Olsen	George	George Olsen	No
Shutta	Ethel	Ethel Shutta	No
Small	Paul	Paul Small	No
Thorgerson	Ed	Ed Thorgerson	No

Songs:

Order	Title	Performers	Vocal
1	Ask Yourself Who Loves You	Ethel Shutta	Yes
1	Ask Yourself Who Loves You	Fran Frey	Yes
2	Moonlight Brings Me You	Paul Small	Yes
3	Oh Say Can't You See	Ethel Shutta	Yes
4	You Can Make My Life a Bed of Roses	Fran Frey	Yes
5	The Night Shall Be Filled with Music	Ethel Shutta	Yes
6	Of Thee I Sing	Fran Frey	Yes

Notes:

Notable	First joking about Jack's movie career

Date: 5/30/1932   **Sponsor:** Canada Dry   **City:** (New York, NY)

Recording Source: None   **Problems:** None

Summary:
Theme song…defining Canada Dry Ginger Ale…endurance test

Cast:

Last name	First name	Roles	Guest star
Benny	Jack	Jack Benny	No
Olsen	George	George Olsen	No
Shutta	Ethel	Ethel Shutta	No
Thorgerson	Ed	Ed Thorgerson	No

Notes:

Notable	No script or recording exists for this show

Date: 6/1/1932   **Sponsor:** Canada Dry   **City:** New York, NY

Recording Source: None   **Problems:** None

First line:
Jack: Hello, every lady...You remember we told you on Monday that this would be
Ladies' Night? Well, we've kept our promise.

Summary:
Ladies' Night...orchestra is dressed in Little Lord Fauntleroy suits...Jack introduces and
describes janitor's wife, Mrs. Kvetch...janitor's wife wants to sing on the show...Paul
Small got a black eye from kissing a bride (two years after the ceremony)...Jack gives
cooking hints...Jack tells women how to attract a man...listener calls who wants to attract
Clark Gable, they'll try to make him a contest prize...leeter from Enchilado Tango,
Embassy of the Republic of Santo Mongo Fongo, they want to start a contest

Cast:

Last name	First name	Roles	Guest star
		Mrs. Kvetch	No
Benny	Jack	Jack Benny	No
Frey	Fran	Fran Frey	No
Olsen	George	George Olsen	No
Shutta	Ethel	Ethel Shutta	No
Small	Paul	Paul Small	No
Thorgerson	Ed	Ed Thorgerson	No

Songs:

Order	Title	Performers	Vocal
1	When Gabriel Blows His Horn	Fran Frey	Yes
2	Lullaby of the Leaves	Paul Small	Yes
3	Under the Old Crow's Nest	Ethel Shutta	Yes
4	Somebody Loves You	Paul Small	Yes
5	Tender Child	Fran Frey	Yes
5	Tender Child	Ethel Shutta	Yes
6	Drums in My Heart	George Olsen	No

Notes:

Notable	First phone call on the show, Jack has Ethel Shutta answer the phone

Date: 6/6/1932   **Sponsor:** Canada Dry   **City:** New York, NY

Recording Source: None   **Problems:** None

First line:
Jack: Hello, you lovers of the classics. This is Jack Benny raving -- Jack Benny -- blue eyes rich wavy hair - both of them - no moustache, not even fuzz -- shoes, size ten -- collar, the same -- hat, size 9 if you laugh at my jokes -- if you don't laugh, size 6 -- born in Illinois -- razzed in Kentucky -- and considered very handsome by parents.

Summary:
Jack reads letters about Ladies' Night (including letter from Leonard Fenchel)...Jack says he can play as well as anyone in Olsen's orchestra...Jack plays a few bars of "Lovable", scratches on violin, starts to sing it, orchestra urges him to play instead...Shutta gave a birthday party for Olsen...Olsen is conservative with money, would give a thousand dollars to be a millionaire...guest star J. Nottingham Leeke, picked up pebble near where Amelia Earhart started Atlantic flight...Leeke only speaks in verse ("Lady Known as Lou" take-off)...sheriff returned contest prizes...contestants should send in a period, first prize is a baby safety razor for the little shaver

Cast:

Last name	First name	Roles	Guest star
		J. Nottingham Leeke	No
Benny	Jack	Jack Benny	No
Frey	Fran	Fran Frey	No
Olsen	George	George Olsen	No
Shutta	Ethel	Ethel Shutta	No
Small	Paul	Paul Small	No
Thorgerson	Ed	Ed Thorgerson	No

Songs:

Order	Title	Performers	Vocal
1	I Love a Parade	George Olsen	No
2	The Clouds Will Soon Roll By	Paul Small	Yes
3	Lovable	Jack Benny	No
4	Is I In Love? I Is	Ethel Shutta	Yes
5	Love You Funny Thing	Fran Frey	Yes
6	Oh What a Thrill	Ethel Shutta	Yes
7	Eat Drink and Be Merry	Fran Frey	Yes

Notes:

Notable	Structure, and even some gags, reused for later post-"Ladies' Night" show
Notable	First time Jack plays the violin on the air

Date: 6/8/1932   **Sponsor:** Canada Dry   **City:** New York, NY

Recording Source: None   **Problems:** None

First line:
Jack: Hello, if you're not too busy.

Summary:
Jack reads fan letter, liked violin playing and neighbors moved away...Jack describes Paul Small...Jack interviews Canada Dry...Jack going away for the weekend to Hay Fever Falls...Jack took boat to Europe last year...Jack talks about Nicaragua...34,765 people tied for contest first place

Cast:

Last name	First name	Roles	Guest star
		151 and fan letter voice	No
		Canada Dry	No
		Large glass	No
Benny	Jack	Jack Benny	No
Borger	Bobby	Bobby Borger	No
Frey	Fran	Fran Frey	No
Olsen	George	George Olsen	No
Rice	Bob	Bob Rice	No
Shutta	Ethel	Ethel Shutta	No
Small	Paul	Paul Small	No
Thorgerson	Ed	Ed Thorgerson	No

Songs:

Order	Title	Performers	Vocal
1	Eat Drink and Be Merry	Fran Frey	Yes
2	If I Were Only Sure of You	Paul Small	Yes
3	Picnic for Two	Ethel Shutta	Yes
3	Picnic for Two	Fran Frey	Yes
4	The Night Shall Be Filled With Music	Ethel Shutta	Yes
5	She's a Cornfed Indiana Gal	Fran Frey	Yes
6	I Beg Your Pardon Mademoiselle	Bob Rice	Yes
6	I Beg Your Pardon Mademoiselle	George Olsen	No
6	I Beg Your Pardon Mademoiselle	Fran Frey	Yes
6	I Beg Your Pardon Mademoiselle	Bobby Borger	Yes

Notes:

Date: 6/13/1932 **Sponsor:** Canada Dry **City:** New York, NY

Recording Source: None **Problems:** None

First line:
Jack: Are you ready -- hmm? As they say in the stock market...high-low, everybody.

Summary:
Coast-to-coast hookup with Alaska and New York...Jack's girlfriend Molly calls...Jack went to Lake Chip-a-munga-chakwa-chobee...played tennis without tennis balls, swatted flies at each other...guest star, Theodolphus T. Snick, professor of Pig Latin...professor stutters badly...tries to get hookup with Alaska...gets Eski-Moe Bimberg and his Igloo Syncopaters...starts contest for Alaska, writing about Canada Dry on dried fish

Cast:

Last name	First name	Roles	Guest star
		Brooklyn voice	No
		Theodolphus T. Snick	No
		Eski-Moe Bimberg	No
Benny	Jack	Jack Benny	No
Coulter	Doug	Phone answerer	No
Frey	Fran	Fran Frey	No
Gardner	Dick Hotcha	Dick Hotcha Gardner	No
Olsen	George	George Olsen	No
Shutta	Ethel	Ethel Shutta	No
Small	Paul	Paul Small	No
Thorgerson	Ed	Ed Thorgerson	No

Songs:

Order	Title	Performers	Vocal
1	Blue Danube	George Olsen	No
2	Rockabye Moon	Ethel Shutta	Yes
3	Scat Song	Dick Hotcha Gardner	Yes
4	Lullaby of the Leaves	Paul Small	Yes
5	Banking on the Weather	Ethel Shutta	Yes
5	Banking on the Weather	Fran Frey	Yes
6	Hi Lee Hi Low	Eski-Moe Bimberg	No
7	I've Got the Potatoes	Fran Frey	Yes

Notes:

Date: 6/15/1932   **Sponsor:** Canada Dry   **City:** New York, NY

Recording Source: None   **Problems:** None

First line:
Jack: Hello, cash customers…this is Jack Benny…Jack as in mule and Benny as in Benny Franklin.

Summary:
Jack calls the roll…winners arguing about prizes (first prize winners claim they got third, etc.)…Jack advertising for a secretary, interviews and hires Smalla Garbo…Jack dictates letter to prize manufacturer, as they haven't sent prizes…Canada Dry boxing for Middleweight Championship, Jack does extensive play-by-play…winner is not yet announced, to be continued

Cast:

Last name	First name	Roles	Guest star
Benny	Jack	Jack Benny	No
Conn	Harry	Philander Kvetch, Mike Angelo	No
Frey	Fran	Fran Frey	No
Gardner	Dick Hotcha	Dick Hotcha Gardner	No
Olsen	George	George Olsen	No
Shutta	Ethel	Ethel Shutta	No
Small	Paul	Paul Small	No
Stewart	Blanche	Smalla Garbo	No
Thorgerson	Ed	Ed Thorgerson	No

Songs:

Order	Title	Performers	Vocal
1	Bugle Call Rag	George Olsen	No
2	Paradise	Paul Small	Yes
3	Crazy People	Fran Frey	Yes
4	Roamin' for Romance	Ethel Shutta	Yes
5	Who Don't You Get Lost	Dick Hotcha Gardner	Yes
6	I'm That Way About Broadway	Ethel Shutta	Yes

Notes:

Date: 6/20/1932 **Sponsor:** Canada Dry **City:** New York, NY

Recording Source: None **Problems:** None

First line:
Jack: By special request…hello, anybody! This is Jack Benny guiding you…are you following?

Summary:
Olsen playing at Hollywood Gardens, had party for cast there…Jack danced with Ethel, she thought he was the head waiter…recap of Canada Dry boxing match…nominating a Presidential candidate for the Canada Dry Made-To-Order ticket, has political convention and delegates arrive…introduces candidate Trafalgar Bee-Fuddle, was President of Mexico for five minutes…Fuddle breaks down in tears and is shot

Cast:

Last name	First name	Roles	Guest star
		Trafalgar Bee-Fuddle	No
Benny	Jack	Jack Benny	No
Frey	Fran	Fran Frey	No
Gardner	Dick Hotcha	Dick Hotcha Gardner	No
Olsen	George	George Olsen	No
Shutta	Ethel	Ethel Shutta	No
Small	Paul	Paul Small	No
Thorgerson	Ed	Ed Thorgerson	No

Songs:

Order	Title	Performers	Vocal
1	Lord You Made the Night Too Long	George Olsen	No
2	My Heart's at Ease	Ethel Shutta	Yes
3	He Didn't Say Yes, He Didn't Say No	Fran Frey	Yes
4	Masquerade	Paul Small	Yes
5	Everything's Going to Be Okay, America	George Olsen	No
6	Keep Away	Dick Hotcha Gardner	Yes

Notes:

Notable	Sahara Desert Canada Dry ad

Partial script of Sahara Desert Canada Dry ad:
And now, while we are on the subject, let me read you a dispatch we received from our representative in North Africa…Sand Dune, a Scotchman. He wires us regarding another severe test of Canada Dry Ginger Ale. Incidentally, this representative of ours has the entire territory of the Sahara Desert…"On my fourth trip across the Desert yesterday afternoon, I discovered a band of eight European tourists who had wandered away from their caravan. They had been deserted on this desert without food…drink…or desert…dessert…for thirty days, no more…no less. Imagine that!…thirty days on the desert without a drink…their throats parched…their tongues hanging out…begging and pleading for any kind of liquid. I came to their rescue," says he, "gave each of them a glass of Canada Dry made-to-order Ginger Ale…and not one of them said he did not like it!" ANOTHER GREAT VICTORY FOR CANADA DRY!

Date: 6/22/1932   **Sponsor:** Canada Dry   **City:** New York, NY

Recording Source: None   **Problems:** None

First line:
Jack: Hello, half of one percent of everybody.

Summary:
Start of summer…Jack saw the Sharkey-Schmelling championship, discusses it at length…Amelia Earhart parade on Monday…guest star Violet Ray who also flew to Ireland…she gives cooking answers to every question

Cast:

Last name	First name	Roles	Guest star
		Dice player	No
Benny	Jack	Jack Benny	No
Frey	Fran	Fran Frey	No
Gardner	Dick Hotcha	Dick Hotcha Gardner	No
Kelcey	?	Violet Ray	No
Olsen	George	George Olsen	No
Shutta	Ethel	Ethel Shutta	No
Small	Paul	Paul Small	No
Thorgerson	Ed	Ed Thorgerson	No

Songs:

Order	Title	Performers	Vocal
1	Marietta	Paul Small	Yes
2	Why Did You Come Along	Ethel Shutta	Yes
3	Yeah Man	Dick Hotcha Gardner	Yes
4	Bring Back Those Dear Old Circus Days	Fran Frey	Yes

Notes:

Date: 6/27/1932   **Sponsor:** Canada Dry   **City:** New York, NY

Recording Source: None   **Problems:** None

First line:
Jack: Hello...hello....hello, there George...hello, Ethel, how are you tonight?...hello, Kvetch!

Summary:
Jack gets fan mail from his tailor, his secretary reviews messages...Jack teases George Olsen about being cheap...Olsen worked for Jack when he owned a café in Chicago (turns out Jack was a waiter)...Jack and Olsen argue, Shutta smooths things...reads telegram from CD salesman in New Jersey...controversy over the Schmelling-Sharkey fight...introduces Homer T. Sass, train conductor (punch expert), to comment...T. Angleworm Smelt, fisherman (knows hooks) comments...Benjamin Listle Hose, hosiery salesman (knows socks) comments...J. Veal Cutlet, butcher (knows uppercuts) comments

Cast:

Last name	First name	Roles	Guest star
		Homer T. Sass	No
		Lucifer Hicks	No
		J. Veal Cutlet	No
		Benjamin Hose	No
		T. Angleworm Smelt	No
Balonin	?	Secretary	No
Benny	Jack	Jack Benny	No
Frey	Fran	Fran Frey	No
Hicks	George	George Hicks	No
Mills Brothers	The	Mills Brothers	Yes
Olsen	George	George Olsen	No
Shutta	Ethel	Ethel Shutta	No
Small	Paul	Paul Small	No

(Balonin may be a typo for Harry Baldwin)

Songs:

Order	Title	Performers	Vocal
1	I Beg Your Pardon Mademoiselle	Fran Frey	Yes
2	A Great Big Bunch of You	Ethel Shutta	Yes
3	It Was So Beautiful	Paul Small	Yes
4	Humming to Myself	Ethel Shutta	Yes
5	Come and Sit Beside the Sea	Fran Frey	Yes

Notes:

Notable	First time an announcer other than Ed Thorgerson (George Hicks) is mentioned

Date: 6/29/1932 **Sponsor:** Canada Dry **City:** New York, NY

Recording Source: None **Problems:** None

First line:
Jack: Don't worry, folks…this is Just Babies' Night…hello, every baby.

Summary:
Babies' Night…reads letter of baby that switched from milk to Canada Dry, got a job in the steel mills…Babe Ruth was there, but had to run home…George Hicks' (announcer) son Lucifer wants to sing Old Man River…Jack gets call from his baby…Shutta and Jack recite nursery rhymes…limerick contest for babies…Jack reads "Little Red Riding Hood"

Cast:

Last name	First name	Roles	Guest star
		Announcer	No
Benny	Jack	Jack Benny	No
Borger	Bobby	Bobby Borger	No
Frey	Fran	Fran Frey	No
Gardner	Dick Hotcha	Dick Hotcha Gardner	No
Mills Brothers	The	The Mills Brothers	Yes
Olsen	George	George Olsen	No
Rice	Bob	Bob Rice	No
Shutta	Ethel	Ethel Shutta	No

Songs:

Order	Title	Performers	Vocal
1	How Can You Say You Love Me	Dick Hotcha Gardner	Yes
2	Hey Diddle Diddle	Bob Rice	Yes
2	Hey Diddle Diddle	Fran Frey	Yes
2	Hey Diddle Diddle	Bobby Borger	Yes
3	Is I In Love? I Is	Ethel Shutta	Yes
4	A Bungalow, a Piccolo, and You	Fran Frey	Yes
5	Unidentified	Mills Brothers	Yes
6	Goodnight, Sweetheart	Ethel Shutta	Yes
6	Goodnight, Sweetheart	Bobby Borger	Yes

Notes:

Notable	First guest stars

Date: 7/4/1932   **Sponsor:** Canada Dry   **City:** New York, NY

Recording Source: None   **Problems:** None

First line:
Jack: Hello...of the people...by the people...and for the people...

Summary:
Fourth of July...Jack's relatives came to visit...will broadcast fireworks over the radio...Jack is very tan, spent two days in Atlantic City...Olsen tried to teach a strange woman how to swim, Shutta upset...Canada Dry political convention goes on...guest star, champion firecracker lighter Pinwheel Klunk...lights fireworks for the audience

Cast:

Last name	First name	Roles	Guest star
		Announcer	No
		Pinwheel Klunk	No
		Shot man	No
Benny	Jack	Jack Benny	No
Frey	Fran	Fran Frey	No
Olsen	George	George Olsen	No
Rice	Bob	Bob Rice	No
Shutta	Ethel	Ethel Shutta	No
Small	Paul	Paul Small	No

Songs:

Order	Title	Performers	Vocal
1	What, You Got No Trouble?	Fran Frey	Yes
2	Talking to You About Me	Ethel Shutta	Yes
3	Songs for Sale	Paul Small	Yes
4	Sipping Soda with Suzie	Ethel Shutta	Yes
5	Cabin in the Cotton	Paul Small	Yes
6	When Gimbel Plays the Cymbal	Bob Rice	Yes

Notes:

Date: 7/6/1932   **Sponsor:** Canada Dry   **City:** New York, NY

Recording Source: None   **Problems:** None

First line:
Jack: Hello, every sunburned body.

Summary:
Jack keeps getting interrupted…fan letter wants to make a special dinner, asks how to make a Fran Frey…tested Canada Dry at the Bronx Zoo, testimonials from the animals…Jack and Olsen discuss Beethoven…giving profit-sharing coupons, 16,000 coupons gets you a pair of ladies' baseball stockings

Cast:

Last name	First name	Roles	Guest star
		Announcer	No
Benny	Jack	Jack Benny	No
Conn	Harry	Interrupting man 1	No
Coulter	Doug	Interrupting man 2	No
Gardner	Dick Hotcha	Dick Hotcha Gardner	No
Olsen	George	George Olsen	No
Shutta	Ethel	Ethel Shutta	No
Small	Paul	Paul Small	No

Songs:

Order	Title	Performers	Vocal
1	Over the Weekend	Ethel Shutta	Yes
2	Rose Room	George Olsen	No
3	Hear the Little German Band	Ethel Shutta	Yes
4	Someone to Care	Paul Small	Yes
5	Margie	Dick Hotcha Gardner	Yes

Notes:

Date: 7/11/1932   **Sponsor:** Canada Dry   **City:** New York, NY

Recording Source: None   **Problems:** None

First line:
Jack: Say, Hicks, this is Amateur Night - isn't it?

Summary:
Jack calls a friend to insure they have one listener…Sharkey won Heavyweight Championship…Olsen tells a joke…train announcer advertises Canada Dry…lion tamer arrives…man who puts "29" on February does impersonations…Allah Bama does psychic routine…mind reader loses her purse and umbrella…

Cast:

Last name	First name	Roles	Guest star
		Male impersonator, Allah Bama mind reader	No
		Announcer	No
Ashe	Ralph	J. Leather Lung	No
Baker	Benny	Olsen Hotcha Benny	No
Benny	Jack	Jack Benny	No
Frey	Fran	Fran Frey, Erlanger Claw	No
Olsen	George	George Olsen	No
Shutta	Ethel	Ethel Shutta	No

Songs:

Order	Title	Performers	Vocal
1	The World Is Waiting For the Sunrise	George Olsen	No
2	I Want to Go Home	Ethel Shutta	Yes
3	That's How We Make Music	George Olsen	Yes
4	Nelly	Benny Baker	Yes
4	Nelly	Jack Benny	Yes
5	I Know You're Lying But I Love It	Fran Frey	Yes
5	I Know You're Lying But I Love It	Ethel Shutta	Yes
6	Three Guesses	Fran Frey	Yes

Notes:

Date: 7/13/1932 **Sponsor:** Canada Dry **City:** New York, NY

Recording Source: None **Problems:** None

First line:
Jack: Hello, summer customers...some are here...some are there...

Summary:
Jack calls Dracula to listen to the program...how Fran Frey got his name...reads letter suggesting Off Night, where they are off the air...Jack went to soda fountain...Harry Conn buys Jack a drink...Jack playing Capitol Theatre next week...giving away $150,000 in gold, three men huddle to decide who gets the money...Ethel wakes up Jack, giving away money was a dream

Cast:

Last name	First name	Roles	Guest star
		Announcer	No
		4 voices	No
		Marshmallow customer	No
Benny	Jack	Jack Benny	No
Conn	Harry	Canada Dry customer, Jay T. Loan, Morris J. Plan, J.K. Leash	No
Frey	Fran	Fran Frey, John T. Rockfellow, Honey Dew	No
Olsen	George	George Olsen	No
Ross	Dorothy	Jelly Bean customer	No
Shutta	Ethel	Ethel Shutta, soda clerk	No
Small	Paul	Paul Small, soda clerk	No

Songs:

Order	Title	Performers	Vocal
1	Stucco in the Sticks	Ethel Shutta	Yes
1	Stucco in the Sticks	Paul Small	Yes
2	Roaming for Romance	Ethel Shutta	Yes
3	Eat, Drink and Be Merry	Fran Frey	Yes
4	Symphony of Love	Paul Small	Yes
5	Get Yourself a Cup of Sunshine	Fran Frey	Yes

Notes:

Date: 7/18/1932   **Sponsor:** Canada Dry   **City:** New York, NY

Recording Source: None   **Problems:** None

First line:
Jack: (sings) Here we are again, Ethel, George and me…

Summary:
Jack says George stuck him with a check…Ethel saw Jack at the Capitol Theatre…Jack explains words to Ethel Shutta…Olympians come to studio…diving competition…running…hammer-throwing…trainer comes and takes athletes because they're supposed to be in bed by 9

Cast:

Last name	First name	Roles	Guest star
		Olympians	No
Benny	Jack	Jack Benny	No
Conn	Harry	Postman, Checko	No
Frey	Fran	Fran Frey, referee	No
Gardner	Dick Hotcha	Dick Hotcha Gardner	No
Havrilla	Alois	Alois Havrilla	No
Olsen	George	George Olsen	No
Ross	Dorothy	Ima Fish	No
Shutta	Ethel	Ethel Shutta, Lady Godiva	No
Small	Paul	Paul Small	No
Wiggin	John	Trainer	No

Songs:

Order	Title	Performers	Vocal
1	Sleep Come On and Take Me	Paul Small	Yes
2	Under the Old Crow's Nest	Ethel Shutta	Yes
3	Talking to You About Me	Ethel Shutta	Yes
4	O.K. America	Fran Frey	Yes
5	Rhumbatism	Dick Hotcha Gardner	Yes

Notes:

Notable	First time cast asks for words to be defined

Date: 7/20/1932   **Sponsor:** Canada Dry   **City:** New York, NY

Recording Source: None   **Problems:** None

First line:
Announcer: Ladies and gentlemen, this is Boarder's Night…the night dedicated to people who are away from their homes and live in boarding-houses.

Summary:
Boarder's Night…introduces boardinghouse owner, Miss Zinc…served Fran Frey to boarders, only seven survived, asks how to make Hotcha Gardner…guest star, Mexican Border (Uncle Don Pedro), fights a bull…Jack collapses, bull is winner…Jack tells bedtime story about a dice game, puts everyone to sleep

Cast:

Last name	First name	Roles	Guest star
		Announcer	No
Ashe	Ralph	Uncle Don Pedro	No
Baldwin	Harry	Man saying "No"	No
Benny	Jack	Jack Benny	No
Frey	Fran	Fran Frey	No
Gardner	Dick Hotcha	Dick Hotcha Gardner	No
Olsen	George	George Olsen	No
Ross	Dorothy	Kitchenette Zinc, Mrs. Phane	No
Shutta	Ethel	Ethel Shutta	No
Small	Paul	Paul Small	No

Songs:

Order	Title	Performers	Vocal
1	Song of India	George Olsen	No
2	Let's Go Out in the Open Air	Ethel Shutta	Yes
2	Let's Go Out in the Open Air	Fran Frey	Yes
3	Little Fraulein	Paul Small	Yes
4	Such is Life	Ethel Shutta	Yes
5	Scat Song	Dick Hotcha Gardner	Yes

Notes:

Date: 7/25/1932   **Sponsor:** Canada Dry   **City:** New York, NY

Recording Source: None   **Problems:** None

First line:
Jack: Hello, anybody…this is Jack Benny, a gentleman, a scholar and a man of letters…

Summary:
Request Night…one listener requests Jack go on vacation…Jack and Olsen change places…Olsen does cheap jokes about Jack…Jack tries to direct orchestra and they sound like they're tuning up…promotes cities in song (e.g., "Akron give you anything but love, baby…")…Jack and Shutta sing commercial…guest star, opera singer Lorraine Gitus…singer can't hit a note, but imitates instruments well

Cast:

Last name	First name	Roles	Guest star
Baldwin	Harry	Prince, man saying "no"	No
Barker	Brad	Trained dogs and chicken	No
Benny	Jack	Jack Benny	No
Caryl	?	Lorraine Gitus	No
Frey	Fran	Fran Frey, Tom	No
Olsen	George	George Olsen	No
Shutta	Ethel	Ethel Shutta	No
Small	Paul	Paul Small	No
Wallington	Jimmy	Jimmy Wallington	No

Songs:

Order	Title	Performers	Vocal
1	Drums in My Heart	George Olsen	No
2	You Can't Tell Love What to Do	Ethel Shutta	Yes
3	Listen to the German Band	Ethel Shutta	Yes
4	Little Blue Canoe	Paul Small	Yes
5	Bugle Call Rag	George Olsen	Yes

Notes:

Notable	First cheap joke about Jack
Notable	Orchestra leading gag was used as late as 1962 Lawrence Welk appearance on TV show

Date: 7/27/1932　　**Sponsor:** Canada Dry　　**City:** (New York, NY)

Recording Source: None　　**Problems:** None

Summary:
"Congratulations" routine…reading wires congratulating Jack on first series…Mary Livingston visits the studio…banquet

Cast:

Last name	First name	Roles	Guest star
		Announcer	No
Benny	Jack	Jack Benny	No
Benny	Sadye	Mary Livingston	No
Olsen	George	George Olsen	No
Shutta	Ethel	Ethel Shutta	No

Notes:

Notable	No script or recording exists for this show
Notable	Mary Livingston's first appearance

Date: 8/1/1932   **Sponsor:** Canada Dry   **City:** New York, NY

Recording Source: None   **Problems:** None

First line:

Jack: Hello, more people han you can get into a rumble seat..

Summary:

Jack discusses how time flies…Novelty Night…Japanese balancing act…Jack describes balancing stunts…trained dogs…Mary Livingston from Plainfield to return, Jack wonders where she is…Ethel reads letter from Mary…Jack and Mary are a little sweet on each other…Jack sends a sack of peanuts to Mary

Cast:

Last name	First name	Roles	Guest star
		Announcer	No
Benny	Jack	Jack Benny	No
Frey	Fran	Fran Frey	No
Gardner	Dick Hotcha	Dick Hotcha Gardner	No
Olsen	George	George Olsen	No
Shutta	Ethel	Ethel Shutta	No
Small	Paul	Paul Small	No

Songs:

Order	Title	Performers	Vocal
1	Marietta	Paul Small	Yes
2	My Little Dreamboat	Ethel Shutta	Yes
3	Circus Days	Fran Frey	Yes
4	Holding My Honey's Hand	Ethel Shutta	Yes
5	Sentimental Gentleman	Dick Hotcha Gardner	Yes

Notes:

Text of Mary's letter to Jack:

Dear Jack: You probably don't remember me, but I'm the girl who came up to the studio Wednesday night. Remember me…Mary? I'm sorry I can't be with you tonight, but you see I have been very busy helping mother with the dishes as she has a sore thumb from trying to tune you out on our radio…and, besides that, our cat had kittens today. I will send you one when they are ripe. Thanks very much for the picture you sent me. I have pictures of all the movie stars…Gable, Montgomery, Chevalier and all of them…your picture looks so sweet. I got it right between Frankenstein and Jimmy Durante……I only wish your picture was a little larger so it could cover the hole in the wall…."

Date: 8/3/1932   **Sponsor:** Canada Dry   **City:** New York, NY

Recording Source: None   **Problems:** None

First line:
Jack: Hello, male, female and fan mail customers…

Summary:
Jack shills a watch, razor blade, etc…Mary shows up with her friend, Dot…Jack gives huge introduction to health expert, Professor J. Quagmire…Professor gives health tips, although coughing profusely…brings Olympic Games to the air…Jack introduces Mary to the cast…Jack introduces left-over novelty, trained fleas…flea pulls ten-ton truck…Jack offers to take Mary home

Cast:

Last name	First name	Roles	Guest star
Baldwin	Harry	Customer 3	No
Benny	Jack	Jack Benny	No
Benny	Sadye	6, Mary Livingston	No
Frey	Fran	Fran Frey, Customer 5	No
Gardner	Dick Hotcha	Dick Hotcha Gardner	No
Herman	Milton	Professor J. Quagmire	No
Olsen	George	George Olsen	No
Ross	Dorothy	Customer 2, Dot	No
Shutta	Ethel	Ethel Shutta, Customer 4	No
Small	Paul	Paul Small, Customer 1	No
Wallington	Jimmy	Jimmy Wallington	No

Songs:

Order	Title	Performers	Vocal
1	Old Man of the Mountain	Dick Hotcha Gardner	Yes
2	Lost in Your Arms	Paul Small	Yes
3	Tender Child	Fran Frey	Yes
3	Tender Child	Ethel Shutta	Yes
4	I'll Never Be the Same	Ethel Shutta	Yes
5	All the World is Waiting for the Sunrise	Ethel Shutta	Yes

Notes:

Notable	Mary is listed as "Sadye" in the script

Date: 8/8/1932   **Sponsor:** Canada Dry   **City:** New York, NY

Recording Source: None   **Problems:** None

First line:
Jack: Say, Hicks, do you think this is a waste of time? I mean, does anyone listen in to our program?

Summary:
Cast feels poorly...guest star Paul Revere, a marathoner...tested Canada Dry in the wilds of Borneo, representative gave natives a glass of Canada Dry and they ate him with it...Mary Livingston returns...Mary's father is a doctor...Jack is jealous of Paul Small...Mary tells a story about a man on a train...he believed in reincarnation (loved flowers)...story goes on and on...Jack takes Mary home again

Cast:

Last name	First name	Roles	Guest star
Benny	Jack	Jack Benny	No
Benny	Sadye	Mary Livingston	No
Conn	Harry	Paul Revere	No
Frey	Fran	Fran Frey	No
Gardner	Dick Hotcha	Dick Hotcha Gardner	No
Hicks	George	George Hicks	No
Olsen	George	George Olsen	No
Shutta	Ethel	Ethel Shutta	No
Small	Paul	Paul Small	No

Songs:

Order	Title	Performers	Vocal
1	The Tartar's Darter	Fran Frey	Yes
2	Another Night Alone	Paul Small	Yes
3	I Love You, Dear	Ethel Shutta	Yes
3	I Love You, Dear	Dick Hotcha Gardner	Yes
4	All-American Girl	Paul Small	Yes
5	So To Bed	Paul Small	Yes
5	So To Bed	Ethel Shutta	Yes

Notes:

Date: 8/10/1932   **Sponsor:** Canada Dry   **City:** New York, NY

Recording Source: None   **Problems:** None

First line:
Jack: Hello, folks of the wave length of the people of the radio network audience...this is Jack Kilocycle, coming to you through 760 Bennys.

Summary:
Reporter wants dope on the program, Jack sends him to Paul Small...reporter interviews Jack and cast...phone call comes in for reporter, he drops them and goes to interview Russ Columbo...listener asks why they don't give out more prizes...starts contest for guessing names of celebrities...another reporter shows up and Jack shoots him

Cast:

Last name	First name	Roles	Guest star
Ashe	Ralph	Shakespearean actor	No
Benny	Jack	Jack Benny	No
Conn	Harry	Lloyd Ribbons	No
Frey	Fran	Fran Frey, reporter 2	No
Gardner	Dick Hotcha	Dick Hotcha	No
Hicks	George	George Hicks	No
Olsen	George	George Olsen	No
Ross	Dorothy	Sister	No
Shutta	Ethel	Ethel Shutta	No
Silvers	Sid	Jessel J. Cantor	No
Small	Paul	Paul Small	No

Songs:

Order	Title	Performers	Vocal
1	Strange Interlude	George Olsen	No
2	We're Dancing Together Again	Paul Small	Yes
3	Let's Knock Knees	Ethel Shutta	Yes
3	Let's Knock Knees	Fran Frey	Yes
4	As Long As I Live	Ethel Shutta	Yes
5	Ol Man of the Mountain	Dick Hotcha Gardner	Yes

Notes:

Date: 8/15/1932   **Sponsor:** Canada Dry   **City:** New York, NY

Recording Source: None   **Problems:** None

First line:
Announcer: And now Jack Benny…just a moment, please, ladies and gentlemen. Say, George, have you seen Jack?

Summary:
Jack is late for the program…George Olsen says that Jack is cheap…Jack shows up and was hit by a truck…Opportunity Night…Three Built-Well Sisters sing "Would You Like to Take a Walk"…man says he's anemic (imitates people), imitates Chevalier, Crosby…Jack chokes him…Shakespearean actor does his bit (was in "Grand-us Hotel-us")…telegram from Mary Livingston, thinks show is swell

Cast:

Last name	First name	Roles	Guest star
		Announcer	No
Benny	Jack	Jack Benny	No
Frey	Fran	Fran Frey	No
Gardner	Dick Hotcha	Dick Hotcha Gardner	No
Olsen	George	George Olsen	No
Shutta	Ethel	Ethel Shutta	No
Small	Paul	Paul Small	No

Songs:

Order	Title	Performers	Vocal
1	Rhumbatism	Dick Hotcha Gardner	Yes
2	Honey Smile at Me	Ethel Shutta	Yes
3	In Old Vienna	Paul Small	Yes
4	Angel Cake Lady	Ethel Shutta	Yes
5	From AM to PM	Fran Frey	Yes

Notes:

Notable	First Sister act ("Chicken Sisters" type) gag

Date: 8/17/1932   **Sponsor:** Canada Dry   **City:** New York, NY

Recording Source: None   **Problems:** None

First line:
Jack: Hello, followers of mystery.

Summary:
The Big Night...Jack asked if Olsen made cracks about him...Jack says he's the "master" of the program...Mary gets upset that other people are giving Jack a rough time...announces winners of brain teaser contest...colleges appreciate intellectual humor...Jack played football at Canada Dry University, he was a nickel-back...introduces Three Little Greeks and other "celebrities"...Mary offers to be Jack's secretary, he hires her at $20 a week...Jack dictates letter to sponsor, Mary writes letter to her mother...Jack offers to take Mary home, but she made a date with "Strange Inter-Luke"

Cast:

Last name	First name	Roles	Guest star
		Luke Warm	No
		Concertino	No
		Alec-trician	No
Baldwin	Harry	Banjo	No
Benny	Jack	Jack Benny	No
Benny	Sadye	Mary Livingston	No
Conn	Harry	Nicholas	No
Frey	Fran	Fran Frey	No
Hicks	George	George Hicks	No
Olsen	George	George Olsen	No
Shutta	Ethel	Ethel Shutta	No
Small	Paul	Paul Small	No

Songs:

Order	Title	Performers	Vocal
1	Libestraum	George Olsen	No
2	I Guess I'll Have to Change My Plans	Ethel Shutta	Yes
3	I'm Yours for Tonight	Ethel Shutta	Yes
3	I'm Yours for Tonight	Fran Frey	Yes
4	After Tonight	Paul Small	Yes
5	Up Down	Ethel Shutta	Yes

Notes:

Notable	Mary offers to be Jack's secretary
Running gag	Mary's mother communication

Date: 8/22/1932   **Sponsor:** Canada Dry   **City:** New York, NY

Recording Source: None   **Problems:** None

First line:
Jack: Hello, fun-seekers...don't be alarmed. This is not a parade passing your house nor a concert in your backyard.

Summary:
Carnival Night...Shutta has her weight guessed...Jack and Olsen want to see dancing girls...Jack and Olsen get hot dogs...hot dog salesman says Jack is rotten, Mary defends him...Mary wants to sit with Jack on the roller coaster...Jack is barker for a side show...interviews Bearded Lady, tattooed boy, and siamese twins...Hotcha Gardner taking Mary home

Cast:

Last name	First name	Roles	Guest star
		Announcer	No
Ashe	Ralph	Hot dog salesman	No
Baldwin	Harry	Carnival barker	No
Benny	Jack	Jack Benny	No
Conn	Harry	Corn salesman, Toto tattooed boy	No
Frey	Fran	Fran Frey, Weight guesser	No
Gardner	Dick Hotcha	Dick Hotcha Gardner, Balloon salesman, rube	No
Livingston	Mary	Mary Livingston	No
Olsen	George	George Olsen	No
Ross	Dorothy	Righta	No
Shutta	Ethel	Ethel Shutta, Lefta	No
Shutta	Jack	Dancing girl barker	No
Small	Paul	Paul Small, Madame Gilletta	No

Songs:

Order	Title	Performers	Vocal
1	Carnival Days are Here Again	Fran Frey	Yes
2	Rockabye Moon	Ethel Shutta	Yes
3	What a Sweet Sensation	Fran Frey	Yes
4	As Long As Love Lives On	Paul Small	Yes
5	The Little German Band	Ethel Shutta	Yes

Notes:

Notable	Mary is now called "Mary" in script, not "Sadye"
Notable	First show where plot takes place almost entirely outside the studio

Date: 8/24/1932   **Sponsor:** Canada Dry   **City:** New York, NY

Recording Source: None   **Problems:** None

First line:
Announcer: Where's Jack Benny?...George, have you seen Jack?

Summary:
Three people waiting for Jack because he hasn't paid them...Jack broadcasting from cellar to avoid them...Request Night...people leave and Jack comes up...fan letter requesting another violin solo from Jack (his father)...announcer does ad over solo, then carpenter starts hammering...fan letter from J. Thespian Legit asks for a play...announces skit...Abercrombie leaves for a trip, Seneca's lover arrives to play bridge...Abercrombie returns for his hat ("It's raining in Havana")

Cast:

Last name	First name	Roles	Guest star
Benny	Jack	Jack Benny, T. Twombley Twilliams	No
Conn	Harry	Groom	No
Coulter	Doug	Tailor	No
Frey	Fran	Fran Frey, barber, carpenter	No
Gardner	Dick Hotcha	Dick Hotcha Gardner	No
Hicks	George	George Hicks	No
Olsen	George	George Olsen, Abercrombie	No
Ross	Dorothy	Landlady	No
Shutta	Ethel	Ethel Shutta, Seneca	No
Small	Paul	Paul Small, Parker	No

Songs:

Order	Title	Performers	Vocal
1	Thou Shalt Not	Dick Hotcha Gardner	Yes
2	Always In My Heart	Ethel Shutta	Yes
3	Soft Lights and Sweet Music	Jack Benny	No
4	Two Poor People	Ethel Shutta	Yes
4	Two Poor People	Fran Frey	Yes
5	Moonlight On the River	Paul Small	Yes
6	I'm That Way about Broadway	Ethel Shutta	Yes

Notes:

Notable	First time Jack plays exercises on violin
Notable	First skit
Skit	She Lived...She Loved...She Learned...She Loafed...He Left...and She Laughed

Date: 8/29/1932   **Sponsor:** Canada Dry   **City:** New York, NY

Recording Source: None   **Problems:** None

First line:
Jack: Hello, John Q. Public…this is er…this is er…

Summary:
Jack has an identity crisis…woman calls asking for Sports Night…introduces Sara Zen, lady golfer…boy came with Mary to play hookey…introduces wrestlers for a match, Jack does play by play, everyone gets mixed up in the match…Jimmy Wallington hurt…Jack dictates letter to Mary, there's no ribbon in her typewriter

Cast:

Last name	First name	Roles	Guest star
		Boy	No
		Wrestler	No
Benny	Jack	Jack Benny	No
Frey	Fran	Fran Frey, Pasha Kamel	No
Gardner	Dick Hotcha	Dick Hotcha Gardner	No
Kelcey	?	Miss Sara Zen	No
Livingston	Mary	Mary Livingston	No
Olsen	George	George Olsen	No
Shutta	Ethel	Ethel Shutta	No
Small	Paul	Paul Small	No
Wallington	Jimmy	Announcer	No

Songs:

Order	Title	Performers	Vocal
1	Wedding of the Painted Doll	George Olsen	No
2	When Mother Played the Organ	Ethel Shutta	Yes
3	All American Girl	Paul Small	Yes
4	My Baby's Gone	Fran Frey	Yes
4	My Baby's Gone	Ethel Shutta	Yes
5	Yeah Man	Dick Hotcha Gardner	Yes

Notes:

Date: 8/31/1932   **Sponsor:** Canada Dry   **City:** New York, NY

Recording Source: None   **Problems:** None

First line:
Announcer: Say, what's the matter with Jack Benny? Looks like he's late again...Grab the mike, Ethel.

Summary:
Indoor Sports Night...Jack late because he got stopped for speeding...cast discusses their favorite indoor sports...Jack and Jimmy argue about emphasis...Mary's favorite is "Who's got the rent?"...Jack interviews cat and fly...skit Three O'Clock in the Morning...parents are awakened by baby crying...parents try to soothe him, but he wants Canada Dry...solar eclipse today, introduces Sun and Moon

Cast:

Last name	First name	Roles	Guest star
Barker	Brad	Meriah the cat, fly, sneezer	No
Benny	Jack	Jack Benny, Mr. Gus Unt-heit	No
Conn	Harry	Motorcycle cop, Sun	No
Frey	Fran	Fran Frey, Moon	No
Livingston	Mary	Mary Livingston	No
Olsen	George	George Olsen	No
Shutta	Ethel	Ethel Shutta, Mrs. Cachoo	No
Small	Paul	Paul Small	No
Wallington	Jimmy	Jimmy Wallington	No

Songs:

Order	Title	Performers	Vocal
1	Let's Have a Party	Fran Frey	Yes
2	When the Sun Kisses the World Good-Bye	Ethel Shutta	Yes
3	Mariella	Paul Small	Yes
4	Another Night Alone	George Olsen	No
5	Harlem Moon	Ethel Shutta	Yes

Notes:

Skit	Three O'Clock in the Morning

Date: 9/5/1932   **Sponsor:** Canada Dry   **City:** New York, NY

Recording Source: None   **Problems:** None

First line:
Jack: Hello, atmosphere customers...remember me?

Summary:
Cast is playing at the Capitol Theatre, invites listeners...Jack and Olson criticize each other's appearance...Jack and Shutta discuss the eclipse...Hicks tells about his vacation...introduces the Meyer of Schenectady, going to fight Schmelling...stages Labor Day Parade...Mary reads poem for Labor Day

Cast:

Last name	First name	Roles	Guest star
Benny	Jack	Jack Benny	No
Benny	Sadye	Mary Livingston	No
Conn	Harry	Meyer McKee Walker	No
Frey	Fran	Fran Frey, street cleaner	No
Gardner	Dick Hotcha	Dick Hotcha Gardner	No
Hicks	George	Announcer	No
Olsen	George	George Olsen	No
Shutta	Ethel	Ethel Shutta	No
Small	Paul	Paul Small	No

Songs:

Order	Title	Performers	Vocal
1	Let's Knock Knees	Ethel Shutta	Yes
1	Let's Knock Knees	Fran Frey	Yes
2	Goodbye to Summer Love	Paul Small	Yes
3	I Can't Believe It's True	Ethel Shutta	Yes
4	I Love a Parade	Fran Frey	Yes
5	You're Telling Me	Fran Frey	Yes

Notes:

Running gag	Mary's poem

Date: 9/7/1932   **Sponsor:** Canada Dry   **City:** New York, NY

Recording Source: None   **Problems:**   None

First line:
Jack: Hello, more people than last week.

Summary:
Welcomes audience back from vacations…Jack upset that Hicks keeps interrupting with a commercial…Jack and Shutta tell corny jokes from Capitol Theatre act…Olsen tells "It's not your father" riddle…Jack reads fan mail, Mrs. Gefilto Fish thinks parade was a fraud…guest star, plane mechanic…mechanic takes off in plane and sends telegrams back to studio, flies around the world…Mary asks if Jack sent her flowers

Cast:

Last name	First name	Roles	Guest star
Baldwin	Harry	"Hooray" man	No
Benny	Jack	Jack Benny	No
Benny	Sadye	Mary Livingston	No
Frey	Fran	Fran Frey	No
Gardner	Dick Hotcha	Dick Hotcha Gardner, telegram boy	No
Hicks	George	Announcer	No
Olsen	George	George Olsen	No
Shutta	Ethel	Ethel Shutta	No
Small	Paul	Paul Small, J. Refuel Tank	No

Songs:

Order	Title	Performers	Vocal
1	You're Just About Right for Me	Dick Hotcha Gardner	Yes
2	Always in My Heart	Ethel Shutta	Yes
3	I Played Fiddle for the Czar	Fran Frey	Yes
4	Three's a Crowd	Paul Small	Yes
5	Angelcake Lady	Ethel Shutta	Yes
5	Angelcake Lady	Fran Frey	Yes

Notes:

Date: 9/12/1932   **Sponsor:** Canada Dry   **City:** New York, NY

Recording Source: None   **Problems:** None

First line:
Jack: Hello, scandal seekers! This is Jack Benny, the Earth Galloper, coming to you with the late news events, thru the courtesy of the Morning Grapefruit.

Summary:
News headlines...new contest for cutting up celebrity pictures...skit School Days...Mary brings teacher a wet sponge because it's swell...Jack introduces Lilyan Tashman

Cast:

Last name	First name	Roles	Guest star
Benny	Jack	Jack Benny, teacher	No
Benny	Sadye	Mary Livingston	No
Conn	Harry	Samuel	No
Frey	Fran	Fran Frey	No
Gardner	Dick Hotcha	Dick Hotcha Gardner	No
Hicks	George	Announcer	No
Olsen	George	George Olsen	No
Shutta	Ethel	Ethel Shutta	No
Small	Paul	Paul Small	No
Tashman	Lilyan	Lilyan Tashman	Yes

Songs:

Order	Title	Performers	Vocal
1	March on to Oregon	George Olsen	No
2	Harlem Moon	Ethel Shutta	Yes
3	So Ashamed	Paul Small	Yes
4	It's Gonna Be You	George Olsen	No
5	And So To Bed	Paul Small	Yes
5	And So to Bed	Ethel Shutta	Yes

Notes:

Skit	School Days

Date: 9/14/1932   **Sponsor:** Canada Dry   **City:** New York, NY

Recording Source: None   **Problems:** None

First line:
Jack: Hello, if I'm not intruding.

Summary:
Jack wants to hear a song about a vest...Jack reads contest entries...announces rodeo...interviews cattle puncher and cowhand...Jack does rodeo play-by-play...announces guy riding the subway...Jack gave Mary a paper box to keep candy in...Mary asks Olsen to put in a good word for her with Jack...Jack offers to take Mary home, but she's going home with Gardner

Cast:

Last name	First name	Roles	Guest star
Ashe	Ralph	Cayenne Pepper, Myer, subway rider	No
Barker	Brad	Dog	No
Benny	Jack	Jack Benny, Rattlesnake Benny	No
Benny	Sadye	Mary Livingston	No
Conn	Harry	Arsenic Pete	No
Frey	Fran	Fran Frey, Willy, bus driver	No
Gardner	Dick Hotcha	Dick Hotcha Gardner	No
Hicks	George	Announcer	No
Olsen	George	George Olsen	No
Ross	Dorothy	Widow Myer	No
Shutta	Ethel	Ethel Shutta	No

Songs:

Order	Title	Performers	Vocal
1	All American Girl	Fran Frey	Yes
2	Stucco In the Sticks	Ethel Shutta	Yes
3	Ten Hours a Day	Fran Frey	Yes
4	It's From Hunger	Ethel Shutta	Yes
5	Keep Away	Dick Hotcha Gardner	Yes

Notes:

Date: 9/19/1932   **Sponsor:** Canada Dry   **City:** New York, NY

Recording Source: None   **Problems:** None

First line:
Jack: Hello, entertainment seekers…this is Jack Benny…not a talking picture…not a phonograph record…not a double…

Summary:
Guest stars Jack invited don't show…Jack calls up talent agency to send talent…Jack and Ethel discuss his work in pictures…talent arrives…chambermaid of the Grand Hotel does imitations…contortionist gets stuck…man sings about his girl Iodine, officer arrests him…Mary says she thinks Jack has romantic appeal

Cast:

Last name	First name	Roles	Guest star
Baldwin	Harry	Officer	No
Benny	Jack	Jack Benny	No
Benny	Sadye	Mary Livingston	No
Borger	Bobby	Bobby Borger	No
Conn	Harry	Ralph Sunz-fran-sanlyz	No
Frey	Fran	Fran Frey, Frank P. Twist	No
Gardner	Dick Hotcha	Dick Hotcha Gardner	No
Hicks	George	George Hicks	No
Olsen	George	George Olsen	No
Shutta	Ethel	Ethel Shutta	No
Stewart	Blanche	Bridget	No

Songs:

Order	Title	Performers	Vocal
1	Eleanor	George Olsen	No
2	Always in Your Heart	Ethel Shutta	Yes
3	Mickey Mouse	Fran Frey	Yes
4	Night Fall	Bobby Borger	Yes
5	Tiger Rag	George Olsen	No

Notes:

Date: 9/21/1932   **Sponsor:** Canada Dry   **City:** New York, NY

Recording Source: None   **Problems:** None

First line:
Announcer: Pardon me a moment, ladies and gentlemen. We seem to be in hot water tonight.

Summary:
Jack and Olsen arrested going 72 miles an hour…Jack talks with other prisoners…Jack tells a story about three lobsters…Mary visits Jack, brings lawyer who questions Jack…Gardiner visits to borrow Jack's car

Cast:

Last name	First name	Roles	Guest star
Ashe	Ralph	Bank robber, lawyer	No
Benny	Jack	Jack Benny	No
Benny	Sadye	Mary Livingston	No
Borger	Bobby	Officer	No
Conn	Harry	Limousine thief	No
Frey	Fran	Fran Frey	No
Gardner	Dick Hotcha	Dick Hotcha Gardner	No
Hicks	George	Announcer	No
Olsen	George	George Olsen	No
Schlossberg	?	Janitor	No
Shutta	Ethel	Ethel Shutta	No

Songs:

Order	Title	Performers	Vocal
1	Liebestraum	George Olsen	No
2	Such is Life	Ethel Shutta	Yes
3	You're Telling Me	Fran Frey	Yes
4	Million Dollar Baby	Ethel Shutta	Yes
4	Million Dollar Baby	Fran Frey	Yes
5	Just Knock At My Door	Dick Hotcha Gardner	Yes

Notes:

Date: 9/26/1932   **Sponsor:** Canada Dry   **City:** New York, NY

Recording Source: None   **Problems:** None

First line:
Jack: Hello, aerial neighbors...you guessed it.

Summary:
Russian Night...Russian dancers perform and get deported...announces skit Chow Service...Vonya waiting for husband, Boris visits...angry at Nicholai because he was drinking (Canada Dry)...Mary going home with boatman

Cast:

Last name	First name	Roles	Guest star
Ashe	Ralph	Vulgar boatman	No
Benny	Jack	Jack Benny, Rubbinoff, Boris Plaster	No
Benny	Sadye	Mary Livingston	No
Frey	Fran	Fran Frey	No
Gardner	Dick Hotcha	Dick Hotcha Gardner	No
Hicks	George	George Hicks, Nicholai	No
Olsen	George	George Olsen, Ivan	No
Shutta	Ethel	Ethel Shutta, Vonya	No

Songs:

Order	Title	Performers	Vocal
1	Pink Elephants	George Olsen	No
2	Come West Little Girl	Ethel Shutta	Yes
3	Thanksgiving	Dick Hotcha Gardner	Yes
4	Just Couldn't Say Goodbye	Ethel Shutta	Yes
5	Fiddle for the Czar	Fran Frey	Yes

Notes:

Date: 9/28/1932   **Sponsor:** Canada Dry   **City:** New York, NY

Recording Source: None   **Problems:** None

First line:
Jack: Well, as Hicks says - we're dedicating our program tonight to the Retail Druggists who are holding their Convention in Boston this week.

Summary:
News headlines...Hicks explains why he has to butt in about Canada Dry all the time...fan letter asks for a picture of Jack falling out of an airplane...Gardner asked Mary to marry him last night, Jack advises against it...Jack upset...description of Mickey Schmelling-Max Walker fight...Jack asks Olsen to send Gardner on vacation, he won't do it

Cast:

Last name	First name	Roles	Guest star
		Walker	No
Benny	Jack	Jack Benny	No
Benny	Sadye	Mary Livingston	No
Conn	Harry	Schmelling	No
Frey	Fran	Fran Frey	No
Gardner	Dick Hotcha	Dick Hotcha Gardner	No
Hicks	George	Announcer	No
Marshall	Dave	Dave Marshall	No
Olsen	George	George Olsen	No
Shutta	Ethel	Ethel Shutta	No

Songs:

Order	Title	Performers	Vocal
1	Song of India	George Olsen	No
2	Sweetheart Hour	Dave Marshall	Yes
3	After Twelve O'Clock	Ethel Shutta	Yes
4	Say It Isn't So	Dave Marshall	Yes
5	Shine On Your Shoes	Fran Frey	Yes

Notes:

Date: 10/3/1932   **Sponsor:** Canada Dry   **City:** New York, NY

Recording Source: None   **Problems:** None

First line:
Jack: Hello, you faithful followers of this what-chu-ma-call-it.

Summary:
World Series Night...Canada Dry Gingeralians and New York Yanks...Jack does play-by-play...interviews people about the game, quizzes Theda Bara on baseball...more play-by-play...Jack hits a home run...game rained out...Jack goes out with Theda Bara, Mary gets mad and breaks up with Gardner

Cast:

Last name	First name	Roles	Guest star
Ashe	Ralph	Bugs Baer, Judge Landis, umpire	No
Benny	Jack	Jack Benny	No
Benny	Sadye	Mary Livingston	No
Conn	Harry	Senor Gomez	No
Frey	Fran	Fran Frey	No
Gardner	Dick Hotcha	Dick Hotcha Gardner	No
Hicks	George	Announcer	No
Lazzeri	?	Italian	No
Marshall	Dave	Dave Marshall	No
Olsen	George	George Olsen	No
Shutta	Ethel	Ethel Shutta, Theda Bara	No

Songs:

Order	Title	Performers	Vocal
1	To Be or Not To Be Collegiate	Fran Frey	Yes
2	It Was Only a Summer Night's Dream	Dave Marshall	Yes
3	I Love You Lizzicato	Ethel Shutta	Yes
4	Walking in the Moonlight	Ethel Shutta	Yes
4	Walking in the Moonlight	Fran Frey	Yes
5	Margy	Dick Hotcha Gardner	Yes

Notes:

Date: 10/5/1932   **Sponsor:** Canada Dry   **City:** New York, NY

Recording Source: None   **Problems:** None

First line:
Jack: Hello, you lucky listeners…this is Jack Benny talking - remember?

Summary:
Jack has a bad cold…Jack says Mary is just a friend…Olsen invited Jack out and didn't pay the check…Jack has a conversation with himself…Jack asks Olsen to try to break up Mary and Hotcha, Olsen does the opposite…Jack describes Dave Marshall…travelogue of China…Jack narrates the film…on departure, hear "Listen to the German Band"…Jack reads a poem about Fall, cast leaves during the reading

Cast:

Last name	First name	Roles	Guest star
		Prop man	No
?	Jake	Jack's alter ego	No
Benny	Jack	Jack Benny	No
Benny	Sadye	Mary Livingston	No
Frey	Fran	Fran Frey	No
Gardner	Dick Hotcha	Dick Hotcha Gardner	No
Hicks	George	Announcer	No
Marshall	Dave	Dave Marshall	No
Olsen	George	George Olsen	No
Shutta	Ethel	Ethel Shutta	No

Songs:

Order	Title	Performers	Vocal
1	What a Sweet Sensation	Fran Frey	Yes
2	Hum a Tune	Ethel Shutta	Yes
3	Three Kisses	Dave Marshall	Yes
4	Harlem Moon	Ethel Shutta	Yes
5	Bugle Call Rag	Ethel Shutta	Yes

Notes:

Skit	Traveling Thru China

Date: 10/10/1932   **Sponsor:** Canada Dry   **City:** New York, NY

Recording Source: None   **Problems:** None

First line:
Mary: Hello, darling public…this is Jack Benny's secretary talking. Remember, hmmm?

Summary:
Mary filling in for Jack because he's late…Jack arrives, tailor kept him waiting…Jack and Ethel discuss Jack's new suit…Fall Program…new contest, send in silk representing the names of celebrities…Canada Dry football team in training…skit Grind Hotel…Boris makes love to dancer Ethel-co-vich…Mary going to Paris with String-a-line

Cast:

Last name	First name	Roles	Guest star
Benny	Jack	Jack Benny, Baron	No
Benny	Sadye	Mary Livingston, operator	No
Frey	Fran	Fran Frey, Ethel's manager	No
Gardner	Dick Hotcha	Dick Hotcha Gardner, bellhop	No
Hicks	George	George Hicks	No
Marshall	Dave	Dave Marshall	No
Olsen	George	George Olsen, String-a-line	No
Ross	Dorothy	Operator	No
Shutta	Ethel	Ethel Shutta, operator, Ethel-co-vitch	No

Songs:

Order	Title	Performers	Vocal
1	Get Yourself a Cup of Sunshine	George Olsen	No
2	My Silver Rose	Ethel Shutta	Yes
3	We're Alone	Dave Marshall	Yes
4	Meanest Gal in Town	Ethel Shutta	Yes
5	Sweet Muchacha	Dick Hotcha Gardner	Yes

Notes:

Skit	Grind Hotel

Date: 10/12/1932   **Sponsor:** Canada Dry   **City:** New York, NY

Recording Source: None   **Problems:** None

First line:
Jack: Hello, steady customers. This is Jack Gibbons Benny…

Summary:
News headlines…Columbus Day, Jack discusses Columbus' voyage…New York was bought from the Indians for one large bottle of Canada Dry…interviews Queen Isabella of Spain…interviews J. Fish-House Clam, first man to eat an oyster…Jack runs for a Chicago train to visit his family, Mary says she'll miss him…Mary goes home with Dave Marshall

Cast:

Last name	First name	Roles	Guest star
Benny	Jack	Jack Benny	No
Conn	Harry	J. Fish-House Clam	No
Frey	Fran	Fran Frey	No
Gardner	Dick Hotcha	Dick Hotcha Gardner	No
Hicks	George	George Hicks	No
Livingston	Mary	Mary Livingston	No
Marshall	Dave	Dave Marshall	No
Olsen	George	George Olsen	No
Shutta	Ethel	Ethel Shutta	No
Stewart	Blanche	Queen Isabella	No

Songs:

Order	Title	Performers	Vocal
1	I Beg Your Pardon Mademoiselle	Fran Frey	Yes
2	When Mother Played the Organ	Ethel Shutta	Yes
3	You'll Get By	Ethel Shutta	Yes
4	How Deep Is the Ocean	Dave Marshall	Yes
5	German Band	Ethel Shutta	Yes

Notes:

Date: 10/17/1932 **Sponsor:** Canada Dry **City:** New York, NY

Recording Source: None **Problems:** None

First line:
Olsen: Say, Hicks - I think we'll have to play another number.

Summary:
Jack is delayed getting to the studio from the train station...fade to train depot...Mary went to depot to meet Jack, they take a cab back to the studio...Olsen gave a party at the Automat...Jack tells Mary he likes her, she thinks he's too good for her...Jack tells about visiting his father in Lake Forest...Jack tells Shutta to put more fire in their love scenes, go over scene from Grind Hotel...Shutta does Garbo for her character...scene at front desk...Baron makes love to Ethelcovich again, String-a-line interrupts, then Prince-a-ling...Ethel keeps having men hide under the bed...travelogue for India, departing song is "I'll Be Glad When You're Dead, You Rascal You"

Cast:

Last name	First name	Roles	Guest star
?	Reggie	Tommy	No
Baldwin	Harry	Dave	No
Benny	Jack	Jack Benny, Baron, desk clerk	No
Frey	Fran	Fran Frey, cabbie	No
Gardner	Dick Hotcha	Dick Hotcha Gardner, porter	No
Hicks	George	George Hicks	No
Livingston	Mary	Mary Livingston, operator, Fraulein Flem-Flem	No
Marshall	Dave	Prince-a-ling-ling	No
Olsen	George	George Olsen, String-a-line	No
Shutta	Ethel	Ethel Shutta, Garbo, operator	No

Songs:

Order	Title	Performers	Vocal
1	All-American Girl	Fran Frey	Yes
2	Cop On the Beat	Ethel Shutta	Yes
3	Fit as a Fiddle	Fran Frey	Yes
4	Thanksgiving	Dick Hotcha Gardner	Yes
5	So to Bed	Ethel Shutta	Yes

Notes:

Notable	In script, some of Mary's lines are listed with the name "Mary" and others with "Sadye"
Notable	First train depot scene

Date: 10/19/1932   **Sponsor:** Canada Dry   **City:** New York, NY

Recording Source: None   **Problems:** None

First line:
Hicks: Who is it? Jack: It's me.

Summary:
Jack tries to tell a joke about Irishmen...Insurance man tries to sell Jack a policy...man tries to sell Jack a car...Mary upset because Jack played a love scene with Shutta...Jack tells Mary he's crazy about her (Hicks keeps interrupting)...Mary slaps him because she thought he said that her mouth reminded her of Canada Dry...the Big Fight between Herbert Hoover and Franklin Roosevelt...Jack does play-by-play...city/state puns...Mary apologizes to Jack, but goes home with Hicks...realtor tries to sell Jack lots

Cast:

Last name	First name	Roles	Guest star
Benny	Jack	Jack Benny	No
Conn	Harry	Death Valley Life Insurance man	No
Frey	Fran	Fran Frey, car salesman, realtor	No
Gardner	Dick Hotcha	Dick Hotcha Gardner	No
Herbert	Charley	Charley Herbert	No
Herbert	Grace	Grace Herbert	No
Hicks	George	George Hicks	No
Livingston	Mary	Mary Livingston	No
Marshall	Dave	Dave Marshall	No
Olsen	George	George Olsen	No
Shutta	Ethel	Ethel Shutta	No

Songs:

Order	Title	Performers	Vocal
1	You're Telling Me	Fran Frey	Yes
2	Now that I've Learned	Ethel Shutta	Yes
3	Let's Put Out the Lights	Charley Herbert	Yes
3	Let's Put Out the Lights	Grace Herbert	Yes
4	What's the Matter No Ice Today	Ethel Shutta	Yes
5	Knock at My Door	Dick Hotcha Gardner	Yes

Notes:

Date: 10/24/1932   **Sponsor:** Canada Dry   **City:** New York, NY

Recording Source: None   **Problems:** None

First line:
Hicks: As chairman of this political rally, I now wish to introduce to you that representative of humanity...a patriot...a social uplifter...for the people...for the people...and I might even say, for the the people...the honorable Jack Benny.

Summary:
Jack running for dog catcher, makes a speech...Jack's opponent makes a speech...Jack not happy with Mary's secretary work...Mary says she was seeing Hotcha to make Jack jealous...going to New Orleans...murder mystery Who Killed Mr. X? (headless victim)...courtroom scene, Jack examines witnesses...Minnie accuses Judge of the murder, he confesses

Cast:

Last name	First name	Roles	Guest star
Baker	Benny	J. Barkingham Mutt, Two Popgun Clarence	No
Benny	Jack	Jack Benny	No
Frey	Fran	Fran Frey, phantom, Blake prisoner	No
Gardner	Dick Hotcha	Dick Hotcha Gardner, Dugan	No
Hicks	George	George Hicks	No
Livingston	Mary	Mary Livingston	No
Marshall	Dave	Dave Marshall, Clerk	No
Olsen	George	George Olsen, Judge	No
Shutta	Ethel	Ethel Shutta, screamer, Minnie Skee	No

Songs:

Order	Title	Performers	Vocal
1	Aintcha Kinda Sorry Now	Fran Frey	Yes
2	Is I In Love I Is	Ethel Shutta	Yes
3	Play Fiddle Play	Dave Marshall	Yes
4	Angelcake Lady and Gingerbread Man	Ethel Shutta	Yes
5	Scat Song	Dick Hotcha Gardner	Yes

Notes:

Skit	Who Killed Mr. X?

Date: 10/26/1932 **Sponsor:** Canada Dry **City:** New York, NY

Recording Source: None **Problems:** None

First line:
Jack: Hello, folks, this is Jack O.O. McIntyre Benny.

Summary:
News headlines…skit Why Girls Leave Home…landlord to foreclose on family…Nellie wants to go to New York to make money, but is five cents shy of the fare…cashes in Canada Dry bottle…finance company comes to take everything…Nellie returns and pays them…Jack says goodbye to the cast

Cast:

Last name	First name	Roles	Guest star
Ashe	Ralph	Landlord	No
Benny	Jack	Jack Benny, father	No
Borger	Bobby	Bobby Borger	No
Frey	Fran	Fran Frey, usher	No
Gardner	Dick Hotcha	Dick Hotcha Gardner	No
Hicks	George	George Hicks	No
Livingston	Mary	Mary Livingston, Nellie Pickens	No
Olsen	George	George Olsen	No
Rice	Bob	Bob Rice, Sheriff	No
Shutta	Ethel	Ethel Shutta	No

Songs:

Order	Title	Performers	Vocal
1	Miss Liza Jane	Fran Frey	Yes
2	German Band	Ethel Shutta	Yes
3	That's How We Make Music	George Olsen	Yes
4	Who	Bobby Borger	Yes
4	Who	Fran Frey	Yes
4	Who	Bob Rice	Yes
5	How Deep Is the Ocean	Ethel Shutta	Yes

Notes:

Skit	Why Girls Leave Home

Date: 10/30/1932   **Sponsor:** Canada Dry   **City:** New Orleans, LA

Recording Source: None   **Problems:** None

First line:
Mary: Jack - oh Jack! Wake up.

Summary:
Mary and Jack on the train to New Orleans...chatty passenger keeps Jack awake...Jack and Mary arrive at studio and meet new cast...Jack describes Ted Weems...Weems introduces Andrea Marsh...Jack narrates travelogue of South America

Cast:

Last name	First name	Roles	Guest star
		Sound effects man	No
		Porter	No
		Vendor	No
Benny	Jack	Jack Benny	No
Conn	Harry	J. Herkimer Tilt	No
Cunliffe	Dick	Dick Cunliffe	No
Livingston	Mary	Mary Livingston	No
Marsh	Andrea	Andrea Marsh	No
Smith	?	Announcer	No
Weems	Ted	Ted Weems	No

Songs:

Order	Title	Performers	Vocal
1	Milenberg Joys	Ted Weems	No
2	Please	Ted Weems	No
3	One Man Band	Dick Cunliffe	Yes
4	Say It Isn't So	Andrea Marsh	Yes
5	Oh Moaner	Ted Weems	No

Notes:

Notable	First show with revised Canada Dry cast, via WSDU New Orleans
Skit	Travelogue of South America

Date: 11/3/1932 **Sponsor:** Canada Dry **City:** New Orleans, LA

Recording Source: None **Problems:** None

First line:
Jack: Hello, you-all...this is Jack Bennah talkin' from down heah in N'Orleans...

Summary:
Jack talks about the food in New Orleans...everyone talks in drawl...Jack argues with Ted Weems over medley, he wanted something southern...Jack had a party and left Weems with the check...skit Uncle Tom's Cabin...Simon Legree going to send Uncle Tom down the river...Eva comes in and dies...Legree wants to sell Tom to Warner Brothers...Legree beats up Tom and Liza runs away...Jack announces departure like a horse race

Cast:

Last name	First name	Roles	Guest star
		Announcer	No
Benny	Jack	Jack Benny, Uncle Tom	No
Conn	Harry	Simon Legree	No
Ingle	Red	Red Ingle, Eva	No
Livingston	Mary	Mary Livingston, Liza	No
Marsh	Andrea	Andrea Marsh	No
Tanner	Elmo	Elmo Tanner, Janitor	No
Washburn	Country	Country Washburn	No
Weems	Ted	Ted Weems	No

Songs:

Order	Title	Performers	Vocal
1	Louisiana Hayride	Ted Weems	No
2	Poor Butterfly/La Veeda/Siren Song	Ted Weems	No
3	Isn't It Romantic	Andrea Marsh	Yes
4	Ploddin' Along	Country Washburn	Yes
5	Sentimental Gentleman from Georgia	Country Washburn	Yes
5	Sentimental Gentleman from Georgia	Elmo Tanner	Yes
5	Sentimental Gentleman from Georgia	Red Ingle	Yes

Notes:

Skit	Uncle Tom's Cabin

Date: 11/6/1932 **Sponsor:** Canada Dry **City:** New Orleans, LA

Recording Source: None **Problems:** None

First line:
Jack: Hello, lots of people. This is Jack Benny, the Earth Galloper.

Summary:
News headlines...Jack describes Elmo Tanner...Mary bought a new dress to go vote...Mary thinks Jack should run for President...Jack makes a speech for the Canada Dry candidate, J. Mississippi Mud (Italian stooge)...Jack asks Mud questions, he is silent...running for President of Sicily...they find the candidate, gives goofy answers...cast tackles him

Cast:

Last name	First name	Roles	Guest star
		J. Mississippi Mud	No
Conn	Harry	J. Nickel Bach Unter-bottle	No
Gregory	Bob	Announcer	No
Gregory	Jack	Jack Benny	No
Ingle	Red	Red Ingle	No
Livingston	Mary	Mary Livingston	No
Marsh	Andrea	Andrea Marsh	No
Tanner	Elmo	Elmo Tanner	No
Weems	Ted	Ted Weems	No

Songs:

Order	Title	Performers	Vocal
1	Way Down Yonder in New Orleans	Ted Weems	No
2	Mimi/Same Old Moon	Elmo Tanner	No
3	Who'd Believe	Andrea Marsh	Yes
4	Don't Tell a Soul	Red Ingle	Yes
5	Picolo Pete	Ted Weems	No

Notes:

Date: 11/10/1932   **Sponsor:** Canada Dry   **City:** New Orleans, LA

Recording Source: None   **Problems:** None

First line:
Jack: Hello, members of our Thursday night club...this is Jack Benny calling the meeting to order

Summary:
Weems showed Jack around New Orleans, Jack will show Weems around New York...Jack likes Andrea Marsh, invites her to a dance...guest star, one man in South who voted for Hoover...happy with administration, hasn't worked in four years...skit The Hills of Old Kentucky...feud of the Diddleberrys and Van Twiffs started over cheating at solitaire...a Diddleberry pays Elvirey for a kiss...Van Twiffs band together and get shot one by one

Cast:

Last name	First name	Roles	Guest star
		Announcer	No
Benny	Jack	Jack Benny, Lem Van Twiff	No
Conn	Harry	Jay Lone Wolf, Abe	No
Conn	Mildred	Andrea Marsh's mother	No
Gibbs	Parker	Parker Gibbs	No
Ingle	Red	Luke	No
Livingston	Mary	Mary Livingston, Elvirey Van Twiff	No
Marsh	Andrea	Andrea Marsh	No
Tanner	Elmo	Elmo Tanner, Zeke	No
Vaughn	Wes	Wes Vaughn	No
Weems	Ted	Ted Weems	No

Songs:

Order	Title	Performers	Vocal
1	All American Girl	Ted Weems	No
2	How Deep Is the Ocean	Andrea Marsh	Yes
3	I Guess I'll Have to Change My Plans/Let's Put Out the Lights and Go to Sleep	Elmo Tanner	Yes
4	Just Another Love Affair	Wes Vaughn	Yes
5	I Cannot Tell You Why	Andrea Marsh	Yes

Notes:

Skit	The Hills of Old Kentucky

Date: 11/13/1932   **Sponsor:** Canada Dry   **City:** New Orleans, LA

Recording Source: None   **Problems:** None

First line:
Mary: Hello, anybody…this is Mary Livingston, of Plainfield, remember, hmmm? Jack is in New York now.

Summary:
Jack in New York producing "Rainbows of 1932"…Mary saw Jack to train and met a man on the way back…Weems asks Mary to have dinner with him, she's booked until April 9…Mary answers fan mail…Harry Conn argues with announcer Bob Gregory…Harry gives Mary guidance on romancing Jack, tells her to make him jealous…telegram from Jack about the show…play now called "Sunbeams of 1932", and Harry Conn describes the plot (sounds a little like Buck Benny)

Cast:

Last name	First name	Roles	Guest star
Conn	Harry	Harry	No
Gibbs	Parker	Parker Gibbs	No
Gregory	Bob	Bob Gregory	No
Ingle	Red	Red Ingle	No
Livingston	Mary	Mary Livingston	No
Marsh	Andrea	Andrea Marsh	No
Washburn	Country	Country Washburn	No
Weems	Ted	Ted Weems	No

Songs:

Order	Title	Performers	Vocal
1	Fit as a Fiddle	Parker Gibbs	Yes
2	Isn't It Romantic	Andrea Marsh	Yes
3	Louisiana Hayride	Red Ingle	Yes
4	This Is No Dream	Elmo Tanner	No
4	This Is No Dream	Red Ingle	Yes
5	Pink Elephants	Red Ingle	Yes
6	Ah, But I've Learned	Andrea Marsh	Yes
7	Lonesome Road	Country Washburn	Yes

Notes:

Notable	Harry Conn takes over most of the show in Jack's absence, even though Mary is official mistress of ceremonies
Notable	Jack does not appear

Date: 11/17/1932   **Sponsor:** Canada Dry   **City:** New York, NY

Recording Source: None   **Problems:** None

First line:
Jack: Remember, the fellow that's been running all over the country broadcasting?

Summary:
Jack talks about producing his show, invites Weems to invest…people waiting to talk to Jack and sell him plays…Douglas has play about Canada Dry…Sid Silvers wants to invest…interviews English comedian…Jack takes Mary home

Cast:

Last name	First name	Roles	Guest star
		Voices	No
		Lady playwright	No
		Jay Ethelbert Haddon-Hall	No
		Stagehand	No
		Eugene O'Neill Fitzwaffle	No
Benny	Jack	Jack Benny	No
Conn	Harry	Sid Silvers, office boy	No
Douglas	Paul	Paul Douglas	No
Livingston	Mary	Mary Livingston	No
Weems	Ted	Ted Weems	No

Songs:

Order	Title	Performers	Vocal
1	Somebody Stole My Girl	Ted Weems	No
2	Here Lies Love	Ted Weems	No
3	Oh Mona	Ted Weems	Yes
4	Please/Make Believe	Ted Weems	No
5	All American Girl	Ted Weems	No

Notes:

Notable	First "Play Ted" call for a music number

Date: 11/20/1932   **Sponsor:** Canada Dry   **City:** New York, NY

Recording Source: None   **Problems:** None

First line:
Jack: Jack Benny speaking with a bad cold...of the International Producing Company.

Summary:
Jack taking calls about his production company...reporter asks about Canada Dry...Weems playing at the Pennsylvania Hotel, Jack dancing with Weems' wife...Mary gives Jack suggestions on his play...Sid Silvers' grandmother died for the second time in four days...backer visits the office, Jack does pitch to him...people keep interrupting and asking for money...Sid has written a play and pitches it

Cast:

Last name	First name	Roles	Guest star
		Renting agent	No
		Messenger boy	No
Ashe	Ralph	MacGregor, Vincent Jay Schlepper	No
Benny	Jack	Jack Benny	No
Conn	Harry	Reporter	No
Douglas	Paul	Paul Douglas	No
Livingston	Mary	Mary Livingston	No
Marsh	Andrea	Andrea Marsh	No
Silvers	Sid	Sid Silvers	No
Weems	Ted	Ted Weems	No

Songs:

Order	Title	Performers	Vocal
1	With a Shine On Your Shoes	Ted Weems	No
2	Sweetheart Hour	Duet	Yes
3	Here Lies Love	Ted Weems	No
4	I'll Follow You	Male chorus	Yes
5	Who'd Believe	Andrea Marsh	Yes
6	What a Lucky Break	Ted Weems	No

Notes:

Date: 11/24/1932   **Sponsor:** Canada Dry   **City:** New York, NY

Recording Source: None   **Problems:** None

First line:
Mary: Hello, International Producing Company. Yes he's here…

Summary:
Call from Jack's father…Mary tying ribbons on everything in the office…play now called "Bubbles of 1932"…Jack discusses play music with Weems…they argue, Weems gets mad and leaves…reads play about woman in a glue factory, college skit…Sid went out to cash Schlepper's $100,000 check and got lost…interviews and hires MacTavish, the stage director from Scotland

Cast:

Last name	First name	Roles	Guest star
Benny	Jack	Jack Benny	No
Douglas	Paul	Paul Douglas	No
Doyle	Bart	MacTavish	No
Livingston	Mary	Mary Livingston	No
Weems	Ted	Ted Weems	No

Songs:

Order	Title	Performers	Vocal
1	Fit as a Fiddle	Ted Weems	No
2	So At Last It's Come to This	Ted Weems	No
3	Home	Ted Weems	No
4	I'm Sure of Everything But You	Ted Weems	No
5	Lucky Little Accident	Ted Weems	No

Notes:

Date: 11/27/1932   **Sponsor:** Canada Dry   **City:** New York, NY

Recording Source: None   **Problems:** None

First line:
Douglas: And now we bring you to Jack Benny and his International Producing Company...Well Jack, how are things going with that producing business of yours?

Summary:
Jack describes crazy ideas for his show...gets refusal telegrams from Barrymore, Chevalier, and Durante...Sid invites Mary to see "Of Thee I Sing"...Jack bets on a horse...Jack wants a big opening number with 30 girls...Jack looks for a theatre for his play, meets Schlepper...Jack wants to build his own theatre

Cast:

Last name	First name	Roles	Guest star
		Hobo	No
		Taxi driver	No
Ashe	Ralph	Vincent Jay Schlepper	No
Benny	Jack	Jack Benny	No
Douglas	Paul	Paul Douglas	No
Livingston	Mary	Mary Livingston	No
Silvers	Sid	Sid Silvers	No
Weems	Ted	Ted Weems	No

Songs:

Order	Title	Performers	Vocal
1	Rise and Shine	Ted Weems	No
2	I've Got a Right to Sing the Blues	Ted Weems	No
3	Same Old Moon	Ted Weems	No
4	Travellin'	Ted Weems	No
5	Pink Elephants	Ted Weems	No

Notes:

Notable	First use of the gag where seats closer to the stage are cheaper

Date: 12/1/1932 **Sponsor:** Canada Dry **City:** New York, NY

Recording Source: None **Problems:** None

First line:
Jack: (Disgusted) Good morning, Mary.

Summary:
Jack so crazy he looked for apples on his coat tree...Jack wants more efficiency in the office...chorus girls in rehearsal hall with Jack...Sid brings in his kid cousin who plays the violin...Mary complains that Jack has forgotten about her...introduces Schlepper to play cast, explains story to all of them...Jack wires his father for money

Cast:

Last name	First name	Roles	Guest star
		Junior	No
?	Helen	Tahellen Bankhead	No
Ashe	Ralph	Vincent Jay Schlepper	No
Benny	Jack	Jack Benny	No
Douglas	Paul	Paul Douglas	No
Livingston	Mary	Mary Livingston	No
Marsh	Andrea	Andrea Marsh	No
Silvers	Sid	Sid Silvers	No
Stewart	Blanche	Chorus girl	No
Weems	Ted	Ted Weems	No

Songs:

Order	Title	Performers	Vocal
1	Louisiana Hayride	Ted Weems	No
2	My River Home	Andrea Marsh	Yes
3	Was Wilst Du Haben	Ted Weems	No
4	Just a Little Home for the Old Folks	Ted Weems	No
5	Hats Off, Here Comes a Lady	Ted Weems	No

Notes:

Date: 12/4/1932   **Sponsor:** Canada Dry   **City:** New York, NY

Recording Source: None   **Problems:** None

First line:
Jack: Hello you lovers of static…

Summary:
Jack offers listeners a share of the show…leading man arriving from Hollywood…Weems demands a contract…leading man arrives (Reno Nevada), Jack interviews him…Nevada plays a love scene with Mary…Sid Silvers went looking for talent, tells corny riddles

Cast:

Last name	First name	Roles	Guest star
		Chorus girls	No
		Bill collector	No
		Reno Nevada	No
Ashe	Ralph	Vincent Jay Schlepper	No
Benny	Jack	Jack Benny	No
Douglas	Paul	Paul Douglas	No
Livingston	Mary	Mary Livingston	No
Silvers	Sid	Sid Silvers	No
Weems	Ted	Ted Weems	No

Songs:

Order	Title	Performers	Vocal
1	Look Who's Here	Ted Weems	No
2	Take Me In Your Arms	Ted Weems	No
3	One Man Band	Ted Weems	No
4	I'll Never Have to Dream Again	Ted Weems	No
5	It's Winter Again	Ted Weems	No

Notes:

Date: 12/8/1932   **Sponsor:** Canada Dry   **City:** New York, NY

Recording Source: None   **Problems:**   None

First line:
Jack: Jackie Benny - remember, hm? You know, the program where I tell a joke and Ted Weems plays a number?

Summary:
Jack has to get rid of his producing company…Jack asks Marsh why she's not been talking much to him…Schlepper shows up for status, Jack tells him he's staying in radio…Schlepper going into automobiles…fan letter demands a play…sequel to "Dinner at Eight" called "Garbage at Nine", Jack describes the whole play…landlord comes for the rent, Mary's French maid has an Irish dialect…chauffeur drives Mary to the poorhouse…repeating Grand Hotel next show

Cast:

Last name	First name	Roles	Guest star
		Chauffeur	No
		Laundry man	No
		Usher	No
		Constant Headache	No
Ashe	Ralph	Schlepper, Thorndike	No
Benny	Jack	Jack Benny	No
Douglas	Paul	Paul Douglas	No
Livingston	Mary	Mary Livingston	No
Marsh	Andrea	Andrea Marsh	No
Stewart	Blanche	Mademoiselle Fifi	No
Weems	Ted	Ted Weems	No

Songs:

Order	Title	Performers	Vocal
1	Shine On Your Shoes	Ted Weems	No
2	A Boy and a Girl Were Dancing	Andrea Marsh	Yes
3	Low Tide	Ted Weems	No
4	My Darling	Ted Weems	No
5	We'll See it Through	Ted Weems	No

Notes:

Date: 12/11/1932   **Sponsor:** Canada Dry   **City:** New York, NY

Recording Source: None   **Problems:** None

First line:
Douglas: Remember Thursday night Jack Benny disposed of his International Producing Company and returned the money to Schlepper?

Summary:
Jack discusses men's fashions…salesman wants Jack to test drive a car, then Weems…skit Grind Hotel…front desk scene…Baron makes love to Rusinskya

Cast:

Last name	First name	Roles	Guest star
		Rusinskya	No
Benny	Jack	Jack Benny, clerk, Baron	No
Conn	Harry	FOB Automobile man	No
Douglas	Paul	Paul Douglas	No
Ingle	Red	Kringelein	No
Livingston	Mary	Mary Livingston, operator, Fraulein Flam-flam	No
Marsh	Andrea	Andrea Marsh, Operator	No
Weems	Ted	Ted Weems, Rusinskya manager	No

Songs:

Order	Title	Performers	Vocal
1	Turn Out the Light	Ted Weems	No
2	Willow, Weep for Me	Ted Weems	No
3	Panhandle Pete	Ted Weems	No
4	Till Tomorrow	Ted Weems	No
5	We'll See It Through	Ted Weems	No

Notes:

Skit	Grind Hotel

Date: 12/15/1932 **Sponsor:** Canada Dry **City:** New York, NY

Recording Source: None **Problems:** None

First line:
Jack: Hello, Christmas shoppers…this is Jack Benny, your boy-friend, talking.

Summary:
Jack talks about Christmas shopping…Mary wasn't paid for being the phone operator…guest star, Vulgarian violinist Senor Mox-Nix-Ouse…does violin tricks…Jack tells a story about a dollar and a penny fighting…Jack and Mary go to the soda fountain…clerk doesn't like the show…Mary asks what Jack is buying her for Christmas

Cast:

Last name	First name	Roles	Guest star
Benny	Jack	Jack Benny	No
Douglas	Paul	Paul Douglas	No
Gibbs	Parker	Clerk	No
Ingle	Red	Canada Dry customer	No
Livingston	Mary	Mary Livingston, Gracie Allen	No
Marsh	Andrea	Andrea Marsh, Lollipop customer	No
Saranoff	?	Senor Mox-Nix-Ouse	No
Stewart	Blanche	1st clerk	No
Tanner	Elmo	Window pane customer	No
Washburn	Country	Jellybean customer	No
Weems	Ted	Ted Weems	No

Songs:

Order	Title	Performers	Vocal
1	Sing (It's Good for You)	Ted Weems	No
2	At the Baby Parade	Vocalist unidentified	Yes
3	I've Got a Right to Sing the Blues	Andrea Marsh	Yes
4	Come to Me	Ted Weems	No
5	Baby	Ted Weems	No

Notes:

Date: 12/18/1932 **Sponsor:** Canada Dry **City:** New York, NY

Recording Source: None **Problems:** None

First line:
Jack: Hello, news seekers…

Summary:
News headlines…Jack compliments everone before Christmas…Weems asks what to get his baby…Mary wants to by a gift (for Georgie Price)…skit Strong Interlude…Nina gets telegram that her husband's plane has crashed…she calls her lover, Sam…Sam comes over and they get engaged…calls Dr. Ned, Nina says she loves him…Kringeline is in the closet

Cast:

Last name	First name	Roles	Guest star
Benny	Jack	Jack Benny, Dr. Ned	No
Douglas	Paul	Paul Douglas	No
Gibbs	Parker	Messenger boy	No
Ingle	Red	Gordon 1, Sam, Kringeline	No
Livingston	Mary	Mary Livingston, Nina Leeds	No
Marsh	Andrea	Andrea Marsh	No
Tanner	Elmo	Elmo Tanner	No
Washburn	Country	Gordon 2	No
Weems	Ted	Ted Weems	No

Songs:

Order	Title	Performers	Vocal
1	Meanest Man in Town	Ted Weems	No
2	Contented	Andrea Marsh	Yes
3	My Favorite Band	Ted Weems	No
4	Wonderful One	Elmo Tanner	No
5	Here it is Monday	Ted Weems	No

Notes:

Skit	Strong Interlude

Date: 12/22/1932 **Sponsor:** Canada Dry **City:** New York, NY

Recording Source: None **Problems:** None

First line:
Jack: Hello, multitude…

Summary:
Jack did his Christmas shopping this afternoon…how would the cast spend $50,000…Jack reads letter from Mary…Weems thinks Jack and Mary should get married…presenting six-day bicycle race participants…Jack does play-by-play of race…show continues over Jack's description

Cast:

Last name	First name	Roles	Guest star
Benny	Jack	Jack Benny	No
Douglas	Paul	Paul Douglas, Jockey	No
Gibbs	Parker	Parker Gibbs, Wheeler Woolsey	No
Ingle	Red	Russian, Kringeline	No
Marsh	Andrea	Andrea Marsh	No
Tanner	Elmo	Elmo Tanner, Frenchy	No
Weems	Ted	Ted Weems	No

Songs:

Order	Title	Performers	Vocal
1	It's Winter Again	Parker Gibbs	Yes
2	I've Told Every Little Star	Andrea Marsh	Yes
3	My Piano and Me	Ted Weems	No
4	When Hearts are Young	Elmo Tanner	No
5	It Don't Mean a Thing	Ted Weems	No

Notes:

Date: 12/25/1932   **Sponsor:** Canada Dry   **City:** New York, NY

Recording Source: None   **Problems:** None

First line:
Douglas: And in the midst of this noise, ladies and gentlemen, stands Jack Benny.

Summary:
Santa left them holding the bag...Paul Douglas looked in his stocking and found his foot...Gibbs gives Jack his laundry as a gift...cast discusses their holiday presents...Mary reads Christmas cards to Jack...guest star, Santa Claus...Santa gives Jack a case of Canada Dry...cast sits down to dinner...Jack does play-by-play of dinner...group makes speeches...Mary reads a poem about winter...mentions Actor's Dinner Club benefit at Waldorf-Astoria

Cast:

Last name	First name	Roles	Guest star
		Jack's dad	No
		Santa Claus	No
		Miss Flittington	No
Benny	Jack	Jack Benny	No
Gibbs	Parker	Parker Gibbs	No
Ingle	Red	Kringaline	No
Livingston	Mary	Mary Livingston	No
Marsh	Andrea	Andrea Marsh	No
Tanner	Elmo	Elmo Tanner	No
Washburn	Country	Country Washburn	No
Weems	Ted	Ted Weems	No

Songs:

Order	Title	Performers	Vocal
1	Fit as a Fiddle	Ted Weems	No
2	Big City Blues	Andrea Marsh	Yes
3	Sitting By the Fire	Trio	Yes
4	Baby	Ted Weems	No
5	Please	Elmo Tanner	No
6	When the Morning Rolls Around	Vocalist unidentified	Yes

Notes:

Running gag	Mary's poem

Date: 12/19/1932   **Sponsor:** Canada Dry   **City:** New York, NY

Recording Source: None   **Problems:** None

First line:
Douglas: Jack Benny hasn't arrived at the Studio yet, so we'll have to tun him in wherever he is.

Summary:
Jack trying to hail a cab...has a conversation with the driver...cop pulls them over, Jack spells his name EDDIE CANTOR...Jack makes the officer cry and he lets them go...Weems is wearing all his Christmas presents...Mary gave Jack a shirt that's too big...Jack gave Mary bank stockings (there's a run in each one)...sequel to "Red Dust" called "Blue Dirt"...husband leaving on business...Twombley arrives to play bridge...husband returns for umbrella

Cast:

Last name	First name	Roles	Guest star
		Woman in audience	No
		Throckmorton	No
Baker	Benny	Cabbie	No
Benny	Jack	Jack Benny, T. Twombley Twilliam	No
Douglas	Paul	Paul Douglas	No
Gibbs	Parker	Cop	No
Ingle	Red	James butler, Kringelein	No
Livingston	Mary	Mary Livingston, Seneca	No
Marsh	Andrea	Andrea Marsh, Fifi	No
Weems	Ted	Ted Weems	No

Songs:

Order	Title	Performers	Vocal
1	Hells Bells	Ted Weems	No
2	After Twelve O'Clock	Ted Weems	No
3	The Old Kitchen Kettle	Ted Weems	No
4	Turn Out the Light	Vocalist unidentified	Yes
5	Say, Young Lady	Ted Weems	No

Notes:

Skit	Blue Dirt

Date: 1/1/1933   **Sponsor:** Canada Dry   **City:** New York, NY

Recording Source: Unknown   **Problems:** Partial show

First line:
Jack: Good evening, ladies and gentlemen. Not to be outdone by the other programs on the air tonight, I want to wish you a all a very happy new year.

Summary:
Father time appears...cast discusses New Year's Resolutions...Violet Ray, pilot and golfer appears...trained dogs, talking dog...Jack to play violin solo, audience calls for Humoresque, plays "How Deep Is the Ocean"...telegram from Kringelein...next Thursday show moves to 8PM

Cast:

Last name	First name	Roles	Guest star
		Father Time	No
Barker	Brad	Dogs	No
Benny	Jack	Jack Benny	No
Douglas	Paul	Paul Douglas	No
Livingston	Mary	Mary Livingston	No
Marsh	Andrea	Andrea Marsh	No
Stewart	Blanche	Violet Ray	No
Weems	Ted	Ted Weems	No

Songs:

Order	Title	Performers	Vocal
1	Rise and Shine	Ted Weems	Yes
2	When It's Darkest on the Delta	Andrea Marsh	Yes
3	Remember Me	Andrea Marsh	Yes
4	Panhandle Pete	Ted Weems	No
5	How Deep Is the Ocean	Jack Benny	No
6	So I Married the Girl	Ted Weems	No

Notes:

Notable	Mary's first recorded show

Date: 1/5/1933 **Sponsor:** Canada Dry **City:** New York, NY

Recording Source: None **Problems:** None

First line:
Mary: Hello friends. This is Mary Livingston from Plainfield - remember, hmm? Yes, I'm still Jack Benny's secretary.

Summary:
Jack late, getting a shave and haircut…Jack gives references for shave, manicure, etc…skit I Am a Fugitive from a Lovely Chain Gang…Jack plans his escape…Mary brings order from the Governor to keep Jack in the gang…keeper tries to throw Jack out, so he becomes a fugitive…Jack goes to work in a jewelry store, in love with proprietor's daughter…Douglas talks Jack into coming back to the chain gang

Cast:

Last name	First name	Roles	Guest star
		Keeper	No
Ashe	Ralph	Conductor	No
Baldwin	Harry	Budd	No
Benny	Jack	Jack Benny	No
Douglas	Paul	Paul Douglas	No
Ingle	Red	Shirtless prisoner, Kringelein	No
Livingston	Mary	Mary Livingston	No
Marsh	Andrea	Andrea Marsh	No
Tanner	Elmo	Hawkins	No
Thomas	?	Stoopnagle	No
Weems	Ted	Ted Weems	No

Songs:

Order	Title	Performers	Vocal
1	Black Eyed Susan Brown	Ted Weems	No
2	The Old Kitchen Kettle	Ted Weems	No
3	Handwriting on the Wall	Andrea Marsh	Yes
4	The Girl in the Little Green Hat	Ted Weems	No
5	I Know a Story	Ted Weems	No

Notes:

Skit	I Am a Fugitive from a Lovely Chain Gang

Date: 1/8/1933   **Sponsor:** Canada Dry   **City:** New York, NY

Recording Source: None   **Problems:** None

First line:
Douglas: And now, ladies and gentlemen, I take great pleasure in introducing to you for the first time on the air tonight that suave, polished, bland, genteel, learned…

Summary:
Weems is eating a hot dog…Jack explains foreign exchange…guest star, Babe, hurdler from Texas…races against Mary and Andrea…Mary stops at a bargain sale…Eddie Cantor calls…Gracie Allen arrives, looking for her brother…Gracie gives a recipe…George Burns arrives, they discuss books

Cast:

Last name	First name	Roles	Guest star
Allen	Gracie	Gracie Allen	Yes
Benny	Jack	Jack Benny	No
Burns	George	George Burns	Yes
Douglas	Paul	Paul Douglas	No
Livingston	Mary	Mary Livingston	No
Stewart	Blanche	Babe	No
Weems	Ted	Ted Weems	No

Songs:

Order	Title	Performers	Vocal
1	Son of the South	Ted Weems	No
2	Lonesome Road	Ted Weems	No
3	Night and Day	Ted Weems	No
4	Chicago	Ted Weems	No
5	My Darling	Ted Weems	No

Notes:

Date: 1/12/1933 **Sponsor:** Canada Dry **City:** New York, NY

Recording Source: None **Problems:** None

First line:
Jack: Hello, everybody...that's listening...

Summary:
Phone call for Mary from Frank, her new boyfriend...call for the janitor...Jack tries to tell a joke about a Hebrew on a train in Texas, keeps getting interrupted...Gibbs argues with his ex-wife about alimony over the joke...Douglas wants to hear a song about January, discuss songs for each month...letter from Jack's father asking for another violin solo...Mary calls her mother to make sure they're listening...next week doing "Rain"...Mary has a date with Frank

Cast:

Last name	First name	Roles	Guest star
		Kvetch the janitor	No
		Frank Glitz	No
Benny	Jack	Jack Benny	No
Douglas	Paul	Paul Douglas	No
Gibbs	Parker	Parker Gibbs	No
Ingle	Red	Red Ingle	No
Livingston	Mary	Mary Livingston	No
Marsh	Andrea	Andrea Marsh	No
Stewart	Blanche	Parker's ex-wife	No
Tanner	Elmo	Elmo Tanner	No
Weems	Ted	Ted Weems	No

Songs:

Order	Title	Performers	Vocal
1	Look Who's Here	Male chorus	Yes
2	Why Can't This Night Go On Forever	Andrea Marsh	Yes
2	Why Can't This Night Go On Forever	Elmo Tanner	Yes
3	Mysterious Moe	Male solo	Yes
4	Just a Little Home for the Old Folks	Male solo	Yes
5	Underneath the Harlem Moon	Jack Benny	No
6	Blues My Naughty Sweetie Gave to Me	Ted Weems	No

Notes:

Notable	Pencil notation on script: "1/18/33 Pd Blanche cash $15.00"
Running gag	Mary's mother communication

Date: 1/15/1933   **Sponsor:** Canada Dry   **City:** New York, NY

Recording Source: None   **Problems:** None

First line:
Douglas: And now for a change, and by way of diversion, we bring you Jack Benny.

Summary:
Jack and Douglas discuss famous quotes…real estate man wants to sell Jack a lot…their version of "Rain" called "Snow"…strangers land on an island…natives talk Yiddish…Davidson tries to send Thompkins back to Canada to dry…later recants and lets her go to Sydney

Cast:

Last name	First name	Roles	Guest star
Benny	Jack	Jack Benny, Red Davidson	No
Conn	Harry	Ernest	No
Douglas	Paul	Paul Douglas	No
Gibbs	Parker	Captain	No
Ingle	Red	Sydney, Kringelein	No
Livingston	Mary	Mary Livingston, Sadie Thompson	No
Marsh	Andrea	Andrea Marsh	No
Stewart	Blanche	Meena, Mrs. Davidson	No
Tanner	Elmo	Sailor	No
Weems	Ted	Ted Weems	No

Songs:

Order	Title	Performers	Vocal
1	Hell's Bells	Ted Weems	No
2	I Told Every Little Star	Andrea Marsh	Yes
3	Suzanne	Ted Weems	No
4	Little Street Where Old Friends Meet	Elmo Tanner	No
5	Claudette	Ted Weems	No

Notes:

Skit	Snow

Date: 1/19/1933   **Sponsor:** Canada Dry   **City:** New York, NY

Recording Source: None   **Problems:** None

First line:
Douglas: Ladies and gentlemen, I was about to present Jack Benny to you, but I just found out that something has happened to him - which I'd rather not mention here. But we'll do the best we can without him, so now Ted Weems…

Summary:
Jack in a sanitarium, cast visits him…goes crazy when Douglas does a Canada Dry commercial…threw Jack out of sanitarium for making too much noise…cast discusses what they're crazy about…Kringelein likes to read (tombstones)…travelogue of France…Jack is still in sanitarium, talking to himself

Cast:

Last name	First name	Roles	Guest star
		Chevalier	No
Benny	Jack	Jack Benny	No
Douglas	Paul	Paul Douglas	No
Gibbs	Parker	Keeper	No
Ingle	Red	Kringelein	No
Livingston	Mary	Mary Livingston, French girl	No
Marsh	Andrea	Andrea Marsh, Fifi	No
Tanner	Elmo	Elmo Tanner, Frenchman	No
Weems	Ted	Ted Weems	No

Songs:

Order	Title	Performers	Vocal
1	Clarinet Marmalade	Ted Weems	No
2	Do You Ever Think of Me	Ted Weems	No
3	Girl In the Little Green Hat	Parker Gibbs	Yes
4	Wait Till I Get You In My Dreams	Elmo Tanner	No
5	There Is a New Day Coming	Ted Weems	No

Notes:

Skit	Travelogue of France

Date: 1/22/1933   **Sponsor:** Canada Dry   **City:** New York, NY

Recording Source: Unknown   **Problems:** Poor sound, partial show

First line:
Jack: Thanks, Paul, thanks…hello, scandal-seekers…

Summary:
News headlines…reviews of "Bertha the Sewing Machine Girl"…Landlord demands rent in ten minutes from Bertha…Bertha decides to go to city to make good, nickel short of fare to New York, cash in Canada Dry bottle…Bertha returns just in time with the money

Cast:

Last name	First name	Roles	Guest star
Ashe	Ralph	Blake the Landlord	No
Benny	Jack	Jack Benny, father	No
Douglas	Paul	Paul Douglas	No
Ingle	Red	Kringelein	No
Livingston	Mary	Mary Livingston, Bertha	No
Marsh	Andrea	Andrea Marsh	No
Weems	Ted	Ted Weems, Sheriff	No

Songs:

Order	Title	Performers	Vocal
1	Roll Up the Carpet	Ted Weems	Yes
2	Echo in the Valley	Andrea Marsh	Yes
3	Twelfth Street Rag	Ted Weems	No
4	Second Honeymoon	Male Duet	Yes
5	I'm in Love with a Great Big Beauty	Jack Benny	Yes
6	Bohemia	Ted Weems	No

Notes:

Notable	First recorded skit show
Skit	Bertha the Sewing Machine Girl

Date: 1/26/1933   **Sponsor:** Canada Dry   **City:** New York, NY

Recording Source: None   **Problems:** None

First line:
Douglas: And now, ladies and gentlemen, it is with great pleasure that I introduce that suave comedian - a man who has reached the pinnacle of success.

Summary:
Douglas does Sunday kids program...Jack and Douglas discuss clothes...guest star, champion ten-cents-a-dancer...Kringelein dances with her...sequel to "Strictly Dishonorable"...husband going away on business...series of lovers arrives, each one hides behind the screen...husband returns and wife says they're her music teachers...Kringeline has bought several coffins...wrestling match between Strangler Lewis and Kringelein, Jack does play-by-play...Kringelein bites Strangler's toe, gets ptomaine poisoning

Cast:

Last name	First name	Roles	Guest star
Benny	Jack	Jack Benny, Clark Benny	No
Douglas	Paul	Paul Douglas, Mr. Raspberry	No
Gibbs	Parker	Sam P. Morgan	No
Ingle	Red	Canada Dry collector, Kringelein	No
Livingston	Mary	Mary Livingston, Mrs. Raspberry	No
Marsh	Andrea	Andrea Marsh	No
Stewart	Blanche	Dimah Twirl, ducks	No
Tanner	Elmo	Elmo Tanner	No
Weems	Ted	Ted Weems	No

Songs:

Order	Title	Performers	Vocal
1	Rise and Shine	Ted Weems	No
2	Rockabye Moon	Andrea Marsh	Yes
3	The Old Kitchen Kettle	Ted Weems	No
4	It Don't Mean a Thing	Ted Weems	No
5	I Know a Story	Ted Weems	No

Notes:

Notable	In last line, Jack calls Mary "Mrs. Benny"
Skit	Strictly It's-Horrible

Date: 3/3/1933   **Sponsor:** Chevrolet   **City:** New York, NY

Recording Source: None   **Problems:** None

First line:
Claney: And now, ladies and gentlemen, for our big surprise of the evening. I take great pleasure in introducing to you for the first time on the Chevrolet program that mirth-provoking, inimitable, suave, polished, bland, genteel, learned…

Summary:
Claney gives Jack a huge introduction…Jack spent his vacation in Miami Beach at the Roney-Plaza…Jack describes Black's orchestra and Frank Black…guest star, greatest traffic-ticket collector…Mary stops by, wants to be on the program…Jack sent her a box of Florida sand…Mary reads Jack telegrams…Jack going to the inauguration tonight

Cast:

Last name	First name	Roles	Guest star
Baker	Benny	Heckler, Major Welcome Scrambel	No
Black	Frank	Frank Black	No
Claney	Howard	Howard Claney	No
Evans	Edith	Edith Evans	No
Livingston	Mary	Mary Livingston	No
Melton	James	James Melton	No

Songs:

Order	Title	Performers	Vocal
1	Strike Me Pink	Frank Black	No
2	Let's Call It a Day	Frank Black	No
3	Little House on the Hill	Edith Evans	Yes
4	Will You Remember	James Melton	Yes
5	Night and Day	Frank Black	No

Notes:

Notable	First show for Chevrolet

Date: 3/10/1933 **Sponsor:** Chevrolet **City:** New York, NY

Recording Source: None **Problems:** None

First line:
Jack: Hello, anybody. This is Jack Brisbane Benny, the Earth Galloper, coming to you with all the late news events thru the courtesy of the Morning Chronic In-Digest.

Summary:
News headlines…Mary flirts with Melton, had a date with Frank Black last night, Claney on Monday…tax man helps Jack figure out his taxes (Jack made $80,000 last year)…Jack describes Grace Hayes' dress…guest star, mind reader Allah Bama…psychic loses her purse and umbrella…Mary says goodnight to everyone

Cast:

Last name	First name	Roles	Guest star
		Mr. Kvetch the Janitor	No
Baker	Benny	Income tax man	No
Benny	Jack	Jack Benny	No
Black	Frank	Frank Black	No
Claney	Howard	Howard Claney	No
Hayes	Grace	Grace Hayes	Yes
Livingston	Mary	Mary Livingston	No
Melton	James	James Melton	No
Stewart	Blanche	Allah Bama	No

Songs:

Order	Title	Performers	Vocal
1	Rise and Shine	Frank Black	No
2	Student Prince medley	James Melton	Yes
3	My Darling	Frank Black	No
4	I Can't Give You Anything But Love	Grace Hayes	Yes
5	You're an Old Smoothie	Frank Black	No

Notes:

Date: 3/17/1933   **Sponsor:** Chevrolet   **City:** New York, NY

Recording Source: None   **Problems:** None

First line:
Jack: This is Jack Benny, the Earth Galloper, coming to you again with the weekly news reports - thru the courtesy of the Durante-Gable News Syndicate, the nose-and-ears of the world.

Summary:
News headlines...Jack interviews Frances Langford...Jack invites Frances to dinner at the Automat (since they're on an auto show)...Jack reads fan mail...travelogue of Ireland...Jack does narration...in County Mayo meets Mayor Jimmy Walker...next week Ladies' Night

Cast:

Last name	First name	Roles	Guest star
		Voice	No
		Bridget	No
		Jimmy Walker	No
Benny	Jack	Jack Benny	No
Black	Frank	Frank Black	No
Claney	Howard	Howard Claney	No
Langford	Frances	Frances Langford	Yes
Livingston	Mary	Mary Livingston	No
Melton	James	James Melton	No

Songs:

Order	Title	Performers	Vocal
1	When the Morning Rolls Around Again	Frank Black	No
2	Hustling and Bustling for Baby	Frances Langford	Yes
3	42nd Street medley	Frank Black	No
4	I Hear You Calling Me	James Melton	Yes
5	Hoch Caroline	Frank Black	No

Notes:

Skit	Travelogue of Ireland

Date: 3/24/1933   **Sponsor:** Chevrolet   **City:** New York, NY

Recording Source: None   **Problems:** None

First line:
Jack: Ladies, ladies -- be gentlemen…

Summary:
Ladies' Night…Jack calls Garbo…Jack describes outfits of cast…Zelma wants to tell story, whispers it to Jack…Jack gives hints on "How to Win a Husband"…demonstration of sawing a woman in half (from Arkansaw)…Ladies' Three Point Two Beer Association wants Jack to play his violin…Mary recites poem over Jack's solo…sponsor telegram, heard Jack's playing and sawed his salary in half

Cast:

Last name	First name	Roles	Guest star
Ashe	Ralph	George Bernard Saw	No
Benny	Jack	Jack Benny	No
Black	Frank	Frank Black	No
Claney	Howard	Howard Claney	No
Livingston	Mary	Mary Livingston	No
Melton	James	James Melton	No
O'Neal	Zelma	Zelma O'Neal	Yes
Stewart	Blanche	Arkansaw woman	No

Songs:

Order	Title	Performers	Vocal
1	There's A New Day Coming	Frank Black	No
2	You're an Old Smoothie	Zelma O'Neal	Yes
3	Black Eyed Susan Brown	Frank Black	No
4	The Bells of St. Mary's	James Melton	Yes
5	Soft Lights and Sweet Music	Jack Benny	No
6	No More Blues	Frank Black	No

Notes:

Running gag	Mary's poem

Date: 3/31/1933   **Sponsor:** Chevrolet   **City:** New York, NY

Recording Source: Unknown   **Problems:** Poor sound

First line:
Jack: Hello optimists…

Summary:
News headlines…discuss Jack's violin solo last Friday for Ladies' Night…reads fan mail about Ladies' Night…"She Done Him Wrong"…Cummings visits Lou, hides in closet and finds Frank Black, James Melton, and Howard Claney hiding there too

Cast:

Last name	First name	Roles	Guest star
Ashe	Ralph	Spider the Bartender	No
Benny	Jack	Jack Benny, Cummings	No
Black	Frank	Frank Black, bar customer	No
Claney	Howard	Howard Claney, bar customer	No
Livingston	Mary	Mary Livingston, Miss Lou	No
Melton	James	James Melton	No
Stewart	Blanche	Miss Lou's maid, chicken	No

Songs:

Order	Title	Performers	Vocal
1	I Like Mountain Music	Frank Black	No
2	Two Tickets to Georgia	Frank Black	No
3	Mavis	James Melton	Yes
4	The Grass is Getting Greener All the Time	Mary Livingston	Yes
5	Dancing the Devil Away	Frank Black	No

Notes:

Notable	First recording of Mary singing
Notable	First recording of Chevrolet Show
Skit	She Done Him Wrong

Date: 4/7/1933   **Sponsor:** Chevrolet   **City:** New York, NY

Recording Source: None   **Problems:** None

First line:
Jack: Hello, folks - is everybody hoppy?...

Summary:
News headlines...contest to see who can tell the funniest story, first prize an inner tube...Jack tells a story about three hermits...Janitor tells story in Hungarian...skit Dr. Jekyll and Mr. Hyde...Jekyll sees patient...takes powders and changes...returns as normal in the morning...Jekyll sees patient Claney...turns into Hyde when Claney discusses Chevrolet and chokes Claney...next week Babies' Night...Mary has date with Dr. Melton and Mr. Black

Cast:

Last name	First name	Roles	Guest star
		Janitor	No
Benny	Jack	Jack Benny, Jekyll/Hyde	No
Black	Frank	Frank Black	No
Claney	Howard	Howard Claney	No
Livingston	Mary	Mary Livingston, Jekyll's secretary Nancy	No
Melton	James	James Melton	No
Stewart	Blanche	Hyde's secretary, Daisy Twilt	No

Songs:

Order	Title	Performers	Vocal
1	Little Me	Frank Black	No
2	Shuffle Off to Buffalo	Frank Black	No
3	A Dream	James Melton	Yes
4	What Have We Got to Lose	Mary Livingston	Yes
5	Mimi	Frank Black	No

Notes:

Running gag	Mary does Mae West
Skit	Dr. Jekyll and Mr. Hyde

Date: 4/14/1933   **Sponsor:** Chevrolet   **City:** New York, NY

Recording Source: None   **Problems:** None

First line:
Claney: And now folks, you remember last Friday Jack Benny promised you that tonight would be Baby's Night - a program just for the little tots - and, here he is!

Summary:
Babies' Night...telegram from Dickie Moore, baby actor...Jack gets a call from his baby...Mary calls George Bernard Shaw, Jack wants him to play Santa Claus...cast recites nursery rhymes...Claney's son wants to sing "Old Man River"...Jack tells of his son Cuthelbert, sings Sonny Boy under commercial...Jack reads "Little Red Riding Hood", puts himself to sleep

Cast:

Last name	First name	Roles	Guest star
?	Bobby	Junior Claney	No
Benny	Jack	Jack Benny	No
Black	Frank	Frank Black	No
Claney	Howard	Howard Claney	No
Livingston	Mary	Mary Livingston	No
Melton	James	James Melton	No

Songs:

Order	Title	Performers	Vocal
1	Strike Me Pink	Frank Black	No
2	Hey Young Fella	Frank Black	No
3	Tommy Lad	James Melton	Yes
4	Kiddie Kapers	Frank Black	No
5	Goodnight Sweetheart	Mary Livingston	Yes

Notes:

Date: 4/21/1933 **Sponsor:** Chevrolet **City:** New York, NY

Recording Source: Unknown **Problems:** Poor sound

First line:
Jack: Hello again, this is Jack Benny the earth galloper, coming to you with all the late news events through the courtesy of the Friday Evening Poll.

Summary:
News headlines...Jack intros E.G. Robinson who talks about his new son...Jack talks about making pictures in Hollywood..."Why Gals Leave Home"...Daughter Nell won't marry and leave home...suitors try their luck until Pete Claney shows up with Chevrolet and Nell accepts

Cast:
Last name	First name	Roles	Guest star
Benny	Jack	Jack Benny, Lemuel Weathersby	No
Black	Frank	Frank Black	No
Claney	Howard	Howard Claney, Pete Claney	No
Livingston	Mary	Mary Livingston, Nell Weathersby	No
Melton	James	James Melton, Zeke Melton	No
Robinson	Edward G.	Edward G. Robinson	Yes
Stewart	Blanche	Salisha Weathersby	No

Songs:
Order	Title	Performers	Vocal
1	The Start of the Big Parade	Frank Black	No
2	Speaking of the Devil	Frank Black	No
3	L'Amour Toujours L'Amour	James Melton	Yes
4	It's Great to Be Alive	Frank Black	No

Notes:
Skit	Why Gals Leave Home

Date: 4/28/1933   **Sponsor:** Chevrolet   **City:** New York, NY

Recording Source: None   **Problems:** None

First line:

Havrilla: And now, ladies and gentlemen, I take great pleasure in introducing to you that talented individual - a man amongst men - a great entertainer - the one and only…

Summary:

Havrilla introduces everyone but Jack…Howard Claney had to leave town and Havrilla takes over as announcer…Jack asks Havrilla not to mention Chevrolet…telegram from Howard Claney…guest star, sea lion from Ringling Brothers…sea lion's wearing moustache to look like Hitler…Mary gives sea lion sardines, forgot to take them out of the can…skit Why Gals Come Back…parents are missing Nell, she's been gone two years…Melton and Black visit, they play bridge…Nell returns with a baby…left Claney and travelled the world…met and married George Bernard Shaw

Cast:

Last name	First name	Roles	Guest star
Barker	Brad	Sea lion, baby	No
Benny	Jack	Jack Benny, Lemuel Weathersby	No
Black	Frank	Frank Black	No
Havrilla	Alois	Alois Havrilla	No
Livingston	Mary	Mary Livingston	No
Melton	James	James Melton, Zeke Melton	No
Stewart	Blanche	Salisha Weathersby	No

Songs:

Order	Title	Performers	Vocal
1	Changing of the Guard	Frank Black	No
2	He's a Son of the South	Frank Black	No
3	Mah Lindy Lou	James Melton	Yes
4	Spring Weather	Frank Black	No
5	Why Can't This Night Go On Forever	Mary Livingston	Yes

Notes:

Skit	Why Gals Come Back

Date: 5/5/1933   **Sponsor:** Chevrolet   **City:** New York, NY

Recording Source: None   **Problems:** None

First line:
Jack: Hello again, this is Jack Benny, the Earth Galloper, coming to you with all the late news events, thru the courtesy of the Joe Brown News Syndicate, the mouth of the world…

Summary:
News headlines…Melton has on a Japanese silk tie…skit Chauve Souris (Russian play)…Cossacks took daughter Vanya…Boris catches a Volga boat…Olga tells Boris what happened to Vanya…Cossacks come and take Olga in a Chevro-sleigh

Cast:

Last name	First name	Roles	Guest star
Ashe	Ralph	Volga boatman, seal	No
Benny	Jack	Jack Benny, Boris Bennovitch, Rubinoff	No
Black	Frank	Frank Black, Frank-sky Blackoff	No
Claney	Howard	Howard Claney, Karloff	No
Livingston	Mary	Mary Livingston, Olga Petroff	No
Melton	James	James Melton, Zekesky Melton	No

Songs:

Order	Title	Performers	Vocal
1	Let's Sing Again	Frank Black	No
2	Stay to the Right of the Road	Frank Black	No
3	The Old Refrain	James Melton	Yes
4	Bright Shines the Moon	Frank Black	No
5	There Is a New Day Coming	Frank Black	No

Notes:

Skit	Chauve-rolet

Date: 5/12/1933   **Sponsor:** Chevrolet   **City:** New York, NY

Recording Source: None   **Problems:** None

First line:
Jack: Hello again…This is Jack Benny, the Earth Galloper, coming to you with some red hot news thru the courtesy of the Transom-Atlantic News Service, the eye and keyhole of the world…

Summary:
News headlines…Chevrolet contest ended last week…limerick contest, fill in last line, first prize is rare old picture of Marlene Dietrich wearing a dress…cast argues about the limerick…after song, announces winners of contest…travelogue of England…meets the Tra-Vulgar Boatman…Mary invites Jack to her house for a surprise Mother's Day party

Cast:

Last name	First name	Roles	Guest star
		Tra-Vulgar Boatman	No
Benny	Jack	Jack Benny	No
Black	Frank	Frank Black	No
Claney	Howard	Howard Claney	No
Livingston	Mary	Mary Livingston	No
Melton	James	James Melton	No

Songs:

Order	Title	Performers	Vocal
1	Tony's Wife	Frank Black	No
2	Gotta Go	Frank Black	No
3	I Heard You Singing	James Melton	Yes
4	My Temptation	Frank Black	No
5	It's Sunday Down in Caroline	Mary Livingston	Yes

Notes:

Running gag	Mary does Mae West
Skit	Travelogue of England

Date: 5/19/1933   **Sponsor:** Chevrolet   **City:** New York, NY

Recording Source: None   **Problems:** None

First line:
Jack: Hello again, this is Jack Benny coming to you with all the latest nonsense, hokum, puns, quips, and salesmen's stories...

Summary:
Reporter wants to get a story from Jack and cast...skit All is Quite Well on the Western Front...soldier on the phone...regiment arrives led by Benny...soldiers settle in...Melton is spy for the enemy...next morning orders men over the top...men are shot, Jack jumps in dugout, Frank Black and his orchestra want in...Jack is shot and Mary sings to him...Mary has date with Melton because she didn't think Jack would live

Cast:

Last name	First name	Roles	Guest star
		Ben Bernie	No
Ashe	Ralph	Vulgar Boatman, soldier, Primo Carnero	No
Baker	Benny	Jay Perspireington Schvitz, Durante	No
Benny	Jack	Jack Benny, Sergeant Benny	No
Black	Frank	Frank Black	No
Claney	Howard	Howard Claney	No
Livingston	Mary	Mary Livingston	No
Melton	James	James Melton	No

Songs:

Order	Title	Performers	Vocal
1	Are You Sure You Love Me	Frank Black	No
2	Let's Sing Again	Frank Black	No
3	Cuban Love Song	James Melton	Yes
4	I Love a Parade	Frank Black	No
5	The Grass is Getting Greener All the Time	Mary Livingston	Yes

Notes:

Skit	All is Quite Well on the Western Front

Date: 5/26/1933 **Sponsor:** Chevrolet **City:** New York, NY

Recording Source: None **Problems:** None

First line:

Jack: Hello, once more. This is your New York correspondent, Jack Benny, the Earth Galloper, coming to you with all the latest news events thru the courtesy of the Friday Evening Fish...

Summary:

News headlines...Jack wonders if Black's orchestra is all American...songwriter (Irving Paris) wants to write a song for Jack...skit Who Killed Mr. X...describes crime scene...courtroom scene...Blake confesses, Jack dismisses him...Greta Gabbo on the stand, Claney questions her about her car...questions Mae East...puts Mr. X on the stand...Mr. X to announce his killer, to be continued

Cast:

Last name	First name	Roles	Guest star
Ashe	Ralph	Four-Gun Blake, Mr. X, Vulgar boatman	No
Baker	Benny	Irving Paris, Bailiff	No
Benny	Jack	Jack Benny	No
Black	Frank	Frank Black, Gas House Clarence	No
Claney	Howard	Howard Claney, States Attorney Claney	No
Livingston	Mary	Mary Livingston, Mae East	No
Melton	James	James Melton	No
Stewart	Blanche	Screamer, Greta Gabbo	No

Songs:

Order	Title	Performers	Vocal
1	Get Yourself a Broom	Frank Black	No
2	My Oh My	Frank Black	No
3	Oh Molly	Benny Baker	Yes
4	Song of Songs	James Melton	Yes
5	Butterflies in the Rain	Frank Black	No
6	In a Second Hand Store	Mary Livingston	Yes

Notes:

Running gag	Mary does Mae West
Skit	Who Killed Mr. X

Date: 6/2/1933   **Sponsor:** Chevrolet   **City:** New York, NY

Recording Source: WEAF   **Problems:** Poor sound

First line:

Jack: Hello some more. This is your New York Correspondent Jack Benny, the Earth Galloper, coming to you with all the late news reports thru the courtesy of the Weekly Wash, the paper that brings out all the dirt...

Summary:

News headlines...part 2 of "Who Killed Mr. X" penthouse murder...review of case facts...Sherlock Holmes brought onto the case...goes to Empire State Building...finds King Kong with Mary Livingston...has Kong arrested for murder of Mr. X...Shadow says they have the wrong suspect

Cast:

Last name	First name	Roles	Guest star
Ashe	Ralph	Shadow, Vulgar boatman	No
Benny	Jack	Jack Benny, Sherlock Holmes	No
Black	Frank	Frank Black, King Kong	No
Claney	Howard	Howard Claney, Detective Claney	No
Hearn	Sam	Dr. Watson	No
Livingston	Mary	Mary Livingston	No
Melton	James	James Melton, Detective Melton	No

Songs:

Order	Title	Performers	Vocal
1	Charley's Home	Frank Black	No
2	My Darling	Frank Black	No
3	Frasquita Serenade	James Melton	Yes
4	Playing with the Devil	Frank Black	No

Notes:

Skit	Who Killed Mr. X

Date: 6/9/1933 **Sponsor:** Chevrolet **City:** New York, NY

Recording Source: WEAF **Problems:** None

First line:
Jack: Hello some more. This is your New York Correspondent Jack Benny, the Earth Galloper, coming to you with all the late news reports thru the courtesy of the Weekly Wash, the paper that brings out all the dirt...

Summary:
Play-by-play of Baer-Smelling fight...Continuation of "Who Killed Mr. X"...Jack as Sherlock Holmes trying to solve the case...takes off in plane which falls apart in the sky...Stool pigeon talks

Cast:

Last name	First name	Roles	Guest star
Ashe	Ralph	Schmelling, Shadow, Stool pigeon	No
Benny	Jack	Jack Benny, Sherlock Holmes	No
Black	Frank	Frank Black	No
Claney	Howard	Howard Claney	No
Hearn	Sam	Watson	No
Livingston	Mary	Mary Livingston, screamer	No
Melton	James	James Melton	No

Songs:

Order	Title	Performers	Vocal
1	Roll Up the Carpet	Frank Black	No
2	Somebody Stole Gabriel's Horn	Frank Black	No
3	Ah Sweet Mystery of Life	James Melton	Yes
4	Petting In the Park	Frank Black	No
5	It's Great to Be Alive	Mary Livingston	Yes

Notes:

Running gag	Mary does Mae West
Skit	Who Killed Mr. X

Date: 6/16/1933   **Sponsor:** Chevrolet   **City:** New York, NY

Recording Source: None   **Problems:** None

First line:
Jack: And now we bring you Heaven's gift to the airwaves - Jack Benny...

Summary:
Jack went to Atlantic City, going to Europe this summer...Jack plays golf in Van Cortland Park...Jack is talking to himself...Jack tells Black a riddle, which is repeated for late cast members...remote broadcast from Chicago for commercial where Al Weeks describes World's Fair...deferring Mr. X because there are no new clues...skit Eight Nights in a Bar Room...Jack says he needs a drink, Melton buys him hot chocolate...daughter and sis come in to bring Jack (father) home...bartender confesses to murder of Mr. X after Jack falls asleep, X was muscling in on the lollipop business in the Bronx...Jack wakes up and arrests him...Mary has a date with Mr. X

Cast:

Last name	First name	Roles	Guest star
		Votson	No
?	Jake	Jake	No
Ashe	Ralph	Shadow, bartender	No
Benny	Jack	Jack Benny, father	No
Black	Frank	Frank Black	No
Claney	Howard	Howard Claney	No
Livingston	Mary	Mary Livingston, daughter	No
Melton	James	James Melton	No
Stewart	Blanche	Baby sister	No

Songs:

Order	Title	Performers	Vocal
1	The Gold Diggers Song	Frank Black	No
2	An Orchid to You	Frank Black	No
3	Give Me One Hour	James Melton	Yes
4	Isn't This a Night for Love	Frank Black	No

Notes:

Skit	Eight Nights in a Bar Room

Date: 6/23/1933   **Sponsor:** Chevrolet   **City:** New York, NY

Recording Source: Unknown   **Problems:** Other

First line:
Jack: Hello again, this is Jack Benny the earth galloper, coming to you with all the late news events through the courtesy of, now get this folks...

Summary:
News headlines...Mary's birthday...how Mary, James, and Jack started in life...end of season gala with Greta Garbo, Clark Gable, Marlene Dietrich, Mahatma Gandhi, Maurice Chevalier, Ed Wynn, Fred Allen, Walter Winchell, Eddie Cantor, Al Smith, Rudy Vallee...Jack and Mary say goodbye to the cast

Cast:

Last name	First name	Roles	Guest star
Benny	Jack	Jack Benny	No
Black	Frank	Frank Black	No
Claney	Howard	Howard Claney, Mahatma Gandhi	No
Livingston	Mary	Mary Livingston	No
Melton	James	James Melton	No
Stewart	Blanche	Garbo, Marlene Dietrich, Irish server	No
Woods	Johnny	Celebrities at gala	No

Songs:

Order	Title	Performers	Vocal
1	Tony's Wife	Frank Black	No
2	My Oh My	Frank Black	No
3	Roses of Picardy	James Melton	Yes
4	Gotta Go	Frank Black	No
5	Sing to Me	Frank Black	No

Notes:

Recording	Circulating recording has end of 6/9/33 show, jumps at last music number
Running gag	Mary does Mae West

Date: 10/1/1933 **Sponsor:** Chevrolet **City:** New York, NY

Recording Source: None **Problems:** None

First line:
Havrilla: And now, ladies and gentlemen, I present to you our master of ceremonies…that suave entertainer and public enemy…that great humoist and international loafer…that hundred percent American…three-quarter comedian and half wit…

Summary:
Crowd of reporters hound Jack…Jack went to Hollywood on his vacation…Frank Black introduces Jack to Alois Havrilla and Frank Parker, Jack introduces Mary to them…Mary and Parker flirt…Jack tries to borrow $20 from Parker…skit The Three Little Pigs…Max Baer is wolf…eats pugs Baer and Schmelling…third pug built house of Chevrolet

Cast:

Last name	First name	Roles	Guest star
Ashe	Ralph	Life story reporter, Primo Carnera	No
Baldwin	Harry	Reporter	No
Benny	Jack	Jack Benny	No
Black	Frank	Frank Black, Max Baer	No
Havrilla	Alois	Alois Havrilla, third pug	No
Livingstone	Mary	Mary Livingstone	No
Parker	Frank	Frank Parker	No
Sorin	Louis	Bugle reporter	No
Stewart	Blanche	Nudist reporter, Schmelling	No

Songs:

Order	Title	Performers	Vocal
1	There Is a New Moon Over My Shoulder	Frank Black	No
2	Get Hot Foot	Frank Black	No
3	My Gypsy Rhapsody	Frank Parker	Yes
4	OK GA	Frank Black	No
5	Football Hero	Frank Black	No

Notes:

Notable	First spelling of Mary Livingstone with an "e"
Skit	Three Little Pigs

Date: 10/8/1933   **Sponsor:** Chevrolet   **City:** New York, NY

Recording Source: None   **Problems:** None

First line:
Jack: Hello again, this is Jack Benny, the Earth Galloper, coming to you with all the latest news events thru the couresy of the Morning Incinerator...

Summary:
News headlines...baseball play-by-play...Jack and Black bet on World Series...Mary and Parker flirt...skit Supper at Six...inviting guests to dinner...at home of Van Brewerys, lover (doctor) shows up...Frank Black comes looking for Jack

Cast:

Last name	First name	Roles	Guest star
?	Janet	Mrs. Van Brewery	No
Ashe	Ralph	Crowd, strike, Wallace Van Brewery	No
Benny	Jack	Jack Benny, Mortimer Van Three Point Two, Doctor	No
Black	Frank	Frank Black	No
Havrilla	Alois	Alois Havrilla	No
Livingston	Mary	Mary Livingston, Zasu Pitts	No
Parker	Frank	Frank Parker	No
Stewart	Blanche	Chicken, duck, Nell, screamer, Gretchen	No

Songs:

Order	Title	Performers	Vocal
1	Gather Lip Rouge While You May	Frank Black	No
2	Shame on You	Frank Black	No
3	Love Is the Sweetest Thing	Frank Parker	Yes
4	Give Me a Roll on the Drum	Frank Black	No
5	There Is a Ring Around My Rainbow	Frank Black	No

Notes:

Skit	Supper at Six

Date: 10/15/1933

Notes:

Notable	No show due to speech of President Roosevelt

Date: 10/22/1933   **Sponsor:** Chevrolet   **City:** New York, NY

Recording Source: None   **Problems:** None

First line:
Havrilla: And now for that irresistible, mirth-provoking, sophisticated delineator of hoko-logical indiosycrasies...our Master of Ceremonies, Jack Benny.

Summary:
No show last week due to Roosevelt speech...cast discusses need to keep up with times...Ruby Wagner comes to see Frank Parker...Alois is worried Mary doesn't like him, Mary is then nasty to him...Havrilla invites Mary to dinner, but she's always busy...Parker has lipstick on his face, Mary gets mad at him and makes date with Havrilla...fight ensues, Parker says he's going to marry Mary...Jack and Black discuss the orchestra, Jack sings about the cornet player from Moscow...Havrilla sings about Chevrolet

Cast:

Last name	First name	Roles	Guest star
Benny	Jack	Jack Benny	No
Black	Frank	Frank Black	No
Havrilla	Alois	Alois Havrilla	No
Livingston	Mary	Mary Livingston	No
Parker	Frank	Frank Parker	No
Stewart	Blanche	Ruby Wagner	No

Songs:

Order	Title	Performers	Vocal
1	Ain't It Marvelous	Frank Black	No
2	I Wanta Ring Bells	Frank Black	No
3	I'll Be Faithful	Frank Parker	Yes
4	Swingee Little Thingee	Frank Black	No
5	There Is a New Day Coming	Frank Black	No

Notes:

Date: 10/29/1933   **Sponsor:** Chevrolet   **City:** New York, NY

Recording Source: None   **Problems:** None

First line:
Havrilla: And now, ladies and gentlemen, who do you think is standing right here at the microphone ready to talk to you?

Summary:
Havrilla listened to other programs...Mary and Parker late...what performers lose on the air...Parker gave Mary a ring, Mary extols his virtues...Jack is jealous...Jack got a letter from his father asking for a violin solo, plays "Humoresque"...Jack calls his father, gets Florence, his father's asleep...next week doing rodeo, talks with participants...changes next week to Romeo and Juliet

Cast:

Last name	First name	Roles	Guest star
Baldwin	Harry	Requestor	No
Benny	Jack	Jack Benny	No
Black	Frank	Frank Black, Cactus Frank	No
Cates	Joe	Roebuck, lost steer	No
Havrilla	Alois	Alois Havrilla	No
Livingston	Mary	Mary Livingston	No
Parker	Frank	Frank Parker	No
Stewart	Blanche	Baby, rooster, Rattlesnake Sarah	No

Songs:

Order	Title	Performers	Vocal
1	Bucking the Wind	Frank Black	No
2	Old Man Harlem	Frank Black	No
3	Softly As In the Morning Sunrise	Frank Parker	Yes
4	Humoresque	Jack Benny	No
5	Sing a Little Lowdown Tune	Frank Black	No
6	That's How Harlem Was Born	Frank Black	No

Notes:

Date: 11/5/1933   **Sponsor:** Chevrolet   **City:** New York, NY

Recording Source: None   **Problems:** None

First line:
Havrilla: And now, ladies and gentlemen, I take great pleasure in introducing to you that all American earache…that illiterate genius…that fourth little pig, Mr. Jack Benny.

Summary:
Jack has lots to tell but no one wants to listen, talks to his alter-ego Jake…alter ego asks if Frank Black is his real name…Jack and Jake discuss Frank Parker…Jack tries to convince Parker to switch programs, he won't do it…Jack asks Black to get rid of Parker…Grabba Contract talks about Chevrolet…skit Romeo and Juliet…Romeo comes to visit Juliet, runs into other characters on the ladder…Romeo and Juliet elope in a Chevrolet-eth…Jack playing in Philadelphia

Cast:

Last name	First name	Roles	Guest star
?	Jake	Jake	No
Benny	Jack	Jack Benny, Romeo	No
Black	Frank	Frank Black, Merchant of Venice	No
Havrilla	Alois	Alois Havrilla, Commercialus Havrillus	No
Hearn	Sam	Father	No
Livingston	Mary	Mary Livingston, Juliet	No
Parker	Frank	Frank Parker, Brutus Parker	No
Stewart	Blanche	Grabba Contract, Cleo, dog, mother	No

Songs:

Order	Title	Performers	Vocal
1	Any Way the Wind Blows	Frank Black	No
2	How Do I Look	Frank Black	No
3	This Time It's Love	Frank Parker	Yes
4	I Love You So Much	Frank Black	No
5	My Temptation	Frank Black	No

Notes:

Skit	Romeo and Juliet

Date: 11/12/1933   **Sponsor:** Chevrolet   **City:** New York, NY

Recording Source: None   **Problems:** None

First line:
Havrilla: And now, ladies and gentlemen, I want to present to you that would-be
humorist...that alleged wit...America's altest annoyance, alias Jack Benny.

Summary:
Jack tries to tell jokes, no one gets them...cast tells jokes...cast discusses repeal of
Prohibition...fan mail criticizing Romeo and Juliet...skit Romeo and Juliet if it was written
today...Frank Black plays Juliet like Garbo...Romeo climbs the fire escape...meets
Brutus...orchestra in the next room...sanitarium man arrests Jack, Black, and Havrilla

Cast:

Last name	First name	Roles	Guest star
?	George	Juliet Black's orchestra	No
Ashe	Ralph	Merchant of Venice, Julius Caesar	No
Benny	Jack	Jack Benny, Romeo	No
Black	Frank	Frank Black, Juliet	No
Havrilla	Alois	Alois Havrilla, Maid	No
Livingston	Mary	Mary Livingston, Father, Miss Ima Luksch	No
Parker	Frank	Frank Parker, Brutus Parker	No

Songs:

Order	Title	Performers	Vocal
1	March of the Musketeers	Frank Black	No
2	Lover Come Back to Me	Frank Black	No
3	Give Me One Hour	Frank Parker	Yes
4	Merry Widow Waltz	Frank Black	No
5	Song of the Flame	Frank Black	No

Notes:

Skit	Romeo and Juliet

Date: 11/19/1933   **Sponsor:** Chevrolet   **City:** New York, NY

Recording Source: None   **Problems:** None

First line:
Havrilla: And now for America's foremost waste of time...Jack Benny.

Summary:
Jack does opening speech in Shakespearean...who said "My kingdom for a horse"...Mary and Parker baby talk...cast discusses their colleges...Jack at Paramount Theatre last week, cast went to see him...Jack tells Parker the tricks of the trade...skit The Shooting of Dan McGrew...guests coming to dinner...guests arrive and shoot dice...McGrew shoots dice well, wins a lot of money then leaves

Cast:

Last name	First name	Roles	Guest star
Benny	Jack	Jack Benny, Herkimer Krotzmere	No
Black	Frank	Frank Black, Mr. Waldorf	No
Havrilla	Alois	Alois Havrilla	No
Hearn	Sam	Dan McGrew	No
Livingston	Mary	Mary Livingston, Gwendolene Krotzmere	No
Parker	Frank	Frank Parker	No
Stewart	Blanche	Bridget	No

Songs:

Order	Title	Performers	Vocal
1	Stout Hearted Men	Frank Black	No
2	Dark Eyes	Frank Black	No
3	Only a Rose	Frank Parker	Yes
4	Rogue Song Fantasy	Frank Black	No
5	I Want to Be Happy	Frank Black	No

Notes:

Skit	The Shooting of Dan McGrew

Date: 11/26/1933   **Sponsor:** Chevrolet   **City:** New York, NY

Recording Source: None   **Problems:** None

First line:
Havrilla: And now I take great pleasure in presenting to you that semi-gentleman, semi-wit, semi-humorist, and semi-Jack Benny.

Summary:
United States recognizes Russia…cast discusses Thanksgiving and what they're thankful for…Mary reads poem about Thanksgiving…skit Switzerland Thru a Keyhole…Liderkranz to celebrate his wedding anniversary by climbing Alps ("alps me feel good")…lover Camembare arrives…husband returns for his golf shoes because it's slippery…finds Camembare and Black in the closet, they all yodel for Chevrolet

Cast:

Last name	First name	Roles	Guest star
Benny	Jack	Jack Benny, Camembare	No
Black	Frank	Frank Black, Merchant of Venice	No
Havrilla	Alois	Alois Havrilla	No
Hearn	Sam	Liederkranz	No
Livingston	Mary	Mary Livingston, Roquefort-Tina	No
Parker	Frank	Frank Parker, Limburger	No

Songs:

Order	Title	Performers	Vocal
1	The Whip	Frank Black	No
2	With a Song In My Heart	Frank Black	No
3	Someday I'll Find You	Frank Parker	Yes
4	Sweet and Lovely	Frank Black	No
5	The Ranger Song	Frank Black	No

Notes:

Skit	Switzerland Thru a Keyhole

Date: 12/3/1933   **Sponsor:** Chevrolet   **City:** New York, NY

Recording Source: None   **Problems:** None

First line:
Havrilla: And now for that great American nuisance, Jack Benny.

Summary:
Jack tells what a gentleman is...man who went to school with Jack arrives, they reminisce...Stubbs Wilbur has a farm...skit School Days...typical schoolroom scene...Parker carrying Mary's books

Cast:

Last name	First name	Roles	Guest star
Benny	Jack	Jack Benny	No
Black	Frank	Frank Black, Merchant of Venice	No
Cates	Joe	Tommy Williams, Percy Fisher Body	No
Havrilla	Alois	Alois Havrilla	No
Hearn	Sam	Joe Schweitzer, Sammy Bloom	No
Livingston	Mary	Mary Livingston	No
Parker	Frank	Frank Parker	No

Songs:

Order	Title	Performers	Vocal
1	You	Frank Black	No
2	Weep No More My Baby	Frank Black	No
3	Where Is the Rainbow	Frank Black	No
4	Moonlight Madonna	Frank Parker	Yes
5	Happy Feet	Frank Black	No

Notes:

Skit	School Days

Date: 12/10/1933 **Sponsor:** Chevrolet **City:** New York, NY

Recording Source: WEAF **Problems:** Poor sound

First line:
Havrilla: And now ladies and gentlemen, I take extreme pleasure in presenting to you once again America's oustanding false alarm, Jack Benny.

Summary:
Jack doesn't like Havrilla's intro and quits…Frank Black stands in for Jack as M.C…Jack fights with Black and gets knocked out…Frank Parker was at Mary's house, and Jack is jealous…"Uncle Tom's Cabin"

Cast:

Last name	First name	Roles	Guest star
Barker	Brad	Dog	No
Benny	Jack	Jack Benny, Uncle Tom	No
Black	Frank	Frank Black, Simon Legree	No
Dressler	Marie	Little Eva	No
Havrilla	Alois	Alois Havrilla	No
Livingston	Mary	Mary Livingston, Liza	No
Parker	Frank	Frank Parker, Captain, Rastus Parker	No
Stewart	Blanche	Topsy	No

Songs:

Order	Title	Performers	Vocal
1	Oo Honey	Frank Black	No
2	Let's Do It	Frank Black	No
3	High Shoes	Frank Black	No
4	Mine	Frank Parker	Yes
5	Memphis in the Morning	Frank Black	No

Notes:

Notable	First recorded Frank Parker and Alois Havrilla appearances
Running gag	Mary does Mae West
Skit	Uncle Tom's Cabin

Date: 12/17/1933   **Sponsor:** Chevrolet   **City:** New York, NY

Recording Source: None   **Problems:** None

First line:
Havrilla: And now for that gentleman of gentlemen…that very fine entertainer and great humorist, Jack Benny.

Summary:
Cast caters to Jack because it's near Christmas…cast discusses what to get for each other…skit inspired by "I'm No Angel"…Jack barks for side show…crowd wants to see Tyra…rube flirts with Tyra…Tyra performs with trained lions…courtroom scene, Tyra sues Luke (rube) for breach of promise

Cast:

Last name	First name	Roles	Guest star
Benny	Jack	Jack Benny, barker	No
Black	Frank	Frank Black, pickpocket, judge	No
Havrilla	Alois	Alois Havrilla	No
Hearn	Sam	Luke Warm	No
Livingston	Mary	Mary Livingston, Garbola, Tyra	No
Parker	Frank	Frank Parker, lion	No

Songs:

Order	Title	Performers	Vocal
1	I'll Be Faithful	Frank Black	No
2	The Song Is You	Frank Parker	Yes
3	Save the Last Dance for Me	Frank Black	No
4	Bright Shines the Moon	Frank Black	No
5	Kashmiri Song	Frank Parker	Yes
6	You Alone	Frank Black	No

Notes:

Notable	Livingston back to no "e"
Running gag	Mary does Mae West
Skit	Who's Afraid of the Big Bad Blonde

Date: 12/24/1933   **Sponsor:** Chevrolet   **City:** New York, NY

Recording Source: None   **Problems:** None

First line:
Havrilla: And now for the Santa Claus of the air...Jack Benny.

Summary:
Jack talks about Christmas shopping...Jack got Mary a diamond ring...packages start arriving...Jack calls his grandfather, grandfather moved to Hollywood seven years ago...calls him there, Mae West voice answers phone...cast visits Mary's family...Mary's father is hard of hearing...sitting down to dinner...Jack starts to play violin solo and everyone starts leaving

Cast:

Last name	First name	Roles	Guest star
?	Andy	Hilliard	No
Benny	Jack	Jack Benny	No
Black	Frank	Frank Black	No
Cates	Joe	Delivery boy 1, J. Herkimer Benny	No
Havrilla	Alois	Alois Havrilla	No
Hearn	Sam	Delivery boy 2, Mary's father	No
Livingston	Mary	Mary Livingston	No
Parker	Frank	Frank Parker	No
Stewart	Blanche	Mary's mother, Babe	No

Songs:

Order	Title	Performers	Vocal
1	New Deal Rhythm	Frank Black	No
2	You've Got Everything	Frank Black	No
3	Arlene	Frank Parker	Yes
4	My Dancin' Lady	Frank Black	No
5	Might Lak a Rose	Jack Benny	No
6	This Is the Missus	Frank Black	No

Notes:

Running gag	Mary does Mae West

Date: 12/31/1933   **Sponsor:**   Chevrolet   **City:**   New York, NY

Recording Source: None   **Problems:**   None

First line:
Havrilla: And now for the Father Time of the Air, Jack Benny.

Summary:
Cast discusses New Years and resolutions...Jack talks about Frank Parker's appearance...Mary gave Jack a shirt that's too big...thanks Mary for dinner, they're missing six knives and forks...guest star, baseball player, bridge player, lady golfer, Mae West, Chinese three little pigs, heavyweight champion, Katharine Heartburn ...telegram from tailor

Cast:

Last name	First name	Roles	Guest star
Baldwin	Harry	J. Photograph Lens	No
Benny	Jack	Jack Benny	No
Black	Frank	Frank Black	No
Edmunds	William	William Fox, Creamo Carnera	No
Havrilla	Alois	Alois Havrilla	No
Livingston	Mary	Mary Livingston, Mae West, pig, Katharine Heartburn	No
Parker	Frank	Frank Parker, pig	No
Stewart	Blanche	Sarah Zen, pig	No

Songs:

Order	Title	Performers	Vocal
1	Roll Out of Bed With a Smile	Frank Black	No
2	You're My Thrill	Frank Black	No
3	My Gypsy Rhapsody	Frank Parker	Yes
4	Keep On Doing What You're Doing	Frank Black	No
5	Music Makes Me	Frank Black	No

Notes:

Running gag	Mary does Mae West

Date: 1/7/1934   **Sponsor:** Chevrolet   **City:** New York, NY

Recording Source: None   **Problems:** None

First line:
Havrilla: (Yawning) And now, ladies and gentlemen, I present to you the world's greatest comedian, Jack Benny.

Summary:
Cast didn't get enough sleep, discusses their dreams…fan letter from woman with 12 children, wants to hear Cinderella…make it into brothers instead of sisters…skit Cinderella…getting ready for the ball…fairy godfather turns Cinderallan into Clark Gable…goes to ball in Chevrolet…Myer rented suit until midnight…repeating Grand Hotel next week

Cast:

Last name	First name	Roles	Guest star
Baldwin	Harry	Narrator	No
Benny	Jack	Jack Benny, Cinderallan	No
Black	Frank	Frank Black, Sasparilla	No
Havrilla	Alois	Alois Havrilla, Haverella	No
Hearn	Sam	King, Myer	No
Livingston	Mary	Mary Livingston	No
Parker	Frank	Frank Parker	No
Shelley	Bill	Fairy godfather	No
Stewart	Blanche	Stepmother, Queen	No

Songs:

Order	Title	Performers	Vocal
1	Keep Young and Beautiful	Frank Black	No
2	Alice in Wonderland	Frank Black	No
3	Smoke Gets In Your Eyes	Frank Parker	Yes
4	Puddin' Head Jones	Frank Black	No
5	Doing the Uptown Lowdown	Frank Black	No

Notes:

Skit	Cinderella

Date: 1/14/1934   **Sponsor:** Chevrolet   **City:** New York, NY

Recording Source: None   **Problems:** None

First line:
Havrilla: And now for a Fool There Was, Jack Benny.

Summary:
Jack found an old joke about a goat without a nose ("How does he smell?...Pretty good for a goat."), but no one will give Jack the cue...cast discusses Durante's nose, Mary still talking about the goat...skit Grind Hotel...front desk scene...Groosinskya will not dance...Baron makes love to Groosinskya, interrupted by Kringalein, Blackovitch, and Havrillavitch...everyone hides under the bed

Cast:

Last name	First name	Roles	Guest star
		Garbo, Groosinskya	No
Ashe	Ralph	Prince-a-ling, Manager	No
Baldwin	Harry	George Bernard Shaw	No
Benny	Jack	Jack Benny, desk clerk, Baron	No
Black	Frank	Frank Black, dining room customer, Blackovitch	No
Havrilla	Alois	Alois Havrilla, Havrillavitch	No
Hearn	Sam	Deaf guy, Kringaline	No
Livingston	Mary	Mary Livingston, operator, Fraulein Flim Flam, Zasu Pitts	No
Parker	Frank	Frank Parker, bellboy	No
Stewart	Blanche	Operator	No

Songs:

Order	Title	Performers	Vocal
1	Poppin the Cork	Frank Black	No
2	Flying Down to Rio	Frank Black	No
3	Everything I Have is Yours	Frank Parker	Yes
4	Two Hearts in Three-Quarter Time	Frank Black	No
5	My Oh My	Frank Black	No

Notes:

Skit	Grind Hotel

Date: 1/21/1934   **Sponsor:** Chevrolet   **City:** New York, NY

Recording Source: None   **Problems:** None

First line:
Havrilla: And now for little King Kong, Junior, Jack Benny!

Summary:
Jack insults everyone, no one understands him…Mary crying all evening about the goat without a nose, Jack explains joke to Mary…gang does old jokes…skit Dinner at Eight (Seven for Chicago listeners)…husband and wife getting ready to go out…go to dinner at diner, ordering dinner…Jack wants to be the chef, Mary becomes waitress…ordering turns into bridge bidding

Cast:

Last name	First name	Roles	Guest star
Baldwin	Harry	Customer	No
Benny	Jack	Jack Benny, Wallace Beery-Harlow, chef	No
Black	Frank	Frank Black	No
Edmunds	William	Chauffeur, chef	No
Havrilla	Alois	Alois Havrilla	No
Hearn	Sam	Joe Miller, waiter	No
Livingston	Mary	Mary Livingston, Jane Beery-Harlow, waitress	No
Parker	Frank	Frank Parker	No
Stewart	Blanche	Hilda, waitress	No

Songs:

Order	Title	Performers	Vocal
1	Better Think Twice	Frank Black	No
2	Carioca	Frank Black	No
3	Suddenly	Frank Parker	Yes
4	You're Gonna Lose Your Gal	Frank Black	No
5	Puttin On the Ritz	Frank Black	No

Notes:

Running gag	Relay
Skit	Dinner at Eight

Date: 1/28/1934   **Sponsor:** Chevrolet   **City:** New York, NY

Recording Source: None   **Problems:** None

First line:
Havrilla: And now for America's pet pest, Jack Benny.

Summary:
Jack says he's a dry comedian…Mary asks about the goat…fan letter requests information about Alois Havrilla…skit Life of Alois Havrilla…Havrilla is born…parents ponder name…Havrilla talks (about Chevrolet)…young Havrilla asks questions…Havrilla an announcer at Grand Central Station…Havrilla goes to War and comes home…gains success with Chevrolet

Cast:

Last name	First name	Roles	Guest star
		Young Alois	No
Barker	Brad	Baby, Fido	No
Benny	Jack	Jack Benny, Squire Jason Havrilla	No
Black	Frank	Frank Black, passenger 2	No
Havrilla	Alois	Alois Havrilla	No
Livingston	Mary	Mary Livingston, Marion Havrilla, Havrilla's wife	No
Parker	Frank	Frank Parker, passenger 1	No

Songs:

Order	Title	Performers	Vocal
1	Extra	Frank Black	No
2	Moonlight On the Water	Frank Black	No
3	Since I First Met Thee	Frank Parker	Yes
4	Kiddie Kapers	Frank Black	No
5	Dixie Lee	Frank Black	No

Notes:

Skit	Life of Alois Havrilla

Date: 2/4/1934   **Sponsor:** Chevrolet   **City:** New York, NY

Recording Source: None   **Problems:** None

First line:
Havrilla: And now for that suave comedian…that elite entertainer…that aristocrat of humor…Mr. Jack Benny.

Summary:
Havrilla gives nice introduction for last week's tribute…Black asks Jack to pay him back ten dollars, they debate…Mary calls Treasury to see how much Jack owes…Opportunity Night (amateurs)…Tibbett sings "Your Time Is My Time"…Wills says he's a humidor, better than Will Rogers…Three Chicken Sisters…second John Barrymore, Shakespearean actor, turns out to be janitor…Mary reads poem about winter

Cast:

Last name	First name	Roles	Guest star
Baldwin	Harry	Rudy Tibbett	No
Benny	Jack	Jack Benny	No
Black	Frank	Frank Black	No
Dallas	?	Chicken Sister	No
Hamilton	?	Second John Barrymore	No
Havrilla	Alois	Alois Havrilla	No
Hearn	Sam	Roger Wills	No
Kelly	Mary	Chicken Sister	No
Livingston	Mary	Mary Livingston	No
Parker	Frank	Frank Parker	No
Sound	?	Double Crosby	No
Stewart	Blanche	Chicken Sister	No

Songs:

Order	Title	Performers	Vocal
1	Old Man Jingle	Frank Black	No
2	You're the Cream in My Coffee	Frank Black	No
3	You Have Taken My Heart	Frank Parker	Yes
4	Did You Ever See a Dream Walking	Chicken Sisters	Yes
5	I'll See You in Church	Frank Black	No
6	Who Walks In When I Walk Out	Frank Black	No

Notes:

Notable	Debut of Chicken Sisters gag
Running gag	Mary's poem

Date: 2/11/1934   **Sponsor:** Chevrolet   **City:** New York, NY

Recording Source: WEAF   **Problems:** Poor sound, music clipped

First line:
(Mary) Dear old winter, dear old winter, with your ice and snow…

Summary:
Mary finishes last week's poem…news headlines…Mary talks about her plans for a vacation in Florida…"Miniature Women"…each daughter has a different dialect…exchanging Christmas gifts…Tom proposes to Jo, but she wants to write poetry…Black, Parker, and Havrilla propose to other sisters…sisters played by the Chicken Sisters from last week's talent show…Jack kisses Mary goodbye

Cast:

Last name	First name	Roles	Guest star
Beach	?	Mrs. Little Woman	No
Benny	Jack	Jack Benny, Tom	No
Black	Frank	Frank Black	No
Dallas	?	Southern (Jean)	No
Havrilla	Alois	Alois Havrilla	No
Kelly	Mary	Irish (June)	No
Livingston	Mary	Mary Livingston, Jo	No
Parker	Frank	Frank Parker	No
Stewart	Blanche	German (Jane)	No

Songs:

Order	Title	Performers	Vocal
1	There's Something About a Soldier	Frank Black	No
2	Without That Certain Thing	Frank Black	No
3	The Touch of Your Hand	Frank Parker	Yes
4	Of Thee I Sing	Frank Black	No
5	I Like It That Way	Frank Black	No

Notes:

Blooper	Jack breaks up over Mary's giggle on the line "I was holding this map upside down"
Running gag	Mary's poem
Skit	Miniature Women

Date: 2/18/1934   **Sponsor:** Chevrolet   **City:** New York, NY

Recording Source: Unknown   **Problems:** Poor sound, partial show, music clipped

First line:
Havrilla: And now for the winner of the World Telegram Radio Editors' Poll, Jack Benny.

Summary:
Mary is in Florida…Jack spent his birthday in Waukegan…gags on Jack's age…Jack tries to tell jokes, but all were told by other comedians…Mary sent a stand-in…Jack reads letters (one attributed to Leonard Fenchel, Jack's real brother-in-law, and another from Cliff Gordon, Jack's real cousin)…"Green Room Murder"…Jack and Alois pulled over on the way to the murder…questions people at the murder…arrests Chicken Sisters

Cast:

Last name	First name	Roles	Guest star
Baldwin	Harry	Telegram boy	No
Benny	Jack	Jack Benny	No
Black	Frank	Frank Black	No
Hamilton	?	Cop	No
Havrilla	Alois	Alois Havrilla	No
Kelly	Mary	Bridge player	No
Parker	Frank	Frank Parker	No
Stewart	Blanche	Mary stand-in, screamer, Maid	No

Songs:

Order	Title	Performers	Vocal
1	Let's Go Places and Do Things	Frank Black	No
2	My Dancing Lady	Frank Black	No
3	You're In My Heart	Frank Parker	Yes
4	South American Medley	Frank Black	No
5	Smiles	Frank Black	No

Notes:

Skit	Green Room Murder

Date: 2/25/1934 **Sponsor:** Chevrolet **City:** New York, NY

Recording Source: Unknown **Problems:** Poor sound, partial show, music clipped

First line:
Havrilla: And now I turn the microphone over to our master of ceremonies, Jack Benny

Summary:
Jack reads letter from Mary...Fan interrupts to ask Jack for $20, Jack gives him $5...telegram from Minnie in Minneapolis asking if Jack was a floorwalker in an Omaha department store...Jack tries to sell a woman her own coat...quits rather than being fired...Mary sends telegram from Miami asking for a goat without a nose...Frank Black defines "vindicated"

Cast:

Last name	First name	Roles	Guest star
?	Eleanor	Miss Kotcha, Greta Garbo	No
?	Rae	Smoking jacket customer	No
Baldwin	Harry	Telegram boy	No
Benny	Jack	Jack Benny	No
Black	Frank	Frank Black, male hat customer	No
Havrilla	Alois	Alois Havrilla, male Chevrolet customer	No
Hearn	Sam	Interrupting fan, Mr. McGillicudy	No
Kelly	Mary	Woman Clerk 2, woman seeking husband	No
Parker	Frank	Frank Parker	No
Parker	Frank	Elevator operator	No
Stewart	Blanche	Mrs. J. Herkimer Stooge Coat customer, umbrella customer	No

Songs:

Order	Title	Performers	Vocal
1	Colonial From Kentucky	Frank Black	No
2	Smoke Gets In Your Eyes	Frank Parker	Yes
3	Carioca	Frank Black	No
4	Take a Chance Medley	Frank Black	No

Notes:

Skit	I Was a Floorwalker In An Omaha Department Store

Date: 3/4/1934   **Sponsor:** Chevrolet   **City:** New York, NY

Recording Source: Unknown   **Problems:** Poor sound, partial show, music clipped

First line:
Havrilla: And now for that vindicated floorwalker, Jack Benny.

Summary:
Why Jack is like Gable…Jack is an outdoorsman…Mary is back from Florida, brings gifts…Jack tells how to become an MC…Jack and Black argue, Frank Black challenges Jack to a duel…gang goes to a graveyard for the duel, reading the gravestones…target practice…end up shooting Havrilla during the commercial…Jack and Frank make up

Cast:

Last name	First name	Roles	Guest star
Baldwin	Harry	Game warden	No
Benny	Jack	Jack Benny	No
Black	Frank	Frank Black	No
Havrilla	Alois	Alois Havrilla	No
Livingston	Mary	Mary Livingston	No
Parker	Frank	Frank Parker	No

Songs:

Order	Title	Performers	Vocal
1	Don't Do It Again	Frank Black	No
2	In a Shelter From a Shower	Frank Black	No
3	Romance	Frank Parker	Yes
4	Louisiana Hayride	Frank Black	No
5	Savage Serenade	Frank Black	No

Notes:

Notable	First recorded "Play Frank" reference

Date: 3/11/1934   **Sponsor:** Chevrolet   **City:** New York, NY

Recording Source: Unknown   **Problems:** Poor sound, music clipped

First line:
Havrilla: And now ladies and gentlemen, I present to you our Master of Ceremonies, but a gentleman nevertheless. Mister Jack Benny!

Summary:
Havrilla says Jack should wear a collar and tie for the broadcast, everyone hassles Jack about his appearance…receive a fan letter from John Dillinger requesting Parker to sing "Home Again"…Alois says his friends think Jack lacks courage…Mary suggests Jack and Frank Black spend the night in a haunted house as a test of courage…Jack loses coin toss and has to spend the first night…ghost of the maid offers Jack a sandwich…Jack gets chased by ghosts…finds Ghostberg on the roof, gives him directions out of the house…turns out to be Frank Black's house

Cast:

Last name	First name	Roles	Guest star
Benny	Jack	Jack Benny	No
Black	Frank	Frank Black	No
Havrilla	Alois	Alois Havrilla	No
Hearn	Sam	Mr. Ghostberg	No
Kent	?	Ghost of Jack Benny	No
Livingston	Mary	Mary Livingston, Sara Livingston	No
Parker	Frank	Frank Parker, bedsheet ghost	No
Stewart	Blanche	Ghost of the maid, ghost of Rin-Tin-Tin, ghost of Garbo	No

Songs:

Order	Title	Performers	Vocal
1	I Hate Myself	Frank Black	No
2	Going to Heaven on a Mule	Frank Black	No
3	With a Song in My Heart	Frank Parker	Yes
4	Mysterious Mose	Frank Black	No
5	What Do Fellows Do	Frank Black	No

Notes:

Running gag	Mary as Mae West

Date: 3/18/1934   **Sponsor:** Chevrolet   **City:** New York, NY

Recording Source: Unknown   **Problems:** Poor sound, partial show, music clipped

First line:
Havrilla: And now ladies and gentlemen, I was about to present Jack Benny to you, but I just found out that something has happened to him which I'd rather not mention here.

Summary:
Jack has been taken to a sanitarium, gang goes to visit him and gets him released...gang discusses each other's obsessions and Jack's coin collection, cheap jokes...gets fan letter from Arizona asking for a play of the West...does play of the Golden West on the Benny D Ranch...Jack's niece coming to stay at the ranch...Sherrif thinks someone rustling Jack's cattle...Jack to visit Rattlesnake Black on Columbus Circle Ranch...has difficulty getting on the horse, falls off...dictates letter to Black instead

Cast:

Last name	First name	Roles	Guest star
Baldwin	Harry	Telegram boy, Ken	No
Barker	Brad	Keeper, Curly, Canyon Pete, horse, Chinese cook, stranger with broken car	No
Benny	Jack	Jack Benny, Kyote Jack	No
Black	Frank	Frank Black, Rattlesnake Black	No
Havrilla	Alois	Alois Havrilla, Sherrif Havrilla	No
Livingston	Mary	Mary Livingston	No
Parker	Frank	Frank Parker, Clarence, 50 cents Jones	No

Songs:

Order	Title	Performers	Vocal
1	I Feel Like a Million Dollars	Frank Black	No
2	Nasty Man	Frank Black	No
3	Flying Down to Rio	Frank Parker	Yes
4	Pony Boy	Frank Black	No
5	Coffee in the Morning	Frank Black	No

Notes:

Notable	First recorded remote (I.e., non-studio-based) opening sequence
Skit	Play of the Golden West

Date: 3/25/1934   **Sponsor:** Chevrolet   **City:** New York, NY

Recording Source: None   **Problems:** None

First line:
Havrilla: And now for that famous Western actor and student of the drama, Jack Benny.

Summary:
Reporter wants to get dope on the program...most of cast is late...cast shows up, having coffee...Mary reads poem about spring...skit Dixie Minstrel Show..."How many hairs on a monkey's face" gag debut...Havrilla sings Chevrolet version of "I Was Strolling Through the Park One Day"...Edmunds tells joke in Italian

Cast:

Last name	First name	Roles	Guest star
Benny	Jack	Jack Benny, Interlocutor	No
Black	Frank	Frank Black, Sambo	No
Edmunds	William	Italian	No
Havrilla	Alois	Alois Havrilla, Hambo	No
Hearn	Sam	George Jean Nathan, Mr. Cohen	No
Livingston	Mary	Mary Livingston, Mirandy Livingston	No
Parker	Frank	Frank Parker	No
Stewart	Blanche	Little Eva	No

Songs:

Order	Title	Performers	Vocal
1	Viva La France	Frank Black	No
2	Hold My Hand	Frank Black	No
3	Love is Love Anywhere	Frank Black	No
4	Silver Threads Among the Gold	Frank Parker	Yes
5	Old Man River	Jack Benny	Yes
6	Dancing in the Moonlight	Frank Black	No

Notes:

Running gag	Mary's poem
Skit	Dixie Minstrel Show

Date: 4/1/1934   **Sponsor:** Chevrolet   **City:** New York, NY

Recording Source: Unknown   **Problems:** Poor sound, music clipped

First line:
Havrilla: And now for that man of mirth, humor, jokes, Rochester, Buffalo, Cleveland, and all points West, Mr. Jack Benny on Track Five.

Summary:
Gang discusses Easter parade...Mary looking for colored eggs in Harlem...Mary reads poem about Easter...April Fools joke on Frank Black - gets him to call aquarium for Mr. Mackerel...skit Eternal Triangle...Kathryn sends Lionel to Boston...lover Clark hides behind radio when Lionel misses train, imitates Jack Benny...last show of series, whole cast loaned money to each other and wants to be paid back...Eddie Cantor comes to claim $10 from Jack, as well as his tie and suit...new Chevrolet series is Victor Young and Orchestra

Cast:

Last name	First name	Roles	Guest star
Benny	Jack	Jack Benny, Clark Benny	No
Black	Frank	Frank Black	No
Cantor	Eddie	Eddie Cantor	Yes
Havrilla	Alois	Alois Havrilla, Lionel Havrilla	No
Livingston	Mary	Mary Livingston, Kathryn Livingston	No
Parker	Frank	Frank Parker	No
Stewart	Blanche	Maid Fifi	No

Songs:

Order	Title	Performers	Vocal
1	Where's That Rainbow	Frank Black	No
2	You're Gonna Lose That Gal	Frank Black	No
3	The House is Haunted	Frank Parker	Yes
4	You've Got Everything	Frank Black	No
5	That's How Rhythm Was Born	Frank Black	No

Notes:

Running gag	Mary's poem
Skit	Eternal Triangle

Date: 4/6/1934   **Sponsor:** General Tire   **City:** New York, NY

Recording Source: Unknown   **Problems:** Poor sound, partial show

First line:
And now, ladies and gentlemen, we bring you that universal favorite...that popular artist...that radiant personality...

Summary:
Don Wilson doesn't recognize Jack as the MC of the show...Jack tells Don not to butt in with advertising...meets Don Bestor, who is an intellectual...Mary got a job as a private secretary...Frank Parker running a music store, Jack and Mary visit and help sell music...Bestor comes in to buy a baton, Wilson comes in for a microphone

Cast:

Last name	First name	Roles	Guest star
Benny	Jack	Jack Benny	No
Bestor	Don	Don Bestor	No
Edmunds	William	Janitor, Don Yonder, dime beggar	No
Hearn	Sam	Don Ginsberg	No
Kelly	Mary	Customer (for "Alice Blue Gown")	No
Livingston	Mary	Mary Livingston	No
Parker	Frank	Frank Parker	No
Stewart	Blanche	Customer (for "Going to Heaven on a Mule")	No
Stewart	Blanche	Customer (for "Sextet from Lucia")	No
Wilson	Don	Don Wilson	No

Songs:

Order	Title	Performers	Vocal
1	You	Don Bestor	No
2	Contented	Don Bestor	No
3	Singing in the Rain/April Showers	Don Bestor	No
4	Orchids in the Moonlight	Frank Parker	Yes
5	Old Watermill	Don Bestor	No

Notes:

Notable	First show for General Tire
Notable	One of two shows that includes part of Frank Parker's song
Notable	First appearance of Don Bestor
Notable	First appearance of Don Wilson

Date: 4/13/1934 **Sponsor:** General Tire **City:** New York, NY

Recording Source: Unknown **Problems:** Poor sound, partial show, music clipped

First line:
And now, ladies and gentlemen, I bring you that international favorite…that world-wide comedian and local nuisance, Jack Benny

Summary:
Gang discusses their home town, everyone from Springfield…Bestor uses big words…Jack dictates a complaint letter to the head of General Tire…bridge gathering at Don Bestor's…whole family is intellectuals…Frank Parker is the butler…Polly the parrot wants matzo…Mary makes silly bids…group mixes bridge bids and food orders

Cast:

Last name	First name	Roles	Guest star
?	Andy	Donald Bestor (son)	No
Benny	Jack	Jack Benny	No
Bestor	Don	Don Bestor	No
Parker	Frank	Frank Parker, Nicholas	No
Stewart	Blanche	Maid	No
Stewart	Blanche	Donita Bestor (wife)	No
Stewart	Blanche	Polly	No
Wilson	Don	Don Wilson	No

Songs:

Order	Title	Performers	Vocal
1	You're My Relaxation	Don Bestor	No
2	Little Dutch Mill	Don Bestor	No
3	Touch of Your Hand	Frank Parker	Yes
4	Riptide	Don Bestor	No
5	Extra	Don Bestor	No

Notes:

Date: 4/20/1934 **Sponsor:** General Tire **City:** New York, NY

Recording Source: None **Problems:** None

First line:
And now, ladies and gentlemen, let me present to you that star of stage, screen and tap-room…Jack Benny.

Summary:
Jack describes Don Wilson…cast discusses whether life begins at forty…Jack suggests that Bestor play more current numbers…Bestor wants to hear Jack play the violin, he plays "Mighty Like a Rose"…sponsor calls and complains…sponsor calls and compliments Frank Parker…Mary reads fan mail from Miss Florence Van Dine Kubelsky…Jack dictates letter, no ribbon in typewriter…skit Jack Benny's Drug Store…cast comes in and looks to buy things…woman wants two shaving brushes because her husband has a double chin

Cast:

Last name	First name	Roles	Guest star
Benny	Jack	Jack Benny	No
Bestor	Don	Don Bestor	No
Kelly	Mary	Three-cent stamp customer, headache pills customer	No
Livingston	Mary	Mary Livingston	No
Parker	Frank	Frank Parker, clock customer	No
Stewart	Blanche	Sandwich customer	No
Wilson	Don	Don Wilson	No

Songs:

Order	Title	Performers	Vocal
1	There Goes My Heart	Frank Black	No
2	Rain or Shine medley	Frank Black	No
3	Might Like a Rose	Jack Benny	No
4	April in Paris	Frank Parker	Yes
5	Easy Come, Easy Go	Frank Black	No
6	You're Devastating	Frank Black	No

Notes:

Skit	Jack Benny's Drug Store

Date: 4/27/1934   **Sponsor:** General Tire   **City:** New York, NY

Recording Source: Unknown   **Problems:** Poor sound, partial show, music clipped

First line:
And now for that effervescent, vivacious, pugnacious master of ceremonies, Mr. Jack Benny.

Summary:
Everyone tells anecdotes...Mary imitates Jimmy Durante...Paris offers to write Jack a team song...Parker has a new suit...skit The Lure of the City...daughter wants to leave home...father sends son to college...four years later, mortgage is overdue...daughter and son come home for more money...Jack and Mary playing Loew's Valencia in Jamaica

Cast:

Last name	First name	Roles	Guest star
Benny	Jack	Jack Benny, Luke Wilkins	No
Bestor	Don	Don Bestor	No
Edmunds	William	Irving Paris	No
Hearn	Sam	Lem Wilkins	No
Livingston	Mary	Mary Livingston, Mariah Wilkins	No
Parker	Frank	Frank Parker	No
Stewart	Blanche	Rooster, mother Wilkins,	No
Wilson	Don	Don Wilson, Zeke	No

Songs:

Order	Title	Performers	Vocal
1	Lovely One	Don Bestor	No
2	How Do I Know It's Sunday	Don Bestor	No
3	Hold My Hand	Frank Parker	Yes
4	Irving Berlin medley	Don Bestor	No
5	A Thousand Good Nights	Don Bestor	No

Notes:

Blooper	Don Wilson misses his cue after Mary imitates Durante
Recording	Only four minutes of show are currently in circulation
Skit	The Lure of the City

Date: 5/4/1934   **Sponsor:**   General Tire   **City:**   New York, NY

Recording Source: Unknown   **Problems:**   Poor sound, music clipped

First line:
And now, ladies and gentlemen, I take great pleasure in introducing that sculptor, painter and chiseler, Mr. Jack Benny.

Summary:
Jack got Don two passes to Central Park...everyone went to a dance...gets telegram from tipster on Derby, gang discuss Kentucky Derby bets...gives reviews of last week's play...skit The Hills of Old Kentucky...ongoing feud between VanTripps and Diddleberrys...Diddleberry insults Elvirie, she rounds up family...Diddleberrys eventually shoot everyone except Elvirie

Cast:

Last name	First name	Roles	Guest star
Baldwin	Harry	Tom (bookie), drummer	No
Benny	Jack	Jack Benny, Old Man Van Twiff	No
Bestor	Don	Don Bestor, Zeke Bestor	No
Livingston	Mary	Mary Livingston, Elviry Van Twiff	No
Parker	Frank	Frank Parker	No
Stewart	Blanche	Annie Van Twiff	No
Wilson	Don	Don Wilson, Clem Van Twiff	No

Songs:

Order	Title	Performers	Vocal
1	You're Welcome	Don Bestor	No
2	Carioca	Don Bestor	No
3	Cocktails for Two	Frank Parker	Yes
4	Hillbilly Medley	Don Bestor	No
5	Why Can't This Night Go On Forever	Don Bestor	No

Notes:

Skit	The Hills of Old Kentucky

Date: 5/11/1934   **Sponsor:** General Tire   **City:** New York, NY

Recording Source: Unknown   **Problems:** Poor sound, partial show

First line:
And now for the face on the tap room floor, Jack Benny.

Summary:
Jack and Don Wilson trade insults and Don leaves...Jack claims he beat up Wilson...Jack's bet on the Derby...Mary reads poem about Mother's Day...Don apologizes and invites Jack to his home in the Bronx for the weekend...Jack and Don get held up...Jack and Don move the piano for Don's mother...no food left for dinner...Jack talks with O'Shaughnessys about weather...Jack and Don move the piano again...Jack wants to go to bed, but O'Shaughnessy have the spare room, mother offers him the garage...Jack leaves and gets held up again

Cast:

Last name	First name	Roles	Guest star
Ashe	Ralph	Final robber	No
Benny	Jack	Jack Benny	No
Bestor	Don	Don Bestor	No
Hearn	Sam	Tom O'Shaughnessy	No
Kelly	Mary	Mrs. O'Shaughnessy	No
Livingston	Mary	Mary Livingston	No
Parker	Frank	Frank Parker	No
Stewart	Blanche	Mrs. Wilson	No
Voght	?	Robber	No
Wilson	Don	Don Wilson	No

Songs:

Order	Title	Performers	Vocal
1	Over Somebody Else's Shoulders	Don Bestor	No
2	Someone to Watch Over Me - S'Wonderful - Thou Swell	Don Bestor	No
3	Love Thy Neighbor	Frank Parker	Yes
4	Fair and Warmer	Don Bestor	No
5	Fare Thee Well	Don Bestor	No

Notes:

Recording	Only 12 minutes of show currently in circulation
Running gag	Mary's poem

Date: 5/18/1934 **Sponsor:** General Tire **City:** New York, NY

Recording Source: Unknown **Problems:** Poor sound, music clipped

First line:
And now for the Spaniard that blighted my life, Jack Benny.

Summary:
Jack is late to the program, catches cab…gang discusses seeing movies…Jack is going to Hollywood next week to make a film…Jack and Mary played two weeks at Capitol Theatre…Jack and Mary go to Frank Parker's house…Everyone in Parker family sings all the time

Cast:

Last name	First name	Roles	Guest star
		Driver	No
		Cabbie	No
		Cop	No
Benny	Jack	Jack Benny	No
Kelly	Mary	Parker mother	No
Miller	?	Parker father	No
Parker	Frank	Frank Parker	No
Stewart	Blanche	Parker sister Jane	No
Wilson	Don	Don Wilson	No

Songs:

Order	Title	Performers	Vocal
1	Lovely One	Don Bestor	No
2	Tea for Two	Don Bestor	No
3	May I	Frank Parker	Yes
4	Old Music Box Review medley	Don Bestor	No
5	What Is the Good in Goodbye	Don Bestor	No

Notes:

Date: 5/25/1934   **Sponsor:** General Tire   **City:** New York, NY

Recording Source: None   **Problems:** None

First line:
And now for the Man on the Flying Trapeze, Jack Benny.

Summary:
Jack makes up all his own jokes…cast tells jokes…Jack leaves to get a shave…Mary and Bestor come down to get Jack…Jack gets a manicure, tries to date the manicurist…manicurist is married to Tony…Jack goes to buy a suit…cast follows to get Jack back to studio…Jack going to Hollywood to make a picture…cast says goodbye to Don Bestor

Cast:

Last name	First name	Roles	Guest star
Benny	Jack	Jack Benny	No
Bestor	Don	Don Bestor	No
Edmunds	William	Tony	No
Hearn	Sam	Mr. Metro	No
Livingston	Mary	Mary Livingston	No
Parker	Frank	Frank Parker	No
Stewart	Blanche	Manicurist	No
Wilson	Don	Don Wilson	No

Songs:

Order	Title	Performers	Vocal
1	Hey Sailor	Frank Black	No
2	Beat of My Heart	Frank Black	No
3	This Is Our Last Night Together	Frank Black	No
4	A Kiss In the Dark	Frank Parker	Yes
5	California Here I Come	Frank Black	No

Notes:

Date: 6/1/1934 **Sponsor:** General Tire **City:** Hollywood, CA

Recording Source: None **Problems:** None

First line:
Hays: Ladies and gentlemen, we are going to cut in on our Chicago World's Fair program for a few minutes to bring to you the General Tire Comedian, Jack Benny...

Summary:
Jack and Don on the train, discuss the World's Fair...Jack tries to buy a blanket from an Indian...Mary writing poem about World's Fair...Mary bought a Pullman blanket from an Indian...Jack talks with train passenger (Nelson), turns out to be Clark Gable

Cast:

Last name	First name	Roles	Guest star
Baker	Benny	Laughing Water, vendor	No
Benny	Jack	Jack Benny	No
Hays	Will	Announcer	No
Livingstone	Mary	Mary Livingstone	No
Nelson	Frank	Clark Gable	No
Underwood	?	Conductor	No
Wilson	Don	Don Wilson	No

Songs:

Order	Title	Performers	Vocal
1	Unidentified		No
2	Unidentified		No
3	Unidentified		No
4	Unidentified		No
5	Unidentified		No

Notes:

Notable	First appearance of Frank Nelson
Running gag	Mary's poem

Date: 6/8/1934   **Sponsor:** General Tire   **City:** Hollywood, CA

Recording Source: None   **Problems:** None

First line:
And now for Hollywood's latest false alarm, Jack Benny.

Summary:
What the cast has been doing in California…Jack introduces Mary and Don to Jimmy Grier…Mary calls Don Bestor in New York so Grier can ask if Jack's checks are good…Mary reads poem about Hollywood…man from Reliance Film Company arrives, asks Jack to take screen test…Jack goes to studio, meets leading lady…Jack tries to play love scene with Hill

Cast:

Last name	First name	Roles	Guest star
?	Georgia	Miss Beverly Hill	No
Benny	Jack	Jack Benny	No
Grier	Jimmy	Jimmy Grier	No
Kane	?	Mr. Stoloff	No
Livingstone	Mary	Mary Livingstone	No
Parker	Frank	Frank Parker	No
Shutan	Harry	Cornet player, Edward Small	No
Wilson	Don	Don Wilson	No

Songs:

Order	Title	Performers	Vocal
1	A Shine On Your Shoes	Jimmy Grier	No
2	Ridin' Around In the Rain	Jimmy Grier	No
3	Just a Little Love, a Little Kiss	Frank Parker	Yes
4	Little Dutch Mill	Jimmy Grier	No
5	This Is the Missus	Jimmy Grier	No

Notes:

Running gag	Mary's poem

Date: 6/15/1934   **Sponsor:** General Tire   **City:** Hollywood, CA

Recording Source: None   **Problems:** None

First line:
And now for America's foremost wind-bag, Jack Benny.

Summary:
Jack and Don discuss California climate…Mary rented bungalow in Beverly Hills…cast discusses where they went to college…Mary reads letter from her mother…skit Who Killed Mr. Stooge…police can't find right door…O'Hare questions maid…interrogates Stooge, finally he starts to confess…to be continued

Cast:

Last name	First name	Roles	Guest star
Benny	Jack	Jack Benny, Sergeant O'Hare	No
Grier	Jimmy	Jimmy Grier, man two flights up	No
Livingston	Mary	Mary Livingston, maid	No
Martin	Minnie	Screamer, neighbor	No
Parker	Frank	Frank Parker, Officer	No
Shutan	Harry	Butler	No
Weber	?	Joe Stooge	No
Wilson	Don	Don Wilson, Officer Clancy	No

Songs:

Order	Title	Performers	Vocal
1	Laugh You Son of a Gun	Jimmy Grier	No
2	Beat of My Heart	Jimmy Grier	No
3	I Never Had a Chance	Frank Parker	Yes
4	Bugle Call Rag	Jimmy Grier	No
5	Christmas Night in Harlem	Jimmy Grier	No

Notes:

Running gag	Hair hair
Running gag	Mary's mother communication
Skit	Who Killed Mr. Stooge

Date: 6/22/1934   **Sponsor:** General Tire   **City:** Hollywood, CA

Recording Source: None   **Problems:** None

First line:
And now I present to you the Kid from Spain, New York and Los Angeles - Jack Benny.

Summary:
Cast discusses society people…Jack shooting Transatlantic Merry-Go-Round…Mary has film scenario for Jack…man tries to sell Jack life insurance…skit Who Killed Mr. Stooge…officers read newspapers about the murder…Stooge still lying there…interrogate man in jail…life insurance salesman in jail with him…letter arrives with address of murderer…to be continued

Cast:

Last name	First name	Roles	Guest star
Baldwin	Harry	Cop	No
Benny	Jack	Jack Benny, Sergeant O'Hare	No
Franz	Joe	Shadow, man parking on wrong side of street	No
Grier	Jimmy	Jimmy Grier	No
Livingston	Mary	Mary Livingston, Miss Donahue	No
Martin	Minnie	Screamer, bridge player	No
Parker	Frank	Frank Parker	No
Silvers	Sid	Death Valley Life Insurance salesman	No
Wilson	Don	Don Wilson, Officer Clancy	No

Songs:

Order	Title	Performers	Vocal
1	Steak and Potatoes	Jimmy Grier	No
2	Do I Love You	Jimmy Grier	No
3	One In a Blue Moon	Frank Parker	Yes
4	Casa Loma Stomp	Jimmy Grier	No
5	Yes Sir I Love Your Daughter	Jimmy Grier	No

Notes:

Running gag	Hair hair
Skit	Who Killed Mr. Stooge

Date: 6/29/1934 **Sponsor:** General Tire **City:** Hollywood, CA

Recording Source: None **Problems:** None

First line:
And now I present to you the late star of Little Women - Jack Hepburn Benny.

Summary:
Don took screen test...cast discusses movie makeup...Grier has a Saxon (same as Olsen in 5/2/32)...Mary wrote a letter to her family...Parker having dinner with Jean Harlow...skit Who Killed Mr. Stooge...Commissioner asks what they're doing about the case...O'Hare takes cab to Stooge home...interrogates Annie, who flirts with him...says she heard Clancy's voice on the night of the murder...to be continued

Cast:

Last name	First name	Roles	Guest star
Benny	Jack	Jack Benny, Sergeant O'Hare	No
Franz	Joe	Shadow, stowaway	No
Grier	Jimmy	Jimmy Grier, Officer	No
Livingston	Mary	Mary Livingston, Miss Donahue	No
Martin	Minnie	Jean Harlow, screamer, Annie	No
Parker	Frank	Frank Parker	No
Wilson	Don	Don Wilson, Officer Clancy	No

Songs:

Order	Title	Performers	Vocal
1	I Wish I Were Twins	Jimmy Grier	No
2	My Hat's On the Side Of My Head	Jimmy Grier	No
3	Someday I'll Find You	Frank Parker	Yes
4	Rise and Shine	Jimmy Grier	No
5	Of Thee I Sing	Jimmy Grier	No

Notes:

Running gag	Mary's mother communication
Running gag	Hair hair
Skit	Who Killed Mr. Stooge

Date: 7/6/1934   **Sponsor:** General Tire   **City:** Hollywood, CA

Recording Source: None   **Problems:** None

First line:
And now I present to you that great comedian, Simple Simon - er, I mean Jack Benny.

Summary:
Jack took his laundry to Graumann's Chinese Theatre…Jack was in San Francisco over July 4th, Grier accuses Jack of stealing the Golden Gate…Mary brings in left over firecrackers…salesman tries to sell Jack a lot…skit Who Killed Mr. Stooge…police need to cut down expenses…Commissioner threatens Sergeant…O'Hare and Clancy go to waterfront…interrogates Old Man River…to be continued

Cast:

Last name	First name	Roles	Guest star
		Salesman	No
Baldwin	Harry	Officer Dugan, narrator	No
Benny	Jack	Jack Benny, Sergeant O'Hare	No
Franz	Joe	Phantom, Old Man River	No
Grier	Jimmy	Jimmy Grier, telegram boy	No
Livingston	Mary	Mary Livingston, Miss Donahue	No
Martin	Minnie	Screamer	No
Parker	Frank	Frank Parker	No
Wilson	Don	Don Wilson, Officer Clancy	No

Songs:

Order	Title	Performers	Vocal
1	Moonlight Parade	Jimmy Grier	No
2	Anything That's Part of You	Jimmy Grier	No
3	Cocktails for Two	Frank Parker	Yes
4	Lady Be Good	Jimmy Grier	No
5	Do I Know What I'm Doing?	Jimmy Grier	No

Notes:

Running gag	Hair hair
Skit	Who Killed Mr. Stooge

Date: 7/13/1934   **Sponsor:** General Tire   **City:** Hollywood, CA

Recording Source: None   **Problems:** None

First line:
And now for that disappointed Beau Brummel, Mister Jack Benny.

Summary:
News headlines…Jack used to lead the Waukegan Symphony Orchestra…tells Jimmy how to get more out of his orchestra…Jack tries to lead Grier's orchestra and they sound like they're tuning up…Jack took a message for Parker but forgot who it was from…call for Sergeant O'Hare, but they're not doing that play…skit Why Gals Depart From Their Residence…parents celebrate daughter's 14th birthday…she works in a glue factory…sponsor calls and asks them to solve the murder…police call man on flying trapeze, interrogate him…to be continued

Cast:

Last name	First name	Roles	Guest star
		Clarinetist	No
Benny	Jack	Jack Benny, Fat-Head, Sergeant O'Hare	No
Franz	Joe	Phantom	No
Grier	Jimmy	Jimmy Grier	No
Livingston	Mary	Mary Livingston, Mary Ellen, Miss Donahue	No
Martin	Minnie	Screamer, Matilda	No
Parker	Frank	Frank Parker	No
Weber	?	Ginsberg, ice man, man on trapeze	No
Wilson	Don	Don Wilson, son, Officer Clancy	No

Songs:

Order	Title	Performers	Vocal
1	Laugh You Son of a Gun	Jimmy Grier	No
2	Varsity Drag	Jimmy Grier	No
3	Moonlight Madonna	Frank Parker	Yes
4	Hallelujah	Jimmy Grier	No
5	A Hut in Old Havana	Jimmy Grier	No

Notes:

Running gag	Hair hair
Skit	Why Gals Depart From Their Residence

Date: 7/20/1934   **Sponsor:** General Tire   **City:** Hollywood, CA

Recording Source: Unknown   **Problems:** Poor sound

First line:
And now for that phoney comedian...uh, funny comedian, Jack Benny.

Summary:
Hollywood news headlines...Jack describes Jimmie Grier...skit Stooge Murder
Case...tries rounding up suspicious characters...O'Hare accuses Phil Baker of murder,
questions Bottle and Beetle...Phil Baker and Jack discuss vaudeville, play duet on
Humoresque

Cast:

Last name	First name	Roles	Guest star
Baker	Phil	Phil Baker	Yes
Baldwin	Harry	Love Thy Neighbor requestor	No
Benny	Jack	Jack Benny, Sgt. O'Hare	No
Franz	Joe	Phantom	No
Grier	Jimmy	Jimmy Grier, Bum	No
Livingston	Mary	Mary Livingston, Miss Donohue	No
Martin	Minnie	Screamer, female arrestee	No
McNaughton	Harry	Nicholas Murray Bottle	No
Parker	Frank	Frank Parker, acrobat	No
Wilson	Don	Don Wilson, Officer Clancy	No
Wilson	Ward	Beetle	No

Songs:

Order	Title	Performers	Vocal
1	Valencia/Barcelona/99 Out of 100	Jimmy Grier	No
2	My Middle Name is Love	Jimmy Grier	No
3	A Pretty Girl is Like a Melody	Frank Parker	Yes
4	I Wish I Were Twins	Jimmy Grier	No
6	Humoresque	Phil Baker	No
6	Humoresque	Jack Benny	No
6	Shine On Your Shoes	Jimmy Grier	No

Notes:

Notable	One of two shows that includes part of Frank Parker's song
Running gag	Hair, hair
Skit	Who Killed Mr. Stooge

Date: 7/27/1934   **Sponsor:** General Tire   **City:** Hollywood, CA

Recording Source: None   **Problems:** None

First line:
And now for the world's most prolific purveyor of imbecilic nonsense, Jack Benny.

Summary:
Reporter comes to interview Jack...Jack tells of the things that Grier did for him...cast says goodbye to Grier...announces skit Over Beverly Hill to the Poor House...Mitzi Green brought up from audience...Jack asks Mitzi to play the maid in their play...film couple worries about money...son working on play (Ed Wynn imitation)...call about the Stooge murder...switch to Mr. Stooge sketch...O'Hare and Donohue catch a train to New York

Cast:

Last name	First name	Roles	Guest star
Benny	Jack	Jack Benny, Graham O'Hare, Sergeant O'Hare	No
Franz	Joe	Phantom	No
Green	Mitzi	Mitzi Green, Zasu, Edwin	Yes
Grier	Jimmy	Jimmy Grier, grocery man	No
Livingston	Mary	Mary Livingston, Gloria O'Hare, Miss Donojue	No
Martin	Minnie	Screamer	No
Parker	Frank	Frank Parker, O'Neil	No
Weber	?	Reporter, Barrymore	No
Wilson	Don	Don Wilson, gas man	No

Songs:

Order	Title	Performers	Vocal
1	Oo That Kiss	Jimmy Grier	No
2	Star Dust	Jimmy Grier	No
3	The Very Thought of You	Frank Parker	Yes
4	Casa Loma Stomp	Jimmy Grier	No
5	Do I Love You	Jimmy Grier	No

Notes:

Skit	Over Beverly Hill to the Poor House

Date: 8/3/1934 **Sponsor:** General Tire **City:** New York, NY

Recording Source: Unknown **Problems:** Partial show, music clipped

First line:
Bestor: Hello everybody, this is Don Bestor speaking.

Summary:
Jack and gang on the 20th Century Limited, returning from Hollywood…Shlepperman is on the train…skit Stooge Murder Case…Shlepperman deputized to look for clues on the train…Slav murderer confesses…gang returns to studio…Mary reads a poem

Cast:

Last name	First name	Roles	Guest star
Benny	Jack	Jack Benny, Sgt. O'Hare	No
Beston	Don	Don Bestor	No
Case	Norman	Opening announcer	No
Green	Eddie?	Porter	No
Hearn	Sam	Irving C. Shlepperman	No
Klein	Vi	Screamer	No
Lee	?	On-train salesman	No
Livingston	Mary	Mary Livingston, Miss Donohue	No
Noa	?	Conductor	No
Parker	Frank	Frank Parker	No
Slattery	?	Slav	No
Wilson	Don	Don Wilson, Clancy, Phantom	No

Songs:

Order	Title	Performers	Vocal
1	Dames	Don Bestor	No
2	Take a Lesson from the Lark	Don Bestor	No
3	I Never Had a Chance	Frank Parker	Yes
4	Ooh You Miser You	Don Bestor	No
5	What Good Is the Good In Goodbye	Don Bestor	No

Notes:

Blooper	Jack cracks up on air after Shlepperman's comment of "Has he got a dialect!"
Notable	First apperance of Shlepperman
Running gag	Mary's poem
Running gag	Hair, hair
Skit	Who Killed Mr. Stooge

Date: 8/10/1934 **Sponsor:** General Tire **City:** New York, NY

Recording Source: None **Problems:** None

First line:
And now I present to you our master of ceremonies, Sergeant O'Hare of Scotland Yard.

Summary:
Jack went to Saratoga Springs…hot in New York, cast competes on hot day stories…Parker asks Jack how to meet beautiful women…call from Mary's mother, she invites them over…Don drives them to Plainfield…serves doughnuts…Mary's father hard of hearing…Bestor brings entire orchesetra

Cast:

Last name	First name	Roles	Guest star
?	Andy	Untermeyer Livingstone	No
Benny	Jack	Jack Benny	No
Bestor	Don	Don Bestor	No
Hearn	Sam	Mary's father	No
Kelly	Mary	Mary's mother	No
Livingstone	Mary	Mary Livingstone	No
Parker	Frank	Frank Parker	No
Stone	?	Cop	No
Wilson	Don	Don Wilson	No

Songs:

Order	Title	Performers	Vocal
1	You Ought to See Sally on Sunday	Don Bestor	No
2	I Wish I Were Twins	Don Bestor	No
3	Two Cigarettes in the Dark	Frank Parker	Yes
4	Oh You Nasty Man	Don Bestor	No
5	Tonight is Mine	Don Bestor	No

Notes:

Running gag	Hair hair
Running gag	Mary's mother communication

Date: 8/17/1934   **Sponsor:** General Tire   **City:** New York, NY

Recording Source: None   **Problems:** None

First line:
And now for the Barney Google of the air, Mr. Jack Benny.

Summary:
Jack tries to tell joke about the woman on a bus with her baby, keeps getting interrupted by cast entering...xylophonist is running a hot dog stand...cast discusses aches and pains...President of General Tire calls to tell them it's not a hospital...Jack reads fan mail...skit The Dunkard...daughter goes out to bring father home...father out dunking doughnuts...run out of doughnuts

Cast:

Last name	First name	Roles	Guest star
Baldwin	Harry	Narrator	No
Benny	Jack	Jack Benny	No
Bestor	Don	Don Bestor	No
Kelly	Mary	Marilyn Kelly, mother	No
Livingstone	Mary	Mary Livingstone, Mariah	No
Parker	Frank	Frank Parker	No
Wilson	Don	Don Wilson	No

Songs:

Order	Title	Performers	Vocal
1	Sweetie Pie	Don Bestor	No
2	Bigger Than the Moon	Don Bestor	No
3	I Only Have Eyes for You	Frank Parker	Yes
4	Panama	Don Bestor	No
5	My Hat's On the Side of My Head	Don Bestor	No

Notes:

Running gag	Hair hair
Skit	The Dunkard

Date: 8/24/1934 **Sponsor:** General Tire **City:** New York, NY

Recording Source: WEAF **Problems:** Poor sound, music clipped

First line:
And now for that master golfer and talented violinist, Jack Benny.

Summary:
Gang just got back from Atlantic City…skit Rise of the House of Rawchild…ushers seating patrons…Meyer loans Prince 20 million gulden…sends sons into worlds to make fortunes…sons return having lost all money, except Sandy who became successful tire salesman…Prince returns to ask for more money

Cast:

Last name	First name	Roles	Guest star
Baldwin	Harry	Steno, impatient audience member	No
Benny	Jack	Jack Benny, Meyer Rawchild	No
Bestor	Don	Don Bestor, Nathan Rawchild	No
Hearn	Sam	Arliss, Prince	No
Kelly	Mary	Audience member, Sarah Rawchild	No
Lee	?	Vendor, late audience member, Goldbergs caller	No
Livingstone	Mary	Mary Livingstone	No
Lytell	Bert	Audience member, Sandy Rawchild	No
Parker	Frank	Frank Parker, Carl Rawchild	No
Wilson	Don	Don Wilson, Solomon Rawchild	No

Songs:

Order	Title	Performers	Vocal
1	We Will All Go Ridin' on a Rainbow	Don Bestor	No
2	There's a House in Harlem for Sale	Don Bestor	No
3	For All We Know	Frank Parker	Yes
4	Farewell to Arms Overture	Don Bestor	No
5	Au Revoir	Don Bestor	No

Notes:

Running gag	Hair hair
Skit	Rise of the House of Rawchild

Date: 8/31/1934   **Sponsor:** General Tire   **City:** New York, NY

Recording Source: WEAF   **Problems:** None

First line:
And now ladies and gentlemen, if you hear any odd noises on your radio, don't worry. It will be Jack Benny.

Summary:
Jack describes Don...Don talks in his sleep...Mary reads a poem about Labor Day...reads fan mail about House of Rawchild, requests House of Benny...Jack is christened (?)...Mary Livingstone comes over to play...Jack runs away to Chicago to get a job on radio...father and sister tune in

Cast:

Last name	First name	Roles	Guest star
?	Andy	Jack at age 8	No
Baldwin	Harry	Prop man, narrator	No
Benny	Jack	Jack Benny	No
Bestor	Don	Don Bestor	No
Kelly	Mary	Jack's sister Florence	No
Livingstone	Mary	Mary Livingstone	No
Parker	Frank	Frank Parker	No
Wilson	Don	Don Wilson, Hiram Benny	No

Songs:

Order	Title	Performers	Vocal
1	My Baby's on Strike	Don Bestor	No
2	Sapphire	Don Bestor	No
3	A New Moon Is Over My Shoulder	Frank Parker	Yes
4	Rain or Shine medley	Don Bestor	No
5	When the New Moon Shines	Don Bestor	No

Notes:

Running gag	Mary's poem

Date: 9/7/1934   **Sponsor:** General Tire   **City:** New York, NY

Recording Source: None   **Problems:** None

First line:
And now if you're not careful, you'll get Jack Benny.

Summary:
Scenery man comes back for Rawchild scenery...author shows up for Rawchild royalties...cast demands money as well...skit School Days...calls roll...quizzes class...last four minutes is long commercial, no show close

Cast:

Last name	First name	Roles	Guest star
Baldwin	Harry	Tommy, Hilliard Marks, Nicholas Murray Butler	No
Benny	Jack	Jack Benny, teacher	No
Bestor	Don	Don Bestor	No
Hearn	Sam	Smith, Sammy	No
Livingston	Mary	Mary Livingston, Babe Ruth	No
Parker	Frank	Frank Parker	No
Simmons	?	Snowball	No
Sorin	Louis	Count Egon Caesar Corti, Tony, George Bernard Shaw	No
Wilson	Don	Don Wilson	No

Songs:

Order	Title	Performers	Vocal
1	Limehouse Nights	Don Bestor	No
2	Ooh You Miser You	Don Bestor	No
3	You're a Builder Upper	Don Bestor	No
4	Love in Bloom	Frank Parker	Yes
5	Why Can't This Night Go On Forever	Don Bestor	No

Notes:

Skit	School Days

Date: 9/14/1934   **Sponsor:** General Tire   **City:** New York, NY

Recording Source: WEAF   **Problems:** None

First line:
Jack and Jill went up the hill to fetch a pail of water, Jack fell down and broke his crown and here he is in person.

Summary:
Show dedicated to the kids...gang talks about how they did in school...Bert Wheeler saw "Transatlantic Merry Go Round"...skit School Days...quizzes class...long closing commercial, no show close

Cast:

Last name	First name	Roles	Guest star
Benny	Jack	Jack Benny, teacher	No
Bestor	Don	Don Bestor	No
Livingston	Mary	Mary Livingston	No
Parker	Frank	Frank Parker	No
Wheeler	Bert	Bert Wheeler	Yes
Wilson	Don	Don Wilson	No
Woods	Johnny	Walter Winchell Jr., Eddie Cantor Jr., Freddy Allen Jr., Rudy Vallee Jr., Stoopnagle and Budd Jr.	No

Songs:

Order	Title	Performers	Vocal
1	Don't Let It Bother You	Don Bestor	No
2	Night and Day	Don Bestor	No
3	Contented	Don Bestor	No
4	It Happened When Your Eyes Met Mine	Frank Parker	Yes
5	Ten Yards to Go	Don Bestor	No

Notes:

Recording	Only first 11 minutes of show currently in circulation, skit is clipped
Skit	School Days

Date: 9/21/1934 **Sponsor:** General Tire **City:** New York, NY

Recording Source: Unknown **Problems:** None

First line:
And now that educator of children, that tower of wisdom, Jack Benny.

Summary:
Discussing Jimmy McLarnin vs Barney Ross boxing match...gang discusses who's the best dressed on the show...letter from a Rhode Island Board of Education...skit School Days...calls roll, quizzes class...long close commercial, no show close

Cast:

Last name	First name	Roles	Guest star
Barker	Brad	Percival E. Clare, Fido	No
Benny	Jack	Jack Benny, teacher	No
Bestor	Don	Don Bestor	No
Gordon	?	Eenie Miney Mo	No
Livingston	Mary	Mary Livingston, Kay Francis	No
Parker	Frank	Frank Parker	No
Wilson	Don	Don Wilson	No
Woods	Johnny	Ben Bernie Jr., Jimmie Durante Jr., Singin Sam Jr., Maurice Chevalier Jr.	No

Songs:

Order	Title	Performers	Vocal
1	Here Come the British	Don Bestor	No
2	You Ain't Been Living Right	Don Bestor	No
3	The Very Thought of You	Frank Parker	Yes
4	Sweetie Pie	Don Bestor	No

Notes:

Blooper	Mary stumbles on "I've got a headache, teacher"
Running gag	Hair hair
Skit	School Days

Date: 9/28/1934   **Sponsor:** General Tire   **City:** New York, NY

Recording Source: None   **Problems:** None

First line:
And now for the last time on this General Tire series, I present to you that great star of stage, screen, radio, hotel lobbies and street corners, Mr. Jack Benny.

Summary:
Jack used to play football...Mary has a date with Bert Wheeler...Jack and Bert argue about his contract...Jack throwing a banquet...guests arrive...food is served...everyone makes speeches

Cast:

Last name	First name	Roles	Guest star
?	Carl	Chef, Guest 2	No
Baldwin	Harry	Guest 1	No
Bestor	Don	Don Bestor	No
Hearn	Sam	Schlepperman	No
Livingston	Mary	Mary Livingston	No
Parker	Frank	Frank Parker	No
Stewart	Blanche	Mrs. Tread	No
Wheeler	Bert	Bert Wheeler	Yes
Wilson	Don	Don Wilson	No

Songs:

Order	Title	Performers	Vocal
1	Twenty-Four Hours in Georgia	Don Bestor	No
2	Valencia	Don Bestor	No
3	The Moon Was Yellow	Frank Parker	Yes
4	La Cucaracha	Don Bestor	No
5	Fare Thee Well	Don Bestor	No

Notes:

Date: 10/14/1934   **Sponsor:** Jell-O   **City:** New York, NY

Recording Source: Unknown   **Problems:** Poor sound, music clipped

First line:
And now, one of the world's greatest assistant comedians, Mr. Jack Benny.

Summary:
Talks about new sponsor…Mary made up a joke about "blowout proof"…tells joke about "not your sister or brother"…starts series of guest stars…this week's guests are the Chicken Sisters from New Orleans, now changed name to Dean Sisters…skit J. Benny grocery store…customers are Dean Sisters…Sam comes in and tells sister/brother joke…asks for ham and says "keep it"…Wilson plays Swede buying "Yello"…promo for Lanny Ross' program

Cast:

Last name	First name	Roles	Guest star
Benny	Jack	Jack Benny	No
Bestor	Don	Don Bestor, Zeke Bestor	No
Hearn	Sam	Sam	No
Kelly	Mary	Nutsy Dean, Prune customer	No
Klein	Vi	Mrs. Goldberg	No
Livingston	Mary	Mary Livingston	No
Parker	Frank	Frank Parker, Zeb Parker	No
Stewart	Blanche	Dizzy Dean, Mrs. Anchovy, Mrs. Borschtmeier	No
Wilson	Don	Don Wilson, Mr. Olsen	No

Songs:

Order	Title	Performers	Vocal
1	Sunny Disposish	Don Bestor	No
2	Who/ Crazy Rhythm medley	Don Bestor	No
3	Rollin Down the Mountain	Dean Sisters	Yes
4	Smoke Gets In Your Eyes	Frank Parker	Yes
5	The Continental	Don Bestor	No
6	Sweetie Pie	Don Bestor	No

Notes:

Notable	First show for Jell-O
Notable	First "Jell-O everybody" opening
Notable	First Sunday at 7 show
Running gag	Hair hair
Skit	J. Benny Grocery Store

Date: 10/21/1934   **Sponsor:** Jell-O   **City:** New York, NY

Recording Source: WJZ   **Problems:** Poor sound, music clipped

First line:
And now we bring the only rival of Popeye the sailor, Jack Benny.

Summary:
Jack tired from rehearsing for "Bring on the Girls", opening in Washington tomorrow..."Transatlantic Merry-Go Round" opening next week...everybody's tired...Mary reads poem "Fall is Here"...guest star is violin virtuoso Senor Hy Fetz...trick violin playing...skit J. Benny Grocery Store part 2...crazy customers...Curtis Mitchell, "Radio Stars" Magazine Editor, awards Jack "Radio Stars Award for Distinguished Service", never before given to a comedian

Cast:

Last name	First name	Roles	Guest star
Benny	Jack	Jack Benny	No
Bestor	Don	Don Bestor, Zeke Bestor	No
Edmunds	William	Squire Angelo Pasquale	No
Kahn	Cy	Caller	No
Kahn	Cy	Hy Fetz	No
Kelly	Mary	Mrs. Schmaltz	No
Livingston	Mary	Mary Livingston	No
Mitchell	Curtis	Curtis Mitchell	Yes
Parker	Frank	Frank Parker, Zeb Parker	No
Stewart	Blanche	Mrs. VanTwitter	No
Stewart	Blanche	Mrs. Borschtmeier	No
Wilson	Don	Don Wilson, Bum caller	No

Songs:

Order	Title	Performers	Vocal
1	It's Fun to Be Fooled	Don Bestor	No
2	Rock and Roll	Don Bestor	No
3	One Night of Love	Frank Parker	Yes
4	Ten Yards to Go	Don Bestor	No
5	Sing	Don Bestor	No

Notes:

Blooper	Mary jumps cue in skit
Blooper	Jack says "damn"
Blooper	Jack and Fetz get lines mixed up
Running gag	Hair hair
Running gag	Mary's poem
Skit	J. Benny Grocery Store

Date: 10/28/1934   **Sponsor:** Jell-O   **City:** New York, NY

Recording Source: WJZ   **Problems:** Poor sound, music clipped

First line:
And now, ladies and gentlemen, I was about to introduce Jack Benny but he hasn't arrived from Washington yet where he played last week...

Summary:
Jack congratulated by his butcher, lawyer, and others...baker's convention...guest star from women's open golf championship, Miss Masha Niblick...hits a golfball off Jack's watch...skit The Bennys of Wimpole Street...mean Papa dominates his daughters, who are pursing romance

Cast:

Last name	First name	Roles	Guest star
Adams	?	Mister Hobgoblin, lawyer	No
Baldwin	Harry	Barber	No
Benny	Jack	Jack Benny, Papa	No
Bestor	Don	Don Bestor, Captain Cook	No
Burns	?	Tailor	No
Kelly	Mary	Landlady, Maureen	No
Lee	?	Butcher, Chauffeur	No
Livingston	Mary	Mary Livingston, Elizabeth	No
Mathews	?	Mister Spook, Doctor	No
Parker	Frank	Frank Parker, Robert Browning	No
Stewart	Blanche	Masha Niblick, cockney maid	No
Wilson	Don	Don Wilson	No

Songs:

Order	Title	Performers	Vocal
1	Don't Let it Bother You	Don Bestor	No
2	Easter Parade - Two Cigarettes in the Dark - You Ought to Be in Pictures	Don Bestor	No
3	It Was Sweet of You	Frank Parker	Yes
4	Serenade to a Wealthy Widow	Don Bestor	No
5	Au Revoir	Don Bestor	No

Notes:

Blooper	Masha misses her cue
Blooper	Dog misses cue in skit
Running gag	Hair hair
Skit	The Bennys of Wimpole Street

Date: 11/4/1934 **Sponsor:** Jell-O **City:** New York, NY

Recording Source: Unknown **Problems:** Poor sound, music clipped

First line:
And now I present to you Mr. Jack Charles Laughton Benny of Wimpole Street.

Summary:
Jack tries to tell a travelling salesman story…everybody saw "Transatlantic Merry Go Round"…guest star, Mrs. Galli Kerchoo, sings "Angela Mia"…doing travelogue on Hawaii…Shlepperman is a Hawaiian…farewell is "Jell-O oe"…turns out they're at Coney Island

Cast:

Last name	First name	Roles	Guest star
Benny	Jack	Jack Benny	No
Bestor	Don	Don Bestor	No
Edmunds	William	Restaurant proprietor	No
Hearn	Sam	Shlepperman	No
Kelly	Mary	Galli Kerchoo, Hula dancer	No
Livingston	Mary	Mary Livingston	No
Parker	Frank	Frank Parker	No
Wilson	Don	Don Wilson	No

Songs:

Order	Title	Performers	Vocal
1	Over My Shoulder	Don Bestor	No
2	I Saw Stars	Don Bestor	No
3	Angela Mia	Mary Kelly	Yes
3	Angela Mia	Jack Benny	Yes
3	Angela Mia	Don Wilson	Yes
4	The Moon was Yellow	Frank Parker	Yes
5	You Gotta Give Credit to Love	Don Bestor	No
6	You're Devastating	Don Bestor	No

Notes:

Running gag	Hair hair

Date: 11/11/1934   **Sponsor:** Jell-O   **City:** New York, NY

Recording Source: Unknown   **Problems:** Poor sound, music clipped

First line:
And now ladies and gentlemen, as it is impossible for me to offer you a cigar, cigarette, or a drink, I can still offer you Jack Benny.

Summary:
Tour of New York ad for Jell-O…news headlines…Don Bestor has an international orchestra…guest star Shakespearean actor J. Barrett Wimpole, since they couldn't get the 4 Marx Bros…fan letter requests that Jack play Charlie Chan…skit Charlie Chan in Radio City…Sam Hearn is Ming Toy Shlepperman to help solve mystery…Jack questions cast to find out who shot Don Wilson…Don does Jell-O plug in Heaven

Cast:

Last name	First name	Roles	Guest star
		Tour guide	No
		Lion	No
		Tourist	No
?	Alice	Screamer	No
Adams	?	J. Barrett Wimpole, Phantom	No
Benny	Jack	Jack Benny, Charlie Chan	No
Bestor	Don	Don Bestor	No
Hearn	Sam	Shlepperman	No
Livingston	Mary	Mary Livingston	No
Parker	Frank	Frank Parker	No
Wilson	Don	Don Wilson	No

Songs:

Order	Title	Performers	Vocal
1	Okay Toots	Don Bestor	No
2	I'll Keep Warm All Winter	Don Bestor	No
3	Water Under the Bridge	Frank Parker	Yes
4	Chinatown My Chinatown	Don Bestor	No
5	Ha-Cha-Cha	Don Bestor	No

Notes:

Running gag	Hair hair
Skit	Charlie Chan in Radio City

Date: 11/18/1934 **Sponsor:** Jell-O **City:** New York, NY

Recording Source: WJZ **Problems:** Poor sound, music clipped

First line:
And now for that great actor, late star of Charlie Chan, the Barretts of Wimpole Street, and the ash cans of 42nd Street, Jack Benny.

Summary:
Fighter knocks out opponent for Jell-O…Jack studies work of other actors (reusing some jokes from E.G. Robinson appearance)…gang shows baby pictures…skit Mrs. Wiggs of the Onion Patch…family is to be evicted…Shlepperman is the long-lost father…Mitzi Green guest stars, does an impersonation of George Arliss imitating Mae West

Cast:

Last name	First name	Roles	Guest star
		Kids	No
Baldwin	Harry	Referee	No
Benny	Jack	Jack Benny, Horace Van Ish	No
Bestor	Don	Don Bestor, evictor, kid	No
Green	Mitzi	Mitzi Green	Yes
Hearn	Sam	Shlepperman	No
Livingston	Mary	Mary Livingston, Mrs. Wiggs	No
Parker	Frank	Frank Parker, Strawberry Wiggs	No
Stewart	Blanche	Miss Toupee, kid	No
Wilson	Don	Don Wilson, kid, mortgage holder	No

Songs:

Order	Title	Performers	Vocal
1	Put on Your Glasses	Don Bestor	No
2	Thief of Baghdad	Don Bestor	No
3	Be Still My Heart	Frank Parker	Yes
4	Hit the Deck Medley	Don Bestor	No
5	If I Had a Million Dollars	Mitzi Green	Yes
6	Isn't It a Shame	Don Bestor	No

Notes:

Running gag	Hair hair
Skit	Mrs. Wiggs of the Onion Patch

Date: 11/25/1934   **Sponsor:** Jell-O   **City:** New York, NY

Recording Source: None   **Problems:** None

First line:
Mary: Gee, that's a swell number Don...what's the name of it?

Summary:
Jack is late, cast fills in...everyone tells jokes...cast discusses what they're thankful for...Mary reads poem about Thanksgiving...Don invites Jack over for Thanksgiving...requests for Grind Hotel...front desk scene...clerk goes up to investigate noise, Wilson making love to Garbo

Cast:

Last name	First name	Roles	Guest star
?	Eleanor	Garbo	No
Baldwin	Harry	Bellman	No
Benny	Jack	Jack Benny, desk clerk	No
Bestor	Don	Don Bestor	No
Edmunds	William	Stringaline	No
Hearn	Sam	Jay Schlepperman Smith	No
Lee	?	Bellboy, bridge player	No
Livingston	Mary	Mary Livingston, operator	No
Parker	Frank	Frank Parker, Cohen	No
Parker	Frank	Frank Parker	No
Stewart	Blanche	Operator	No
Wilson	Don	Don Wilson	No
Wilson	Don	Don Wilson	No

Songs:

Order	Title	Performers	Vocal
1	Congratulate Me	Don Bestor	No
2	You're Not the Only Oyster in the Stew	Don Bestor	No
3	I'll Follow My Secret Heart	Frank Parker	Yes
4	Okay and Connecticut Yankee medley	Don Bestor	No
5	Out of a Clear Blue Sky	Don Bestor	No

Notes:

Running gag	Mary's poem
Skit	Grind Hotel

Date: 12/2/1934 **Sponsor:** Jell-O **City:** New York, NY

Recording Source: WJZ **Problems:** Poor sound, music clipped

First line:
And now for that self-made man who could have done a better job, Jack Benny.

Summary:
Jack and gang saw new movies...Mary calls an agent for new talent..."Bring on the Girls" is playing in Boston...new talent arrives and performs...skit Rose of the Rio Grande...Jack and posse go after Mary and Frank Parker...Shlepperman is a Mexican

Cast:

Last name	First name	Roles	Guest star
Baldwin	Harry	Carlos	No
Benny	Jack	Jack Benny	No
Bestor	Don	Don Bestor, Don Jose Bestor	No
Hearn	Sam	Shlepperman	No
Kahn	Cy	W.C. Jones, Lopez	No
Livingston	Mary	Mary Livingston, Rose	No
Parker	Frank	Frank Parker, Don Franco Parker	No
Stewart	Blanche	Imitator, Carioca	No
Wilson	Don	Don Wilson	No

Songs:

Order	Title	Performers	Vocal
1	Okay Toots	Don Bestor	No
2	You Ain't Been Living Right	Don Bestor	No
3	Blame It On My Youth	Frank Parker	Yes
4	La Cucaracha	Don Bestor	No
5	Love is Just Around the Corner	Don Bestor	No

Notes:

Running gag	Hair hair
Skit	Rose of the Rio Grande

Date: 12/9/1934   **Sponsor:** Jell-O   **City:** New York, NY

Recording Source: None   **Problems:** None

First line:
And now for the jokel boy who made good in the city - Jack Benny!

Summary:
Cast discusses colorful people...Jack playing in Boston a second week...songwriter wants to sell Jack a song about Jell-O...skit Shuv Soree...Boris goes to Moscow on business...lovers show up...Boris returns, missed bus

Cast:

Last name	First name	Roles	Guest star
?	Walter	Park-your-Carcass	No
Benny	Jack	Jack Benny, Boris	No
Bestor	Don	Don Bestor, Ivan	No
Hearn	Sam	Schlepperman	No
Kahn	Cy	Victor Herbert Ira Gershwin Berlin	No
Livingstone	Mary	Mary Livingstone, Vonya	No
Parker	Frank	Frank Parker, Petroff	No
Stewart	Blanche	Sonya	No
Wilson	Don	Don Wilson	No

Songs:

Order	Title	Performers	Vocal
1	Yes to You	Don Bestor	No
2	I've Got Rhythm/Fascinating Rhythm/Lady Be Good	Don Bestor	No
3	The World is Mine	Frank Parker	Yes
4	Dark Eyes	Don Bestor	No
5	One Little Kiss	Don Bestor	No

Notes:

Skit	Shuv Soree

Date: 12/16/1934 **Sponsor:** Jell-O **City:** New York, NY

Recording Source: Unknown **Problems:** Poor sound, music clipped

First line:
And now ladies and gentleman, I present to you that wizard of mirth and wit, that
gentleman of gentlemen…

Summary:
Everyone is making out their Christmas lists…Jack talks about the orchestra at the
Barrison Theatre in Waukegan…Jack wants to play a violin solo for his father, who is
visiting from Waukegan…skit Russia Through a Keyhole…Mary's sister, Natasha, taken
by Cossacks…Cossacks take Mary to the Automat

Cast:

Last name	First name	Roles	Guest star
Benny	Jack	Jack Benny, Boris	No
Bestor	Don	Don Bestor	No
Eddy	?	Violinist	No
Hearn	Sam	Volga boatman	No
Livingston	Mary	Mary Livingston, Olga	No
Parker	Frank	Frank Parker, Scarface Parker	No
Sorin	Louis	Karloff	No
Wilson	Don	Don Wilson	No

Songs:

Order	Title	Performers	Vocal
1	Take It Easy	Don Bestor	No
2	Music Box Revue medley	Don Bestor	No
3	If I Had a Million Dollars	Jack Benny	No
4	Some Day I'll Find You	Frank Parker	Yes
5	A Needle In a Haystack	Don Bestor	No
6	Stars Fell on Alabama	Don Bestor	No

Notes:

Running gag	Hair hair
Skit	Russia Through A Keyhole

Date: 12/23/1934 **Sponsor:** Jell-O **City:** New York, NY

Recording Source: None **Problems:** None

First line:
And here is Jack Benny who has just arrived, ready to start our big Christmas program!...Hey Jack, where are you?

Summary:
Jack finished Christmas shopping...Mary reads poem about Christmas...Jack gives Mary a ribbon for her wrist...everyone gives Jack "Anthony Adverse"...cast exchanges gifts...need to try out skit in Philadelphia...skit Christmas Eve in Iowa...family celebrates Christmas...father tells kids about Santa Claus...everyone goes to bed...Schlepperman is Santa Claus...Jack playing the Stanley Theatre in Jersey City next Friday

Cast:

Last name	First name	Roles	Guest star
?	Walter	Junior	No
Benny	Jack	Jack Benny, Poppa	No
Bestor	Don	Don Bestor	No
Hearn	Sam	Schlepperman	No
Livingston	Mary	Mary Livingston	No
Parker	Frank	Frank Parker	No
Stewart	Blanche	Mechanical doll, mother	No
Wilson	Don	Don Wilson	No

Songs:

Order	Title	Performers	Vocal
1	Night and Day	Don Bestor	No
2	A Bolt From the Blue	Don Bestor	No
3	June in January	Frank Parker	Yes
4	The Object of My Affection	Don Bestor	No
5	Sweet Madness	Don Bestor	No

Notes:

Running gag	Mary's poem
Skit	Christmas Eve in Iowa

Date: 12/30/1934   **Sponsor:** Jell-O   **City:** New York, NY

Recording Source: None   **Problems:** None

First line:
And now I present to you Father Time in person - Jack Benny!

Summary:
Cast discusses gifts…Door guy wishes Jack happy new year (repeatedly)…outstanding people of 1934 are guest stars…man who sold Carnera ticket from Italy…man who bet against Calvacade (race horse)…woman who lived near Kate Hepburn…stork who brought Dione Quintuplets…Mary's mother calls, invites cast over for New Years…cast goes to Plainfield…gang has dinner and all Jell-O flavors…cast makes resolutions

Cast:

Last name	First name	Roles	Guest star
Benny	Jack	Jack Benny	No
Bestor	Don	Don Bestor	No
Ducky	?	Abner J. Klunk, Willie	No
Edmunds	William	J. Angelo Potchagaloop	No
Hearn	Sam	Mary's father	No
Kelly	Mary	Mary's mother	No
Lee	?	Door guy	No
Livingston	Mary	Mary Livingston	No
Parker	Frank	Frank Parker	No
Stewart	Blanche	Mrs. Otto Graf, Tirley Shemple, stork, rooster	No
Wilson	Don	Don Wilson	No

Songs:

Order	Title	Performers	Vocal
1	Don't Let it Bother You	Don Bestor	No
2	College Rhythm	Don Bestor	No
3	Orchids in the Moonlight	Frank Parker	Yes
4	Rain or Shine medley	Don Bestor	No
5	Stay as Sweet as You Are	Don Bestor	No

Notes:

Notable	First appearance of "Door guy"-type character
Running gag	Mary's mother communication
Running gag	Hair hair

Date: 1/6/1935   **Sponsor:** Jell-O   **City:** New York, NY

Recording Source: Unknown   **Problems:** Poor sound, music clipped

First line:
And now I'm on the air in the year 1935, I present to you that famous...that well-known...a fellow whom you all...a man that's...

Summary:
Gang discusses what they did New Year's Eve...guy tries to sell Jack a bulldog...Jack still doesn't know what to buy Don Bestor for Christmas..."The day that Wilson doesn't eat Jell-O, you'll know it's Yom Kippur"...skit The Count of Monte Cristo...Dante conspires with prisoner to tunnel out of prison...encounter Shlepperman in tunnel...treasure ends up being Jell-O...opening at Stanley Theatre in Pittsburgh next Friday

Cast:

Last name	First name	Roles	Guest star
Baldwin	Harry	Telegram boy, narrator	No
Benny	Jack	Jack Benny, Edward Dante	No
Bestor	Don	Don Bestor, bellboy	No
Granby	?	Bank robber	No
Hearn	Sam	Shlepperman	No
Lee	?	Bulldog seller	No
Livingston	Mary	Mary Livingston, Mercedes Ginsburg, bat	No
Parker	Frank	Frank Parker, Frank P. Mondego	No
Wilson	Don	Don Wilson, French Foreign Legion officer	No

Songs:

Order	Title	Performers	Vocal
1	Anything Goes	Don Bestor	No
2	Some of These Days	Don Bestor	No
3	With Every Breath I Take	Frank Parker	Yes
4	Flirtation Walk	Don Bestor	No
5	Say When	Don Bestor	No

Notes:

Blooper	Frank Parker stumbles on "I thought the noise was mice in my apartment"
Blooper	Jack says "Alexander Dumont" instead of "Alexander Dumas"
Running gag	Hair hair
Skit	Count of Monte Cristo

Date: 1/13/1935   **Sponsor:** Jell-O   **City:** New York, NY

Recording Source: None   **Problems:** None

First line:
And now, ladies and gentlemen, I present to you that…just a minute, folks…Say Bestor, where is Jack?

Summary:
Jack and Mary playing in Pittsburgh…Jack is late, gang discusses why they don't need Jack…Jack arrives, still doesn't know what to get Bestor for Christmas…man with ticket to show doing Door guy routine, asking when show starts…Bestor is bossed by his wife…Jack wants Bestor to get rid of his violinist…Mary calls her mother to get them to listen…telegram from man who wrote "Object of My Affection" asking Jack to play "Love in Bloom"…telegram from man who wrote "Love in Bloom" requests "You're the Top"…Parker calls his grandfather to listen (in England)…Jack tunes up…Jack tries to play and keeps getting interrupted for silly comments…Jack and Mary need to catch train to Pittsburgh…Jack plays "Love in Bloom" in the cab to the train, but still can't finish it…Mary writes poem to Pittsburgh on the train

Cast:

Last name	First name	Roles	Guest star
		Violinist	No
Benny	Jack	Jack Benny	No
Bestor	Don	Don Bestor	No
Ducky	?	Man with ticket	No
Hearn	Sam	Schlepperman	No
Livingston	Mary	Mary Livingston	No
Parker	Frank	Frank Parker	No
Wilson	Don	Don Wilson, train announcer	No

Songs:

Order	Title	Performers	Vocal
1	Unidentified	Don Bestor	No
2	Sweetie Pie	Don Bestor	No
3	One Night of Love	Frank Parker	Yes
4	Sapphire	Don Bestor	No
5	Love in Bloom	Jack Benny	No
6	June in January	Don Bestor	No

Notes:

Notable	First time Jack plays "Love in Bloom"
Running gag	Mary's mother communication
Running gag	Mary's poem

Date: 1/20/1935   **Sponsor:** Jell-O   **City:** Chicago, IL

Recording Source: None   **Problems:** None

First line:
And now let us welcome back to Chicago that local boy who not only made good in the big city, but came bck to pay his bills...Jack Benny!

Summary:
From Chicago, Bob Brown stands in for Don Wilson...Mary went to see World's Fair, it closed three months ago...Don Bestor seeing his grandmother...Jack, Mary and Parker playing at Chicago Theatre...skit The Sixth Guest...Don Wilson calls...man invites six guests to dinner, one will die...guests arrive...Mr. B announces that in three minutes someone will be murdered, guests try to leave...Mr. B asks each guest why they shouldn't be murdered...shoots Brown as he starts commercial

Cast:

Last name	First name	Roles	Guest star
		Butler	No
Benny	Jack	Jack Benny, Mr. B	No
Bestor	Don	Don Bestor, guest 5	No
Brown	Bob	Bob Brown, guest 6	No
Horan	Tommy	Herman	No
Kelly	Mary	Guest 1	No
Lee	?	Door guy	No
Livingstone	Mary	Mary Livingstone, guest 4	No
Parker	Frank	Frank Parker, guest 2	No
Stewart	Blanche	Guest 3	No

Songs:

Order	Title	Performers	Vocal
1	Smooth Sailing	Don Bestor	No
2	Sweet Music	Don Bestor	No
3	Isle of Capri	Frank Parker	Yes
4	Mysterious Mose	Don Bestor	No
5	I Woke Up Too Soon	Don Bestor	No

Notes:

Running gag	Hair hair
Skit	The Sixth Guest

Date: 1/27/1935   **Sponsor:** Jell-O   **City:** New York, NY

Recording Source: None   **Problems:** None

First line:
And now, folks, I want to announce that Jack Benny has just finished a theatrical engagement in Chicago and is rushing East by train…

Summary:
Jack on train from Chicago…Mary reading "The Private Life of a Goldfish"…Jack and Mary play poker with Oy-Oy…Oy-Oy wins money from them and gets off the train…Jack calls Don from station…Jack's sister borrowed stockings from Mary…Jack wants to finally play "Love in Bloom"…Bestor changed violinist to cornetist…Jack starts to play, gets interrupted again…finally starts to play and carpenters arrive to fix Bestor's platform, hammering over Jack's solo…Jack says it's the last time he'll play "Love in Bloom"…promo for infantile paralysis donations

Cast:

Last name	First name	Roles	Guest star
Ashe	Ralph	Carpenter	No
Baldwin	Harry	Train announcer, carpenter	No
Benny	Jack	Jack Benny	No
Bestor	Don	Don Bestor	No
Hearn	Sam	Oy-Oy MacIntyre, William Parker	No
Kelly	Mary	Parker's wife	No
Lee	?	Vendor on train	No
Livingston	Mary	Mary Livingston	No
Noa	?	Conductor	No
Parker	Frank	Frank Parker	No
Wilson	Don	Don Wilson	No

Songs:

Order	Title	Performers	Vocal
1	If It's Love	Don Bestor	No
2	I'm a Hundred Percent for You	Don Bestor	No
3	Blue Moon	Frank Parker	Yes
4	All Thru The Night	Don Bestor	No
5	Love in Bloom	Jack Benny	No
6	I Believe in Miracles	Don Bestor	No

Notes:

Date: 2/3/1935 **Sponsor:** Jell-O **City:** New York, NY

Recording Source: None **Problems:** None

First line:
And now we bring to you that hundred percent comedian…fifty per cent gentleman..and ten per cent violinist…Jack Benny!

Summary:
Jack came over from Staten Island on ice skates…Jack playing Baltimore this weekend…gang discusses how cold it is…Mary reads a poem about Baltimore

Cast:

Last name	First name	Roles	Guest star
Benny	Jack	Jack Benny	No
Bestor	Don	Don Bestor	No
Hearn	Sam	Door guy	No
Livingston	Mary	Mary Livingston	No
Parker	Frank	Frank Parker	No
Wilson	Don	Don Wilson	No

Songs:

Order	Title	Performers	Vocal
1	I'm Going Shopping With You	Don Bestor	No
2	Believe It, Beloved	Don Bestor	No

Notes:

Notable	Script is missing pages 7 to the end
Running gag	Mary's poem
Skit	Emperor Jones

Date: 2/10/1935 **Sponsor:** Jell-O **City:** New York, NY

Recording Source: None **Problems:** None

First line:
And now ladies and gentlemen, I present to you our Master of Ceremonies - one of the
sweetest guys in the whole world…

Summary:
Telegram from Eugene O'Neill about last week's skit…Jack appearing at Mastbaum
Theatre in Philadelphia this week…gang discusses Philadelphia…Mary thinks filly of sole
comes from Philadelphia…Bestor explains necessity of orchestra
conductor…Schlepperman brings his son to the studio…skit Romeo and Jello-
ett…Romeo visits…Jello-ett's mother tries to talk her out of Romeo…Romeo interrupted
by other characters…Wilson makes love to Jello-ett…Romeo says Wilson is only
interested because Jello-ett is twice as rich as ever before…Jack voted best comedian
and Jell-O show best program on the air in New York World-Telegram…Jack gives
significant recognition to Harry W. Conn…opening at Earle Theatre in Washginton next
Friday

Cast:

Last name	First name	Roles	Guest star
		John Quincy Schlepperman	No
Benny	Jack	Jack Benny, Romeo	No
Bestor	Don	Don Bestor, Merchant of Venice	No
Hearn	Sam	Schlepperman, Jello-ett's father	No
Kelly	Mary	Jello-ett's mother	No
Livingston	Mary	Mary Livingston, Jello-ett	No
Parker	Frank	Frank Parker, Brutus Parker	No
Stewart	Blanche	Ophelia, MacDuff	No
Wilson	Don	Don Wilson	No

Songs:

Order	Title	Performers	Vocal
1	March Winds and April Showers	Don Bestor	No
2	Throwing Stones at the Sun	Don Bestor	No
3	Isle of Capri	Frank Parker	Yes
4	Love for Sale	Don Bestor	No
5	Zing Went the Strings of My Heart	Don Bestor	No

Notes:

Running gag	Hair hair
Skit	Romeo and Jello-ett

Date: 2/17/1935   **Sponsor:** Jell-O   **City:** New York, NY

Recording Source: None   **Problems:** None

First line:
And now we bring you...a fellow whom you all know...he'll make you glad you came...Jack Benny is the name.

Summary:
Jack and Wilson sing opera...Jack and Wilson discuss government changes...Mary stubbed her toe on the Washington Monument...Jack offers to play with Bestor's orchestra, Jack has plumber's union card...Jack starts to play "Love in Bloom", gets interrupted by girl duo, the O.K. Sisters (bow-legged and knock-kneed)...skit George Washington...father gives Washington a hatchet at age 10...George talks to Martha, girl next door...George chops down cherry tree...father angry because he only has five flavors left...Hearn announces that the Yiddish are coming

Cast:

Last name	First name	Roles	Guest star
Baldwin	Harry	Man from other studio	No
Benny	Jack	Jack Benny	No
Bestor	Don	Don Bestor	No
Hearn	Sam	Paul Revere	No
Kelly	Mary	Zasu	No
Livingston	Mary	Mary Livingston, Martha	No
Parker	Frank	Frank Parker, Washington as a boy	No
Stewart	Blanche	Agnes, baby, chicken	No
Wilson	Don	Don Wilson, Washington's father	No

Songs:

Order	Title	Performers	Vocal
1	In My Country That Means Love	Don Bestor	No
2	You Are a Heavenly Thing	Don Bestor	No
3	Take a Number from One to Ten	Blanche Stewart	Yes
3	Take a Number from One to Ten	Mary Kelly	Yes
4	I Get a Kick Out of You	Frank Parker	Yes
5	Exactly Like You - Memories of You – On the Sunny Side of the Street	Don Bestor	No
6	Where Were You on the Night of June 3rd	Don Bestor	No

Notes:

Running gag	Hair hair
Skit	George Washington

Date: 2/24/1935   **Sponsor:** Jell-O   **City:** New York, NY

Recording Source: None   **Problems:** None

First line:
Oh! He talks on the air with the greatest of ease. His hair all mussed up, and he has baggy knees. He tells a joke that's only a wheeze...

Summary:
Gang discusses circuses, they all worked in one...Jack suggests that Bestor play the classics...Jack calls Mr. Brownlee of Jell-O to discuss Bestor's music...Brownlee asks for "Hold That Tiger"...Jack says Parker looks terrible, says he should move to the country...skit City and Country Life...lazy day and slow life in country...fast-paced city life where the same things happen but much faster, son meets girl, gets marries and comes home with baby in one scene...playing Chicago Theatre starting Friday

Cast:

Last name	First name	Roles	Guest star
Benny	Jack	Jack Benny	No
Bestor	Don	Don Bestor, doctor	No
Hearn	Sam	Chicken, grandpa	No
Kelly	Mary	Gretchen	No
Livingston	Mary	Mary Livingston, Mrs. Schmaltz	No
Parker	Frank	Frank Parker, Egbert	No
Stewart	Blanche	Rooster, grandma	No
Wilson	Don	Don Wilson, grocer	No

Songs:

Order	Title	Performers	Vocal
1	I Was Lucky	Don Bestor	No
2	Panama	Don Bestor	No
3	Dinah	Frank Parker	Yes
4	Diga-Diga-Doo - I Can't Give You Anything But Love Baby	Don Bestor	No
5	Clouds	Don Bestor	No

Notes:

Skit	City and Country Life

Date: 3/3/1935   **Sponsor:** Jell-O   **City:** Chicago, IL

Recording Source: None   **Problems:** None

First line:
Old Man Benny, that Old Man Benny, he keeps on talkin', he don't say nothin', that Old Man Benny, He jes keeps rollin' along.

Summary:
Gang discusses how great Chicago is…Lupe Velez comes from the Loop…Jack not talking to Bestor, Mary relays statements for them…Mary's mother calls, she won the Irish Sweepstakes…skit The Bennys of Wimpole Street…Elizabeth is sick, confined to bed…mean father lords over his daughters…doesn't like Elizabeth being with Browning, she's sick and she'll get verse…Browning visits…Maureen entertaining Bestor's orchestra

Cast:

Last name	First name	Roles	Guest star
Benny	Jack	Jack Benny, Old Man Benny	No
Bestor	Don	Don Bestor, Captain Cook	No
Kelly	Mary	Maureen	No
Livingstone	Mary	Mary Livingstone, Elizabeth Benny	No
Parker	Frank	Frank Parker, Robert Browning	No
Stewart	Blanche	Screamer, maid, Flush (dog)	No
Wilson	Don	Don Wilson	No

Songs:

Order	Title	Performers	Vocal
1	Who's Honey Are You	Don Bestor	No
2	Needle in a Haystack	Don Bestor	No
3	You and the Night and the Music	Frank Parker	Yes
4	Sweet Music	Don Bestor	No
5	Unidentified	Don Bestor	No

Notes:

Running gag	Mary's mother communication
Running gag	Hair hair
Skit	The Bennys of Wimpole Street

Date: 3/10/1935   **Sponsor:** Jell-O   **City:** New York, NY

Recording Source: None   **Problems:** None

First line:
And now, ladies and gentlemen, we bring to you a man who has made a name for himself...a fellow who is a credit to his community...beloved by his neighbors...but in my opinion is just a ham...Jack Benny!

Summary:
Wilson talks about his children...gang discusses their childhoods...Jack still hasn't given Bestor a Christmas present...Jack giving a party, invites gang but not Bestor...tax expert comes to help Jack with his taxes...Jack says he's 38...discusses play "Rain"...skit Bad Weather...guests arrive and rent rooms...missionary Javidson sends Sadie back to San Francisco, sailor taking her to Sydney...Schlepperman is Big Chief...natives eating Frank Parker for dinner...Sadie finally agrees to go to San Francisco, Governor is under her bed

Cast:

Last name	First name	Roles	Guest star
Benny	Jack	Jack Benny, Javidson	No
Bestor	Don	Don Bestor, Governor	No
Hearn	Sam	Big Chief	No
Kelly	Mary	Ameena	No
Laurie	?	Tax expert, guest 1, native	No
Livingston	Mary	Mary Livingston, Sadie Johnson	No
Parker	Frank	Frank Parker, Sailor	No
Stewart	Blanche	Mrs. Javidson, screamer	No
Wilson	Don	Don Wilson, Joe Horn	No

Songs:

Order	Title	Performers	Vocal
1	Not Bad	Don Bestor	No
2	Rhumbola	Don Bestor	No
3	When I Grow Too Old to Dream	Frank Parker	Yes
4	Rain on the Roof/Singing In the Rain/Rain, Rain Go Away	Don Bestor	No
5	Pardon My Love	Don Bestor	No

Notes:

Running gag	Hair hair
Skit	Bad Weather

Date: 3/17/1935   **Sponsor:** Jell-O   **City:** New York, NY

Recording Source: None   **Problems:** None

First line:
And now, just a minute, folks, who is this entering the Studio?

Summary:
Don introduces Jack in Irish dialect...jokes about Irish, Ireland, etc...Mary's diamond ring is like the Irish national emblem because it's a sham rock...Mary wrote a poem about Ireland...Jack and Bestor still at odds...Bestor quits and takes orchestra...Mary calls Boston Philharmonic Symphony...Bestor accompanies Parker from Staten Island Ferry...Schlepperman shows up with his band to replace Bestor...Jack asks them to audition with "Love in Bloom", they play "The Object of My Affliction"...announces skit The Rocky Road to Dublin, but not enough actors...Bea Lillie comes up from audience...Jack offers to take Bea home...telegrams Frank Parker on his appearance at Century Theatre in Baltimore

Cast:

Last name	First name	Roles	Guest star
?	Carl	Thorndyke	No
Baldwin	Harry	Cabbie	No
Benny	Jack	Jack Benny	No
Bestor	Don	Don Bestor	No
Hearn	Sam	Schlepperman	No
Lillie	Beatrice	Beatrice Lillie	Yes
Livingstone	Mary	Mary Livingstone	No
Parker	Frank	Frank Parker	No
Wilson	Don	Don Wilson	No

Songs:

Order	Title	Performers	Vocal
1	Lost My Rhythm, Lost My Music, Lost My Man	Don Bestor	No
2	Lookie Lookie Lookie Here Comes Cookie	Don Bestor	No
3	Sweetheart Darlin	Frank Parker	Yes
4	Alexander's Ragtime Band	Don Bestor	No
5	So Close to the Forest	Don Bestor	No

Notes:

Running gag	Mary's poem
Running gag	Hair hair

Date: 3/24/1935   **Sponsor:** Jell-O   **City:** New York, NY

Recording Source: None   **Problems:** None

First line:
And now we bring to you for the first time on the air…this week…Jack Benny!

Summary:
Jack flew to California and back…going to make "Broadway Melody of 1935"…gang discusses plane travel…Jack auditions replacement orchestra…Marion is a German orchestra…Jack and Bestor make up…Jack and Bestor discuss Bestor's spats…skit Are Gentlemen Born…Van Pelts expecting a child…Mr. Mortgage arrives and throws them out for non-payment…redo same scene in East Side setting, quintuplets arrive, mother goes to Roseland…Schlepperman is landlord…Marion's German band starts playing in back yard…promo to send three ends from packages of Jell-O to get autographed photo of Jack

Cast:

Last name	First name	Roles	Guest star
Benny	Jack	Jack Benny, Van Pelt, Spike	No
Bestor	Don	Don Bestor, Mr. Mortgage	No
Hearn	Sam	Dugan	No
Livingston	Mary	Mary Livingston, nurse	No
Marion	Sid	Sid Marion	Yes
Parker	Frank	Frank Parker, Throndyke	No
Stewart	Blanche	Mrs. Renssalaire Twig	No
Wilson	Don	Don Wilson, baby	No

Songs:

Order	Title	Performers	Vocal
1	That's the Reason	Don Bestor	No
2	You're a Heavenly Thing	Don Bestor	No
3	Life is a Song	Frank Parker	Yes
4	Sweet Madness/Angry	Don Bestor	No
5	It's Easy to Remember	Don Bestor	No

Notes:

Notable	First time Jack's entrance played in with "Love in Bloom"
Running gag	Hair hair
Skit	Are Gentlemen Born

Date: 3/31/1935   **Sponsor:** Jell-O   **City:** Boston, MA

Recording Source: None   **Problems:** None

First line:
And now we welcome to Boston that national wit, comm…humorist, period…and violinist, question-mark - Jack Benny!

Summary:
Jack asks Wilson if he can walk down Washington Street…gang discusses famous Boston sites…Jack gives Bestor a Christmas present, everyone makes speeches…Jack gives gift to Bestor and leaves for appointment…long present unwrapping, finds note reminding him that tomorrow is April 1…skit Dr. Jello and Mr. Hyde…Jekyll arrives…diagnoses dizzy spell woman with sprained ankle…Jekyll takes powders, becomes Hyde…dictates demand letter to Dracula…Jekyll returns to normal in morning…Don Wilson is a patient, swallowed a microphone…sees hard-of-hearing rube, gives him powder, turns into Schlepperman…repeated offer for Jack's picture

Cast:

Last name	First name	Roles	Guest star
Benny	Jack	Jack Benny	No
Bestor	Don	Don Bestor	No
Hearn	Sam	Hiram Oats, Schlepperman	No
Kelly	Mary	Miss Daisy Twilt	No
Livingston	Mary	Mary Livingston, Jekyll operator	No
Parker	Frank	Frank Parker	No
Stewart	Blanche	Hyde operator	No
Wilson	Don	Don Wilson	No

Songs:

Order	Title	Performers	Vocal
1	Go Into Your Dance	Don Bestor	No
2	Valencia	Don Bestor	No
3	Star Dust	Frank Parker	Yes
4	She's a Latin from Manhattan	Don Bestor	No
5	According to the Moonlight	Don Bestor	No

Notes:

Running gag	Hair hair
Skit	Dr. Jello and Mr. Hyde

Date: 4/7/1935 **Sponsor:** Jell-O **City:** New York, NY

Recording Source: None **Problems:** None

First line:
And now we bring to you our hero who is broadcasting from New York tonight, and next Sunday from Hollywood -- Mr. William Powell Benny!

Summary:
Jack talks about the Hollywood cutting room...gang talks about being in pictures...Bestor bought a dog to keep him company in California...Schlepperman brings his wife to the studio...Parker running around with various women...Mary reads poem about California...announces skit From Rags to Riches...gang gives Jack send off...cancels skit, have a banquet for Jack...gang eats like a boardinghouse...Don makes a speech about Jack...Dionne Quintuplets call to wish jack a happy trip...gang gives Jack a tie with initials "D.B." (originally for Don Bestor)...Jack plays Love in Bloom

Cast:

Last name	First name	Roles	Guest star
		Telegram boy	No
		Flowers boy	No
		Package boy	No
Benny	Jack	Jack Benny	No
Bestor	Don	Don Bestor	No
Hearn	Sam	Schlepperman	No
Livingstone	Mary	Mary Livingstone	No
Parker	Frank	Frank Parker	No
Stewart	Blanche	Mrs. Schlepperman	No
Wilson	Don	Don Wilson, dog	No

Songs:

Order	Title	Performers	Vocal
1	I Won't Dance	Don Bestor	No
2	April Showers	Don Bestor	No
3	Lovely to Look At	Frank Parker	Yes
4	Believe It Beloved	Don Bestor	No
5	Love in Bloom	Jack Benny	No
6	Things Might Have Been So Different	Don Bestor	No

Notes:

Running gag	Mary's poem
Running gag	Hair hair

Date: 4/14/1935 **Sponsor:** Jell-O **City:** Hollywood, CA

Recording Source: None **Problems:** None

First line:
Special announcement, ladies and gentlemen - Jack Benny has not arrived in Hollywood yet, owing to a stop-over in Chicago to visit his folks, but we will try and get him for you...

Summary:
Jack and Mary on the train...Wilson driving, Parker flying, Bestor coming by way of Panama Canal...car tried to climb a telegraph pole, it's Don Wilson...hear Parker in the distance...gang arrives in California...Jack wants to play the violin, interrupted by reporter...MGM calls, wants Jack over right away...Jack tries to get into MGM but Miss Jones (receptionist) hassles him...Jack falls asleep and dreams of gang as different movie stars

Cast:

Last name	First name	Roles	Guest star
?	Margaret	Miss Jones	No
Baker	Benny	Hollywood Snoop reporter	No
Baldwin	Harry	Boy	No
Benny	Jack	Jack Benny	No
Franz	Joe	Okay man	No
Grier	Jimmy	Jimmy Grier	No
Livingstone	Mary	Mary Livingstone, Miss Crawford	No
McIntire	?	Opening commercial announcer, radio passenger, Mr. Gable	No
Parker	Frank	Frank Parker	No
Underwood	?	Opening announcer	No
Wilson	Don	Don Wilson	No
Young	?	Orange salesman	No

Songs:

Order	Title	Performers	Vocal
1	I Know That You Know	Jimmy Grier	No
2	The Martinique	Jimmy Grier	No
3	Tell Me That You Love Me	Frank Parker	Yes
4	Hallelujah	Jimmy Grier	No
5	Of Thee I Sing	Jimmy Grier	No

Notes:

Running gag	Hair hair

Date: 4/21/1935   **Sponsor:** Jell-O   **City:** Hollywood, CA

Recording Source: None   **Problems:** None

First line:
And now we bring to you that famous radio star...that well known stage star...and that questionable screen star, Jack Benny.

Summary:
Jack talks about the place he rented on Beverly Boulevard...Mary bought Easter Eggs and dyed them white...Mary reads poem about Easter...guest star, Garbo's delivery boy...Jack goes back to MGM, receptionist hassles him again...Jack compliments her and she lets him in...LeMaire's secretary shows Jack around, introduces him to stars...Bestor is new janitor...gang is there working on Jack's picture, they rehearse...scene goes on and on without an entrance for Jack...Mary wrote the script...Bestor sweeps up the script

Cast:

Last name	First name	Roles	Guest star
?	Cecil	Under-undersecretary, Mr. Silvey	No
?	Fred	William Powell, Robert Montgomery, Jean Harlow	No
?	Margaret	Miss Jones	No
Baker	Benny	Douglas Menjou Figg	No
Baldwin	Harry	Boy, undersecretary	No
Benny	Jack	Jack Benny	No
Bestor	Don	Don Bestor	No
Livingston	Mary	Mary Livingston	No
McIntire	?	Mr. LeMaire's secretary	No
Parker	Frank	Frank Parker	No
Wilson	Don	Don Wilson	No

Songs:

Order	Title	Performers	Vocal
1	It's an Old Southern Custom	Don Bestor	No
2	All Thru the Night	Don Bestor	No
3	Soon	Frank Parker	Yes
4	Chloe	Don Bestor	No
5	So Red the Rose	Don Bestor	No

Notes:

Running gag	Mary's poem

Date: 4/28/1935 **Sponsor:** Jell-O **City:** Hollywood, CA

Recording Source: None **Problems:** None

First line:
Again we bring to you America's best dressed man and worst actor - Jack Benny!

Summary:
News headlines...reads fan mail (including from Florence Fenchel, Lake Forest, IL)...Mary reads a letter from her mother, sends separate note for Jack...Jack and Parker discuss how the climate is good for their voices, Jack sings a bit of "Love in Bloom"...start shooting "Broadway Melody" next week...gang discusses playing golf...Jack, Mary, and Parker catch a cab to the golf course...caddy came out to make a picture, left holding the bag...Jack gives Sarazen golf guidance...Jack breaks a window in the clubhouse behind him...Jack gets in the rough, swings and breaks his club...Jack says he got a birdie 12...Jack hits it into the woods...Jack loses caddy, hears tom-toms (Paramount making a jungle picture)...Jack hits into a ditch, changes places with caddy...promo for Tony and Gus...next Sunday switching to 7:30 Pacific Standard Time

Cast:

Last name	First name	Roles	Guest star
?	Fred	Gene Sarazen, Emperor Jones	No
Baker	Benny	Caddy	No
Baldwin	Harry	Hawkins	No
Benny	Jack	Jack Benny	No
Bestor	Don	Don Bestor	No
Livingston	Mary	Mary Livingston	No
Parker	Frank	Frank Parker	No
Rome	Betty	83 year old golfer	No
Wilson	Don	Don Wilson	No

Songs:

Order	Title	Performers	Vocal
1	Anything Goes	Don Bestor	No
2	Lullaby of Broadway	Don Bestor	No
3	When I Grow Too Old to Dream	Frank Parker	Yes
4	Good News medley	Don Bestor	No
5	Every Day	Don Bestor	No

Notes:

Running gag	Mary's mother communication

Date: 5/5/1935   **Sponsor:** Jell-O   **City:** Hollywood, CA

Recording Source: None   **Problems:** None

First line:
And now we bring to you for the first time in the month of May a fellow who, though no Sarazen at golf and no Heifetz on the fiddle, is still a great guy...

Summary:
Don gives Jack long introduction and breaks down in tears...Jack played in with "Love in Bloom"...Jack and Wilson discuss suburbs...Jack coaches Mary on Mexican pronunciation...Parker went to Kentucky Derby...Bestor playing at St. Francis Hotel...postman delivers mail, it's almost all for Parker...Jack gets a prosperity chain letter...Don gets chain letter with Jell-O flavors...MGM Casting Director stops by...Jack says that in some script, the villain should get the girl...skit The Fatal Wedding...parents prepare for daughter's wedding...ceremony starts, need to take keys off the ring...Jack's landlord interrupts and demands rent, marries Tillie instead...Mary gets chains in response to chain letter

Cast:

Last name	First name	Roles	Guest star
Baker	Benny	Postman, butler	No
Baker	Wally	Landlord	No
Benny	Jack	Jack Benny, Mr. Flit	No
Bestor	Don	Don Bestor, best man	No
Livingston	Mary	Mary Livingston, Sarah Flit	No
MacIntire	John	Billy Grady	No
Parker	Frank	Frank Parker, Elmer Brown	No
Rome	Betty	Tillie Flit	No
Wilson	Don	Don Wilson, Deacon Wilson	No

Songs:

Order	Title	Performers	Vocal
1	Fare Thee Well, Annabelle	Don Bestor	No
2	Love for Sale	Don Bestor	No
3	Easy to Remember	Frank Parker	Yes
4	You Fit Into the Picture	Don Bestor	No
5	Sunday at Sundown	Don Bestor	No

Notes:

Skit	The Fatal Wedding

Date: 5/12/1935   **Sponsor:** Jell-O   **City:** Hollywood, CA

Recording Source: None   **Problems:** None

First line:
And now, folks, this being Mother's Day, we bring you Jack Benny!

Summary:
Jack's father made him practice the violin so he could play "Love in Bloom"...gang talks about mothers and Mother's Day...Mary reads poem about Mother's Day...Opportunity Night...guest star, barber Stanwyck sings...Zasu Shvitz, ribbon saleswoman, wants to be an actress...dentist McQuade imitates Frank Parker...Jack and Parker fight...Thomas Thumb, hitch-hiker...Carrie Dish, a waitress, carries eight cups of coffee in one hand (crash)...ventriloquist uses the Voice of Experience, dummy only says "I'm all right"...amateurs dismissed with a gong...asks audience to vote for best amateur...Jack sends everyone away...wants to play "Love in Bloom" for the mothers of America...Jack plays "Love in Bloom" and amateur gong keeps ringing

Cast:

Last name	First name	Roles	Guest star
?	Margaret	Zasu Shvitz	No
Baker	Wally	John Stanwyck	No
Benny	Jack	Jack Benny	No
Bestor	Don	Don Bestor	No
Livingston	Mary	Mary Livingston	No
Parker	Frank	Frank Parker, Jay Mantague McQuade	No
Pearson	?	Jay C. Klippen	No
Rome	Betty	Carrie Dish	No
Wilson	Don	Don Wilson	No
Young	?	Thomas Thumb	No

Songs:

Order	Title	Performers	Vocal
1	Mister and Missus Is the Name	Don Bestor	No
2	She's a Latin from Manhattan	Don Bestor	No
3	Ah Sweet Mystery of Life	Frank Parker	Yes
4	I Want to Be Happy	Don Bestor	No
5	Love in Bloom	Jack Benny	No
6	Zing Went the Strings Of My Heart	Don Bestor	No

Notes:

Running gag	Mary's poem

Date: 5/19/1935   **Sponsor:** Jell-O   **City:** Hollywood, CA

Recording Source: None   **Problems:** None

First line:
And now we bring to you the Eyes and Ears of Hollywood - Jack Benny!

Summary:
News headlines...gang discusses each other's appearance..Parker says he's a comedian that sings...skit Walking Down to Rio...Don Hosay visits Chinchilla...introduces him to her father, Ricoro...father wants her to marry a Mexican...bullfighter Manuelo proposes to Chinchilla, she asks him to kill a bull for her...kills a Boston Bull for her

Cast:

Last name	First name	Roles	Guest star
Benny	Jack	Jack Benny, Ricoro Corona	No
Bestor	Don	Don Bestor, Don Hosay Sox	No
Livingstone	Mary	Mary Livingstone, Chinchilla	No
MacIntire	John	Dog	No
Parker	Frank	Frank Parker, Manelo Panatella	No
Rome	Betty	Mosquita	No
Wilson	Don	Don Wilson, baby, Enrico Rspberro	No

Songs:

Order	Title	Performers	Vocal
1	I Hate to Talk About Myself	Don Bestor	No
2	Out For No Good	Don Bestor	No
3	Bon Jour Mamselle	Frank Parker	Yes
4	You're the Top	Don Bestor	No
5	You Opened My Eyes	Don Bestor	No

Notes:

Running gag	Hair hair
Skit	Walking Down to Rio

Date: 5/26/1935   **Sponsor:** Jell-O   **City:** Hollywood, CA

Recording Source: None   **Problems:** None

First line:
And now we bring to you a fellow who is to radio what Nero was to Rome, what Shakespeare was to England, what Bismarck was to Germany, and what corn beef is to cabbage - Jack Benny!

Summary:
Wilson's family has many ribbers...gang discusses ribbers in their family (robber, rubber, spare ribs)...Jack is a legitimate actor in "Broadway Melody"...Una Merkel is in the audience...Merkel says she never misses the program, but hasn't heard it in a while...Mary is jealous of Merkel...Merkel starts doing Labor Day poem...skit The Great Hollywood Pearl Robbery...Mrs. Van Payne's pearls stolen...police are called and come over...new catch phrase "We have no time to lose!" repeated...police call oysters, get a clam...find a dead man in the bedroom...sponsor calls and tells them to mention Jell-O...policeman comes in and searches everyone, finds Jell-O on Don...Bestor playing at the Palomar Hotel

Cast:

Last name	First name	Roles	Guest star
?	Margaret	Screamer, Mrs. Van Payne	No
Baker	Wally	Guest, policeman	No
Benny	Jack	Jack Benny, Sergeant McCue	No
Bestor	Don	Don Bestor	No
Franz	Joe	Phantom	No
Livingstone	Mary	Mary Livingstone, Miss McKee	No
Merkel	Una	Una Merkel	Yes
Parker	Frank	Frank Parker	No
Wilson	Don	Don Wilson	No

Songs:

Order	Title	Performers	Vocal
1	Footloose and Fancy Free	Don Bestor	No
2	Parade of the Wooden Soldiers	Don Bestor	No
3	Tell Me Tonight	Frank Parker	Yes
4	Kiss Me Goodnight	Don Bestor	No
5	Ninon	Don Bestor	No

Notes:

Skit	The Great Hollywood Pearl Robbery

Date: 6/2/1935   **Sponsor:** Jell-O   **City:** Hollywood, CA

Recording Source: None   **Problems:** None

First line:
And now we bring to you the first Son of the Bride of Frankenstein - Jack Benny!

Summary:
Jack compares California and New York valleys...Wilson caught an 84-pound tuna with a radio ("you just tuna-in on them")...Mary went to San Diego Exposition...Parker caught a filet of sole ("why catch the parts you don't eat?")...Jack says Bestor is playing old tunes...gang discusses the importance of good acting...continuation of The Great Hollywood Pearl Robbery...McCann saw three guys with scars hanging around pawn shop...sends out police to clean up the town, four stay behind to play bridge...man driving 70 miles an hour turns himself in...interrogates man found loitering in front of Van Payne house...Bestor brings in Mrs. Van Payne...man reports pearls are at Brown Derby (Mr. And Mrs. Jack Pearl)

Cast:

Last name	First name	Roles	Guest star
?	Margaret	Screamer, Mrs. Van Payne	No
Baldwin	Harry	McCloud, McDowell	No
Benny	Jack	Jack Benny, Sergeant McCue	No
Bestor	Don	Don Bestor, McBestor	No
Franz	Joe	Phantom, McDuff, Derby caller	No
Livingston	Mary	Mary Livingston, Miss McKee	No
Marks	Hilliard	McHorovitz	No
McIntire	?	McQuade, driver	No
Parker	Frank	Frank Parker, lawyer, tough guy	No
Wilson	Don	Don Wilson, McCann	No

Songs:

Order	Title	Performers	Vocal
1	Footloose and Fancy Free	Don Bestor	No
2	Sometimes I'm Happy/Hallelujah	Don Bestor	No
3	Lovely to Look At	Frank Parker	Yes
4	East of the Sun	Don Bestor	No
5	Flowers for Madame	Don Bestor	No

Notes:

Skit	The Great Hollywood Pearl Robbery

Date: 6/9/1935 **Sponsor:** Jell-O **City:** Hollywood, CA

Recording Source: None **Problems:** None

First line:
And now we bring to you that great scavenger of wit and humor, Jack Benny!

Summary:
Jack lost 10 pounds, discusses his diet...Parker gives Jack a peanut, tells him to go to the park and people throw them at you...Jack asks Bestor to play an operatic number...skit The Great Hollywood Pearl Robbery...prisoner in cell 14 goes out for cup of coffee...think of the bride of Frankenstein, might have taken pearls for his wife...go to Frankenstein's house...son is Frankenparker...McCue searches the place...Napoleon starts to tell who has the pearls, but gets interrupted by gun shot...Frank Parker introduces Bobby Breen as his kid brother

Cast:

Last name	First name	Roles	Guest star
Baker	Wally	Frankenstein	No
Benny	Jack	Jack Benny	No
Bestor	Don	Don Bestor, Doctor Frankenspats	No
Breen	Bobby	Frankenstein's grandfather, Bobby Breen	Yes
Franz	Joe	Phantom, Napoleon	No
Klein	Vi	Screamer	No
Livingston	Mary	Mary Livingston, Miss McKee	No
Marks	Hilliard	Cell 14 prisoner	No
Parker	Frank	Frank Parker, lawyer, Frankenparker	No
Rome	Betty	Mrs. Frankenstein	No
Wilson	Don	Don Wilson, McCann	No

Songs:

Order	Title	Performers	Vocal
1	I'll Never Say Never Again	Don Bestor	No
2	You Are So Lovely and I Am So Lonely	Don Bestor	No
3	Why Do They Call It Gay Paree	Frank Parker	Yes
4	Exactly Like You/On the Sunny Side of the Street/Memories of You	Don Bestor	No
5	Stay as Sweet As You Are	Bobby Breen	Yes
6	Seein' Is Believin'	Don Bestor	No

Notes:

Skit	The Great Hollywood Pearl Robbery

Date: 6/16/1935 **Sponsor:** Jell-O **City:** Hollywood, CA

Recording Source: None **Problems:** None

First line:
Jello again, this is Jack Benny, coming to you with some hot weather jokes and funny sayings. Are you at home, folks, or listening in your automobiles?

Summary:
Gang discusses whether there's anything new under the sun...Bestor wearing spats on his wrists to keep up with the times...gang changes things around (e.g., "Don play")...Jack wants Bestor to play new songs...continuation of The Great Hollywood Pearl Robbery...stone comes through window with note saying pearls are in the hands of Gravy-Face Gordon...police go to Pajama Inn...break into wrong place...machine gun shoot-out...Gordon says he doesn't have the pearls, they arrest him...they search Gordon and find the pearls...Mrs. Van Payne calls and says she found the pearls in her vault, but now her diamond bracelet is gone...interrogate Gordon about bracelet, he starts to tell who took it, but is interrupted by a gun shot...introduces Miss Wynn Davis, winner of Annual Allied Arts Festival of Southern California...announces upcoming contest

Cast:

Last name	First name	Roles	Guest star
?	Margaret	Screamer, Mrs. Van Payne	No
Baldwin	Harry	Property man	No
Benny	Jack	Jack Benny, Sarge	No
Bestor	Don	Don Bestor	No
Davis	Wynn	Wynn Davis	Yes
Franz	Joe	Phantom, Gum Drop Inn man	No
Livingstone	Mary	Mary Livingstone, Miss McCue	No
Parker	Frank	Frank Parker, Shyster, Gravy-Face Gordon	No
Wilson	Don	Don Wilson, McCann	No

Songs:

Order	Title	Performers	Vocal
1	Zing Went the Strings Of My Heart	Don Bestor	No
2	What a Little Moonlight Can Do	Don Bestor	No
3	In the Middle of a Kiss	Frank Parker	Yes
4	Let's Swing It	Don Bestor	No
5	My Hero	Wynn Davis	Yes
6	Tina	Don Bestor	No

Notes:

Skit	The Great Hollywood Pearl Robbery

Date: 6/23/1935   **Sponsor:** Jell-O   **City:** Hollywood, CA

Recording Source: None   **Problems:** None

First line:
And now, folks, you are in for a little treat. We are taking you to the MGM Studio where Jack is finishing his picture, "Broadway Melody of 1936"...Hey Cecil, turn in the Studio and get Rehearsal Hall "C".

Summary:
Jack tries to give tips to choreographer...gang is in the chorus...not doing skit tonight, starting a contest...contest is to guess the name of a dessert and flavors...first prize is parking for two nights in Culver City...gives answers to contest after Parker's song...Jack sent Mary out for cigars, plans surprise birthday party for Mary...serves cake with Jell-O Ice Cream Powder...Bestor gives Mary a lavalier with rubies and diamonds...Mrs. Van Payne calls and says she's missing a lavalier with rubies and diamonds...Mary reads poem about life

Cast:

Last name	First name	Roles	Guest star
?	Alice	James Cagney	No
?	Margaret	Bowlegged chorus girl, screamer, Mrs. Van Payne	No
Baker	Benny	Mr. Gould	No
Benny	Jack	Jack Benny	No
Bestor	Don	Don Bestor, Doneeta Bestor	No
Franz	Joe	Phantom	No
Livingston	Mary	Mary Livingston	No
Parker	Frank	Frank Parker, Franceeta Parker	No
Rome	Betty	Gwendolyn Smythe	No
Ross	Dorothy	Joan Blondell	No
Wilson	Don	Don Wilson, Dolores Wilson	No

Songs:

Order	Title	Performers	Vocal
1	Revelation	Don Bestor	No
2	All Thru the Night	Don Bestor	No
3	Storm in My Soul	Frank Parker	Yes
4	You're a Heavenly Thing	Don Bestor	No
5	I'm In Love All Over Again	Don Bestor	No

Notes:

Running gag	Mary's poem

Date: 6/30/1935   **Sponsor:** Jell-O   **City:** Hollywood, CA

Recording Source: None   **Problems:** None

First line:
And now we bring to you that sunburned comedian with the hot weather jokes - Jack Benny.

Summary:
Gang discusses where to go on vacation…Parker going to Lake Potch-in-Ponem (Indian word for Slap-in-the-Face)…Jack says he's given up "Love In Bloom" for "Life Is a Song"…Parker leaving for New York tonight…skit is comparison of New York and California life…shoemaker in Brooklyn and his family pines for Hollywood…same scene is played out where Hollywood stars are tired of their work…option is picked up and they're disappointed…Ricardo shoots Wilson because of his dog impersonation…Radio Guide's Martin Lewis announces that Jack is favorite performer, Jack thanks Harry W. Conn

Cast:

Last name	First name	Roles	Guest star
?	Margaret	Lena, Edna Mae	No
Baldwin	Harry	Telegram boy	No
Benny	Jack	Jack Benny, son, Ricardo	No
Bestor	Don	Don Bestor, son, Spats Karloff	No
Lewis	Martin	Martin Lewis	Yes
Livingston	Mary	Mary Livingston, daughter	No
Parker	Frank	Frank Parker, August, Gary Barrymore	No
Wilson	Don	Don Wilson, Emil, Fido, Douglas Fairplug	No

Songs:

Order	Title	Performers	Vocal
1	At Last	Don Bestor	No
2	Let's Swing It	Don Bestor	No
3	I Wished On the Moon	Frank Parker	Yes
4	Fair and Warmer	Don Bestor	No
5	You're So Darn Charming	Don Bestor	No

Notes:

Notable	Frank Parker leaves for New York and gang says they'll see him back there, but this is his last performance

Date: 7/7/1935   **Sponsor:** Jell-O   **City:** Hollywood, CA

Recording Source: None   **Problems:** None

First line:
And now we bring you the man who holds a record for staying on the air six hundred and fifty-four hours without refueling - Jack Benny.

Summary:
News headlines…gang discusses Frank Parker…Mary reads a letter from her mother…skit Less Miserable..paroled Zhon shows up at Bishop's house, they give him food and shelter…five years later, Zhon is Monsieur Madlon…Cosette asks for work…Wilson makes Madlon Mayor, but thinks he recognizes him…Madlon and Cosette go to Paris…ten years later, Madlon is Jack Val Jack…revolutionary flirts with Cosette…Wilson comes to arrest Zhon, Zhon wants to shoot him but can't, revolutionary shoots him instead

Cast:

Last name	First name	Roles	Guest star
Benny	Jack	Jack Benny, Zhon Valzhon, Monsieur Madlon	No
Bestor	Don	Don Bestor, Bishop Roo de la Pay	No
Flick	Patsy	Revolutionary	No
Livingston	Mary	Mary Livingston, Cosette	No
Wilson	Don	Don Wilson, Patty de Fois Gras	No

Songs:

Order	Title	Performers	Vocal
1	Poopchen	Don Bestor	No
2	Young Ideas	Don Bestor	No
3	Alexander's Ragtime Band	Don Bestor	No
4	Unidentified	Don Bestor	No

Notes:

Running gag	Mary's mother communication
Skit	Less Miserable

Date: 7/14/1935   **Sponsor:** Jell-O   **City:** Hollywood, CA

Recording Source: None   **Problems:** None

First line:
And now, ladies and gentlemen, for the last broadcast of this series we bring you that sterling humorist, a fellow who is a credit to everything except "Love in Bloom" -- Jack Benny!

Summary:
Gang discusses what they're doing for the summer…people interrupt to remind cast of bills…Jack is making another MGM movie on location in Arizona…Jack finally gives Bestor his Christmas present, a pair of earmuffs…Fred(dy) Allen appears, out to make a movie "Sing, Governor, Sing"…Portland and Mary are competitive…Portland reads poem about Summertime…skit The Hills of Kentucky feud between Zeke Allens and Ebenezer Bennys…families "shoot" each other with corny riddles…only Jack and Fred are left standing, so they dance…summer replacement is "State Fair Concerts" with Lanny Ross and Howard Barlow's Symphony Orchestra

Cast:

Last name	First name	Roles	Guest star
Allen	Fred	Fred Allen, Zeke Allen	Yes
Baldwin	Harry	Pacific Coast Spat Company rep	No
Benny	Jack	Jack Benny, Ebenezer Benny	No
Bestor	Don	Don Bestor	No
Hoffa	Portland	Portland Hoffa	Yes
Lee	?	Garage man, shot Allen	No
Livingstone	Mary	Mary Livingstone, Mariah Benny	No
Marks	Hilliard	Beverly Hand Laundry rep	No
Parker	Frank	Frank Parker	No
Rome	Betty	Wilshire Beauty Parlor rep	No
Wilson	Don	Don Wilson	No

Songs:

Order	Title	Performers	Vocal
1	A Little Door, a Little Lock, a Little Key	Don Bestor	No
2	One In a Million	Don Bestor	No
3	You've Got Me Doing Things	Don Wilson	Yes
3	You've Got Me Doing Things	Jack Benny	Yes
3	You've Got Me Doing Things	Mary Livingstone	Yes
4	Come On Home	Don Bestor	No
5	Love in Bloom	Don Bestor	No

Notes:

Notable	First mention of feud between Allen and Benny
Skit	The Hills of Kentucky

Date: 9/29/1935   **Sponsor:** Jell-O   **City:** Hollywood, CA

Recording Source: None   **Problems:** None

First line:
And now ladies and gentlemen, after a long rest we bring to you that prince of humorists...that man of mirth...Major...I mean Freddie...Say, what is your name again, feller?

Summary:
Jack and Don don't recognize each other...Mary reads stanza of poem about September to prove who she is...each cast member enters as an amateur performer...Green introduces his orchestra...entire gang is staying at Beverly-Wilshire hotel in room 404, but doesn't know it...skit Follies of a Grocery Store...opening the store...customers come in to buy things...Bartlett comes by to take out Mariah...Mary thinks Bartlett is handsome

Cast:

Last name	First name	Roles	Guest star
Baker	Benny	Mr. Wheelspoke	No
Bartlett	Michael	Michael Barlett	No
Benny	Jack	Jack Benny, Ebenezer Benny	No
Green	Johnny	Johnny Green, Mr. Fetzmeyer	No
Livingstone	Mary	Mary Livingstone, Mariah Living-feather	No
Stewart	Blanche	Rooster, chicken, Miss Loganberry, mouse	No
Wilson	Don	Don Wilson, cow, Luke	No

Songs:

Order	Title	Performers	Vocal
1	Sing Before Breakfast	Johnny Green	No
2	On a Sunday Afternoon	Johnny Green	No
3	Love Me Forever	Michael Bartlett	Yes
4	Broadway Rhythm	Johnny Green	No
5	I've Got a Feelin' You're Foolin	Johnny Green	No

Notes:

Notable	Mary's name is now consistently spelled "Livingstone" in the scripts
Notable	First "Well!" when Jack is being introduced to orchestra members
Running gag	Mary's poem
Skit	Follies of a Grocery Store

Date: 10/6/1935   **Sponsor:** Jell-O   **City:** Hollywood, CA

Recording Source: None   **Problems:** None

First line:
And now it is with great pleasure I introduce that Jello good fellow - Jack Benny!

Summary:
Gang discusses the importance of applause...Mary brags about herself...Bartlett and Mary do cutesy talk to each other...Jack making "It's In the Air"...Jack recreates a love scene from "Broadway Melody" with Mary...skit Groceries of 1936...customers come in to buy things...MGM orders a ham...tunes in a baseball game on the radio

Cast:

Last name	First name	Roles	Guest star
Baker	Benny	Baseball announcer	No
Bartlett	Michael	Michael Barlett	No
Benny	Jack	Jack Benny, Ebenezer Benny	No
Green	Johnny	Johnny Green, Clem	No
Livingstone	Mary	Mary Livingstone, Mariah	No
Stewart	Blanche	Mary's mother, rooster, Miss Loganberry, tomato customer	No
Wilson	Don	Don Wilson, Luke Wilson	No

Songs:

Order	Title	Performers	Vocal
1	No Strings	Johnny Green	No
2	Page Miss Glory	Johnny Green	No
3	Tell Me That You Love Me Tonight	Michael Bartlett	Yes
4	Quarter to Nine	Johnny Green	No
5	Double Trouble	Johnny Green	No

Notes:

Running gag	Mary does Mae West
Skit	Groceries of 1936

Date: 10/13/1935 **Sponsor:** Jell-O **City:** Hollywood, CA

Recording Source: None **Problems:** None

First line:
And now we bring to you the late star of Broadway Jellody of 1936 - Jack Benny!

Summary:
Gang discusses about European war news, Jack tells of being in World War I...sings Jell-O version of K-K-K-Katy...Jack reads and responds to fan mail...Jack describes Johnny Green...skit School Days...call roll...quizzes class...1st anniversary of Jell-O sponsorship...Jack asks Mary what "parlay vous Francais" means, she answers "Do you speak French?" ("No!"), sort of Abbott-and-Costelloish

Cast:

Last name	First name	Roles	Guest star
Baldwin	Harry	Eddy Mannix, George Jean Nathan	No
Bartlett	Michael	Michael Barlett, Mickey Bartlett	No
Benny	Jack	Jack Benny	No
Flick	Patsy	Sammy Genzel	No
Green	Johnny	Johnny Green	No
Livingstone	Mary	Mary Livingstone	No
Stewart	Blanche	Jenny Zipper, Savannah Georgia	No
Wilson	Don	Don Wilson, Dinky Dean	No

Songs:

Order	Title	Performers	Vocal
1	Truckin	Johnny Green	No
2	Sweet Sue	Johnny Green	No
3	I'm In the Mood for Love	Michael Bartlett	Yes
4	Top Hat, White Tie and Tails	Johnny Green	No
5	I'd Love to Take Orders from You	Johnny Green	No

Notes:

Skit	School Days

Date: 10/20/1935   **Sponsor:** Jell-O   **City:** Hollywood, CA

Recording Source: None   **Problems:** None

First line:
And now we bring to you the fellow who makes funny every Sunday night - Jack Benny!

Summary:
Gang discusses football...Mary borrowed $10 from a coach, made a touch-down...guest star, famous mind reader Pisha Paysha...mind reader gag with her guessing objects and names (with hints from Jack)...skit All's Quiet on the Western Sandwich...regiment arrives looking for accomodations...Mary brings mind reader to predict what the enemy is doing, she is shot...soldiers settle down to sleep...enemy spy reports planned attack in 10 seconds...orders soldiers over the top, soldiers are shot...Jack jumps in dugout, finds Johnny Green and his orchestra...Jack is shot, Mary sings "I've Got a Feeling you're Foolin'" to him

Cast:

Last name	First name	Roles	Guest star
Baldwin	Harry	Warnecke	No
Bartlett	Michael	Michael Barlett	No
Benny	Jack	Jack Benny, Sergeant Benny	No
Flick	Patsy	Soldier on phone, spy	No
Green	Johnny	Johnny Green, Private Green	No
Livingstone	Mary	Mary Livingstone	No
Stewart	Blanche	Miss Pisha Paysha	No
Wilson	Don	Don Wilson	No

Songs:

Order	Title	Performers	Vocal
1	From the Top of Your Head	Johnny Green	No
2	I Get a Kick Out of You	Johnny Green	No
3	How Can I Hold You Close Enough	Michael Bartlett	Yes
4	Let's Swing It	Johnny Green	No
5	Everything is Okey Dokey	Johnny Green	No

Notes:

Skit	All's Quiet on the Western Sandwich

Date: 10/27/1935   **Sponsor:** Jell-O   **City:** Hollywood, CA

Recording Source: None   **Problems:** None

First line:
Ladies and gentlemen, kindly stand by. Jack Benny just called up to say he was detained at the Picture Studio but is rushing right over. He should be here in a few minutes.

Summary:
Jack and Mary driving to studio...Jack doing 50 on Sunset Boulevard (25 is the limit), driving a Whippet...gets pulled over by a cop...skit Way out East...Jack announces that Michael Bartlett is leaving the program to star in a Columbia picture opposite Grace Moore...parents debate whether to let son go from the farm...Mary O'Grady arrives looking for work...Gabby reports that Mary was seen two years ago in Boston smoking a cigarette...Thorndyke planning to marry Squire's niece...Squire confronts Mary, throws her out...Jonathan follows her...Squire orders everyone out...sponsor calls and orders Jack out

Cast:

Last name	First name	Roles	Guest star
Bartlett	Michael	Michael Barlett	No
Bennett	?	Officer	No
Benny	Jack	Jack Benny, Squire Meyer	No
Flick	Patsy	Bakery wagon driver, Thorndyke	No
Green	Johnny	Johnny Green, Jonathan Meyer	No
Higby	?	Hannah Meyer	No
Livingstone	Mary	Mary Livingstone, Mary O'Grady	No
Stewart	Blanche	Dog, Gabby	No
Underwood	?	Sponsor	No
Wilson	Don	Don Wilson, Deacon	No

Songs:

Order	Title	Performers	Vocal
1	No Other One	Johnny Green	No
2	I Feel a Song Coming On	Johnny Green	No
3	Ah Sweet Mystery of Life	Michael Bartlett	Yes
4	The Daughter of Rosie O'Grady	Mary Livingstone	Yes
5	Dinah	Johnny Green	No
6	Thanks a Million	Johnny Green	No

Notes:

Skit	Way Out East

Date: 11/3/1935   **Sponsor:** Jell-O   **City:** Hollywood, CA

Recording Source: Unknown   **Problems:** None

First line:
And now we bring to you the cheerleader of this program, Jack Benny.

Summary:
Jack getting a shave…discusses sports with Pasquale…gang laughs at Jack's short haircut…Kenny Baker introduced..."It's a thrill"…fan mail from Flora Fenchel, Lake Forest, IL, wants to get into pictures and become a star…skit on Metro Pathamount Studios, called Open Up that Golden Gate…routine of relaying question and answer from person to person ("Paging Eugene O'Wilson" - "Eugene O.Wilson" - "Eugene O. Wilson" - "He's out to lunch" - "He's out to lunch"…)…keeps changing location of movie and ordering different animals…elephants show up anyway because elephants never forget…Jack says "Play John" instead of "Play Don"

Cast:

Last name	First name	Roles	Guest star
Baker	Kenny	Kenny Baker	No
Baldwin	Harry	Pager, Mr. Lemaire	No
Benny	Jack	Jack Benny, Mr. Paradise/Parasite	No
Conrad	?	Pasquale	No
Green	Johnny	Johnny Green, thespian	No
Livingstone	Mary	Mary Livingstone, Miss Klutz	No
Stewart	Blanche	Pager, Atlantic City beauty contest winner	No
Wilson	Don	Don Wilson, Eugene O. Wilson	No

Songs:

Order	Title	Performers	Vocal
1	Eenie Meenie Miney Mo	Johnny Green	No
2	Anything Goes	Johnny Green	No
3	A Rose In Her Hair	Kenny Baker	Yes
4	Cheek to Cheek	Johnny Green	No
5	You've Got What it Takes	Johnny Green	No

Notes:

Notable	First appearance of Kenny Baker
Running gag	Relay question and answer

Date: 11/10/1935   **Sponsor:** Jell-O   **City:** Hollywood, CA

Recording Source: None   **Problems:** None

First line:
And now we bring to you the life of the party - Jack Benny!

Summary:
Man from Here-Today-and-Gone-Tomorrow Insurance Company tries to sell Jack a policy...insurance man and Don compete to sell their products...Green hires his relatives for the orchestra...Kenny Baker has no will power...skit Barbary Toast...patrons gather at the Hunky Dorey bar...Trigger looking to marry a woman from New York who just arrived...Mary came out to marry Frisco Pete...Jack calls Edward G. Robinson...Mary flirts with prospector...Vigilantes coming after Trigger...playing roulette with prospector...Mary lets prospector win no matter what number he plays...vigilantes come to hang Trigger...insurance man interrupts them again...Barbara Stanwyck calls to say she didn't like the play

Cast:

Last name	First name	Roles	Guest star
Baker	Kenny	Kenny Baker	No
Baldwin	Harry	Cable car driver, gin patron, roulette player	No
Bennett	?	Vigilante	No
Benny	Jack	Jack Benny, Trigger Benny	No
Flick	Patsy	Insurance salesman	No
Green	Johnny	Johnny Green, prospector	No
Lee	?	Spike, roulette player	No
Livingstone	Mary	Mary Livingstone, Manhattan Mary	No
Stewart	Blanche	Ming Toy (dog), Mazie	No
Wilson	Don	Don Wilson, Captain	No

Songs:

Order	Title	Performers	Vocal
1	At Your Service, Madame	Johnny Green	No
2	Got a Brand-New Suit	Johnny Green	No
3	To Call You My Own	Kenny Baker	Yes
4	Mile a Minute	Johnny Green	No
5	The Milky Way	Johnny Green	No

Notes:

Running gag	Mary does Mae West
Skit	Barbary Toast

Date: 11/17/1935   **Sponsor:** Jell-O   **City:** Hollywood, CA

Recording Source: None   **Problems:** None

First line:
And now, ladies and gentlemen, we bring to you…for your Sunday evening
entertainment…that noted violin virtuoso…Mr. Jack Benny!

Summary:
Jack complains that he doesn't get enough respect as a violinist…Mary says the same
about her poetry…Mary reads poem about winter…Kenny brings his girlfriend to the
studio…Freeda sent a fan letter to Crosby and Kenny answered it…skit The Blue Room
Murder Case…host Katz is killed during his party, police are called…police arrive and
question guests…garcon explains in French what happens (line is accurate French, not
double-talk)…inspection of body, but still alive ("a Katz has nine lives")

Cast:

Last name	First name	Roles	Guest star
Baker	Kenny	Kenny Baker, bum	No
Baldwin	Harry	Drinker	No
Bennett	?	Lloyd Pantages	No
Benny	Jack	Jack Benny, Sergeant O'Nertz	No
Green	Johnny	Johnny Green, Jacques Brujos Marquise de Poop-Poop	No
Lee	?	Wallace Beery	No
Livingstone	Mary	Mary Livingstone, Lady in Red	No
Stewart	Blanche	Freeda Grepsmeyer, drinker, dog	No
Wilson	Don	Don Wilson, Officer O'Shaughnessy	No

Songs:

Order	Title	Performers	Vocal
1	How Do I Rate With You	Johnny Green	No
2	Why	Johnny Green	No
3	I Wished on the Moon	Kenny Baker	Yes
4	Jockey on the Carrousel	Johnny Green	No
5	Lulu's Back in Town	Johnny Green	No

Notes:

Running gag	Mary's poem
Skit	The Blue Room Murder Case

Date: 11/24/1935   **Sponsor:** Jell-O   **City:** Hollywood, CA

Recording Source: None   **Problems:** None

First line:
And now we bring to you as fine a fellow as ever stooped to pick up a cigar butt - Jack Benny!

Summary:
Jack went to San Diego on a fishing trip…gang discusses fish and fishing (and tons of fish puns)…Jack reads a note from Kenny's folks, they think it's his show…gang goes over to Kenny's follks for Thanksgiving…gang crowds into Kenny's car…Jack tries to fix a blowout…pick up a hitchhiker…run out of gas…Mary reads poem about Thanksgiving…Jack goes for gas and gets held up…Jack carries his money in his shoe…gas station is out of gas…Jack gets caught in the rain…turns out Kenny had gas but forgot to turn on the ignition…Kenny gets lost and they stop at a barbecue stand

Cast:

Last name	First name	Roles	Guest star
Baker	Kenny	Kenny Baker	No
Baker	Wally	Robber	No
Baldwin	Harry	Hitchhiker	No
Barton	?	Gas station attendant	No
Benny	Jack	Jack Benny	No
Flick	Patsy	Barbecue attendant (Max)	No
Green	Johnny	Johnny Green	No
Livingstone	Mary	Mary Livingstone	No
Stewart	Blanche	Baby, molested woman, dog, Kenny's mother	No
Wilson	Don	Don Wilson, baby	No

Songs:

Order	Title	Performers	Vocal
1	Love Makes the World Go Round	Johnny Green	No
2	Wild Rose	Johnny Green	No
3	Not Bad	Johnny Green	No
4	Here's to Romance	Kenny Baker	Yes
5	The International	Johnny Green	No

Notes:

Running gag	Mary's poem

Date: 12/1/1935   **Sponsor:** Jell-O   **City:** Hollywood, CA

Recording Source: None   **Problems:** None

First line:
And now on our anniversary, we bring to you for the two hundredth consecutive time on the air, Jack Benny!

Summary:
Mary wrote a song for Jack's anniversary (ala M-O-T-H-E-R), gang sings it...Jack reminisces about his program...reporter interviews Jack...telegrams on Jack's anniversary...Kenny eats Jell-O to sing well...skit Charlie Chansky in Russia...husband returns from Moscow and his 200th pogrom...pumpernickel is stolen...Chansky investigates...lover Baker arrives...telegram from Flank Parker...people keep hiding in the closet as more people arrive...reporter returns, took pumpernickel instead of his hat...thanks everyone associated with the show, and Harry W. Conn is first on the list (Beloin and Morrow not mentioned)

Cast:

Last name	First name	Roles	Guest star
Baker	Benny	Sam Winchell	No
Baker	Kenny	Kenny Baker, Kennovitch Baker	No
Baldwin	Harry	Telegram boy	No
Benny	Jack	Jack Benny, Charlie Chansky, Ming Toy-ovitch	No
Flick	Patsy	Boris Vestoff	No
Green	Johnny	Johnny Green, son Vestoff, Ivan Greenavitch	No
Livingstone	Mary	Mary Livingstone, Natasha Vestoff	No
Wilson	Don	Don Wilson, Jelloff	No

Songs:

Order	Title	Performers	Vocal
1	Keep Your Fingers Crossed	Johnny Green	No
2	Just One of Those Things	Johnny Green	No
3	Midnight in Paris	Kenny Baker	Yes
4	Two Guitars	Johnny Green	No
5	Unidentified	Johnny Green	No

Notes:

Notable	When Benny Baker and Kenny Baker are on the program, BB is prompted as "Baker" and KB is "Kenny" in the script (KB is usually prompted as Baker)
Skit	Charlie Chansky in Russia

Date: 12/6/1935   **Sponsor:** Jell-O   **City:** Hollywood, CA

Recording Source: None   **Problems:** None

First line:
And now we bring to you the star of stage, screen, radio, soapbox, street corner and cocktail lounge - Jack Benny!

Summary:
Jack playing the Paramount Theatre for 4-5 shows a day…Jack faints from exhaustion…Mary reads a letter from her mother…encloses a blank check for Jack to autograph…Mary calls for a doctor for Jack…Doctor checks Jack and advises him to rest…Green suggests a Dude Ranch…Jack dreams of being on the dude ranch…Jack steps on a rattlesnake, plays "Love in Bloom" to make him go away…Kiyote says they just lost 100 herd of cattle…go to McIntyre Ranch, as they suspect them of rustling…find Schlepperman at the ranch…Jack playing Orpheum Theatre in San Francisco next week

Cast:

Last name	First name	Roles	Guest star
		Dr. Blum	No
Baker	Kenny	Kenny Baker	No
Benny	Jack	Jack Benny	No
Green	Johnny	Johnny Green, Kiyote Van Dillingwater, Strawberry Pete	No
Hearn	Sam	Rooster, Schlepperman	No
Livingstone	Mary	Mary Livingstone, Annie Oakley, Raspberry Kate	No
Wilson	Don	Don Wilson, Cactus	No

Songs:

Order	Title	Performers	Vocal
1	All's Well	Johnny Green	No
2	Footloose and Fancy Free	Johnny Green	No
3	That's You Sweetheart	Kenny Baker	Yes
4	The Piccolino	Johnny Green	No
5	I've Got a Feelin' You're Foolin'	Johnny Green	No

Notes:

Running gag	Mary's mother communication

Date: 12/15/1935 **Sponsor:** Jell-O **City:** San Francisco, CA

Recording Source: None **Problems:** None

First line:
And now we welcome to San Francisco, Jack Benny and his troupe of aerial artists.

Summary:
Locksmith gives Jack key to city…man gives Jack pass to walk across Bay Bridge (it's only half-finished)…Mary breaks down door…gang discusses how they got to town and where they're staying…girls to audition, the Jello-fornians…sing "Oh Canada" (Love in Bloom: "Oh! Canada be the trees That fill the breeze…")…Jack sends them to work for Freddy Allen…skit for tips on shopping, I Found Stella Parish at the Ribbon Counter…customers shopping and asking floorwalker for direction…Shlepperman is doing Christmas shopping…Wilson calls floor for Jell-O and customers rush him

Cast:

Last name	First name	Roles	Guest star
?	Bobby	Bass, hosiery customer	No
?	Doris	Bundle woman	No
?	Kay	Beatrice Jones, baby woman	No
Baker	Kenny	Kenny Baker	No
Baldwin	Harry	Bridge pass guy, smoked glasses shopper	No
Benny	Jack	Jack Benny, floorwalker Mr. Red Schnozzle	No
Green	Johnny	Johnny Green, glove shopper	No
Hearn	Sam	Locksmith, Shlepperman[]	No
Livingstone	Mary	Mary Livingstone, Miss Schultz	No
Stewart	Blanche	Fanny, shopper 1, underwear customer, baby Edna Mae Oliver	No
Wilson	Don	Don Wilson, elevator man	No

Songs:

Order	Title	Performers	Vocal
1	Sugar Plum	Johnny Green	No
2	Love is a Dancing Thing	Johnny Green	No
3	Love in Bloom	Jello-fornians	Yes
4	Where Am I	Kenny Baker	Yes
5	Let's Swing It	Johnny Green	No
6	Yankee Doodle Never Went to Town	Johnny Green	No

Notes:

Skit	I Found Stella Parish at the Ribbon Counter

Date: 12/22/1935 **Sponsor:** Jell-O **City:** Hollywood, CA

Recording Source: None **Problems:** None

First line:
And now we bring to you for the first time in this new and beautiful N.B.C. Studio in Hollywood…Sir Jack Benny, Esquire.

Summary:
Jack sings "Love in Bloom" on his entrance…new studio is very swanky…gang discusses each other's appearance…Green's orchestra chipped in to buy Jack a cigar lighter…Mary wants Clark Gable for Christmas…Jack gives Mary pierced earrings ("Go put holes in your own ears, I'm no cannibal.")…gang exchanges Christmas gifts…Jack tries to sell earrings to Kenny for his girl…skit I've Got Those Back-Home-Again-Indiana on Chrirstmas Eve Blues…and Scratches Your Back in the Morning…parents think of their kids on Christmas Eve…Kenny brings home cactus and a wife…Green comes back from France, Timothy from Moscow…Timothy gives his mother an oyster, since she loves pearls…Santa brings Jell-O

Cast:

Last name	First name	Roles	Guest star
Baker	Kenny	Kenny Baker	No
Baldwin	Harry	Usher	No
Benny	Jack	Jack Benny, father	No
Green	Johnny	Johnny Green	No
Hearn	Sam	Rooster, Timothy	No
Livingstone	Mary	Mary Livingstone, Jenny	No
Stewart	Blanche	Tess	No
Wilson	Don	Don Wilson, Santa Claus	No

Songs:

Order	Title	Performers	Vocal
1	Don't Give Up the Ship	Johnny Green	No
2	Out of Sight Out of Mind	Johnny Green	No
3	Carry Me Back to the Lone Prairie	Kenny Baker	Yes
4	Broadway Rhythm	Johnny Green	No
5	You Hit the Spot	Johnny Green	No

Notes:

Skit	I've Got Those Back-Home-Again-Indiana on Chrirstmas Eve Blues…and Scratches Your Back in the Morning

Date: 12/29/1935   **Sponsor:** Jell-O   **City:** Hollywood, CA

Recording Source: None   **Problems:** None

First line:
And now we will wash out the old year with Jack Benny!

Summary:
Jack wearing all his Christmas presents…Kenny's girl didn't like the ring, exchanged him for another guy…Mary exchanged earrings for a can opener…Mary writes New Years poems to people…Jack and Green argue and fight…Mary calls her mother to wish her a Happy New Year…Mary's father hard of hearing, thinks Jack is Mary and vice-versa…outstanding personalities of 1935…prize fighter, Joe N. Louis, turns out to be Joe Johnson, Johnny Green's chauffeur…golf player Doolittle demostrates his swing…interviews race horse, Discovery…swimmer Gefilta Trout…she dives into tank, but they forgot to fill it with water…hog caller Herkimer Sow…man who runs Army and Navy Store in Keokuk, Iowa, Shlepperman

Cast:

Last name	First name	Roles	Guest star
Baker	Kenny	Kenny Baker	No
Benny	Jack	Jack Benny	No
Cates	Joe	Jay Herkimer Sow	No
Green	Johnny	Johnny Green, Discovery	No
Hearn	Sam	Mary's father, Shlepperman	No
Klein	Al	Lawton Doolittle	No
Livingstone	Mary	Mary Livingstone	No
Moore	?	Joe N. Louis, Joe Johnson	No
Stewart	Blanche	Mary's mother, Gefilta Trout	No
Wilson	Don	Don Wilson, Discovery	No

Songs:

Order	Title	Performers	Vocal
1	I've Got My Fingers Crossed	Johnny Green	No
2	I'm Building Up to an Awful Let Down	Johnny Green	No
3	Madonna Mia	Kenny Baker	Yes
4	Begin the Beguine	Johnny Green	No
5	Twenty Four Hours a Day	Johnny Green	No

Notes:

Notable	Mary has a call with her mother where both sides are heard
Running gag	Mary's poem
Running gag	Mary's mother communication

Date: 1/5/1936 **Sponsor:** Jell-O **City:** Hollywood, CA

Recording Source: None **Problems:** None

First line:
And now we usher in our 1936 radio season with Jack Benny.

Summary:
Jack is laying on couch with ice on his head, been knocked out for three days...Jack wakes up and can't find the microphone...managers of clubs come in and demand payment for Jack's damages...skit Mutiny on the Jello...Captain arrives and they set sail...Wilson confesses to Green about mutiny plans...Captain overhears and makes Green lash Wilson, who cries out "Jell-oh!"...crew mutinies and makes Captain walk the plank, Wilson takes over...Fisherman picks up Captain...Wilson lands on south sea island, meets native girls Wickey and Wackey...fisherman talks in Yiddish to a native on the same island...Captain orders men back to ship...Captain, Schlep, and girls dance

Cast:

Last name	First name	Roles	Guest star
		Hotsy-Totsy manager	No
Baker	Kenny	Kenny Baker	No
Benny	Jack	Jack Benny, Captain Benny	No
Green	Johnny	Johnny Green, Second Mate Green	No
Hearn	Sam	Blue Mouse Café manager, fisherman Schlepperman	No
Klein	Al	Cotton Club Manager, native	No
Livingstone	Mary	Mary Livingstone, Wickey	No
Stewart	Blanche	Wackey	No
Wilson	Don	Don Wilson	No

Songs:

Order	Title	Performers	Vocal
1	I'm Sitting High on a Hilltop	Johnny Green	No
2	Why	Johnny Green	No
3	If I Should Lose You	Kenny Baker	Yes
4	I Want to Learn to Speak Hawaiian	Johnny Green	No
5	These and That and Those	Johnny Green	No

Notes:

Skit	Mutiny on the Jell-O

Date: 1/12/1936   **Sponsor:** Jell-O   **City:** Hollywood, CA

Recording Source: None   **Problems:** None

First line:
Don't be surprised, folks, for tonight his broadcast is being dedicated to the children of this country...to all the little kiddies who listen to our program.

Summary:
Children's Night...interviews Humpty Dumpty, other nursery rhyme characters...Jack changes "Little Boy Blue" to Little Boy Green...Schlepperman brings his son to the studio to recite poetry...skit Little Red Riding Hood...Red sent with goodies to her grandma...wolf eats grandma...Schlepperman steps in as Red's father, won't kill the wolf because he ate his mother-in-law and he'll die of indigestion...introduces Tillie the Talking Doll

Cast:

Last name	First name	Roles	Guest star
?	Sidney	Maxwell	No
Baker	Kenny	Kenny Baker, Peter Piper	No
Benny	Jack	Jack Benny, wolf	No
Green	Johnny	Johnny Green, Humpty Dumpty, bees	No
Hearn	Sam	Schlepperman, Red's father	No
Livingstone	Mary	Mary Livingstone, pretty maid, Red Riding Hood	No
Stewart	Blanche	Dog, Mother Goose, Red's mother, grandma, Tillie (mechanical doll)	No
Wilson	Don	Don Wilson, cuckoo	No

Songs:

Order	Title	Performers	Vocal
1	Too Much Imagination	Johnny Green	No
2	I Feel Like a Feather In the Breeze	Johnny Green	No
3	Shooting High	Kenny Baker	Yes
4	Little Bit Independent	Johnny Green	No
5	Noon at Midnight	Johnny Green	No

Notes:

Skit	Little Red Riding Hood

Date: 1/19/1936   **Sponsor:** Jell-O   **City:** Hollywood, CA

Recording Source: Unknown   **Problems:** Poor sound

First line:
Ladies and gentlemen, I'm terribly sorry to announce that Mary Livingstone will be unable to appear on tonight's program, owing to a very sudden attack of laryngitis which has resulted in the complete loss of her voice. But she will be with us again next Sunday night.

Summary:
Jack and Johnny Green missing…they were arrested for speeding and knocking over a telegraph pole…Mary's sister, Mamie, comes to get Jack and Johnny out of jail…Kenny and Don visit Jack and Johnny…Jack tells a story about three lobsters…orchestra is thrown into jail…Shlepperman is a lawyer who has come to get Jack out of jail…Shlepperman and Jack discuss his story…the trial begins, questions witnesses…puts orchestra on the stand

Cast:

Last name	First name	Roles	Guest star
Baker	Kenny	Kenny Baker	No
Baker	Wally	Keeper	No
Baldwin	Harry	Underwood	No
Benny	Jack	Jack Benny	No
Green	Johnny	Johnny Green	No
Hearn	Sam	Shlepperman	No
Muse	Clarence	Bank robber	No
Shields	Fred	Judge	No
Stewart	Blanche	Mamie Livingstone	No
Wilson	Don	Don Wilson	No

Songs:

Order	Title	Performers	Vocal
1	My Sweet	Johnny Green	No
2	Little Rose of the Rancho	Kenny Baker	Yes
3	I Got a Brand New Suit	Johnny Green	No
4	Music Goes Round and Round	Johnny Green	No
5	When You Took My Breath Away	Johnny Green	No

Notes:

Date: 1/26/1936   **Sponsor:** Jell-O   **City:** Hollywood, CA

Recording Source: None   **Problems:** None

First line:
And now we bring to you that vivacious comedian, La Petite Jack Benny.

Summary:
Mary over her laryngitis...reads request letter to know lowdown on movie stars...gang decides to produce their own picture...Mary calls up friend Mac to finance their picture...Jack plays "Love in Bloom" and has pennies thrown at him...gang has meeting to discuss the picture...starts shooting with no actors...gang brings in their relatives to audition...tells Clark Gable to leave his name in the waste basket...tries to shoot a love scene, but everyone's acting is bad...shooting scene where couple elopes...Egbert climbs into father's room by mistake, Schlepperman is father

Cast:

Last name	First name	Roles	Guest star
Baker	Kenny	Kenny Baker	No
Baldwin	Harry	Clark Gable	No
Benny	Jack	Jack Benny, Mr. Cecil B. de Benny/Lubitsch/Zannuck/Lasky	No
Green	Johnny	Johnny Green, Mr. Firstsky	No
Hearn	Sam	Snorer, Schlepperman	No
Klein	Al	Ricardo, Egbert	No
Livingstone	Mary	Mary Livingstone, Anita Loosehead	No
Stewart	Blanche	Mamie Livingstone, Minerva, duck	No
Wilson	Don	Don Wilson, Mr. Goldwyn	No

Songs:

Order	Title	Performers	Vocal
1	The Day I Let You Get Away	Johnny Green	No
2	Love in Bloom	Jack Benny	No
3	Eeni Meeni Mini Mo	Johnny Green	No
4	The Night is Beginning	Kenny Baker	Yes
5	Top Hat, White Tie, and Tails	Johnny Green	No
6	Everything's in Rhythm With My Heart	Johnny Green	No

Notes:

Date: 2/2/1936   **Sponsor:** Jell-O   **City:** Hollywood, CA

Recording Source: None   **Problems:** None

First line:
And now, ladies and gentlemen, this being our last broadcast from Hollywood, we take you to Jack Benny, who is in his apartment pacing up and getting ready to leave for New York.

Summary:
Jack and Mary packing...Jack tells Kenny about New York...train porter comes to the studio to take everyone's bags...Mary reads poem about Hollywood...Jack and Johnny Green go shopping...Shlepperman is clothing salesman...gang at the train station...Mayor gives Jack key OUT of the city

Cast:

Last name	First name	Roles	Guest star
		Moe	No
Baker	Kenny	Kenny Baker	No
Baldwin	Harry	Vendor	No
Benny	Jack	Jack Benny	No
Franz	Joe	Train announcer	No
Green	Johnny	Johnny Green	No
Hearn	Sam	Shlepperman[]	No
Livingstone	Mary	Mary Livingstone	No
Muse	Clarence	Porter	No
Shields	Fred	Mayor	No
Stewart	Blanche	Landlady, handkerchief saleswoman	No
Wilson	Don	Don Wilson	No

Songs:

Order	Title	Performers	Vocal
1	Broken Record	Johnny Green	No
2	So This is Heaven	Johnny Green	No
3	With All My Heart	Kenny Baker	Yes
4	Rhythmatic	Johnny Green	No
5	Alone	Johnny Green	No

Notes:

Notable	Clarence Muse plays a character that is essentially Rochester
Running gag	Mary's poem

Date: 2/9/1936   **Sponsor:** Jell-O   **City:** New York, NY

Recording Source: None   **Problems:** None

First line:
And now let us welcome back to New York from California that sun-kissed comedian, Jack Benny.

Summary:
Kenny has never been out of California before…Sixth Avenue bum welcomes Jack back to New York…Mary's mother calls…Otto won 100-yard dachshund in German Olympics…gets fan letter from Regina, Saskatchewan, requests a play of the Northwest…Mary writes the play…skit Sergeant Benny of the Northwest Mounted Police…police nab the Irishman/Greek…Jack tries to announce a contest, but keeps getting interrupted..Jell-O congratulates gang on performance in National Radio Editors' poll, voted favorite show on the air for second consecutive year, and Jack is outstanding comedian

Cast:

Last name	First name	Roles	Guest star
Baker	Kenny	Kenny Baker, Pierre	No
Baldwin	Harry	Sixth Avenue bum, ice cream seller	No
Benny	Jack	Jack Benny	No
Green	Johnny	Johnny Green, Jean	No
Livingstone	Mary	Mary Livingstone	No
Nazzaro	Cliff	Reporter	No
Rubin	Benny	Irishman/Greek	No
Wilson	Don	Don Wilson, Andre	No

Songs:

Order	Title	Performers	Vocal
1	Co si Co sa	Johnny Green	No
2	Love is a Dancing Thing	Johnny Green	No
3	Carry Me Back to the Lone Prairie	Kenny Baker	Yes
4	Mile a Minute	Johnny Green	No
5	I'm Gonna Sit Right Down and Write Myself a Letter	Johnny Green	No

Notes:

Notable	First recording where Jack's entrance is played on with "Love in Bloom"
Running gag	Mary's mother communication
Skit	Sergeant Benny of the Northwest Mounted Police

Date: 2/16/1936   **Sponsor:** Jell-O   **City:** New York, NY

Recording Source: None   **Problems:** None

First line:
And now we bring to you a man who took Horace Greeley's advice and went West...then took Jello's advice and came back East, Jack Benny.

Summary:
Jack played on with "Love in Bloom"...Don asks Jack how old he is, says life begins at 40, Jack says he's 2 years old...gang wishes Jack a happy birthday...Kenny made 90 cents at Roseland...Beulah Barefax gives advice on love...avoid love at first sight by not looking at anybody...fan letter asks what Jack does in his spare time...dictates response to Mary, but there's no ribbon in the typewriter...skit Jack Benny's Drugstore...customers come in to buy things...tries to sell Irish Stew to Rubin, turns from Jewish to Irish dialect...everyone turns Irish...Rubin opening at Michigan Theatre in Detroit next Friday

Cast:

Last name	First name	Roles	Guest star
Baker	Kenny	Kenny Baker	No
Baldwin	Harry	Aspirin customer	No
Benny	Jack	Jack Benny	No
Green	Johnny	Johnny Green, razor blade customer	No
Klein	Vi	Three-cent stamp customer	No
Livingstone	Mary	Mary Livingstone	No
Rubin	Benny	Rubin	No
Stewart	Blanche	Beulah Barefax, screamer, sandwich customer	No
Wilson	Don	Don Wilson	No

Songs:

Order	Title	Performers	Vocal
1	Life Begins When You're in Love	Johnny Green	No
2	Dancing Feet	Johnny Green	No
3	Moon Over Miami	Kenny Baker	Yes
4	Joan of Arkansas	Johnny Green	No
5	Every Time I Look At You	Johnny Green	No

Notes:

Skit	Jack Benny's Drugstore

Date: 2/23/1936   **Sponsor:** Jell-O   **City:** New York, NY

Recording Source: Unknown   **Problems:** Poor sound

First line:
And now we bring to you late of the Ringling Brothers' Circus, Jack Benny and his troupe of aerial artists.

Summary:
Starting a contest...door guy asks for the time...Mary wanted to stay home to take care of her father...Kenny Baker doesn't want to come over from his hotel...Johnny Green says he has laryngitis and doesn't want to come to the show...Jack introduces Don as guest star...Jell-O ad in the home of Mr. And Mrs. Cecil Underwood...guest star opera singer, Mr. I.L. Trovatore...skit Eternal Triangle...wife sends husband to Pittsburgh...lovers keep showing up to the house...same scene is repeated 50 years later...Jack had to cancel appearance in Cleveland, Jack and Mary appearing at the Stanley Theatre in Pittsburgh beginning 2/28

Cast:

Last name	First name	Roles	Guest star
Baker	Kenny	Kenny Baker	No
Baldwin	Harry	Door guy	No
Benny	Jack	Jack Benny, Cecil Underwood	No
Edmunds	William	I.L. Trovatore	No
Green	Johnny	Johnny Green	No
Hearn	Sam	Old Kenny Baker	No
Livingstone	Mary	Mary Livingstone, Mrs. Cecil Underwood	No
Stewart	Blanche	Hetta Lettuce, maid Lena, Mary's mother	No
Wilson	Don	Don Wilson	No

Songs:

Order	Title	Performers	Vocal
1	Goody Goody	Johnny Green	No
2	Dancing Feet	Johnny Green	No
3	Alone	Kenny Baker	Yes
4	The Piccolino	Johnny Green	No
5	Breaking In a New Pair of Shoes	Johnny Green	No

Notes:

Blooper	Jack puts wrong inflection on "It's me, Lena."
Skit	Eternal Triangle

Date: 3/1/1936   **Sponsor:** Jell-O   **City:** Pittsburgh, PA

Recording Source: None   **Problems:** None

First line:
And now we bring to you from Pittsburgh that smokey jokey comedian, Jack Benny.

Summary:
Jack played on with "Love in Bloom"...Pitts welcomes Jack to Pittsburgh...from station KDKA...gang compares Pittsburgh and California...harmony girls waiting to perform, the Penn Sisters...gang discusses to what they attribute their success...skit The Life of Diamond Jim...Jim Brady is born...works on the railroad...re-sells idea of trains running on two tracks (which they already do)...meets actress Lillian Jessel in restaurant, finances her play...stock market crashes...Jack playing at Stanley Theatre in Pittsburgh through Thursday, then Loew's State in New York

Cast:

Last name	First name	Roles	Guest star
Baker	Kenny	Kenny Baker	No
Baldwin	Harry	Pitts (door guy), broke man	No
Benny	Jack	Jack Benny, baby,	No
Fess?	Dave	Pittsburgh boy	No
Green	Johnny	Johnny Green, Mr. Brady	No
Klein	Vi	Motza soprano	No
Lee	Kathrine	Piggy Penn	No
Livingstone	Mary	Mary Livingstone, Lillian Jessel	No
Stewart	Blanche	Fountain Penn, nurse	No
Wilson	Don	Don Wilson, waiter	No

Songs:

Order	Title	Performers	Vocal
1	Haystraw	Johnny Green	No
2	I'm Shootin' High	Johnny Green	No
3	The Music Goes Round and Round	Mary Kelly	Yes
3	The Music Goes Round and Round	Blanche Stewart	Yes
3	The Music Goes Round and Round	Vi Klein	Yes
4	What's the Name of That Song	Kenny Baker	Yes
5	Thanks a Million	Johnny Green	No
6	Say the Word and It's Yours	Johnny Green	No

Notes:

Skit	The Life of Diamond Jim

Date: 3/8/1936   **Sponsor:** Jell-O   **City:** New York, NY

Recording Source: None   **Problems:** None

First line:
And now, ladies and gentlemen, we bring to you - Jack Benny!
Jack: Hm, a fine way to introduce a lot of hokum.

Summary:
Don says "Jello again" is getting monotonous…Jack and Don exchange parts, Mary and Kenny switch parts…Kenny reads a poem about spring…skit to help people fill out their income tax…people come to Jack for tax guidance…race horse Top Row made $104,000…Kenny asks Jack to show him around…takes gang to the zoo…Irish guide shows them around…guide hits giraffe on back to raise lumps and turn him into a camel…parrot asks for Jell-O flavors…Jewish keeper shows them wild animals…gives them back to Irish guide to see wild pigs…Green gets stuck in the monkey cage…playing Loew's Fox Theatre in Washington starting Friday

Cast:

Last name	First name	Roles	Guest star
Baker	Kenny	Kenny Baker	No
Baldwin	Harry	Vendor	No
Benny	Jack	Jack Benny	No
Edmunds	William	Guiseppe Antonio Farmargeeno	No
Green	Johnny	Johnny Green, Top Row	No
Livingstone	Mary	Mary Livingstone	No
Rubin	Benny	Irish guide, Jewish keeper	No
Stewart	Blanche	Old lady, chicken, parrot	No
Wilson	Don	Don Wilson, Top Row	No

Songs:

Order	Title	Performers	Vocal
1	Don't Say a Word, Just Dance	Johnny Green	No
2	We Saw the Sea	Johnny Green	No
3	Let's Face the Music and Dance	Kenny Baker	Yes
4	Let Yourself Go	Johnny Green	No
5	Wake Up and Sing	Johnny Green	No

Notes:

Running gag	Mary's poem
Skit	Income Tax

Date: 3/15/1936   **Sponsor:** Jell-O   **City:** Washington, DC

Recording Source: Unknown   **Problems:** Music clipped

First line:
And this week we bring to you from Washington that national comedian and his entire cabinet, Jack Benny.

Summary:
Broadcasting a mile from the White House...isn't it amazing how a big city like this crossed the Delaware...gang is seeing the sights in Washington...Mary reads poem about St. Patrick's Day...Jack is guest of honor at a French Embassy banquet...gang crashes the party...Jack plays "Love in Bloom"...Jack and Mary appearing all next week at Loew's Century in Baltimore, MD starting Friday, 3/20

Cast:

Last name	First name	Roles	Guest star
Baker	Kenny	Kenny Baker	No
Baldwin	Harry	Announcer	No
Benny	Jack	Jack Benny	No
Fess?	Dave W.	Benjamin Franklin	No
Green	Johnny	Johnny Green	No
Lee	Kathrine	Senarita, wife	No
Livingstone	Mary	Mary Livingstone	No
McIlevey	Hugh	Secretary of Interior	No
Metaxa	Georges	Ambassador from Spain	No
Stewart	Blanche	Hostess	No
Wilson	Don	Don Wilson	No

Songs:

Order	Title	Performers	Vocal
1	I Don't Know Your Name But You're Beautiful	Johnny Green	No
2	You Hit the Spot	Johnny Green	No
3	A Little Town in the Old County Down	Kenny Baker	Yes
4	Great Day	Johnny Green	No
5	Love in Bloom	Jack Benny	No
6	Early Bird	Johnny Green	No

Notes:

Blooper	Mary stumbles on "If I can't meet the bosses, then skip 'em."
Blooper	Jack says "hand graved invitation"
Blooper	Don cracks up at Smithsonian joke
Running gag	Mary's poem

Date: 3/22/1936   **Sponsor:** Jell-O   **City:** Baltimore, MD

Recording Source: Unknown   **Problems:** Partial show

First line:
And now we bring to you from the heart of Maryland, that comedian with the heartless jokes - Jack Benny.

Summary:
Officer gives Jack a ticket...gang discusses hospitality in Baltimore...the "nude eel" is a Democratic fish...Block and Sully appear from audience, Jack introduces them to the gang...skit Why Nell Left Home...eventually leaves with man who has Jell-O...two years later, daughter comes home married to Hollywood star and with baby...Jack tries to get a date with Eve Sully...from WBAL

Cast:

Last name	First name	Roles	Guest star
Baker	Kenny	Kenny Baker	No
Baldwin	Harry	Officer	No
Benny	Jack	Jack Benny, Lemuel Weathersby	No
Block	Jesse	Jesse Block	Yes
Fess?	Dave W.	Mayor of Philadelphia	No
Green	Johnny	Johnny Green, Zeke Green	No
Livingstone	Mary	Mary Livingstone, Nell Weathersby	No
Stewart	Blanche	Salisha Weathersby	No
Sully	Eve	Eve Sully	Yes
Wilson	Don	Don Wilson	No

Songs:

Order	Title	Performers	Vocal
1	Saddle Your Blues to a Wild Mustang	Johnny Green	No
2	Rhythm in My Nursery Rhymes	Johnny Green	No
3	Lovely Lady	Kenny Baker	Yes
4	I Feel a Song Coming On	Johnny Green	No
5	I'm Putting All My Eggs in One Basket	Johnny Green	No

Notes:

Skit	Why Nell Left Home

Date: 3/29/1936   **Sponsor:** Jell-O   **City:** New York, NY

Recording Source: Unknown   **Problems:** None

First line:
And now let us welcome back to New York that wandering boy, that prodigal son, that vagabond lover, Jack Benny.

Summary:
Gang compares things in the East to things in the West...joke about a baby grand (Jack says it's two years old, and Joan would have been about two at this time)...violinist interrupts and wants to be on the show, turns out to be Shlepperman...plays Klezmer version of "Love in Bloom"...gets fan letter from Constantinople, SD, asks for a play for her 12 children...they don't have enough women to do Cinderella, so skit is Cinderallen...fairy godfather turns boxes of Jell-O into horses...Horatio takes tuxedo from Cinderallen at midnight

Cast:

Last name	First name	Roles	Guest star
Baker	Kenny	Kenny Baker	No
Baldwin	Harry	Narrator	No
Benny	Jack	Jack Benny	No
Green	Johnny	Johnny Green	No
Hearn	Sam	Fritz Packard/Shlepperman, Horatio	No
Livingstone	Mary	Mary Livingstone, Princess	No
Shelley	Bill	Fairy godfather	No
Stewart	Blanche	Stepmother	No
Wilson	Don	Don Wilson	No

Songs:

Order	Title	Performers	Vocal
1	Wahoo	Johnny Green	No
2	So This is Heaven	Johnny Green	No
3	Awake in a Dream	Kenny Baker	Yes
4	Doin' the Prom	Johnny Green	No
5	I Got to Go To Work Again	Johnny Green	No

Notes:

Date: 4/5/1936   **Sponsor:** Jell-O   **City:** New York, NY

Recording Source: Unknown   **Problems:** Poor sound

First line:
And now we start off the spring season by bringing you that flowery speaker, that gilded lily, that budding genius, Jack Benny.

Summary:
Mary reads a poem about spring…Kenny gives Jack a carnation…fan letter asks Jack to change places with Fred Allen so they can hear his program (they work on Wednesday nights)…Jack puts clothespin on his nose to impersonate Fred Allen…skit Clown Hall Tonight…does Clown Hall News...Mighty Benny Art Players do "Charlie Chan in China"…amateurs include a talking bird, woman who puts bloomers on lamb chops…Shlepperman sings "Home on the Range", wins amateur contest

Cast:

Last name	First name	Roles	Guest star
Baker	Kenny	Kenny Baker	No
Benny	Jack	Jack Benny, Fred Benny	No
Brown	John	Bed salesman, husband, George A. Gumpelmeyer	No
Green	Johnny	Johnny Green, Peter Van Green, Luke	No
Hearn	Sam	Zeke	No
Hearn	Sam	Doctor	No
Hearn	Sam	Shlepperman	No
Livingstone	Mary	Mary Livingstone, Portland Livingstone	No
Stewart	Blanche	Wife	No
Stewart	Blanche	Polled woman, nurse	No
Wilson	Don	Don Wilson	No

Songs:

Order	Title	Performers	Vocal
1	You	Johnny Green	No
2	Breaking in a Pair of Shoes	Johnny Green	No
3	I'll Follow My Secret Heart	Kenny Baker	Yes
4	Cheek to Cheek	Johnny Green	No
5	It's Been So Long	Johnny Green	No

Notes:

Blooper	Jack and Don go for the same line of "And now, ladies and gentlemen…"
Blooper	Jack cracks up on air at start of Clown Hall News
Notable	First Beloin-Morrow script
Running gag	Mary as Mae West
Running gag	Mary's poem
Skit	Clown Hall Tonight

Date: 4/12/1936   **Sponsor:** Jell-O   **City:** Cleveland, OH

Recording Source: WJZ   **Problems:** None

First line:
And now we bring to you from Cleveland the pride of Waukegan, the idol of California,
Ohio's favorite son, Jack Benny of New York.

Summary:
Jack and Mary performing at Loew's State Theatre…reading review of Jack's
performance…Mary wrote a poem about Easter, Jack interrupts her reading it…skit Ah
Wilderness…parents are worried about their son, Wilderness…Forrest teaches son the
facts of life…Uncle takes Annabelle Simpson away from Wilderness

Cast:

Last name	First name	Roles	Guest star
Baker	Kenny	Kenny Baker, Wilderness	No
Benny	Jack	Jack Benny, Forrest	No
Green	Johnny	Johnny Green	No
Hearn	Sam	Uncle Ferncliff	No
Livingstone	Mary	Mary Livingstone, Treesa	No
Stewart	Blanche	Rooster	No
Wilson	Don	Don Wilson	No

Songs:

Order	Title	Performers	Vocal
1	It's No Fun	Johnny Green	No
2	Goody Goody	Johnny Green	No
3	In the Hills of Old Wyoming	Kenny Baker	Yes
4	I'm Gonna Sit Right Down and Write Myself a Letter	Jack Benny	Yes
4	I'm Gonna Sit Right Down and Write Myself a Letter	Sam Hearn	Yes
4	I'm Gonna Sit Right Down and Write Myself a Letter	Kenny Baker	Yes
5	I Don't Want to Make History	Johnny Green	No

Notes:

Blooper	Mary stumbles on the line "That suit looks like you forgot to take it off the hanger"
Notable	1st show has commercial for Jell-O, 2nd show has close commercial for Jell-O Ice Cream Powder
Running gag	Mary's poem
Skit	Ah Wilderness

Date: 4/19/1936 **Sponsor:** Jell-O **City:** New York, NY

Recording Source: WJZ **Problems:** Poor sound, partial show

First line:
And now we bring to you our weekly bogey man, Jack Benny.

Summary:
Jack tells what a gentleman is…fan letter from parents who want their son to grow up like Jack, but he'd rather have a bicycle…Mrs. Otis Elevator asks to hear the story of Jack's life…Jack says he will present his life, 39 years in all--Don notes that Jack is 42…skit Jack's Life Story…Jack is born…Jack takes violin lessons…Jack meets Mary in a park, both feel like failures but Jack says he'll conquer the world and come back to marry Mary…Jack plays "Love in Bloom" in the trenches of World War I…Mary accepts Jack's proposal

Cast:

Last name	First name	Roles	Guest star
Baker	Kenny	Kenny Baker	No
Benny	Jack	Jack Benny	No
Brown	John	Doctor	No
Green	Johnny	Johnny Green	No
Hearn	Sam	Schlepperman, violin teacher	No
Livingstone	Mary	Mary Livingstone, nurse	No
Stewart	Blanche	Agatha, teacher	No
Wilson	Don	Don Wilson, Zeke Benny	No

Songs:

Order	Title	Performers	Vocal
1	Everything Stops for Tea	Johnny Green	No
2	Swing Mister Charlie	Johnny Green	No
3	Maria My Own	Kenny Baker	Yes
4	I've Got a Heavy Date	Johnny Green	No

Notes:

Notable	First association of 39 with Jack's age
Recording	Only 11 minutes of show currently in circulation; opening comedy segment seems lost…extensive jumping during skit
Skit	Jack's Life Story

Date: 4/26/1936   **Sponsor:** Jell-O   **City:** Boston, MA

Recording Source: WJZ   **Problems:** None

First line:
And now we bring to you not the hero of Bunker Hill, not the catch of Cape Cod, not the Dean of Harvard University, but who do you think?

Summary:
Pat Weaver subs for Don Wilson...gang discusses seeing the sights in Boston...dishwasher welcomes Jack to Boston...Kenny stopped at Harvard to pick up a degree, but they're closed on Sunday...Mary thinks Pat Weaver is asking her for a date...Johnny Green throwing a party, hasn't invited Jack...no one has a car to go to the party except Jack...party is on a boat...meets Johnny's relatives...Uncle makes Jack drink tea, then Jack gets thrown overboard...special announcement to New York area listeners about limited release of Jell-O ice cream mix...originated from WBZ in Boston

Cast:

Last name	First name	Roles	Guest star
Baker	Kenny	Kenny Baker	No
Baldwin	Harry	Dishwasher, Joe the cornetist, Captain	No
Benny	Jack	Jack Benny	No
Green	Johnny	Johnny Green	No
Hearn	Sam	Officer 215, Uncle Kensington	No
Livingstone	Mary	Mary Livingstone	No
Stewart	Blanche	Aunt Clementine	No
Weaver	Pat	Pat Weaver	No

Songs:

Order	Title	Performers	Vocal
1	Yours Truly is Truly Yours	Johnny Green	No
2	Lost	Johnny Green	No
3	You	Kenny Baker	Yes
4	Let's Face the Music and Dance	Johnny Green	No
5	You'd Better Play Ball with Me	Johnny Green	No

Notes:

Blooper	Johnny Green says they "have to take a robot out to the party"

Date: 5/3/1936 **Sponsor:** Jell-O **City:** New York, NY

Recording Source: WJZ **Problems:** None

First line:
Ladies and gentlemen, tonight marks Jack Benny's 4th anniversary on the air. Radio marches back!

Summary:
Jack's 4th anniversary on radio...Don Bestor visits and is introduced to the cast...Frank Parker visits...skit Code of the Hills...Jake Bennys vs. Bestor Parkers...Kenny is shot...Shlepperman buys Benny land...Don is shot doing commercial

Cast:

Last name	First name	Roles	Guest star
Baker	Kenny	Kenny Baker, Ken Benny	No
Baldwin	Harry	Voice on phone	No
Benny	Jack	Jack Benny, Jake Benny	No
Bestor	Don	Don Bestor	Yes
Green	Johnny	Johnny Green, Jake Green	No
Hearn	Sam	President of Chevrolet, Shlepperman	No
Livingstone	Mary	Mary Livingstone, Mariah Benny	No
McGowan	John	President of General Tire	No
Parker	Frank	Frank Parker	Yes
Shelley	Bill	President of Canada Dry	No
Stewart	Blanche	Sara Benny	No
Wilson	Don	Don Wilson	No

Songs:

Order	Title	Performers	Vocal
1	At the Codfish Ball	Johnny Green	No
2	She Shall Have Music	Johnny Green	No
3	Small Hotel	Kenny Baker	Yes
4	She'll Be Comin' Round the Mountain	Johnny Green	No
5	The Right Somebody to Love	Johnny Green	No

Notes:

Blooper	Don Bestor says "I just wear spats"
Recording	Announcement for Jell-O ice cream mix inserted over closing commercial for New York/New England area listeners
Skit	Code of the Hills

Date: 5/10/1936   **Sponsor:** Jell-O   **City:** Detroit, MI

Recording Source: WJZ   **Problems:** None

First line:
Ladies and gentlemen, this is most embarassing. Jack Benny hasn't arrived yet, and we just learned that he still has his act to do at the Fox Theatre here in Detroit where he's appearing all this week.

Summary:
Tunes into Fox Theatre where Jack is performing..."do you serve shrimps here?"...Jack argues with a heckler...Mary gets huge reception...Jack and Mary return to studio...Kenny's mother sent him a check for Mother's Day...gang reminisces about their youth...Mary calls her mother...Mary reads poem to her mother...Kenny leaves for a date...salesman tries to get Jack to buy a car...Jack test drives the Synthetic Seven, has accident...gang visits him in the hospital...Shlepperman is the doctor...Don volunteers for a transfusion for Jack, Jack starts doing Jell-O commercial...show originates from Venetian Room of Book-Cadillac Hotel over WXYZ

Cast:

Last name	First name	Roles	Guest star
		Emcee	No
		Female trio	No
Baker	Kenny	Kenny Baker	No
Baldwin	Harry	Special delivery boy, heckler, Sam	No
Beloin	Ed	Applauder	No
Benny	Jack	Jack Benny	No
Green	Johnny	Johnny Green	No
Hearn	Sam	Shlepperman	No
Livingstone	Mary	Mary Livingstone	No
Robertson	Guy	Chester C. Chiselwood	No
Stewart	Blanche	Nurse	No
Wilson	Don	Don Wilson	No

Songs:

Order	Title	Performers	Vocal
1	I've Got a Heavy Date	Johnny Green	No
2	Eenie Meenie Miney Mo	Mary Livingstone	Yes
3	Take Your Time	Johnny Green	No
4	The Touch of Your Lips	Kenny Baker	Yes
5	It's You I'm Talking About	Johnny Green	No
6	I Can Pull a Rabbit Out of a Hat	Johnny Green	No

Notes:

Recording	Announcement for Jell-O ice cream mix inserted over closing commercial (may be for New York/New England area listeners only)
Running gag	Mary's poem
Running gag	Mary's mother communication

Date: 5/17/1936   **Sponsor:** Jell-O   **City:** New York, NY

Recording Source: Unknown   **Problems:** Poor sound, partial show

First line:
And now we bring to you that star of stage, screen, and Jell-O, Jack Benny.

Summary:
Jack is feeling tired and run down...Mary criticizes Jack's appearance...Kenny being bothered by millionaire's daughter...Jack says he's learning "Moon Over Miami" to replace "Love in Bloom", telegram from Mayor of Miami asking Jack not to switch...Jack going to California to make "Big Broadcast of 1937"...Kenny asks for Jack's advice in making pictures...gang flies to Hollywood, goes to Paramount...gang meets with Gensler, movie executive...Gensler says he needs more people, gang tries to get parts...Schlepperman is assistant director...they are ready to shoot (dice)...gang goes back to New York

Cast:

Last name	First name	Roles	Guest star
?	Terry	Mitchell Leisen	No
Baker	Kenny	Kenny Baker	No
Baldwin	Harry	Telegram boy, Mr. Lewis, plane announcer	No
Benny	Jack	Jack Benny	No
Brown	John	Mr. Gensler	No
Green	Johnny	Johnny Green	No
Hearn	Sam	Schlepperman	No
Livingstone	Mary	Mary Livingstone	No
Stewart	Blanche	Paramount operator	No
Wilson	Don	Don Wilson	No

Songs:

Order	Title	Performers	Vocal
1	Robins and Roses	Johnny Green	No
2	It's Got to Be Love	Johnny Green	No
3	Stardust	Kenny Baker	Yes
4	I'd Rather Lead a Band	Johnny Green	No
5	Spring in Vienna	Johnny Green	No

Notes:

Recording	Only 15 minutes of show currently in circulation...middle section and end are missing

Date: 5/24/1936 **Sponsor:** Jell-O **City:** New York, NY

Recording Source: Unknown **Problems:** Partial show

First line:
And now we bring to you the boss of our program who leaves for California tomorrow, Jack Benny.

Summary:
Jack interrupted by salesmen...guest star, Pat Button, lady golfer...Jack making a picture in California...fan letter in Yiddish dialect...skit Tour of New York City...walks on Broadway...goes to Automat...salesman tries to get Jack to go to California by steamship...meets gang at Automat

Cast:

Last name	First name	Roles	Guest star
Baker	Kenny	Kenny Baker	No
Baldwin	Harry	Beggar	No
Beloin	Ed	Tom at Automat	No
Benny	Jack	Jack Benny	No
Brown	John	H&H Railroad salesman, cabbie, Rolling Steamship representative	No
Cantor	Charles	Dashund Bus Company rep	No
Green	Johnny	Johnny Green	No
Hearn	Sam	Nervous Aircraft representative, George M. Cohan, Shlepperman	No
Livingstone	Mary	Mary Livingstone	No
Stewart	Blanche	Pat Button, Operator	No
Stewart	Blanche	Change girl at Automat	No
Wilson	Don	Don Wilson	No

Songs:

Order	Title	Performers	Vocal
1	I'll Bet You Tell That to All the Girls	Johnny Green	No
2	Love Is Like a Cigarette	Johnny Green	No
3	No Regret	Kenny Baker	Yes
4	Great Day	Johnny Green	No
5	Rhythm Saved the World	Johnny Green	No

Notes:

Recording	Only 14 minutes of show currently in circulation...middle segment before Kenny's song lost

Date: 5/31/1936   **Sponsor:** Jell-O   **City:** Hollywood, CA

Recording Source: None   **Problems:** None

First line:
And now we welcome back to California that sun-kissed comedian with the sun-sational jokes...Jack Sunny-boy Benny!

Summary:
Gang discusses being back in Hollywood...Mary reads poem about Hollywood...reporter shows up to interview Jack about his next picture, "The Big Broadcast of 1937"...Jack has switched to Paramount...Green is sore because he wasn't in the first segment...Jack and Green fight...cop comes along and they break it up...skit Murder at the Hokum-Plaza...guests check in...several men with weapons ask about a woman in black with jewels, ask to be near her room...lady in 303 is dead...clerk investigates, finds lots of people in 303, questions them...clerk grills himself, makes himself confess

Cast:

Last name	First name	Roles	Guest star
Baker	Kenny	Kenny Baker	No
Baldwin	Harry	Stalker 3	No
Benny	Jack	Jack Benny, desk clerk	No
Franz	Joe	Cop, stalker 1	No
Green	Johnny	Johnny Green, stalker 2	No
Kelly	Mary	Screamer, corpse	No
Livingstone	Mary	Mary Livingstone, operator	No
Robertson	Guy	Sidney Slotsky	No
Wilson	Don	Don Wilson	No

Songs:

Order	Title	Performers	Vocal
1	You Can't Pull the Wool Over My Eyes	Johnny Green	No
2	Let Yourself Go	Johnny Green	No
3	I Heard You Calling Me	Kenny Baker	Yes
4	You	Johnny Green	No
5	One Rainy Afternoon	Johnny Green	No

Notes:

Notable	First permanent California broadcast
Running gag	Mary's poem
Skit	Murder at the Hokum-Plaza

Date: 6/7/1936 **Sponsor:** Jell-O **City:** Hollywood, CA

Recording Source: Unknown **Problems:** Partial show

First line:
And now folks, I am sorry to state you won't hear the familiar "Jello Again" tonight because Jack Benny is at the Paramount Studio discussing the story for his forthcoming picture

Summary:
Jack and Mary conferencing with Gensler on story...Jack says part isn't big enough and Gensler threatens to get Fred Allen...Jack walked out of Paramount for a bigger role...Leo Robin and Ralph Rainger in audience, authors of "Love in Bloom"...Robin and Rainger smash Jack's violin...Jack's cook (a woman) calls, Jack wants bacon and eggs...Jack decides to start his own film company, Bennymount Films...Jack looks for good story, hires Irish tenor and director...Gensler calls for Fred Allen's phone number

Cast:

Last name	First name	Roles	Guest star
Baker	Kenny	Kenny Baker, Teeto Ruffo	No
Baldwin	Harry	Builder	No
Benny	Jack	Jack Benny	No
Blanc	Mel	Gensler	No
Flick	Patsy	Mr. Mulcahey	No
Green	Johnny	Johnny Green, Sir Guy Sitting	No
Livingstone	Mary	Mary Livingstone	No
Rainger	Ralph	Ralph Rainger	Yes
Robin	Leo	Leo Robin	Yes
Wilson	Don	Don Wilson	No

Songs:

Order	Title	Performers	Vocal
1	Take Your Time	Johnny Green	No
2	I Don't Want to Make History	Johnny Green	No
3	I Don't Want to Make History	Jack Benny	No
4	You Started Me Dreaming	Kenny Baker	Yes
5	I've Got a Heavy Date	Johnny Green	No
6	There Isn't Any Limit to My Love	Johnny Green	No

Notes:

Notable	First permanent California broadcast
Recording	Only 15 minutes of show currently in circulation

Date: 6/14/1936   **Sponsor:** Jell-O   **City:** Hollywood, CA

Recording Source: KFI   **Problems:** Partial show, music clipped

First line:
And now we bring to you the eyes and ears of Hollywood, that rambling reporter who brings you all the news, Jack "Scoop" Benny.

Summary:
Jack still concerned that Paramount hasn't called after he walked out...Jack does Hollywood news headlines...Phil Baker is coming to Hollywood to make a film, Jack is worried Baker is going to replace him...Mary calls Paramount and imitates Mae West...Phil Baker calls, Jack tries to talk him out of the part...Bennymount Films, Jack still looking for a story...Shlepperman shows up as an author...Jack gets telegram from Paramount, they added a line to his part...Jack disbands his studio...Jell-O ice cream powder now advertised nationally

Cast:

Last name	First name	Roles	Guest star
Baker	Kenny	Kenny Baker	No
Baldwin	Harry	Telegram boy	No
Benny	Jack	Jack Benny	No
Green	Johnny	Johnny Green, Pierre	No
Hearn	Sam	Shlepperman	No
Livingstone	Mary	Mary Livingstone	No
Wilson	Don	Don Wilson	No

Songs:

Order	Title	Performers	Vocal
1	Let's Sing Again	Johnny Green	No
2	I Can't Understand	Johnny Green	No
3	Gee It's a Thrill	Kenny Baker	Yes
4	Robins and Roses	Johnny Green	No
5	All My Life	Johnny Green	No

Notes:

Blooper	Mary stumbles on "San Luis Obispo Pedro Don Martinez Junior"
Notable	Time stamp 10 seconds before 8PM
Recording	Only 20 minutes of show currently in circulation...middle section after Kenny's song is missing

Date: 6/21/1936 **Sponsor:** Jell-O **City:** Hollywood, CA

Recording Source: KFI **Problems:** Poor sound, partial show

First line:
And now we bring to you for the last time this season, that worn-out Master of Ceremonies, Jack Benny.

Summary:
Don is MC on Jell-O summer show…it's Father's Day…gang discusses what they're doing this summer…Jack is going to take violin lessons…Jack on the set making "The Big Broadcast of 1937"…Shlepperman demonstrates how to read Jack's line properly…Jack takes a nap…Svengali hypnotizes Jack into being world's greatest violinist…Tim Ryan and Irene Noblette on Jell-O summer show with Don Voorhees Orchestra…Jack thanks Harry Conn and says Ed Beloin and Bill Morrow have helped to write the program for the last 12 weeks due to "Mr. Conn's illness"…won Radio Guide contest again this year

Cast:

Last name	First name	Roles	Guest star
?	Joe	Svengali	No
Baker	Kenny	Kenny Baker	No
Baldwin	Harry	Sparky the cameraman	No
Benny	Jack	Jack Benny	No
Green	Johnny	Johnny Green	No
Hearn	Sam	Shlepperman	No
Hicks	Russell	Mitchell Leisen	No
Livingstone	Mary	Mary Livingstone	No
Wilson	Don	Don Wilson	No

Songs:

Order	Title	Performers	Vocal
1	She Shall Have Music	Johnny Green	No
2	Would You	Kenny Baker	Yes
3	Lost	Johnny Green	No
4	Glory of Love	Johnny Green	No

Notes:

Notable	On-air thanks to Harry Conn and acknowledgement of Ed Beloin and Bill Morrow writing show for past 12 weeks
Recording	Kenny Baker's song is clipped

Date: 10/4/1936   **Sponsor:** Jell-O   **City:** Hollywood, CA

Recording Source: KFI   **Problems:** None

First line:
And now ladies and gentlemen, after four months vacation we present to you the man the whole world is waiting to hear.

Summary:
Jack went to the races at Saratoga Springs…Radio Guide reporter wants to talk to Kenny Baker…Mary had tonsils out, fell in love with her doctor…Phil Harris introduced…Play Frank/Don/John/Phil…Kenny was locked in closet…Kenny brought his girlfriend, Lina, to the studio…guest star is guy who drove the truck that carried the gas for the transatlantic plane…next week's skit is "Anthony Adverse"…Jell-O chocolate pudding is a new product

Cast:

Last name	First name	Roles	Guest star
		Jack's father	No
?	Bobby	Denver child	No
Baker	Benny	Truck driver Samuel T. Butchlina?	No
Baker	Benny	Samuel T. Botchvinner	No
Baker	Kenny	Kenny Baker	No
Baldwin	Harry	Lewis Radio Guide reporter	No
Beloin	Ed	Denver man	No
Benny	Jack	Jack Benny	No
Harris	Phil	Phil Harris	No
Klein	Vi	Glasgow woman	No
Klein	Vi	New York woman	No
Livingstone	Mary	Mary Livingstone	No
Mather	?	Glasgow man, New York man	No
Stewart	Blanche	Woman with Jack's father	No
Stewart	Blanche	Lena Cat, screamer, gramma	No
Wilson	Don	Don Wilson	No

Songs:

Order	Title	Performers	Vocal
1	Here's Love in Your Eye	Phil Harris	No
2	Bye Bye Baby	Phil Harris	No
3	The Way You Look Tonight	Kenny Baker	Yes
4	Sing Baby Sing	Phil Harris	No
5	Rose Room	Phil Harris	No

Notes:

Blooper	Mary misses cue for "So why didn't you stop him?"
Blooper	Jack calls Phil "the romantic tripe"
Notable	First toupee joke
Notable	First appearance of Phil Harris
Notable	First appearance of Lena, Kenny's girlfriend

Date: 10/11/1936 **Sponsor:** Jell-O **City:** Hollywood, CA

Recording Source: KFI **Problems:** None

First line:
And now we bring to you the man who returned to the air last Sunday with a deluge of merriment, a gale of laughter, and a worried look, Jack Benny.

Summary:
Reading reviews of previous week's show...telegram from New York Giants...congratulations wire from Freddy Bartholomew...skit Anthony Adverse...Anthony is a boy looking for work...Anthony sent to Cuba...Carlos gives Anthony a rubber plantation in Africa...Anthony gets drunk with power on plantation, dreams of Angela with another man...Mary does show close

Cast:

Last name	First name	Roles	Guest star
Baker	Kenny	Kenny Baker, African servant	No
Baldwin	Harry	Telegram boy, Captain	No
Benny	Jack	Jack Benny, Anthony Adverse	No
Cates	Joe	Angela	No
Flick	Patsy	Carlos Ceboe	No
Harris	Phil	Chocolate sundae	No
Harris	Phil	Phil Harris	No
Irwin	Charles	John Bonnyfeather	No
Livingstone	Mary	Mary Livingstone, Angela	No
Stewart	Blanche	Operator	No
Wilson	Don	Don Wilson	No

Songs:

Order	Title	Performers	Vocal
1	Tain't No Use	Phil Harris	No
2	Sing Sing Sing	Phil Harris	No
3	Did I Remember	Kenny Baker	Yes
4	Siboney	Phil Harris	No
5	When I'm With You	Phil Harris	No

Notes:

Blooper	Phil Harris says, "I've heard some awfully things about you."
Notable	Jack listed from 8:30 to 9:00 in San Francisco Examiner
Notable	First credit of Mary in opening announcement
Skit	Anthony Adverse

Date: 10/18/1936 **Sponsor:** Jell-O **City:** Hollywood, CA

Recording Source: Unknown **Problems:** None

First line:
And now ladies and gentlemen, we bring you that rising young movie star, Jack Benny.

Summary:
"The Big Broadcast of 1937" just released, Jack brags about his performance…gang punctures Jack's performance, then Jack's father calls from Waukegan and bolsters him again…skit Anthony Adverse (continued)…Jack recaps the story…Anthony returns to Europe…Angela has become a famous opera singer in Paris and Napoleon's lover…Angela sends Anthony away to America

Cast:

Last name	First name	Roles	Guest star
Baker	Kenny	Kenny Baker, African servant	No
Baldwin	Harry	Animal counter	No
Beloin	Ed	Joe	No
Benny	Jack	Jack Benny, Anthony Adverse	No
Flick	Patsy	Napoleon	No
Franz	Joe	Frank Buck	No
Harris	Phil	Phil Harris, Bombo	No
Klein	Vi	Hope	No
Livingstone	Mary	Mary Livingstone, Angela	No
Marks	Babe	Charity	No
Morrow	Bill	Hervey Allen	No
Stewart	Blanche	Faith	No
Wilson	Don	Don Wilson, ship captain	No

Songs:

Order	Title	Performers	Vocal
1	Swing the Jinx Away	Phil Harris	No
2	A Night in Manhattan	Phil Harris	No
3	When Did You Leave Heaven	Kenny Baker	Yes
4	I'll Sing You a Thousand Love Songs	Phil Harris	No

Notes:

Blooper	Jack misses his cue on Kenny Baker's entrance
Skit	Anthony Adverse

Date: 10/25/1936   **Sponsor:** Jell-O   **City:** Hollywood, CA

Recording Source: KFI   **Problems:** None

First line:
And now, ladies and gentlemen, we bring you the star of two Paramount pictures - Jack Benny.

Summary:
Jack went to the Paramount Theatre every night to see his own movie...Sam Harris offered Jack $4000 a week to play Anthony Adverse on stage...Loretta Young in audience...Jack keeps retelling Sam Harris story and increasing salary...Mr. Blue is Phil's arranger, cracks up on every line...Jack annouces "Romeo and Juliet" as next week's play, present previews...Mr. Campbell, head of General Foods, calls...Campbell doesn't want them to do "Romeo and Juliet", and Jack gets mad and hangs up on him...Jack eventually calls him back and pretends he was kidding, Campbell suggests they do an old-fashioned minstrel show

Cast:

Last name	First name	Roles	Guest star
Baker	Kenny	Kenny Baker	No
Baldwin	Harry	"So are you" guy, guy in mezzanine	No
Beloin	Ed	"Hooray" guy	No
Benny	Jack	Jack Benny	No
Blue	Ben	Ben Blue	No
Harris	Phil	Phil Harris	No
Livingstone	Mary	Mary Livingstone	No
Stewart	Blanche	Grandma	No
Wilson	Don	Don Wilson	No

Songs:

Order	Title	Performers	Vocal
1	Bojangles of Harlem	Phil Harris	No
2	Falling in Love With a Brand New Baby	Phil Harris	No
3	Make Believe	Kenny Baker	Yes
4	South Sea Island Magic	Phil Harris	No
5	A Fine Romance	Phil Harris	No

Notes:

Notable	Blue cracks up on every line in the show, but there's no indication to do this in the script; unclear if this is intentional or a blooper

Date: 11/1/1936   **Sponsor:** Jell-O   **City:** Hollywood, CA

Recording Source: KFI   **Problems:** None

First line:
And now ladies and gentleman, we bring you that leftover ghost from Halloween, Jack Benny.

Summary:
Jack played "Love in Bloom" under all the windows at Halloween...gang went to a masquerade party at Phil Harris' house...Kenny Baker asks about voting...skit Doc Benny's Minstrels...Johnny Green has gone to Fred Astaire's show...Minstrel parade through town...Mary taking tickets...Harris and Baker quarrel...Jack and Mississippi Four sing "Asleep In the Deep"...do "Romeo and Juliet" as an afterpiece...announces "Girls' Dormitory" as next week's skit

Cast:

Last name	First name	Roles	Guest star
Baker	Kenny	Kenny Baker, Macbeth	No
Baldwin	Harry	Asks for Mary, vendor	No
Beloin	Ed	Asks for Johnny Green	No
Benny	Jack	Jack Benny, Romeo	No
Harris	Phil	Phil Harris, Anthony	No
Livingstone	Mary	Mary Livingstone, Juliet	No
Morrow	Bill	Sweet Sue requestor	No
Nazarro	Cliff	Parade leader, guy on a horse, Tarzan	No
Stewart	Blanche	Mother, laugher	No
Wilson	Don	Don Wilson, Othello Jell-O	No

Songs:

Order	Title	Performers	Vocal
1	Alabama Barbecue	Phil Harris	No
2	When a Lady Meets a Gentleman Down South	Phil Harris	No
3	Can't Yo Hear Me Callin' Caroline	Kenny Baker	Yes
4	Asleep in the Deep	Jack Benny	Yes
5	The Night is Young and You're So Beautiful	Phil Harris	No

Notes:

Notable	First glimpse of ultimate Phil Harris character
Skit	Doc Benny's World Renowned Minstrels

Date: 11/8/1936   **Sponsor:** Jell-O   **City:** Hollywood, CA

Recording Source: Unknown   **Problems:** Partial show

First line:
And now, ladies and gentlemen, we bring you that outstanding stage comedian...that outstanding radio personality...that outstanding screen star - Jack Benny!...Mary, where's Jack?

Summary:
Jack is different since he started playing romantic roles...Kenny carrying a trunk, lost an election bet...Mary reads a letter from her mother...Kenny sings Mary's mother's request...skit Girls' Dormitory...Mr. Blue still cracks up on his lines...calls roll...quizzes class...Mary confesses she's in love with Haire Benny, he sings "When Did You Leave New Haven" to her

Cast:

Last name	First name	Roles	Guest star
Baker	Kenny	Kenny Baker	No
Baldwin	Harry	Jellogram boy, special delivery boy, Margaret Sullivan, Maureen O'Sullivan	No
Benny	Jack	Jack Benny, Haire Benny	No
Blue	Ben	Ben Blue, Betty Blue	No
Flick	Patsy	Doormat salesman	No
Harris	Phil	Phil Harris, Phyllis Harris	No
Livingstone	Mary	Mary Livingstone, Mary Mary	No
Stewart	Blanche	Student	No
Wilson	Don	Don Wilson, Dolores Wilson	No

Songs:

Order	Title	Performers	Vocal
1	You	Phil Harris	No
2	Did You Mean It	Phil Harris	No
3	Blue Eyes	Kenny Baker	Yes
4	Swing for Sale	Phil Harris	No
5	Did You Mean It	Phil Harris	No

Notes:

Recording	Only 8 minutes of show currently in circulation...opening and end are missing
Running gag	Mary's mother communication
Skit	Girls' Dormitory

Date: 11/15/1936 **Sponsor:** Jell-O **City:** Hollywood, CA

Recording Source: KFI **Problems:** Partial show

First line:
Jack: That was the last number of the sixth program in the new Jell-O series.

Summary:
Jack does closing of previous week's show since they omitted it...Don restarts show...Jack reminisces about his school days...Kenny's first anniversary on the program, planning a surprise for him...gang gives Kenny roller skates, he makes a speech...?...skit Buck Benny Rides Again...interrupted because Kenny skated into Tony's Pushcart...Jack settles the issue for $25...Mary steals Kenny's skates and runs into Tony's pushcart again

Cast:

Last name	First name	Roles	Guest star
?	Joe	Officer	No
Baker	Kenny	Kenny Baker	No
Baldwin	Harry	"You said it" guy	No
Benny	Jack	Jack Benny, Buck Benny	No
Flick	Patsy	Kenny's lawyer	No
Harris	Phil	Phil Harris, Frank Carson	No
Livingstone	Mary	Mary Livingstone, Daisy Carson	No
Royale	William	Tony	No
Stewart	Blanche	Lena, dog	No
Wilson	Don	Don Wilson	No

Songs:

Order	Title	Performers	Vocal
1	You On My Mind	Phil Harris	No
2	With Thee I Swing	Phil Harris	No
3	Talking Through My Heart	Kenny Baker	Yes
4	You Do the Darndest Things	Phil Harris	No
5	Pennies from Heaven	Phil Harris	No

Notes:

Blooper	Don says, "Gee I can just see how...his face...when it'll be red when he finds out..."
Notable	First Buck Benny skit
Recording	Section between Kenny's song and next Phil Harris number missing
Skit	Buck Benny Rides Again

Date: 11/22/1936   **Sponsor:** Jell-O   **City:** Hollywood, CA

Recording Source: Unknown   **Problems:** None

First line:
And now ladies and gentlemen, we bring to you your friend, my friend, and Jack Benny's friend, Jack Benny.

Summary:
Jack went to Palm Springs for a rest, parked his trailer in front of the El Mirador and hung his wash in the lobby...Mary reads a poem about Thanksgiving...Mary's Aunt Ruby calls, invites Jack and his turkey for Thanksgiving...Phil is late for the next number, Jack stands in for him...everyone has seen Phil with a different girl...Phil shows up and Jack chastizes him...skit continuation of Buck Benny Rides Again...Carole Lombard phones for Phil, and he makes a date with her...Carson's cow is stolen...Rattlesnake stole the cow...Ginger Rogers calls for Phil, Jack tries to get Phil off the phone so they can finish the skit...the cows come home anyway

Cast:

Last name	First name	Roles	Guest star
Baker	Kenny	Kenny Baker	No
Baldwin	Harry	Trumpeter	No
Benny	Jack	Jack Benny, Buck Benny	No
Blue	Ben	Ben Blue, Rattlesnake Rawler?	No
Harris	Phil	Phil Harris, Frank Carson	No
Livingstone	Mary	Mary Livingstone, Daisy Carson	No
Wilson	Don	Don Wilson	No

Songs:

Order	Title	Performers	Vocal
1	Plenty of Money and You	Phil Harris	No
2	One Two Button Your Shoe	Phil Harris	No
3	Your Eyes Have Told Me So	Kenny Baker	Yes
4	I'm Sorry Dear	Phil Harris	No
5	Who	Phil Harris	No

Notes:

Blooper	Sounds effects for phone ringing and picking up are door opening and closing
Running gag	Mary's poem
Skit	Buck Benny Rides Again

Date: 11/29/1936   **Sponsor:** Jell-O   **City:** Hollywood, CA

Recording Source: KFI   **Problems:** None

First line:
And now ladies and gentlemen, through the courtesy of NBC, we bring you our Master of Ceremonies through the courtesy of Paramount, Jack Benny, through the courtesy of Jell-O.

Summary:
Jack and Don being very polite to each other...Phil is late again...gang was at Jack's for Thanksgiving...Jack calls up Phil and pretends to be Mae West...discusses forthcoming picture "College Holiday"...Phil knew it was Jack calling because he was with Mae West...Phil gets his permanent at the same place Jack gets his toupee...fan letter from Mrs. Westover asking Jack to complete the Buck Benny skit...Buck asks Daisy to marry him...Cactus Face rustled some of Carson's cows...goes to Ike Muller's saloon to find Cactus Face...shootout with Cactus Face

Cast:

Last name	First name	Roles	Guest star
		Special delivery boy	No
Baker	Kenny	Kenny Baker, Partner	No
Baldwin	Harry	Special delivery boy, Curly	No
Beloin	Ed	Thanksgiving card seller	No
Benny	Jack	Jack Benny, Buck Benny	No
Flick	Patsy	Cactus Face Elmer	No
Franz	Joe	British guy	No
Harris	Phil	Phil Harris, Frank Carson	No
Livingstone	Mary	Mary Livingstone, Daisy Carson	No
Stewart	Blanche	Operator, Kate	No
Wilson	Don	Don Wilson, Slim Wilson	No

Songs:

Order	Title	Performers	Vocal
1	Curly Top	Phil Harris	No
2	Who's That Knockin' At My Heart	Phil Harris	No
3	I'll Sing You a Thousand Love Songs	Kenny Baker	Yes
4	Just a Rhyme for Love	Phil Harris	No
5	I Know That You Know	Phil Harris	No

Notes:

Skit	Buck Benny Rides Again

Date: 12/6/1936   **Sponsor:** Jell-O   **City:** Hollywood, CA

Recording Source: KFI   **Problems:** None

First line:
And now ladies and gentlemen, we bring you that uh...hey Jack...

Summary:
Don asks Jack about his eye...Jack had an argument with a gas station attendant...Phil is late again...California gas stations are swanky...Kenny comes in late with Phil...Jack mad at Phil and doesn't want to talk with him...Phil and Jack argue...Mary's mother calls...Jack says he's just a stooge on the show...had to discontinue Buck Benny skit because they can't find Cactus Face...skit Money Ain't Everything, a society drama...on a ship cruising the Mediterranean...Princes to fight a duel for Schnorrer's daughter...gets a cablegram from Frank Carson, they've located Cactus Face...Jack in Phoenix next Tuesday, invites everyone to a party except Phil

Cast:

Last name	First name	Roles	Guest star
Baker	Kenny	Kenny Baker, Prince Morris	No
Baldwin	Harry	Iceberg caller, radiogram boy	No
Benny	Jack	Jack Benny, J. Stuyvestant Schnorrer	No
Harris	Phil	Phil Harris, Prince Boris	No
Livingstone	Mary	Mary Livingstone, daughter	No
Stewart	Blanche	Mrs. Van deVeer, dog	No
Wilson	Don	Don Wilson, Captain	No

Songs:

Order	Title	Performers	Vocal
1	I'm in a Dancing Mood	Phil Harris	No
2	I'm in Love with a Brand New Baby	Phil Harris	No
3	Close to Me	Kenny Baker	Yes
4	Vote for Mr. Rhythm	Phil Harris	No
5	Just One of Those Things	Phil Harris	No

Notes:

Blooper	Jack cracks up on announcing his character's name
Running gag	Mary's mother communication
Skit	Money Ain't Everything

Date: 12/13/1936   **Sponsor:** Jell-O   **City:** Hollywood, CA

Recording Source: KFI   **Problems:** None

First line:
And now ladies and gentlemen, we present the man who every week spreads a little joy, a little cheer, a little sunshine, Jack "Pollyana" Benny.

Summary:
Jack is late…Don calls up Jack's house…Jack has a Chinese butler…Jack is mad and says that the gang can get along without him…Phil stands in for Jack…Jack shows up…Carole Lombard calls to talk to Jack, asks if Phil can get out early…continuing Buck Benny Rides Again…gang sings "I'm an Old Cowhand" theme….Cactus Face is cornered in a theatre…meets Sheriff Andy Devine…Buck is shot…Andy Devine does show close…show ends in chaos, five seconds long

Cast:

Last name	First name	Roles	Guest star
Baker	Kenny	Kenny Baker	No
Baldwin	Harry	Dead Eye	No
Benny	Jack	Jack Benny, Buck Benny	No
Devine	Andy	Andy Devine	No
Harris	Phil	Phil Harris, Frank Carson	No
Livingstone	Mary	Mary Livingstone, Daisy Carson	No
Royale	William	Chinese butler, Ike	No
Stewart	Blanche	Ticket vendor, audience member	No
Wilson	Don	Don Wilson	No

Songs:

Order	Title	Performers	Vocal
1	All's Fair in Love and War	Phil Harris	No
2	Frost on the Moon	Phil Harris	No
3	Night and Day	Kenny Baker	Yes
4	It's De-Lovely	Phil Harris	No
5	I Get a Kick Out of You	Phil Harris	No

Notes:

Blooper	Andy Devine says "the Jell-Y series"
Notable	First apperance of Andy Devine
Notable	May be longest laugh with Andy's blooper at the end of the program
Skit	Buck Benny Rides Again

Date: 12/20/1936   **Sponsor:** Jell-O   **City:** Hollywood, CA

Recording Source: KFI   **Problems:** None

First line:
And now we bring you a man who stands for good, wholesome entertainment, who stands for bright, sparkling humor, in fact, a man who stands for almost anything, Jack Benny.

Summary:
Jack still mad at Phil…everyone has a split personality…Don encourages Jack to make up with Phil…Mary, Kenny, and Don bought Jack a gold buttonhook…Jack gives Kenny a red silk necktie, Don a box of genuine Jell-O…gives Mary an earring ("there'll be other Christmases")…gives Phil a curling iron…Flick brings Jack a suit vest and pants, coat will cost him $75…Andy Devine arrives, can't do Buck Benny until next week…Andy is stuck on Mary…Phil gives Jack a platinum watch with diamonds…Jack and Phil make up, everyone starts crying…gang goes out for the evening

Cast:

Last name	First name	Roles	Guest star
Baker	Kenny	Kenny Baker	No
Benny	Jack	Jack Benny	No
Devine	Andy	Andy Devine	No
Flick	Patsy	Pat C. Flick	No
Harris	Phil	Phil Harris	No
Livingstone	Mary	Mary Livingstone	No
Wilson	Don	Don Wilson	No

Songs:

Order	Title	Performers	Vocal
1	I Feel a Song Coming On	Phil Harris	No
2	You Can Tell She Comes from Dixie	Phil Harris	No
3	Summer Night	Kenny Baker	Yes
4	Mutiny in the Brass Section	Phil Harris	No
5	Here's Love in Your Eye	Phil Harris	No

Notes:

Date: 12/27/1936 **Sponsor:** Jell-O **City:** Hollywood, CA

Recording Source: KFI **Problems:** None

First line:
And now ladies and gentlemen, Christmas being over, we are left with broken ornaments, tattered tinsel, burned-out bulbs, and Jack Benny.

Summary:
Don is wearing a loud Christmas tie...Jack talks about Christmas gifts...Phil is late again...Kenny got a necktie with sleeves from his girlfriend...Mary got a letter from her mother...they got a washing machine with a built-in radio...Hilliard home from barber college...Jack gets a holiday telegram from stars back east...Phil shows up...people saw previews of "College Holiday"...continuing Buck Benny skit...New Year's Eve at Sheriff's office...go over to Frank Carson's for party...Cactus Face sends a cowhide travel bag...Jack falls off his horse

Cast:

Last name	First name	Roles	Guest star
		Guest at Carsons	No
Baker	Kenny	Kenny Baker	No
Baldwin	Harry	Telegram boy	No
Benny	Jack	Jack Benny, Buck Benny	No
Devine	Andy	Andy Devine	No
Harris	Phil	Phil Harris, Frank Carson	No
Livingstone	Mary	Mary Livingstone, Daisy Carson	No
Stewart	Blanche	Florabelle	No
Wilson	Don	Don Wilson	No

Songs:

Order	Title	Performers	Vocal
1	Hallelujah	Phil Harris	No
2	The Night Is Young and You're So Beautiful	Kenny Baker	Yes
3	A Fine Romance	Phil Harris	No
4	Sing Baby Sing	Mary Livingstone	Yes
4	Sing Baby Sing	Andy Devine	Yes
4	Sing Baby Sing	Don Wilson	Yes
4	Sing Baby Sing	Phil Harris	Yes
5	Hallelujah	Phil Harris	No

Notes:

Notable	First use of joke about someone giving a tie with sleeves, "she started to knit a sweater and changed her mind'
Running gag	Mary's mother communication
Skit	Buck Benny Rides Again

Date: 1/3/1937 **Sponsor:** Jell-O **City:** Hollywood, CA

Recording Source: KFI **Problems:** None

First line:
And now ladies and gentlemen, we bring you that... Jack: Uh, ho...hold it a minute, Don.

Summary:
Jack asks for nice introduction...Door guy wishes Jack Happy New Year...gang talks about what they did New Year's Eve...Mary forgot to write a New Year's poem, writes it during the show...Mary reads "Oh You 1937"...Kenny brings Lina to the studio...continuing Buck Benny skit...Buck in hospital, visited by Deputies and Daisy...Cactus Face is doctor...Jack has Mary take a wire to Fred Allen--"I am not ashamed of myself"

Cast:

Last name	First name	Roles	Guest star
Baker	Kenny	Kenny Baker	No
Baldwin	Harry	Door guy	No
Benny	Jack	Jack Benny, Buck Benny	No
Flick	Patsy	Doctor/Cactus Face Elmer	No
Harris	Phil	Phil Harris, Frank Carson	No
Livingstone	Mary	Mary Livingstone, Daisy Carson	No
Stewart	Blanche	Lena, nurse, hen, screamer	No
Wilson	Don	Don Wilson	No

Songs:

Order	Title	Performers	Vocal
1	One in a Million	Phil Harris	No
2	Under the Spell of the Voodoo Drums	Phil Harris	No
3	The Sweetheart Waltz	Kenny Baker	Yes
4	Lorelei	Phil Harris	No
5	A Pretty Girl is Like a Melody	Phil Harris	No

Notes:

Notable	First show after Fred Allen has Stuart Canin play "The Bee" on his show, considered the start of the feud
Running gag	Mary's poem
Skit	Buck Benny Rides Again

Date: 1/10/1937   **Sponsor:** Jell-O   **City:** Hollywood, CA

Recording Source: Unknown   **Problems:** None

First line:
And now ladies and gentlemen, we bring you America's boyfriend who can't get a date, Jack Benny.

Summary:
Everyone heard Fred Allen's show...Door guy is back to wish Jack Happy New Year...Jack was at Paramount's silver jubilee for Adolph Zukor, took out Carole Lombard (and Clark Gable)...Buckingham Benny says Buck Benny series causing him problems...continuing Buck Benny skit...town up in arms because Cactus Face hasn't been caught...Sheriff Andy Devine has Cactus Face cornered in a hotel...the hotel is haunted, they search it...find Buckingham in hotel and gives him directions back to Pomona

Cast:

Last name	First name	Roles	Guest star
Baker	Benny	Buckingham Benny	No
Baldwin	Harry	Door guy, Bogey man	No
Benny	Jack	Jack Benny, Buck Benny	No
Devine	Andy	Andy Devine	No
Franz	Joe	Hotel doorman	No
Harris	Phil	Phil Harris, Frank Carson	No
Livingstone	Mary	Mary Livingstone, Daisy Carson	No
Stewart	Blanche	Wolf	No
Wilson	Don	Don Wilson	No

Songs:

Order	Title	Performers	Vocal
1	Gee But You're Swell	Phil Harris	No
2	When My Dreamboat Comes Home	Phil Harris	No
3	Kashmiri Song	Kenny Baker	Yes
4	Mysterious Mose	Phil Harris	No
5	Who Loves You	Phil Harris	No

Notes:

Blooper	Jack says, "One sniff of monoxnoid and I'm a new person."
Blooper	Sound man misses his cue to knock on the door during the skit
Blooper	Jack misses his cue from Mary, "You ought to put a Mickey Finn in their oats."
Notable	First extensive exchange of barbs with Fred Allen
Notable	Jack is calling the piece "Flight of the Bumblebee" when Canin actually played Schubert's "The Bee"
Skit	Buck Benny Rides Again

Date: 1/17/1937 **Sponsor:** Jell-O **City:** Hollywood, CA

Recording Source: KFI **Problems:** None

First line:
And now ladies and gentlemen, we bring you that violinist with the accent on vile, Jack Benny.

Summary:
Gang discusses Fred Allen's program...Jack has a photo of himself at age 10 playing "The Bee"...Jack won't stoop to argue with a toothpaste salesman (Fred was sponsored by Ipana)...Door guy returns with New Year's Greetings...guest star Mr. Oscar T. Foretoo/Mush, hit in face by Harry Cooper's divot...continuation of Buck Benny skit...prisoners broke out of Buck's jail...Buck asks Daisy to marry him, but she's sweet on Andy...Buck Jones saw Cactus Face in Ensenada...Andy had a radio built into his horse...Buck and Andy meet Buck Jones at a hotel in Ensenada...Cactus Face is bartender, Jack asks questions in Spanish, bartender answers in Yiddish)...shootout ensues

Cast:

Last name	First name	Roles	Guest star
		Senorita	No
Baker	Kenny	Kenny Baker	No
Baldwin	Harry	Door guy, horse	No
Benny	Jack	Jack Benny, Buck Benny	No
Devine	Andy	Andy Devine	No
Flick	Patsy	Bartender/Cactus Face Elmer	No
Harris	Phil	Phil Harris, Frank Carson	No
Jones	Buck	Buck Jones	Yes
Livingstone	Mary	Mary Livingstone, Daisy Carson	No
Marks	Hilliard	Desk clerk	No
Morrow	Bill	Horse	No
Nazarro	Cliff	Oscar T. Foretoo/Mush	No
Stewart	Blanche	Screamer	No
Wilson	Don	Don Wilson	No

Songs:

Order	Title	Performers	Vocal
1	Life Begins When You're in Love	Phil Harris	No
2	Chapel In the Moonlight	Kenny Baker	Yes
3	Lady Be Good	Phil Harris	No
4	Mama Inez	Phil Harris	No
5	The Way You Look Tonight	Phil Harris	No

Notes:

Blooper	Jack calls the male desk clerk a "senorita"
Blooper	Kenny Baker says, "Can I see the picture too too Jack?"
Skit	Buck Benny Rides Again

Date: 1/24/1937   **Sponsor:** Jell-O   **City:** Hollywood, CA

Recording Source: KFI   **Problems:** None

First line:
And now ladies and gentlemen, we bring you a man who as a child had whooping cough, measles, and violin lessons, Jack Benny.

Summary:
Mary opens the show because Jack is out practicing "The Bee"...telegram says town in Florida renamed for Jack, Off-Key West...Jack throws barbs at Fred Allen, "Allen isn't even his right name" Mary: "Is Benny yours?"...Door guy returns again with New Year's greetings...Phil's mother and sister in town, gang rides Buck Benny horses to see them...Jack is infatuated with Phil's sister, but she thinks Fred Allen is wonderful...shows pictures of Phil as a baby...Jack stays behind to say goodnight to Lucy-Belle...next week to use jokes for Fourth of July, since the show is not on during the summer

Cast:

Last name	First name	Roles	Guest star
?	Claudia	Lucy-Belle Harris	No
Baker	Kenny	Kenny Baker	No
Baldwin	Harry	Door guy	No
Beloin	Ed	Telegram boy	No
Benny	Jack	Jack Benny	No
Devine	Andy	Andy Devine	No
Felton	Verna	Mrs. Harris	No
Harris	Phil	Phil Harris	No
Livingstone	Mary	Mary Livingstone	No
Morrow	Bill	Chamber of Commerce representative	No
Wilson	Don	Don Wilson	No

Songs:

Order	Title	Performers	Vocal
1	Right or Wrong	Phil Harris	No
2	I've Got You Under My Skin	Kenny Baker	Yes
3	Goodnight My Love	Phil Harris	No
4	It's DeLovely	Andy Devine	Yes
4	It's DeLovely	Phil Harris	Yes
4	It's DeLovely	Mary Livingstone	Yes
5	Whispering	Phil Harris	No

Notes:

Date: 1/31/1937   **Sponsor:** Jell-O   **City:** Hollywood, CA

Recording Source: KFI   **Problems:** None

First line:
And now we bring you our radiant Master of Ceremonies with warmth in his heart and a cold in his head, Jack Benny.

Summary:
Jack has a cold, got it at Santa Anita…horse quit cold, came to the rail, and asked Jack if he'd heard Fred Allen's program…Kenny and Mary went to the races too…Lucy-Belle likes Jack…letter arrives from Mary's mother…Door guy brings New Year's greetings again…Lucy-Belle arrives, has a date with the boy next door…Jack is not in a Fourth of July mood tonight…Jack sends everyone home except Phil Harris…wants Phil to add 30 guys to his orchestra because he's going to play "The Bee" next week…Jack takes a nap, and dreams of shooting Fred Allen…telegram from Alton Cook, Radio Editor of the New York World Telegram, Jack wins favorite radio comedian for the fourth consecutive year, Jell-O show all-around favorite show, Don Wilson best announcer…announcement for Red Cross donations for flood victims

Cast:

Last name	First name	Roles	Guest star
?	Claudia	Lucy-Belle Harris	No
Baker	Kenny	Kenny Baker	No
Baldwin	Harry	Door guy, newspaper seller	No
Beloin	Ed	Special delivery guy	No
Benny	Jack	Jack Benny	No
Harris	Phil	Phil Harris	No
Hayes	Peter Lind	Fred Allen	No
Livingstone	Mary	Mary Livingstone	No
Stewart	Blanche	Screamer	No
Wilson	Don	Don Wilson	No

Songs:

Order	Title	Performers	Vocal
1	Everything is Rhythm in My Heart	Phil Harris	No
2	St. Louis Blues	Phil Harris	No
3	Sweetheart Let's Grow Old Together	Kenny Baker	Yes
4	Remember	Phil Harris	No
5	Lonesome and Sorry	Phil Harris	No

Notes:

Running gag	Mary's mother communication

Date: 2/7/1937   **Sponsor:** Jell-O   **City:** Hollywood, CA

Recording Source: KFI   **Problems:** None

First line:
And now ladies and gentlemen, after a week in the desert we bring you that sun-baked comedian with the warmed-over jokes, Jack Benny.

Summary:
Jack spent the week in Palm Springs…Jack going to play "The Bee" tonight…Kenny bought a raffle ticket on a car…Door guy wishes Jack a successful performance…Jack makes a secret phone call to Lucy-Belle…new villain for Buck Benny, Rattlesnake Allen…gang makes Fred Allen anemia jokes…Phil's family arrives…Jack gets good luck telegram from Ching Ling Allen…Jack gives a speech about Fred Allen…receives telegram from Mancel Talcott, Mayor of Waukegan, going to hang a picture of Jack in City Hall…Jack's violin is stolen…Mysterious stranger knows who stole the violin…telegram from Cactus Face Elmer volunteering to give up if Jack forgets the violin

Cast:

Last name	First name	Roles	Guest star
Baker	Kenny	Kenny Baker	No
Baldwin	Harry	Door guy, earmuff salesman	No
Beloin	Ed	Popcorn salesman	No
Benny	Jack	Jack Benny	No
Devine	Andy	Andy Devine	No
Felton	Verna	Mrs. Harris	No
Franz	Joe	Mysterious Stranger	No
Harris	Phil	Phil Harris	No
Livingstone	Mary	Mary Livingstone	No
Morrow	Bill	Program salesman	No
Stewart	Blanche	Lena, screamer	No
Wilson	Don	Don Wilson	No

Songs:

Order	Title	Performers	Vocal
1	Boo Hoo	Phil Harris	No
2	Swing High Swing Low	Phil Harris	No
3	Goodnight My Love	Kenny Baker	Yes
4	Slumming on Park Avenue	Phil Harris	No
5	Do You Ever Think of Me	Phil Harris	No

Notes:

Blooper	Kenny misses his entrance cue

Date: 2/14/1937   **Sponsor:** Jell-O   **City:** Hollywood, CA

Recording Source: KFI   **Problems:** None

First line:
Ladies and gentlemen, on this same Valentine's Day many years ago in the little town of Waukegan, Illinois, there was cause for great rejoicing.

Summary:
Everyone sings "Happy Birthday" to Jack…Mary gives Jack kiss…Jack says he's "in the neighborhood of 35"…everyone chipped in to see Jack's picture "College Holiday"…Kenny baked Jack a cake, Mary baked Jack a potato…Mary wrote a poem for Jack…telegram from the Metropolitan Life Insurance Company…ad placed for Jack's missing violin…Andy gives Jack a combination necktie and suspenders…Jack gets a valentine from Fred Allen…telegram from Jack's father…Ben Bernie gives Jack half a box of cigars…Kenny tries to get on Ben Bernie's show, Andy Devine volunteers to replace him…Bernie and Walter Winchell making "Wake Up and Live"…presents highlights in the life of Fred Allen (dead silence)…Bernie brought Jack his violin, Ben Bernie kidnapped…Jack doing "Brewster's Millions" tomorrow night

Cast:

Last name	First name	Roles	Guest star
Baker	Kenny	Kenny Baker	No
Baldwin	Harry	Western Union man	No
Beloin	Ed	Telegram boy	No
Benny	Jack	Jack Benny	No
Bernie	Ben	Ben Bernie	Yes
Devine	Andy	Andy Devine	No
Harris	Phil	Phil Harris	No
Livingstone	Mary	Mary Livingstone	No
Morrow	Bill	Special delivery boy	No
Wilson	Don	Don Wilson	No

Songs:

Order	Title	Performers	Vocal
1	Swing the Jinx Away	Phil Harris	No
2	Ridin' High	Phil Harris	No
3	Carry Me Back to the Lone Prairie	Kenny Baker	Yes
4	Goona Goo	Phil Harris	No
5	I Cried for You	Phil Harris	No

Notes:

Running gag	Mary's poem

Date: 2/21/1937   **Sponsor:** Jell-O   **City:** Hollywood, CA

Recording Source: KFI   **Problems:** None

First line:
And now ladies and gentlemen, we bring you Waukegan's gift to the amusement world, that star of screen, radio, and Brewster's Millions, Jack Benny.

Summary:
Gang talks about "Brewster's Millions"...Mary now thinks she's Katharine Hepburn...everyone starts using British accents...Jack has hired a private detective to find his violin...Mary going for a rest because she read in Winchell's column that she's sick...Jack will be in New York in two weeks...cheap jokes about Fred Allen...going to do Lady Guenevere's Bracelet, a high English drama...Mr. Campbell of General Foods calls, tells Jack to look for Cactus Face or a new job...continuation of Buck Benny skit...Cactus Face collected his own reward...Cactus Face seen at Bucket o' Blood Barber Shop...Buck visits Daisy, Frank Carson working on his still...Buck takes Daisy to the depot...Jack will play the Bee next Sunday

Cast:

Last name	First name	Roles	Guest star
Baker	Kenny	Kenny Baker, rooster	No
Baldwin	Harry	Skeeter	No
Baldwin	Harry	Door guy	No
Benny	Jack	Jack Benny, Buck Benny	No
Harris	Phil	Phil Harris, Frank Carson	No
Livingstone	Mary	Mary Livingstone, Daisy Carson	No
Stewart	Blanche	Buck Benny's mother	No
Wilson	Don	Don Wilson	No

Songs:

Order	Title	Performers	Vocal
1	Blow Gabriel Blow/Alabama Barbecue	Phil Harris	No
2	When My Dreamboat Comes Home	Kenny Baker	Yes
3	He Ain't Got Rhythm	Phil Harris	No
4	Dear Old Southland	Phil Harris	No
5	Moonlight and Roses	Phil Harris	No

Notes:

Skit	Buck Benny Rides Again

Date: 2/28/1937 **Sponsor:** Jell-O **City:** Hollywood, CA

Recording Source: KFI **Problems:** None

First line:
Jack: Arrived in New York okay, but the train trip was terrible as there was nothing but trunks and suitcases in my car.

Summary:
Reading letter from Mary...she saw her family and ran into Fred Allen...Kenny brought girlfriend Lena to help with the show...detective found Jack's violin, gives him a dollar reward...Andy Devine wanted to kiss Mary goodbye...Jack to be accompanied by pianist Rachmaninoff T. Smith...Jack warms up with Kreutzer exercises...Jack plays "The Bee", switches to "Plenty of Money and You" in the middle of it..."What NOW Mister Allen?"...Mary telephones...Jack wants gang to secretly come and join Mary in New York...Jack going to drop in on Ben Bernie's program on Tuesday

Cast:

Last name	First name	Roles	Guest star
		Rachmaninoff T. Smith	No
Baker	Kenny	Kenny Baker	No
Benny	Jack	Jack Benny	No
Devine	Andy	Andy Devine	No
Flick	Patsy	Detective	No
Harris	Phil	Phil Harris	No
Stewart	Blanche	Lena	No
Wilson	Don	Don Wilson	No

Songs:

Order	Title	Performers	Vocal
1	Gee But You're Swell/I've Got My Love to Keep Me Warm	Phil Harris	No
2	Melancholy Baby	Phil Harris	No
3	The Night is Young and You're So Beautiful	Kenny Baker	Yes
4	The Bee – Plenty of Money and You	Jack Benny	No
5	Panamania	Phil Harris	No
6	I've Got My Love to Keep Me Warm/Gee But You're Swell	Phil Harris	No

Notes:

Notable	Jack plays "The Bee"
Notable	May be first time Jack plays Kreutzer exercises on the air

Date: 3/7/1937 **Sponsor:** Jell-O **City:** New York, NY

Recording Source: KFI **Problems:** None

First line:
And now ladies and gentlemen, we bring you the man who made "The Bee" Public Insect Number One, Jack Benny.

Summary:
From the grand ballroom of the Waldorf-Astoria…Jack sent his violin to Honolulu for a rest…Waldorf-Astoria is so swanky that Jack had to shave before going to the barber shop…Mary tells what she's been doing in New York…Abe Lyman directed orchestra with a blackjack…Mary describes Abe Lyman…Jack asked Stuart Canin to come to the show, wants to see if he's really ten years old…Shlepperman visits, has little Gypsy Tea Room and hotel…five-year-old girl played "The Bee" on the piano on Fred Allen's program…Stuart Canin says he doesn't give lessons…Jack interrogates Canin…Don interrogates Canin about Jell-O…Canin confesses to being ten years and four months old…Shlepperman defends Canin

Cast:

Last name	First name	Roles	Guest star
?	George	Vice President in charge of removing dishes	No
Baker	Kenny	Kenny Baker	No
Benny	Jack	Jack Benny	No
Canin	Stuart	Stuart Canin	Yes
Hearn	Sam	Schlepperman	No
Livingstone	Mary	Mary Livingstone	No
Lyman	Abe	Abe Lyman	Yes
Wilson	Don	Don Wilson	No

Songs:

Order	Title	Performers	Vocal
1	Plenty of Money and You	Abe Lyman	No
2	Slumming on Park Avenue	Abe Lyman	No
3	When the Poppies Bloom Again	Kenny Baker	Yes
4	Shine on Your Shoes/Louisiana Hayride	Abe Lyman	No
5	One in a Million	Abe Lyman	No

Notes:

Blooper	Mary stumbles on "You've either got a loud heart or a cheap watch."

Date: 3/14/1937   **Sponsor:** Jell-O   **City:** New York, NY

Recording Source: KFI   **Problems:** None

First line:

And now ladies and gentlemen, we bring you a fellow who is a big man in Hollywood, a giant in Waukegan, but just another actor in New York, Jack Benny.

Summary:

From the grand ballroom of the Hotel Pierre...hotel representative asks Jack not to mingle with the guests...Fred Allen is a scaredy cat ("Boo" Allen)...Kenny had to go to Hollywood to finish his picture, got off in St. Louis instead of Hollywood...Abe Lyman is a sensitive guy...Lyman's band is tough, feeds them meat and cream puffs...Mary never paid income tax, thought government letters were fan mail...Shlepperman comes to audition as a singer, say with Goy Lombardo...Fred Allen arrives, says Jack makes Andy Devine sound like Lawrence Tibbett...huge argument ensues..."anything you say accidentally will be better than the script"...Shlepperman tries to break up the fight...Jack asks Fred to step out in the hall...after a band number, Jack and Fred re-enter reminiscing about vaudeville...Fred brought Jack a box of candy with Ipana...Fred tells Abe Lyman to lay off his pal, Jack

Cast:

Last name	First name	Roles	Guest star
Allen	Fred	Fred Allen	Yes
Baldwin	Harry	Hotel Pierre representative	No
Benny	Jack	Jack Benny	No
Hearn	Sam	Schlepperman	No
Livingstone	Mary	Mary Livingstone	No
Lyman	Abe	Abe Lyman	Yes
Wilson	Don	Don Wilson	No

Songs:

Order	Title	Performers	Vocal
1	You	Abe Lyman	No
2	I Got Rhythm	Abe Lyman	No
3	You Do the Darndest Things	Mary Livingstone	Yes
3	You Do the Darndest Things	Jack Benny	Yes
4	Hallelujah/Love and Learn	Abe Lyman	No
5	You Do the Darndest Things	Fred Allen	Yes
5	You Do the Darndest Things	Jack Benny	Yes
6	Love and Learn/Hallelujah	Abe Lyman	No

Notes:

Date: 3/21/1937 **Sponsor:** Jell-O **City:** New York, NY

Recording Source: Unknown **Problems:** None

First line:
And now we bring you the man who came to New York for a rest and has to go back to Hollywood to get it, Jack "Playboy" Benny.

Summary:
Jack has been carousing...Jack and Phil will be in the same movie...Abe Lyman recommends that Jack have a Striker's Cocktail...returning to Hollywood next week...Mayor Mancel "Bidey" Talcott of Waukegan appears...Jack's nickname was "Toughie" Benny...Jack asks about Julius Sinykin, Stubbs Wilbur, Aunt Josephine, and others...planning Jack Benny Day in Waukegan...introduces Talcott to gang...Jack re-enacts helping his father in the Waukegan store, Jack plays his own father...store is Emporium on South Genesee...Jack's father tells him to practice "The Bee"...Don is 19 months old, weighs 210 pounds..."Stwawbewwy, chewwy" gag...Kenny and Mancel show up to play ball with Jack, want to use his violin as a bat...Abe Lyman throws a stone through the window because it's his last week...Shlepperman appears as a travelling salesman, selling men's bathing suit tops ("the trunks missed the boat")

Cast:

Last name	First name	Roles	Guest star
Baker	Kenny	Kenny Baker	No
Baldwin	Harry	Customer for suit	No
Benny	Jack	Jack Benny, Jack's father	No
Hearn	Sam	Shlepperman	No
Kelly	Mary	Mrs. Wilson	No
Livingstone	Mary	Mary Livingstone, Mary Thompson	No
Lyman	Abe	Abe Lyman	Yes
O'Day	Junior	Young Jackie Benny	No
Talcott	Mancel	Mancel Talcott	Yes
Wilson	Don	Don Wilson, baby	No

Songs:

Order	Title	Performers	Vocal
1	Gee But You're Swell	Abe Lyman	No
2	I've Got My Love to Keep Me Warm	Abe Lyman	No
3	It's De-Lovely	Abe Lyman	No
4	For You	Kenny Baker	Yes
5	Who	Abe Lyman	No

Notes:

Blooper	Sound man misses cue to toot the horn
Running gag	Baby talk Jell-O flavors

Date: 3/28/1937 **Sponsor:** Jell-O **City:** Hollywood, CA

Recording Source: KFI **Problems:** None

First line:
And now ladies and gentlemen, we take you to the Debron Street Station in Chicago where we find Jack and the rest of the gang about to board the train for California.

Summary:
Phil's band in Hollywood...gang is boarding the train for California...porter calls Jack "Mr. Bunny" (it's Easter)...took Jack's bags to the drawing room, but the lady keeps throwing them out...goofy train announcements...Kenny taking snow to California for his mother to see it...Mary stayed up half the night writing an Easter poem...joke about "Does the train stop in Albuquerque?"...woman has daughter Millicent sing for Jack...Yiddish Indian running bargain store...Jack wants to buy a pair of moccasins...Andy and Phil waiting for gang's arrival...Jack brings back menu from Waldorf-Astoria...Jack tipped the Waldorf-Astoria waiter a dime...Mary asks autograph seeker in Kansas City to return her gold pencil in person

Cast:

Last name	First name	Roles	Guest star
		Opening announcer	No
?	Sidney	Little papoopsie Rain in the Face	No
Anderson	Eddie	Porter	No
Baker	Kenny	Kenny Baker	No
Baldwin	Harry	Conductor 1	No
Benny	Jack	Jack Benny	No
Devine	Andy	Andy Devine	No
Felton	Verna	Autograph seeker 1	No
Flick	Patsy	Indian bargain seller	No
Franz	Joe	Transfer man, information clerk, conductor 2	No
Gibson	John	Train announcer	No
Livingstone	Mary	Mary Livingstone	No
Marks	Hilliard	Program seller	No
Nelson	?	Redcap	No
Royale	William	Chinaman, indian	No
Stewart	Blanche	Millicent	No
Wilson	Don	Don Wilson	No

Songs:

Order	Title	Performers	Vocal
1	I'm Bubbling Over	Phil Harris	No
2	Too Marvelous for Words	Phil Harris	No
3	Trust In Me	Kenny Baker	Yes
4	Swing High Swing Low	Phil Harris	No
5	Life Begins When You're In Love	Phil Harris	No

Notes:

Notable	Eddie Anderson's lines are indicated for "Eddy" in the script
Notable	First appearance of Eddie Anderson
Running gag	Mary's poem

Date: 4/4/1937   **Sponsor:** Jell-O   **City:** Hollywood, CA

Recording Source: KFI   **Problems:** None

First line:
And now ladies and gentlemen, spring is here, ah beautiful spring, spring with its butterflies, blossoms, wildflowers, April showers, and...
Jack: Jack Benny.

Summary:
Jack has filled his swimming pool with water and relatives...people working on their gardens, Mary plants mashed potatoes...Waukegan planted the Jack Benny Elm in his honor...Abe Lyman is a friend of Phil...Jack says the feud with Fred Allen was all in fun...gang alternately cricizes and defends Allen...Mary's mother calls, father set bear traps all over the house...Andy showed Waldorf-Astoria menu to his chickens, now they want to live in the house...in response to audience requests, Jack gives list of 1936 plays for listeners to vote on one for encore performance...shows elk's tooth to Andy Devine

Cast:

Last name	First name	Roles	Guest star
Baker	Kenny	Kenny Baker	No
Benny	Jack	Jack Benny	No
Devine	Andy	Andy Devine	No
Harris	Phil	Phil Harris	No
Livingstone	Mary	Mary Livingstone	No
Stewart	Blanche	Dog, lady in Racine	No
Wilson	Don	Don Wilson	No

Songs:

Order	Title	Performers	Vocal
1	Boo Hoo	Phil Harris	No
2	That Foolish Feeling	Phil Harris	No
3	Turn Off the Moon	Kenny Baker	Yes
4	Ridin' High	Phil Harris	No
5	One in a Million	Phil Harris	No

Notes:

Running gag	Mary's mother communication

Date: 4/11/1937   **Sponsor:** Jell-O   **City:** Hollywood, CA

Recording Source: KFI   **Problems:** None

First line:
And now ladies and gentlemen, we bring you that Hollywood fashion plate whose pockets bulge from his tailor's bills, Jack Benny.

Summary:
Jack talks about his new spring suit...Phil's coat is loud ("first time I ever saw a sunset with a belt in the back")...Mary gets a letter from her mother...Kenny's suit isn't finished yet...George Burns sent Gracie to deliver a message to Jack, which she can't remember...Gracie thought Don was a box of Jell-O...continuing Buck Benny skit...George Burns reminds Gracie that she was to give Jack tickets to their new Grape Nuts show...Cactus Face has stolen every cow in the county...Buck locks up George and Gracie in jail...Gracie keeps interrupting the skit...go to hideout of Cactus Face...Radio Editor's show at the Shrine Auditorium next Saturday night

Cast:

Last name	First name	Roles	Guest star
Allen	Gracie	Gracie Allen	Yes
Baker	Kenny	Kenny Baker	No
Baldwin	Harry	Special delivery boy	No
Benny	Jack	Jack Benny, Buck Benny	No
Burns	George	George Burns	Yes
Harris	Phil	Phil Harris, Frank Carson	No
Livingstone	Mary	Mary Livingstone, Daisy Carson	No
Wilson	Don	Don Wilson	No

Songs:

Order	Title	Performers	Vocal
1	All's Fair in Love and War	Phil Harris	No
2	Moonlight and Shadows	Kenny Baker	Yes
3	This Year's Crop of Kisses	Phil Harris	No
4	You	Phil Harris	No

Notes:

Running gag	Mary's mother communication
Skit	Buck Benny Rides Again

Date: 4/18/1937   **Sponsor:** Jell-O   **City:** Hollywood, CA

Recording Source: KFI   **Problems:** None

First line:
And now ladies and gentlemen…oh, Phil, has our guest star arrived yet?

Summary:
Jack acts like a famous film actor as guest star…considering Jack for the lead in "Gone With the Wind"…Jack says he's 31…gang introduces themselves to Jack…Kenny didn't realize it was the real Jack Benny…Jack was guest of honor at Phil Harris' opening at the Coconut Grove Tuesday…Mary and Don danced the rhumba…Andy can't get his dress shirt off…skit Lady Millicent's Husband, an English drawing room drama…Sir Ronnie has died and made Lady Millicent his sole heir…all of Millicent's ex-husbands show up and want to remarry her…Sir Ronnie appears and is not dead…"We're a little late, so cheerio folks."

Cast:

Last name	First name	Roles	Guest star
Baker	Kenny	Kenny Baker, Sir Ronnie	No
Benny	Jack	Jack Benny, Lord Stanley Puffypusses	No
Devine	Andy	Andy Devine, Sir Andrew Oliver Archibald Clambake	No
Flick	Patsy	Lord Cedric Warwick Patrick Flick	No
Harris	Phil	Phil Harris, Sir Philip Harris Algernon Chatsworth	No
Livingstone	Mary	Mary Livingstone, Lady Millicent	No
Wilson	Don	Don Wilson, Heaves, Sir Jell-O	No

Songs:

Order	Title	Performers	Vocal
1	Jamboree	Phil Harris	No
2	Southern Hospitality	Phil Harris	No
3	Will You Remember	Kenny Baker	Yes
4	Big Boy Blue	Phil Harris	No
5	Wanted	Phil Harris	No

Notes:

Blooper	Jack misses his cue for "That's all right, Mr. Wilson."
Notable	First recorded occasion of "We're a little late" sign-off
Notable	Youngest age Jack ever claims: 31
Skit	Lady Millicent's Husband

Date: 4/25/1937 **Sponsor:** Jell-O **City:** Hollywood, CA

Recording Source: KFI **Problems:** None

First line:
Jack: Hey Mary, Mary come here. Don't you love the way Phil wiggles around when he leads the orchestra? Look at him.

Summary:
Jack and Mary talk over the opening music...Phil is mad at Jack for talking during the music...everyone starts arguing...Jack accuses Phil of picking fights to get his watch back...Thelma Snodgrass stops by to see Mary, brings new husband Sam...they start arguing, Jack tells Sam to assert himself...everyone attacks Jack...everyone progressively gets mad and leaves...Jack gives up on skit "In the Spring Tra La", plays "Love in Bloom"...Andy calls and invites Jack to come over to the ranch...Andy's family gets mad at Jack...Jack falls down the stairs, finds liniment at the bottom...next week is Jack's 5th anniversary in radio

Cast:

Last name	First name	Roles	Guest star
Baker	Kenny	Kenny Baker	No
Baldwin	Harry	Eskimo	No
Benny	Jack	Jack Benny	No
Block	Jesse	Sam Clunk	No
Devine	Andy	Andy Devine	No
Harris	Phil	Phil Harris	No
Livingstone	Mary	Mary Livingstone	No
Nazarro	Cliff	Andy's father	No
Stewart	Blanche	Andy's mother	No
Sully	Eve	Thelma Snodgrass	No
Wilson	Don	Don Wilson	No

Songs:

Order	Title	Performers	Vocal
1	Hallelujah Things Look Rosy Now	Phil Harris	No
2	Let's Get Together	Phil Harris	No
3	Sweet Is the Word for You	Kenny Baker	Yes
4	Panamania	Phil Harris	No
5	I Get a Kick Out of You	Phil Harris	No

Notes:

Date: 5/2/1937   **Sponsor:** Jell-O   **City:** Hollywood, CA

Recording Source: KFI   **Problems:** None

First line:
Ladies and gentlemen, today, May 2nd 1937, marks an important occasion: the 5th anniversary of the radio debut of a man who has established himself in the hearts of millions.

Summary:
Jack's 5th anniversary in radio...Mary wrote a poem for Jack...gets congratulations telegram from Fibber McGee...Andy Devine gives Jack a billfold with a banana cream pie inside ("maybe a dollar will slip out")...reporter shows up to interview Jack and the gang...takes picture, makes Jack stand behind Don Wilson...special episode of Buck Benny...gets a congratulatory telegram from the sponsor...Buck hasn't paid his phone bill...Buck's 5th anniversary as Sheriff of Cactus County, party at Busy Bee Restaurant and Pool Parlor...gang tries to figure out what to order, Pierre dissuades them from everything, recommend the hash ("it ain't fatal")...winner of repeat play contest to be announced next Sunday

Cast:

Last name	First name	Roles	Guest star
Anderson	Eddie	Pierre	No
Baker	Kenny	Kenny Baker	No
Baldwin	Harry	Door guy, phone man	No
Beloin	Ed	Telegram boy	No
Benny	Jack	Jack Benny, Buck Benny	No
Devine	Andy	Andy Devine	No
Gibson	John	Brown with Hollywood Scoop	No
Harris	Phil	Phil Harris, Frank Carson	No
Livingstone	Mary	Mary Livingstone, Daisy Carson	No
Morrow	Bill	Dead Eye	No
Wilson	Don	Don Wilson	No

Songs:

Order	Title	Performers	Vocal
1	Honey Bunch	Phil Harris	No
2	September in the Rain	Kenny Baker	Yes
3	How Could You	Phil Harris	No
4	Let's Call the Whole Thing Off	Mary Livingstone	Yes
4	Let's Call the Whole Thing Off	Andy Devine	Yes
4	Let's Call the Whole Thing Off	Jack Benny	Yes
4	Let's Call the Whole Thing Off	Don Wilson	Yes
5	Looking for Romance	Phil Harris	No

Notes:

Notable	Second appearance of Eddie Anderson, first time he calls Jack "Boss"
Running gag	Mary's poem
Skit	Buck Benny Rides Again

Date: 5/9/1937   **Sponsor:** Jell-O   **City:** Hollywood, CA

Recording Source: Unknown   **Problems:** None

First line:
Ladies and gentlemen, if you don't feel like taking a walk or going to a movie, and you're not in the mood for a nap, that is, if you haven't anything else to do, you might as well listen to Jack Benny.

Summary:
Jack is mad about Don's introduction…it's Mother's Day, gang discusses what they got for their mothers…gang discusses Kentucky Derby bets…Phil's band isn't alert…telegram from Mrs. Otis Elevator with six children, wants schoolroom play to set an example…Pat C. Flick is a lifeguard…skit The Bump on Teacher's Head…calls roll, morning exercises…calls for Donald and gets Donald Duck…Phil keeps throwing spitballs…asks who was father of our country ("George…Olsen") and the mother ("Ethel Shutta")…Phil wrote "Teacher is a loose" on the blackboard (can't spell "louse")…repeat play next week is "Ah Wilderness", does previews

Cast:

Last name	First name	Roles	Guest star
Baker	Kenny	Kenny Baker	No
Baldwin	Harry	Telegram boy, Fred Allen	No
Beloin	Ed	Arthur Jean	No
Benny	Jack	Jack Benny, teacher	No
Devine	Andy	Andy Devine	No
Flick	Patsy	Pat C. Flick	No
Harris	Phil	Phil Harris	No
Livingstone	Mary	Mary Livingstone	No
Marks	Hilliard	Man Mountain Dean	No
Stewart	Blanche	Jean Arthur, wolf, screamer	No
Wilson	Don	Don Wilson	No

Songs:

Order	Title	Performers	Vocal
1	You're Number One on My Love Parade	Phil Harris	No
2	Study in Brown	Phil Harris	No
3	Where Are You	Kenny Baker	Yes
4	Ridin High	Phil Harris	No
5	I'm Bubbling Over	Phil Harris	No

Notes:

Blooper	Mary cracks up on "Last year, he didn't take his pants off for a week."
Blooper	Jack says "how many hairs" instead of "how many pairs"
Notable	First Phil can't spell/read joke
Notable	Fred Allen is done by Harry Baldwin holding his nose
Skit	The Bump on Teacher's Head

Date: 5/16/1937 **Sponsor:** Jell-O **City:** Hollywood, CA

Recording Source: Unknown **Problems:** None

First line:
And now ladies and gentlmen, Jack Benny.

Summary:
Don running out of adjectives for introducing Jack...gang discusses where Jack should go for his vacation, he's concerned about cost...Phil not in the play because he threw spitballs last week...skit Ah Wilderness...parents are concerned about their son staying out late...Forest decides he needs to teach Wilderness the facts of life...Wilderness wrote a love letter to Annabelle Thompson...Ferncliff takes Annabelle away from Wilderness...telegram from Eugene O'Neill

Cast:

Last name	First name	Roles	Guest star
Baker	Kenny	Kenny Baker, Wilderness	No
Benny	Jack	Jack Benny, Forest	No
Devine	Andy	Andy Devine, Uncle Ferncliff	No
Harris	Phil	Phil Harris, Paul Revere	No
Livingstone	Mary	Mary Livingstone, Treeza	No
Stewart	Blanche	Rooster	No
Wilson	Don	Don Wilson	No

Songs:

Order	Title	Performers	Vocal
1	Shall We Dance	Phil Harris	No
2	One Alone	Kenny Baker	Yes
3	The Love Bug Will Bite You If You Don't Watch Out	Phil Harris	No
4	I'm Gonna Sit Right Down and Write Myself a Letter	Jack Benny	Yes
4	I'm Gonna Sit Right Down and Write Myself a Letter	Andy Devine	Yes
4	I'm Gonna Sit Right Down and Write Myself a Letter	Kenny Baker	Yes
5	I Can't Lose that Longing for You	Phil Harris	No

Notes:

Blooper	Don forgets lemon in Jell-O flavors..."lime and...uh...limonberry"
Skit	Ah Wilderness

Date: 5/23/1937   **Sponsor:** Jell-O   **City:** Hollywood, CA

Recording Source: KNX   **Problems:** None

First line:
Good evening ladies and gentlmen, this is Don Wilson speaking. I'd like nothing better than to introduce Jack Benny at this point for a half hour of fun. But I am indeed sorry to have to tell you that Jack is confined to a bed with a severe case of flu, and will not be able to appear tonight.

Summary:
Jack is sick, all music program

Cast:

Last name	First name	Roles	Guest star
Baker	Kenny	Kenny Baker	No
Harris	Phil	Phil Harris	No
Wilson	Don	Don Wilson	No
Wood	Trudy	Trudy Wood	Yes

Songs:

Order	Title	Performers	Vocal
1	Song of the Marines	Phil Harris	No
2	You Are My Love	Kenny Baker	Yes
3	Cause My Baby Says It's So	Phil Harris	No
4	Never In a Million Years	Trudy Wood	Yes
5	On the Isle of Kitchymikoko	Phil Harris	No
6	That Foolish Feeling	Phil Harris	No
7	Nobody	Phil Harris	Yes
8		Phil Harris	No
9	September in the Rain	Kenny Baker	Yes
10		Phil Harris	No

Notes:

Blooper	Phil stumbles on "that broken-down compliment"
Notable	Jack does not appear

NOTE: The show broadcast on 5/23/1937 was an all music program due to Jack's illness, as indicated above. However, a script for the planned show does exist, and is described below. Notice that it was split into halves and used for the two subsequent shows.

Date: 5/23/1937   **Sponsor:** Jell-O   **City:** Hollywood, CA

First line:
And now ladies and gentlemen, we bring you a man were he a flower, he'd be an orchid...were he a bird, he'd be a lark...were he a tree, he'd be an oak...

Summary:
Jack lost Phil's watch...Mary has started shooting a picture at Paramount...Door guy asks about Jack's watch...telegram from Jack's father about the wristwatch...man shows up with Jack's watch, asks for reward...found it at the Acme Hot Dog Parlor...skit Death at Midnight...Krotzmeer reports that he thinks he's going to be murdered...wife calls back and says he's been shot...police go to home and interrogate the wife...Credit Jewelry Store man interrupts and reposesses Jack's watch

Cast:

Last name	First name	Roles	Guest star
Anderson	Eddie	Man who found Jack's watch, chauffeur	No
Baker	Kenny	Kenny Baker, J. Wellington Krotzmeer	No
Baker	Wally	Credit Jewelry Store man	No
Baldwin	Harry	Door guy, Lieutenant	No
Beloin	Ed	Telegram boy	No
Benny	Jack	Jack Benny, Detective O'Benny	No
Harris	Phil	Phil Harris	No
Livingstone	Mary	Mary Livingstone, Mrs. Krotzmeer	No
Stewart	Blanche	Screamer, French maid	No
Wilson	Don	Don Wilson, butler	No

Songs:

Order	Title	Performers	Vocal
1	Song of the Marines	Phil Harris	No
2	On the Isle of Kitchymikoko	Phil Harris	No
3	You Are My Love	Kenny Baker	Yes
4	Make Way for Tomorrow	Phil Harris	No

Notes:

Notable	Eddie Anderson now referred to as "Ed" in script
Running gag	Mary does Mae West
Skit	Death at Midnight

Date: 5/30/1937 **Sponsor:** Jell-O **City:** Hollywood, CA

Recording Source: Unknown **Problems:** Poor sound

First line:
And now ladies and gentlemen, let us hail the return of a man who last week was flat on his back but is now standing here flat on his feet, Jack Benny.

Summary:
Jack talks about being sick...Mary sent Jack a third of a dozen roses...Doctor keeps interrupting to give Jack medicine...Phil is flirting with nurse in the hallway, prescription is her phone number...Jack compliments Don on last week's commercial...Mary's mother calls, she wants to take over the summer show...skit Death at Midight...Proxmire calls and says he thinks he's going to be murdered...Mrs. Proxmire calls and says her husband is dead...drives to murder scene but still at police headquarters (forgot to release the break)...goes to Proxmires...interrogates Mrs. Proxmire...call comes in from Cactus Face, they have the wrong last script page

Cast:

Last name	First name	Roles	Guest star
Baker	Kenny	Kenny Baker, J. Wellington Proxmire	No
Baldwin	Harry	Dr. Baldy	No
Benny	Jack	Jack Benny, Detective O'Benny	No
Harris	Phil	Phil Harris, Sergeant Harris	No
Livingstone	Mary	Mary Livingstone, Mrs. Proxmire	No
Morrow	Bill	Lieutenant	No
Stewart	Blanche	Screamer, Fifi Foofoo	No
Wilson	Don	Don Wilson, butler	No

Songs:

Order	Title	Performers	Vocal
1	Ooh Aah	Phil Harris	No
2	Blue Lou	Phil Harris	No
3	Was It Rain	Kenny Baker	Yes
4	You Can't Run Away From Love	Phil Harris	No
5	Tomorrow Is Another Day	Phil Harris	No

Notes:

Blooper	Jack cracks up after Mary's mother's call
Running gag	Mary's mother communication
Skit	Death at Midnight

Date: 6/6/1937   **Sponsor:** Jell-O   **City:** Hollywood, CA

Recording Source: Unknown   **Problems:** None

First line:
And now ladies and gentlemen, we bring you the man who has thrown away his medicine, hot water bottle and doctor's bills, Jack Benny.

Summary:
Jack is nervous because he lost Phil's watch...Mary is making her first picture, "This Way Please"...Door guy asks about Jack's watch...gang discusses worms...Don gets a call about Jell-O...gets telegram from Jack's father about the watch...two guys found Jack's watch, and try to negotiate the reward...talk Jack into $50, his pocketbook sounds like Inner Sanctum, moth flies out...found watch at the Acme Hot Dog Parlor...Phil arrives because he overslept and had a flat tire...Jack admits he lost the watch, Phil doesn't care...continuation of Death at Midnight...Mrs. Proxmire calls and asks police to come over and investigate...Proxmire flirts with Captain...decides to re-enact the crime...interrogates Mrs. Proxmire again, she confesses...man comes to repossess Jack's watch because Phil's last payment was one week after Christmas

Cast:

Last name	First name	Roles	Guest star
Anderson	Eddie	Watch finder 1	No
Baker	Kenny	Kenny Baker, J. Wellington Proxmire	No
Baker	Wally	Credit jewelry store man	No
Baldwin	Harry	Door guy	No
Beloin	Ed	Telegram boy	No
Benny	Jack	Jack Benny, Captain O'Benny	No
Harris	Phil	Phil Harris, Sergeant Harris	No
Livingstone	Mary	Mary Livingstone, Mrs. Proxmire	No
Morrow	Bill	Murdering male	No
Stewart	Blanche	Murdered woman, Fifi Foofoo	No
Wilson	Don	Don Wilson	No

Songs:

Order	Title	Performers	Vocal
1	When	Phil Harris	No
2	September in the Rain/Shades of Hades	Phil Harris	No
3	Blue is the Night	Kenny Baker	Yes
4	Dardanella	Phil Harris	No
5	I'm Hatin' This Waiting Around	Phil Harris	No

Notes:

Blooper	Don stumbles on the line "I just happened to think of something"
Notable	Jack says "You're blushing, Don" and Don ad-libs "That's the strawberry."
Skit	Death at Midnight

Date: 6/13/1937 **Sponsor:** Jell-O **City:** Hollywood, CA

Recording Source: Unknown **Problems:** None

First line:
And now ladies and gentlemen, we bring you a man who looks twice as good as ever before, but oh how he looked before, Jack Benny.

Summary:
Jack is devoted to exercise…Kenny's personal trainer is an animal trainer ("You should see me bury a bone")…Phil is embarassed about Jack's repossessed watch…Mary gets a call from Mr. Shauer, Paramount producer, he wants her to come to the studio immediately to shoot an important scene…Don wants her to change the movie name to "This Way Jell-O"…Phil says he'll give Jack something to replace the watch…Andy Devine was going to send Jack flowers when he was sick, but his mother told to him to "see which way it goes"…Andy making a picture with Bing Crosby…Jack starting "Artists and Models" soon, but Phil says they've been shooting it for six weeks…Jack calls Mr. Gensler at Paramount, he's saving Jack for the climax…gang goes to visit Mary at the studio…Jack claims to know all the stars, Marlene Dietrich won't say hello, Gary Cooper calls Jack "Sam"…Mary is in a bad mood, acts like a prima donna…everyone shouts sandwich orders to Andy

Cast:

Last name	First name	Roles	Guest star
Baker	Kenny	Kenny Baker	No
Baldwin	Harry	Information man	No
Beloin	Ed	Quiet caller, cameraman	No
Benny	Jack	Jack Benny	No
Devine	Andy	Andy Devine	No
Gibson	John	Stage boy	No
Harris	Phil	Phil Harris	No
Hicks	Russell	Robert Florey	No
Livingstone	Mary	Mary Livingstone	No
Morrow	Bill	Gary Cooper, quiet caller	No
Stewart	Blanche	Paramount operator, chorus girl	No
Wilson	Don	Don Wilson	No

Songs:

Order	Title	Performers	Vocal
1	Fine and Dandy	Phil Harris	No
2	They All Laughed	Phil Harris	No
3	I Know Now	Kenny Baker	Yes
4	Unidentified	Phil Harris	No

Notes:

Notable	First show where music numbers are reduced from five to four
Running gag	Relay

Date: 6/20/1937   **Sponsor:** Jell-O   **City:** Hollywood, CA
Recording Source: Unknown   **Problems:** None

First line:
And now ladies and gentlemen, this being Father's Day, we bring you Jack Benny.

Summary:
Gang considers Jack like a father...gang talks about what they sent their fathers...Phil at the Paramount Theatre...Jack gets call from Paramount to run over to shoot his scene...Mary reads a poem for her father...Jack's dressing room at Paramount, getting made up by Wally Westmore...Rochester pressing Jack's suit...Jack calls Mr. Walsh to see if he's ready for him...gang visits Jack in his dressing room...Jack explains the story of "Artists and Models", very confusing...Jack is nervous on the set, develops hiccoughs...Andy gives Jack pointers on love scenes, tells him to be rough with women...Rochester brings Jack sports shoes to go with his dress suit...Jack has to hide in a barrel, has one line: "Hey!"...Jack forgets his line...Jack introduces Charlie Winninger, starts July 8 with "Maxwell House Show Boat"

Cast:

Last name	First name	Roles	Guest star
Anderson	Eddie	Rochester	No
Baker	Kenny	Kenny Baker	No
Baldwin	Harry	Wally Westmore	No
Beloin	Ed	Stage caller, cameraman	No
Benny	Jack	Jack Benny	No
Devine	Andy	Andy Devine	No
Harris	Phil	Phil Harris	No
Keane	Robert Emmett	Raoul Walsh	No
Livingstone	Mary	Mary Livingstone	No
Morrow	Bill	Bill	No
Nelson	Frank	Richard Arlen	No
Stewart	Blanche	Ida Lupino	No
Wilson	Don	Don Wilson	No
Winninger	Charlie	Charlie Winninger	Yes

Songs:

Order	Title	Performers	Vocal
1	Jericho	Phil Harris	No
2	Never In a Million Years	Kenny Baker	Yes
3	Swing Low, Sweet Harriet	Phil Harris	No
4	I Get a Kick Out of You	Phil Harris	No

Notes:

Blooper	Eddie Anderson answers "Yes sir" instead of saying "You mean the one with the red stripes?" when Jack asks if he laid out his full dress suit
Notable	Eddie Anderson's lines are prompted as both "Eddy" and "Eddie" in the script
Notable	First appearance of Eddie Anderson as Rochester
Running gag	But but but
Running gag	Mary's poem

Date: 6/27/1937 **Sponsor:** Jell-O **City:** Hollywood, CA

Recording Source: Unknown **Problems:** None

First line:
And now ladies and gentlemen, for his final voyage of the season we bring you that worn-out Captain of the good ship Jello...Jack Benny!

Summary:
Last show of the season, Jack is tired...Phil explains to Jack that he only works 13 minutes a week...Andy Devine is taking singing lessons...Jack is going to Waukegan and Europe...Door guy wishes Jack a good trip to Europe, says he's the Queen Mary...Jack and Mary going to Dallas, TX to appear at the Pan American Exposition on July 3, 4, and 5...Mary wants to meet a cowboy...Andy Devine tells them to look up his aunt, who's a blacksmith...Don is making a picture for Universal ("Behind the Mike")...Kenny got a new car, wants to drive to Honolulu...Jack gets sentimental...Johnny Green arranged "Body and Soul" for violin, plays piano with Jack on violin, almost all piano...Jane Frohman on Jell-O summer show...received Radio Guide award again

Cast:

Last name	First name	Roles	Guest star
Baker	Kenny	Kenny Baker	No
Baldwin	Harry	Door guy	No
Benny	Jack	Jack Benny	No
Devine	Andy	Andy Devine	No
Green	Johnny	Johnny Green	Yes
Harris	Phil	Phil Harris	No
Livingstone	Mary	Mary Livingstone	No
Morrow	Bill	Clark Gable	No
Wilson	Don	Don Wilson	No

Songs:

Order	Title	Performers	Vocal
1	Who Put that Moon in the Sky/Yours for the Asking	Phil Harris	No
2	I'm Yours For the Asking/Sweet Like You	Phil Harris	No
3	Here Comes the Sandman	Kenny Baker	Yes
4	The Love Bug Will Bite You If You Don't Watch Out	Mary Livingstone	Yes
5	Body and Soul	Jack Benny	No
5	Body and Soul	Johnny Green	No
6	Why	Phil Harris	No

Notes:

Blooper	Jack says "come in" before the door knock sound effect (notation: this is actually in the script)

Date: 10/3/1937   **Sponsor:** Jell-O   **City:** Hollywood, CA

Recording Source: None   **Problems:** None

First line:
And now ladies and gentlemen, after a holiday of thirteen weeks, we bring you a man whose vacation is over and so is yours…Jack Benny!

Summary:
Jack tells of his trip to Europe…Don says Jack put on weight, he forgot to take off his life belt…Phil went fishing in Texas, caught a 110-pound blonde…Mary went to Paris over the summer, now wants to be called Marie…went over on the Queen Mary Livingstone…Jack brought everyone perfume from Paris…Mary reads poem about Paris…Kenny is growing up, wants to kiss Mary…Door guy welcomes Jack back, says he missed himself…Andy went to Catalina…Abe Lyman says that Jack promised to use his band this season…Lyman is angry and threatens everyone…Jack tells him they'll talk this over in a couple days…"This Way Please" opening at Paramount Theatre this week…promo for Jack Haley doing a show for Log Cabin Syrup

Cast:

Last name	First name	Roles	Guest star
Baker	Kenny	Kenny Baker	No
Baldwin	Harry	Door guy	No
Beloin	Ed	Mike	No
Benny	Jack	Jack Benny	No
Devine	Andy	Andy Devine	No
Harris	Phil	Phil Harris	No
Livingstone	Mary	Mary Livingstone	No
Lyman	Abe	Abe Lyman	Yes
Wilson	Don	Don Wilson	No

Songs:

Order	Title	Performers	Vocal
1	High Wide and Handsome	Phil Harris	No
2	Stop You're Breaking My Heart	Phil Harris	No
3	Remember Me	Kenny Baker	Yes
4	Yours and Mine	Phil Harris	No

Notes:

Notable	Kenny Baker is now announced as "Courtesy of Mervyn LeRoy Productions"
Running gag	Mary's poem

Date: 10/10/1937 **Sponsor:** Jell-O **City:** Hollywood, CA

Recording Source: Unknown **Problems:** None

First line:
And now ladies and gentlemen, for the second broadcast of the new series we bring you by popular demand and public acclaim, our latest discovery...Jack What's-his-Name!

Summary:
Jack was nervous on the first program of the season, smoking his cigar sideways...Mary gets great review in The Hollywood Reporter...Phil has to wake up his band...Don gets great review in Radio Guide...Jack got good review in Waukegan Sun-Gazette...Kenny has chocolate cigar, stopped off for slug of root beer, says he's growing up...Andy Devine calls, has a cold...read reviews of last week's program...announces skit High, Wide, Tall, Dark and Handsome...Shlepperman came to California in a trailer, no car...Jack didn't show to meeting with Lyman about using his orchestra instead of Phil's...Lyman threatens Phil and he leaves, then threatens Shlepperman...Lyman falls down the stairs...Jack saw Mary's picture

Cast:

Last name	First name	Roles	Guest star
Baker	Kenny	Kenny Baker	No
Benny	Jack	Jack Benny	No
Devine	Andy	Andy Devine	No
Harris	Phil	Phil Harris	No
Hearn	Sam	Schlepperman	No
Livingstone	Mary	Mary Livingstone	No
Lyman	Abe	Abe Lyman	Yes
Wilson	Don	Don Wilson	No

Songs:

Order	Title	Performers	Vocal
1	You Can't Have Everything	Phil Harris	No
2	Am I In Love	Phil Harris	No
3	Whispers in the Dark	Kenny Baker	Yes
4	Yours and Mine	Phil Harris	No

Notes:

Blooper	Jack omits his line to cue Kenny to say "Boy, have I got a hangover"...
Notable	Show is now announced as on National Broadcasting Company, no "red network" designation

Date: 10/17/1937   **Sponsor:** Jell-O   **City:** Hollywood, CA

Recording Source: None   **Problems:** None

First line:
And now ladies and gentlemen, for the third broadcast of the series, we bring you a man with a twinkle in his eye, a smile on his face, and a toupee on his head…Jack Benny!

Summary:
Jack listened to Don on the Packard Program…Jack is jealous of Charlie Butterworth…Jack and Don argue…Kenny upset because his girl asked him to put his arms around her because she was cold, but she wasn't…Andy Devine calls, he still has a cold…skit If you don't see what you want, blame it on the dust…Zeke Benny opens the grocery store…customers come in to buy things…Clark Gable wants to be a clerk…Abe Lyman stops by for cigars, says he'll be waiting when the store closes

Cast:

Last name	First name	Roles	Guest star
Baker	Kenny	Kenny Baker	No
Baldwin	Harry	Clark Gable	No
Beloin	Ed	Sun	No
Benny	Jack	Jack Benny, Zeke Benny	No
Devine	Andy	Andy Devine	No
Harris	Phil	Phil Harris, Clem Harris	No
Hearn	Sam	Hezekiah	No
Livingstone	Mary	Mary Livingstone, Nancy	No
Lyman	Abe	Abe Lyman	Yes
Stewart	Blanche	Mrs. Baker	No
Wilson	Don	Don Wilson	No

Songs:

Order	Title	Performers	Vocal
1	Goodbye Jonah	Phil Harris	No
2	Have You Got Any Castles, Baby	Phil Harris	No
3	Lovely One	Kenny Baker	Yes
4	On With the Dance	Phil Harris	No

Notes:

Skit	If you don't see what you want, blame it on the dust

Date: 10/24/1937   **Sponsor:** Jell-O   **City:** Hollywood, CA

Recording Source: Unknown   **Problems:** None

First line:
And now ladies and gentlemen, we bring you that favorite of men, women and children...especially men and children...Jack Benny

Summary:
Jack isn't as romantic as other Hollywood stars...Jack traded in his car, a Stanley Steamer, for a Maxwell...Don says they haven't made Maxwells in 10 years...Jack says there's no radio, but there's a victrola on the steering wheel...Jack and Mary drove to Santa Barbara and back...gets telegram from vaudeville agent offering Jack's car three weeks at the Paramount Theatre...Jack tells cast not to make fun of his car...announces skit Wife, Doctor, and Nurse...Jack invited Loretta Young to play the wife, she refused...guitar player marcels Phil's hair...Andy Devine plays Jack's wife...Don keeps repeating Jell-O flavors...Jack operates on Don...Shlepperman is a patient, sick with everything...Loretta Young calls

Cast:

Last name	First name	Roles	Guest star
Baker	Kenny	Kenny Baker	No
Beloin	Ed	Telegram boy	No
Benny	Jack	Jack Benny, Dr. Benny	No
Devine	Andy	Andy Devine, Wife	No
Harris	Phil	Phil Harris	No
Hearn	Sam	Shlepperman	No
Livingstone	Mary	Mary Livingstone	No
Wilson	Don	Don Wilson	No

Songs:

Order	Title	Performers	Vocal
1	Something to Sing About	Phil Harris	No
2	That Old Feeling	Kenny Baker	Yes
3	You Can't Stop Me from Dreaming	Phil Harris	No
4	You Can't Have Everything	Jack Benny	Yes
4	You Can't Have Everything	Sam Hearn	Yes
5	Love Me	Phil Harris	No

Notes:

Blooper	Jack says "diagraph" instead of "diaphragm"
Blooper	Mary says "He's down at Mid-sky's studying anatomy"
Notable	First mention of the Maxwell
Notable	First mention of Remley, though not by name
Skit	Wife, Doctor, and Nurse

Date: 10/31/1937   **Sponsor:** Jell-O   **City:** Hollywood, CA

Recording Source: Unknown   **Problems:** None

First line:
And now ladies and gentlemen, we bring you that prominent comedian, musician and after-dinner speaker, Jack Benny.

Summary:
Jack was at Eddie Cantor's anniversary last Thusday night, Jack is jealous because no one has given him a dinner...Kenny was in the next studio talking to Charlie McCarthy (no Bergen, just Charlie)...Bergen asked Charlie to sing and put Kenny in a suitcase...Laughton Campbell of General Foods calls...Western Costume Company wires Jack for the suit he wore at Cantor's dinner...Phil was at a fiesta in Phoenix...Jack was behind a truck on Wilshire Boulevard, motor dropped out when truck backfired...Halloween party at Andy Devine's...gang goes in Jack's car...Phil got there first, he walked...all of Andy's animals are at the party...Jack plays violin and animals start caterwauling

Cast:

Last name	First name	Roles	Guest star
Baker	Kenny	Kenny Baker	No
Baldwin	Harry	Telegram boy	No
Benny	Jack	Jack Benny	No
Devine	Andy	Andy Devine	No
Harris	Phil	Phil Harris	No
Hearn	Sam	Mr. Devine	No
Livingstone	Mary	Mary Livingstone	No
Stewart	Blanche	Mrs. Devine, pig, dog	No
Wilson	Don	Don Wilson, horse	No

Songs:

Order	Title	Performers	Vocal
1	Love Is On the Air Tonight	Phil Harris	No
2	Rosita	Kenny Baker	Yes
3	Blue Bonnet	Phil Harris	No
4	Have You Got Any Castles, Baby	Jack Benny	No
4	Have You Got Any Castles, Baby	Mary Livingstone	Yes
4	Have You Got Any Castles, Baby	Phil Harris	Yes
4	Have You Got Any Castles, Baby	Andy Devine	Yes
5	Goodnight Kisses	Phil Harris	No

Notes:

Notable	First time the Maxwell is heard
Running gag	But but but

Date: 11/7/1937 **Sponsor:** Jell-O **City:** Hollywood, CA

Recording Source: Unknown **Problems:** None

First line:
And now we bring you Jack Benny from Waukegan.

Summary:
Jack drove to Palm Springs for a rest…hitchhikers thumbing at the Maxwell…letter from Mary's mother…brother Hilliard went to jail for signing Mary's check…parents threatened to be taken out of the blue book because Mary's riding in Jack's Maxwell…Murray and Lozmo had a bet on whether Jack's car runs…Jack stopped for a gallon of gas, says he has too much invested in the car already…roasting peanuts in the radiator…Cactus Face throws a taunting note through the window…continuation of Buck Benny…Sheriff's office a week before election day, running against Dead Eye Cassidy…planning campaign speech…Frank Carson gave up drinking, has had milk for three weeks but feeds the cow gin…shootout after campaign speeches

Cast:

Last name	First name	Roles	Guest star
?	Henry	Henry	No
Anderson	Eddie	Lord Mouth	No
Baker	Kenny	Kenny Baker	No
Benny	Jack	Jack Benny, Buck Benny	No
Franz	Joe	Town Hall man	No
Harris	Phil	Phil Harris, Frank Carson	No
Hearn	Sam	Dead Eye Cassidy	No
Livingstone	Mary	Mary Livingstone, Daisy Carson	No
Stewart	Blanche	Screamer	No
Wilson	Don	Don Wilson	No

Songs:

Order	Title	Performers	Vocal
1	Who Knows	Phil Harris	No
2	Roses in December	Kenny Baker	Yes
3	Old King Cole	Phil Harris	No
4	Delighted to Meet You	Phil Harris	No

Notes:

Running gag	Mary's mother communication
Skit	Buck Benny Rides Again

Date: 11/14/1937   **Sponsor:** Jell-O   **City:** Hollywood, CA

Recording Source: None   **Problems:** None

First line:
And now ladies and gentlemen...hey Phil, where's Jack?

Summary:
Jack is late, calls Don to tell him that he and Mary are coming over in the Maxwell...Jack can't start the car, Mary steps through the running board...kids and women make fun of Jack's car...kids steal Jack's headlights...officer questions Jack about the car, gives him a ticket for stalling out next to a fire plug...Mary brings over mechanic to look at the Maxwell...mechanic leaves, Jack starts the car...Jack tells gang he got a ticket for speeding...Door guy says he's from the Acme Car Washing Company...skit Buck Benny Rides Again...Pinto Pete calls to ask how much Buck is paying for votes...Buck offers to let Rochester out of jail if he'll vote for him...Frank Carson voted for Buck four times...they tune in radio to hear election returns...Buck wins

Cast:

Last name	First name	Roles	Guest star
		Kid 2	No
		Radio announcer	No
		Kid 1	No
Allman	Elvia	Mamie	No
Anderson	Eddie	Rochester	No
Baker	Kenny	Kenny Baker, Deputy Baker	No
Baldwin	Harry	Door guy	No
Benny	Jack	Jack Benny, Buck Benny	No
Colvig	Pinto	Maxwell	No
Harris	Phil	Phil Harris, Frank Carson	No
Kendall	Cy	Officer, Pinto Pete	No
Livingstone	Mary	Mary Livingstone, Daisy Carson	No
Rubin	Benny	Joe mechanic	No
Stewart	Blanche	Gertie	No
Wilson	Don	Don Wilson, Deputy Wilson	No

Songs:

Order	Title	Performers	Vocal
1	Rosalie	Phil Harris	No
2	Have You Met Miss Jones	Phil Harris	No
3	Moon Got In My Eyes	Kenny Baker	Yes
4	Have You Ever Been in Heaven	Phil Harris	No

Notes:

Notable	Specific commercial for Montreal-Toronto announcing new Jell-O Chocolate Pudding
Skit	Buck Benny Rides Again

Date: 11/21/1937 **Sponsor:** Jell-O **City:** Hollywood, CA

Recording Source: Unknown **Problems:** Partial show

First line:
And now ladies and gentlemen, we bring you a man who owns a watch comma, a violin comma, and an automobile question mark...Jack Benny.

Summary:
Jack had a flat tire on the way to the studio, didn't change it because he gave the tools to his sister as a charm bracelet...car broke down in front of the finance company...Andy's mom sent Jack a live turkey...skit Lost Horizon...Mary asks Kenny what "Lost Horizon" means, he gives an intelligent answer and faints...Jack goes to Mary's apartment because he's nervous and upset...Jack saw "Lost Horizon", wishes he could go there...Mary gives Jack a pill to sleep...Chang takes Jack to Shangri-La...Jack drinks water from the fountain to make his voice better...High Lama is Shlepperman...sells birthday candles, is making a fortune, his wife sells matches...Mary is Lama's daughter, shows Jack around...Jack wakes up thinking he's drowning, he's in Mary's apartment with his head in the goldfish bowl

Cast:

Last name	First name	Roles	Guest star
Baker	Kenny	Kenny Baker	No
Beloin	Ed	Sound man	No
Benny	Jack	Jack Benny	No
Brown	?	Chang	No
Devine	Andy	Andy Devine	No
Harris	Phil	Phil Harris	No
Hearn	Sam	High Lama	No
Livingstone	Mary	Mary Livingstone, Mary Lama	No
MacKaye	Fred	Andy in Shangri-La	No
Stewart	Blanche	Mrs. Chang	No
Wilson	Don	Don Wilson, Clambake Chang	No

Songs:

Order	Title	Performers	Vocal
1	Swing is Here to Sway	Phil Harris	No
2	Bob White	Phil Harris	No
3	Veeny Veeny Veeny	Kenny Baker	Yes
4	Unidentified	Phil Harris	No

Notes:

Recording	Kenny Baker's song is clipped, along with part of the show
Skit	Lost Horizon

Date: 11/28/1937   **Sponsor:** Jell-O   **City:** Hollywood, CA

Recording Source: **Problems:** None

First line:
And now ladies and gentlemen, we bring you a man who, every Sunday nite at this same time, walks up to the microphone, looks it square in the eye, and says…

Summary:
Jack and Don balance each other well…Jack had the gang over for Thanksgiving dinner…everyone kids Jack's cooking…Jack may get rid of the Maxwell, someone wrote on it "Lulu Loves Butch"…Jack advertising the show on a sign on the back of his car…Kenny and Door guy interested in buying the Maxwell…Jack wants $95 for his car…Kenny sings in the bathtub every morning…announces skit The Private Life of a Bumblebee…Shlepperman's wife's brother, Anatole Ginsburg, wants to buy Jack's car…Jack takes Shlepperman and his brother-in-law for a ride, fall out going over a bump…Jack wanted two gallons of gas, attendant gives him two and a half and they argue over eight cents for the half gallon…Jack hits the car behind him

Cast:

Last name	First name	Roles	Guest star
Baker	Kenny	Kenny Baker	No
Baldwin	Harry	Door guy	No
Beloin	Ed	Phil, gas attendant	No
Benny	Jack	Jack Benny	No
Colvig	Pinto	Maxwell	No
Flick	Patsy	Anatole Ginsburg	No
Harris	Phil	Phil Harris	No
Hearn	Sam	Shlepperman	No
Livingstone	Mary	Mary Livingstone	No
Marr	Eddie	Driver	No
Wilson	Don	Don Wilson	No

Songs:

Order	Title	Performers	Vocal
1	Go South Young Man	Phil Harris	No
2	You Can't Stop Me From Dreaming	Phil Harris	Yes
3	Moon of Manakoora	Kenny Baker	Yes
4	Mama, that Moon's Here Again	Phil Harris	No
5	Unidentified	Phil Harris	No

Notes:

Date: 12/5/1937 **Sponsor:** Jell-O **City:** Hollywood, CA

Recording Source: Unknown **Problems:** None

First line:
And now, ladies and gentlemen, we bring you a rag, a bone and a hank of gray hair...Jack Benny.

Summary:
Don quotes Shakespeare, but it was written by Kipling...Jack's gray hair...Kenny had a fight with his girl, she won't put nuts in the fudge she makes him...Kenny's girl wants to play Post Office ("but it's not open at night")...Jack tries to teach Kenny how to play Post Office...Andy is interested in Jack's car...gang discusses what they said as kids...Andy shows a picture of himself at six months...Jack gets philosophical...Door guy offers to show his baby pictures...skit The Big Game...Flatfoot vs. Meatball College...Phil wears a steel helmet so he doesn't muss his hair...Flash Benny runs for a touchdown, gets pulled over...cop knocks out Flash, so Meatball wins...Mary's mother calls, Mary and mother do show close

Cast:

Last name	First name	Roles	Guest star
Baker	Kenny	Kenny Baker	No
Baldwin	Harry	Door guy, "Come on" man	No
Benny	Jack	Jack Benny, Flash Benny, Coach	No
Brown	?	Sports announcer	No
Devine	Andy	Andy Devine	No
Harris	Phil	Phil Harris	No
Livingstone	Mary	Mary Livingstone, Butch	No
Marks	Hilliard	"Yeah" 2	No
Marr	Eddie	Cop	No
Marr	Eddie	"Yeah" 1	No
Wilson	Don	Don Wilson	No

Songs:

Order	Title	Performers	Vocal
1	Over Night	Phil Harris	No
2	Blossoms on Broadway	Kenny Baker	Yes
3	Who	Phil Harris	No
4	I Hit a New High	Phil Harris	No

Notes:

Blooper	Don stumbles on Jack's name
Running gag	Mary's mother communication
Skit	The Big Game

Date: 12/12/1937   **Sponsor:** Jell-O   **City:** Hollywood, CA

Recording Source: Unknown   **Problems:** None

First line:
And now ladies and gentlemen, we bring you that all around swell guy, a man I'm proud to call my friend, one of the sweetest fellows I've ever been associated with, Jack Benny.

Summary:
Gang compliments Jack for Christmas presents…Jack kissed Mary at the Trocadero…Jack wanted to bet Phil on the Rose Bowl…show is long tonight, so gang abbreviates…Kenny's girl has another fellow…Mary gets a letter from her mother…it's so cold they have to milk the cow with an ice pick…sending Jack's Christmas gift COD…Jack and Mary go Christmas shopping…Jack wants to buy a keychain for Phil…Kenny tries to buy hosiery…Mary wants to buy dolls…find an Andy Devine doll…Shlepperman is Santa Claus

Cast:

Last name	First name	Roles	Guest star
Allman	Elvia	Woman in elevator, perfume customer, Tilly, doll	No
Anderson	Eddie	Elevator man	No
Baker	Kenny	Kenny Baker	No
Baldwin	Harry	Harry, Christmas card customer	No
Beloin	Ed	Pen Clerk	No
Benaderet	Bea	Hosiery woman	No
Benny	Jack	Jack Benny	No
Devine	Andy	Andy Devine	No
Harris	Phil	Phil Harris	No
Hearn	Sam	Shlepperman	No
Livingstone	Mary	Mary Livingstone	No
Miller	?	Shlepperman's son Pincus	No
Nelson	Frank	Floorwalker Woo Woo Smith, creepy floorwalker	No
Stewart	Blanche	Dog, Doll saleswoman	No
Stewart	Blanche	Mother of lost child	No
Wilson	Don	Don Wilson	No

Songs:

Order	Title	Performers	Vocal
1	Life Begins at Sweet Sixteen	Phil Harris	No
2	Dipsy Doodle	Phil Harris	No
3	Am I in Love	Kenny Baker	Yes
4	Comin' Down the Chimney	Sam Hearn	Yes
4	Comin' Down the Chimney	Mary Livingstone	Yes
5	I'm In My Glory	Phil Harris	No

Notes:

Notable	First Christmas shopping show
Notable	First "We're a little late, so goodnight folks"
Running gag	Mary's mother communication

Date: 12/19/1937 **Sponsor:** Jell-O **City:** Hollywood, CA

Recording Source: Unknown **Problems:** None

First line:
And now ladies and gentlemen, we bring you the only adult in the world who wrote a letter to Santa Claus, Jack Benny.

Summary:
Jack has been acting like a kid…Jack gives Don a combination electric razor and shoe brush…gives Phil hair tonic…sent Mary a charm bracelet…gang forgot to get Jack anything…Door guy recites a poem…Jack gives band a pint of California wine…Mary knitted sweaters for band's instruments…Jack got Kenny a musical collar button…Kenny bought his girl a travelling bag because she's going to elope with another man…special delivery for Jack of twin waffle irons…skit Little Red Riding Hood…send Red over with soup for Grandma…Jack howls over commercial…Jack going to visit Fred Allen about a business deal

Cast:

Last name	First name	Roles	Guest star
Baker	Kenny	Kenny Baker, Robin	No
Baldwin	Harry	Door guy	No
Beloin	Ed	Delivery guy	No
Benny	Jack	Jack Benny, Old Man Hood, Wolf	No
Devine	Andy	Andy Devine, Grandma	No
Harris	Phil	Phil Harris, Woodchopper	No
Livingstone	Mary	Mary Livingstone, Red	No
Stewart	Blanche	Ma Hood	No
Wilson	Don	Don Wilson	No

Songs:

Order	Title	Performers	Vocal
1	I Double Dare You	Phil Harris	No
2	She's Tall, She's Tan, She's Terrific	Phil Harris	No
3	Once In a While	Kenny Baker	Yes
4	Unidentified	Phil Harris	No

Notes:

Blooper	Jack puts wrong inflection on "Where's your sister at?"
Skit	Little Red Riding Hood

Date: 12/26/1937   **Sponsor:** Jell-O   **City:** Hollywood, CA

Recording Source: None   **Problems:** None

First line:
The Jello program, coming to you direct from Jack Benny's home in Beverly Hills, where he is celebrating the holidays with a little party for the gang.

Summary:
Party at Jack's home…Jack hired a detective to protect the silverware…Rochester's wife calls…Jack and Rochester were taking turns answering the phone, but "that's off during the party"…Jack and Mary on Fred Allen's program Wednesday night…Allen uses cheap microphones, Jack was broadcasting through a tomato can…Phil says Jack snores…Mary reads New Year's poem…Shlepperman brings his wife and son to the party…Don has Rochester do the commercial…Andy brought his sister to the party…cook quit, won Bank Night at the movies…Jack credits "Eddy Anderson" at the end of the show

Cast:

Last name	First name	Roles	Guest star
?	Sidney	Pincus	No
Allman	Elvia	Camille Devine	No
Anderson	Eddie	Rochester	No
Baker	Kenny	Kenny Baker	No
Baldwin	Harry	Houlihan	No
Benaderet	Bea	Lupe Shlepperman	No
Benny	Jack	Jack Benny	No
Devine	Andy	Andy Devine	No
Harris	Phil	Phil Harris	No
Hearn	Sam	Shlepperman	No
Livingstone	Mary	Mary Livingstone	No
Stewart	Blanche	Lena	No
Wilson	Don	Don Wilson	No

Songs:

Order	Title	Performers	Vocal
1	You've Got Something There	Phil Harris	No
2	I'm Like a Fish Out of Water	Phil Harris	No
3	Rolling Plains	Kenny Baker	Yes
4	How Many Rhymes Can You Get	Don Wilson	Yes
4	How Many Rhymes Can You Get	Jack Benny	Yes
4	How Many Rhymes Can You Get	Sam Hearn	Yes
4	How Many Rhymes Can You Get	Phil Harris	Yes
4	How Many Rhymes Can You Get	Mary Livingstone	Yes
4	How Many Rhymes Can You Get	Eddie Anderson	Yes
5	Unidentified	Phil Harris	No

Notes:

Running gag	Mary's poem

Date: 1/2/1938 **Sponsor:** Jell-O **City:** Hollywood, CA

Recording Source: Unknown **Problems:** None

First line:
And now ladies and gentlemen, 1938 is with us, and who do you think is standing here at the microphone waiting to greet you one and all?

Summary:
24 Canadian stations being added tonight…Jack going to pay off his old debts…Jack went on blind date with Phil on New Year's Eve, his girl "looked like a smudge pot with rouge"…Mary went out with a jockey from Santa Anita, he wanted to dance piggy-back…Jack claims he sang last week, but everyone disputes it…Phil tried to set Kenny up with Jack's ugly date, he's not that dumb…Kenny went out with his girl and her boyfriend…Andy's father flying to Reno for a divorce…mother put her wedding ring in the bull's nose…broadcasting from San Francisco next week…Rochester calls…packing for San Francisco…guest star Goldie Sponge, the only woman in Hollywood who hasn't tested for Scarlett O'Hara…Goldie has a strange vocal affectation…Door guy offers to be a bum…guest star, J. Rutherford Munch who ate the most Jell-O in 1937…guest star Three Krotzmer Sisters, Jack shoos them off the stage when they sing…Andy's father shows up

Cast:

Last name	First name	Roles	Guest star
		Three Krotzmer Sisters	No
?	Billy	J. Rutherford Munch	No
Anderson	Eddie	Rochester	No
Baker	Kenny	Kenny Baker	No
Baldwin	Harry	Door guy	No
Benny	Jack	Jack Benny	No
Devine	Andy	Andy Devine	No
Harris	Phil	Phil Harris	No
Livingstone	Mary	Mary Livingstone	No
Royale	William	Andy's father	No
Stewart	Blanche	Goldie Sponge	No
Wilson	Don	Don Wilson	No

Songs:

Order	Title	Performers	Vocal
1	Don't Cry Sweetheart, Don't Cry	Phil Harris	No
2	Have You	Phil Harris	No
3	Rolling Plains	Kenny Baker	Yes
4	The Lady is a Tramp	Phil Harris	No
5	Swing Is Here to Stay	Three Krotzmer Sisters	Yes
6	San Francisco/I Live the Life I Love	Phil Harris	No

Notes:

Date: 1/9/1938   **Sponsor:** Jell-O   **City:** San Francisco, CA

Recording Source: KFI   **Problems:** None

First line:
And now ladies and gentlemen, we bring you a man who has been in San Francisco a whole week and has just found out that the Gold Rush is over, Jack Benny.

Summary:
From Western Women's Club in San Francisco…Jack brought a pick and shovel in case the Gold Rush repeats itself…what's great about San Francisco…Phil tried to get a room at the Western Women's Club…Chamber of Commerce asks Jack to keep the Maxwell off the new bridge…Gladys calls to say Phil will be late…Jack calls Mary May-ry…Mary went to Chinatown…Mary writes poem about San Francisco…Jack gets enthusiastic about the new bridges…Door guy wants to know where the women are…Mary reads her poem…Phil shows up, drove in from Sacramento gig…Andy and his parents came up on the train…Jack takes the gang to Ling Fu Chop Suey…Ling Fu is Shlepperman, serves egg foo young with matzo balls

Cast:

Last name	First name	Roles	Guest star
Baker	Kenny	Kenny Baker	No
Baldwin	Harry	Door guy	No
Beloin	Ed	Chamber of Commerce representative	No
Benny	Jack	Jack Benny	No
Devine	Andy	Andy Devine	No
Harris	Phil	Phil Harris	No
Hearn	Sam	Shlepperman, Ling Foo	No
Kroenke?	Carl	Chinese guy	No
Livingstone	Mary	Mary Livingstone	No
Stewart	Blanche	Gladys, operator	No
Wilson	Don	Don Wilson	No

Songs:

Order	Title	Performers	Vocal
1	San Francisco	Phil Harris	No
2	When the Organ Played "Oh Promise Me"	Kenny Baker	Yes
3	Bei Mir Bist Du Schoen	Phil Harris	Yes
4	Chinatown My Chinatown	Phil Harris	No

Notes:

Blooper	Phil stumbles on "Bei Mir Bist Du Schoen"
Blooper	Don stumbles on "Bei Mir Bist Du Schoen" at close
Running gag	Mary's poem

Date: 1/16/1938 **Sponsor:** Jell-O **City:** Hollywood, CA

Recording Source: Unknown **Problems:** None

First line:
And now ladies and gentlemen, for a little surprise. Jack and Mary are driving back from San Francisco where we did our last broadcast, so we'll pick them up in the Maxwell en route to Hollywood.

Summary:
Rochester falls asleep at the wheel driving back from San Francisco...man on bike wants to pass...Maxwell gets a flat...Jack and Mary go to the lunch counter...they tune in Kenny's song on the radio...Jack and Mary finally arrive...Rochester forgot to pack the bags...reporter asks Jack to verify rumors that he's retiring from radio, Jack says he intends to keep working in radio and maybe even television...Mary makes a date with Beetle...Jack imagines what he'll be doing 40 years from now...everyone is still on the show but old...Phil Harris is bald...Andy's voice hasn't changed...Jack slams the door on the Door guy...presenting "Hurricane" in two weeks

Cast:

Last name	First name	Roles	Guest star
Anderson	Eddie	Rochester	No
Baker	Kenny	Kenny Baker	No
Baldwin	Harry	Door guy	No
Beloin	Ed	Station attendant, writer	No
Benny	Jack	Jack Benny	No
Devine	Andy	Andy Devine	No
Harris	Phil	Phil Harris	No
Livingstone	Mary	Mary Livingstone	No
Morrow	Bill	Lem the cook	No
Ruick	Mel	Bicyclist, Evans Plummer	No
Stewart	Blanche	Emmy the lunch counter waitress	No
Wilson	Don	Don Wilson	No
Wilson	Ward	Beetle	No

Songs:

Order	Title	Performers	Vocal
1	Fifi	Phil Harris	No
2	Rosalie	Kenny Baker	Yes
3	Home Town	Phil Harris	No
4	I Could Use a Dream	Phil Harris	No

Notes:

Date: 1/23/1938 **Sponsor:** Jell-O **City:** Hollywood, CA

Recording Source: Unknown **Problems:** None

First line:
And now ladies and gentlemen, we bring you a man who doesn't sing like Crosby, who doesn't photograph like Gable, who cannot act like Muni, yet he's in the movies, Jack Benny.

Summary:
Restaurants serving Jell-O can display an autographed picture of Jack Benny…Jack is starting a new picture soon, script captures the "inner Benny"…Franciska Gaal is leading lady…Mary has idea for a movie: Jack is on a desert island and women keep leaving him ("Little Swimmin")…Kenny was eating in the drug store…Jack calls Franciska Gaal to read the script, she asks him to bring Phil Harris with him…skit Behind the Front Page…Scoop is firing everyone for being bad reporters…Door guy has the measles…Scoop decides to print that Nails Mulligan killed a banker…gets a package that's ticking…tries to get Charlie Chan on the phone…package explodes…presenting "Hurricanne" next week

Cast:

Last name	First name	Roles	Guest star
Baker	Kenny	Kenny Baker	No
Baldwin	Harry	Door guy, measles guy	No
Benny	Jack	Jack Benny, Scoop Benny	No
Harris	Phil	Phil Harris	No
Livingstone	Mary	Mary Livingstone	No
Stewart	Blanche	Ms. Stewart operator	No
Wilson	Don	Don Wilson	No

Songs:

Order	Title	Performers	Vocal
1	Be a Good Sport	Phil Harris	No
2	Nice Work If You Can Get It	Phil Harris	No
3	Love Walked In	Kenny Baker	Yes
4	One Song	Phil Harris	No

Notes:

Blooper	Jack stumbles on the line "It's vital evidence."
Skit	Behind the Front Page

Date: 1/30/1938 **Sponsor:** Jell-O **City:** Hollywood, CA

Recording Source: Unknown **Problems:** None

First line:
And now ladies and gentlemen, we bring you that human dynamo, that bundle of energy who is always bubbling over with pep and vitality, Jack Benny.

Summary:
Jack is tired from rehearsing and setting up for his movie…Jack has same makeup man as Fred MacMurray…Jack spent the evening teaching Franciska Gaal how to do the Big Apple…Phil sent Jack out for ice cream…Andy's mother thinks he's too delicate to be in "The Hurricane"…skit The Hurricane…Governor sent a popular native to prison for stealing a coconut…Captain and the Doctor ask Governor to pardon him…wind starts picking up…Shlepperman is Terangi…stops the hurricane for a Jell-O commercial…Door guy wants to sell Jack an electric fan…telegram from Alton Cook, radio editor of the New York World-Telegram, Jack most popular comedian 5th consecutive year, Don Wilson most popular announcer, Kenny Baker second in singers

Cast:

Last name	First name	Roles	Guest star
Baker	Kenny	Kenny Baker, Terangi's brother	No
Baldwin	Harry	Door guy	No
Benny	Jack	Jack Benny, Governor De Laage	No
Devine	Andy	Andy Devine	No
Harris	Phil	Phil Harris, Doctor Kersaint	No
Hearn	Sam	Shlepperman, Terangi	No
Livingstone	Mary	Mary Livingstone, Germaine De Laage	No
Wilson	Don	Don Wilson, Captain Nagle	No

Songs:

Order	Title	Performers	Vocal
1	I Double Dare You	Phil Harris	No
2	Sweet Someone	Kenny Baker	Yes
3	Snake Charmer	Phil Harris	No
4	Rosalie	Phil Harris	No

Notes:

Skit	The Hurricane

Date: 2/6/1938   **Sponsor:** Jell-O   **City:** Hollywood, CA

Recording Source: Unknown   **Problems:** None

First line:
And now ladies and gentlemen, we bring you…
Phil: Hold it, Don. Jack isn't here yet.

Summary:
Jack is late to the broadcast…Don calls Jack's home and gets Rochester, Jack is still in bed…Rochester wakes up Jack…Phil teaches the cast a card game…Rochester hocked Jack's wristwatch…Jack forgets to put on his pants…Don conducted orchestra during card game, so Phil does commercial…letter from Mary's mother…brother Hilliard swallowed his harmonica…requests "Bei Mir Bist Du Schoen"…Jack didn't bet the horse that paid big at Santa Anita…scene shift to Santa Anita…Jack goes to bet on horse Playmay…Crosby's horse stopped in the home stretch and sang "I Surrender Dear"…tout talks Jack out of betting on Playmay…Mary changed her bet to Playmay…tout shows up at studio with another tip…Jack's horse finally comes in

Cast:

Last name	First name	Roles	Guest star
Anderson	Eddie	Rochester	No
Baker	Kenny	Kenny Baker	No
Baldwin	Harry	Special delivery guy	No
Baldwin	Harry	Race track tout	No
Beloin	Ed	Delivery guy, clerk, betting window agent, hot dog vendor	No
Benny	Jack	Jack Benny	No
Harris	Phil	Phil Harris	No
Livingstone	Mary	Mary Livingstone	No
Marks	Hilliard	Customer in line	No
Morrow	Bill	Jell-O salesman	No
Nelson	Frank	Pickpocket, race announcer	No
Stewart	Blanche	Operator	No
Stewart	Blanche	Customer in line	No
Wilson	Don	Don Wilson	No

Songs:

Order	Title	Performers	Vocal
1	In Old Chicago	Phil Harris	No
2	Let That Be a Lesson to You/You Do Something to Me	Phil Harris	No
3	Bei Mir Bist Du Schoen	Kenny Baker	Yes
4	Let That Be a Lesson to You	Phil Harris	No

Notes:

Blooper	Rochester steps on a laugh with "Next time I'll go with you."
Notable	First racetrack sequence
Running gag	Mary's mother communication

Date: 2/13/1938   **Sponsor:** Jell-O   **City:** Hollywood, CA

Recording Source: Unknown   **Problems:** None

First line:
And now ladies and gentlemen, we bring you America's latest fashion plate, that Beau Brummell of Beverly Hills, Jack Benny.

Summary:
Tailors of America selected Jack as one of the Ten Best Dressed Men in the Country--Jack was second, Gable was first...Phil can't understand why he's not on the list...Jack has "Hooray for Waukegan" tatooed on his chest...Kenny remembers Jack's birthday, brought a cake with 50 candles on it...Jack claims he's not even 40 yet...Jack's father wires congratulations on Jack's 25th birthday, since he couldn't afford a telegram back then...Jack going over to Franciska Gaal's house...Mary runs lines with Jack...Robert Taylor offers Jack guidance on his performance...Jack introduces Taylor to the gang...Door guy asks if Taylor's really on the program...Robert Taylor plays Jack's scene with Mary, gives her a big kiss...Robert Taylor plays the cello, Jack and Taylor duet with comic banter

Cast:

Last name	First name	Roles	Guest star
Baker	Kenny	Kenny Baker	No
Baldwin	Harry	Door guy	No
Beloin	Ed	Telegram boy	No
Benny	Jack	Jack Benny	No
Harris	Phil	Phil Harris	No
Livingstone	Mary	Mary Livingstone	No
Taylor	Robert	Robert Taylor	Yes
Wilson	Don	Don Wilson	No

Songs:

Order	Title	Performers	Vocal
1	I've Taken a Fancy to You	Phil Harris	No
2	You're An Education	Phil Harris	No
3	New Moon	Kenny Baker	Yes
4	Mighty Lak a Rose	Jack Benny	No
4	Mighty Lak a Rose	Robert Taylor	No
5	Unidentified	Phil Harris	No

Notes:

Notable	Andy Devine appearance deleted from script

Date: 2/20/1938   **Sponsor:** Jell-O   **City:** Hollywood, CA

Recording Source: East coast   **Problems:** None

First line:
And now ladies and gentlemen, we bring you a man who celebrated his birthday last Monday, February the 14th, and his age was exactly…

Summary:
Jack won't tell his age…how Jack got into the service in World War I…Phil wishes him happy 44 (which is right)…Jack says he's 33…gang discusses astrology…telegrams from Jack's father and doctor who delivered Jack…Jack was on Maxwell House "Good News" program, says Allan Jones has a good voice…Kenny Baker thinks Virginia Bruce plays Baby Snooks…skit Submarine D-1…Rochester doesn't want to go on a U-boat…off to Panama…sea horse goes by with sign of "Santa Anita or Bust"…submarine running out of gas, find a submerged gas station…Shlepperman runs the gas station…Shlepperman offers to introduce Jack to a Mermaid…Mary is looking for a he-mermaid

Cast:

Last name	First name	Roles	Guest star
Anderson	Eddie	Rochester	No
Baker	Kenny	Kenny Baker, Lucky Baker	No
Beloin	Ed	Telegram boy 1	No
Benny	Jack	Jack Benny, Butch O'Benny	No
Harris	Phil	Phil Harris, Sock Harris	No
Hearn	Sam	Shlepperman	No
Livingstone	Mary	Mary Livingstone, Slug Livingstone	No
Morrow	Bill	Telegram boy 2	No
Wilson	Don	Don Wilson, Slim Wilson	No

Songs:

Order	Title	Performers	Vocal
1	Go South Young Man	Phil Harris	No
2	Rose Marie I Love You	Kenny Baker	Yes
3	You Do Something to Me	Phil Harris	No
4	Who Knows	Phil Harris	No

Notes:

Blooper	Phil delivers a line slowly and Jack says, "You can deliver that faster tonight"
Blooper	Jack stumbles on the line "ship's steering"
Skit	Submarine D-1

Date: 2/27/1938 **Sponsor:** Jell-O **City:** Hollywood, CA

Recording Source: None **Problems:** None

First line:
And now ladies and gentlemen, as is customary every Sunday night at this time, we bring you…
Jack: Hello Don.

Summary:
Gang greets each other…gang discusses changes to the program…Andy Devine stops by, didn't want to be on with Robert Taylor because they're both crazy about Barbara Stanwyck…Jack says he kept "Love in Bloom" alive a long time, Jack says "Thanks for the Memory" is going to be his new theme song…Rochester was in the war armed with a razor…skit Submarine D1…calls roll…sailing to San Diego Harbor…battleship crashes into them…Rochester calls out depth like an elevator…phone rings, it's a woman wanting the Orpheum Theatre…Door guy asks if Jack is sorry he saved all his money…promo for Lum and Abner joining General Foods family for Postum this week

Cast:

Last name	First name	Roles	Guest star
Anderson	Eddie	Rochester Van Jones	No
Baker	Kenny	Kenny Baker, Lucky Baker	No
Baldwin	Harry	Door guy	No
Benny	Jack	Jack Benny, Butch O'Benny	No
Devine	Andy	Andy Devine, steam whistle	No
Harris	Phil	Phil Harris, Sock Harris	No
Livingstone	Mary	Mary Livingstone, Slug Livingstone	No
Stewart	Blanche	Screamer, caller	No
Wilson	Don	Don Wilson, Slim Wilson	No

Songs:

Order	Title	Performers	Vocal
1	Be Myself	Phil Harris	No
2	Thanks for the Memory	Kenny Baker	Yes
3	How'd You Like to Love Me	Phil Harris	No
4	Some Day My Prince Will Come	Phil Harris	No

Notes:

Notable	First time Rochester is given the last name of "Van Jones"
Skit	Submarine D1

Date: 3/6/1938   **Sponsor:** Jell-O   **City:** Hollywood, CA

Recording Source: Unknown   **Problems:** None

First line:
And now ladies and gentlemen… Jack: Wait a minute, Don, wait a minute. This one's on me.

Summary:
Don's 15th year on radio, started in radio as a singer…Phil went from drummer to leader when he lost one stick…Mary reads a poem for Don…Jack and Phil argue…Kenny's girlfriend and her boyfriend are going to get married, Kenny's going to be the flower girl…Jack hired another announcer to do the middle commercial…Jack plays "Thanks for the Memory" and Robin and Rainger show up…they offer Jack $300 not to play their song

Cast:

Last name	First name	Roles	Guest star
Baker	Kenny	Kenny Baker	No
Beloin	Ed	Mischa	No
Benny	Jack	Jack Benny	No
Harris	Phil	Phil Harris	No
Livingstone	Mary	Mary Livingstone	No
Morrow	Bill	Yascha	No
Nazarro	Cliff	Announcer substitute	No
Rainger	Ralph	Ralph Rainger	Yes
Robin	Leo	Leo Robin	Yes
Wilson	Don	Don Wilson	No

Songs:

Order	Title	Performers	Vocal
1	Hooray for Hollywood	Phil Harris	No
2	Darktown Strutters' Ball/Alexander's Ragtime Band	Phil Harris	Yes
3	Ti Pi Tin	Kenny Baker	Yes
4	Thanks for the Memory	Jack Benny	No
5	Some Day My Prince Will Come	Phil Harris	No

Notes:

Running gag	Mary's poem

Date: 3/13/1938   **Sponsor:** Jell-O   **City:** Hollywood, CA

Recording Source: East coast   **Problems:** None

First line:
And now ladies and gentlemen, we bring you…
Jack: Hold it a minute, Don. How about letting me introduce myself tonight, just for a change?

Summary:
Jack gives himself an egotistical introduction…Phil has to match coins with Jack for his salary, Jack using a two-headed half dollar…Jack is building a new house…Jack carries his money in his sock…Kenny is upset because he didn't get the Academy Award for Best Actor…Door guy congratulates Jack on winning the Academy Award…skit Death In the Nightclub…last day of the trial of Three Tonsil Devine, accused of murder…Shlepperman is the judge…Andy's mother is a chorus girl at the Hotsy Totsy Club…District Attorney drives Andy into a crying jag…someone shoots the judge

Cast:

Last name	First name	Roles	Guest star
Baker	Kenny	Kenny Baker	No
Baldwin	Harry	Door guy	No
Beloin	Ed	Hot dog salesman	No
Benny	Jack	Jack Benny, Fearless John Benny	No
Devine	Andy	Andy Devine, Three Tonsil Devine	No
Franz	Joe	Bailiff	No
Harris	Phil	Phil Harris, Corny Harris	No
Hearn	Sam	Shlepperman	No
Livingstone	Mary	Mary Livingstone, Millicent Livingstone, Gertie La Strip	No
Nazarro	Cliff	Bartender	No
Wilson	Don	Don Wilson	No

Songs:

Order	Title	Performers	Vocal
1	I Love to Whistle	Phil Harris	No
2	Dipsy Doodle	Phil Harris	No
3	Sweet Someone	Kenny Baker	Yes
4	Whistle While You Work	Phil Harris	No

Notes:

Skit	Death in the Nightclub

Date: 3/20/1938   **Sponsor:** Jell-O   **City:** Hollywood, CA

Recording Source: Unknown   **Problems:** None

First line:
And now ladies and gentlemen, tomorrow being the first day of spring, we bring you sulfur, molasses, and Jack Benny.

Summary:
The beginning of spring…Jack is leaving for New York tomorrow, Harry Von Zell to be announcer…Jack borrowed a suitcase from Kenny that has legs--made from fresh alligators…Jack gets a telegram collect from Abe Lyman, threatens Jack if he doesn't use his orchestra in New York…Kate Smith will stand in for Kenny…Mary made a hat based on a vegetable plate…Fred Allen calls and wants Jack's Boy Scout knife…packing for New York…Jack has a goldfish and a canary, Mary and Kenny pack them…Rochester glued earmuffs on Jack's toupee…Rochester walked in his sleep, Jack put a vacuum in his hand…Andy's family doing spring cleaning…Shlepperman brings Jack's tuxedo from cleaning and pressing…tries to put old tuxedo in trunk, but the new suits keep throwing it out…Kenny gets locked in the trunk…Jack going over to Phil Baker's show to congratulate him on his 5th anniversary

Cast:

Last name	First name	Roles	Guest star
Anderson	Eddie	Rochester	No
Baker	Kenny	Kenny Baker	No
Beloin	Ed	Telegram boy	No
Benny	Jack	Jack Benny	No
Devine	Andy	Andy Devine	No
Harris	Phil	Phil Harris	No
Hearn	Sam	Shlepperman	No
Livingstone	Mary	Mary Livingstone	No
Wilson	Don	Don Wilson	No

Songs:

Order	Title	Performers	Vocal
1	Midnight in Paris	Phil Harris	No
2	I See Your Face Before Me	Kenny Baker	Yes
3	Who Stole the Jam	Phil Harris	No
4	Unidentified	Phil Harris	No

Notes:

Blooper	Jack puts the wrong inflection on "Who does he think he's bluffing anyway?"
Notable	No Mervyn LeRoy mention in the closing announcement; announcement is spotty in subsequent shows

Date: 3/27/1938   **Sponsor:** Jell-O   **City:** New York, NY

Recording Source: Unknown   **Problems:** None

First line:
And now ladies and gentlemen, we bring you a man who travelled all the way from California to New York, that gypsy of the airwaves, Jack Benny.

Summary:
From Radio City...Jack took a streamlined train out, very full service...all the girls are asking for Phil Harris...Lyman gives Jack flowers with a tarantula in them...Ripley interviews Jack as a curiosity...Door guy acts like he knows Jack...Harry Von Zell messes up the commercial...Kate Smith reads a letter from Mary...Kenny Baker calls, upset that Smith is taking his place...Jack is staying at the Waldorf-Astoria...Rochester asks for a salary advance...Fred demands Jack's Boy Scout knife...Jack saw "Sally, Irene, and Mary"...Fred Allen threatens Rochester...Jack and Fred argue...flute player bumped into Allen, got Jack's knife back--offers him Fred's watch too...Door guy asks if the program is over...Jack says "Goodnight Doll."

Cast:

Last name	First name	Roles	Guest star
		Mischa the Monk	No
Allen	Fred	Fred Allen	Yes
Anderson	Eddie	Rochester	No
Baldwin	Harry	Door guy 2	No
Benny	Jack	Jack Benny	No
Brown	John	Door guy 1	No
Lyman	Abe	Abe Lyman	Yes
Ripley	Robert	Robert Ripley	Yes
Smith	Kate	Kate Smith	Yes
Von Zell	Harry	Harry Von Zell	Yes

Songs:

Order	Title	Performers	Vocal
1	I Double Dare You	Abe Lyman	No
2	Hallelujah	Abe Lyman	No
3	This Time It's Real	Kate Smith	Yes
4	Who	Abe Lyman	No

Notes:

Blooper	Jack puts wrong inflection on "Well Harry, Ripley seems to be..."
Blooper	Fred Allen stumbles on "I'll hit you on top of your head so hard, you'll think your feet are bookends for your head."
Notable	First recorded "Goodnight, Doll" to Mary.

Date: 4/3/1938 **Sponsor:** Jell-O **City:** Hollywood, CA

Recording Source: Unknown **Problems:** None

First line:
And now ladies and gentlemen, we have a little surprise for you. Jack wired us that owing to a slight delay on the train, he'll be just a few minutes late.

Summary:
Georgie Jessel stands in for Jack…Jessel hopes that Jack will pay him…Rochester got off in Albuquerque and Jack went to look for him…scene shifts to the train…Jack says that Jessel looks like an anteater…Jessel and Jack started in same theatre…cast insults Jack to Jessel…Kenny Baker thinks Gracie Allen should be President…Kenny Baker says he saw a movie with Jessel and Bette Davis, "Jesselbelle"…Jack arrives, Jessel demands his $500…Jack postdates the check…Door guy bounces in, he's the check…gang didn't listen to Jack's program…Phil claims he heard Whiteman on it ("I coulda been drunk you know")…Shlepperman bought some of Andy's ranch…sold Shlepperman a cow, "only one faucet works"…Andy is going to buy an airplane for his father…Jack's home was robbed

Cast:

Last name	First name	Roles	Guest star
Anderson	Eddie	Rochester	No
Baker	Kenny	Kenny Baker	No
Baldwin	Harry	Door guy	No
Beloin	Ed	Train announcer	No
Benny	Jack	Jack Benny	No
Devine	Andy	Andy Devine	No
Harris	Phil	Phil Harris	No
Hearn	Sam	Shlepperman	No
Jessel	George	Georgie Jessel	Yes
Livingstone	Mary	Mary Livingstone	No
Stewart	Blanche	Lady on train	No
Wilson	Don	Don Wilson	No

Songs:

Order	Title	Performers	Vocal
1	Heigh Ho	Phil Harris	No
2	Swinging Annie Laurie Through the Rye	Phil Harris	No
3	I Can Dream Can't I	Kenny Baker	Yes
4	Tonight We Love	Phil Harris	No

Notes:

Blooper	Jack stumbles on the line "I'm not infallible."
Blooper	Georgie Jessel stumbles on the line "My wife thinks she is."
Notable	First drunk joke about Phil

Date: 4/10/1938   **Sponsor:** Jell-O   **City:** Hollywood, CA

Recording Source: Unknown   **Problems:** None

First line:
And now ladies and gentlemen, we bring you a man who has just become Beverly Hills' latest taxpayer and homeowner, Jack Benny.

Summary:
Jack's home is still under construction, Carlton Burgess is architect...a lighthouse in the swimming pool...Mary picked out Jack's wallpaper...Jack's dog Fido...red tulips in the front spelling out Jell-O...Kenny sees carpenters selling Jack's lumber...Phil calls to "Frank" and "Charlie" to find out the tune they played...Fred Allen barbs restart, says Allen has his toothbrush rebristled...skit A Yank at Oxford...set in Waukegan...town turns out to see Speedy off...Speedy rows across the Atlantic Ocean...Innkeeper encourages Jack to have Jell-O for dessert...Speedy wanders around looking for Oxford...Cliff Nazarro tries to give Speedy directions...Speedy gives up and goes back to America to look for Yale

Cast:

Last name	First name	Roles	Guest star
?	Ernie	Innkeeper	No
Bagby	Charley	Charley	No
Baker	Kenny	Kenny Baker	No
Baldwin	Harry	Train announcer	No
Beloin	Ed	Stanislaus	No
Benny	Jack	Jack Benny, Robert "Speedy" Benny	No
Harris	Phil	Phil Harris, George Pritchard?	No
Livingstone	Mary	Mary Livingstone, Maureen O'Livingstone	No
Morrow	Bill	Shark	No
Nazarro	Cliff	American	No
Nazarro	Cliff	Lionel Kvetz	No
Remley	Frank	Frankie	No
Stewart	Blanche	Cockney woman	No
Stewart	Blanche	Mrs. Bunker	No
Wilson	Don	Don Wilson	No

Songs:

Order	Title	Performers	Vocal
1	Something Tells Me	Phil Harris	No
2	Joseph, Joseph	Phil Harris	No
3	Good Night Angel	Kenny Baker	Yes
4	Who Are We to Say	Phil Harris	No

Notes:

Notable	First mention of Frankie Remley and Charlie Bagby by name
Skit	A Yank at Oxford

Date: 4/17/1938 **Sponsor:** Jell-O **City:** Hollywood, CA

Recording Source: Unknown **Problems:** None

First line:
And now ladies and gentlemen, we bring you a man who is celebrating Easter with a new suit, new shirt, new tie, and new shoes that squeak, Jack Benny.

Summary:
Gang discusses Easter outfits…Kenny suggests that Jack bump off Fred Allen…Mary writes and reads a poem about Easter…Jack got passes to the circus by letting them put posters on his new house…Andy's aunt is the Bearded Lady…Door guy asks Phil if he has a blind date…meet Rochester at the circus…watch barker for side show…Jack's passes are only good for matinee…Jack gets mad and crawls under tent with Mary and Kenny, they end up in the lions' cage…next week doing Snow White

Cast:

Last name	First name	Roles	Guest star
?	Matty	Band member	No
Anderson	Eddie	Rochester	No
Baker	Kenny	Kenny Baker	No
Baldwin	Harry	Door guy	No
Beloin	Ed	Balloon/hot dog salesman	No
Benny	Jack	Jack Benny	No
Devine	Andy	Andy Devine	No
Franz	Joe	Wild Man of Borneo	No
Harris	Phil	Phil Harris	No
Hearn	Sam	Ticket taker	No
Livingstone	Mary	Mary Livingstone	No
Nazarro	Cliff	Side show barker	No
Stewart	Blanche	Snake charmer	No
Wilson	Don	Don Wilson	No

Songs:

Order	Title	Performers	Vocal
1	Cry Baby Cry	Phil Harris	No
2	Donkey Serenade	Kenny Baker	Yes
3	Don't Be That Way	Phil Harris	No
4	When the Stars Go to Sleep	Phil Harris	No

Notes:

Notable	First mention of Rochester's girl Josephine
Running gag	Mary's poem

Date: 4/24/1938   **Sponsor:** Jell-O   **City:** Hollywood, CA

Recording Source: Unknown   **Problems:** None

First line:
And now ladies and gentlemen, this being the first day of Daylight Saving Time, we bring you a man who saves time, money, and old pieces of string - Jack Benny!

Summary:
First day of Daylight Saving Time...Jack was almost late to the program...Don imitates Edward G. Robinson for commercial...skit Snow White and the Seven Gangsters...gangsters plan on holding up the 12th National Bank...Dopey spent 2 hours trying to pick Fred Allen's pocket...Prince Charming visits Snow White, has a castle in the Catskills...Prince says "Hi ho Silverstein"...Snow White runs away from home...Snow White happens upon gangsters and talks them out of their plans...Prince arrives to take Snow White to his castle...Mary sings "I'm Wishing" and Andy Devine plays the echo

Cast:

Last name	First name	Roles	Guest star
Baker	Kenny	Kenny Baker, Dopey	No
Baker	Wally	Grumpy	No
Baldwin	Harry	Dynamite delivery	No
Beloin	Ed	Deer	No
Beloin	Ed	Sneezy	No
Benny	Jack	Jack Benny, Doc Benny	No
Devine	Andy	Andy Devine, Bashful	No
Harris	Phil	Phil Harris, Sleepy	No
Hearn	Sam	Shlepperman, Prince Charming	No
Livingstone	Mary	Mary Livingstone, Snow White	No
Stewart	Blanche	Agatha Witch	No
Wilson	Don	Don Wilson, Happy	No

Songs:

Order	Title	Performers	Vocal
1	Hooray for Hollywood	Phil Harris	No
2	One Song	Kenny Baker	Yes
3	Heigh Ho	Jack Benny	Yes
4	Some Day My Prince Will Come	Sam Hearn	Yes
4	Some Day My Prince Will Come	Mary Livingstone	Yes
5	Whistle While You Work	Jack Benny	Yes
6	Some Day My Prince Will Come (reprise)	Mary Livingstone	Yes
6	Some Day My Prince Will Come (reprise)	Sam Hearn	Yes
7	Whistle While You Work	Phil Harris	No
8	I'm Wishing	Andy Devine	Yes
8	I'm Wishing	Mary Livingstone	Yes

Notes:

Notable	One of the longest laughs on the Benny show when Mary gets raspberry from bird in the forest
Skit	Snow White and the Seven Gangsters

Date: 5/1/1938 **Sponsor:** Jell-O **City:** Hollywood, CA

Recording Source: Unknown **Problems:** None

First line:
And now ladies and gentlemen, we bring you a man who hasn't made a picture in over a year and still thinks he's a movie star, Jack Benny.

Summary:
Jack has a four-year contract with Paramount…Jack's raise was going from the 45-cent lunch to the 60-cent lunch…work with Franciska Gaal called off, Jack wanted to be her lover and Paramount wanted him to be her father…Graumann asked Jack to put his footprints at the Chinese Theatre…Jack stepped in the cement in his bare feet, took so many bows that the cement hardened…starting a new picture next week, "Artists and Models Abroad"…Kenny is reading about higher mathematics, gives his opinion on Einstein…Jack congratulates cast on performance last week…Walt Disney liked Mary so much he wants her to do a Silly Symphony…Don does the Highland Fling over Jell-O…Carlton Burgess out of control, built 8 stories on Jack's house…Phil flying to Louisville for Kentucky Derby ("are you going to take a plane or use your ears?")…Mary and Kenny accompany Jack to his house site…Burgess gives them a tour of the house…Jack falls off the balcony…Ed VandeVere drove Jack's Maxwell in the Fresno State College Hat Race last Thursday

Cast:

Last name	First name	Roles	Guest star
Baker	Kenny	Kenny Baker	No
Baldwin	Harry	Deauville	No
Beloin	Ed	Foreman, program seller	No
Benny	Jack	Jack Benny	No
Harris	Phil	Phil Harris	No
Livingstone	Mary	Mary Livingstone	No
Morrow	Bill	Onion worker	No
Nelson	Frank	Carlton Burgess	No
Stewart	Blanche	Jezebel (dog)	No
Wilson	Don	Don Wilson	No

Songs:

Order	Title	Performers	Vocal
1	Latin Quarter/Life Begins When You're in Love	Phil Harris	No
2	Love Walked In	Kenny Baker	Yes
3	Ti Pi Tin	Phil Harris	No
4	Who Do You Think I Saw Last Night	Phil Harris	No

Notes:

Date: 5/8/1938   **Sponsor:** Jell-O   **City:** Hollywood, CA

Recording Source: Unknown   **Problems:** None

First line:
And now ladies and gentlemen, this being Mother's Day, we bring you the mother of the Jell-O program, Jack Benny.

Summary:
Jack is a mother hen and the gang are his chicks…Phil sent his mother a picture of him with his orchestra…Mary calls her mother…sent her mother a bathing suit and she was elected Miss Plainfield…Phil had a Mint Julep at Kentucky Derby…everyone tells riddles…Don Wilson sings M-O-T-H-E-R with Jell-O lyrics…Jack and Mancel Talcott (Mayor of Waukegan) reminisce about school days in Waukegan…fire department has a hose now…special skit in Talcott's honor…Jack and Mary play husband and wife, everyone else is a lover…husband pretends to go to Altoona, lovers then arrive…Talcott keeps jumping his cues…Talcott offers Faith a honeymoon to Waukegan Falls, the WPA just built them…Talcott will go back to Waukegan if he can't get into movies

Cast:

Last name	First name	Roles	Guest star
Baker	Kenny	Kenny Baker	No
Benny	Jack	Jack Benny	No
Harris	Phil	Phil Harris	No
Livingstone	Mary	Mary Livingstone, Faith	No
Talcott	Mancel	Mayor Mancel Talcott, Mortimer J. Bookend	Yes
Wilson	Don	Don Wilson	No

Songs:

Order	Title	Performers	Vocal
1	Day Dreams	Phil Harris	No
2	Morocco	Phil Harris	No
3	M-O-T-H-E-R	Don Wilson	Yes
4	Lost and Found	Kenny Baker	Yes
5	Unidentified	Phil Harris	No

Notes:

Blooper	Jack does a spoonerism of "I'm not really a ken, Henny."
Running gag	Mary's mother communication
Skit	Eternal Triangle rehash

Date: 5/15/1938   **Sponsor:** Jell-O   **City:** Hollywood, CA

Recording Source: Unknown   **Problems:** None

First line:
And now ladies and gentlemen, we bring you a man who has joined the ranks of Hollywood Turfmen and bought himself a racehorse, Jack Benny.

Summary:
Jack wants to put his horse in Crosby's stable, but he charges too much...horse is named Buck Benny, 2 years old in January...Phil quizzes Jack about his horse...Jack shows a picture of the horse, Phil finds "Man of War" stamped on the back...Shlepperman struck oil last week and it ruined his potatoes...Jack decides to split his horse's time on Andy and Shlepperman's farms...skit Murder in the Library...phone calls in Captain O'Benny's office...someone passing phone dollar bills...get called to a murder and Captain forgets to get the address...interrogating Mrs. Clunkenbush on how she killed each of her eight husbands...Phil engaged to be her next husband...Clunkenbush turns out to be alive and tries to tell who tried to kill him...Captain gives him a glass of water and he falls over dead...Mary does double-talk...next week, Adventures of Tom Sawyer

Cast:

Last name	First name	Roles	Guest star
Baker	Kenny	Kenny Baker	No
Baldwin	Harry	Police radio announcer	No
Beloin	Ed	Audience	No
Benny	Jack	Jack Benny, Captain O'Benny	No
Devine	Andy	Andy Devine	No
Harris	Phil	Phil Harris	No
Hearn	Sam	Shlepperman	No
Livingstone	Mary	Mary Livingstone, Sugar Klunkenbush	No
Nazarro	Cliff	Mr. Klunkenbush	No
Wilson	Don	Don Wilson, Blimp the Butler	No

Songs:

Order	Title	Performers	Vocal
1	Life Begins when You're In Love	Phil Harris	No
2	I Fall in Love With You Every Day	Kenny Baker	Yes
3	Something Tells Me	Phil Harris	No
4	I Know That You Know	Phil Harris	No

Notes:

Blooper	Don says "Jell-O freezing milk" instead of "Jell-O freezing mix"
Skit	Murder in the Library

Date: 5/22/1938   **Sponsor:** Jell-O   **City:** Hollywood, CA

Recording Source: Unknown   **Problems:** None

First line:
And now ladies and gentlemen, put on your carpet slippers, move your chairs up to the fireplace and throw the radio on the fire, 'cause here comes…Jack Benny!

Summary:
Jack is irritable because he's on a diet, starting a picture next week…Jack photographs plaid in Technicolor…Joan Bennett is Jack's leading lady…Phil talks about his mother's cooking…Kenny has Jack hold his chocolate bar…gang reminisces about being a kid…Kenny smoked his first cigarette last night, swallowed it when his mother came in…Andy Devine elected Mayor of Van Nuys…skit The Adventures of Tom Sawyer…Sawyer boys eat breakfast…Tom wants to take Becky to the show to see Jack Benny and his violin…Freddie Allen just moved into town, Tom beats him up…"We're a little late, so goodnight folks"

Cast:

Last name	First name	Roles	Guest star
Baker	Kenny	Kenny Baker, Skinny Baker	No
Benny	Jack	Jack Benny, Tom Sawyer	No
Devine	Andy	Andy Devine, Huckleberry Finn	No
Felton	Verna	Aunt Polly	No
Harris	Phil	Phil Harris, Sidney Sawyer	No
Hayes	Peter Lind	Freddie Allen	No
Livingstone	Mary	Mary Livingstone, Becky Thatcher	No
Stewart	Blanche	Mrs. Newton	No
Wilson	Don	Don Wilson, Puddin Head Wilson	No

Songs:

Order	Title	Performers	Vocal
1	In Old Chicago	Phil Harris	No
2	Lovelight in the Starlight	Kenny Baker	Yes
3	Cry Baby Cry	Phil Harris	No
4	Unidentified	Phil Harris	No

Notes:

Notable	Exchange with Shlepperman at end of show deleted from script, he announces that he's going to Pittsburgh, Philadelphia, Baltimore, and Washington on personal appearances
Skit	The Adventures of Tom Sawyer

Date: 5/29/1938   **Sponsor:** Jell-O   **City:** Hollywood, CA

Recording Source: Unknown   **Problems:** None

First line:
And now ladies and gentlemen, as is customary every Sunday at this time, we bring you a man who…uh…a man who…uh…oh say, Phil, where's Jack?

Summary:
Jack is running lines with Rochester standing in for Joan Bennett…gang eavesdrops on them…Jack plays Conrad Bagel in the movie…Andy made his father head of Sanitation in Van Nuys, he took a bath…makes Don Wilson Chief of Police…continuing Tom Sawyer skit…Mr. Dobbins leads class, typical classroom skit…Parkyakarkus saved John Smith…Tom Sawyer sneaks into school but then runs away again

Cast:

Last name	First name	Roles	Guest star
Anderson	Eddie	Rochester Van Jones	No
Baker	Kenny	Kenny Baker, Skinny Baker	No
Baldwin	Harry	Scarlett No-Haira	No
Benny	Jack	Jack Benny, Tom Sawyer, Mr. Dobbins	No
Devine	Andy	Andy Devine, Huckleberry Finn	No
Harris	Phil	Phil Harris, Sidney Sawyer	No
Livingstone	Mary	Mary Livingstone, Becky Thatcher	No
Nazarro	Cliff	Sylvester Worm	No
Stewart	Blanche	Marlene DeTruck	No
Stewart	Blanche	Scarlett O'Hara	No
Stewart	Blanche	Mrs. Newton	No
Wilson	Don	Don Wilson, Puddin Head Wilson	No

Songs:

Order	Title	Performers	Vocal
1	Everything's in Rhythm With My Heart	Phil Harris	No
2	You Couldn't Be Cuter	Phil Harris	No
3	Silver on the Sage	Kenny Baker	Yes
4	Unidentified	Phil Harris	No

Notes:

Blooper	Jack stumbles on "Huckleberry Finn"
Blooper	Jack stumbles on the line "School is about to begin."
Notable	Marlene DeTruck sequence deleted from previous week's show
Skit	The Adventures of Tom Sawyer

Date: 6/5/1938   **Sponsor:** Jell-O   **City:** Hollywood, CA

Recording Source: Unknown   **Problems:** None

First line:
Jack: Yes...yes...what's that? Now look, Mr. Hornblow, I know you're the producer of the picture, but I'm the star, and after all, I have some rights.

Summary:
Jack doesn't want to do a scene hanging out of a window...producer says it's too dangerous to have a stuntman do it...Zucker of Paramount calls, Jack argues with him...Mr. Winkler, Joan Bennett's manager calls...Mitch Leisen calls...continuing Tom Sawyer...Sawyer boys get ready to go to the school picnic and Indian cave...Mr. Hornblow calls and interrupts skit...Tom, Becky, and Skinny go into the cave and get lost...encounter an Eskimo...Tom hangs by his heels to help get kids out of the cave, Paramount says that he should do it in the picture then...Phil slaps Jack, Jack runs to Aunt Polly

Cast:

Last name	First name	Roles	Guest star
Baker	Kenny	Kenny Baker, Skinny Baker	No
Baldwin	Harry	Echo	No
Beloin	Ed	Eskimo	No
Beloin	Ed	Telegram boy	No
Benny	Jack	Jack Benny, Tom Sawyer	No
Colvig	Pinto	Moaner, sound effects	No
Felton	Verna	Aunt Polly	No
Harris	Phil	Phil Harris, Sidney Sawyer	No
Livingstone	Mary	Mary Livingstone, Becky Thatcher	No
Stewart	Blanche	Mrs. Newton	No
Stewart	Blanche	Bat	No
Wilson	Don	Don Wilson, Puddin Head Wilson	No

Songs:

Order	Title	Performers	Vocal
1	I've Got a Heartful of Music	Phil Harris	No
2	Jungle Love	Phil Harris	No
3	Let's Sail to Dreamland	Kenny Baker	Yes
4	Unidentified	Phil Harris	No

Notes:

Running gag	But but but
Skit	The Adventures of Tom Sawyer

Date: 6/12/1938   **Sponsor:** Jell-O   **City:** Hollywood, CA

Recording Source: Unknown   **Problems:** None

First line:
And now ladies and gentlemen, we take you to Jack Benny's dressing room at the Paramount Studio. It's Jack's first day in his new picture.

Summary:
Jack is expecting Joan Bennett to visit him in his dressing room...makeup man says Jack doesn't need makeup because his coat will hang down over his face...gang visits Jack...Jack's dressing room is a dump...Joan Bennett arrives, Jack introduces her to the gang...Mary insults Joan...Jack rehearses a scene with Joan...Jack always bought his own production film...Joan complains to Leisen that Jack can't play a love scene...Jack hangs upside down and loses change out of his pockets...cast breaks in the middle of the scene, leaves Jack hanging

Cast:

Last name	First name	Roles	Guest star
Anderson	Eddie	Rochester	No
Baker	Kenny	Kenny Baker	No
Baldwin	Harry	Stage caller	No
Beloin	Ed	Chuck soundman	No
Beloin	Ed	Newt the makeup man	No
Bennett	Joan	Joan Bennett	Yes
Benny	Jack	Jack Benny	No
Bunker	?	Mr. Zukor	No
Harris	Phil	Phil Harris	No
Leisen	Mitchell	Mitchell Leisen	Yes
Livingstone	Mary	Mary Livingstone	No
Morrow	Bill	Teddy Tetslab cameraman	No
Wilson	Don	Don Wilson	No

Songs:

Order	Title	Performers	Vocal
1	I'm Taking a Fancy to You	Phil Harris	No
2	I've Told Every Little Star	Kenny Baker	Yes
3	Says My Heart	Phil Harris	No
4	Did an Angel Kiss Me	Phil Harris	No

Notes:

Date: 6/19/1938 **Sponsor:** Jell-O **City:** Hollywood, CA

Recording Source: Unknown **Problems:** None

First line:
And now ladies and gentlemen, this being our next-to-the-last broadcast of the season, we bring you a little man who had a busy year, Jack Benny.

Summary:
Jack tells how he keeps in good condition…Kenny is exhausted, but doesen't sound it…Jack had long eyelashes as a kid…gang brags about themselves…Door guy has beautiful eyes…Kenny going to New York, sailing to England to do "The Mikado"…how Jack pays the cast…Jack was on the Normandy last year…Andy held a beauty contest in Van Nuys…skit Back Home in Indiana…Door guy says he's boiled now…kids bring home gifts for Father's Day, Kenneth has gone Hollywood…Petunia brings a grandson…"We're a little late, so goodnight folks."

Cast:

Last name	First name	Roles	Guest star
Baker	Kenny	Kenny Baker, Kenneth Benny	No
Baldwin	Harry	Door guy	No
Benny	Jack	Jack Benny, Clem Benny	No
Devine	Andy	Andy Devine, Petunia Benny	No
Harris	Phil	Phil Harris, Stub Benny	No
Livingstone	Mary	Mary Livingstone, Mariah Benny	No
Wilson	Don	Don Wilson, grandson	No

Songs:

Order	Title	Performers	Vocal
1	Latin Quarter	Phil Harris	No
2	Let Me Whisper	Kenny Baker	Yes
3	What Do You Hear from the Mob in Scotland	Phil Harris	No
4	I Fall in Love With You Every Day	Phil Harris	No

Notes:

Notable	Hand-written addition to end of script: "And I also want to announce that Mayor Andy Devine has proclaimed next week, June 20th to 25th, as Jello Week in Van Nuys.
Skit	Back Home in Indiana

Date: 6/26/1938   **Sponsor:** Jell-O   **City:** Hollywood, CA

Recording Source: Unknown   **Problems:** None

First line:
Cliff Nazarro: And now ladies and gentlemen, for the last time this season, we bring you our Master of Ceremonies, a man who…(doubletalk)

Summary:
Jack decided to go to Spain for a vacation, but there's a war going on…Phil quizzes Jack on current events…Phil became the leader of his orchestra because he was the only guy who looked good from the back…Mary reads poem "Fare Thee Well and Toodle-Oo"…Kenny not there, he's sailing to England…Don is going to write a book about Jell-O…Door guy asks if it's the last program of the season…Andy going to Honolulu…Jack invites gang to his house for a party…Jack's Chinese cook is Swing Hi…Rochester put Jack's raccoon coat in the icebox for cold storage…Jack decides to take gang to Trocadero instead…Jack and Don high in Radio Guide poll again…Hobby Lobby is summer replacement

Cast:

Last name	First name	Roles	Guest star
Anderson	Eddie	Rochester	No
Baldwin	Harry	Door guy	No
Benny	Jack	Jack Benny	No
Devine	Andy	Andy Devine	No
Elman	Dave	Dave Elman	Yes
Harris	Phil	Phil Harris	No
Livingstone	Mary	Mary Livingstone	No
Nazarro	Cliff	Opening announcer	No
Royale	William	Swing Hi	No
Wilson	Don	Don Wilson	No

Songs:

Order	Title	Performers	Vocal
1	Hooray for Hollywood	Phil Harris	No
2	You Couldn't Be Cuter	Phil Harris	Yes
3	Says My Heart	Mary Livingstone	Yes
4	It's Raining Sunshine	Phil Harris	No

Notes:

Blooper	Jack says "you haven't an ounce of sediment" instead of "sentiment" (note: "sediment" is written in pencil on the script)
Running gag	Mary's poem

Date: 10/2/1938   **Sponsor:** Jell-O   **City:** Hollywood, CA

Recording Source: Unknown   **Problems:** None

First line:
Mrs. Harris: "Oh Phil, Phil Harris!"
Phil: "What do you want, Mom?"

Summary:
Gang getting ready for the program...Jack cut his vacation short for American Legion Convention, he belongs to the Lake Forest, IL branch...Phil hasn't had a drink in four months...Phil's orchestra played in Waukegan, bought clothes from Julius Sinykin...Mary kissees Don and Phil hello...gang discusses Jack's performance in "Seven Keys to Baldpate"...Door guy welcomes Jack back...Kenny returns speaking with a British accent...going to do "Yellow Jack" next Sunday, does previews...telegram from Fred Allen

Cast:

Last name	First name	Roles	Guest star
?	Paula	Lucy Wilson	No
?	Reggy	Higgins the valet	No
Anderson	Eddie	Rochester	No
Baker	Kenny	Kenny Baker	No
Baldwin	Harry	Door guy	No
Beloin	Ed	Telegram boy	No
Beloin	Ed	Mosquito	No
Benny	Jack	Jack Benny	No
Felton	Verna	Mrs. Harris	No
Harris	Phil	Phil Harris	No
Livingstone	Mary	Mary Livingstone	No
Morrow	Bill	Microphone	No
Stewart	Blanche	Mrs. Baker, screamer	No
Wilson	Don	Don Wilson	No

Songs:

Order	Title	Performers	Vocal
1	Confidentially	Phil Harris	No
2	What Goes On Here in My Heart	Phil Harris	No
3	Remember	Kenny Baker	Yes
4	I Married an Angel	Phil Harris	No

Notes:

Notable	Non-standard opening, scenes from each cast member getting ready for the program
Notable	First opening crediting most cast members, "Jack Benny, with Mary Livingstone, Phil Harris, Kenny Baker, and yours truly, Don Wilson."

Date: 10/9/1938 **Sponsor:** Jell-O **City:** Hollywood, CA

Recording Source: Unknown **Problems:** None

First line:
And now ladies and gentlemen, we bring you our Master of Ceremonies. I could say he's one of the greatest comedians of all time…

Summary:
Gang reads reviews of last week's program…Higgins is taking Kenny's girl to the movies…Jack and Mary went skating, Jack helped Hedy Lamarr on with her skates…skit Yellow Jack…Dr. Nazarro has discovered the cause of yellow fever…looking for volunteer to be infected by a mosquito, Dr. Benny volunteers…mosquito shoots Dr. Benny with a machine gun…Stage Relief Fund picnic at World's Fair…promoting Al Pearce show starting tomorrow night

Cast:

Last name	First name	Roles	Guest star
Anderson	Eddie	Rochester, Private Van Jones	No
Baker	Kenny	Kenny Baker, Private O'Baker	No
Baldwin	Harry	Mosquito (speaking)	No
Beloin	Ed	Laundry man	No
Benny	Jack	Jack Benny, Dr. Benny	No
Colvig	Pinto	Mosquito sound effects	No
Harris	Phil	Phil Harris, Sgt. O'Harris	No
Livingstone	Mary	Mary Livingstone, Nurse Blake	No
Nazarro	Cliff	Dr. Nazarro	No
Nelson	Frank	Police radio announcer	No
Stewart	Blanche	Mosquito	No
Wilson	Don	Don Wilson, Dr. O'Wilson	No

Songs:

Order	Title	Performers	Vocal
1	How Can I Thank You	Phil Harris	No
2	So Help Me	Kenny Baker	Yes
3	I've Got a Pocketful of Dreams	Phil Harris	No
4	The Night is Filled with Music	Phil Harris	No

Notes:

Skit	Yellow Jack

Date: 10/16/1938   **Sponsor:** Jell-O   **City:** Hollywood, CA

Recording Source: Unknown   **Problems:** None

First line:
And now ladies and gentlemen, I'd like to announce that next week this program will move to the new NBC studios on Sunset Boulevard in Hollywood...

Summary:
Gang gets sentimental about their studio...Mary reads a poem to the old studio...Jack brags about his love scenes in "Artists and Models Abroad"...Don tells how to order Jell-O in French...Jack kicks Kenny in the rear...Kenny was delayed because the movers kept packing him...Andy went to Honolulu with his parents, brings Jack a pineapple...Rochester calls, his friends stopped over and ate all the food...Rochester asks Jack to bring his fan mail home...movers flip Jack off of the rug..."We ran over time, so goodnight folks."

Cast:

Last name	First name	Roles	Guest star
Anderson	Eddie	Rochester	No
Baker	Kenny	Kenny Baker	No
Beloin	Ed	Mervyn	No
Benny	Jack	Jack Benny	No
Devine	Andy	Andy Devine	No
Harris	Phil	Phil Harris	No
Lewis	Elliott	LaVerne	No
Livingstone	Mary	Mary Livingstone	No
Wilson	Don	Don Wilson	No

Songs:

Order	Title	Performers	Vocal
1	For No Rhyme or Reason	Phil Harris	No
2	What Have You Got That Gets Me?	Phil Harris	No
3	I've Got a Date With a Dream	Kenny Baker	Yes
4	Don't Cross Your Fingers, Cross Your Heart	Phil Harris	No

Notes:

Notable	Eddie Anderson's lines now prompted as "Rochester" in the script
Notable	Jack says "We ran over time, so goodnight folks."
Running gag	Mary's poem

Date: 10/23/1938   **Sponsor:** Jell-O   **City:** Hollywood, CA

Recording Source: Unknown   **Problems:** None

First line:
And now ladies and gentlemen, for the first time from the new NBC building in Hollywood with its new studios, its new facilities, and its new equipment, we bring you that old foof, Jack Benny.

Summary:
New studios are very swanky...now have a door chime instead of a knock on the door...some parts of the building not done yet...tour group comes through...audience is 325...Jack does his own laundry...another tour group, Kenny's in it...Kenny yells back at Jack...skit Algiers...le Moko sends Phil to Beverly-Algiers Hotel to steal jewels...Inspector tells le Moko that the police are looking for him...Ines is jealous, goes to kill Pepe but interrupted by tour group...Ines shoots Pepe...Door guy wanted to play Hedy Lamarr role

Cast:

Last name	First name	Roles	Guest star
Baker	Kenny	Kenny Baker, Bubbles Baker	No
Baldwin	Harry	Tour member man (1), Door guy	No
Beloin	Ed	Tour guide	No
Benaderet	Bea	Mamie	No
Benny	Jack	Jack Benny, Pepe le Moko	No
Devine	Andy	Andy Devine, Gaby	No
Harris	Phil	Phil Harris, Three-Fingered Harris	No
Livingstone	Mary	Mary Livingstone, Ines	No
Nazarro	Cliff	Tour member man (2)	No
Stewart	Blanche	Tour member woman (1&2), Woman in audience	No
Wilson	Don	Don Wilson, Inspector	No

Songs:

Order	Title	Performers	Vocal
1	From Alpha to Omega	Phil Harris	No
2	The Yam	Phil Harris	No
3	Two Sleepy People	Kenny Baker	Yes
4	There's a Brand New Picture in My Picture Frame	Phil Harris	No

Notes:

Skit	Algiers

Date: 10/30/1938   **Sponsor:** Jell-O   **City:** Hollywood, CA

Recording Source: Unknown   **Problems:** None

First line:
And now ladies and gentlemen, tonight we take you to Jack Benny's new home in
Beverly Hills where he's throwing a Halloween party for his whole gang.

Summary:
Rochester is making sandwiches...kids tore down admission sign in front of Jack's
house, Ronald Colman was one of the kids...Rochester's brother September is
helping...Jack serving a squab for dinner...Kenny boobytrapped his own house...Jack
catches a bear in his backyard...Phil brings his girlfriend Barbara to the party..."Jack
wouldn't buy champagne if Sally Rand was behind every bubble"...Jack flirts with
Barbara...Jack being stingy with food, fight breaks out over deviled egg...Andy was going
to come as a geranium, but he looks lousy in a flower pot...September threw squab at
the cook, caught it in his open mouth...gang finds Jack's Thanksgiving turkey in the
icebox

Cast:

Last name	First name	Roles	Guest star
		September	No
?	Barbara	Barbara Whitney	No
Anderson	Eddie	Rochester	No
Baker	Kenny	Kenny Baker	No
Benny	Jack	Jack Benny	No
Devine	Andy	Andy Devine	No
Harris	Phil	Phil Harris	No
Livingstone	Mary	Mary Livingstone	No
Wilson	Don	Don Wilson	No

Songs:

Order	Title	Performers	Vocal
1	Rainbow	Phil Harris	No
2	Change Partners and Dance	Kenny Baker	Yes
3	What Have You Got That Gets Me	Mary Livingstone	Yes
3	What Have You Got That Gets Me	Don Wilson	Yes
3	What Have You Got That Gets Me	Andy Devine	Yes
3	What Have You Got That Gets Me	Phil Harris	Yes
3	What Have You Got That Gets Me	Jack Benny	Yes
4	Unidentified	Phil Harris	No

Notes:

Blooper	Jack stumbles on the line "The way you hear this gang talk"
Notable	First mention of Ronald Colman being in Jack's neighborhood

Date: 11/6/1938 **Sponsor:** Jell-O **City:** Hollywood, CA

Recording Source: Unknown **Problems:** None

First line:
And now ladies and gentlemen, we bring you that genial host of Beverly Hills, a man who is famous for his lavish and extravagant parties, Jacques Benny.

Summary:
Gang discusses Jack's party last week...served hot dogs and gang had nightmares...Jack saw Phil in a patrol wagon, he thought it was a sightseeing bus...Jack makes his own Grape Nuts...Kenny dreamed he was President, Maxie Rosenbloom was Vice-President...Door guy doesn't want Jack to be a prize fighter...Stinky wants to be a prizefighter, not a violinist...becomes Killer Benny...Harris sets up a fight between Killer and Kid Baker...Killer knocked out by Kid...Killer settles down on a farm, calls hogs with his violin

Cast:

Last name	First name	Roles	Guest star
Arquette	Cliff	Stinky's father	No
Baker	Kenny	Kenny Baker, Kid Baker	No
Baldwin	Harry	Door guy	No
Benny	Jack	Jack Benny, Stinky Killer Benny	No
Franz	Joe	Fight announcer (weight)	No
Harris	Phil	Phil Harris, Curly Harris manager	No
Livingstone	Mary	Mary Livingstone, Sheila	No
Nazarro	Cliff	Referee	No
Wilson	Don	Don Wilson, fight announcer	No

Songs:

Order	Title	Performers	Vocal
1	The Riddle Song	Phil Harris	No
2	If I Loved You More	Kenny Baker	Yes
3	F.D.R. Jones	Phil Harris	No
4	Unidentified	Phil Harris	No

Notes:

Notable	Someone in the brass section is WAY off on the last note of the final Jell-O call
Skit	The Crowd Roars

Date: 11/13/1938 **Sponsor:** Jell-O **City:** Hollywood, CA

Recording Source: Unknown **Problems:** None

First line:
And now ladies and gentlemen, the political excitement being over, we bring you that prominent citizen of Beverly Hills who was just elected dogcatcher, Jack Benny.

Summary:
Jack thought he was running for mayor, he was elected dogcatcher...Jack giving violin lessons on Tuesdays...Jack going out with Phil's girl, Barbara...Jack and Phil argue about Barbara...Jack and Barbara (and her Uncle Louie) went to Wilshire Bowl, where Phil was playing...Jack and Mary go to a fortune teller to see how Jack stands with Barbara...Maxwell doesn't have brakes, Rochester throws out anchor...Madame Zombie looks into crystal ball and sees Barbara with a man in her arms...man is Uncle Louie...Jack says that Madame Zombie is a fake...Zombie sets dogs on Jack and Mary, they run down stairs and Jack breaks his ankle...Rochester does show close

Cast:

Last name	First name	Roles	Guest star
		Madame Zombie	No
Anderson	Eddie	Rochester	No
Baker	Kenny	Kenny Baker	No
Beloin	Ed	Peanuts/program seller	No
Benny	Jack	Jack Benny	No
Harris	Phil	Phil Harris	No
Livingstone	Mary	Mary Livingstone	No
Nelson	Frank	Butler of Madame Zombie, Butch	No
Wilson	Don	Don Wilson	No

Songs:

Order	Title	Performers	Vocal
1	It Serves You Right	Phil Harris	No
2	Ya Got Me	Phil Harris	No
3	Umbrella Man	Kenny Baker	Yes
4	Unidentified	Phil Harris	No

Notes:

Notable	First song take-off, "A-Tisket A-Tasket", when Jack asks questions and Madame Zombie answers "no no no no"
Notable	Fortune teller lives at "1002 Dracula Drive", as opposed to Jack's real-life address of 1002 N. Roxbury Drive
Notable	First mention of Wilshire Bowl as Phil's orchestra venue

Date: 11/20/1938   **Sponsor:** Jell-O   **City:** Hollywood, CA

Recording Source: East coast   **Problems:** None

First line:
And now ladies and gentlemen, hey Jack, Jack? Oh Phil, where's Jack?

Summary:
Jack talking to Barbara Whitney on the phone, makes a date with her for Thursday night...Jack claims he was talking to his tailor in Santa Barbara...Kenny saw Jack in a jewelry store...Barbara calls back and cancels date...Phil complains that Jack always takes lead in skits...Door guy asks if Jack is going to the jungle...skit Too Hot to Handle...Clark was sent to China, went to Chinatown...was on S.S. Roxbury last year...Clark's last chance is to help Myrna find her brother, Ignatz...gets lost in Africa...find Ignatz with a bunch of cannibals...Clark and Myrna dance to jungle music instead of rescuing Ignatz..."We're a little over time, so good night folks"

Cast:

Last name	First name	Roles	Guest star
Baker	Kenny	Kenny Baker, cannibal	No
Baldwin	Harry	Door guy	No
Beloin	Ed	Baboon	No
Benny	Jack	Jack Benny, Clark Benny	No
Harris	Phil	Phil Harris, Phil Fathead	No
Livingstone	Mary	Mary Livingstone, Myrna Livingstone	No
Nazarro	Cliff	Ignatz	No
Stewart	Blanche	Ms. Stewart operator	No
Wilson	Don	Don Wilson, cannibal	No

Songs:

Order	Title	Performers	Vocal
1	No Wonder	Phil Harris	No
2	Little Town in Old County Down	Kenny Baker	Yes
3	Jeepers Creepers	Phil Harris	No
4	Tell Me With Your Kisses	Phil Harris	No

Notes:

Blooper	Don Wilson says "desert saucers" instead of "dessert saucers"
Blooper	Kenny stumbles on line, "I'm selling some tickets for a turkey raffle"
Blooper	Jack stumbles on the line, "Come on, Myrna"
Notable	East coast broadcast, Jack mentions getting "a better joke for tonight"
Skit	Too Hot to Handle

Date: 11/27/1938 **Sponsor:** Jell-O **City:** Hollywood, CA

Recording Source: Unknown **Problems:** Wrong speed

First line:
And now ladies and gentlemen, we bring you a man who after lying flat on his back for three days with a bad cold, threw off the covers and said, "Good Heavens, it's Sunday! The show must go on!"

Summary:
Jack's doctor is a chiropodist...Jack told Phil he was sick as a dog, so Phil sent him a can of Ken-L-Ration...Kenny won his own turkey raffle...Jack painted a red cross on Rochester's coat...Don and Phil help Jack remove the mustard plaster from his chest...next week broadcasting from Radio City in New York...Jack has an appointment with a New York producer who wants him to appear in "Romeo and Juliet"...Jack teases Mary about her hat...Rochester calls, Jack's cough medicine was hair tonic...skit Hold That Line...Coach Benny peps the team in the locker room, he'll play himself in the second half...skit interrupted by telegram from the Acme Hotel in New York...Wilson misses kicking ball, kicks Kenny...running with the ball turns into a horse race...Lone Ranger wins the race

Cast:

Last name	First name	Roles	Guest star
Anderson	Eddie	Rochester	No
Baker	Kenny	Kenny Baker	No
Beloin	Ed	Telegram boy, Lone Ranger	No
Benny	Jack	Jack Benny, Flash Benny	No
Harris	Phil	Phil Harris	No
Livingstone	Mary	Mary Livingstone, Butch Livingstone	No
Nelson	Frank	Football announcer	No
Wilson	Don	Don Wilson, Big Boy Wilson	No

Songs:

Order	Title	Performers	Vocal
1	This Can't Be Love	Phil Harris	No
2	My Reverie	Kenny Baker	Yes
3	Girl Friend of the Whirling Dervish	Phil Harris	No
4	I Can't Say It Too Many Times	Phil Harris	No

Notes:

Blooper	Mary stumbles on the line, "You better buy some galoshes"
Notable	First mention of the Acme Hotel in New York
Skit	Hold That Line

Date: 12/4/1938   **Sponsor:** Jell-O   **City:** New York, NY

Recording Source: Unknown   **Problems:** None

First line:
And now ladies and gentlemen, let us welcome to New York that little ray of California sunshine, that shimmering, quivering, ice-kissed comedian, Jack Benny.

Summary:
From Radio City, New York...Jack is having a hard time dealing with the cold...Jack was invited to Fred Allen's for dinner, he served sardines...Phil is staying at the Astor Bar...Jack teases Mary about her hat...Jack's old girlfriend shows up...Jack and Mary play husband and wife for commercial...Kenny is late, Jack explains snow to Kenny Baker...skit Murder at the Movies...need to clean up the cops in the town...Mamie calls to report a murder at Bijou Theatre...killer ran into theatre, gun was smoking so Kenny made him sit in loge...police spot killer, but O'Benny stops them when "Artists and Models" starts screening...killer confesses because he doesn't want to sit through the picture..."We're a little late, so good night folks"

Cast:

Last name	First name	Roles	Guest star
?	Erik	Killer	No
Baker	Kenny	Kenny Baker	No
Baldwin	Harry	Ticket taker	No
Beloin	Ed	Police announcer, man who wants to lie down	No
Benny	Jack	Jack Benny, Mr. Homer T. Griddle, Captain O'Benny	No
Brown	John	Newsreel announcer	No
Harris	Phil	Phil Harris, Sergeant Harris	No
Kelly	Mary	Rosie Nicholson	No
Livingstone	Mary	Mary Livingstone, Mrs. Homer T. Griddle, Mamie Livingstone	No
Morrow	Bill	Ticket seller	No
Wilson	Don	Don Wilson, Lieutenant Wilson	No

Songs:

Order	Title	Performers	Vocal
1	For No Rhyme or Reason	Phil Harris	No
2	Pocketful of Dreams	Phil Harris	No
3	Say It With a Kiss	Kenny Baker	Yes
4	Simple and Sweet	Phil Harris	No

Notes:

Blooper	Jack answers phone with "Hello, police headquarters" but is speaking away from the mike and has to repeat the line
Notable	Although never discussed on the show, Jack had to return to New York for these shows due to the hearings on his smuggling case. Kenny Baker was also called as a witness during these hearings.
Skit	Murder at the Movies

Date: 12/11/1938   **Sponsor:** Jell-O   **City:** New York, NY
Recording Source: Unknown   **Problems:** None

First line:
And now ladies and gentlemen, we bring you a man who came to New York in the middle of winter without an overcoat and still hasn't bought one, Jack Benny.

Summary:
From Radio City, New York...Phil hired an orchestra that belongs to Fred Allen...Jack saw Olsen and Johnson's "Heckzapoppin"...Mary visits her family, they're having trouble with the landlord...Mary reads a letter from her mother...Kenny borrowed $10 from Don to see the World's Fair...Jack wants to play a violin solo, can't get together with orchestra...Door guy is sorry Jack isn't playing the violin...Jack keeps his money in his sock...Jack needs to complete his Christmas shopping...Rochester calls, he's in Harlem...Rochester's friends threw a banquet in his honor last Wednesday, it isn't over...Rochester borrowed Jack's full dress suit...Jack and Mary go shopping...Jack shops for perfume...Jack gets hassled by floorwalker...Mary talks Jack into buying an overcoat...meet Rochester and his girlfriend shopping...salesmen try to sell Jack a coat that's too big...salesmen shoot Mary's new hat that looks like a wild duck...Jack really does have a coat

Cast:

Last name	First name	Roles	Guest star
?	Amanda	Lucille Garbo	No
Anderson	Eddie	Rochester	No
Baldwin	Harry	Door guy	No
Beloin	Ed	Piano player, necktie clerk, Joe	No
Benny	Jack	Jack Benny	No
Brown	John	Mr. Peters	No
Cantor	Charles	Floorwalker	No
Harris	Phil	Phil Harris	No
Kelly	Mary	Perfume clerk	No
Livingstone	Mary	Mary Livingstone	No
Morrow	Bill	Pickpocket	No
Wilson	Don	Don Wilson	No

Songs:

Order	Title	Performers	Vocal
1	Hooray for Hollywood	Phil Harris	No
2	Pocketful of Dreams	Phil Harris	Yes
3	F.D.R. Jones	Phil Harris	No
4	All Ashore	Phil Harris	No

Notes:

Blooper	Phil jumps his cue on the line "Maybe they jumped their cue"
Blooper	Pickpocket misses his cue for line "You do too"
Blooper	Jack stumbles on the line, "Don, I'll see you later"
Notable	Kenny was called as a witness against Jack in his smuggling case...not sure if there's a connection between that and his absence on this show
Running gag	Mary's mother communication

Date: 12/18/1938 **Sponsor:** Jell-O **City:** Hollywood, CA
Recording Source: Unknown **Problems:** None

First line:
And now ladies and gentlemen, Jack Benny and his gang, who are en route from New York to Hollywood, have reached Chicago. So we pick them up at the station where they are about to board the train going west. Take it away!

Summary:
Opening done by Mel Ruick…Jack and Rochester at Chicago train station…boy hassles Jack about his coat…redcaps are picketing Rochester for carrying Jack's bags…Jack is wearing Rochester's coat…Jack got a shave and haircut from a lady barber…Rochester checked Kenny Baker in as a parcel so he doesn't get lost…Jack going to play Julius Caesar in the spring…Kenny riding half fare, conductor questions whether he's 12 years old…Mary chats with psychiatrist…Don talks in his sleep about Jell-O…Rochester tells porter Sylvester that he writes Jack's radio program…Jack claims he doesn't take things from hotels…Jack tips porter $10, didn't have his glasses on…Andy Devine meets gang at the station…smart-mouth kid turns out to be Andy Devine's nephew…Andy's parents are decorating their Christmas tree…final train announcement has train going to Mars…Jack going to give Mary tickets to "Artists and Models Abroad" which opens next week

Cast:

Last name	First name	Roles	Guest star
?	Eric	Boy	No
Anderson	Eddie	Rochester	No
Baker	Kenny	Kenny Baker	No
Beloin	Ed	Train announcer	No
Benny	Jack	Jack Benny	No
Devine	Andy	Andy Devine	No
Franz	Joe	Conductor	No
Harris	Phil	Phil Harris	No
Livingstone	Mary	Mary Livingstone	No
Nelson	Frank	Magazine seller	No
Ruick	Mel	Mr. Thompson	No
Ruick	Mel	Opening announcer	No
Stewart	Blanche	Flossie	No
Taylor	?	Sylvester	No
Wilson	Don	Don Wilson	No

Songs:

Order	Title	Performers	Vocal
1	Your Eyes are Bigger Than Your Heart	Phil Harris	No
2	I Go For That	Phil Harris	No
3	Diane	Kenny Baker	Yes
4	Unidentified	Phil Harris	No

Notes:

Date: 12/25/1938   **Sponsor:** Jell-O   **City:** Hollywood, CA

Recording Source: Unknown   **Problems:** None

First line:
And now ladies and gentlemen, this being Christmas Day, we look in on Jack Benny's home in Beverly Hills where he's holding open house for all his friends. Take it away!

Summary:
Jack is decorating the tree...drying his socks on the tree...finds squirrel in the top of the tree...Phil's orchestra shows up...Jack invited a number of celebrities and Barbara Whitney...Kenny gives Jack musical handkerchiefs...Jack got Rochester a vacuum cleaner...regret telegram from Robert Taylor and Barbara Stanwyck...regret telegram from Ronald Colman ("Dear Sir")...Jack falls off the ladder when Barbara arrives with Don...Jack gets Andy Devine to play Santa Claus...regret telegram from Clark Gable and Carole Lombard...Jack can't get anyone to dance with him...Phil shows up with Joan Bennett as his date...Jack falls off the ladder again...every time Rochester lights the gas, the turkey blows it out...Jack went to see his own movie 12 times...Jack kisses Joan Bennett under the mistletoe...Andy Devine gets stuck in the chimney

Cast:

Last name	First name	Roles	Guest star
?	Barbara	Barbara Whitney	No
Anderson	Eddie	Rochester	No
Baker	Kenny	Kenny Baker	No
Baldwin	Harry	Squirrel	No
Bennett	Joan	Joan Bennett	Yes
Benny	Jack	Jack Benny	No
Devine	Andy	Andy Devine	No
Harris	Phil	Phil Harris	No
Livingstone	Mary	Mary Livingstone	No
Wilson	Don	Don Wilson	No

Songs:

Order	Title	Performers	Vocal
1	This Can't Be Love	Phil Harris	No
2	Oh Little Town of Bethlehem - Away in a Manger - Oh Come All Ye Faithful	Kenny Baker	Yes
3	I Go For That	Phil Harris	No
4	Love I'd Give My Life for You	Phil Harris	No

Notes:

Blooper	Andy Devine stumbles on line "That's for your hair as you're going by", has trouble regaining composure
Notable	First time Ronald Colman is presented as Jack's neighbor, in back of Jack's house

Date: 1/1/1939   **Sponsor:** Jell-O   **City:** Hollywood, CA

Recording Source: Unknown   **Problems:** None

First line:
And now ladies and gentlemen, this being the first day of the new year, it behooves me to introduce the star of this program in a manner befitting his dignity and position.

Summary:
Gang discusses how they spent New Year's Eve…Jack took Mary to the Wilshire Bowl where Phil Harris is playing…Jack complains about their table at the Wilshire Bowl…Mary writes and reads poem "Goodbye 1938, Hello 1939"…Door guy recites poem…Phil gave Jack a porthole for Christmas…Kenny slept in folding bed, forgot to pull it down…last year at the Rose Bowl, Jack waved a pennant for Waukegan High School…Phil wants to bet Jack on the Rose Bowl…Rochester calls, can't find Jack's tickets to the Rose Bowl…Rochester claims he needs tomorrow off to go to a wedding in Pasadena…still trying to pick out Scarlett O'Hara…next week going to redo "Snow White and the Seven Dwarves" with Andy as Prince Charming

Cast:

Last name	First name	Roles	Guest star
?	Billy	New Year 1939	No
Anderson	Eddie	Rochester	No
Baker	Kenny	Kenny Baker	No
Baldwin	Harry	Door guy	No
Beloin	Ed	Moon	No
Benny	Jack	Jack Benny, 1938	No
Devine	Andy	Andy Devine, Old Man Mars	No
Harris	Phil	Phil Harris	No
Livingstone	Mary	Mary Livingstone, Mrs. 1938	No
Wilson	Don	Don Wilson	No

Songs:

Order	Title	Performers	Vocal
1	No Wonder	Phil Harris	No
2	Say It With a Kiss	Phil Harris	No
3	I Promise You	Kenny Baker	Yes
4	It's the Strangest Thing	Phil Harris	No

Notes:

Blooper	Jack blows the line, "They're still wearing single-breasted tuxedos"
Notable	First "new tenant" skit
Running gag	Mary's poem
Skit	The New Tenant

Date: 1/8/1939 **Sponsor:** Jell-O **City:** Hollywood, CA

Recording Source: Unknown **Problems:** None

First line:
And now ladies and gentlemen, we bring you that Don Juan, that Casanova, that answer to a maiden's prayer, Jack Benny.

Summary:
Jack talks about the girls he dates...Kenny was in a phone booth talking to his girl, but someone wanted to use the phone and they had to get out...none of the gang heard Jack announce Snow White last week...giving listeners genuine solid gold soup knife...skit Snow White and the Seven Gangsters...gangsters plan to rob a bank...Prince Charming says that he'll take Snow White to his castle in Van Nuys...Prince's horse, "Heigh ho, Sliver"...Snow White runs away from Agatha Witch, runs into woods...Snow White stumbles on gangsters, talks them out of holding up bank...Harry Baldwin takes over as Prince Charming...Prince Charming offers to take Snow White to the booby hatch...Jack had to run to another broadcast, so Mary does show close

Cast:

Last name	First name	Roles	Guest star
Baker	Kenny	Kenny Baker, Dopey	No
Baldwin	Harry	Dynamite deliverer, Prince Charming (2)	No
Beloin	Ed	Sneezy, silver fox	No
Benny	Jack	Jack Benny, Doc, worm	No
Devine	Andy	Andy Devine, Prince Charming (1)	No
Harris	Phil	Phil Harris, Sleepy	No
Livingstone	Mary	Mary Livingstone, Snow White	No
Morrow	Bill	Grumpy	No
Nazarro	Cliff	Bashful	No
Stewart	Blanche	Agatha Witch	No
Wilson	Don	Don Wilson, Happy	No

Songs:

Order	Title	Performers	Vocal
1	It Serves You Right	Phil Harris	No
2	One Song	Kenny Baker	Yes
3	Heigh Ho	Jack Benny	Yes
4	Some Day My Prince Will Come	Mary Livingstone	Yes
4	Some Day My Prince Will Come	Andy Devine	Yes
5	Whistle While You Work	Jack Benny	Yes
6	Some Day My Prince Will Come	Mary Livingstone	Yes
6	Some Day My Prince Will Come	Harry Baldwin	Yes
7	Simple and Sweet	Phil Harris	No
8	I'm Wishing	Mary Livingstone	Yes
8	I'm Wishing	Andy Devine	Yes

Notes:

Skit	Snow White and the Seven Gangsters

Date: 1/15/1939 **Sponsor:** Jell-O **City:** Hollywood, CA

Recording Source: Unknown **Problems:** None

First line:
And now ladies and gentlemen, we turn back the clock and take you to the drug store across the street from the NBC building here in Hollywood. The time is exactly fifteen minutes before this broadcast. Take it away, drug store.

Summary:
Jack and Mary at the drug store before the broadcast...Gilroy and Radcliffe are drug store clerks...they refuse to serve Jack a businessman's lunch because he's not a businessman...Door guy gets aspirin repeatedly...Jack gets Don to get on the scale, it breaks...gang discusses Fred Allen hassling Jack on last program...woman brought her dog to the broadcast...Phil calls Jack "Jackson" because it's as close as he can get to "jackass" and still be polite...Jack performed on "Screen Actors' Guild" with Joan Crawford last week...Jack bent Joan over to kiss her, his toupee fell in her face and she fainted...Kenny counts his toes...Phil and Mary decide to have their own show, Phil asks Kenny to be the singer on it...writers on Phil's show will be Noel Coward and Maxie Rosenbloom...Kenny asks if Joan Crawford is as beautiful as she looks...next week's skit is Encyclopedia Britannica...Jack gets perfume for Joan Crawford...Rochester can't pick up Jack, tires are flat..."We're a little late, so goodnight folks"

Cast:

Last name	First name	Roles	Guest star
Anderson	Eddie	Rochester	No
Baker	Kenny	Kenny Baker	No
Baldwin	Harry	Door guy	No
Beloin	Ed	Radcliffe	No
Benny	Jack	Jack Benny	No
Gilly	?	Dog	No
Harris	Phil	Phil Harris	No
Livingstone	Mary	Mary Livingstone	No
Nelson	Frank	Opening announcer, Gilroy	No
Stewart	Blanche	Dog owner	No
Wilson	Don	Don Wilson	No

Songs:

Order	Title	Performers	Vocal
1	Go South Young Man/Joobalai	Phil Harris	No
2	Could Be/This Can't Be Love	Phil Harris	No
3	Deep in a Dream	Kenny Baker	Yes
4	Unidentified	Phil Harris	No

Notes:

Blooper	Kenny says, "Boy, have I been put onning weight"
Notable	First time Phil calls Jack "Jackson"

Date: 1/22/1939   **Sponsor:** Jell-O   **City:** Hollywood, CA

Recording Source: Unknown   **Problems:** None

First line:
And now ladies and gentlemen, we bring you a man who used to be a beautiful baby, Jack Benny.

Summary:
Don looked at Jack's family album…Jack's father ran a combination meat market and clothing store…Kenny says he was a smart kid…Phil is going to leave Jack's program, Jack gets concerned…Phil had offer for sponsorship from a corn plaster ("half the time you're corny, and the other half you're plastered")…Andy's girlfriend weighs 300 pounds, she's a plumber in Van Nuys…Jack starts praising Phil…Fred Allen challenged Jack to a fight…Jack says he saved Fred Allen's life 12 years ago in vaudeville…flashback, Jack encourages Allen as he follows Fink's Mules…Fred drops a cannonball on his foot, Jack takes him to a hospital…Jack donates his blood to save Fred's life..Fred starts thinking of jokes after getting Jack's blood…Jack promos March of Dimes

Cast:

Last name	First name	Roles	Guest star
Baker	Kenny	Kenny Baker	No
Baldwin	Harry	Audience member 2	No
Beloin	Ed	Audience member 1, stagehand	No
Benny	Jack	Jack Benny	No
Devine	Andy	Andy Devine	No
Harris	Phil	Phil Harris	No
Hayes	Peter Lind	Fred Allen	No
Livingstone	Mary	Mary Livingstone	No
Nelson	Frank	Doctor	No
Stewart	Blanche	Screamer, nurse	No
Wilson	Don	Don Wilson	No

Songs:

Order	Title	Performers	Vocal
1	This Is It	Phil Harris	No
2	Penny Serenade	Kenny Baker	Yes
3	This Can't Be Love	Phil Harris	No
4	This Night Will Be My Souvenir	Phil Harris	No

Notes:

Date: 1/29/1939   **Sponsor:** Jell-O   **City:** Hollywood, CA

Recording Source: Unknown   **Problems:** None

First line:
And now ladies and gentlemen, in this corner at 143 pounds we bring you that Waukegan bomber, Jack Benny.

Summary:
Jack trying to get back into shape...Fred Allen has been making threats, alluding to boxing match...Phil still working on getting his own program...Phil sings theme song for Bixby's Bubble Gum...Mary sings middle song, "Thanks for the Bubble Gum"...Jack saw Fred Allen wearing Portland's gown...Door guy is a female impersonator...Don has written a play...Fred Allen was ashamed to be a juggler in vaudeville...Jack goes to work out in Andy Devine's barn...Rochester drives Jack and Mary, runs Maxwell into the barn...Rochester and Jack box, Rochester knocks out Jack's bridge work

Cast:

Last name	First name	Roles	Guest star
Anderson	Eddie	Rochester	No
Baker	Kenny	Kenny Baker	No
Baldwin	Harry	Door guy	No
Beloin	Ed	Oliver	No
Benny	Jack	Jack Benny, Mr. Average American	No
Devine	Andy	Andy Devine	No
Harris	Phil	Phil Harris	No
Livingstone	Mary	Mary Livingstone, Mrs. Average American	No
Stewart	Blanche	Screamer	No
Wilson	Don	Don Wilson	No

Songs:

Order	Title	Performers	Vocal
1	Joobalai	Phil Harris	No
2	Umbrella Man	Phil Harris	No
3	I Dream of Jeannie With the Light Brown Hair	Kenny Baker	Yes
4	It's the Strangest Thing	Phil Harris	No

Notes:

Date: 2/5/1939   **Sponsor:** Jell-O   **City:** Hollywood, CA

Recording Source: Unknown   **Problems:** None

First line:
And now ladies and gentlemen, tonight we bring you…oh, just a moment folks. Mary, Mary, where's Jack?

Summary:
Jack trying to send a telegram to Fred Allen to threaten him…gang talks about how stingy Fred Allen is…Phil had trouble with his sponsor, decided not to leave…Kenny finally made a date with the waitress…announces skit Hop-a-Lung Cassidy…Jack has a bodyguard, Aubrey Mulligan…Aubrey reads middle commercial…Rochester calls, Fred Allen sent collect telegram to his home…man is prowling around Jack's back yard…Aubrey's car runs out of gas, Jack and Mary have to walk home…three mugs hold up Jack, rip off his pants…Jack runs home in his BVDs, runs into Barbara Stanwyck…New York World Telegram poll again honored Jack

Cast:

Last name	First name	Roles	Guest star
Anderson	Eddie	Rochester	No
Baker	Kenny	Kenny Baker	No
Baker	Wally	Professor Kingsley	No
Beloin	Ed	Western Meat Market guy, telegram boy	No
Benaderet	Bea	Western Union operator	No
Benny	Jack	Jack Benny	No
Harris	Phil	Phil Harris	No
Lewis	Elliott	Aubrey Mulligan	No
Livingstone	Mary	Mary Livingstone	No
Ross	?	Dr. Thorndyke	No
Stewart	Blanche	Operator, Barbara Stanwyck	No
Wilson	Don	Don Wilson	No

Songs:

Order	Title	Performers	Vocal
1	Just One of Those Things	Phil Harris	No
2	One O'Clock Jump	Phil Harris	No
3	Please Come Out of Your Dream	Kenny Baker	Yes
4	Jeepers Creepers	Phil Harris	No
5	I Cried for You	Phil Harris	No

Notes:

Date: 2/12/1939   **Sponsor:** Jell-O   **City:** Hollywood, CA

Recording Source: Unknown   **Problems:** None

First line:
And now ladies and gentlemen, Tuesday being Valentine's Day and also Jack Benny's birthday, let us welcome our little cupid with that old familiar greeting. Are you ready?

Summary:
Crowd sings "Happy Birthday" to Jack...Jack discusses how it's hard to be outstanding with other significant birthdays in February...gang guesses Jack's age...Mary brings Jack a silk tie with a silkworm because it's not finished yet...Mary reads a poem for Jack...Door guy wishes Jack a happy birthday...Remley taught Phil a new word...Kenny brought Jack a box of candy...Fred Allen has poor blood circulation...Rochester calls, a large box arrived containing a polar bear...skit Love Finds Annie Hardy...Baker consents to marry Annie...Annie returns from beauty parlor already married to travelling salesman...Jack congratulates Boy Scouts on 29th birthday

Cast:

Last name	First name	Roles	Guest star
Anderson	Eddie	Rochester	No
Baker	Kenny	Kenny Baker, Daffy Baker	No
Baldwin	Harry	Door guy	No
Beloin	Ed	Frankie Remley	No
Benny	Jack	Jack Benny, Zeke Hardy	No
Harris	Phil	Phil Harris, Twitch Harris	No
Livingstone	Mary	Mary Livingstone, Ma Hardy	No
Nazarro	Cliff	Travelling salesman	No
Stewart	Blanche	Miss Mildew, Annie Hardy	No
Wilson	Don	Don Wilson, Tubby Wilson	No

Songs:

Order	Title	Performers	Vocal
1	Sing My Heart	Phil Harris	No
2	I'd Better Get Some Shut Eye	Phil Harris	No
3	Thanks for Everything	Kenny Baker	Yes
4	Unidentified	Phil Harris	No

Notes:

Notable	First mention of polar bear
Running gag	Mary's poem
Skit	Love Finds Annie Hardy

Date: 2/191939 **Sponsor:** Jell-O **City:** Hollywood, CA

Recording Source: Unknown **Problems:** None

First line:
And now ladies and gentlemen, next Thursday evening, February the 23rd, the winners of the annual Academy Awards for distinguished achievement in motion pictures will be announced.

Summary:
Jack discusses his chances at the Academy Awards...no one saw "Artists and Models Abroad"...Don gets mad and goes out for a smoke...telegram from Jack's father in Miami Beach, says everyone there thinks Jack will win an Academy Award...Fred Allen is a ham in movies...Jack keeps bragging about his acting, Kenny gets mad and leaves...Andy brings Jack and hand-painted sofa pillow from his mother...Jack is trying to train the polar bear...not sure who sent the bear, but he turned off Fred Allen's program...next week going to do "Jesse James", presents previews...Rochester calls, wants to quit because of polar bear...Rochester locks Carmichael in the garage, he's now driving the car...finally returns with car and a policeman in his mouth

Cast:

Last name	First name	Roles	Guest star
Anderson	Eddie	Rochester	No
Baker	Kenny	Kenny Baker	No
Beloin	Ed	Telegram boy	No
Beloin	Ed	Jesse James' sidekick	No
Benny	Jack	Jack Benny	No
Devine	Andy	Andy Devine	No
Harris	Phil	Phil Harris	No
Livingstone	Mary	Mary Livingstone, Zerelda	No
Stewart	Blanche	Jesse James' mother	No
Wilson	Don	Don Wilson	No

Songs:

Order	Title	Performers	Vocal
1	It's All Yours	Phil Harris	No
2	Stardust	Kenny Baker	Yes
3	Hold Tight	Phil Harris	No
4	We'll Never Know	Phil Harris	No

Notes:

Notable	First show where polar bear is named Carmichael

Date: 2/26/1939 **Sponsor:** Jell-O **City:** Hollywood, CA

Recording Source: Unknown **Problems:** None

First line:
And now ladies and gentlemen, last Sunday night we brought you a man who thought he was going to win the Motion Picture Academy Award this year, and he didn't.

Summary:
Jack upset that he didn't win an Academy Award...Fred Allen has worn the same shoes since he was 12 years old...skit Jesse James...Jesse and Juicy James are brothers...Jesse milks the cow...Zerelda tells them that railroad men are trying to buy the farm...Jesse faces down railroad men...railroad builds tracks through James' house, trains keep coming through the living room during breakfast...trains coming opposite directions collide in living room...Jesse decides to move...Carmichael has a cold

Cast:

Last name	First name	Roles	Guest star
Baker	Kenny	Kenny Baker, President St. Louis Midland Railroad	No
Beloin	Ed	Sound effects man, Sam the engineer	No
Benny	Jack	Jack Benny, Jesse James	No
Devine	Andy	Andy Devine, Juicy James	No
Felton	Verna	Jesse James' mother	No
Harris	Phil	Phil Harris, Marshee	No
Livingstone	Mary	Mary Livingstone, Zerelda	No
Wilson	Don	Don Wilson	No

Songs:

Order	Title	Performers	Vocal
1	San Francisco	Phil Harris	No
2	This Night Will Be My Souvenir	Kenny Baker	Yes
3	I've Been Working on the Railroad/Oh Susanna	Phil Harris	No
4	I Long to Belong to You	Phil Harris	No

Notes:

Blooper	Don says "Jell-er" in the closing commercial
Skit	Jesse James

Date: 3/5/1939 **Sponsor:** Jell-O **City:** Hollywood, CA

Recording Source: Unknown **Problems:** None

First line:
And now ladies and gentlemen, we bring you that well-known plunger who lost $2 on the big race at Santa Anita yesterday, grief-stricken Jack Benny.

Summary:
Jack lost $2 at Santa Anita, tried to get it back by telling the man he was under 21...Jack tells Don he'll have a satchel full of something during play, Don guesses it's Grape Nuts...Jack says he has to strap Phil's guitar player (Remley) down before he says "Hello" to him, he laughs so much...Darryl Zanuck is in the third row...Rochester calls, Carmichael is scratching everything in the house...turns out Mary had $1 of Jack's bet, and Rochester had the other $1...skit Jesse James...Jesse has become a train robber, wife Zerelda is knitting him a bullet-proof sweater...Juicy brings "Wanted" poster of Jesse...horses have to stop for stoplights...Juicy makes noise like a train whistle to get the train to stop...Fred Allen is on train, carrying $150,000 in pennies...Phil Harris holds up and shoots Jesse

Cast:

Last name	First name	Roles	Guest star
Anderson	Eddie	Rochester	No
Baker	Kenny	Kenny Baker, President St. Louis Midland Railroad	No
Baldwin	Harry	Program seller	No
Beloin	Ed	Darryl Zanuck	No
Benny	Jack	Jack Benny, Jesse James	No
Devine	Andy	Andy Devine, Juicy James	No
Harris	Phil	Phil Harris	No
Hayes	Peter Lind	Gangbuster, Fred Allen	No
Livingstone	Mary	Mary Livingstone, Zerelda	No
Stewart	Blanche	Screamer, Old maid	No
Wilson	Don	Don Wilson, salesman	No

Songs:

Order	Title	Performers	Vocal
1	Mr. And Mrs. America	Phil Harris	No
2	Memory Lane	Kenny Baker	Yes
3	Casey Jones	Phil Harris	No
4	Dying Zerelda	Andy Devine	Yes
4	Dying Zerelda	Jack Benny	Yes
5	Old Drum	Phil Harris	No

Notes:

Blooper	Jack calls Andy Devine "Jesse" instead of "Juicy"
Notable	First time you can distinctly hear Remley's laugh, after jokes about him laughing so much
Skit	Jesse James

Date: 3/12/1939   **Sponsor:** Jell-O   **City:** Hollywood, CA

Recording Source: Unknown   **Problems:** None

First line:
Jack: That was Fine and Dandy played by the orchestra. And now ladies and gentlemen, I bring you a man...

Summary:
Don's 16th anniversary in radio, wants a raise...Don was known as "Happy Don, the Muscle Builder"...Phil started in radio with hillbilly band, the Blue Ridge Blue Blowers...Mary reads letter from her mother...Mary's sister married a tree surgeon...Kenny's mother thinks he's Frank Parker...gang discusses income tax, Mary wrote a poem on the back of her check...Jack was on cover of Radio Guide, training to fight Allen...Rochester calls, tried to give Carmichael a bath since he has a cold...Jack decides to go home to take care of Carmichael...Jack drives Mary and Kenny in the Maxwell...Jack runs a stoplight and gets pulled over...Jack tells cop about Carmichael, he thinks he's drunk...gets ticket for running light, talking back, and expired license plates...Rochester put Jack's pajamas on Carmichael...Jack tries to give Carmichael cough medicine...Carmichael chases everyone out of the room...25th anniversary of the American Legion

Cast:

Last name	First name	Roles	Guest star
Anderson	Eddie	Rochester	No
Baker	Kenny	Kenny Baker	No
Benny	Jack	Jack Benny	No
Blanc	Mel	Carmichael	No
Harris	Phil	Phil Harris	No
Lewis	Elliott	Officer	No
Livingstone	Mary	Mary Livingstone	No
Wilson	Don	Don Wilson	No

Songs:

Order	Title	Performers	Vocal
1	Fine and Dandy	Phil Harris	No
2	Begin the Beguine	Kenny Baker	Yes
3	My Heart Belongs to Daddy	Phil Harris	No
4	We've Gone a Long Way Together	Phil Harris	No

Notes:

Blooper	Mary jumps her cue with "What's that, a mockingbird?"
Notable	First time Carmichael speaks
Running gag	Mary's poem
Running gag	Mary's mother communication

Date: 3/19/1939   **Sponsor:** Jell-O   **City:** Hollywood, CA

Recording Source: Unknown   **Problems:** None

First line:
And now ladies and gentlemen, every Sunday at this time, it is my custom to bring you Jack Benny. Tonight however, Jack is confined to his house with a slight cold.

Summary:
Jack caught a cold from Carmichael…Rochester caring for Carmichael and Jack in twin beds…nurse is in the kitchen playing cards with Swing Hi, the cook…Jack playing checkers with Carmichael…Mary stops by to see Jack…Phil hosting the show with hipster talk…Fred had the "real Jack Benny" on his program, says Jack is Maxwell Stroud…nurse asks Mary if she's still with the May Company…Jack questions Rochester about accounts…Jack can't fire Rochester because he has letters Jack wrote to Garbo…Phil forward announces song as "Mother Feeds the Baby Garlic So She Can Find Him In the Dark"…doing a skit called "Buck Harris Rides Again", Kenny Baker to play Daisy…doctor taps Jack's chest with a polo mallet…doctor diagnoses Carmichael and Jack with measles

Cast:

Last name	First name	Roles	Guest star
Baker	Kenny	Kenny Baker, Daisy Carson	No
Benny	Jack	Jack Benny	No
Blanc	Mel	Carmichael	No
Harris	Phil	Phil Harris, Buck Harris	No
Livingstone	Mary	Mary Livingstone	No
Nelson	Frank	Doctor Nelson	No
Stewart	Blanche	Minnie LaToosh nurse	No
Wilson	Don	Don Wilson	No

Songs:

Order	Title	Performers	Vocal
1	This is It	Phil Harris	No
2	A Little Bit of Heaven	Kenny Baker	Yes
3	Honolulu	Phil Harris	No
4	In a Moment of Weakness	Phil Harris	No

Notes:

Notable	First goofy song title

Date: 3/26/1939 **Sponsor:** Jell-O **City:** Hollywood, CA

Recording Source: Unknown **Problems:** None

First line:
And now ladies and gentlemen, we bring you our Master of Ceremonies, that suave comedian and sophisticated humorist, Maxwell Stroud.

Summary:
Spring weather has improved Jack's cold...Jack taking Carmichael for walks on Hollywood Boulevard, Jack plays his violin and Carmichael has a tin cup...Mary reads poem about spring...Kenny upset because he didn't win the Irish sweepstakes...Ed Sullivan stops by, Jack introduces him to the gang...Ed wants the low-down on Maxwell Stroud...Ed says his real name was Edward Hooligan...Waukegan planted elm tree for Jack, Jack tells Sullivan to call Mancel Talcott for proof that he's the real Jack Benny, Sullivan says he tried but Talcott won't come down out of the tree...skit hotel murder mystery...Hotel Chafing Dish in Sterno, PA...guests arrive...Mary keeps saying "Yes" into phone, Jack asks who it is, Mary answers "My darling daughter", Jack says, "How is Joanie?"...guest arrives on way to New York, it's Maxwell Stroud going to expose Fred Allen...Ed Sullivan shows up looking for Maxwell Stroud...Stroud is killed in his room, murderer jumps out window and drops derby with initials "F.A"...murderer shoots Jack..."We're a little late folks, good night."

Cast:

Last name	First name	Roles	Guest star
Baker	Kenny	Kenny Baker, Waldemar	No
Baldwin	Harry	Mr. Baldome	No
Benny	Jack	Jack Benny, clerk	No
Harris	Phil	Phil Harris	No
Lewis	Elliott	Maxwell Stroud	No
Livingstone	Mary	Mary Livingstone, operator Miss LaVonce	No
Nelson	Frank	Napoleon guest	No
Stewart	Blanche	Screamer, Sophie	No
Sullivan	Ed	Ed Sullivan	Yes
Wilson	Don	Don Wilson, Junior Wilson	No

Songs:

Order	Title	Performers	Vocal
1	Jericho	Phil Harris	No
2	I'm Gonna Get Some Shut Eye	Phil Harris	No
3	Deep Purple	Kenny Baker	Yes
4	This Night Will Be My Souvenir	Phil Harris	No

Notes:

Blooper	Phil misses his cue for "You just ain't mod-ren, that's all."
Notable	First mention of Joan Benny by name
Running gag	Mary's poem
Running gag	Baby talk Jell-O flavors
Skit	Hotel murder mystery

Date: 4/2/1939   **Sponsor:** Jell-O   **City:** Hollywood, CA

Recording Source: Unknown   **Problems:** None

First line:
And now folks, you all know last Wednesday night, Clark Gable and Carole Lombard eloped to Kingman, Arizona and were married. So tonight ladies and gentlemen, we bring you the man that held the ladder, Jack Benny.

Summary:
Jack thought Lombard wanted to elope with him...Jack isn't talking to Rochester...Jack started making "Man About Town"...Mark Sandrich directed Rogers-Astaire pictures, has Jack jumping over furniture...Kenny played April Fool's Gags...telegram from Fred Allen about Jack's new movie...Fred Allen ad libs because he can't read his script...Don has written a play...starving man decides to hold out for Jell-O...Phil comes in late with British accent...Door guy asks Jack if he's Maxwell Stroud...Kenny upset that people other than him sang...Jack mad because Rochester hocked Carmichael...announces skit Topper Takes an Aspirin...Shlepperman has been touring as a musician in vaudeville, opened a nightclub...Rochester calls, got Carmichael out of hock...traded Jack's violin for Carmichael..."We're a little late, so good night folks"

Cast:

Last name	First name	Roles	Guest star
Anderson	Eddie	Rochester	No
Baker	Kenny	Kenny Baker	No
Baldwin	Harry	Door guy	No
Beloin	Ed	Telegram boy	No
Benny	Jack	Jack Benny, Luke Miller	No
Harris	Phil	Phil Harris	No
Hearn	Sam	Schlepperman	No
Lewis	Elliott	Prospector	No
Livingstone	Mary	Mary Livingstone, Tess Miller	No
Wilson	Don	Don Wilson	No

Songs:

Order	Title	Performers	Vocal
1	Mr. And Mrs. America	Phil Harris	No
2	Little Old Hot Dog Stand	Kenny Baker	Yes
3	I Go For That	Phil Harris	Yes
3	I Go For That	Jack Benny	Yes
3	I Go For That	Mary Livingstone	Yes
4	This Night Will Be My Souvenir	Phil Harris	No

Notes:

Blooper	Jack stumbles on the line "I saw a screen test"

Date: 4/9/1939   **Sponsor:** Jell-O   **City:** Hollywood, CA

Recording Source: Unknown   **Problems:** None

First line:
And now ladies and gentlemen, we bring you a man who was the sensation of the Easter parade this morning in his frock coat, white spats, and beanie, Jack Benny.

Summary:
Jack took Carmichael on the Easter Parade with him...Phil and Rochester have the same tailor, Neon Cohen...Mary got a new Easter dress, met a man named Wendell Kendall...Jack and Phil argue about Phil's work in pictures...Phil is going to conduct with his hands like Stokowski...Door guy reads easter poem...Kenny had Easter Egg hunt at his house...Wendell calls Mary, makes a date...skit Four Girls in White...classroom sketch...Dolores breaks Phyllis' arm, class wraps it in gauze, wraps Peaches up too...Doctor has class perform operation on patient with sliver in his finger...patient is Shlepperman...Shlepperman sings as the anesthetic is applied, wakes up with an Irish brogue

Cast:

Last name	First name	Roles	Guest star
Baker	Kenny	Kenny Baker, Peaches Baker	No
Baldwin	Harry	Door guy	No
Beloin	Ed	Program/ticket salesman	No
Benny	Jack	Jack Benny, Dr. DeShnook	No
Harris	Phil	Phil Harris, Phyllis Harris	No
Hearn	Sam	Shlepperman	No
Livingstone	Mary	Mary Livingstone, Marie Livingstone	No
Stewart?	Blanche	Miss Pasadena/LaRose	No
Wilson	Don	Don Wilson, Dolores Wilson	No

Songs:

Order	Title	Performers	Vocal
1	It's All Yours	Phil Harris	No
2	Hold Tight	Phil Harris	No
3	I'm Building a Sailboat of Dreams	Kenny Baker	Yes
4	Little Skipper	Phil Harris	No

Notes:

Notable	First show after the smuggling case verdict
Skit	Four Girls in White

Date: 4/16/1939   **Sponsor:**   Jell-O   **City:**   Hollywood, CA

Recording Source: Unknown   **Problems:**   None

First line:
And now ladies and gentlemen, we bring you our sun-kissed Master of Ceremonies who has just returned from a week's vacation in Palm Springs.

Summary:
Jack stayed at the Bellevue Auto Court...the waffles have numbers on them so you can play bingo until your eggs come...Kenny was in Palm Springs but didn't see much, bought a cowboy hat that was too big for him...stopped production on Jack's picture for a week and suggested Jack go away for a rest...Jack discusses Phil's acting ability...Door guy asks Jack if he thinks Dorothy Lamour is beautiful...Phil sold Kenny a joke for $10...Phil wrote a hipster Jell-O commercial...Phil is late because he's been shooting love scenes at Paramount, Jack upset because he thought they'd suspended production...Jack calls Mr. Hornblow to complain...Rochester drives Jack to Paramount in the Maxwell, has to shut off the engine because the car has no brakes...Jack and Rochester discuss the Joe Louis-Jack Roper fight...Rochester punches out the windshield, crashes car into drive-in...Jack and Mary walk to Paramount, see Mr. Hornblow walking the other way, Jack runs after him

Cast:

Last name	First name	Roles	Guest star
Baker	Kenny	Kenny Baker	No
Baldwin	Harry	Door guy	No
Benny	Jack	Jack Benny	No
Harris	Phil	Phil Harris	No
Livingstone	Mary	Mary Livingstone	No
Stewart	Blanche	Waitress	No
Wilson	Don	Don Wilson	No

Songs:

Order	Title	Performers	Vocal
1	Just One of Those Things	Phil Harris	No
2	Heaven Can Wait	Kenny Baker	Yes
3	Penny Serenade	Phil Harris	No
4	Unidentified	Phil Harris	No

Notes:

Running gag	But but but

Date: 4/23/1939 **Sponsor:** Jell-O **City:** Hollywood, CA

Recording Source: Unknown **Problems:** None

First line:
And now laides and gentlemen, as you all know, Jack Benny and Phil Harris are busy working on a new Paramount picture, "Man About Town", and will not be here today.

Summary:
Rochester helping Jack get dressed at Paramount…Phil has a snooty English butler…Roper lost the fight…Jack tries to borrow a collar button from Phil…Mary comes to watch them work…Phil has a better dressing room than Jack…Jack won't pay his bet on the Louis-Roper fight…Kenny gets in to see Jack by saying he's his business manager…Phil told Kenny that Jack is playing the part of a janitor…Jack has almost nothing to do in a scene with Phil, gets mad and walks off

Cast:

Last name	First name	Roles	Guest star
		Stage caller	No
?	Paula	Claudette Colbert	No
Anderson	Eddie	Rochester	No
Baker	Kenny	Kenny Baker	No
Beloin	Ed	Twinkle makeup man	No
Benny	Jack	Jack Benny	No
Campbell	?	Elkins	No
Harris	Phil	Phil Harris	No
Hicks	Russell	Mark Sandrich	No
Livingstone	Mary	Mary Livingstone	No
Milford	?	Lady Trumley	No
Stewart	Blanche	Screamer, Binnie Barnes	No
Wilson	Don	Don Wilson	No

Songs:

Order	Title	Performers	Vocal
1	That's What We Do Over Here	Phil Harris	No
2	Strange Enchantment	Kenny Baker	Yes
3	Honolulu	Phil Harris	No
4	Tears from My Inkwell	Phil Harris	No

Notes:

Running gag	But but but

Date: 4/30/1939   **Sponsor:** Jell-O   **City:** Hollywood, CA

Recording Source: Unknown   **Problems:** None

First line:
And now ladies and gentlemen, I would like to announce that this occasion is a gala event on our Jell-O program. Today marks the seventh radio anniversary of our illustrious and beloved Master of Ceremonies.

Summary:
Mary gives Jack socks with a zipper on the side...telegram from Jack's sister, Florence...Kenny is getting corny from hanging around Phil...Jack and Don reminisce about their first broadcasts, then argue...Door guy says he's cured of being nuts...congratulations wire from Fred Allen...Phil is late because he lives in Encino...Phil throwing a party in honor of Jack's anniversary, going to Shlepperman's Hawaiian nightclub...drunk hassles Jack...everyone calls for a violin solo...drunk falls apart as Jack plays "Love in Bloom"...drunk turns out to be a ruse, Phil hired him...congratulations telegram from Lloyd's of London

Cast:

Last name	First name	Roles	Guest star
Baker	Kenny	Kenny Baker	No
Baldwin	Harry	Door guy	No
Beloin	Ed	Telegram boy	No
Benny	Jack	Jack Benny	No
Harris	Phil	Phil Harris	No
Hearn	Sam	Shlepperman	No
Livingstone	Mary	Mary Livingstone	No
Marr	Eddie	Drunk	No
Morrow	Bill	Cab driver	No
Stewart	Blanche	Shlepperman's wife Lotus Blossom	No
Wilson	Don	Don Wilson	No

Songs:

Order	Title	Performers	Vocal
1	Man About Town	Phil Harris	No
2	Our Love	Kenny Baker	Yes
3	Rose of Washington Square	Phil Harris	No
4	I Want to Go Back To My Little Grass Shack	Sam Hearn	Yes
4	I Want to Go Back To My Little Grass Shack	Mary Livingstone	Yes
5	Love in Bloom	Jack Benny	No
6	I'm Building a Sailboat of Dreams	Phil Harris	No

Notes:

Blooper	Jack says, "Hey Shlep, how about the feud?" instead of "how about the food?"
Blooper	Mary says that a telegram just came "from" Jack instead of "for" Jack

355

Date: 5/7/1939 **Sponsor:** Jell-O **City:** Hollywood, CA

Recording Source: Unknown **Problems:** None

First line:
And now ladies and gentlemen, that spring is here and well underway, we bring you a big dose of sulphur and molasses, Jack Benny.

Summary:
Jack talks about taking sulphur and molasses as a kid…Phil Harris sang "Three Little Fishies" on the radio last night…Kenny flirting with the waitress at the sandwich shop…Jack has a dog named Baskerville who guards his lunch…Door guy asks if Phil is going to sing "Three Little Fishies"…Phil wants more brass in his band…Jack takes waitress' phone number away from Kenny…yesterday was running of the Kentucky Derby…waitress is Andy's girlfriend…announces play Weather Clear, Track Fast, Fine Play, Bum Cast…everyone plays horses…Shlepperman plays Abdul the Third, out of Gefilte Girl by Bagel Boy…horses discuss race…Johnstown wins…On Location last, courtesy of Mervyn LeRoy…next week doing Gunga Din

Cast:

Last name	First name	Roles	Guest star
Baker	Kenny	Kenny Baker, On Location	No
Baldwin	Harry	Door guy	No
Beloin	Ed	Horsefly	No
Benny	Jack	Jack Benny, Technician	No
Devine	Andy	Andy Devine, Johnstown	No
Harris	Phil	Phil Harris, El Chico	No
Hearn	Sam	Abdul the Third	No
Livingstone	Mary	Mary Livingstone, Featherbroom	No
Nelson	Frank	Race announcer	No
Stewart	Blanche	Dog	No
Wilson	Don	Don Wilson, Shaladon	No

Songs:

Order	Title	Performers	Vocal
1	Sing My Heart	Phil Harris	No
2	Rose of the Rio Grande	Phil Harris	No
3	Penny Serenade	Kenny Baker	Yes
4	I Cried for You	Phil Harris	No

Notes:

Blooper	Don cracks up on closing announcement
Skit	Weather Clear, Track Fast, Fine Play, Bum Cast

Date: 5/14/1939   **Sponsor:** Jell-O   **City:** Hollywood, CA

Recording Source: Unknown   **Problems:** None

First line:
And now ladies and gentlemen, this being Mothers' Day, we bring you that little old lady, Jack Benny.

Summary:
Jack says he's not fussy...Jack was a Boy Scout...Phil sent his mother a corncob pipe...Kenny doesn't know what day it is...piano player is shaving while Jack introduces the skit...Rochester is teaching Carmichael to skate for vaudeville...skit Gunga Din...Mary reads narration...Gunga doesn't want to be a magician, he wants to be a bugler...Captain sends Gunga and Baker to cross the desert and look for thieves...Gunga Din goes mad after five days in the desert...they find Carmichael on roller skates in the desert...no closing announcements

Cast:

Last name	First name	Roles	Guest star
Anderson	Eddie	Rochester	No
Baker	Kenny	Kenny Baker, Private Baker	No
Baldwin	Harry	Gunga Din's father	No
Beloin	Ed	Lemonade seller	No
Benny	Jack	Jack Benny, Gunga Din	No
Harris	Phil	Phil Harris, Captain Harris	No
Livingstone	Mary	Mary Livingstone, narrator	No
Stewart	Blanche	Mrs. Din	No
Wilson	Don	Don Wilson, Major Wilson	No

Songs:

Order	Title	Performers	Vocal
1	Hooray for Hollywood	Phil Harris	No
2	For My Mother	Kenny Baker	Yes
3	Hindustan/Tiger Rag	Phil Harris	No
4	If I Were Sure of You	Phil Harris	No

Notes:

Skit	Gunga Din

Date: 5/21/1939   **Sponsor:** Jell-O   **City:** Hollywood, CA

Recording Source: Unknown   **Problems:** None

First line:
And now ladies and gentlemen, we bring you our own movie star who has just finished another epic at Paramount and is nervously awaiting the preview, Jack Benny.

Summary:
Jack still complaining that Phil has too much to do in "Man About Town"...Kenny upset because he put a nickel in the apple machine and a worm came out...Mary gets a letter from her mother, thanks Mary for Mother's Day perfume...Phil says that Dorothy Lamour doesn't like doing love scenes with Jack because he's too much of a brute...Mr. Hornblow calls for Jack, wants Rochester in the picture...skit Gunga Din...Gunga and Kenny still in the desert...Gunga and Kenny find bandits...Gunga blows bugle and they are captured by bandits...take prisoners into leader's temple, Wilshire Bowl...leader tortures Gunga and Kenny by singing "Three Little Fishies"...everyone starts talking baby talk...promo for "We the People" on Tuesday night, sponsored by Jell-O Ice Cream Powder

Cast:

Last name	First name	Roles	Guest star
Baker	Kenny	Kenny Baker, Private Baker	No
Beloin	Ed	Special delivery boy, guy on camel	No
Benny	Jack	Jack Benny, Gunga Din	No
Harris	Phil	Phil Harris, leader of Hindu bandits	No
Livingstone	Mary	Mary Livingstone, narrator	No
Wilson	Don	Don Wilson	No

Songs:

Order	Title	Performers	Vocal
1	Roller Skating on a Rainbow	Phil Harris	No
2	Little Skipper	Kenny Baker	Yes
3	The Lady's In Love	Phil Harris	No
4	If I Were Sure of You	Phil Harris	No

Notes:

Running gag	But but but
Running gag	Mary's mother communication
Skit	Gunga Din

Date: 5/28/1939 **Sponsor:** Jell-O **City:** Hollywood, CA

Recording Source: Unknown **Problems:** None

First line:
And now ladies and gentlemen, we bring you Hollywood's newest glamour boy, Jack Benny.

Summary:
Jack is the "Oomph Man"...Rochester has been putting on airs since he's in "Man About Town"...Jack couldn't lift Dorothy Lamour, so she carried him across the threshold...Don's wife calls, wants to know what flavor of Jell-O to serve...Rochester says someone stole Jack's car, doesn't want to go to the police station because he's behind on his alimony...skit Alexander Graham Bell...Bell and assistant Harris working on the telephone...Harris wants Bell to finish the telephone because he got a blonde's number this morning...Door guy interrupts laboratory...Bell and Harris ask for four million dollars from financeer, he starts counting out one dollar at a time...finally paid four years later...Bell tries to demonstrate telephone, calls Baltimore and gets the Boston Meat Market...Shlepperman answers in Baltimore...Jack going to get J. Edgar Hoover to help look for his car

Cast:

Last name	First name	Roles	Guest star
Anderson	Eddie	Rochester	No
Baker	Kenny	Kenny Baker, financeer	No
Baldwin	Harry	Door guy	No
Beloin	Ed	Jo Jo/Sugar Foot, heckler, Darryl Zanuck	No
Benny	Jack	Jack Benny, Alexander Graham Bell	No
Harris	Phil	Phil Harris	No
Hearn	Sam	Shlepperman, Professor Osgood	No
Livingstone	Mary	Mary Livingstone, Mrs. Bell	No
Stewart	Blanche	Boston Meat Market/Melrose Grotto operator	No
Wilson	Don	Don Wilson	No

Songs:

Order	Title	Performers	Vocal
1	You Got Everything	Phil Harris	No
2	Melancholy Mood	Kenny Baker	Yes
3	Snug as a Bug in a Rug	Phil Harris	Yes
4	This is My Dream	Phil Harris	No

Notes:

Notable	Indication that Rochester was married, owes alimony
Skit	Alexander Graham Bell

Date: 6/4/1939 **Sponsor:** Jell-O **City:** Hollywood, CA

Recording Source: Unknown **Problems:** None

First line:
And now ladies and gentlemen, may I present our versatile Master of Cermonies, a comedian who with one subtle gesture, one wistful look, can plumb the depths of your emotions.

Summary:
Gang lauds Jack's acting ability, say he's as good as Paul Muni and Spencer Tracy...turns out to be a conspiracy...Door guy compliments Jack too...gang discusses their cheap date histories...Andy invites gang to his parents' golden wedding anniversary...Andy brings Happy Callahan, a car salesman...Callahan tries to sell Jack a car in China...next week presenting Hound of the Baskervilles, present previews...Jack shorted Rochester on his paycheck, deducted portion because car was stolen and Rochester couldn't be a chauffeur...Rochester shaved all the hair off of Carmichael..."We're a little late, so good night folks."

Cast:

Last name	First name	Roles	Guest star
Anderson	Eddie	Rochester	No
Baker	Kenny	Kenny Baker, Dr. Watson	No
Baldwin	Harry	Door guy	No
Benny	Jack	Jack Benny	No
Cleary	Leo	Happy Callahan	No
Devine	Andy	Andy Devine	No
Harris	Phil	Phil Harris	No
Livingstone	Mary	Mary Livingstone, Lady Beryl	No
Stewart	Blanche	Screamer, dogs	No
Wilson	Don	Don Wilson	No

Songs:

Order	Title	Performers	Vocal
1	Hallelujah	Phil Harris	No
2	New Moon and an Old Serenade	Kenny Baker	Yes
3	My Heart Stood Still	Phil Harris	No
4	Strange Enchantment	Phil Harris	No

Notes:

Blooper	Andy stumbles on line "I was awful sorry when I heard your car was stolen", has trouble regaining composure

Date: 6/11/1939   **Sponsor:** Jell-O   **City:** Hollywood, CA

Recording Source: Unknown   **Problems:** None

First line:
And now ladies and gentlemen, greetings from Hollywood. In just a moment, you will hear from your Hollywood reporter with his frank comments about motion pictures, radio, and their glamourous stars. A man who will startle you with his sensational scoops, and here he is folks, that human dynamo, Jimmy Fiddler Benny.

Summary:
Jack does Hollywood news headlines, recommends "Man About Town"...Kenny fell down an elevator shaft...will be in Waukegan in two weeks...Mary's mother calls, Mary invites her parents to Waukegan...skit Hound of the Baskervilles...Sherlock Holmes complains his cases are too easy...Lady Beryl reports that Sir Hugo Baskerville has been murdered...Madame Zaracky holds a séance so Sir Hugo can say who murdered him...Operator interrupts séance...Phillip confesses to the murder...Jack forgot about the hound

Cast:

Last name	First name	Roles	Guest star
?	Olga	Madame Zaracky	No
Baker	Kenny	Kenny Baker, Dr. Watson	No
Benny	Jack	Jack Benny, Sherlock Holmes	No
Devine	Andy	Andy Devine, hound	No
Harris	Phil	Phil Harris, Phillip Baskerville	No
Livingstone	Mary	Mary Livingstone, Lady Beryl	No
Nazarro	Cliff	Sir Hugo Baskerville	No
Nelson	Frank	Butch the butler	No
Stewart	Blanche	Screamer, operator	No
Wilson	Don	Don Wilson, Dr. Wilson	No

Songs:

Order	Title	Performers	Vocal
1	From Alpha to Omega	Phil Harris	No
2	Hooray for Spinach/Tears From My Inkwell	Phil Harris	No
3	And the Angels Sing	Kenny Baker	Yes
4	Unidentified	Phil Harris	No

Notes:

Running gag	Mary's mother communication
Skit	Hound of the Baskervilles

Date: 6/18/1939 **Sponsor:** Jell-O **City:** Hollywood, CA

Recording Source: Unknown **Problems:** None

First line:
And now ladies and gentlemen, this being Father's Day, we bring you a man who is "Daddy" to a polar bear, Jack Benny.

Summary:
Don is going on a diet...gang criticizes each other's looks...Jack says that he'll stay at Aunt Clara's, Aunt Molly's or Cousin Sudie's in Waukegan...rest of gang staying at the Hotel Wau-ke-GAN...Mary's mother can't come to Waukegan, Mary's father working for an escort service...Mary reads a poem to her father...Kenny put "J. Edgar Hoover" on his suitcase so no one steals it...Door guy wishes Jack a good trip to Waukegan...Jack saw Kenny in "The Mikado" last night...Jack says Heifetz tried to shoot him once...announces skit Lavender and Old Louse...Rochester burned a hole in Jack's new white flannel trousers...Jack wants to take Carmichael to Waukegan...don't have time for skit, need to get to new Union Station...Jack tries to buy tickets to Waukegan...Jack tries to buy a mystery book, ends up with Saturday Evening Post...Andy Devine inquires about train's facilities...Jack's violin teacher is Charlie Lindsay...Rochester shows up at the last minute

Cast:

Last name	First name	Roles	Guest star
Anderson	Eddie	Rochester	No
Baker	Kenny	Kenny Baker	No
Baldwin	Harry	Door guy, train announcer	No
Beloin	Ed	Ticket clerk	No
Benny	Jack	Jack Benny	No
Devine	Andy	Andy Devine	No
Harris	Phil	Phil Harris	No
Livingstone	Mary	Mary Livingstone	No
Nazarro	Cliff	Book salesman	No
Nelson	Frank	Airplane passenger	No
Stewart	Blanche	Aunt Rosie	No
Wilson	Don	Don Wilson	No

Songs:

Order	Title	Performers	Vocal
1	Confidentially	Phil Harris	No
2	Don't Worry About Me	Kenny Baker	Yes
3	If It's Good	Phil Harris	No
4	White Sails In the Sunsest	Phil Harris	No

Notes:

Blooper	Jack loses his place after Mary says, "Jack brought sandwiches"
Running gag	Mary's poem
Running gag	Mary's mother communication

Date: 6/25/1939   **Sponsor:** Jell-O   **City:** Waukegan, IL
Recording Source: Unknown   **Problems:** None

First line:
And now ladies and gentlemen, greetings from Waukegan. Our last broadcast of the season is coming to you from the stage of the Genesee Theatre in Waukegan, Illinois.

Summary:
From the Genesee Theatre in Waukegan, IL...Jack visiting his old hang-outs...mentions Ollie Eimerman, Stubbs Wilbur, Cliff Gordon, Bobby O'Farrell's pool room...went to Julius Sinykin's clothing store...Phil and orchestra got put in jail, palled around with Mayor Bidey Talcott...Jack's birthplace turned into a fish market...Mary saw elm tree planted in Jack's honor...Jack saw Vivan Thompson, his old girlfriend...Mary reads poem about Waukegan...Door guy reads his own poem about Waukegan...Jack and Mary going to Nolan's restaurant to fill up Jack's meal ticket...Mark Sandrich, Dorothy Lamour, and Hedda Hopper in the audience...Mayor Talcott talks like a hipster after being around Phil...Kenny Baker was called back to Hollywood...Talcott told Andy Devine that Chicago was South Waukegan...Jack's father and sister in the audience...Rochester is tired of being cooped up in the hotel...Carmichael putting marmalade on a bellboy...Jack going to New York to see the Louis-Galento fight (June 28)...gang goes into audience to see the movie...The Aldrich Family is Jack's summer replacement, were a feature on Kate Smith show

Cast:

Last name	First name	Roles	Guest star
Anderson	Eddie	Rochester	No
Baldwin	Harry	Door guy	No
Beloin	Ed	Charlie Lindsay	No
Benny	Jack	Jack Benny	No
Devine	Andy	Andy Devine	No
Harris	Phil	Phil Harris	No
Livingstone	Mary	Mary Livingstone	No
Talcott	Mancel	Mayor Mancel "Bidey" Talcott	No
Wilson	Don	Don Wilson	No

Songs:

Order	Title	Performers	Vocal
1	Man About Town	Phil Harris	No
2	Rose of Washington Square	Phil Harris	No
3	The Lady's In Love	Phil Harris	Yes
3	The Lady's in Love	Mary Livingstone	Yes
4	You Grow Sweeter As the Years Go By	Phil Harris	No

Notes:

Blooper	Jack loses his place in the script when Talcott is to start telling jokes
Notable	On previous show, it sounds like Kenny is coming to Waukegan; however, he does not appear. The fact that he was not continuing with the show may have come to light during the intervening week and caused or contributed to this fact.
Running gag	Mary's poem

Date: 10/8/1939   **Sponsor:** Jell-O   **City:** Hollywood, CA

Recording Source: Unknown   **Problems:** None

First line:
Jack: Rochester, step on it or we'll be late for the broadcast.

Summary:
Rochester driving Jack in the Maxwell, going to pick up the gang…1920 Maxwell…Phil picked up at Maizie's Beauty Parlor, hasn't rehearsed his orchestra…see Kenny Baker sitting on his front porch, he's on another program…Don Wilson's mother selling Jell-O in the front yard…Don bought a yacht, lost five pounds…Jack and Rochester toured the country this summer…Door guy looking for the Aldrich Family…heat wave in Hollywood…Mary met a lifeguard in Laguna Beach, Barracuda Jones…Phil makes big entrance…getting a new tenor, Jack tried to use his canary (Dickie Boy) to save money…Dennis Day's mother calls, Dennis is taking a bath…Jack studied the violin for 15 years…Jack asks gang to show him courtesy while Dennis is there…Dennis is 19 years old, shows up with his mother…mother says Dennis was born in Cairo, IL…mother coaches Dennis on singing…Mary wonders what to do on her next vacation

Cast:

Last name	First name	Roles	Guest star
Anderson	Eddie	Rochester	No
Baldwin	Harry	Door guy	No
Benny	Jack	Jack Benny	No
Day	Dennis	Dennis Day	No
Felton	Verna	Mrs. Day	No
Harris	Phil	Phil Harris	No
Livingstone	Mary	Mary Livingstone	No
Stewart	Blanche	Don Wilson's mother	No

Songs:

Order	Title	Performers	Vocal
1	Merry Old Land of Oz	Phil Harris	No
2	Go Fly a Kite	Phil Harris	No
3	Goodnight My Beautiful	Dennis Day	Yes
4	The Lamp is Low	Phil Harris	No

Notes:

Notable	Dennis is not yet announced in the leading credits
Notable	First appearance of Dennis Day
Notable	Maxwell is said to be a 1920 model

Date: 10/15/1939   **Sponsor:** Jell-O   **City:** Hollywood, CA

Recording Source: Unknown   **Problems:** None

First line:
And now folks as you all know, 447 years ago last Thursday, Christopher Columbus discovered America.

Summary:
Jack is tired of cracks about him being cheap...Jack threw a party at the Coconut Grove, took home a tree for lumber...Mary had a strap break during last week's show...Phil graduated from Cornpone Tech...Jack says he doesn't wear a toupee...Jack has Dennis mowing his lawn...Andy drove his parents to the Pomona Fair last week...Andy's mother disappointed, she thought Andy would be the new tenor...Phil got a rave review in the "Musical Courier", says music is "abominable"..."Grocers' Journal" gave Don a good review...Dennis and his mother arrive...Dennis framed his first check from Jack...Jack explains "abominable" to Phil in hipster language...Jack and Mrs. Day argue over what song Dennis will sing...next week presenting "Stanley and Livingston"...Rochester calls, Carmichael has a toothache...Rochester wants to borrow Jack's top hat because he has a date with a tall girl...Door guy says he'll see Jack in the jungle next week...promos Aldrich Family

Cast:

Last name	First name	Roles	Guest star
Anderson	Eddie	Rochester	No
Baldwin	Harry	Door guy	No
Benny	Jack	Jack Benny	No
Day	Dennis	Dennis Day	No
Devine	Andy	Andy Devine	No
Felton	Verna	Mrs. Day	No
Harris	Phil	Phil Harris	No
Livingstone	Mary	Mary Livingstone	No
Wilson	Don	Don Wilson	No

Songs:

Order	Title	Performers	Vocal
1	Baby Me	Phil Harris	No
2	Put That Down in Writing	Phil Harris	No
3	Cinderella Stay In My Arms	Dennis Day	Yes
4	It's a Hundred To One	Phil Harris	No

Notes:

Notable	First announcement of Dennis Day in opening credits
Notable	First use of Dennis' "Yes please?"

Date: 10/22/1939　　**Sponsor:** Jell-O　　　**City:** Hollywood, CA

Recording Source: Unknown　　**Problems:** None

First line:
And now ladies and gentlemen, for the third time this season, we bring you our Master of Ceremonies. A man who smokes a cigar so short that it finally becomes an inlay, Jack Benny.

Summary:
Jack to play Stanley in skit...Dennis is late again...Mary calls a number Jack gives her, it's Gladys...Dennis has been bad and his mother won't let him come to the program, won't eat his carrots...Don finds a cigarette case under the piano, Jack says he'll hold it until the owner comes...Jack wants Dennis to play a cannibal, his mother wants him to have a more dignified part...Kay Kyser shows up for his cigarette case...Phil is jealous of Kay Kyser...Kyser making a picture called "That's Right, You're Wrong"...Jack quizzes Kay to identify his cigarette case...parody of Kay Kyser's Kollege of Musical Knowledge...Lucky Strikes in the case...Jack gives Kyser the cigarettes, but not the case...Mrs. Day wants Kyser to conduct the orchestra...skit Stanley and Livingston...editor yells at Stanley, tells him to find Livingston or he's fired...gets native guide Zombie...find a sign in Africa for Wilshire Bowl, 9,000 miles away..."Man About Town" stars Rochester in Africa...cannibals eat Jell-O...Kay Kyser plays cannibal and demands his cigarette case..."We're a little late, so good night folks."

Cast:

Last name	First name	Roles	Guest star
Beloin	Ed	Young Dr. Kildare	No
Benny	Jack	Jack Benny, Jack Stanley	No
Day	Dennis	Dennis Day, Zombie	No
Felton	Verna	Mrs. Day	No
Harris	Phil	Phil Harris, newspaper editor	No
Kyser	Kay	Kay Kyser, cannibal	Yes
Livingstone	Mary	Mary Livingstone, Mary LaTush	No
Wilson	Don	Don Wilson, cannibal	No

Songs:

Order	Title	Performers	Vocal
1	Good Morning	Phil Harris	No
2	Are You Having Any Fun	Phil Harris	No
3	South of the Border	Dennis Day	Yes
4	Seventeen	Phil Harris	No

Notes:

Blooper	Mary steps on the laugh with line "Just worry about the ones you've got"
Notable	Nice Wayne Songer solo on "Are You Having Any Fun"
Notable	First mention of Gladys Zybysko
Running gag	But but but
Skit	Stanley and Livingston

Date: 10/29/1939   **Sponsor:** Jell-O   **City:** Hollywood, CA

Recording Source: Unknown   **Problems:** None

First line:

And now ladies and gentlemen, tonight Jack Benny officially opens his social season with a Halloween masquerade party at his house for the whole gang. So without further ado, we whisk you to Jack's hpme in Beverly Hills. Take it away!

Summary:

Jack is going as Romeo for Halloween...Mary comes as Campfire Girl...Jack invited a lot of stars, but they can't come because they have a headache...Dennis' mother helping in the kitchen...Jack invites Mrs. Day to call him Jack, she invites Jack to call her Lucretia...Mary thinks Mrs. Day might poison Jack...Rochester tries to spike punch bowl...Dennis wears a tuxedo to be a Hollywood tramp...Mrs. Day asks for iodine, she cut her finger...Don comes as a dish of Jell-O...Dennis asks to see Carmichael...Carmichael is upstairs reading "Grapes of Wrath"...Phil comes as a college professor, brings orchestra...Rochester puts rum in the punch, Phil's band attacks it...Mrs. Day made a special pumpkin pie just for Jack...Andy Devine comes as a ghost...Mrs. Day puts out a big buffet...Phil takes a bite out of Jack's pie...Mrs. Day wants to play Post Office...Carmichael gets hold of Dennis, gang tries to save him...Mrs. Day yells at Carmichael and he faints...promo Aldrich Family

Cast:

Last name	First name	Roles	Guest star
Anderson	Eddie	Rochester	No
Benny	Jack	Jack Benny	No
Blanc	Mel	Carmichael	No
Day	Dennis	Dennis Day	No
Devine	Andy	Andy Devine	No
Felton	Verna	Mrs. Lucretia Day	No
Harris	Phil	Phil Harris	No
Livingstone	Mary	Mary Livingstone	No
Wilson	Don	Don Wilson	No

Songs:

Order	Title	Performers	Vocal
1	All In Favor Say Aye	Phil Harris	No
2	I Poured My Heart Into a Song	Dennis Day	Yes
3	Make With the Kisses	Mary Livingstone	Yes
3	Make With the Kisses	Jack Benny	Yes
3	Make With the Kisses	Don Wilson	Yes
3	Make With the Kisses	Phil Harris	Yes
4	Twilight Interlude	Phil Harris	No

Notes:

Blooper	Jack stumbles on line "Mary, look what you dropped on my new Chinese rug."
Notable	First mention of Mrs. Day's first name (Lucretia)
Notable	Apparently Dennis' father is no longer with his mother, based on her flirting

Date: 11/5/1939   **Sponsor:** Jell-O   **City:** Hollywood, CA

Recording Source: Unknown   **Problems:** None

First line:
And now ladies and gentlemen, this being the first Sunday in November, we bring you the last rose of summer, Jack Benny.

Summary:
Jack asks Phil if he's boring him…Dennis going on eating spree in drug store because his mother isn't with him…Jack announces skit, makes Dennis five-year-old Denice…Rochester to play Jack's maid…woman calls for Graumann's Chinese Theatre, Don tells her about Jell-O…skit The Women…Phyllis calls Jacqueline with gossip, saw Jacqueline's husband, Updike, at the Silver Slipper…Phyllis and Donna wait for Jacqueline at Park Villa Hotel…they see Frieda Allen…Andrea Devine arrives, came back from Paris to marry a cowboy…Phyllis accuses Jacqueline of her marriage being over, Jacqueline slaps Phyllis…Updike returns for his long underwear

Cast:

Last name	First name	Roles	Guest star
Anderson	Eddie	Rochester, Rochelle	No
Baldwin	Harry	Updike	No
Benny	Jack	Jack Benny, Jacqueline	No
Day	Dennis	Dennis Day, Denise	No
Devine	Andy	Andy Devine, Andrea Devine	No
Harris	Phil	Phil Harris, Phyllis	No
Livingstone	Mary	Mary Livingstone	No
Stewart	Blanche	Woman caller	No
Wilson	Don	Don Wilson, Donna	No

Songs:

Order	Title	Performers	Vocal
1	Billy	Phil Harris	No
2	Last Night	Dennis Day	Yes
3	An Apple For the Teacher	Phil Harris	No
4	Goodie Goodbye	Phil Harris	No

Notes:

Skit	The Women

Date: 11/12/1939   **Sponsor:** Jell-O   **City:** Hollywood, CA

Recording Source: Unknown   **Problems:** None

First line:
And now ladies and gentlemen...oh Jack, Jack?

Summary:
Jack has a toothache...Phil's orchestra has a slogan...piano player will knock out Jack's painful tooth...Rochester makes Jack's toothache drops...Jack and Don rhyme for Jell-O...Mrs. Day is mad at Jack because he called her a pest...Mary takes Jack to the dentist...screams ensuing from the office...Dr. Nelson straps Jack into a chair...Nelson finds cavity and offers to fill it with gold or silver, Jack wants cement...Jack wants tooth pulled...gives Jack gas...Jack asks Mary to keep an eye on his money...dreams dentist is Fred Allen and assistant is Mrs. Day...dreams Phil takes over the show...dreams he is Carmichael, Rochester tries to turn him into a fur rug...joke about "You don't know when Thanksgiving is" "Who does?"...Allen takes a machine gun to Jack's tooth...charges Jack $35 to pull his tooth, Jack passes out again...promo for Red Cross Roll Call and Aldrich Family

Cast:

Last name	First name	Roles	Guest star
Anderson	Eddie	Rochester	No
Benny	Jack	Jack Benny	No
Day	Dennis	Dennis Day	No
Felton	Verna	Mrs. Day	No
Harris	Phil	Phil Harris	No
Hayes	Peter Lind	Fred Allen	No
Kelly	Mary	Secretary	No
Livingstone	Mary	Mary Livingstone	No
Nelson	Frank	Dr. Frank Nelson	No
Stewart	Blanche	Mrs. Stewart patient	No
Wilson	Don	Don Wilson	No

Songs:

Order	Title	Performers	Vocal
1	Oh Johnnie	Phil Harris	No
2	Stop It's Wonderful	Phil Harris	No
3	A Man and His Dream	Dennis Day	Yes
4	I've Got My Eye on You	Phil Harris	No

Notes:

Blooper	Mary cracks up on the line "Stop complaining and go to a dentist"

Date: 11/19/1939   **Sponsor:** Jell-O   **City:** Hollywood, CA

Recording Source: Unknown   **Problems:** None

First line:
And now ladies and gentlemen, once again we bring you our Master of Ceremonies, that bubbling personality, that effervescent comedian, that fizz, Jack Benny.

Summary:
Jack got a gag from Virgil, the sound man...Jack tells a joke about a guy leading a pink alligator...Dennis' mother is across the street in a bowling alley...Mary tells a joke she heard from Phil Harris...fraternity makes initiates go to Harris for hazing...Phil sold the corny painting on his bass drum to the Metropolitan Museum of New York, will be hanging next to the "Mona Lu Lu"...Jack says he's not paying Dennis in order to teach him how to save money...Mary wrote a poem about Thanksgiving...Phil says his relatives came over on the Mayflower...Mary insists that Jack let her read her poem or she won't buy Christmas cards from him this year...Door guy asks if Jack is mixed up about two Thanksgivings this year...Jack invites gang to his house for Thanksgiving...Jack has a live turkey roosting in the Maxwell...Jack makes Don guess Jell-O flavor to be served...Rochester calls, says Thursday's his night off, offers his twin brother...Rochester thinks turkey is an ostrich, it ate the headlights off the car...promo for Aldrich Family

Cast:

Last name	First name	Roles	Guest star
Anderson	Eddie	Rochester	No
Baldwin	Harry	Door guy	No
Benny	Jack	Jack Benny	No
Day	Dennis	Dennis Day	No
Felton	Verna	Mrs. Day	No
Harris	Phil	Phil Harris	No
Livingstone	Mary	Mary Livingstone	No
Wilson	Don	Don Wilson	No

Songs:

Order	Title	Performers	Vocal
1	It's a Whole New Thing	Phil Harris	No
2	I Dream of Jeannie with the Light Brown Hair	Dennis Day	Yes
3	Ciribiribin	Phil Harris	No
4	Bluebirds in the Moonlight	Phil Harris	No

Notes:

Blooper	Don flubs closing commercial, saying "It's quick and easy to make with...and mother will appreciate it. After working, uh...cooking a big Thanksgiving dinner..."
Notable	First time Phil uses "Lu Lu" as a gag
Running gag	Mary's poem

Date: 11/26/1939   **Sponsor:** Jell-O   **City:** Hollywood, CA

Recording Source: Unknown   **Problems:** None

First line:
And now ladies and gentlemen, once again we bring you our Master of Ceremonies, that genial host of Beverly Hills whose Thanksgiving Party last Thursday will never be forgotten.

Summary:
Gang discusses Jack's party…Phil says he got a hangover from the turkey…Beverly Hills Citizen covered the party, guest list included Homer T. Shmenk who delivered ice cream and wouldn't go home…Citizen column turns out to be an ad that Jack bought…Phil asks about cute girl in ermine wrap he was dancing with, it was Carmichael…Phil says he's at the pinochle of his career…Jack starts ordering everyone around…gang was kidding Jack about his dinner…Jack didn't serve turkey, it was wild duck he shot while hunting with Andy Devine…in Waukegan they called him "Bulls-Eye Benny"…flashback: Andy tries to wake Jack up at 4AM to go duck hunting…Jack goes to wake up Rochester…can't shoot ducks until 7AM…Jack tries to shoot a tin can off Rochester's head…Andy warns Jack that the gun has a kick…Jack drops his gun, it goes off, and he hits a duck…Jack gets upset over the fact that he killed a duck…everyone starts crying…Jack bought Thanksgiving ducks at the market…"We're a little late, so good night folks"

Cast:

Last name	First name	Roles	Guest star
Benny	Jack	Jack Benny	No
Day	Dennis	Dennis Day	No
Devine	Andy	Andy Devine	No
Harris	Phil	Phil Harris	No
Livingstone	Mary	Mary Livingstone	No
Wilson	Don	Don Wilson	No

Songs:

Order	Title	Performers	Vocal
1	I Must Have One Kiss Kiss Kiss	Phil Harris	No
2	Faithful Forever	Dennis Day	Yes
3	South of the Border	Phil Harris	No
4	Does Your Heart Beat for Me	Phil Harris	No

Notes:

Blooper	Jack says "I consider that a very lovely nurtice" instead of "a very lovely notice"

Date: 12/3/1939   **Sponsor:** Jell-O   **City:** Hollywood, CA

Recording Source: Unknown   **Problems:** None

First line:
And now ladies and gentlemen, we bring you a man who officially opened the Christmas season last week by leading the Santa Claus Lane parade down Hollywood Boulevard, Jack Benny.

Summary:
Jack talks about his horsemanship skills, he plays polo…Jack was riding a stuffed horse…Phil enters with hipster talk, Jack threatens to take away his "chicken inspector" badge…Dennis shows up with hipster talk…Door guy thought Jack's horse was beautiful…gang offers Chinese proverbs…Don does Jell-O flavors in Chinese…brings in Dynamite Dugan, star fullback of the Hermosa Beach Grunions…Phil and Dynamite greet each other with big words…skit Murder on the Gridiron…Coach gives team pep talk at halftime…didn't have a quarterback in first half…brick comes through the window with a message saying Dugan is going to be bumped off…Dugan runs for touchdown and is shot…"We're a little late, so good night folks"

Cast:

Last name	First name	Roles	Guest star
Baldwin	Harry	Door guy	No
Benny	Jack	Jack Benny, Coach Flash Benny	No
Day	Dennis	Dennis Day	No
Felton	Verna	Mrs. Day, Butch	No
Harris	Phil	Phil Harris	No
Lewis	Elliott	Dynamite Dugan	No
Livingstone	Mary	Mary Livingstone	No
Nelson	Frank	Sports announcer	No
Wilson	Don	Don Wilson	No

Songs:

Order	Title	Performers	Vocal
1	Down in the Alley and Over the Fence	Phil Harris	No
2	My Prayer	Dennis Day	Yes
3	In My Merry Oldsmobile	Phil Harris	No
4	It's a Hap Hap Happy Day	Phil Harris	No

Notes:

Skit	Murder on the Gridiron

Date: 12/10/1939 **Sponsor:** Jell-O **City:** Hollywood, CA

Recording Source: Unknown **Problems:** None

First line:
And now folks, once again we bring you that genial personality who guides the destiny of this program, a man I am proud to be associated with, and whose friendship I shall always cherish, that grand artist, Jack Benny.

Summary:
Gang kisses up to Jack for their Christmas gift...Mary asks if they moved Christmas...Jack is going to give Mary nail polish...Mary gets a letter from her mother...had a crowd at their house for Thanksgiving, but not same list of celebrities Jack always invites...Babe working on a bullet-proof vest...Rochester calls and offers to pick Jack up in the Maxwell...Trudy laid an egg and threw it in Carmichael's face...Carmichael put glue in Trudy's bucket of sand...skit The Murder of Dynamite Dugan...office of Captain O'Benny...Dean kept Toots after school, made her write "Wilshire Bowl" 100 times on the board...group returns to football stadium because murderer always returns to the scene of the crime...35 years go by and Dean finally confesses...promo for Aldrich Family

Cast:

Last name	First name	Roles	Guest star
Anderson	Eddie	Rochester	No
Baker	Kenny	Kenny Baker	No
Beloin	Ed	Special delivery, police announcer	No
Benny	Jack	Jack Benny, Detective O'Benny, Coach Flash Benny	No
Day	Dennis	Dennis Day, Officer O'Day	No
Harris	Phil	Phil Harris, Dean of Flatfoot	No
Livingstone	Mary	Mary Livingstone, Toots Livingstone	No
Nazarro	Cliff	Professor	No
Wilson	Don	Don Wilson, Sergeant Wilson	No

Songs:

Order	Title	Performers	Vocal
1	I Want to Wrap You Up	Phil Harris	No
2	Oh Johnnie	Phil Harris	No
3	Lilacs in the Rain	Dennis Day	Yes
4	All the Things You Are	Phil Harris	No

Notes:

Notable	First loud "Yipe!" from Jack
Notable	First time ostrich is given the name Trudy
Running gag	Mary's mother communication
Skit	The Murder of Dynamite Dugan

Date: 12/17/1939   **Sponsor:** Jell-O   **City:** Hollywood, CA

Recording Source: Both   **Problems:** None

First line:
And now ladies and gentlemen, I bring you our worn-out Master of Ceremonies.
Between his broadcast at NBC, his picture at Paramount, and Christmas shopping at the
five and ten, he's the busiest little man in Hollywood, Jack Benny.

Summary:
Jack fell asleep on his pool table...Jack doing a western movie at Paramount ("Buck Benny Rides
Again")...Paramount thought that Jack was the only person who could stand in for Gary
Cooper...Jack and Phil bet on the USC-UCLA game, but only 15 cents...Jack's uncle, "Shoot the
Works" Benny ("Stand Back You Bother Me Boys" Benny on later show), was one of the biggest
gamblers in Waukegan...(west coast - Gladys is the pin girl at bowling alley)...Don has written a
play...Mr. And Mrs. Santa Claus read letters from the kids...Mrs. Claus tells Santa to "just fill Ann
Sheridan's stocking and git"...Don Wilson asks for Jell-O...Jack and Mary need to go Christmas
shopping...Dennis' mother told him to ask Jack when's he's going to start getting paid, they've got
enough Jell-O for 25 years...Dennis is giving Jack a pair of socks...Floorwalker won't tell Jack
where the watch counter is...shows Jack a Venus de Milo watch with no hands (west coast - "You
call Ulrich 8-900")...Jack buys a watch with an unbreakable crystal, saleswoman has him hit it with
a hammer and he smashes it...saleswoman won't refund Jack's money...mooley guy is selling
perfume (he's "the only mug in the joint that can speak French")...Jack buys perfume for his
sister...Rochester is buying an 89-cent necktie for Jack..."We're a little late, so good night folks."

Cast:

Last name	First name	Roles	Guest star
Beloin	Ed	Special delivery boy, Mr. Chambers floorwalker	No
Benny	Jack	Jack Benny, Santa Claus	No
Day	Dennis	Dennis Day	No
Harris	Phil	Phil Harris	No
Kelly	Mary	Miss Kelcy watch saleswoman	No
Lewis	Elliott	Perfume salesman	No
Livingstone	Mary	Mary Livingstone, Mrs. Claus	No
Stewart	Blanche	Offended woman	No
Tuttle	Lurene	Hosiery saleswoman	No
Wilson	Don	Don Wilson	No

Songs:

Order	Title	Performers	Vocal
1	Goody Goodbye	Phil Harris	No
2	Make With the Kisses	Phil Harris	No
3	Tomorrow Night	Dennis Day	Yes
4	Baby Me	Phil Harris	No

Notes:

Blooper	(West coast) Jack stumbles on line "I wish I knew what it was, I'd like to get some more lines"
Notable	Mary plays a wife jealous of Ann Sheridan, she later insulted Sheridan in real life for the same reason
Running gag	Baby talk Jell-O flavors

Date: 12/24/1939 **Sponsor:** Jell-O **City:** Hollywood, CA

Recording Source: Unknown **Problems:** None

First line:

And now ladies and gentlemen, as is always his custom on Christmas Eve, Jack Benny is holding open house tonight for all the members of his cast. So without further ado, we whisk you to Jack's home in Beverly Hills. Take it away!

Summary:

Commercial is take-off on "Night Before Christmas", reindeer become flavors…Trudy ate ornaments off one side of the tree…cook is still Swing Hi…Jack got Don a belt, Phil an oil painting ("Birth of Venus" by Botticelli)…selling ostrich plumes for 15 cents…Dennis and his mother arrive, Jack and Mrs. Day are friends again…Don brings six packages, gives Rochester hair tonic…Trudy galloping through the house…Jack serving turkey hash…Jack's sister Florence and her husband, Leonard, driving in from Waukegan…Leonard is an interior decorator…Jack gives Phil the oil painting, Phil tells Jack to keep it…Trudy escapes from garage and gallops through house…Leonard says Hollywood is over-rated…Jack wants Florence and Leonard to stay in the guest room, Rochester asks where the border will sleep (he'll sleep in the den)…Andy brings Jack a combination sock, sweater, and ear lap that his mother knitted…Fred Allen says he's going to make a picture with Jack…Jack is upset, calls Mark Sandrich…Jack tells Mr. Billingsley to sleep in the den…Trudy gallops through with Carmichael chasing her…show ends in chaos…promo for Aldrich Family

Cast:

Last name	First name	Roles	Guest star
		Leonard Fenchel	No
?	Dorothy	Florence Fenchel	No
Anderson	Eddie	Rochester	No
Beloin	Ed	Mr. Billingsley	No
Benny	Jack	Jack Benny	No
Blanc	Mel	Carmichael	No
Day	Dennis	Dennis Day	No
Devine	Andy	Andy Devine	No
Felton	Verna	Mrs. Day	No
Harris	Phil	Phil Harris	No
Livingstone	Mary	Mary Livingstone	No
Wilson	Don	Don Wilson	No

Songs:

Order	Title	Performers	Vocal
1	A Happy, Happy Holiday	Phil Harris	No
2	Oh Little Town of Bethlehem - The First Noel - Away in a Manger	Dennis Day	Yes
3	Unidentified	Phil Harris	No
4	Unidentified	Phil Harris	No

Notes:

Notable	Trudy is heard
Running gag	But but but

Date: 12/31/1939   **Sponsor:** Jell-O   **City:** Hollywood, CA

Recording Source: Unknown   **Problems:** None

First line:
And now ladies and gentlemen, in just a few short hours we will welcome in the new year 1940. So without further ado, we bring you a man who was once 19 and once 40, Jack Benny.

Summary:
Everyone sent Jack calendars…Wilshire Bowl is sending a calendar with Phil Harris' picture on it…Mary got a calendar from the May Company that says, "Come back, all is forgiven"…Jack gave Mary a pewter saucer for Christmas, Don a golf ball…Phil says he got a cashier sweater…Door guy sent Jack a calendar of Lady Godiva on a horse…Don going to see Sally Rand…Mary going to Ginger Rogers' house…Jack is going out with Gladys…Dennis is taking his girl to a midnight show…Gladys tested for Scarlett O'Hara…everyone talks with Southern accents…next week will do "Golden Boy"…Andy's Pa writes all of Phil's material…Gladys calls and cancels date with Jack…Jack goes to Ginsberg's for a cup of coffee…waitress at Ginsberg's is Gladys…Jack catches cab, driver has date with the woman Gladys is subbing for…everyone is out except Rochester…Jack says the world needs more peace…Billingsley comes in…Jack turns on radio and hears Mary reading a New Year's poem…Jack left his cane at Ginsberg's…Mary does program close…promo for Aldrich Family

Cast:

Last name	First name	Roles	Guest star
Baldwin	Harry	Door guy	No
Beloin	Ed	Mr. Billingsley	No
Benny	Jack	Jack Benny	No
Day	Dennis	Dennis Day	No
Devine	Andy	Andy Devine	No
Harris	Phil	Phil Harris	No
Livingstone	Mary	Mary Livingstone	No
Marr	Eddie	New Year's celebrator, Joe the Cabbie	No
Rubin	Benny	Mike the Irish guard, Sam Ginsberg	No
Stewart	Blanche	Gladys Zybysko	No
Wilson	Don	Don Wilson	No

Songs:

Order	Title	Performers	Vocal
1	Do I Love You	Phil Harris	No
2	All The Things You Are	Dennis Day	Yes
3	Unidentified	Phil Harris	No
4	Unidentified	Phil Harris	No

Notes:

Notable	First time Gladys Zybysko speaks
Running gag	Mary's poem

Date: 1/7/1940   **Sponsor:** Jell-O   **City:** Hollywood, CA

Recording Source: Unknown   **Problems:**   None

First line:
And now ladies and gentlemen…
Jack: Oh Don, Don…did Phil get here yet?

Summary:
Jack and Phil wagered on the Rose Bowl and Phil lost…Phil pays easily, but Jack says he's a sore loser and refuses to take the money…Jack switched the skit from "Golden Boy" to "Rulers of the Sea"…flashback: Jack and Mary went to the Wilshire Bowl since Gladys had to work…cigarette girl selling locks of Phil Harris' hair…Phil says he's the star of "Man About Town"…Barbara Stanwyck introduces Jack as Ben Bernie to her companions…Jack wants to ask Barbara to appear in "Golden Boy", badgers Stanwyck into dancing with him…Stanwyck finally acquiesces to playing the role…Jack ordering Rochester around when Stanwyck is coming for rehearsal…Jack forgot to put his pants on…Mary tells Stanwyck, "I knew Bob Taylor before you did", Stanwyck says that Mary used to sell her hose at the May Company…Jack rehearses a dramatic scene with Stanwyck…Jack's performance is too bad and Stanwyck leaves…Jack has Rochester read Stanwyck's lines

Cast:

Last name	First name	Roles	Guest star
Anderson	Eddie	Rochester	No
Baldwin	Harry	Waiter	No
Beloin	Ed	Mr. Kendall	No
Benny	Jack	Jack Benny	No
Day	Dennis	Dennis Day	No
Harris	Phil	Phil Harris	No
Kelly	Mary	Lillian Kendall	No
Livingstone	Mary	Mary Livingstone	No
Stanwyck	Barbara	Barbara Stanwyck	Yes
Stewart	Blanche	Cigarette girl	No
Werner	Mort	Mort Werner	Yes
Wilson	Don	Don Wilson	No

Songs:

Order	Title	Performers	Vocal
1	Pinch Me	Phil Harris	No
2	With the Wind and the Rain In Your Hair	Dennis Day	Yes
3	Tea for Two	Phil Harris	No
4	Penthouse for Rent	Phil Harris	No

Notes:

Date: 1/14/1940   **Sponsor:** Jell-O   **City:** Hollywood, CA

Recording Source: Unknown   **Problems:** None

First line:
And now ladies and gentlemen, this being the second week of leap year, we bring you a man who hasn't leaped in years, Jack Benny.

Summary:
Don and Jack argue over Jack not being the athletic type...Phil says that Gladys still thinks Jack is wonderful...Gladys is a candidate for Miss Vine Street, Jack gets the cast to vote for her...Jack shows Phil how to make a "Z"...Olivia deHun to play Ingrid Bergman's role, she was last a caboose for Union Pacific...Jack gets a call from Gladys to see how many votes Jack got for her...winner gets a trip to Boulder Dam...Don asks Jack to define "Intermezzo", Phil found the definition in a Chinese cookie...skit Intermezzo...Leslie practices "Souvenir"...Leslie going on a tour, he's in love with his accompanist...Edna put a dictaphone in Leslie's fiddle...manager booked him into Wilshire Bowl, the cultural center of Southern California...plays "Love in Bloom" in Waukegan...accompanist is in love with Jack's manager...Leslie wants to give up violin when accompanist leaves him, Edna bolsters him again...plays "Meditation" from "Thaiis" at Carnegie Hall...Don does closing commercial over "Meditation"...Radio Editors of New York World Telegram honor show again

Cast:

Last name	First name	Roles	Guest star
Beloin	Ed	Telegram boy	No
Benny	Jack	Jack Benny, Leslie Benny	No
Day	Dennis	Dennis Day, Pizzicato Benny	No
Harris	Phil	Phil Harris, manager	No
Kelly	Mary	Olivia DeTroit Street, Anita	No
Livingstone	Mary	Mary Livingstone, Edna Benny	No
Wilson	Don	Don Wilson	No

Songs:

Order	Title	Performers	Vocal
1	Ma He's Making Eyes At Me	Phil Harris	No
2	Down By the River	Dennis Day	Yes
3	Rhumba Jumps	Phil Harris	No
4	Meditation	Jack Benny	No

Notes:

Notable	First time Gladys is given the last name of "Zybysko"
Notable	Jack and Mary Kelly play lovers and she leaves him for another man, and he finds solace with Mary Livingstone; Jack, Kelly, and Livingstone had their real lives run similar to this story in the 1920s
Running gag	But but but
Skit	Intermezzo

Date: 1/21/1940 **Sponsor:** Jell-O **City:** Hollywood, CA

Recording Source: Unknown **Problems:** None

First line:
And now ladies and gentlemen, we bring you our genial master of ceremonies...a man who each Sunday night at this time...

Summary:
Jack talking on the telephone, trying to reach Gladys...Gladys is visiting her folks in Azusa...Gladys' father Zeke works for the Zenith Zipper Company...Don introduces Phil instead...Jack says Gladys is his fiancee...Phil tells jokes...Jack reaches Gladys' mother, but Gladys is at neighbors' house taking a bath...Jack tries to give operator a slug for a quarter...Gladys winked at Don when she brought him a sandwich at Ginsberg's, Jack says her eye twitches...Jack took Gladys to the Trocadero and ordered fried chicken, Gladys went to the kitchen and got it...Jack won Academy Award from Spencer Tracy in a crap game...next week doing show from Oakland, CA for the benefit of F.D.R.'s Infantile Paralysis Fund...Jack goes home to pack because he's leaving early in the morning...Jack gets phone call from Azusa, gets cut off from Gladys...pay phone ejects change...Jack takes cab home, Ronald Colman looking at them out of his window...Rochester writing a play with his cousin, "Gone With the Gin"...Carmichael and Trudy staying at a pet shop...Mr. Billingsley has been on the wagon for two weeks because he saw a polar bear and an ostrich...Gladys calls but Rochester hangs up on her...Jack tries to get her on the phone again...letter from Andy Devine, he's making personal apperances in Dayton, Ohio this week and Chicago next week

Cast:

Last name	First name	Roles	Guest star
Anderson	Eddie	Rochester	No
Beloin	Ed	Mr. Billingsley	No
Benny	Jack	Jack Benny	No
Day	Dennis	Dennis Day	No
Harris	Phil	Phil Harris	No
Lewis	Elliott	Cab driver	No
Livingstone	Mary	Mary Livingstone	No
Morrow	Bill	Page boy	No
Wilson	Don	Don Wilson	No

Songs:

Order	Title	Performers	Vocal
1	Night After Night	Phil Harris	No
2	Unidentified	Phil Harris	No
3	Careless	Dennis Day	Yes
4	Unidentified	Phil Harris	No

Notes:

Blooper	Mary says "Oh Mary" instead of "Oh Jack"

Date: 1/28/1940 **Sponsor:** Jell-O **City:** Oakland, CA
Recording Source: Unknown **Problems:** None

First line:
And now ladies and gentlemen, we bring you our Master of Ceremonies, a man who was so anxious to appear at this benefit tonight that he drove all the way from Los Angeles to Oakland in his 1923 Maxwell.

Summary:
From Oakland Civic Auditorium for March of Dimes...Jack describes his trip to Oakland in the Maxwell like the Donner Party...Phil thinks he drew the entire audience...Phil and Don staying in the Bridal Suite of the Hotel Oakland...Jack has rooms in San Francisco and Oakland...Mary enters with a poem...woman wants to enter her French Poodle in the dog show, that's at the San Francisco Civic Auditorium...Dennis went to Treasure Island to see the World's Fair...Jack tells Dennis the story of his trip, Don does the commercial over it...Rochester still in San Jose getting the Maxwell fixed...Jack tells Rochester to get money for repairs from the truck driver who hit them...Door guy looking for the dog show...skit Murder on the Bay Bridge...murder is reported...O'Day snarls traffic at Fifth and Main...Mrs. Smith confesses to murdering her husband, then her lawyer confesses...O'Benny gets dizzy on high bridge...Rochester arrives in the Maxwell, they let him on the bridge without a toll..."We're a little late folks, and it was swell being here. Good night everybody."

Cast:

Last name	First name	Roles	Guest star
Anderson	Eddie	Rochester	No
Baldwin	Harry	Door guy	No
Beloin	Ed	Man in last row, Fifi, police radio announcer	No
Benny	Jack	Jack Benny, Captain O'Benny	No
Day	Dennis	Dennis Day, Officer O'Day	No
Harris	Phil	Phil Harris, lawyer	No
Livingstone	Mary	Mary Livingstone, Mrs. Smith	No
Stewart	Blanche	Fifi owner	No
Wilson	Don	Don Wilson, Sergeant Wilson	No

Songs:

Order	Title	Performers	Vocal
1	Billy	Phil Harris	No
2	Pinch Me	Phil Harris	No
3	Goodnight My Beautiful	Dennis Day	Yes
4	All the Things You Are	Phil Harris	No

Notes:

Blooper	Jack says "Phil, if you were the only traction here tonight" instead of "attraction here tonight"
Blooper	Mary laughs through line "I couldn't get a veil, Vine Street is closed today"
Notable	Maxwell is now a 1923 model
Running gag	Mary's poem
Skit	Murder on the Bay Bridge

Date: 2/4/1940 **Sponsor:** Jell-O **City:** Hollywood, CA

Recording Source: Unknown **Problems:** None

First line:
And now ladies and gentlemen as you all know, last Sunday our broadcast came to you from Oakland, California, where we gave a benefit performance for the March of Dimes. So now we would like to show you exactly what happened at the conclusion of that program.

Summary:
Gang discusses how the Oakland show went...Phil and Jack argue about who was the hit of the show...Phil says he's bringing his own writer, Belly Laugh Barton...Barton is now working for Fred Allen...leaving in the morning for Yosemite, gang discusses clothing and equipment to take...everyone has to get up at 7AM...Jack and Mary go to sporting goods store, clerk tries to talk Jack out of buying stuff...Mary is grouchy...Jack goes out with Gladys on Wednesday and Saturday, bowls to midnight Thursday...Phil got his own car to go to Yosemite...Jack holds Dennis on his lap in lieu of a windshield...Don mumbles commercial in his sleep...Rochester falls asleep at the wheel...Phil Harris passes them...gang stops at an Auto Court to spend the night, Phil got the last cabin

Cast:

Last name	First name	Roles	Guest star
Anderson	Eddie	Rochester	No
Beloin	Ed	Sporting goods clerk	No
Benny	Jack	Jack Benny	No
Day	Dennis	Dennis Day	No
Harris	Phil	Phil Harris	No
Kelly	Mary	Auto court proprietress	No
Livingstone	Mary	Mary Livingstone	No
Marks	Hilliard	Male autograph seeker (Mary)	No
Stewart	Blanche	Female autograph seeker (Phil), sporting goods clerk wife	No
Wilson	Don	Don Wilson	No

Songs:

Order	Title	Performers	Vocal
1	I've Got My Eyes on You	Phil Harris	No
2	Blue World	Dennis Day	Yes
3	Where is Love	Phil Harris	No
4	Unidentified	Phil Harris	No

Notes:

Blooper	Ed Beloin says, "I've had just about enough for you" rather than "enough of you"
Notable	First mention of Belly Laugh Barton
Notable	Yosemite show

Date: 2/11/1940   **Sponsor:** Jell-O   **City:** Hollywood, CA

Recording Source: Unknown   **Problems:** None

First line:
And now ladies and gentlemen, our program tonight will be devoted to a further description of our trip to Yosemite.

Summary:
Following morning travelling to Yosemite...Jack has Rochester sing for him, "At 8:00 he wants me to imitate Amos 'n Andy!"...Jack, Don, and Dennis shared a bed...gang stops at a lunchroom...Jack talks with parrot Polly, parrot hits on Mary...waitress has Jack autograph Ry-Krisp...parrot likes Fred Allen, Jack argues with parrot...Rochester kicked tire and it blew out...haywagon passes Maxwell...Jack won't let Phl pass, hogs road...gets pulled over by cop, Jack talks his way out of a ticket...arrive at 10PM, park is closed and they can't get to the hotel...it starts to rain and gang has to sleep in the car...30th anniversary of the Boy Scouts...promo for Aldrich Family

Cast:

Last name	First name	Roles	Guest star
Anderson	Eddie	Rochester	No
Beloin	Ed	Gas attendant	No
Benny	Jack	Jack Benny	No
Day	Dennis	Dennis Day	No
Harris	Phil	Phil Harris	No
Hiestand	John	Ranger	No
Lewis	Elliott	Cook, cop	No
Livingstone	Mary	Mary Livingstone	No
Pullen	A. Purvis?	Parrot	No
Stewart	Blanche	Waitress	No
Wilson	Don	Don Wilson	No

Songs:

Order	Title	Performers	Vocal
1	Relax	Phil Harris	No
2	Darn That Dream	Dennis Day	Yes
3	Unidentified	Phil Harris	No
4	It's a Blue World	Phil Harris	No

Notes:

Blooper	Jack mildly cracks up on closing announcement, makes others start laughing
Notable	Yosemite show

Date: 2/18/1940   **Sponsor:** Jell-O   **City:** Hollywood, CA

Recording Source: East coast   **Problems:** None

First line:
And now ladies and gentlemen, once again we continue with the description of our trip to Yosemite in Jack's Maxwell. As you remember last week, our little party finally reached the gates of Yosemite National Park, only to find it was closed for the night.

Summary:
Recreation of last week's ending...Mary keeps complaining...Jack wakes everyone up at 6AM...find a sign for the Wishire Bowl in Yosemite...get directions from an Indian...Jack thinks he sees geyser, it's the radiator...Jack puts on three sweaters...Jack still mad at Phil, Phil offers to pay his own expenses and Jack relents...Phil saw a guy break his leg skiing, and Jack starts to chicken out...gang goes up to ski, Jack wants hot chocolate...Phil introduces Jack to ski instructor...gang urges Jack to go skiing...Jack puts his skis on backwards...Jack gets going down the hill and forgets what to do...runs into ski house and gets his hot chocolate...Mary does show close...promo for Aldrich Family

Cast:

Last name	First name	Roles	Guest star
Anderson	Eddie	Rochester	No
Beloin	Ed	Indian	No
Benny	Jack	Jack Benny	No
Day	Dennis	Dennis Day	No
Harris	Phil	Phil Harris	No
Hiestand	John	Ranger	No
Kelly	Mary	Waitress	No
Livingstone	Mary	Mary Livingstone	No
Nelson	Frank	Larson the ski instructor	No
Stewart	Blanche	Old woman skier	No
Wilson	Don	Don Wilson	No

Songs:

Order	Title	Performers	Vocal
1	How High the Moon	Phil Harris	No
2	Do I Love You? Do I?	Phil Harris	No
3	Jingle Bells	Phil Harris	No
4	Unidentified	Phil Harris	No

Notes:

Notable	Mary treats Jack very harshly throughout the show
Notable	Dennis appears on the show, but doesn't sing
Notable	Yosemite show

Date: 2/25/1940 **Sponsor:** Jell-O **City:** Hollywood, CA

Recording Source: Unknown **Problems:** None

First line:
And now ladies and gentlemen, for the last installment of our recent journey to Yosemite National Park in Jack's Maxwell. The trip will go down in history with the adventures of Marco Polo, the exploits of Admiral Byrd, the voyage of Christopher Columbus.

Summary:
Several days after Jack's accident on his birthday...Rochester reading Jack a romantic story...last month Jack got a sliver in his tongue from a Good Humor...Mary brings Jack a bottle of rubbing alcohol for his birthday...Jack lost $80 to Rochester playing Casino...Jack's nurse out skiing with Phil...Don contemplates verbiage for next week's commercial...Dr. Nelson asks how everyone is doing except Jack...doesn't remember anything about Jack's injury...nurse finally shows up, tries to take Jack's pulse through her mittens...Jack is released to go home...birthday wire from Fred Allen...Rochester won doctor's stethescope in Casino...desk clerk charges Jack 40 cents extra for towel sticking out of his suitcase...singing birthday telegram from Jack's father in Miami Beach...gang goes home...promo for Aldrich Family

Cast:

Last name	First name	Roles	Guest star
Anderson	Eddie	Rochester	No
Baldwin	Harry	Desk clerk	No
Beloin	Ed	Eddie	No
Benny	Jack	Jack Benny	No
Day	Dennis	Dennis Day	No
Harris	Phil	Phil Harris	No
Kelly	Mary	Miss Kelly the nurse	No
Livingstone	Mary	Mary Livingstone	No
Marks	Hilliard	Telegram boy	No
Morrow	Bill	Bill	No
Nelson	Frank	Dr. Nelson	No
Sportsmen Quartet?	The	Singing telegram backup	No
Stewart	Blanche	Western Union, singer lead	No
Wilson	Don	Don Wilson	No

Songs:

Order	Title	Performers	Vocal
1	Let's All Sing Together	Phil Harris	No
2	The Isle of May	Dennis Day	Yes
3	Confucius Say	Phil Harris	No
4	Give a Little Whistle	Phil Harris	No

Notes:

Notable	First appearance of the Sportsmen?
Running gag	Relay question and answer

Date: 3/3/1940   **Sponsor:** Jell-O   **City:** Hollywood, CA

Recording Source: Unknown   **Problems:** None

First line:
And now ladies and gentlemen, we're back in Hollywood after enjoying the winter sports in Yosemite. So without further ado, we bring you our Master of Ceremonies, that outdoor man with an indoor body, Jack Benny.

Summary:
Gang ribs Jack about his skiing accident...rather than getting a night nurse, Jack hired a girl with insomnia...Jack upset that he didn't win the Academy Award for Best Actor...Andy Devine has been off doing vaudeville, did an adagio act with his Ma and Pa...wire from Jack's father, says newspapers got Academy Award winner wrong...Frankie remley used to be a tout, gave Jack tips on horses...Gracie Allen is running for President, asks gang to vote for her...Gracie kisses Phil for a baby...were going to do Mr. Smith Goes to Washington, now doing Mr. Smith goes to Glendale...Rochester calls, Carmichael and Trudy are fighting...no show close

Cast:

Last name	First name	Roles	Guest star
Allen	Gracie	Gracie Allen	Yes
Anderson	Eddie	Rochester	No
Baldwin	Harry	Telegram boy	No
Beloin	Ed	Eddie	No
Benny	Jack	Jack Benny	No
Day	Dennis	Dennis Day	No
Devine	Andy	Andy Devine	No
Harris	Phil	Phil Harris	No
Livingstone	Mary	Mary Livingstone	No
Morrow	Bill	Bill	No
Wilson	Don	Don Wilson	No

Songs:

Order	Title	Performers	Vocal
1	Little Girl	Phil Harris	No
2	Make Love With a Guitar	Dennis Day	Yes
3	I've Got My Eyes on You	Phil Harris	No
4	Where Was I?	Phil Harris	No

Notes:

Running gag	Relay question and answer

Date: 3/10/1940 **Sponsor:** Jell-O **City:** Hollywood, CA
Recording Source: Unknown **Problems:** None

First line:
And now ladies and gentlemen…
Jack: Just a second, Don. Wait a minute, wait a minute.

Summary:
Don's 17th anniversary in radio…Phil says Jack should give Don a raise…Mary gives Don a musical cigarette case…Mary reads a poem for Don Wilson…Phil says Dennis should sing because his band hasn't rehearsed yet…gang thought they were going to do "Goodbye Mr. Chips"…Rochester calls, working on his income tax…skit Mr. Benny Goes to Washington…Waukegan seeing off Jefferson Benny, who has just been elected to the Senate…promises fresh ink and new blotters in post office…Benny tours Washington…jumps off bus to find dollar Washington threw…Senator Wilson makes a speech for Jell-O…Senator Harris advocates Panama Canal…Benny speaks for 12 days about Waukegan ink and blotters…secretary gives Benny violin to turn filibuster into a fiddlebuster, plays "Love in Bloom"…Senate relents and gives Benny ink and blotters…promo for Aldrich Family

Cast:

Last name	First name	Roles	Guest star
Anderson	Eddie	Rochester	No
Baldwin	Harry	Train announcer	No
Beloin	Ed	Eddie, Cousin Boo Boo	No
Benny	Jack	Jack Benny, Jefferson Benny	No
Day	Dennis	Dennis Day, Vice President	No
Harris	Phil	Phil Harris, Senator Harris	No
Livingstone	Mary	Mary Livingstone, Jean Livingstone	No
Morrow	Bill	Bill, "nothin but promises" man	No
Nazarro	Cliff	Tour guide	No
Nelson	Frank	Narrator	No
Stewart	Blanche	Eleanor Roosevelt	No
Wilson	Don	Don Wilson, Senator Wilson	No

Songs:

Order	Title	Performers	Vocal
1	Run Rabbit Run	Phil Harris	No
2	Some Day You'll Find Your Bluebird	Dennis Day	Yes
3	Woodpecker Song	Phil Harris	No
4	Love in Bloom	Jack Benny	No
5	Bluebirds in the Moonlight	Phil Harris	No

Notes:

Notable	At the start of the skit, Jack says "Take it, Mr. Merrick"…may indicate that Mahlon Merrick was conducting orchestra by this time
Running gag	Mary's poem
Running gag	Relay question and answer
Skit	Mr. Benny Goes to Washington

Date: 3/17/1940   **Sponsor:** Jell-O   **City:** Hollywood, CA

Recording Source: West coast   **Problems:** None

First line:
And now ladies and gentlemen, we bring you our Master of Ceremonies, a man…
Phil: Hold it, Don, hold it. Just a minute. Jack isn't here yet.

Summary:
Jack talking to Orson Welles on the phone to get coaching for heavy drama since Jack didn't win the Academy Award…Jack speaking in clipped British tones…Jack says he needs no introduction because he's so well known…Mary in bed with the flu…Jack claims he went to high school with Welles because Welles graduated at age five…Welles' secretaries arrive…call comes in for Welles and Jack forgets to get the name of the caller…Jack introduces Welles to the gang…Welles tells Jack he's selecting the wrong parts, suggests "Hunchback of Notre Dame"…tailor comes in and measures Welles for a suit…call comes in from London for Welles…play scenes where Jack only has to groan…when Jack has a speech, Welles drowns it out with bells, then a phone call…Welles invites Jack to perform on "June Moon"…"Goodnight Doll"

Cast:

Last name	First name	Roles	Guest star
Beloin	Ed	Sam	No
Benny	Jack	Jack Benny	No
Day	Dennis	Dennis Day	No
Harris	Phil	Phil Harris	No
Mather	?	Mr. Stone	No
Rubin	Benny	Max the tailor	No
Stone	Ann	Miss Wentworth	No
Welles	Orson	Orson Welles	Yes
Wilson	Don	Don Wilson	No

Songs:

Order	Title	Performers	Vocal
1	Night After Night	Phil Harris	No
2	Phil the Fluter's Ball	Dennis Day	Yes
3	Woodpecker Song	Phil Harris	No
4	Day Dreams Come True At Night	Phil Harris	No

Notes:

Notable	First time Jack says "Goodnight Doll"
Notable	Jack says "Can you hear that, Doll?" after Dennis' song
Notable	First time Dennis does dialect

Date: 3/24/1940   **Sponsor:** Jell-O   **City:** Hollywood, CA

Recording Source: Unknown   **Problems:** None

First line:
And now ladies and gentlemen, I bring you a man who last Sunday gave us his interpretation of "The Hunchback of Notre Dame". Now, I will not say that his performance surpassed Charles Laughton.

Summary:
Jack reads review from Ed Sullivan, has many copies...Jack suggests that Phil play classical music...Mary returns, fell in love with her doctor...Jack trying to be a serious actor by walking around Beverly Hills with a cane...Dennis says he has a sore throat and can't sing, Phil and Mary fill in...Don wrote a play...newlywed wife worries about her mother-in-law who gets her son to come home with Jell-O...Andy models his new Easter suit...Fred Allen says Jack is a straight man to Orson Welles, Jack says he'd rather be that than a perch for an eagle...next week doing Pinocchio...Rochester calls, taking Carmichael to see "Grapes of Wrath"...sending Sullivan review to everyone Jack knows...Welles giving Jack's dramatic lessons...previews of Pinocchio (Jack plays all parts)...Mary does close, Jack ran over to do "June Moon"...promo for Aldrich Family

Cast:

Last name	First name	Roles	Guest star
Anderson	Eddie	Rochester	No
Benny	Jack	Jack Benny, Oliver J. Snodgrass	No
Day	Dennis	Dennis Day	No
Devine	Andy	Andy Devine	No
Harris	Phil	Phil Harris	No
Livingstone	Mary	Mary Livingstone, Myrtle Snodgrass	No
Wilson	Don	Don Wilson	No

Songs:

Order	Title	Performers	Vocal
1	There's Yes Yes In Your Eyes	Phil Harris	No
2	Holy Smoke	Mary Livingstone	Yes
2	Holy Smoke	Phil Harris	Yes
3	Do I Love You	Phil Harris	No
4	You, You Darling!	Phil Harris	No

Notes:

Notable	First time Phil says "that was a lu-lu!"

Date: 3/31/1940　　**Sponsor:** Jell-O　　**City:** Hollywood, CA
Recording Source: Unknown　**Problems:** None

First line:

And now ladies and gentlemen, in the last two weeks a new star has loomed over the dramatic horizon, a young man who is destined to become one of the first names in the American theatre. So without further ado, we bring you the man who startled the world last Sunday with his amazing performance in "June Moon", Jack Benny.

Summary:

Don compliments Jack on his performance on "June Moon"...Jack split up with Gladys Zybysko because she charged him five cents for cheese on his apple pie...Jack says he's going back to the stage because radio won't last due to sun spots...Jack wonders if Orson Welles caused sun spots, calls and accuses him...skit Pinnochio...Old Man Benny is building Pinocchio...Blue Fairy brings Pinocchio to life...Mary Cricket and Pinocchio go to school, Mary tells him to stay away from Freddy Allen...Pinocchio wooed by Harris and Day into vaudeville...Pinocchio finally comes home, his father missing, goes in search of him...swallowed by Donstro the whale, finds father...the Blue Fairy rescues them..."We're a little late, so good night folks"

Cast:

Last name	First name	Roles	Guest star
Baldwin	Harry	Echo	No
Beloin	Ed	Eddie, pickled herring	No
Benny	Jack	Jack Benny, Pinocchio Benny	No
Day	Dennis	Dennis Day, vaudeville agent	No
Harris	Phil	Phil Harris, vaudeville agent	No
Kelly	Mary	Blue Fairy	No
Livingstone	Mary	Mary Livingstone, Mary Cricket	No
Morrow	Bill	Bill	No
Sportsmen Quartet?	The	Backup quartet	No
Wilson	Don	Don Wilson, Donstro the whale	No
Wright	?	Spencer Tracy, Old Man Benny	No

Songs:

Order	Title	Performers	Vocal
1	Playmates	Phil Harris	No
2	Relax	Phil Harris	No
3	When You Wish Upon a Star	Dennis Day	Yes
4	Give a Little Whistle	Mary Kelly	Yes
5	Hi Diddle Dee Dee	Jack Benny	Yes
5	Hi Diddle Dee Dee	Mary Livingstone	Yes
5	Hi Diddle Dee Dee	Dennis Day	Yes
5	Hi Diddle Dee Dee	Phil Harris	Yes
5	Hi Diddle Dee Dee	Don Wilson	Yes
6	When You Wish Upon a Star	Quartet	Yes
7	Give a Little Whistle/Where Was I	Phil Harris	No

Notes:

Blooper	Jack stumbles on the line "a young songwriter from Schenectady"
Running gag	But but but
Running gag	Relay question and answer
Skit	Pinocchio

Date: 4/7/1940   **Sponsor:** Jell-O   **City:** Hollywood, CA

Recording Source: Unknown   **Problems:** None

First line:
And now ladies and gentlemen, as you all know, this is the beginning of Spring. Tiny blades of grass are peeping through the soil, blossoms are bursting into bloom, the harsh winds of winter have changed into soft, balmy breezes. So without further ado, we bring you a man who is still wearing his longies, Jack Benny.

Summary:
Jack says his underwear is his own business...Jack waxes poetic to gang on loyalty...Mary and Don respond with poems..."Buck Benny" world premiere in two weeks, going to broadcast from there...Jack's horse tried to steal every scene from him...Jack brings back Buck Benny as Dennis doesn't know it...Rochester calls, asks if Jack will take him to New York...tells Mr. Billingsley to make his own coffee...considering what to do with Carmichael and Trudy...skit Buck Benny...gets a call that Dead Eye's dad died...still looking for Cactus Face...gets haircut at Dead Eye's...visits Daisy Carson, proposes to her, she turns him down again...Cactus Face robbed First National Bank...Blue Fairy returns, she didn't get paid...promo for Aldrich Family

Cast:

Last name	First name	Roles	Guest star
Anderson	Eddie	Rochester	No
Benny	Jack	Jack Benny, Buck Benny	No
Day	Dennis	Dennis Day, Deputy Day	No
Harris	Phil	Phil Harris, Frank Carson	No
Kelly	Mary	Blue Fairy	No
Lewis	Elliott	Dead Eye	No
Livingstone	Mary	Mary Livingstone, Daisy Carson	No
Stewart	Blanche	Goldie, screamer	No
Wilson	Don	Don Wilson, Deputy Wilson	No

Songs:

Order	Title	Performers	Vocal
1	Ma He's Makin Eyes at Me/Little Girl	Phil Harris	No
2	My Kind of Country	Dennis Day	Yes
3	I Hear Bluebirds	Phil Harris	No
4	Where Was I	Phil Harris	No

Notes:

Running gag	Mary's poem
Skit	Buck Benny Rides Again

Date: 4/14/1940 **Sponsor:** Jell-O **City:** Hollywood, CA

Recording Source: Unknown **Problems:** None

First line:
And now ladies and gentlemen, as we announced last week, next Sunday the Jell-O
Program will originate from New York City, where Paramount is holding the premiere of
its new picture, "Buck Benny Rides Again". So without further ado, we whisk you to Jack
Benny's home in Beverly Hills, where Jack is in the throes of last-minute packing. Take it
away!

Summary:
Rochester and Jack are packing…put mothballs in the trunk, the bats threw them
out…wants to give suit to cousin Marvin…finds Orpheum vaudeville review in old San
Francisco Chronicle…Mr. Billingsley won back two weeks' rent at dice…Jack says
goodbye to Ronald Colman…stops at drug store, is challenged by pushy French
clerk…meets Rochester at the station…Jack's trunk fell off the truck, his high silk hat is
now a beanie…everyone says goodbye to their mothers, Phil's mother uses hipster
talk…Mary wants to buy a mink coat on Paramount's tab…promo for Aldrich Family

Cast:

Last name	First name	Roles	Guest star
		Ronald Colman	No
		Mrs. Harris	No
Anderson	Eddie	Rochester	No
Baldwin	Harry	Train station drug store clerk	No
Beloin	Ed	Mr. Billingsley, Eddie	No
Benny	Jack	Jack Benny	No
Day	Dennis	Dennis Day	No
Feld	Fritz	Drug store clerk	No
Felton	Verna	Mrs. Day	No
Harris	Phil	Phil Harris	No
Lewis	Elliott	Express company	No
Livingstone	Mary	Mary Livingstone	No
Marr	Eddie	Cabbie	No
Morrow	Bill	Bill, train announcer	No
Stewart	Blanche	Mrs. Wilson	No
Wilson	Don	Don Wilson	No

Songs:

Order	Title	Performers	Vocal
1	My Wonderful One, Let's Dance	Phil Harris	No
2	Too Romantic	Dennis Day	Yes
3	Dreams in the Night	Phil Harris	No
4	I Walk With Music	Phil Harris	No

Notes:

Running gag	Relay question and answer

Date: 4/21/1940   **Sponsor:** Jell-O   **City:** New York, NY

Recording Source: Unknown   **Problems:** Partial show

First line:
And now ladies and gentlemen, we bring you a man who arrived here Tuesday morning at Grand Central Station, and was greeted by thousands and thousands of his loyal fans.

Summary:
From Ritz Theatre...Jack staying at the Sherry Netherland...reporter wants story from Jack...Jack spied on Fred Allen's program, Allen wears breakaway suspenders...Dennis went to burlesque shows, has a date with Fifi LaRose, a chorus girl...Phil arrives late...Logan Jerkfinkle says he's one of Jack's biggest fans, wants to shake hands with Frank Parker...Phil brought Frankie from Hollywood to press his pants...Jack says he's making a picture with Fred Allen in the summer...Rochester calls, claims he didn't know where Jack was staying...Jack looking for his cowboy suit

Cast:

Last name	First name	Roles	Guest star
Anderson	Eddie	Rochester	No
Baldwin	Harry	Porter, door guy	No
Beloin	Ed	Hotel bellboy	No
Benny	Jack	Jack Benny	No
Brown	John	Brown of Staten Island Bugle	No
Cantor	Charles	Logan Jerkfinkle	No
Day	Dennis	Dennis Day	No
Harris	Phil	Phil Harris	No
Livingstone	Mary	Mary Livingstone	No
Morrow	Bill	Streetcar driver	No
Wilson	Don	Don Wilson	No

Songs:

Order	Title	Performers	Vocal
1	My Little Girl	Phil Harris	No
2	Last Night's Gardenias	Dennis Day	Yes
3	My Kind of Country	Phil Harris	No
4	You Darling	Phil Harris	No

Notes:

Blooper	Door guy stumbles on "Can you tell me how to get to Ripley's Believe It or Not Auditorium?"
Blooper	Rochester says, "I just pointed...I thought I just pointed."
Notable	First time Jack describes how blue his eyes are ("Alice blue")
Recording	Ending clipped in middle of Jack-Rochester dialogue

Date: 4/28/1940   **Sponsor:** Jell-O   **City:** New York, NY

Recording Source: West coast   **Problems:** None

First line:
And now ladies and gentlemen, I bring you the latest and greatest of Western heroes, a rugged, two-fisted cowboy who rides like Roy Rogers, hoots like Hoot Gibson, hops like Hopalong Cassidy, and skips like Alison Skipworth, Jack Benny.

Summary:
From Ritz Theatre...Jack is an usher at Paramount so he can see his picture six times a day, Jack claims it's his cousin Boo-Boo...Mark Sandrich hyptonized Jack to make him a good actor...Frankie wrote a letter to the editor praising Phil...Peter Van Steeden asks Mary to go out with him...Jack was asked to appear on "Information Please", but he turned it down...Jack took Dennis' girlfriend, Fifi LaRose, away from him...Logan Jerkfinkle says he's a Don Wilson fan...next week parodying Fred Allen...Rochester was on Fred Allen's program last week...Jack calls Rochester about his appearance...Allen wants Rochester to be his valet..."Goodnight Joanie, be a good girl"...Marty Lewis of Radio Guide, Jack most popular comedian, Don is outstanding announcer

Cast:

Last name	First name	Roles	Guest star
Anderson	Eddie	Rochester	No
Benny	Jack	Jack Benny	No
Cantor	Charles	Logan Jerkfinkle	No
Day	Dennis	Dennis Day	No
Green	Eddie	Mr. DeWitt	No
Harris	Phil	Phil Harris	No
Lewis	Marty	Marty Lewis	Yes
Livingstone	Mary	Mary Livingstone	No
Van Steeden	Peter	Peter Van Steeden	Yes
Wilson	Don	Don Wilson	No

Songs:

Order	Title	Performers	Vocal
1	I Hear Bluebirds	Phil Harris	No
2	Woodpecker Song	Phil Harris	No
3	Say It	Dennis Day	Yes
4	I Got My Eyes on You	Phil Harris	No

Notes:

Blooper	Jack says "Good thing I've got my uniform during my...under my suit."
Notable	First "Goodnight Joanie"
Running gag	But but but

Date: 5/5/1940   **Sponsor:** Jell-O   **City:** New York, NY
Recording Source: East coast   **Problems:** None

First line:
And now ladies and gentlemen, I would like to announce that tonight marks the ninth radio anniversary of our Master of Ceremonies. So without further ado, we bring you a man who for nine long years in the field of radio has worked, slaved, worried, and looks it, Jack Benny.

Summary:
Jack discusses his start in radio for Bixby's Bonnie Biscuit Batter from 7 to 7:05AM...Phil can't find his hotel...Jack was on for Newton's Non-Roll Nightshirts at 5AM...Mary calls her mother...Dennis brings Jack a cake, he can't blow out the candles...Jack puts a clothespin on his nose to imitate Allen...skit The Fred Allen Show...News of the Week interviews Rochester...guest is an amateur street cleaner...question of the week panel introduced...runs out of time due to too much ad-libbing

Cast:

Last name	First name	Roles	Guest star
Anderson	Eddie	Rochester	No
Baldwin	Harry	Tommy, Abner J. Lum (East coast)	No
Beloin	Ed	Eddie, Arlington Brew (West coast)	No
Benny	Jack	Jack Benny, Fred Allen	No
Brown	John	Amateur street cleaner, Merry Mucks	No
Cantor	Charles	Logan Jerkfinkle, Merry Mucks	No
Day	Dennis	Dennis Day, bottle of Sal Hepatica	No
Harris	Phil	Phil Harris, Peter Van Harris	No
Livingstone	Mary	Mary Livingstone, Portland Hoffa	No
Morrow	Bill	Bill	No
Pious	Minerva	Lulu, Merry Mucks, Miss Minnie Tonka/Ruby Stevens	No
Wilson	Don	Don Wilson, Harry Von Wilson	No

Songs:

Order	Title	Performers	Vocal
1	Oh Gee Oh Gosh Oh Golly, I'm in Love	Phil Harris	No
2	Bixby's Batter jingle	Jack Benny	Yes
3	How High the Moon	Dennis Day	Yes
4	Alice Blue Gown	Phil Harris	No
5	Ma He's Making Eyes at Me	Charles Cantor	Yes
5	Ma He's Making Eyes at Me	Minerva Pious	Yes
5	Ma He's Making Eyes at Me	John Brown	Yes
6	Playmates	Phil Harris	No

Notes:

Notable	Jack's anniversary is announced as his ninth, but it is really his eighth. Previous years' discussions of Jack's anniversary were correct.
Running gag	Relay question and answer
Running gag	Mary's mother communication
Skit	Fred Allen Show

Date: 5/12/1940   **Sponsor:** Jell-O   **City:** Hollywood, CA

Recording Source: East coast   **Problems:** None

First line:
And now ladies and gentlemen, for our program tonight, we're going to re-enact the events which occurred on our recent airplane trip from New York to Los Angeles. The time is last Monday morning, and as the scene opens, a taxicab carrying Jack and Mary is approaching the New York Municipal Airport on Long Island.

Summary:
Jack and Mary discuss the expenses…18-hour flight to California…gang discusses what it's like to fly…Phil says goodbye to a girl…Rochester is afraid of flying…Jack buys up magazines with his picture on the front…gang looks at view from the air…stewardess helps the gang…Jack swallows to get his ears to pop…Jack looks at Waukegan from the air…Phil asks for help with his crossword puzzle…little old lady drew a moustache on Jack's picture…hit an air pocket and Jack throws soup all over himself…Jack gets sick in turbulence, falls asleep until they get to Los Angeles…promo for Aldrich Family

Cast:

Last name	First name	Roles	Guest star
Anderson	Eddie	Rochester	No
Beloin	Ed	Cabbie	No
Benny	Jack	Jack Benny	No
Day	Dennis	Dennis Day	No
Harris	Phil	Phil Harris	No
Livingstone	Mary	Mary Livingstone	No
Milford	?	Minnie Jerkfinkle/Jennie Jerkfinkle	No
Morrow	Bill	Newsstand boy, Bidey Talcott	No
Nelson	Frank	Plane announcer	No
Stewart	Blanche	Little old lady	No
Stone	Ann	Miss Rutherford	No
Wilson	Don	Don Wilson	No

Songs:

Order	Title	Performers	Vocal
1	My Wonderful One Let's Dance	Phil Harris	No
2	Unidentified	Phil Harris	No
3	Little Mother of Mine	Dennis Day	Yes
4	Unidentified	Phil Harris	No

Notes:

Date: 5/19/1940 **Sponsor:** Jell-O **City:** Hollywood, CA

Recording Source: Unknown **Problems:** None

First line:
And now ladies and gentlemen, we bring you a man who after three hectic weeks in New York, has returned to the simple life in Southern California, and resumed his favorite hobby of raising flowers.

Summary:
Jack's petunias won an award at the Beverly Hills Flower Show...Jack has created a cactus with no needles...Jack throwing a party for Mr. Mortimer of General Foods, they haven't picked up his option for next season...Dennis is Mr. Mortimer's nephew...Don explains why a woman was out in the wind and rain...Jack gives Dennis the lead in the play, then takes it away when it turns out he's not related to Mr. Mortimer...skit Northwest Passage...Rangers plan to raid Abernathy Indiana...find Mary, who was captured by Indians...Rangers get lost and can't find Indians for six months..."We're a little late, so good night folks"

Cast:

Last name	First name	Roles	Guest star
Baldwin	Harry	Big Chief	No
Beloin	Ed	Snapdragon, Red Feather	No
Benny	Jack	Jack Benny, Major Rogers	No
Day	Dennis	Dennis Day, Konkapot	No
Harris	Phil	Phil Harris, Private Harris	No
Livingstone	Mary	Mary Livingstone	No
Morrow	Bill	Thundercloud	No
Nelson	Frank	Narrator	No
Wilson	Don	Don Wilson, company of Rangers	No

Songs:

Order	Title	Performers	Vocal
1	Where Do I Go From You	Phil Harris	No
2	With the Wind and the Rain in Her Hair	Dennis Day	Yes
3	Meet the Sun Half Way	Phil Harris	No
4	Where Was I	Phil Harris	No

Notes:

Notable	First "Now cut that out"
Notable	Jack calls Ed Beloin "Beloin"
Running gag	Relay question and answer
Skit	Northwest Passage

Date: 5/26/1940 **Sponsor:** Jell-O **City:** Hollywood, CA

Recording Source: Unknown **Problems:** None

First line:
And now ladies and gentlemen, Mr. Charles G. Mortimer of General Foods, the sponsor of this program, happens to be visiting the coast. So without further ado, we take you to Jack Benny's home in Beverly Hills where Jack is giving a dinner party in Mr. Mortimer's honor. Here we go!

Summary:
Rochester giving Jack a haircut…Rochester makes cocktails with Bay Rum…Jack is nervous about Mr. Mortimer's visit…new cook, Mrs. Nichols, asks for key to the icebox…Mr. Mortimer calls and can't come, Jack gets him to change his mind…everyone teases Jack about his haircut…Mr. Mortimer arrives, gang sings "For He's a Jolly Good Fellow"…Mortimer wishes Mary good luck on her Presidential campaign…Jack tries to cater to Mr. Mortimer…Jack pretends to be drunk…Billingsley says he's on the wagon (hic)…fired old Chinese cook…Mortimer surprised because they're serving apple pie for dessert…Jack fires Rochester and Don Wilson faints…Mortimer picks up Jack's option, Jack asks how he knows he's available…promo for Aldrich Family

Cast:

Last name	First name	Roles	Guest star
Anderson	Eddie	Rochester	No
Beloin	Ed	Mr. Billingsley	No
Benny	Jack	Jack Benny	No
Day	Dennis	Dennis Day	No
Harris	Phil	Phil Harris	No
Hicks	Russell	Mr. Mortimer	No
Kelly	Mary	Mrs. Nichols	No
Livingstone	Mary	Mary Livingstone	No
Wilson	Don	Don Wilson	No

Songs:

Order	Title	Performers	Vocal
1	Let's Have Another One	Phil Harris	No
2	You Can't Brush Me Off	Phil Harris	No
3	Violetta	Dennis Day	Yes
4	Believing	Phil Harris	No

Notes:

Date: 6/2/1940   **Sponsor:** Jell-O   **City:** Hollywood, CA

Recording Source: Unknown   **Problems:** None

First line:
And now ladies and gentlemen, we bring you our Master of Ceremonies, a man who had his option picked up last Sunday and now looks ten years younger, Jack Benny.

Summary:
Gang teases Jack about being nervous with Mr. Mortimer…Mortimer won every game of Bingo…gang went to fortune teller Madame Zuzu…Zuzu says Jack will win the Academy Award…Jack criticizes Phil's band…Jack and Dennis go out to negotiate Dennis' contract…gang keeps eavesdropping on negotiations…Dennis asks for $500 a week, Jack offers $37.50…Rochester calls, he bought a racehorse…Rochester's new contract says a week is 14 days…Don has written a play, "Code of the Hills"…feud between Jake Bennys and Fud Allens…feud started over question about how many hairs on a monkey's face…Linda Lou went to buy a girdle…Don comes in and does Jell-O commercial, Zeke shoots him on the "O"

Cast:

Last name	First name	Roles	Guest star
Anderson	Eddie	Rochester	No
Baldwin	Harry	Wilson responder 1	No
Beloin	Ed	Clem	No
Benny	Jack	Jack Benny, Jake Benny	No
Day	Dennis	Dennis Day, Zeb Benny	No
Harris	Phil	Phil Harris, Twitch Harris	No
Kelly	Mary	Linda Lou	No
Livingstone	Mary	Mary Livingstone, Ma Benny	No
Morrow	Bill	Zeke	No
Wilson	Don	Don Wilson, Porky Wilson	No

Songs:

Order	Title	Performers	Vocal
1	I Hear Bluebirds	Phil Harris	No
2	Alice Blue Gown	Phil Harris	No
3	Where Was I	Dennis Day	Yes
4	You're Lonely, I'm Lonely	Phil Harris	No

Notes:

Notable	Show runs long, close cut off
Running gag	Relay question and answer
Skit	Code of the Hills

Date: 6/9/1940   **Sponsor:** Jell-O   **City:** Hollywood, CA

Recording Source: Unknown   **Problems:** None

First line:
And now ladies and gentlemen, I would like to announce that...uh...next week marks our final appearance on the air for this season. So tonight we bring you our Master of Ceremonies who has one more Sunday to greet you.

Summary:
Jack going to Honolulu, staying at the Sweet Leilani Auto Court...Don says Jack should stay at the Royal Hawaiian...Jack bought an old swimsuit from his father, he also sold Don a sarong and Mary a sailor suit...going on the Luralene...Jack got Sandrich to eliminate Fred Allen from upcoming movie...Phil wants to sit on the beach with a couple papayas...Remley sits in Phil's rumble seat with a lasso for women...Jack asks gang to come to boat to see him off...Don does commercial in Hawaiian...Jack charges Phil $5 for listening to Fred Allen...announces skit Number Please, based on Los Angeles telephone directory...Andy Devine drives a horse and buggy to town...Andy wants to have the summer show (Aldrich Family is summer show)...Fred Allen is in town to make a picture with Jack...Jack calls Mark Sandrich to complain, but Sandrich won't relent...Don does show close, solicits donations to Red Cross due to "destruction in Europe"

Cast:

Last name	First name	Roles	Guest star
Benny	Jack	Jack Benny	No
Day	Dennis	Dennis Day	No
Devine	Andy	Andy Devine	No
Harris	Phil	Phil Harris	No
Livingstone	Mary	Mary Livingstone	No
Wilson	Don	Don Wilson	No

Songs:

Order	Title	Performers	Vocal
1	Goodnight Moonlight	Phil Harris	No
2	Cecilia	Phil Harris	No
3	Say It	Dennis Day	Yes
4	How Can I Ever Be Alone	Phil Harris	No

Notes:

Notable	Jack ad libs to Mary "Gee, you're cute tonight"
Running gag	But but but

Date: 6/16/1940 **Sponsor:** Jell-O **City:** Hollywood, CA

Recording Source: Unknown **Problems:** None

First line:
Soda jerk 1: One cherry phosphate!

Summary:
Gang gathers at drug store...Don sits on Jack's straw hat...sandwich is the Jack Benny three-decker delight...Paramount put Jack and Fred in adjoining dressing rooms...Jack compromised with Mark Sandrich, Fred Allen has to be the straight man...customer tells Jack he didn't like his program...Phil going on the road next week...Don pursues Jell-O thieves...Mrs. Day thinks Dennis should have more jokes...Jack gets intimidated by Henry Aldrich replacing him...Aldrich shows up and Jack is cold to him, Aldrich pays him compliments and Jack softens...Jack and Aldrich go to the drug store for a sandwich...Jack suggests that Aldrich does a dramatic or adventure show

Cast:

Last name	First name	Roles	Guest star
Baldwin	Harry	Time customer	No
Beloin	Ed	Soda jerk 1, Eddie	No
Benny	Jack	Jack Benny	No
Day	Dennis	Dennis Day	No
Felton	Verna	Mrs. Day	No
Harris	Phil	Phil Harris	No
Livingstone	Mary	Mary Livingstone	No
Morrow	Bill	Soda jerk 2, Bill	No
Rubin	Benny	Mooley customer	No
Stone	Ezra	Henry Aldrich	No
Wilson	Don	Don Wilson	No

Songs:

Order	Title	Performers	Vocal
1	Down by the Ohio	Phil Harris	No
2	Blue Lovebird	Dennis Day	Yes
3	Make Believe Island	Phil Harris	No

Notes:

Running gag	Relay question and answer

Date: 10/6/1940 **Sponsor:** Jell-O **City:** Hollywood, CA

Recording Source: Unknown **Problems:** Music clipped

First line:
Nelson: Fall is here. It is the sixth day of October, and Jell-O is back on the air. But where are all our little playmates?

Summary:
Narrator says that all the cast is asleep, Blue Fairy awakens them one by one...gang discusses the opening...Phil discusses this summer's tour...Dennis wants a raise because Kenny Baker has a yacht...Jack gives entire cast a raise...man shows up to interview Jack, asks about when he's going to be out of town (he's a burglar)...Jack wrote corny Jell-O commercial...Jack leaves to go home and write an article for the Saturday Evening Post...Rochester asks if he's getting a raise too...Jack has Rochester stop the car to pick up a girl, but she won't speak to him...Mary does show close...Phil is taking the Blue Fairy to the Wilshire Bowl

Cast:

Last name	First name	Roles	Guest star
Anderson	Eddie	Rochester	No
Baldwin	Harry	Will Jack wake voice 1	No
Beloin	Ed	Eddie, Gross	No
Benny	Jack	Jack Benny	No
Day	Dennis	Dennis Day	No
Felton	Verna	Mrs. Day	No
Harris	Phil	Phil Harris	No
Kelly	Mary	Blue Fairy	No
Livingstone	Mary	Mary Livingstone	No
Morrow	Bill	Bill	No
Nelson	Frank	Opening narrator	No
Wilson	Don	Don Wilson	No

Songs:

Order	Title	Performers	Vocal
1	Awake, awake, awake	Mary Kelly	Yes
2	Shout I am an American	Phil Harris	No
3	When the Swallows Come Back to Capistrano	Dennis Day	Yes
4	Our Love Affair	Phil Harris	No
5	Unidentified	Phil Harris	No

Notes:

Notable	Unusual opening, Blue Fairy awakens the cast
Running gag	Relay question and answer

Date: 10/13/1940   **Sponsor:** Jell-O   **City:** Hollywood, CA

Recording Source: Unknown   **Problems:** Music clipped

First line:
And now ladies and gentlemen, I bring you a man who returned to the air last Sunday, happy as a June bride and just as nervous, Jack Benny.

Summary:
Jack says that he wasn't nervous…Ed Sullivan liked last week's show, Jack reads the review…got a good review in "The Alcatraz Herald"…Jack wants to play violin with Phil's band…Jack owes Phil $10 on World Series…Jack doesn' t carry his money in his sock since a midget picked his ankle…Jack won $5 from Don…clipping from Mary's mother…Dennis wants to change the day he mows Jack's lawn because he needs to register for the draft…Jack explains the draft to Phil…Rochester elected Mayor of Central Avenue…Jack and Mary playing a benefit for the British Red Cross at the El Capitan…Jack calls Rochester to have him pick him up at the El Capitan…Rochester encourages Jack to trade in the Maxwell at the Auto Show…Jack made so many bets on the World Series that he broke even…Log Cabin ad is show close

Cast:

Last name	First name	Roles	Guest star
		Tommy	No
Anderson	Eddie	Rochester	No
Baldwin	Harry	Special delivery boy	No
Benny	Jack	Jack Benny	No
Day	Dennis	Dennis Day	No
Harris	Phil	Phil Harris	No
Livingstone	Mary	Mary Livingstone	No
Wilson	Don	Don Wilson	No

Songs:

Order	Title	Performers	Vocal
1	Ferry Boat Serenade	Phil Harris	No
2	Get the Moon Out of Your Eyes	Jack Benny	No
2	Get the Moon Out of Your Eyes	Phil Harris	No
3	The Nearness of You	Dennis Day	Yes
4	In a Moon Boat	Phil Harris	No

Notes:

Blooper	Rochester misses his entrance cue
Notable	Gag about reading a bad review and thinking it's good…originally used with Phil Harris, now with Jack
Notable	Log Cabin Syrup ad substituted for show close
Running gag	Mary's mother communication

Date: 10/20/1940 **Sponsor:** Jell-O **City:** Hollywood, CA

Recording Source: West coast **Problems:** Other

First line:
And now ladies and gentlemen, this being the hottest week of the year in Southern California, we bring you a man who can hardly stand it in his long underwear, Jack Benny.

Summary:
Jack discusses his schedule (on Gulf Screen Guild tonight)...Mary teases Jack about having so much medicine...Jack made kids sign a lease to put a lemonade stand in his front yard...Jack explains the draft to Dennis...Mark Sandrich calls for Jack, Jack wants top billing in "Love Thy Neighbor"...Jack talks about working with Mary Martin...Door guy heard last week's show...Mary tells what happened when Jack tried to trade in Maxwell...flashback: Mary, Jack, and Rochester going to trade in car...Jack thinking of getting a Rio or Chandler (haven't made either in years)...Jack considering buying a Packard...says it's a 1921 Maxwell...Vandemere appraises Jack's Maxwell, Collins offers him $40...new Packard is $1450...Jack making out the check, gets upset when they go to junk the Maxwell, calls off the deal...Mary does show close

Cast:

Last name	First name	Roles	Guest star
Anderson	Eddie	Rochester	No
Baldwin	Harry	Door guy	No
Beloin	Ed	Mr. Collins the Packard dealer	No
Benny	Jack	Jack Benny	No
Day	Dennis	Dennis Day	No
Harris	Phil	Phil Harris	No
Livingstone	Mary	Mary Livingstone	No
Rubin	Benny	Mr. Vandermeer	No
Wilson	Don	Don Wilson	No
Wright	?	Officer	No

Songs:

Order	Title	Performers	Vocal
1	The Sun Will Be Up In the Morning	Phil Harris	No
2	Trade Winds	Dennis Day	Yes
3	The World Is In My Arms	Phil Harris	No
4	Once In a Love	Phil Harris	No

Notes:

Recording	Dennis' and Phil's songs clipped

Date: 10/27/1940   **Sponsor:** Jell-O   **City:** Hollywood, CA

Recording Source: Unknown   **Problems:** Other

First line:
And now ladies and gentlemen, without further ado, we bring you our modest, unassuming Master of Ceremonies, a man who is never too busy to say "Hello"...

Summary:
Jack is friendly to strangers...Mary is out with a cold, Dennis to read Mary's lines...Blue Fairy appears to stand in for Mary, Jack says she's too fat...Phil goes to night school, starts spewing facts...includes Rochester as water boy in football sketch...skit Hold That Line...Coach Benny gives team a pep talk at halftime...water boy mixes Tom Collins in bucket...brings in sensational new player (Butch Shlepperman)...Shlepperman is tackled hard and is carried off...Blue Fairy offers to carry the ball...she carries 21 footballs simultaneously over the goal line and Flatfoot wins...Jack talks on phone with Mary, "Good night, Doll." (in the script)

Cast:

Last name	First name	Roles	Guest star
Anderson	Eddie	Rochester, water boy	No
Baldwin	Harry	Ejected player	No
Benny	Jack	Jack Benny, Coach Flash Benny	No
Day	Dennis	Dennis Day	No
Harris	Phil	Phil Harris	No
Hearn	Sam	Butch Shlepperman	No
Kelly	Mary	Blue Fairy	No
Nelson	Frank	Announcer	No
Wilson	Don	Don Wilson	No

Songs:

Order	Title	Performers	Vocal
1	Just Like Taking Candy From a Baby	Phil Harris	No
2	That's for Me	Phil Harris	No
3	He's My Uncle	Dennis Day	Yes
4	One Look at You	Phil Harris	No

Notes:

Recording	Part of Phil's song clipped, Dennis' song clipped
Skit	Hold That Line

Date: 11/3/1940 **Sponsor:** Jell-O **City:** Hollywood, CA

Recording Source: Unknown **Problems:** Wrong speed

First line:
And now ladies and gentlemen, as you all know, last Thursday evening was Halloween, and Jack celebrated by throwing his annual costume party for the Jell-O gang. So this evening we will turn back the clock. The time, last Thursday night. The place, Jack's home in Beverly Hills. Take it away!

Summary:
Jack going as a hula girl...Jack has a tatoo for Waukegan...Dennis comes in a Navy suit because his girlfriend goes with a sailor...Jack suggests that Mary wear one of his old vaudeville suits...Dennis asks why he only got 35 cents for mowing Jack's lawn last week ("it's the winter rate")...Don comes as a skeleton, Phil as Julius Caesar...Dennis has sweet cider and thinks he's drunk...Mary finds a program from the Globe Theatre in Kansas City, MO (all others are animal acts)...Mr. Billingsley took cord of rope to his room, playing a flute to it...Mary finds an old love letter from Lupe Herman in the suit pocket...Mary says Phil isn't so dumb...Billingsley is going as Napoleon, doesn't know it's Halloween...Jack does the hula, his grass skirt catches fire from his cigar...Jack jumps in the swimming pool, but Rochester drained the pool...reminder to vote on November 5...Log Cabin Syrup ad

Cast:

Last name	First name	Roles	Guest star
Anderson	Eddie	Rochester	No
Beloin	Ed	Mr. Billingsley	No
Benny	Jack	Jack Benny	No
Day	Dennis	Dennis Day	No
Harris	Phil	Phil Harris	No
Livingstone	Mary	Mary Livingstone	No
Wilson	Don	Don Wilson	No

Songs:

Order	Title	Performers	Vocal
1	Let's Be Buddies	Phil Harris	No
2	Do You Know Why	Dennis Day	Yes
3	You Catch on Quick	Mary Livingstone	Yes
3	You Catch on Quick	Jack Benny	Yes
3	You Catch on Quick	Don Wilson	Yes
3	You Catch on Quick	Phil Harris	Yes
4	Dream Valley	Phil Harris	No

Notes:

Blooper	Mary stutters on "They t-tomatoed him in Toledo"
Notable	First "Oh Rohhh-chester..."

Date: 11/10/1940   **Sponsor:** Jell-O   **City:** Hollywood, CA

Recording Source: Unknown   **Problems:** Other

First line:
The orchestra opens the program with…
Phil: Wait a minute, Don. Hold it. Hold it. We can't start the show yet.

Summary:
Jack out in the hall talking to Mark Sandrich, wants premiere in Waukegan…no one will let Dennis get a word in edgewise…Jack is elected dog catcher of Beverly Hills…Phil corrects Jack's pronunciation…Mr. LeBaron calls for Jack, Mary plays Jack's secretary…LeBaron doesn't support a debut in Waukegan either…Door guy asks if Jack is dog catcher…announces skit Murder at the Soda Fountain…Mr. Freeman calls, he wants debut in Greenville, GA…Jack needs to leave for Paramount and summarizes play…makes Rochester deputy dog catcher…Jack tells Rochester to put his money in real estate, but Rochester doesn't have a shovel…see Mr. Freeman leaving just as they arrive at Paramount, crash the Maxwell into his Cadillac…"Good night, folks"…Log Cabin Syrup ad

Cast:

Last name	First name	Roles	Guest star
Anderson	Eddie	Rochester	No
Baldwin	Harry	Door guy	No
Beloin	Ed	Man in hall	No
Benny	Jack	Jack Benny	No
Day	Dennis	Dennis Day	No
Harris	Phil	Phil Harris	No
Livingstone	Mary	Mary Livingstone	No
Nelson	Frank	Sightseeing bus guide	No
Wilson	Don	Don Wilson	No

Songs:

Order	Title	Performers	Vocal
1	I Just Want to Be With You	Phil Harris	No
2	Blueberry Hill	Dennis Day	Yes
3	Bad Humor Man	Phil Harris	No
4	So You're the One	Phil Harris	No

Notes:

Blooper	Mary stumbles of "Root for Roosevelt"
Recording	Phil's band number clipped
Running gag	But but but

Date: 11/17/1940   **Sponsor:** Jell-O   **City:** Hollywood, CA

Recording Source: Unknown   **Problems:** None

First line:
And now ladies and gentlemen, I'd like to explain why Jack Benny is not here for his customary introduction. As you may remember, Jack has been having a lot of trouble lately with Paramount regarding the premiere of his picture that he recently made with Fred Allen.

Summary:
Jack and Mary waiting to see Mark Sandrich...talks with mooley writer...Rochester gets a ticket for pulling in a 10-minute zone for 3 hours...people keep going ahead of Jack into Sandrich's office...Jack gets mad and goes to look for Mr. LeBaron...mooley writer is waiting for LeBaron too, wrote "Desire Like Anything"...Jack brought his own box lunch...mooley writer plugs Jell-O...Mary Martin comes into the office, Mary Livingstone insults her...Mary Martin goes in to sing a song for LeBaron...Jack leaves to see Mr. Freeman...shaves in Freeman's office...Jack gave all his confederate money to Dennis...Jack gets angry and throws a fit, then leaves...Jack decides to solicit Martin's support for a Waukegan premiere

Cast:

Last name	First name	Roles	Guest star
Anderson	Eddie	Rochester	No
Baldwin	Harry	Program seller	No
Beloin	Ed	Mr. Welch	No
Benny	Jack	Jack Benny	No
Blanc	Mel	Mr. Lopez	No
Day	Dennis	Dennis Day	No
Harris	Phil	Phil Harris	No
Kelly	Mary	Miss Brecker	No
Lewis	Elliott	Oinest Hemingway	No
Livingstone	Mary	Mary Livingstone	No
Martin	Mary	Mary Martin	Yes
Nelson	Frank	Mr. Nelson	No
Rubin	Benny	Benjamin Rubin	No
Rubin	Benny	Colonel Beaumont	No
Stewart	Blanche	Miss Wellman	No
Wilson	Don	Don Wilson	No

Songs:

Order	Title	Performers	Vocal
1	You Walked By	Phil Harris	No
2	Ferry Boat Serenade	Phil Harris	No
3	Isn't That Just Like Love	Mary Martin	Yes
4	I'd Know You Anywhere	Phil Harris	No

Notes:

Recording	Open and closinig commercials clipped

Date: 11/24/1940   **Sponsor:** Jell-O   **City:** Hollywood, CA

Recording Source: Unknown   **Problems:** Other

First line:
And now ladies and gentlemen, as is customary every Sunday night…
Jack: Wait a minute, Don, wait a minute. Hold Everything.

Summary:
Jack introduces Don as a bridegroom…spent honeymoon in Coronado Beach…Jack gave Don a bowl of wax fruit that lights up…Phil says he envies Don…Dennis thinks he has the goods on Don…Door guy plays cupid…Phil wrote a ballad…Don does Jell-O commercial in Eskimo…movie debut will be in New York City…Don invites gang over to the house to meet his new wife, Peggy, Jack tells him to call his wife…Rochester calls, extols cultural virtues of New York…Jack captured two great danes, Darryl Zanuck says one of them is his polo pony…Phil and Dennis fight to pay for the cab…Don has gang hide in rose bushes so his wife isn't upset…Don brings in Phil and Mary…Jack complains that he told Don to "Call up the little woman"…Don says he saw Dennis ride up on his bicycle…it starts to rain with Jack outside…burglar holds up Jack, and Jack continues to complain

Cast:

Last name	First name	Roles	Guest star
Anderson	Eddie	Rochester	No
Baldwin	Harry	Door guy, passerby at Don's	No
Benny	Jack	Jack Benny	No
Day	Dennis	Dennis Day	No
Harris	Phil	Phil Harris	No
Livingstone	Mary	Mary Livingstone	No
Max	Ed	Burglar	No
Morrow	Bill	Cabbie	No
Stone	Ann	Peggy Wilson	No
Wilson	Don	Don Wilson	No

Songs:

Order	Title	Performers	Vocal
1	Meet the People	Phil Harris	No
2	Two Dreams Met	Dennis Day	Yes
3	Ferry Boat Serenade	Phil Harris	No
4	Not So Long Ago	Phil Harris	No

Notes:

Blooper	Phil ad libs "Reading isn't going to help this any"
Blooper	Phil loses his place during the talk of his song
Recording	Opening commercial, Dennis' song, Phil's song, part of end commercial clipped

Date: 12/1/1940 **Sponsor:** Jell-O **City:** Hollywood, CA

Recording Source: Unknown **Problems:** None

First line:
And now ladies and gentlemen, I regret to announce that Jack Benny has been confined to his bed for the past week with a severe cold, due to an unfortunate occurrence at my house last Sunday. It seems that I invited Jack and the rest of the gang over to meet my wife, and while Jack was waiting outside, it started to rain…

Summary:
Jack still complaining about Don not calling his wife…Dorothy Lamarr calls to see how Jack is, she's the Colman's cook…Mary makes Jack an omelet with Vap-O-Rub…Rochester took four cigars out of the humidor…Dennis sings Jack to sleep…Rochester breaks the humidor…going to New York next week…Billingsley wove a magic carpet…Phil brings flowers for Jack's nurse…girl from bowling alley calls, Phil says she's homely…Jack's cough syrup is 60% alcohol, Phil starts coughing…Billingsley is under the bed looking for his cloud…Jack still mad at Don…Jack and Don argue…Doctor was up all night with Gene Autry's horse…puts corks in Jack's nostrils, Jack sneezes them out…Jack gets held up in his own bedroom, wants his mattress…Jack grabs his gun and shoots him…turns out to be a dream…no show close...ad for Sanka

Cast:

Last name	First name	Roles	Guest star
Anderson	Eddie	Rochester	No
Beloin	Ed	Mr. Billingsley	No
Benny	Jack	Jack Benny	No
Day	Dennis	Dennis Day	No
Harris	Phil	Phil Harris	No
Livingstone	Mary	Mary Livingstone	No
Max	Ed	Burglar	No
Nelson	Frank	Doctor LeRoy	No
Wilson	Don	Don Wilson	No

Songs:

Order	Title	Performers	Vocal
1	You Say the Sweetest Things	Phil Harris	No
2	A Nightingale Sang in Berkeley Square	Dennis Day	Yes
3	Isn't That Just Like Love	Phil Harris	No
4	Johnny Peddler	Phil Harris	No

Notes:

Date: 12/8/1940 **Sponsor:** Jell-O **City:** Hollywood, CA

Recording Source: Unknown **Problems:** None

First line:
And now ladies and gentlemen, it gives me great pleasure to present a man I have been associated with for many years, and whom I'm proud to call my friend.

Summary:
Don gets mad and walks out...Jack says he used to pose for muscle magazines...Phil talks about songs his trumpet player wrote...Door guy says there was a song written about him...leaving tomorrow for New York...Phil says he can't go to New York because he doesn't want to leave night school...Don and Jack continue to argue...Phil says he's going to be a shrub in the night school play...Don tells Mr. Swallow that Jack put a slug in the apple machine, Swallow bawls Jack out...Bob Hope told Brenda and Cobina not to go out with Jack...Fred Allen still making cracks about Jack...Doctor visits Jack, gives Jack a shot, leaves needle in his arm...Jack and Don make up...Rochester calls, burned Jack's pants...threw mothballs in with Jack's overcoat, the moths juggled them...can't catch Jack's coonskin cap...ad for Sanka

Cast:

Last name	First name	Roles	Guest star
Anderson	Eddie	Rochester	No
Baldwin	Harry	Door guy	No
Benny	Jack	Jack Benny	No
Cleary	Leo	Mr. Swallow	No
Day	Dennis	Dennis Day	No
Harris	Phil	Phil Harris	No
Livingstone	Mary	Mary Livingstone	No
Nelson	Frank	Dr. LeRoy	No
Wilson	Don	Don Wilson	No

Songs:

Order	Title	Performers	Vocal
1	You Walked By	Phil Harris	No
2	Bad Humor Man	Phil Harris	No
3	I'd Know You Anywhere	Dennis Day	Yes
4	If You Were Mine	Phil Harris	No

Notes:

Blooper	Jack says "You little trainer" instead of "You little traitor"

Date: 12/15/1940 **Sponsor:** Jell-O **City:** New York, NY
Recording Source: Unknown **Problems:** None

First line:
And now ladies and gentlemen, as you all know, this week our program originates from
New York City.

Summary:
From the Ritz Theatre, New York...Jack has a bodyguard (Killer Hogan), so he isn't afraid
of Fred Allen...Killer Hogan very effeminate...Don is on honeymoon in New York...Jack
offers to pay his hotel bill, Don's at the Ritz, gives Don a handful of nickels to eat...Mary
took Hogan's blackjack away...Don and Mary thought Ed Wynn was great, Jack is
jealous...Dennis' uncle is house detective at Sherry-Netherland...Door guy gets knocked
out by Hogan...Dennis waiting at stage entrance for burlesque girls...Phil followed a
blonde to Staten Island...Jack's doctor followed him to New York...doctor has Jack hold
his breath and Don does Jell-O commercial...Mayor of Waukegan drops in, thinks Dennis
is Kenny Baker...Talcott thought that the movie was debuting in Waukegan...Jack makes
calls to find Rochester in Harlem...no closing commercial

Cast:

Last name	First name	Roles	Guest star
Baldwin	Harry	Door guy	No
Beloin	Ed	Sylvester	No
Benny	Jack	Jack Benny	No
Cantor	Charles	Killer Hogan	No
Day	Dennis	Dennis Day	No
Green	Eddie	Radcliffe Sayles Jr.	No
Harris	Phil	Phil Harris	No
Huey	?	Harlem Benevolent Club operator	No
James	Gee Gee	Susan Brown	No
Livingstone	Mary	Mary Livingstone	No
Morrow	Bill	Pancake	No
Nelson	Frank	Dr. LeRoy	No
Talcott	Mancel	Mayor Mancel "Bidey" Talcott	Yes
Wilson	Don	Don Wilson	No

Songs:

Order	Title	Performers	Vocal
1	Cheerio	Phil Harris	No
2	There I Go	Dennis Day	Yes
3	So You're the One	Phil Harris	No
4	Unidentified	Phil Harris	No

Notes:

Blooper	Mary calls Don "Dan"
Blooper	Talcott says "Kenny Bakee" instead of "Kenny Baker"
Notable	Open commercial maintains that listeners had never been offered a recipe book, but "Jack and Mary's Jell-O Cookbook" is dated 1937
Running gag	Relay question and answer

Date: 12/22/1940   **Sponsor:** Jell-O   **City:** Hollywood, CA
Recording Source: West coast   **Problems:** None

First line:
And now ladies and gentlemen, there being just two more shopping days till Christmas, we bring you that fugitive from Gimbel's basement, Jack Benny.

Summary:
From the Ritz Theatre, New York...shopping women tore up Jack at Gimbel's...Mary calls Jack "Doll" because his hair is glued on...Jack asks Don for an opinion on Fred Allen's performance...Phil got Jack a box of nuts...Phil's band sells potato peelers, etc...Dennis cleaned up at Roseland...Dennis and Kenny Baker seeing the town...Jack says Dennis shouldn't be a cheapskate...Rochester calls, Jack bawls him out for disappearing...Rochester tells what he's been doing...Rochester tells Susan that he'll be back in a half hour, but forgot to hang up the phone...Jack, Phil, and Mary go shopping...wants to buy a compact for Aunt Molly, gets harassed by cosmetics clerk...customer saw Jack's picture and thinks he's a floorwalker...Jack says "She looks like Babe Marks"...Jack wants to buy a collar button...meet Kenny Baker buying a camera...Kenny says that Allen pays him every week...Jack and Kenny reminisce..."Merry Christmas, see you Wednesday Miss Benny"...ad for Sanka

Cast:

Last name	First name	Roles	Guest star
Anderson	Eddie	Rochester	No
Baker	Kenny	Kenny Baker	Yes
Beloin	Ed	Cosmetics clerk	No
Benny	Jack	Jack Benny	No
Brown	John	Collar button clerk	No
Day	Dennis	Dennis Day	No
Harris	Phil	Phil Harris	No
James	Gee Gee	Susan Brown	No
Kelly	Mary	Camera clerk	No
Livingstone	Mary	Mary Livingstone	No
Pious	Minerva	Evening gown customer	No
Wilson	Don	Don Wilson	No

Songs:

Order	Title	Performers	Vocal
1	Tookie/This and That	Phil Harris	No
2	Jingle Bells	Phil Harris	No
3	The First Noel/Oh Come All Ye Faithful	Dennis Day	Yes
4	Harris Number #1	Phil Harris	No

Notes:

Blooper	Phil slow on his cue for "Yeah?"
Blooper	Rochester says "Our weekend ended up the Harlem" instead of "up the Hudson"; Roch later gets a big laugh and Jack says, "That makes up for the one you muffed!"
Notable	Rochester breaks character for a moment on his blooper
Notable	Kenny Baker says "Yes please?"
Notable	Jack wishes Joan Merry Christmas, calls her "Miss Benny"

Date: 12/29/1940 **Sponsor:** Jell-O **City:** Hollywood, CA

Recording Source: East coast **Problems:** None

First line:
And now ladies and gentlemen, as you all know, our program last Sunday came to you from New York City. Immediately after the broadcast, the entire Jell-O gang left for Hollywood, and Christmas found us aboard a Union-Pacific train passing through Nebraska.

Summary:
Jack purchased a tree in Chicago, decorating it with items on the train...conductor tells them to stop tearing up timetables for snow...Rochester gave himself Jack's watch for Christmas...Mary scavenging for items for Jack...Phil trying to make a date with a girl, but it's Dennis...kid hassles Jack...Phil didn't know they were on a train, Remley went out to play golf...conductor asks Jack to return ladder for people to get into upper berths...Jack gave Don and his wife a pickle fork, Dennis a bottle of white shoe polish...Jack says that Gladys Zybysko hasn't worked since a steam table fell on her foot (apparently they're back together)...Jack gave Door guy a toupee...skit Father Time Rides Again...Phil tries to explain the play to Dennis...things have been quite a mess in 1940..."lucky we got that swimmin' pool" (Atlantic Ocean)...Fred Allen looks like Father Time...Radio Daily honored Jack's program

Cast:

Last name	First name	Roles	Guest star
Anderson	Eddie	Rochester, Cloud	No
Baldwin	Harry	Door guy	No
Benny	Jack	Jack Benny, Old Man 1940	No
Cleary	Leo	Conductor	No
Conrad	?	Baby 1941	No
Day	Dennis	Dennis Day	No
Harris	Phil	Phil Harris, Moon	No
Kelly	Mary	Venus	No
Livingstone	Mary	Mary Livingstone, Mariah 1940	No
Tetley	William?	Smart aleck kid	No
Wilson	Don	Don Wilson	No

Songs:

Order	Title	Performers	Vocal
1	Encino Madness*/So and So	Phil Harris	No
2	Perfidia	Dennis Day	Yes
3	You Walked By	Phil Harris	No
4	Unidentified	Phil Harris	No

Notes:

Notable	Possibly first time a fake song title is used at the opening of the show
Skit	Father Time Rides Again (New Tenant)

Date: 1/5/1941 **Sponsor:** Jell-O **City:** Hollywood, CA

Recording Source: Unknown **Problems:** None

First line:
And now, ladies and gentlemen, this being the fifth day of January, we bring you a man who is still doing his Christmas shopping, Jack Benny!

Summary:
Jack and Don discuss exchanging gifts…Phil gave Jack an Indian suit…Jack took Mary to the Wilshire Bowl for New Year's Eve…Dennis went to see Jack's picture every night to bolster audience laughter…Phil is late, made New Year's resolution to stop smoking, drinking, gambling, and staying up late…Phil gives Jack his New York expense report, mentions Charlie Bagby…Mary tells about Jack going to the Rose Bowl with Gladys…Schlepperman is selling hot dogs ("You ain't hep till you dine with Schlep")…every guy knows Gladys, including the entire Stanford team…Jack gets mad and leaves…"We're a little late, so goodnight folks."

Cast:

Last name	First name	Roles	Guest star
		Gladys Zybysko	No
Baldwin	Harry	Program seller	No
Beloin	Ed	Ticket taker Eddie	No
Benny	Jack	Jack Benny	No
Day	Dennis	Dennis Day	No
Harris	Phil	Phil Harris	No
Hearn	Sam	Shlepperman	No
Livingstone	Mary	Mary Livingstone	No
Marks	Hilliard	Lexy Flanagan/Mickey Rooney	No
Morrow	Bill	Lefty	No
Norton	?	Drunk	No
Rubin	Benny	Nick	No
Wilson	Don	Don Wilson	No

Songs:

Order	Title	Performers	Vocal
1	Moon Over Tarzana*/Bagby Stomp	Phil Harris	No
2	I'm Going to Round Up My Love	Dennis Day	Yes
3	There'll Be Some Changes Made	Phil Harris	No
4	Harris Spec. #3	Phil Harris	No

Notes:

Date: 1/12/1941   **Sponsor:** Jell-O   **City:** Hollywood, CA

Recording Source: Unknown   **Problems:** None

First line:
And now, ladies and gentlemen, it gives me great pleasure to bring…Phil: Hold it, hold it, Don. Jack isn't here yet.

Summary:
Jack talks with his writers, they have no script for tonight's show…Phil's writer parks cars at the Wilshire Bowl…Mary gets a letter from her mother…they went to see Jack's picture…writers can't write because they thought there was no lead in automatic pencil…Phil suggests gang talk about current events…Rochester calls, Billingsley built a mechanical man…Jack takes partial play from the writers…skit The Murder of Malcolm Smith…wife reports murder…Captain accuses wife of the murder…gang keeps running out of script, getting more pages from writers…Doctor confesses to murder, breaks down and cries

Cast:

Last name	First name	Roles	Guest star
Anderson	Eddie	Rochester	No
Baldwin	Harry	Special delivery guy	No
Beloin	Ed	Eddie	No
Benny	Jack	Jack Benny, Captain O'Benny	No
Day	Dennis	Dennis Day, Sergeant O'Day	No
Harris	Phil	Phil Harris, Doctor Philo Harris	No
Livingstone	Mary	Mary Livingstone, Mrs. J. Malcolm Smith	No
Morrow	Bill	Bill	No
Wilson	Don	Don Wilson, butler	No

Songs:

Order	Title	Performers	Vocal
1	Grounded in Glendale*	Phil Harris	No
2	The Rose of Tralee	Dennis Day	Yes
3	Nellie Bly	Phil Harris	No
4	Unidentified	Phil Harris	No

Notes:

Blooper	Jack stumbles on line "The Benny when we act you better like…uh… act like you enjoy it players"
Running gag	Mary's mother communication
Skit	The Murder of Malcolm Smith

Date: 1/19/1941   **Sponsor:** Jell-O   **City:** Hollywood, CA

Recording Source: Unknown   **Problems:** None

First line:
And now, ladies and gentlemen, I would like to announce that last Monday, a great and well-deserved honor was bestowed upon our illustrious master of ceremonies.

Summary:
Jack put his footprints in Graumann's, tries to be humble about it...Phil got a gold star for spelling in night school...writers went to Catalina to write the script, pinned it on a seagull...Jack jumped into wet cement and Graumann's and disappeared, they were filling in a manhole...gang says Jack can't play Jimmy Cagney role in City for Conquest...Rochester calls, Billingsley's mechanical man is breaking everything in the house...mechanical man fell in love with electric refrigerator, is wearing Jack's toupee...skit City for Conquest...Eddie is a drummer, composing symphony of New York...Danny becomes Kid Sampson, prize fighter, to raise money for his brother...Danny going to fight Dennis "Killer" Day...Day knocks out Danny...Jack upset because Dennis hit him in the eye...Jack and Mary go to Ciro's to get a steak for Jack's eye

Cast:

Last name	First name	Roles	Guest star
Anderson	Eddie	Rochester	No
Benny	Jack	Jack Benny, Danny	No
Day	Dennis	Dennis Day, Killer Day	No
Harris	Phil	Phil Harrism, Eddie	No
Livingstone	Mary	Mary Livingstone, Peggy	No
Nazarro	Cliff	Lefty	No
Nelson	Frank	Clem McNulty	No
Wilson	Don	Don Wilson	No

Songs:

Order	Title	Performers	Vocal
1	On the Road to Pismo Beach*	Phil Harris	No
2	I Hear a Rhapsody	Dennis Day	Yes
3	You Walked By	Phil Harris	No
4	Unidentified	Phil Harris	No

Notes:

Skit	City for Conquest

Date: 1/26/1941   **Sponsor:** Jell-O   **City:** Hollywood, CA

Recording Source: Unknown   **Problems:** None

First line:
And now, ladies and gentlemen, I would like to announce that Jack Benny is at home this evening, where he is packing for a sudden and unexpected trip to New York City...

Summary:
Jack packing for New York...Jack is considering a part in a Broadway play...Jack tells of playing the Glow Worm in his vaudeville act...Mr. Billingsley put on a fur coat and said he was a beaver, built a dam across the swimming pool...Phil loans Jack a suitcase...Jack is packing everything in sight...Jack sends Rochester to borrow Ronald Colman's evening cape, he's borrowed lots of stuff from Colman...Billingsley offers Jack his magic carpet to fly to New York...Mr. MacDougal is the mechanical man...Jack sits on suitcase for Phil to latch it, pinches Jack in the latch...there's no needle on the speedometer of the Maxwell...Fred Allen's shoes are so thin he could stand on a lawn and feel the grass growing...gang sees Dennis on his bicycle, but he's going too fast for them...pass Dennis going downhill...Jack's luggage is overweight, so Jack makes everyone take everything out...Mary does show close, promo for March of Dimes

Cast:

Last name	First name	Roles	Guest star
Anderson	Eddie	Rochester	No
Baldwin	Harry	Plane announcer	No
Beloin	Ed	Mr. Billingsley	No
Benny	Jack	Jack Benny	No
Day	Dennis	Dennis Day	No
Harris	Phil	Phil Harris	No
Livingstone	Mary	Mary Livingstone	No
Wilson	Don	Don Wilson	No

Songs:

Order	Title	Performers	Vocal
1	You Should Be Set to Music	Phil Harris	No
2	It All Comes Back to Me	Dennis Day	Yes
3	You're the One	Phil Harris	No
4	Love Is	Phil Harris	No

Notes:

Blooper	Jack says "I'll become one of the leading interpretators" instead of "leading interpretors"
Blooper	Mary says "Hey Rome-ah" instead of "Hey Romeo"
Blooper	Don says, "Here's those ice cream puffs...er...those cream puffs you asked me to bring over."
Blooper	Rochester says, "I want to pass that catalog...Cadillac!"
Notable	On the comment of the May Company, Jack ad libs, "We ought to get something from them pretty soon," referring to practice of mentioned companies sending celebrities free stuff

Date: 2/2/1941   **Sponsor:** Jell-O   **City:** Hollywood, CA

Recording Source: Unknown   **Problems:** None

First line:
And now, ladies and gentlemen, I would like to announce that Jack Benny has not yet returned from his trip to New York City…

Summary:
Phil wants to take over the show in Jack's absence…Jack got Herbert Marshall to take over the show…gang excited about Marshall…Marshall is late because he was picked up in a Maxwell…Don introduces Marshall to the gang…Phil confuses Marshall with hipster talk…Marshall knows Jack from buying Christmas Cards from him…Jack calls from New York, won't pay Marshall for appearing but will give him free Christmas cards…Dennis upset because he's not in the play…skit The Letter…Leslie is found not guilty of the murder of her lover…Phil talked a blackmailer down from $10,000 to 85 cents for incriminating letter…Robert demands to hear letter…Mary asks Marshall to drop her off, but stop at Ciro's on the way…Don does show close, 31st anniversary of Boy Scouts…Mary says "Good night, Jack"

Cast:

Last name	First name	Roles	Guest star
Day	Dennis	Dennis Day	No
Harris	Phil	Phil Harris, lawyer	No
Livingstone	Mary	Mary Livingstone, Leslie	No
Marshall	Herbert	Herbert Marshall, Robert	Yes
Wilson	Don	Don Wilson	No

Songs:

Order	Title	Performers	Vocal
1	Way Down Yonder in Seattle*	Phil Harris	No
2	That's What I Like About the South	Phil Harris	Yes
3	Yours	Dennis Day	Yes
4	Keep an Eye on Your Heart	Phil Harris	No
5	Poor Moon	Phil Harris	No

Notes:

Notable	First mention of "That's What I Like About the South"
Notable	Jack does not appear
Skit	The Letter

Date: 2/9/1941   **Sponsor:** Jell-O   **City:** Hollywood, CA

Recording Source: Unknown   **Problems:** None

First line:
Jack: Better step on it, Rochester.

Summary:
Jack and Rochester driving to studio in the Maxwell, Billingsley in back seat (magic carpet is at the cleaners)...Rochester driving on side street because on weekends and holidays they have to keep the Maxwell off the main drag...Billingsley going to bowling alley to have ball removed from his thumb...Rochester enthusiastic about Marshall...Jack is jealous of Herbert Marshall...waiter at Ciro's gave separate checks to Mary and Marshall...Jack tells how he took Mary home to Plainfield once...gang continues to talk about Marshall, Jack sulks...Jack doesn't understand "That's What I Like About the South"...Phil defines "gastronomical"...Dennis still saying Hubert Marshall...Fred Allen said last week's show was the first to have any class...Dennis didn't mow Jack's lawn while he was in New York...Herbert Marshall returns...Jack insists on doing "The Letter" again...sponsor calls to talk to Marshall...run out of time, Jack faded out as he does the skit introduction...World-Telegram honored Jack's program again

Cast:

Last name	First name	Roles	Guest star
Beloin	Ed	Mr. Billingsley	No
Benny	Jack	Jack Benny	No
Day	Dennis	Dennis Day	No
Harris	Phil	Phil Harris	No
Livingstone	Mary	Mary Livingstone	No
Marshall	Herbert	Herbert Marshall	Yes
Wilson	Don	Don Wilson	No

Songs:

Order	Title	Performers	Vocal
1	Emporia Kansas Stomp*/Phil Harris Tune #2	Phil Harris	No
2	You Can Depend on Me	Phil Harris	No
3	You Should Be Set to Music	Dennis Day	Yes
4	You Made a Touchdown In My Heart	Phil Harris	No

Notes:

Date: 2/16/1941 **Sponsor:** Jell-O **City:** Hollywood, CA

Recording Source: West coast **Problems:** None

First line:
And now, ladies and gentlemen, last Friday the 14th which was Valentine's Day, was also the birthday of our master of ceremonies, Jack Benny, who was exactly...

Summary:
Jack's birthday dinner at home...Jack taking Mary to a movie, building up all the food at dinner...Billingsley is eating the centerpiece, wearing a fife and drum because they're having Yankee Pot Roast...plate is hot, Jack throws the pot roast up on the chandelier...crowd of people surprises Jack for his birthday...Phil wants to make a speech...gang gives Jack a bicycle pump...Rochester rings doorbell to give Jack an idea of what he goes through...gang wants to play games, decide on Blind Man's Bluff...Jack gets a comic valentine from New York...Jack says he'll never see 36 again...Rochester yells at himself to answer the door...Andy's parents send him two jugs of cider...Herbert Marshall gives Jack cufflinks...serves Marshall sardines and popovers...Marshall recognizes punch bowl as Ronald Colman's

Cast:

Last name	First name	Roles	Guest star
Beloin	Ed	Mr. Billingsley	No
Benny	Jack	Jack Benny	No
Day	Dennis	Dennis Day	No
Devine	Andy	Andy Devine	No
Harris	Phil	Phil Harris	No
Livingstone	Mary	Mary Livingstone	No
Marshall	Herbert	Herbert Marshall	Yes
Wilson	Don	Don Wilson	No

Songs:

Order	Title	Performers	Vocal
1	San Diego Serenade*	Phil Harris	No
2	Little Brown Jug	Phil Harris	No
3	I'll Take You Home Again, Kathleen	Dennis Day	Yes
4	Here's My Heart	Phil Harris	No

Notes:

Blooper	Rochester says, "It's pretty tough meat...it's a pretty tough piece of meat, Boss"
Blooper	Phil says "great pwide" instead of "great pride"
Blooper	Mary stumbles on the line "now I'm down to a gardenia"
Blooper	Don (in closing commercial) says, "The moment you lays eye...eh...lay eyes on it"

Date: 2/23/1941 **Sponsor:** Jell-O **City:** Palm Springs, CA

Recording Source: Unknown **Problems:** None

First line:
And now, ladies and gentlemen, we bring you our master of ceremonies, toughened by the desert wind, tanned by the desert sun, and frightened by the desert prices, Jack Benny.

Summary:
From Plaza Theatre...Jack staying at the Teepee Motel in Arizona, run by T.P. Ginsberg...door guy welcomes Jack on behalf of Palm Springs Chamber of Commerce...Jack sublet his house, only going to be in Palm Springs five days...Don walking around in sun shorts, Jack walking around in cowboy suit...Jack and Mary rode a horse, horse is Dennis...Jack explains the Palm Springs climate to Dennis...Paramount studios sends wire asking Jack to return cowboy suit...Mary says Rochester took out Jack's tonsils...Phil says he's living at a "dud" ranch (no dames)...Jack says Phil looks better in Palm Springs, tells Phil he should get more exercise...Jack teaching Dennis gin rummy...Phil offers to call Charlie Farrell at Racquet Club to get Jack closer room...Dennis owes Jack $30,000 from gin rummy...Remley got a tan from passing out in front of a fireplace... Mary reads a poem about Palm Springs...Jack acquiesces to getting a room at the Racquet Club, then says he forgot his tennis shoes...Rochester calls from motel, an Indian shot an arrow through the gas tank of the Maxwell, thought the Maxwell was a buffalo ("they're both darn near extinct")...Rochester sitting under a sun lamp...Rochester won a gross of peace pipes from Indians

Cast:

Last name	First name	Roles	Guest star
Anderson	Eddie	Rochester	No
Baldwin	Harry	Door guy	No
Benny	Jack	Jack Benny	No
Day	Dennis	Dennis Day	No
Harris	Phil	Phil Harris	No
Livingstone	Mary	Mary Livingstone	No
Morrow	Bill	Telegram boy	No
Wilson	Don	Don Wilson	No

Songs:

Order	Title	Performers	Vocal
1	When the Midnight Choo Choo Leaves for Beaumont and Banning*	Phil Harris	No
2	Perfidia	Dennis Day	Yes
3	There'll Be Some Changes Made	Phil Harris	No
4	Keep an Eye On Your Heart	Phil Harris	No

Notes:

Blooper	Mary says "please return cow suit immediately" instead of "cowboy suit"
Blooper	Mary cracks up in the middle of her poem
Notable	First mention of Charlie Farrell
Running gag	Mary's poem

Date: 3/2/1941 **Sponsor:** Jell-O **City:** Palm Springs, CA

Recording Source: West coast **Problems:** None

First line:
And now, ladies and gentlemen, for our second broadcast from Palm Springs, we're going to show you how Jack and all of us have been enjoying our vacation here on the desert...

Summary:
From Plaza Theatre...Jack rented a house with a pool, gang comes to visit...Rochester working on a Navajo rug for Jack's father...Rochester giving Jack swimming lessons...Jack contemplates high or low board dive, finally dives in and doesn't come up...Rochester won a canoe from an Indian...Billingsley flew in from Hollywood on his magic carpet...Jack gives Mary oil that still has a sardine in it...Dennis plays one of his records...Jack wants to hike to Taquitz Falls, got an Indian guide...Phil picks an orange and sets off alarm...Billingsley brought drum along for the hike...gang argues about who should carry water jug...Jack thinks he's found gold, it's his bridgework...gang arrives at Taquitz Falls..."Good night, Joanie"...ad for Sanka, sponsors "We the People"

Cast:

Last name	First name	Roles	Guest star
Anderson	Eddie	Rochester	No
Baldwin	Harry	Echo	No
Beloin	Ed	Mr. Billingsley	No
Benny	Jack	Jack Benny	No
Day	Dennis	Dennis Day	No
Harris	Phil	Phil Harris	No
Livingstone	Mary	Mary Livingstone	No
Max	Ed	Eagle Puss	No
Wilson	Don	Don Wilson	No

Songs:

Order	Title	Performers	Vocal
1	I'm Going to El Centro with a Banjo on My Knee*	Phil Harris	No
2	It All Comes Back to Me Now	Dennis Day	Yes
3	Keep An Eye On Your Heart	Phil Harris	No
4	We Go Together	Phil Harris	No

Notes:

Notable	Good night, Joanie.

Date: 3/9/1941   **Sponsor:** Jell-O   **City:** Palm Springs, CA

Recording Source: East coast   **Problems:** None

First line:
And now, ladies and gentlemen, as you may remember, three weeks ago a certain young man came to Palm Springs run down, anemic, and pale…

Summary:
From Plaza Theatre…Jack has three white spots on his forehead, Rochester left change there…Don has lost four pounds…Jack fell off a horse when he was trying to pick up a handkerchief…Phil told Dennis he'd get 10 years for parking in front of a fire plug (east coast only)/Door guy reminds Jack to get his writers at the Chee-Chee Bar (west coast only)…Guadalajara Trio hasn't been paid…Jack didn't join racquet club because they don't take actors…Phil is late, he tried to pick up a date picker in Indio...skit Murder at the Racquet Club…jail cells rented out to tourists at this time of the season…Carey Carew (actor) has been murdered…Guadalajara Trio call for payment…doorman won't let police into Racquet Club because they're not members, will throw the body over the fence to them…Charlie Farrell mentions "Seventh Heaven"…O'Day tries to sell dates to the corpse…Butterworth was to play tennis with Carew…Peter Lorre asks if he can be the murderer…Guadalajara Trio throw a rock through the window with a note asking for payment…O'Benny starts to arrest Lorre, but Farrell says he put him up to the murder to get Jack to come join their club…body is dummy from Bullock's window…charges Jack $12 for a Coca-Cola…"We're a little late, folks, so good night."

Cast:

Last name	First name	Roles	Guest star
?	Jesus	Guadalajara Trio member	No
?	Lamberto	Guadalajara Trio member	No
?	Mario	Guadalajara Trio member	No
Baldwin	Harry	Door guy, police radio announcer	No
Benny	Jack	Jack Benny, Captain O'Benny	No
Butterworth	Charles	Charles Butterworth	Yes
Day	Dennis	Dennis Day, Sergeant O'Day	No
Farrell	Charlie	Charlie Farrell	Yes
Harris	Phil	Phil Harris, doorman	No
Livingstone	Mary	Mary Livingstone, Mitzi LaRue	No
Lorre	Peter	Peter Lorre	Yes
Wilson	Don	Don Wilson, Sergeant Wilson	No

Songs:

Order	Title	Performers	Vocal
1	The Phil Harris Concerto #6 for Oboe and Drum*	Phil Harris	No
2	Frenesi	Dennis Day	Yes
2	Frenesi	Guadalajara Trio	Yes
3	Wise Old Owl	Phil Harris	No
4	Slowly But Surely	Phil Harris	No

Notes:

Skit	Murder at the Racquet Club

Date: 3/16/1941 **Sponsor:** Jell-O **City:** Hollywood, CA

Recording Source: Unknown **Problems:** None

First line:
And now ladies and gentlemen, after a month's vacation in Palm Springs, we bring you a man who looks a month younger--as if that made any difference--Jack Benny.

Summary:
Jack shows off his muscle...Jack, Mary, and Dennis took four days to get back from Palm Springs in the Maxwell...Jack tries to beat up Dennis...Don claims to do dialects...Phil happy to be back in the city...Jack, Mary, and Dennis argue about cities where they had car trouble...Phil missed four weeks of night school, teacher now going around with another man...Guadalajara Trio comes back for more money...next week doing "Tobacco Road"...Phil says he lived on Tobacco Road...Rochester calls, is in Pasadena to pick up Maxwell from engine repairs...Jack signed a contract to make another picture...highlights of "Tobacco Road"

Cast:

Last name	First name	Roles	Guest star
Anderson	Eddie	Rochester	No
Benny	Jack	Jack Benny, Jeeter Lester	No
Benny	Jack	Jack Benny	No
Boardman	?	Guadalajara Trio	No
Day	Dennis	Dennis Day	No
Harris	Phil	Phil Harris	No
Livingstone	Mary	Mary Livingstone, Ellie Mae Lester	No
Morrison	?	Guadalajara Trio	No
Perez	?	Guadalajara Trio	No
Wilson	Don	Don Wilson	No

Songs:

Order	Title	Performers	Vocal
1	I See the Moon at Noon	Phil Harris	No
2	In Dublin's Fair City (aka Cockles and Mussels)	Dennis Day	Yes
3	Darling Nellie Gray	Phil Harris	No
4	You Walked By	Phil Harris	No

Notes:

Blooper	Jack stumbles on "We will be with you again"

Date: 3/23/1941   **Sponsor:**   Jell-O   **City:**   Hollywood, CA

Recording Source: Unknown   **Problems:**   None

First line:
And now ladies and gentlemen, it is with great pleasure that I bring you a man with whom I have been associated for many years. A man whose friendship and…

Summary:
Jack interrupts Don's introduction because they have a long play…Don gets mad because Jack forgot his 8th anniversary on the program…Jack says his writers are illiterate…Jack sends reminder telegrams before his birthday…Dennis across the street shooting pool…Guadalajarah Trio comes back for more money…Phil's band dives for cigars…Don refuses to read commercial…Dennis is chewing tobacco…says Heather Noodleman is too heavy to play Ellie Mae…has cast take off shoes to get in the mood…Jack takes off his shoe and money comes off…skit Tobacco Road…Ada Lester tells Jeeter to go find food, haven't eaten in a month…Dude drove the car to sell a load of wood, got $1.50 for the wood and the car…tell Dude to have ice cream, but it's cotton…want to marry off Ellie Mae to get money to save the farm…try to convince Twitch Harris to marry her…Banker Wilson comes and demands $8 (because it's his 8th anniversary)…marries Ellie Mae to Skeeter, who pays the $8…Sam "Shlepperman" Hearn opening at Seattle Paramount tomorrow

Cast:

Last name	First name	Roles	Guest star
Beloin	Ed	Skeeter	No
Benny	Jack	Jack Benny, Jeeter Lester	No
Day	Dennis	Dennis Day, Dude Lester	No
Harris	Phil	Phil Harris, Twitch Harris	No
Kelly	Mary	Heather Noodleman, Ellie Mae Lester	No
Livingstone	Mary	Mary Livingstone, Ada Lester	No
Wilson	Don	Don Wilson, Banker Wilson	No

Songs:

Order	Title	Performers	Vocal
1	Goodbye Broadway, Hello Figueroa Street*/To a Wild Petunia	Phil Harris	No
2	You Walked By	Phil Harris	No
3	High on a Windy Hill	Dennis Day	Yes
4	You Walked By	Phil Harris	No

Notes:

Blooper	Jack says "At the same band" instead of "At the same time", Mary then giggles through her lines afterwards
Notable	Dennis Day appears, but does not sing
Skit	Tobacco Road

Date: 3/30/1941 **Sponsor:** Jell-O **City:** Hollywood, CA
Recording Source: Unknown **Problems:** None

First line:
And now ladies and gentlemen, spring has come to Southern California. Birds are twittering in the treetops, buds are bursting on the branches, all nature is in tune.

Summary:
Flashback to Jack's backyard this afternoon...Rochester wants Jack to plant more watermelon...Billingsley thought the hose was a snake and shot it...Dennis mowing the lawn, Jack agents him to mow Claudette Colbert's lawn...Mary brings cucumber seeds...Jack put cheese on the ground to grow potatoes au gratin...Jack shoos away Ronald Colman's chickens...Bill brings Jack the script, it's Tobacco Road again...Rochester steals one of Colman's chickens...Billingsley is wearing a turban, it's a bedsheet ("I slept like a top last night")...Dennis is suing Jack because he bumped his head in the Maxwell...Rochester drives Jack, Mary, and Dennis to the studio...Rochester leaves to take his girl for a drive, has a chicken under the front seat, Jack takes it from him...Jack, Mary, and Dennis stop at the drug store for a bite to eat...Dennis wants peanut brittle on whole wheat...Heather Noodleman orders leg of lamb for a late breakfast...Don has a new picture ("The Round Up")...Colman chicken lays an egg, Jack has them put it in his malted milk...Phil is abrupt...end of program is start of program...Jack is leaving for Chicago tomorrow, performing in Greek War Relief benefit, bringing Quiz Kids back with him...ad for Sanka

Cast:

Last name	First name	Roles	Guest star
Anderson	Eddie	Rochester	No
Beloin	Ed	Mr. Billingsley	No
Benny	Jack	Jack Benny	No
Blanc	Mel	Chicken	No
Day	Dennis	Dennis Day	No
Harris	Phil	Phil Harris	No
Kelly	Mary	Heather Noodleman	No
Livingstone	Mary	Mary Livingstone	No
Morrow	Bill	Bill	No
Nelson	Frank	Mervyn	No
Rubin	Benny	Chicken, LaVerne	No
Wilson	Don	Don Wilson	No

Songs:

Order	Title	Performers	Vocal
1	Way Down Upon the Los Angeles River*/Phil Harris Special #3	Phil Harris	No
2	High on a Windy Hill	Dennis Day	Yes
3	Even Steven	Phil Harris	No
4	What This Country Needs is More Love	Phil Harris	No

Notes:

Date: 4/6/1941   **Sponsor:** Jell-O   **City:** Hollywood, CA

Recording Source: Unknown   **Problems:** None

First line:
And now ladies and gentlemen, we bring you our Master of Ceremonies who has just returned from a quick trip to Chicago, Jack Benny.

Summary:
Jack took the Streamliner train to Chicago…Jack brags about his reception in Chicago…redcaps resistant to take Jack's bags ("If you can do a benefit, I can.")…Dennis late because he was kissing his girl goodbye on the phone and got his lips caught in the mouthpiece…Quiz Kids are on the show…Jack to guest on Quiz Kids a week from Wednesday…Don flunked everything in school but cooking…Rochester calls, Carmichael came out of hibernation and apparently ate the gas man…Rochester suggests that Jack ask the Quiz Kids what happened to the gas man…the Quiz Kids vs. the Jell-O Kids…both teams introduce themselves…Jack asks the Jell-O Kids much easier questions…Phil spells "fish" F-I-S-C-H…Jell-O Kids beat Quiz Kids 3 to 2…"We're a little late, so good night folks."

Cast:

Last name	First name	Roles	Guest star
Anderson	Eddie	Rochester	No
Beloin	Ed	Eddie	No
Benny	Jack	Jack Benny	No
Bishop	Joan	Joan Bishop	Yes
Brenner	Claude	Claude Brenner	Yes
Darrow	Gerard	Gerard Darrow	Yes
Day	Dennis	Dennis Day	No
Harris	Phil	Phil Harris	No
Livingstone	Mary	Mary Livingstone	No
Morrow	Bill	Bill	No
Quiz Kids	The	Quiz Kids	Yes
Williams	Richard	Richard Williams	Yes
Wilson	Don	Don Wilson	No

Songs:

Order	Title	Performers	Vocal
1	Silver Threads Among the Brass Section*/Phil Harris #3	Phil Harris	No
2	Two Hearts That Pass in the Night	Dennis Day	Yes
3	Wise Old Man	Phil Harris	No
4	Once Upon a Time	Phil Harris	No

Notes:

Notable	Carmichael eats the gas man
Running gag	Relay question and answer
Running gag	Gas man

Date: 4/13/1941   **Sponsor:** Jell-O   **City:** Hollywood, CA
Recording Source: Unknown   **Problems:** None

First line:
And now ladies and gentlemen, once again I bring you our Master of Ceremonies, a man who last Sunday night referreed that famous battle of wits between the Quiz Kids of Chicago and the Jell-O Kids…

Summary:
Mary says Jack won't be on the show because he's worried about his Quiz Kids appearance…Jack frets over going into vaudeville instead of going to college…says Taj Mahal is an auto court on Ventura Boulevard…three Quiz Kids staying at Jack's house…Rochester makes notes on Kids' conversation, says he's not a Caucasian…Jack tells Rochester to show Carmichael to two of the Kids…Claude is memorizing Hamlet…Jack asks Claude if the Kids can miss on a few questions, but he refuses…asks Claude if he knows the theatre manager at the Penn Theatre in Wilkes-Barre…Rochester says gas company doesn't know where the gas man is either…Richard thinks they're paying as much to stay at Jack's house as for a hotel…Jack tries a sympathy ploy to get the Kids to miss questions…Billingsley's watch's hands have mittens on them…Jack and Mary have dinner with the Kids…couple wants to rent a room…Jack goes to bed, dreams about the Quiz Kids program…Jell-O pudding ad by Frank Bingham…show cut off on Jack's closer

Cast:

Last name	First name	Roles	Guest star
Anderson	Eddie	Rochester	No
Beloin	Ed	Mr. Billingsley	No
Benny	Jack	Jack Benny	No
Bingman	Frank	Jell-O pudding announcer	No
Brenner	Claude	Claude Brenner	Yes
Darrow	Gerard	Gerard Darrow	Yes
Day	Dennis	Dennis Day	No
Harris	Phil	Phil Harris, Sir Isaac Newton	No
Kelly	Mary	Lady Godiva	No
Lewis	Elliott	Quiz Kids announcer, gas man	No
Livingstone	Mary	Mary Livingstone	No
Morrow	Bill	Homer	No
Nelson	Frank	William Shakespeare	No
Quiz Kids	The	Quiz Kids	Yes
Stewart	Blanche	Sam, screamer	No
Williams	Richard	Richard Williams	Yes
Wilson	Don	Don Wilson	No

Songs:

Order	Title	Performers	Vocal
1	Wyoming, Why Do You Being with W*/Phil Harris #5	Phil Harris	No
2	Unidentified	Phil Harris	No
3	Ciribiribin	Phil Harris	No
4	We Go Together	Phil Harris	No

Notes:

Notable	Show cut off in the middle of Jack's closing announcements

Date: 4/20/1941 **Sponsor:** Jell-O **City:** Hollywood, CA

Recording Source: Unknown **Problems:** None

First line:
Jack: No, no Mary. I've made up my mind. I am not going into that studio and broadcast tonight.

Summary:
Mary tries to cajole Jack into going on the air, he's upset about his showing on the Quiz Kids…Jack says he's 34 years old…Mary says Jack tried to hang himself (he was hanging laundry)…Clara Bow was mad at Jack because her garter got caught in his wristwatch during a Charleston contest…Dennis used to be as smart as the Quiz Kids…Quiz Kids are leaving Jack's house tonight…wire from Waukegan, Cousin Boo-Boo disgusted with Jack due to Quiz Kids performance…Jack makes Don do commercial with a lisp, Don gets mad and goes home…Phil is playing at the Paramount Theatre, hits Remley with a blueberry pie…Jack taking Quiz Kids to the station in the Maxwell…horn on Maxwell is an old atomizer…Jack talks with kids about their California visit…see Don on the street, he says he's not speaking to Jack…Kids want to settle up their bill, Jack says to forget it…Kids insist, but Mary stops them…Kids talk about Jack on the train…Jack wonders what to do in his spare time, Rochester suggests looking for the gas man…Frank Bingman promotes Jell-O pudding…"We're a little late, good night folks"

Cast:

Last name	First name	Roles	Guest star
		Girl autograph seeker	No
Anderson	Eddie	Rochester	No
Baldwin	Harry	Telegram boy	No
Benny	Jack	Jack Benny	No
Bingman	Frank	Jell-O pudding announcer	No
Brenner	Claude	Claude Brenner	Yes
Darrow	Gerard	Gerard Darrow	Yes
Day	Dennis	Dennis Day	No
Harris	Phil	Phil Harris	No
Livingstone	Mary	Mary Livingstone	No
Nelson	Frank	Foreign Legion recruiting officer	No
Quiz Kids	The	Quiz Kids	Yes
Williams	Richard	Richard Williams	Yes
Wilson	Don	Don Wilson	No

Songs:

Order	Title	Performers	Vocal
1	The Vine Street Viggle*/Phil Harris #6	Phil Harris	No
2	Once Upon a Summertime	Dennis Day	Yes
3	Blues My Naughty Sweetie Taught Me	Phil Harris	No
4	Unidentified	Phil Harris	No

Notes:

Date: 4/27/1941   **Sponsor:** Jell-O   **City:** Hollywood, CA

Recording Source: Unknown   **Problems:** None

First line:
And now ladies and gentlemen, as there are only five more weeks left in the current Jell-O series, at this time I would like to pay tribute to a man who, for the past 30 weeks has brought joy and happiness into millions of American homes.

Summary:
Don's wife thinks he's not getting a big enough raise…Mary's contract has her mending Jack's socks…Phil using fresh material, hitting Frankie with a strawberry shortcake…telegram from Dennis Day saying that he's out in the hall…Phil's lawyers don't like his new contract…Rochester calls, wants to discuss his contract…Jack says that he's giving him a substantial raise…Rochester asks if Jack's playing a dectetive, suggests he find out what happened to the gas man…Jack makes Don pretend he's out of breath for the commercial...skit Murder at the Movies…man killed in front of box office…police investigate…man came in with smoking gun, so Dennis made him sit in the loge…Phil tells very old jokes…complaining patron says that he bumped off the man who wrote Harris' material…Benny wants to arrest him after Phil's act, killer says he'll wait for Captain at the station because he can't stand to listen to more of Harris' act…"We're a little late, so goodnight folks"

Cast:

Last name	First name	Roles	Guest star
Anderson	Eddie	Rochester	No
Baldwin	Harry	Telegram boy, balcony ticket taker	No
Beloin	Ed	Police announcer, man who wants to lie down	No
Benny	Jack	Jack Benny, Captain Benny	No
Bingman	Frank	Jell-O pudding announcer	No
Day	Dennis	Dennis Day, ticket taker	No
Harris	Phil	Phil Harris, Sergeant	No
Kelly	Mary	Woman patron	No
Lewis	Elliott	Killer	No
Livingstone	Mary	Mary Livingstone, Mamie Livingstone	No
Wilson	Don	Don Wilson	No

Songs:

Order	Title	Performers	Vocal
1	I'm Building a Palace for Alice in Dallas*/Phil Harris Special #1	Phil Harris	No
2	Why Cry, Baby	Phil Harris	No
3	Amapola	Dennis Day	Yes
4	Unidentified	Phil Harris	No

Notes:

Blooper	Jack stumbles on "Captain Benny is seated at his desk"
Skit	Murder at the Movies

Date: 5/4/1941   **Sponsor:** Jell-O   **City:** Hollywood, CA

Recording Source: KFI   **Problems:** None

First line:
And now ladies and gentlemen, it is with great pride and pleasure that I present to you a man who next Friday, May the 9th, celebrates his 10th anniversary in radio, Jack Benny.

Summary:
Jack gets repeated fanfare for his 10th anniversary...Jack reminisces about his first broadcast...on air for Burger's Black Beauty Buggy Whips, then The Heartbreak of Hortense Hooligan...telegram from Fred Allen...Dennis takes issue with being called a nightingale...Don wrote play for commercial, husband and wife overdo the "dears", son comes out of closet...Jack tells about playing violin in vaudeville...men bring in giant crate with gang's present to Jack, cigarette lighter with 50 gallons of fluid... Mary reads poem for Jack's anniversary...Rochester calls, Billingsley wearing dinner jacket (nothing else)...Billingsley waltzing with the hall tree...gas man showed up, wanted to know what happened to the other gas man...Jack gets another fanfare

Cast:

Last name	First name	Roles	Guest star
Anderson	Eddie	Rochester	No
Benny	Jack	Jack Benny, Mr. Boyle Heights	No
Bingman	Frank	Jell-O pudding announcer	No
Day	Dennis	Dennis Day	No
Harris	Phil	Phil Harris	No
Livingstone	Mary	Mary Livingstone, Mrs. Boyle Heights	No
Rubin	Benny	Telegram boy	No
Wilson	Don	Don Wilson	No

Songs:

Order	Title	Performers	Vocal
1	I Wonder Who's Kissing Her Now That I'm Drafted*/Phil Harris Spec. #2	Phil Harris	No
2	My Sister and I	Dennis Day	Yes
3	Ida Sweet as Apple Cider	Phil Harris	Yes
3	Ida Sweet as Apple Cider	Jack Benny	Yes
4	Sweet Dreaming	Phil Harris	No

Notes:

Running gag	Mary's poem

431

Date: 5/11/1941   **Sponsor:** Jell-O   **City:** Hollywood, CA

Recording Source: Unknown   **Problems:** None

First line:
And now ladies and gentlemen, we bring you one of Hollywood's most versatile movie stars, whose new picture has just gone into production. An actor whose roles extend from leading man in "Love Thy Neighbor" to leading lady in "Charley's Aunt", Jack Benny.

Summary:
Jack went into production for "Charley's Aunt" this week...Jack Oakie made a pass at Jack in costume...Dennis says Jack has been like a mother to him (it's Mother's Day)...gang discusses Jack's 10th anniversary banquet...Rochester calls, Maxwell broke down (on Central Avenue)...the life of Jack Benny in music...Jack's father is called Meyer Benny

Cast:

Last name	First name	Roles	Guest star
		Young Jack Benny	No
?	Harry	Meyer Benny	No
?	Johnny	Socks customer	No
?	Martha	"Threw out our hero"	No
?	Mercedes	Teacher, Mary	No
Anderson	Eddie	Rochester	No
Benny	Jack	Jack Benny	No
Bingman	Frank	Jell-O pudding announcer	No
Carpenter	Ken	Ken Carpenter	Yes
Day	Dennis	Dennis Day	No
Harris	Phil	Phil Harris	No
Jenkins	Gordon	Gordon Jenkins	Yes
Lescoulie	Jack	Dennis, Rochester	No
Livingstone	Mary	Mary Livingstone	No
Wilson	Don	Don Wilson	No

Songs:

Order	Title	Performers	Vocal
1	Brown Eyes, Why Are You So Close to My Nose*/Phil Harris Special #3	Phil Harris	No
2	Amapola	Phil Harris	No
3	The Life of Jack Benny	Gordon Jenkins	Yes
4	Once In a Love Time	Phil Harris	No

Notes:

Date: 5/18/1941 **Sponsor:** Jell-O **City:** Hollywood, CA

Recording Source: East coast **Problems:** None

First line:
And now ladies and gentlemen, as we mentioned last week, Jack Benny has started production on his new picture, "Charley's Aunt", in which he masquerades as a woman. So without further ado, let us eavesdrop on Jack's dressing room at 20th Century Fox studio, where he's getting ready to go on the set. Take it away!

Summary:
Rochester helping Jack get into his "Charley's Aunt" costume…Dennis takes a shower in Jack's dressing room, sings…Phil got married, gang agrees not to say anything about it…Phil acts like he doesn't know who Alice Faye is…Don asks if they can color Jack's curls to coincide with Jell-O…Jack goes on the set…Jack offers to introduce Phil to Kay Francis, he says he's too weak…Jack introduces Mary to Kay…Mary makes fun of her, Kay says she used to shop at the May Company…Jack encourages Kay to include a kiss in their scene, director nixes it…Jack and Kay rehearse…Jack can't get the right voice or accent…Jack starts arguing with the director about everything…"We're a little late, but thanks Miss Francis and Mr. Mayo"

Cast:

Last name	First name	Roles	Guest star
Anderson	Eddie	Rochester	No
Baldwin	Harry	Baldy	No
Beloin	Ed	Mr. Zanuck, Baldy	No
Benny	Jack	Jack Benny	No
Bingman	Frank	Jell-O Ice Cream announcer	No
Day	Dennis	Dennis Day	No
Francis	Kay	Kay Francis	Yes
Harris	Phil	Phil Harris	No
Livingstone	Mary	Mary Livingstone	No
Max	Ed	Caesar Romero	No
Mayo	Archie	Mr. Mayo	Yes
Morrow	Bill	Glide (East coast)/Schnitz (West Coast)	No
Nelson	Frank	Mr. Carnagel	No
Wilson	Don	Don Wilson	No

Songs:

Order	Title	Performers	Vocal
1	The Knot Was Tied in Ensenotta*/Special #5	Phil Harris	No
2	I Do, Do You	Dennis Day	Yes
3	Wise Old Owl	Phil Harris	No
4	Here's My Heart	Phil Harris	No

Notes:

Date: 5/25/1941   **Sponsor:** Jell-O   **City:** Hollywood, CA

Recording Source: Unknown   **Problems:** None

First line:
And now ladies and gentlemen for the next to the final broadcast of the season, we bring you a man who came to you last October fresh as a daisy, and is now standing here faded as a fuschia, Jack Benny.

Summary:
Jack says he's worn out...bought his writers a typewriter, they did a maypole dance with the ribbon...one writer demonstrated hair tonic, the other drank it...gang says Jack has no reason to be worn out...Phil explains that Jack works only 13 minutes a week...Door guy wants to buy hair tonic...Jack calls Dennis Kenny Baker...Don wrote a play about Mr. And Mrs. Philbert Harris...Phil upset because he thinks it's about him, Jack claims it's ficticious...Jack going to Eagle Nook Lodge in Sierras to fish this summer...summer replacement is "Reg'lar Fellas"...Door guy says he lost his hair by pulling off a tight hat too quickly...Jack reminisces about being in the Navy...Rochester calls, says Billingsley plans to swim to Australia...Billingsley thinks he's a boat, wants Rochester to break champagne over his head...says if the Maxwell can make it to San Diego, Billingsley's a cinch for Australia...Thomas E. Dewey pitches for the USO

Cast:

Last name	First name	Roles	Guest star
Anderson	Eddie	Rochester	No
Baldwin	Harry	Door guy	No
Benny	Jack	Jack Benny, Philbert Harris	No
Bingman	Frank	Jell-O Freezing Mix announcer	No
Day	Dennis	Dennis Day	No
Dewey	Thomas E.	Thomas E. Dewey	Yes
Harris	Phil	Phil Harris	No
Livingstone	Mary	Mary Livingstone, Alyce Harris	No
Wilson	Don	Don Wilson	No

Songs:

Order	Title	Performers	Vocal
1	Beat Me Daddy With a Pickled Beet*/Special #4	Phil Harris	No
2	You and I	Dennis Day	Yes
3	There'll Be Some Changes Made	Phil Harris	No
4	I See the Moon at Noon	Phil Harris	No

Notes:

Date: 6/1/1941 **Sponsor:** Jell-O **City:** San Diego, CA

Recording Source: Unknown **Problems:** None

First line:
And now ladies and gentlemen, from the Naval Training Station here in San Diego, California, we bring you our master of ceremonies, that ex-sailor who doesn't know a porthole from a donut, Jack Benny.

Summary:
Jack wears his 1917 Navy uniform…Jack reminisces about his Navy days, says he enlisted when he was 14 years old because of his gray hair…Jack tells Dennis that he'll be able to get girls with his sailor suit…Door guy says he had gray hair when he was in the Navy…Dennis has a song prepared for next week…Phil touring with his band this summer…Phil and Alice had an argument, both wanted to use the curling iron…Jack got permission to tour a battleship…Rochester calls, packing for fishing trip to June Lake…Rochester asks if battleship goes all around the world, suggests they keep an eye out for the gas man…gang catches shore boat to get out to battleship…gang complains that the water's choppy, Jack admonishes them and becomes queasy himself…Jack acts like he knows everything about the ship, says that the galley is where they steer the ship…Jack takes Mary's picture by the guns, gets arrested…battleship shoves off with Jack aboard…Don does show close

Cast:

Last name	First name	Roles	Guest star
Anderson	Eddie	Rochester	No
Baldwin	Harry	Door guy	No
Beloin	Ed	Boat ferryman	No
Benny	Jack	Jack Benny	No
Day	Dennis	Dennis Day	No
Harris	Phil	Phil Harris	No
Lewis	Elliott	Arresting officer	No
Livingstone	Mary	Mary Livingstone	No
Morrow	Bill	Officer	No
Wilson	Don	Don Wilson	No

Songs:

Order	Title	Performers	Vocal
1	Coronado Corn*/Special #6	Phil Harris	No
2	Till Reveille	Dennis Day	Yes
3	With a Twist of the Wrist	Phil Harris	No
4	Here is My Heart	Phil Harris	No

Notes:

Blooper	Mary says, "I came here to visit a battleship and I want to BE one"
Notable	First military base broadcast

Date: 10/5/1941 **Sponsor:** Jell-O **City:** New York, NY

Recording Source: KFI **Problems:** None

First line:
Jack: Jell-O again…darnit, I forgot how I used to say that.

Summary:
Jack rehearses "Jell-O again" before the show…writers are at Roseland dancing with each other…Jack is very nervous…Phil is in a contemplative mood since he married Alice…Mr. Mortimer of the sponsor drops by…writers won a dancing cup…Don lost eight pounds…Jack went to game at Ebbets Field…Dennis says Yankees are scared of the Dodgers (gets boos)…Rochester calls, wants an advance from Jack because he's behind in dice…Jack left his glasses in Hollywood…flashback to Jack and Mary going to the game, Jack can't see anything…Jack tries to catch DiMaggio foul ball, gets hit in the head with it…Mr. Mortimer is asleep in the audience

Cast:

Last name	First name	Roles	Guest star
Anderson	Eddie	Rochester	No
Baker	?	Hot dog salesman	No
Baldwin	Harry	Stage caller, Madame	No
Beloin	Ed	Ed writer	No
Benny	Jack	Jack Benny	No
Day	Dennis	Dennis Day	No
Harris	Phil	Phil Harris	No
Jameson	Bud	Mr. Mortimer	No
Livingstone	Mary	Mary Livingstone	No
Morrow	Bill	Bill writer	No
Pious	Minerva	Kill the umpire woman	No
Shirley	Tom	Policeman	No
Wilson	Don	Don Wilson	No

Songs:

Order	Title	Performers	Vocal
1	Hi Neighbor	Phil Harris	No
2	You and I	Dennis Day	Yes
3	A Romantic Guy I	Phil Harris	No

Notes:

Blooper	Don stumbles on "imitation cherry flavor" in the closing commercial
Notable	"Goodnight Joanie" is in the script
Notable	Sponsorship is now Jell-O and Jell-O pudding

Date: 10/12/1941 **Sponsor:** Jell-O **City:** New York, NY

Recording Source: KFI **Problems:** None

First line:
Ladies and gentlemen, exactly 449 years ago today, Christopher Columbus first set foot in the new world after a perilous ocean voyage of 40 days and 40 nights...

Summary:
Gang discusses reviews of opening show...Jack's cousin Boo-Boo arrested...Alice thinks the show is too corny for Phil...Dennis didn't know lady in Charley's Aunt was Jack, sent him a love letter...Jack took Mary to see "Arsenic and Old Lace"...gang discusses shows they saw...Rochester sends note asking Jack to give the bearer $50...Jack hands out train tickets...Smith returns and asks Jack to call Rochester...Jack calls Rochester, operator wants to know if Rochester has a girlfriend in California...Jack finally agrees to cover the $50, Rochester offers to make it $100 or nothing..."We're a little late folks, goodnight Joanie"

Cast:

Last name	First name	Roles	Guest star
Anderson	Eddie	Rochester	No
Baldwin	Harry	Door guy	No
Benny	Jack	Jack Benny	No
Day	Dennis	Dennis Day	No
Green	Eddie	Columbus Smith	No
Harris	Phil	Phil Harris	No
Huey	?	Metropolitan M. Spears	No
James	Gee Gee	Theresa Hotel operator	No
Livingstone	Mary	Mary Livingstone	No
Wilson	Don	Don Wilson	No

Songs:

Order	Title	Performers	Vocal
1	What'll We Do	Phil Harris	No
2	Time Was	Dennis Day	Yes
3	I Don't Want to Set the World On Fire	Phil Harris	No
4	Unidentified	Phil Harris	No

Notes:

Blooper	Mary stumbles on "I got caught in some cobwebs"

Date: 10/19/1941   **Sponsor:** Jell-O   **City:** Hollywood, CA

Recording Source: Unknown   **Problems:** None

First line:
And now ladies and gentlemen, this evening we would like to re-enact for you the events that occurred on our recent trip from New York to Hollywood. As you all know, we did our last show from New York City, and the following day, the whole Jell-O gang left for the coast...

Summary:
Jack and Rochester check out of the hotel...Jack says his father gave him his trunk for his 16th birthday...Jack analyzes his bill, discovers $68 for calls to Birmingham, Alabama...Dennis complains about Jack's snoring...Miss Whipple (Mary's berth-mate) is wider than Wilson...Jack praises the simple life...Jack had to give away dishes with his autographed photos...Phil studying etiquette in night school...Don's wife not letting him eat because their berth is too crowded...Jack overhears that Rochester's old girlfriend is in Birmingham, bawls him out for phone calls...all the men in the washroom getting ready for bed at the same time...boy says he's going to be a gag man for Bob Hope...Jack tells Dennis a bed time story to get him to sleep...Jack wonders about hiring the boy gag writer...Jack snores and Dennis counts sheep..."We're a little late, so goodnight folks"

Cast:

Last name	First name	Roles	Guest star
?	Anne	Peggy Wilson	No
?	Grace	Miss Whipple	No
Anderson	Eddie	Rochester	No
Beloin	Ed	Train caller	No
Benny	Jack	Jack Benny	No
Corni	?	Sylvester	No
Davis	Dix	Boy	No
Day	Dennis	Dennis Day	No
Harris	Phil	Phil Harris	No
Livingstone	Mary	Mary Livingstone	No
Nelson	Frank	Desk clerk	No
Wilson	Don	Don Wilson	No

Songs:

Order	Title	Performers	Vocal
1	A Romantic Guy I	Phil Harris	No
2	Unidentified	Phil Harris	No
3	Unidentified	Phil Harris	No
4	Unidentified	Phil Harris	No

Notes:

Blooper	Frank Nelson says "good wait-up" instead of "good write-up"
Notable	First appearance of Belly Laugh Barton character (but not by name)

Date: 10/26/1941   **Sponsor:** Jell-O   **City:** Hollywood, CA

Recording Source: KFI   **Problems:** None

First line:
And now ladies and gentlemen, as you all know, next Friday, October 31st, is Halloween, and will be celebrated by gay parties throughout the land…

Summary:
Mary is mad because the guy at the front desk winked at her…Jack reminisces about Halloween pranks when he was a kid…Phil wears short pants to night school, he's in third grade…Dennis has been asleep since they got back from New York…Don's wife made a cake for Jack…tomorrow is Navy Day, so doing skit Dive Bomber…Jack keeps switching cast parts when he finds more important parts…Jack trying to sign up boy gag writer, Belly Laugh Barton…play to be done in Technicolor, because they're on the red and blue network with a green cast…Doctor grounds Dennis…Jack upset that other people have more acting opportunities…Doctors start experiment on flying belt…Dr. Bellamy falls asleep in plane flown by Dennis…Dennis counts sheep and joins him…no show close, inset Jell-O pudding announcement

Cast:

Last name	First name	Roles	Guest star
Baldwin	Harry	Dr. Kildare pager	No
Beloin	Ed	Dive	No
Benny	Jack	Jack Benny, Dr. Bellamy	No
Davis	Dix	Belly Laugh Barton	No
Day	Dennis	Dennis Day, Dennis MacMurray	No
Harris	Phil	Phil Harris, Dr. Flynn	No
Livingstone	Mary	Mary Livingstone, nurse Miss Krotzmeer	No
Wilson	Don	Don Wilson, Commander Wilson	No

Songs:

Order	Title	Performers	Vocal
1	Are You Ready	Phil Harris	No
2	Poet and Peasant Overture	Phil Harris	No
3	I Don't Want to Set the World on Fire	Dennis Day	Yes
4	Hi Neighbor	Phil Harris	No

Notes:

Skit	Dive Bomber

Date: 11/2/1941   **Sponsor:** Jell-O   **City:** Hollywood, CA

Recording Source: KFI   **Problems:** None

First line:
And now ladies and gentlemen, at this time we would like to turn the clock back to last Friday night, and show you what happened when Jack and the rest of our gang went out and celebrated Halloween. The time, 7:30 Friday evening, the place, Jack's house in Beverly Hills. Take it away!

Summary:
Rochester helping Jack to dress for the party, he's going as the devil...Mary going as Pochahontas in a mink coat ("John Smith was nice to me")...Don is a kangaroo, Dennis is in his pouch...Billingsley was supposed to tune piano, cleaned the keys with dental floss, pulled out black keys because they were decayed...Phil being kept after night school because he gave the teacher a hotfoot...Jack impersonates Phil's father to get the teacher to let him go...Jack made donuts with huge holes in them...Rochester perked up the cider...Billingsley is dressed as Marie Antoinettte ("My head aches, so I'm going to have it cut off")...gang goes out to play pranks on Ronald Colman...Colman isn't home, so they go to Basil Rathbone's...Don wrote a Jell-O ad on Jack's sidewalk...gang sneaks into Rathbone's backyard...Jack knocks on his door and runs...Jack throws a rock and breaks Rathbone's window, Phil tied Jack's tail to the bush so he can't run...Rathbone finds Jack and bawls him out...Rathbone decides to join the gang in tipping over flower pots at Charles Laughton's house...promo for Community Chest

Cast:

Last name	First name	Roles	Guest star
Anderson	Eddie	Rochester	No
Beloin	Ed	Mr. Billingsley	No
Benny	Jack	Jack Benny	No
Davis	Dix	Belly Laugh Barton	No
Day	Dennis	Dennis Day	No
Harris	Phil	Phil Harris	No
Lewis	Elliott	Policeman	No
Livingstone	Mary	Mary Livingstone	No
Rathbone	Basil	Basil Rathbone	Yes
Wilson	Don	Don Wilson	No

Songs:

Order	Title	Performers	Vocal
1	Mama	Phil Harris	No
2	I Know Why	Dennis Day	Yes
3	I Guess I'll Have to Dream the Rest	Phil Harris	No
4	Be Young Again	Phil Harris	No

Notes:

Date: 11/9/1941   **Sponsor:** Jell-O   **City:** Hollywood, CA

Recording Source: KFI   **Problems:** None

First line:
And now ladies and gentlemen, we bring you our versatile master of ceremonies who started work this week on a new motion picture.

Summary:
Jack upset because Don didn't see "Charley's Aunt", charges him...Jack tells gang about his new picture with Lubitsch and Lombard...Dennis says he goes with a girl who's better-looking than movie stars...Belly Laugh Barton calls with gag about how many hairs on a monkey's face, says younger generation never heard it...Phil is late, was in the car listening to the program, says Jack needs him...gang discusses how Jack ended up working with Ernst Lubitsch...Jack forgets answer to monkey's face joke...Rochester calls, Mr. Billingsley crawled into suit of armor and thinks he's King Arthur...put a saddle on Carmichael for his horse...Phil Harris has two pianists because they're Siamese twins...announces skit next week about the gridiron...Phil wants to leave early to have dinner with Leo Durocher...Durocher staying at George Raft's house because it's cheaper than Jack's house...Jack asks Durocher how the Dodgers lost the World Series to the Yankees...Mary says "We're a little late, so goodnight folks"

Cast:

Last name	First name	Roles	Guest star
Anderson	Eddie	Rochester	No
Benny	Jack	Jack Benny	No
Davis	Dix	Belly Laugh Barton	No
Day	Dennis	Dennis Day	No
Durocher	Leo	Leo Durocher	Yes
Harris	Phil	Phil Harris	No
Livingstone	Mary	Mary Livingstone	No
Wilson	Don	Don Wilson	No

Songs:

Order	Title	Performers	Vocal
1	Free for All	Phil Harris	No
2	Carry Me Back to the Lone Prairie	Dennis Day	Yes
3	Chatanooga Choo Choo	Phil Harris	No
4	Unidentified	Phil Harris	No

Notes:

Date: 11/16/1941   **Sponsor:** Jell-O   **City:** Hollywood, CA

Recording Source: KFI   **Problems:** None

First line:
And now ladies and gentlemen, as you all know, next Thursday is Thanksgiving and no doubt most of you will have turkey for dinner.

Summary:
Jack says he went hunting yesterday and brought home 3 ducks for Thanksgiving...gang discusses duck hunting...Phil hands out tickets to his night school's play, Phil is playing Priscilla...telegram from Mary's mother...Dennis is late, couldn't find a parking place...Jack and Don were on NBC's 15th anniversary show last night, Dennis says they were lousy...Rochester calls, says ducks Jack shot were pigeons...skit He Fumbled the Ball...Flash Benny lectures his team at half time...score is 65-0...Flash to play in second half...announcer leaves, replaced by Radcliff (gruff Elmer Fudd type)...Day is tackled hard and starts talking like Radcliff...Jack invited lots of stars to his home for Thanksgiving

Cast:

Last name	First name	Roles	Guest star
Anderson	Eddie	Rochester	No
Baldwin	Harry	Telegram boy	No
Benny	Jack	Jack Benny, Flash Benny	No
Bryan	Arthur Q.	Raymond Radcliff	No
Day	Dennis	Dennis Day	No
Harris	Phil	Phil Harris	No
Livingstone	Mary	Mary Livingstone, Livvy	No
Nelson	Frank	Football announcer	No
Wilson	Don	Don Wilson	No

Songs:

Order	Title	Performers	Vocal
1	Jump for Joy	Phil Harris	No
2	This Time the Dream's on Me	Phil Harris	No
3	Shepherd's Serenade	Dennis Day	Yes
4	Unidentified	Phil Harris	No

Notes:

Running gag	Mary's mother communication
Skit	He Fumbled the Ball

Date: 11/23/1941 **Sponsor:** Jell-O **City:** Hollywood, CA

Recording Source: KFI **Problems:** None

First line:
And now ladies and gentlemen, we would like to take you back three days and show you how Jack Benny entertained the gang on Thanksgiving. The time, 2PM last Thursday, the scene, the kitchen of Jack's home in Beverly Hills where we find Jack, Mary, and Rochester preparing the dinner. Take it away!

Summary:
Jack sorting out one olive per guest…Jack has a combination on his icebox…Dennis borrows Colman's punch bowl for Jack…Jack has Dennis rub burnt cork on to pretend to be Rochester's brother, Sylvester…Billingsley has his arm in a sling, fell off ladder while putting on long underwear…Rochester shoots ducks again…Phil and Alice arrive, Mary is jealous of Alice…Jack asks Mary to call Louella Parsons to tell her that Alice Faye is there…Alice reads Phil an alphabet book…Jack offers to show Carmichael to Alice…gang goes into the music room…Rochester suggests they turn over the buckshot from the ducks for national defense…Alice calls Jack "Jackson"

Cast:

Last name	First name	Roles	Guest star
?	Anne	Peggy Wilson	No
Anderson	Eddie	Rochester	No
Beloin	Ed	Mr. Billingsley	No
Benny	Jack	Jack Benny	No
Day	Dennis	Dennis Day, Sylvester	No
Faye	Alice	Alice Faye	Yes
Harris	Phil	Phil Harris	No
Livingstone	Mary	Mary Livingstone	No
Wilson	Don	Don Wilson	No

Songs:

Order	Title	Performers	Vocal
1	One on the House	Phil Harris	No
2	Chatanooga Choo Choo	Phil Harris	Yes
3	Tropical Magic	Alice Faye	Yes
4	Everything I Love	Phil Harris	No

Notes:

Notable	ID at end just says "National Broadcasting Company", not red network

Date: 11/30/1941 **Sponsor:** Jell-O **City:** Hollywood, CA

Recording Source: Unknown **Problems:** None

First line:
And now ladies and gentlemen, there being only 24 shopping days till Christmas, we bring you that 24-karat comedian with a heart of gold, Jack Benny.

Summary:
Jack gave Don a sarong last Christmas, mixed up present with Dorothy Lamour's who got a 54-inch girdle...gang discusses Christmas gifts...Phil's band played in San Diego last night, played street corners on the way back...got 15 halibut in Seal Beach, storing them in the piano...Belly Laugh Barton is supposed to be a writer, actor, and publicity man...Phil selling fish to the audience...Phil comments that boys in Army camps all over were listening to his number...skit Dr. Jekyll and Mr. Hyde...Jekyll has nice secretary, Hyde has gruff secretary...Fred Allen can't pay his bill, he gets paid by the laugh...patient Fingerwave walks in his sleep...Jekyll visits patients during the day...takes powders in the evening, turns into Hyde...dictates letter to Fred Allen threatening to put his adenoids back in...Dr. Jekyll returns in the morning...cowboy actor has too beautiful of a speaking voice...gives him powders and he turns into Andy Devine...Jack tells Phil to lower the price on his fish

Cast:

Last name	First name	Roles	Guest star
Baldwin	Harry	Ice man	No
Benny	Jack	Jack Benny, Dr. Jekyll/Mr. Hyde	No
Davis	Dix	Belly Laugh Barton, Johnny the newsboy	No
Day	Dennis	Dennis Day, Otis J. Fingerwave	No
Devine	Andy	Andy Devine	No
Harris	Phil	Phil Harris	No
Lewis	Elliott	Tex Beaumont	No
Livingstone	Mary	Mary Livingstone, Miss Jones	No
Stewart	Blanche	Mr. Hyde's secretary	No
Wilson	Don	Don Wilson	No

Songs:

Order	Title	Performers	Vocal
1	Be Young Again	Phil Harris	No
2	Magnolias in the Moonlight	Dennis Day	Yes
3	Keep Em Smiling	Phil Harris	No
4	Are You Ready	Phil Harris	No

Notes:

Skit	Dr. Jekyll and Mr. Hyde

Date: 12/7/1941 **Sponsor:** Jell-O **City:** Hollywood, CA

Recording Source: KFI **Problems:** None

First line:
And now ladies and gentlemen, it is my very great honor to bring you a man who last Sunday on this program gave you what was undoubtedly the finest performance of his acting career.

Summary:
Don didn't think Jack was as good as Spencer Tracy in last week's skit...Jack threatens to exchange Mary's Christmas gift for something cheaper ("They don't dig a bargain basement that deep")...Dennis compliments Jack on his performance...Jack makes list of what Dennis wants, he asks for a bird on a stick...Door guy says Jack's performance frightened him so that his (one) hair stood on end...Jack reminisces about his girl, Gussie Bageltwist...Phil said that Jack's acting was putrid...Phil says he's buying Alice a roadster (roaster) for Christmas...gang continues to rib Jack about his performance last week...Don wrote play of "Mr. Hyde and Dr. Jekyll"...husband comes home in bad mood...wife gives husband Jell-O, he turns into nice guy...gang asks Jack how to play the crazy Mr. Hyde, he demonstrates and dislocates his jaw...Don snaps Jack's jaw back...Phil still selling fish...Rochester calls, can't get Carmichael to go to sleep, he's sitting in bed reading Esquire...Carmichael wrote a letter to Santa asking for a fat boy to read the meter...Jack still eating his Thanksgiving ducks

Cast:

Last name	First name	Roles	Guest star
Anderson	Eddie	Rochester	No
Baldwin	Harry	Door guy	No
Benny	Jack	Jack Benny, Mr. Homer D. Hyde	No
Day	Dennis	Dennis Day, Otto	No
Harris	Phil	Phil Harris, Blotto	No
Livingstone	Mary	Mary Livingstone, Mrs. Homer D. Hyde	No
Wilson	Don	Don Wilson	No

Songs:

Order	Title	Performers	Vocal
1	A Gay Ranchero	Phil Harris	No
2	Everything I Love - All the Things You Are	Dennis Day	Yes
3	Nango	Phil Harris	No
4	Sweet Dreaming	Phil Harris	No

Notes:

Notable	Station break-ins during both musical numbers for war announcements
Notable	First Dennis Day's "What a perFAWmance!"
Running gag	Baby talk Jell-O flavors

Date: 12/14/1941 **Sponsor:** Jell-O **City:** Hollywood, CA
Recording Source: KFI **Problems:** None

First line:
And now ladies and gentlemen, this being the height of the Christmas shopping season, let us leave the studio and journey two blocks north to Hollywood Boulevard, where we find Jack Benny's Maxwell cruising along and holding up traffic, as usual.

Summary:
Promo for defense bonds before show open...Jack, Mary, and Rochester looking for a street parking place...Dennis wearing a sign that says he's not Japanese because he mows Jack's lawn...gets pulled over, Jack acts like a rube...parking attendant isn't sure that Jack will come back for the Maxwell...Jack leaves Rochester to sell horseradish from the back yard, Dennis to sing to attract a crowd...Billingsley took apart Colman's vacuum cleaner, made it into a bagpipe...Mary's sable from Jack is rabbit (snapped at a head of lettuce)...Billingsley getting Jack a 100-pound sack of fertilizer...Mary goes to buy perfume, knows the clerk...Phil waiting for Alice, who's in the beauty salon...Jack wants to go to bargain basement to get ties for Phil's orchestra...pandemonium and gunshots in bargain basement...Jack tries to buy Dennis a bird on a stick...salesman tries to sell Jack a chemistry set...salesman cries remembering his own mama doll...Jack tries out bird on a stick, gets confronted by floorwalker who accuses him of breaking it...chaos ensues

Cast:

Last name	First name	Roles	Guest star
Anderson	Eddie	Rochester	No
Baldwin	Harry	Pickpocket	No
Beloin	Ed	Angry driver, Mr. Billingsley	No
Benny	Jack	Jack Benny	No
Day	Dennis	Dennis Day	No
Harris	Phil	Phil Harris	No
Lewis	Elliott	Toy salesman	No
Livingstone	Mary	Mary Livingstone	No
Max	Ed	Policeman	No
Nelson	Frank	Floorwalker	No
Rubin	Benny	Parking attendant	No
Stewart	Blanche	Dolly Dinkelhoff	No
Wilson	Don	Don Wilson	No

Songs:

Order	Title	Performers	Vocal
1	Thank Your Lucky Stars and Stripes	Phil Harris	No
2	Rose O'Day	Dennis Day	Yes
3	Take the A Train/Be Honest With Me	Phil Harris	No
4	I Love You More and More Every Day	Phil Harris	No

Notes:

Blooper	Don chokes or coughs during closing commercial
Blooper	Phil starts to say "in the booty saloon" instead of "the beauty saloon"
Notable	Ed Beloin and Bill Morrow credited at end of the show, periodically on subsequent shows
Notable	First encounter with classic Frank Nelson character, sans "yessss"

Date: 12/21/1941   **Sponsor:** Jell-O   **City:** Hollywood, CA

Recording Source: KFI   **Problems:** None

First line:
And now ladies and gentlemen, once again the Yuletide season is here with all its joy and gaiety. So without further ado, we bring you a star to place atop your Christmas tree, Jack Benny.

Summary:
Don explains why Jack resembles a star...Mary asks what stars are going to be at Jack's holiday party, he says Rodney Dangerfield...Jack goes over lots of stars that aren't coming, Barney Dean is coming...Phil was late, doubling his salary shooting pool...Jack and Phil act like cowboys (a-bang, a-bang, a-bang)...Door guy wants to know if he's invited to Jack's party...Dennis came to studio to watch Jack do a love scene with Carole Lombard...Mary gets a letter from her mother...her sister's new baby looks like Popeye...of Jack's Dr. Jekyll, she says "What a pew-formance"...Jack and Mary leave to go decorate Jack's tree...Jack matches cabbie double or nothing on the fare, loses $3...Jack fines Roch $3 for being late answering the door...Billingsley carrying a hatchet ("When I say chopped chicken livers, that's what I mean!")...Jack has socks drying on his tree...goes to pick oranges in his backyard for ornaments...meets Carolyn Lee, who just moved in next to Colman's...Jack invites her over for Christmas morning...Billingsley chops down Christmas tree..."We're a little late, so goodnight folks and Merry Christmas to all"

Cast:

Last name	First name	Roles	Guest star
Anderson	Eddie	Rochester	No
Baldwin	Harry	Door guy	No
Beloin	Ed	Mr. Billingsley	No
Benny	Jack	Jack Benny	No
Day	Dennis	Dennis Day	No
Harris	Phil	Phil Harris	No
Lee	Carolyn	Carolyn Lee	Yes
Livingstone	Mary	Mary Livingstone	No
Morrow	Bill	Special delivery boy	No
Rubin	Benny	Cabbie	No
Wilson	Don	Don Wilson	No

Songs:

Order	Title	Performers	Vocal
1	Relax	Phil Harris	No
2	Popocataptl	Phil Harris	No
3	The First Noel - Away In a Manger - Hark the Herald Angels Sing (first two flipped in script)	Dennis Day	Yes
4	You Go Your Way and I'll Go Crazy	Phil Harris	No

Notes:

Blooper	Don says, "Mary's mother...er...she's just...uh...a riot"
Running gag	Rodney Dangerfield
Running gag	Mary's mother communication

Date: 12/28/1941   **Sponsor:** Jell-O   **City:** Hollywood, CA

Recording Source: Unknown   **Problems:** Partial show, other

First line:
And now ladies and gentlemen, we bring you a man who gave a big party last Thursday at his home in Beverly Hills, a host whose Christmas dinner was the greatest thing since Harper's Bazarre diet, Jack Benny.

Summary:
Jack served ham hocks and celery (nothing else)...Mary gave Jack a nutcracker for coconuts...Dennis upset because his girl slapped him for swallowing one of her earrings...Mary reads write up of Jack's party...Dennis gave Jack anchovy paste, Jack thought it was shaving cream...Phil opening tomorrow night at Biltmore Bowl...Phil and Mary will sing a duo, Jack offers to play his violin...Rochester calls, asks for tomorrow night off for New Year's Eve...Jack tells Rochester he should stick to ginger ale...Jack gave Roch a bottle of ink, so Roch is going to buy a fountain pen...skit The New Tenant...Jack tries to explain the skit to Dennis behind Don's commercial...Texas has new airfields to show Uncle Sam...Sam angry about adopted daughter Lulu (Hawaii)...Russian bear chasing Mad Dog Adolph...Old Year advises New Year to take care of Franklin, Winston, Chiang Kai-Shek

Cast:

Last name	First name	Roles	Guest star
Anderson	Eddie	Rochester	No
Baldwin	Harry	Door guy	No
Benny	Jack	Jack Benny, Old Man 1941	No
Blanc	Mel	Mad Dog Adolph, Benito	No
Davis	Dix	New Year, Belly Laugh Barton	No
Day	Dennis	Dennis Day	No
Harris	Phil	Phil Harris, Uncle Sam	No
Livingstone	Mary	Mary Livingstone, Columbia	No
Wilson	Don	Don Wilson, Texas	No

Songs:

Order	Title	Performers	Vocal
1	We Did It Before	Phil Harris	No
2	Who Calls	Dennis Day	Yes
3	How About You	Jack Benny	No
3	How About You	Mary Livingstone	Yes
3	How About You	Phil Harris	Yes
4	Jealous	Phil Harris	No

Notes:

Blooper	Jack says "You're getting New Year's off Eve"
Recording	Dennis' song clipped, Phil/Mary's song partially clipped, ending clipped after skit
Skit	The New Tenant

Date: 1/4/1942   **Sponsor:** Jell-O   **City:** Hollywood, CA
Recording Source: Unknown   **Problems:** None

First line:
And now ladies and gentlemen, let us take you back to last Wednesday night and show you how Jack and the rest of us celebrated New Year's Eve. Our little story opens at Jack's house around 7 PM, where Jack assisted by Rochester is getting…

Summary:
Rochester wore Jack's pearl cufflinks to his lodge meeting, lost them playing dice…Mary insists on taking a cab, won't ride in the Maxwell…Stella Buggenhaven broke a date with Jack…Carolyn Lee stops by to see Jack all dressed up…Carolyn hid Jack's toupee, gave it to a bird for a nest…Jack falls down the steps, Billingsley thinks he's drunk…Dennis doesn't have a date because his girl is a welder at Lockheed…Jack demands a paper hat from the waiter…Rodney Dangerfield comes in with Stella Buggenhaven, they join Jack's table…Phil introduces people from the stage…Jack tunes up when he thinks Phil will introduce him, introduces Dennis instead…Jack finally gets Phil's attention, volunteers for violin solo…Jack starts to play "Love in Bloom", gets interrupted by New Year

Cast:

Last name	First name	Roles	Guest star
Anderson	Eddie	Rochester	No
Beloin	Ed	Mr. Billingsley	No
Benny	Jack	Jack Benny	No
Day	Dennis	Dennis Day	No
Gilroy	Gwen	Stella Buggenhaven	No
Harris	Phil	Phil Harris	No
Lee	Carolyn	Carolyn Lee	Yes
Lewis	Elliott	Rodney Dangerfield	No
Livingstone	Mary	Mary Livingstone	No
Mather	?	Baron Long, Drunk	No
Nelson	Frank	Waiter	No
Rubin	Benny	Cabbie	No
Wilson	Don	Don Wilson	No

Songs:

Order	Title	Performers	Vocal
1	Be Young Again/Thumbs Up	Phil Harris	No
2	Be Honest With Me	Phil Harris	No
3	Rose O'Day/I See Your Eyes Before Me - I'm In the Mood for Love - The Way You Look Tonight	Dennis Day	Yes
4	A Gay Ranchero	Phil Harris	No

Notes:

Notable	First use of gag where Jack interrupts conversation to read the cab meter
Recording	Opening ad clipped
Running gag	Rodney Dangerfield

Date: 1/11/1942   **Sponsor:** Jell-O   **City:** March Field, CA

Recording Source: Unknown   **Problems:** Ads clipped

First line:
And now ladies and gentlemen, inasmuch as our program today is coming to you from March Field, California, it is with great pleasure that I bring you that emminent authority on aviation, flying Jack Benny.

Summary:
Jack says that he thought of the airplane before the Wright Brothers...Jack rode his bicycle off his father's barn, became a comedian...Mary had a date with a military man, waiting for blackout to kiss her...Phil says he has a Webster under the bridge dictionary...Door guy gives Jack a 100-pound bomb...Mary says for Jack to let her read her poem or she'll tell everyone that Jack owes $8 on his toupee...Dennis had his camera confiscated, thinks he's going to be shot at sunrise, Jack asks Dennis to take Phil with him...Mary reads poem about March Field...Door guy welcomes Jack to the pearly gates ("Didn't that bomb go off yet?")...Dennis took out his girl, and the soldiers took her away...Alice doesn't allow Phil out of the house on windy days...introduces August Stackwell as the biggest soldier in the US Army (407 pounds), calls Don Wilson "Skinny"...Wilson gets jealous...Andy Devine was on Fred Allen's program, claims Jack owes back salary...Rochester calls, ran into an orange truck...cut up spare tire when Jack needed rubber heels..."We're a little late, so goodnight folks."

Cast:

Last name	First name	Roles	Guest star
Anderson	Eddie	Rochester	No
Baldwin	Harry	Door guy	No
Benny	Jack	Jack Benny	No
Day	Dennis	Dennis Day	No
Harris	Phil	Phil Harris	No
Livingstone	Mary	Mary Livingstone	No
Stackwell	August	Sergeant August Stackwell	Yes
Wilson	Don	Don Wilson	No

Songs:

Order	Title	Performers	Vocal
1	Wings of America	Phil Harris	No
2	Tonight We Love	Phil Harris	No
3	We Did It Before	Dennis Day	Yes
4	America I Love You	Phil Harris	No

Notes:

Notable	First disclaimer of no endorsement of the product by the War Department
Recording	Opening ad clipped
Running gag	Mary's poem

Date: 1/18/1942 **Sponsor:** Jell-O **City:** Hollywood, CA

Recording Source: KFI **Problems:** None

First line:
Ladies and gentlemen, this is Don Wilson. Jack Benny will not be with us tonight, but he hopes you will enjoy the program we have prepared for you. Jack wants you to know that he will be back with us again next week.

Summary:
All music due to Carole Lombard's death

Cast:

Last name	First name	Roles	Guest star
Day	Dennis	Dennis Day	No
Merrick	Mahlon	Mahlon Merrick	No
Sportsmen Quartet	The	Sportsmen Quartet	No
Wilson	Don	Don Wilson	No

Songs:

Order	Title	Performers	Vocal
1	Me and My Buddy Next Door	Mahlon Merrick	No
2	On My Pony	Mahlon Merrick	Yes
3	Madeleine	Dennis Day	Yes
4	La Cumparsita	Mahlon Merrick	No
5	Rhumba on the Tuba	Sportsmen Quartet	Yes
6	Unidentified	Mahlon Merrick	No
7	Phil the Fluter's Ball	Dennis Day	Yes
8	Blue Room	Mahlon Merrick	No
9	Little Brown Jug	Sportsmen Quartet	Yes
10	Shepherd's Serenade	Dennis Day	Yes
11	America the Beautiful	Dennis Day	Yes
12	Unidentified	Mahlon Merrick	No

Notes:

Notable	First credited appearance of Sportsmen Quartet
Notable	First inclusion of Rochester in listing of Jell-O cast in closing announcement
Notable	Script page says "Musical Program Regular show cancelled on account of Carole Lombard air crash"

Date: 1/25/1942   **Sponsor:** Jell-O   **City:** Hollywood, CA
Recording Source: KFI   **Problems:** Other

First line:

And now ladies and gentlemen, once again I bring you our master of ceremonies, a man who...
Mary: Hold it, Don. Jack isn't here yet.

Summary:

Jack talking to his lawyers on the phone about Rochester's accident...Phil passed mid-term at night school, he's now a semaphore...Phil studying French, knows how to say "I ate the window"...Jack says that Phil's band plays too loud...skit Frightwig Murder Case...wife calls to report that her husband has been shot...drives to scene but still at police headquarters, forgot to release emergency brake...questions help and wife...wife admits she killed her husband because he was always singing "Shortnin' Bread"...Jack's lawyers (the Sportsmen) show up to discuss Rochester's case in song

Cast:

Last name	First name	Roles	Guest star
Baldwin	Harry	Chauffeur, police radio announcer	No
Benny	Jack	Jack Benny, Detective Captain O'Benny	No
Day	Dennis	Dennis Day, Homer J. Frightwig	No
Days	Bill	Droop	No
Harris	Phil	Phil Harris, Sergeant Phil O'Reilly	No
Livingstone	Mary	Mary Livingstone, Mrs. Frightwig	No
Rarig	John	Harrington 1	No
Ravenscroft	Thurl	Harrington 3	No
Smith	Max	Harrington 2	No
Sportsmen Quartet	The	Sportsmen Quartet	No
Vonn	Veola	Screamer, French maid	No
Wilson	Don	Don Wilson, butler O'Ruly	No

Songs:

Order	Title	Performers	Vocal
1	Boy Oh Boy	Phil Harris	No
2	Hi Neighbor	Phil Harris	No
3	The White Cliffs of Dover	Dennis Day	Yes
4	Goodbye Mama	Phil Harris	No

Notes:

Notable	First inclusion of Rochester in cast of opening announcement
Notable	First classic Sportsmen Quartet interaction
Notable	Performances are very subdued at the start, Mary's continues that way through the show (apparently she has a cold)
Notable	Writing credit to Bill Morrow and Ed Beloin at the end
Recording	Opening ad clipped
Running gag	Mary does Mae West
Running gag	But but but
Skit	Frightwig Murder Case

Date: 2/1/1942   **Sponsor:** Jell-O   **City:** Hollywood, CA

Recording Source: KFI   **Problems:** None

First line:
And now ladies and gentlemen, inasmuch as this evening marks the halfway point of our radio season, I think it only fair that we pay tribute to the man who has contributed his invaluable services to the Jell-O show.

Summary:
Don announces sound effects man, Virgil Reimer...Virgil tells a story with tons of sound effects...Phil now can say "I sleep in the inkwell" in French...Jack announces that Humphrey Bogart will be one of his assistants in tonight's skit...Jack introduces Bogart to the gang...Bogart asks for Rochester, Jack says he has a cold...Bogart not happy with script casting, he insists on being Captain...Virgil keeps butting in...Bogart announces skit Frightwig Murder Case...police discuss details of the case...wife invites police over to investigate...Jack asks Virgil to break down the door, he insists on an apology...O'Bogart interrogates wife...finds O'Benny in the closet, he confesses to the murder...O'Bogart, O'Harris, and wife go out for coffee...O'Benny plays gin with Homer Frightwig

Cast:

Last name	First name	Roles	Guest star
Baldwin	Harry	Police radio announcer	No
Benny	Jack	Jack Benny, O'Benny	No
Bogart	Humphrey	Humphrey Bogart, Detective Captain O'Bogart	Yes
Day	Dennis	Dennis Day, Homer J. Frightwig	No
Harris	Phil	Phil Harris, Sergeant O'Harris	No
Livingstone	Mary	Mary Livingstone, Mrs. Frightwig	No
Nelson	Frank	Virgil Reimer	No
Vonn	Veola	Fifi	No
Wilson	Don	Don Wilson, butler Jurgen	No

Songs:

Order	Title	Performers	Vocal
1	Call Out the Marines	Phil Harris	No
2	Popocatepetl	Phil Harris	No
3	Unidentified	Phil Harris	No

Notes:

Notable	Dennis Day appears but does not sing
Running gag	Mary does Mae West
Skit	Frightwig Murder Case

Date: 2/8/1942   **Sponsor:** Jell-O   **City:** Hollywood, CA

Recording Source: KFI   **Problems:** None

First line:
And now ladies and gentlemen, as you all know, Daylight Saving Time goes into effect tomorrow, and clocks throughout the country will be moved one hour ahead.

Summary:
Jack upset because he never won a prize at his theatre...Billingsley was playing soldier outside Jack's bedroom door, wouldn't let Jack in because he didn't know the password...Jack docking cast one hour's pay due to Daylight Saving Time...Phil can now say "My orchestra works in the soup tureen" in French (as close as he could get to Biltmore Bowl)...Door guy says he shouldn't have taken the ring out of his nose...Phil's band played three months in Van Horn because Frankie was arrested for stealing a cow...Don wrote a Jell-O play...bride makes first dinner for her husband (Virgil keeps butting in)...husband has indigestion but wants Jell-O...Dennis say he isn't a kid anymore because he fell in a manhole...Dennis gives Jack a clipping that Fred Allen is moving to Sunday nights to replace the Symphony Hour...Jack upset about the change and calls John Swallow...Swallow says censor has been complaining about Jack...Jack going to form the S.A.A.L.C. (Sunday Artists Against Low Comedy) to protest Allen's move...Jack fires Dennis because he likes Fred Allen...Rochester calls, Billingsley playing soldier and locked Rochester in his room for three hours...Billingsley printing $5 with Rochester's picture on them...Billingsley squeezes orange juice by nailing an orange on the wall and backing the Maxwell into it..."We're a little late, so goodnight folks."

Cast:

Last name	First name	Roles	Guest star
Anderson	Eddie	Rochester	No
Baldwin	Harry	Door guy	No
Beloin	Ed	Police announcer	No
Benny	Jack	Jack Benny, Mr. Typical American	No
Day	Dennis	Dennis Day	No
Harris	Phil	Phil Harris	No
Keane	Robert	Mr. Swallow	No
Livingstone	Mary	Mary Livingstone, Mrs. Typical American	No
Nelson	Frank	Virgil Reimer	No
Wilson	Don	Don Wilson	No

Songs:

Order	Title	Performers	Vocal
1	Free For All	Phil Harris	No
2	The Eyes of Texas Are Upon You - Deep In the Heart of Texas	Phil Harris	No
3	This Love of Mine	Dennis Day	Yes
4	Fooled	Phil Harris	No

Notes:

Blooper	Both Jack and Mary go for the line to talk to Mr. Swallow

Date: 2/15/1942 **Sponsor:** Jell-O **City:** Hollywood, CA

Recording Source: KFI **Problems:** None

First line:
And now ladies and gentlemen, yesterday, February 14th, was not only Valentine's Day, but also the birthday of Jack Benny who was exactly (ding) years of age. So let us show you what happened. The time, 7 o'clock last night, the place, Jack's home in Beverly Hills. Take it away!

Summary:
Jack trying to figure out what to do on his birthday...Jack and Rochester sing "Blues in the Night"...Jack kicked the tubes out of the radio because Fred Allen had a good program...Jack decides to see "Charley's Aunt" at the Bijou...Jack calls Scheherezade Crump for a date, she turns him down...Carolyn Lee brings Jack fudge for his birthday, her mother told her she mustn't use sugar...Jack gives up on getting a date, decides to read Radio Guide...Rochester gives Jack a haircut...puts goldfish bowl on top of Jack's head, has to smash it to get it off...Mary tells Rochester that they're planning a surprise party and to keep Jack home...Dennis comes in shouting "Surprise!" and Mary tries to cover...Jack figures out the surprise...Mary asks Rochester to make sandwiches, but Jack says the people giving the party are supposed to bring the food...Billingsley is playing soldier, demands to see visitors' passes...gang arrives to surprise Jack...Jack breaks down in tears...gang gives Jack a can of crabmeat...Shlepperman arrives to deliver a singing telegram...Jack discovers the goldfish went down his back

Cast:

Last name	First name	Roles	Guest star
Anderson	Eddie	Rochester	No
Beloin	Ed	Mr. Billingsley	No
Benny	Jack	Jack Benny	No
Day	Dennis	Dennis Day	No
Harris	Phil	Phil Harris	No
Hearn	Sam	Shlepperman	No
Lee	Carolyn	Carolyn Lee	Yes
Livingstone	Mary	Mary Livingstone	No
Wilson	Don	Don Wilson	No

Songs:

Order	Title	Performers	Vocal
1	Marine's Hymn	Phil Harris	No
2	Blues In the Night	Phil Harris	No
3	Abe Lincoln Had Just One Country	Dennis Day	Yes
4	Happy Birthday	Sam Hearn	Yes
5	Miss You	Phil Harris	No

Notes:

Notable	Opening and closing commercials are inset

Date: 2/22/1942   **Sponsor:** Jell-O   **City:** San Francisco, CA

Recording Source: KFI   **Problems:** None

First line:
And now ladies and gentlemen, inasmuch as we are broadcasting from the U.S. Army Post at the Presidio in San Francisco, and this being the birthday of George Washington, it is only fitting that we bring you a man who fought heroically for that great General at Valley Forge, Jack Benny.

Summary:
Don and his wife staying in a suite at the Fairmont...Jack and Dennis staying on a ferry boat at an auto court in Alameda...gang discusses whether Jack or Fred Allen is older...Dennis has been sightseeing, left his hat in Chinatown...Dennis went to Treasure Island to see the World's Fair (been closed for 2 years)...Door guy gives Jack an Army uniform...Jack thrown out of Streets of Paris café...Phil has a suite at the Palace Hotel...Phil started at Rose Room in St. Francis Hotel, Frankie only member still with him...Mary reads a poem about soldiers...Jack announces that tonight's show is being shortwaved around the world...Phil says his band played at the Biltmore Bowl last night and took a bus to San Francisco, he makes it sound like an epic...Don has to use Berkeley in Jell-O flavors...Rochester calls, tide came in and Jack's hotel went out...Rochester left Jack's trunks on the boat..."We're a little late, so goodnight folks."

Cast:

Last name	First name	Roles	Guest star
Anderson	Eddie	Rochester	No
Baldwin	Harry	Door guy	No
Benny	Jack	Jack Benny	No
Day	Dennis	Dennis Day	No
Harris	Phil	Phil Harris	No
Livingstone	Mary	Mary Livingstone	No
Wilson	Don	Don Wilson	No

Songs:

Order	Title	Performers	Vocal
1	Caissons Go Rolling Along	Phil Harris	No
2	Private Buckeroo	Dennis Day	Yes
3	How About You	Phil Harris	No
4	San Francisco	Phil Harris	No

Notes:

Blooper	Jack and Mary crack up during her poem
Blooper	Closing commercial announcer stumbles multiple times
Notable	Opening and closing commercials are inset
Notable	Jack announces that tonight's show is being shortwaved around the world
Notable	Network cuts away from show during Don's closing announcements
Running gag	Mary's poem

Date: 3/1/1942 **Sponsor:** Jell-O **City:** Hollywood, CA

Recording Source: Unknown **Problems:** None

First line:
And now ladies and gentlemen, as is my custom every Sunday night at this time, I bring you a man who… Mary: Hold it a second, Don. Jack isn't here yet.

Summary:
Jack in a daze because he didn't win the Best Actor Academy Award…Dennis says Jack is dunking donuts and splashed coffee all over him…Jack explains that in "Charley's Aunt", people didn't know whether to award him Best Actor or Actress…wire from Jack's father on Academy Award…Jack quizzes Don on what he loves…Dennis' suit keeps shrinking…Jack says he's as good an actor as Gary Cooper, but he's taller…Jack gets upset and goes home…Rochester says that he could catch the mouse if Jack would let him put cheese in the trap…Billingsley is under Jack's bed, doesn't want to come out lest he see his shadow and cause 40 more days of winter…Jack wants to go to sleep, has Rochester sing to him…dreams of Academy Awards in St. Joe ("They love me in St. Joe")…Fred Allen gives Jack the award, Jack does Hamlet…Warner Brothers sing to him…Gary Cooper crying because he lost the award, Jack grows to over ten feet tall…Jack wakes up, put his head through the foot of the bed…Mary does show close

Cast:

Last name	First name	Roles	Guest star
Anderson	Eddie	Rochester	No
Baldwin	Harry	Telegram boy	No
Beloin	Ed	Mr. Billingsley, Mervyn LeRoy	No
Benny	Jack	Jack Benny	No
Day	Dennis	Dennis Day	No
Days	Bill	Darryl Zanuck	No
Harris	Phil	Phil Harris	No
Hayes	Peter Lind	Academy Award announcer, Gary Cooper, Fred Allen	No
Livingstone	Mary	Mary Livingstone, Miss LaMarr	No
Sportsmen Quartet	The	Sportsmen Quartet	No
Wilson	Don	Don Wilson	No

Songs:

Order	Title	Performers	Vocal
1	Captains of the Clouds	Phil Harris	No
2	Everything I Love - All the Things You Are	Dennis Day	Yes
3	I Said No	Phil Harris	No
4	Wherever You Are	Phil Harris	No

Notes:

Notable	Opening and closing commercials are inset

Date: 3/8/1942   **Sponsor:** Jell-O   **City:** San Diego, CA

Recording Source: Unknown   **Problems:** None

First line:
And now ladies and gentlemen, as I announced before, our program this evening comes to you from the United States Marine Corps Base in San Diego.

Summary:
From Marine Corps Base in San Diego…Don quizzes Jack on his military record…Jack tells how he competed with a Marine for Eva Slatkoe…Mary says she's black and blue from riding down in the Maxwell…had blowout, Jack bought 1,000 packages of gum, asked Rochester to chew it into a tire…Phil and Frankie went to Tiajuana on a goodwill tour…Door guy asks if Jack wants to join the Marines…Dennis saw a baboon at the zoo who looked like Fred Allen…Mary reads poem about Marines…Marine shows up who competed with Jack for Eva, he and Jack reminisce…Joan Bennett sat on Dennis' lap in the Maxwell…Jack wants to know why he hasn't made another picture with Joan ("I don't eat salami any more")…Joan Bennett says she can't believe Jack playing Hamlet…Jack's legs are prettier than Betty Grable's…Rochester calls, wants night off to go to a party…Joan Bennett says hello to General MacArthur

Cast:

Last name	First name	Roles	Guest star
Anderson	Eddie	Rochester	No
Baldwin	Harry	Door guy	No
Bennett	Joan	Joan Bennett	Yes
Benny	Jack	Jack Benny	No
Clarke	Cliff	Bull-Face Hurley	No
Day	Dennis	Dennis Day	No
Harris	Phil	Phil Harris	No
Livingstone	Mary	Mary Livingstone	No
Wilson	Don	Don Wilson	No

Songs:

Order	Title	Performers	Vocal
1	Call Out the Marines	Phil Harris	No
2	He's 1-A in the Army and A-1 In My Heart	Phil Harris	No
3	Always In My Heart	Dennis Day	Yes
4	Original Music	Phil Harris	No

Notes:

Notable	Opening and closing commercials are inset
Running gag	Mary's poem

Date: 3/15/1942 **Sponsor:** Jell-O **City:** Hollywood, CA

Recording Source: KFI **Problems:** None

First line:
And now ladies and gentlemen, as you all know, next Tuesday, March the 17th, is St. Patrick's Day. So instead of my usual hackneyed introduction this evening...uh, you can sit down now, Jack.

Summary:
Don introduces Dennis Day for St. Patrick's Day, he does Irish dialect...Dennis wants to be Master of Ceremonies, Jack won't let him...gang considering offers from Baxter Beauty Clay...Jack recites poem about loyalty...Jack threatened by Baxter trying to take his cast, say he'll quit radio...Baxter ends up being a gag...Rochester calls for income tax guidance...Fred Allen presented his life story last week...skit The Life of Jack Benny...Jack is born...Jack takes violin lessons...Jack plays violin in WWI trenches...Jack plays "Love in Bloom" in vaudeville...in St. Joe, Fred Allen begs a nickel from Jack, he gives him $10...3 years later, Fred is playing the Palace and Jack begs a nickel from him, Fred refuses...Jack beats up Fred Allen

Cast:

Last name	First name	Roles	Guest star
Anderson	Eddie	Rochester	No
Benny	Jack	Jack Benny	No
Day	Dennis	Dennis Day, Zeke Benny	No
Harris	Phil	Phil Harris, Mr. Lindsay	No
Hayes	Peter Lind	Fred Allen	No
Livingstone	Mary	Mary Livingstone, nurse	No
Wilson	Don	Don Wilson	No

Songs:

Order	Title	Performers	Vocal
1	I Am an American	Phil Harris	No
2	The Garden Where the Praties Grow	Dennis Day	Yes
3	I Said No	Phil Harris	No
4	Sing Me a Song of the Islands	Phil Harris	No

Notes:

Notable	Opening and closing commercials are inset
Skit	The Life of Jack Benny

Date: 3/22/1942   **Sponsor:** Jell-O   **City:** Hollywood, CA

Recording Source: KFI   **Problems:** None

First line:
And now ladies and gentlemen, spring is here once again and warm weather has returned to Southern California.

Summary:
Jack talks about his morning routine, spars with Rochester…gang discusses how good they feel now that Spring is here…Phil has a victory garden…Dennis doesn't want to mow Jack's lawn any more because it's not dignified…next Sunday to do minstrel show…Jack wants to play golf at Hillcrest…Jack and Phil played golf, Mary as scorekeeper…Phil says he's very tired, so Jack bets with him on the game…Phil hits a beautiful drive, Jack fans the ball three times…Jack finally hits the ball, breaks window in the clubhouse behind him…after 7, Phil is 28 and Jack is 128 (Jack keeps fanning the ball)…Jack and Rochester looking for the ball into the night

Cast:

Last name	First name	Roles	Guest star
Anderson	Eddie	Rochester	No
Beloin	Ed	"pants on" guy	No
Benny	Jack	Jack Benny	No
Day	Dennis	Dennis Day	No
Harris	Phil	Phil Harris	No
Lacey	Charlie	Charlie Lacey	Yes
Livingstone	Mary	Mary Livingstone	No
Morrow	Bill	Artie Stebbens	No
Stewart	Blanche	Old lady golfer	No
Wilson	Don	Don Wilson	No

Songs:

Order	Title	Performers	Vocal
1	One On the House	Phil Harris	No
2	I'll Pray For You	Dennis Day	Yes
3	How Do You Fall in Love	Phil Harris	No
4	Miss You	Phil Harris	No

Notes:

Notable	Opening and closing commercials are inset

Date: 3/29/1942   **Sponsor:** Jell-O   **City:** Hollywood, CA
Recording Source: Unknown   **Problems:** None

First line:
Jack: Rochester, I'm sure that golfball sliced over here to the right. No...no, it's not here.

Summary:
Jack and Rochester still searching for Jack's golfball...Dennis trying to talk like Amos n Andy, comes out like Lum and Abner...Virgil Reimer to pass out tambourines, passed out tangerines...skit Doc Benny's minstrels...parade on Main Street of St. Joe, MO...audience is seated...typical minstrel exchange and songs (some reuse of gags from 1936 version)...Rochester sings a Bert Williams song...afterpiece is Romeo and Juliet...encounters other Shakespeare characters on the ladder...Mary does show close because Jack left for Motion Picture Relief Fund benefit

Cast:

Last name	First name	Roles	Guest star
Anderson	Eddie	Rochester	No
Baldwin	Harry	Sandwich vendor	No
Beloin	Ed	Doc Benny caller, man in B-2, requestor	No
Benny	Jack	Jack Benny, Romeo	No
Clarke	Cliff	Song seller	No
Day	Dennis	Dennis Day	No
Harris	Phil	Phil Harris, Julius Mushmouth Caesar	No
Kilbride	Percy	Constabule	No
Livingstone	Mary	Mary Livingstone, ticket taker, Juliet	No
Nelson	Frank	Virgil Reimer	No
Sportsmen Quartet	The	Alabama Four	No
Stewart	Blanche	Mrs. Farrel, woman in B-2	No
Wilson	Don	Don Wilson, boy, Othello Jell-O	No

Songs:

Order	Title	Performers	Vocal
1	Deep In the Heart of Encino*/Harris Spec. #3	Phil Harris	No
2	On the Mississippi - I Dream of Jeannie - Waiting for the Robert E. Lee	Cast	Yes
3	Can't You Hear Me Callin' Caroline	Dennis Day	Yes
4	Asleep In the Deep	Jack Benny	Yes
5	Somebody Else Not Me	Eddie Anderson	Yes
6	Bring Back Those Minstrel Days	Phil Harris	No

Notes:

Blooper	Mary cracks up during Dennis' song
Blooper	Phil says "I am the local and this is the express comin' through" instead of "You are the local"
Blooper	Rochester calls Jack "Mr. Benny" instead of "Mr. Interlocutor"
Notable	Closing commercial is inset
Skit	Doc Benny's minstrels

Date: 4/5/1942 **Sponsor:** Jell-O **City:** Hollywood, CA

Recording Source: Unknown **Problems:** None

First line:
And now ladies and gentlemen, we bring you a man who was the sensation of the Easter Parade this morning, when his suspenders gave way-a at Sunset and La Brea, Jack Benny!

Summary:
When Jack lost his pants, he had on his "Charley's Aunt" bloomers on…gang discusses each other's Easter outfits…Dennis hid in his girl's refrigerator, but she didn't come home that night…Don gets mad over goofy commercial and leaves…special delivery boy harasses Jack and Mary over postal regulations…Mary reads a letter from her mother…Hilliard in the Army, sent home a kangaroo…Mary's parents saw "To Be or Not to Be"…Don comes back, tries to read commercial, leaves again…next week doing quiz program where five people get $24, to be called "Try and Get It"…Fred Allen was quizmaster on Quiz Kids…Jack says he'll knock out Fred's teeth (tooth)…Don comes back in and leaves immediately…Rochester calls, Billingsley chasing him with a bow and arrow, thinks he's William Tell…Don finally reads commercial, breaks door…"A little late, next week at Camp Haan."

Cast:

Last name	First name	Roles	Guest star
Anderson	Eddie	Rochester	No
Benny	Jack	Jack Benny	No
Day	Dennis	Dennis Day	No
Harris	Phil	Phil Harris	No
Keighly	William	William Keighly	No
Kilbride	Percy	Special delivery boy	No
Livingstone	Mary	Mary Livingstone	No
Wilson	Don	Don Wilson	No

Songs:

Order	Title	Performers	Vocal
1	Lovely Little Lady	Phil Harris	No
2	In an Old Cathedral Garden	Dennis Day	Yes
3	Easter Parade	Phil Harris	No
4	Wherever You Are	Phil Harris	No

Notes:

Notable	Opening commercial is inset (Don's network announcement can be heard momentarily under open commercial)
Running gag	Mary's mother communication

Date: 4/12/1942 **Sponsor:** Jell-O **City:** Camp Haan, CA

Recording Source: Unknown **Problems:** None

First line:
And now ladies and gentlemen, from Camp Haan California, we bring you a man who pedalled here all the way from Hollywood on the rear end of a tandem bicycle, Jack Benny!

Summary:
Jack and Rochester came down on a bicycle...Jack's girlfriend, Myrtle Minkelhoffer, a deep sea diver, loaned Jack her helmet for the trip...Mary came down on a bus with Phil's orchestra, Phil sunbathing on the roof...Dennis came down on Jack's handlebars...Mary reads a poem about Camp Haan...Rochester calls, lost Jack's bicycle in a dice game...telegram from Fred Allen asking about Jack giving away money, selects telegram boy as game show contestant...skit Try and Get It, game show...double-or-nothing style show...$24 questions are either very hard or trick questions, Jack won't let people quit before the $24 question

Cast:

Last name	First name	Roles	Guest star
Anderson	Eddie	Rochester	No
Benny	Jack	Jack Benny	No
Day	Dennis	Dennis Day	No
Harris	Phil	Phil Harris	No
Kilbride	Percy	Telegram boy	No
Livingstone	Mary	Mary Livingstone	No
Nelson	Frank	Virgil Reimer	No
Stewart	Blanche	Myrtle Minkelhoffer	No
Wilson	Don	Don Wilson	No

Songs:

Order	Title	Performers	Vocal
1	Let's Be Buddies	Phil Harris	No
2	She'll Always Remember - Memories	Dennis Day	Yes
3	Someday Sweetheart	Phil Harris	No
4	Happy in Love	Phil Harris	No

Notes:

Notable	Opening commercial is inset
Notable	Video clip exists for the first part of this program, but is a different broadcast than the circulating recording
Running gag	Mary's poem
Skit	Try and Get It

Date: 4/19/1942 **Sponsor:** Jell-O **City:** Hollywood, CA

Recording Source: Unknown **Problems:** None

First line:
And now ladies and gentlemen, we turn back the clock and take you to the drug store across the street from the NBC building here in Hollywood. The time is exactly 15 minutes before this broadcast. Take it away drug store!

Summary:
Gang converges at the drug store for food before the show...Jack won't go to the Brown Derby until they put his picture in the main dining room instead of the men's room...Jack Benny special on the menu...Phil put on Alice's pants...Virgil Reimer brags about his fan mail...Dennis weighed himself at the drug store, stripped...Jack just started production of his movie with Ann Sheridan...clerk won't sell Jack shaving cream without turning in an old tube...scene shifts to studio...Jack talks about his movie and playing love scenes with Ann Sheridan...Door guy tries to sell Jack a toupee...Jack charged Dennis 25 cents to meet Barbara Stanwyck...Don wrote Jell-O play about couple that lives on the edge of the Mojave Desert...starving prospector refuses all food except Jell-O...next week to do first broadcast from NBC San Francisco studios...Jack checks gang's train reservations, Phil, Dennis, and Don in the same berth...Rochester calls, Carmichael came out of hibernation and the gas man is missing again...men in uniform coming in after the show

Cast:

Last name	First name	Roles	Guest star
Anderson	Eddie	Rochester	No
Baldwin	Harry	Door guy	No
Beloin	Ed	Gilroy	No
Benny	Jack	Jack Benny, Rufus LaMer	No
Day	Dennis	Dennis Day, prospector	No
Harris	Phil	Phil Harris	No
Kilbride	Percy	Shaving cream clerk	No
Livingstone	Mary	Mary Livingstone, Saree LaMer	No
Nelson	Frank	Virgil Reimer	No
Wilson	Don	Don Wilson	No

Songs:

Order	Title	Performers	Vocal
1	The Fleet's In	Phil Harris	No
2	Jersey Bounce	Phil Harris	No
3	I Remember You	Dennis Day	Yes
4	Full Moon	Phil Harris	No

Notes:

Notable	Opening commercial is inset

Date: 4/26/1942   **Sponsor:** Jell-O   **City:** San Francisco, CA

Recording Source: KFI   **Problems:** None

First line:
And now ladies and gentlemen, as you all know, we are assembled here today to dedicate the new NBC building in San Francisco.

Summary:
Jack and Don interrupted for mike tests...new studios are swanky, worms in apple machine wearing tuxedos...Mary comes in with tour guide...NBC paying all expenses, so Jack decides to get a room...Dennis comes in with tour group...Phil comes in with tour group...Phil and Frankie staying in the bridal suite of the Fairmont...Jack and Dennis have been staying at an all-night movie...Rochester calls from Oakland, wants to spend the week...asks if Mary needs a new maid (he's found a girl)...Jack went with a lady barber (Christina) in Waukegan...skit Jack "Ace" Hawkin's Revenge...man tells Hawkins that they've found gold...Hawkins and Lulu go to the bar, plays high card with prospector...interrupted by tour group...end of show is cut off by the network

Cast:

Last name	First name	Roles	Guest star
Anderson	Eddie	Rochester	No
Beloin	Ed	Tour guide Abercrombie	No
Benny	Jack	Jack Benny, Jack "Ace" Hawkins	No
Day	Dennis	Dennis Day, prospector	No
Harris	Phil	Phil Harris, bartender Curly	No
Kirkwood	Jack	"Hello Mack" guy, gold finder	No
Livingstone	Mary	Mary Livingstone, Lulu Davenport	No
Morrow	Bill	Frankie	No
Wilson	Don	Don Wilson, Slim	No

Songs:

Order	Title	Performers	Vocal
1	We Did It Before/Keep Em Flying	Phil Harris	No
2	Always In My Heart	Dennis Day	Yes
3	Don't Sit Under the Apple Tree	Phil Harris	No
4	Johnny Doughboy Found a Rose in Ireland	Phil Harris	No

Notes:

Blooper	Jack stumbles on the word "emanate"
Notable	Show runs long, is cut off by the network
Notable	Opening commercial is inset
Running gag	Relay question and answer
Skit	Jack "Ace" Hawkins' Revenge

Date: 5/3/1942   **Sponsor:** Jell-O   **City:** Hollywood, CA

Recording Source: KFI   **Problems:** None

First line:
And now ladies and gentlemen, as you all know, Jack Benny has started work on his new picture with Ann Sheridan. So tonight we would like to show you what happened when the whole gang paid Jack a visit at Warner Brothers' studio yesterday. Jack told us to come over to his dressing room about 9 AM...

Summary:
Jack promo for war bonds before show opening...Jack wants to rehearse his scene with Ann Sheridan, with Rochester standing in for Ann...Jack is squatting in Errol Flynn's dressing room...makeup man arrives ("Are we ready for our daily tussle with father time?")...woman calls for Errol Flynn, Jack tries to make a date with her...Rochester wears Flynn's watch...Dennis wants to kiss Jack after he kisses Ann Sheridan...gang goes to movie set...Keighley (director) asks Jack if he's visiting...Jack has been bringing tour groups through...Jack sending violets to Ann every day...Jack introduces Ann to the gang...Ann seen Phil so often she feels like she knows him (at Masie's Beauty Parlor)...Dennis is overwhelmed...Ann and Mary compare notes on Jack...Jack learned the wrong scene...Jack ad libs his way through the scene, kisses Ann Sheridan, she faints

Cast:

Last name	First name	Roles	Guest star
Anderson	Eddie	Rochester	No
Baldwin	Harry	Stage caller, Warner Brother	No
Beloin	Ed	Gordon, Warner Brother	No
Benny	Jack	Jack Benny	No
Day	Dennis	Dennis Day	No
Harris	Phil	Phil Harris	No
Keighley	William	William Keighley	Yes
Kilbride	Percy	Passes demander	No
Livingstone	Mary	Mary Livingstone	No
Morrow	Bill	Warner Brother, Ernie	No
Sheridan	Ann	Ann Sheridan	Yes
Wilson	Don	Don Wilson	No

Songs:

Order	Title	Performers	Vocal
1	Jump for Joy	Phil Harris	No
2	Somebody Else Is Taking My Place	Phil Harris	No
3	Don't Sit Under the Apple Tree	Phil Harris	No
4	Unidentified	Phil Harris	No

Notes:

Notable	Dennis appears, but does not sing
Notable	Mary and Ann Sheridan compare notes on Jack, some time thereafter Mary gave a harsh insult to Sheridan when she suspected her of having relations with Jack
Notable	Jack kisses Ann Sheridan, huge audience reaction
Notable	Opening commercial is inset

Date: 5/10/1942   **Sponsor:** Jell-O   **City:** Mather Field, CA

Recording Source: KFI   **Problems:** None

First line:
And now ladies and gentlemen, our broadcast today originates from Mather Field near Sacramento, Mather Field where Uncle Sam's eagles of the sky are trained.

Summary:
Jack's father gave him a kite when he was a seven, he tied it to his waist and landed in St. Joe...Mary says the boys there are bashful...Dennis came up in a crate in the baggage car...gang discusses Mother's Day...Jack explains what a navigator is...Mary reads poem about pilots...man sells Jack a war bond to send to Fred Allen ("the shock would kill him")...Jack announces that this is the last season for Jell-O...flashback to Rochester driving Jack, Mary, and Don to see sponsor, Mr. Mortimer...Jack worries about being fired...Mortimer tells him that General Foods wants him to broadcast for another product...Jack tells Don, and he breaks down in tears...Jack consoles Don

Cast:

Last name	First name	Roles	Guest star
Anderson	Eddie	Rochester	No
Beloin	Ed	Bond seller	No
Benny	Jack	Jack Benny	No
Day	Dennis	Dennis Day	No
Harris	Phil	Phil Harris	No
Kirkwood	Jack	Mr. Mortimer	No
Livingstone	Mary	Mary Livingstone	No
Stewart	Blanche	Miss Stewart	No
Wilson	Don	Don Wilson	No

Songs:

Order	Title	Performers	Vocal
1	Army Air Corps/Buckle Down, Buck Private	Phil Harris	No
2	Johnny Doughboy	Dennis Day	Yes
3	I Can't Give You Anything But Love Baby	Phil Harris	No
4	I'll Pray for You	Phil Harris	No

Notes:

Notable	Opening commercial is inset
Running gag	Mary's poem

Date: 5/17/1942   **Sponsor:** Jell-O   **City:** Santa Ana, CA

Recording Source: Unknown   **Problems:** None

First line:
And now ladies and gentlemen, from the United States Army Air Base at Santa Ana, we bring you a man who drove up here in his old tin canna, Jack Benny.

Summary:
Gang insists on paying for his share of the gas...Dennis thought he had the mumps, but it was a tennis ball...Phil says he's a breath of spring, audience laughs over Jack's response...Jack explains what a bombardier is...special delivery for Mary, letter from Hutchison at Mater Field...he thinks Jack is Mary's father...Rochester calls, Billingsley came on trip and thinks he's a bombardier...sitting on Maxwell radiator dropping ping-pong balls on an anthill...George M. Cohan medley in honor of "I Am an American" Day...Fred has been opening his show with a comical analysis of the Benny show...Jack impersonates Fred Allen and predicts what he will say..."We're a little late, so thanks Colonel Robinson and all the boys, good night."

Cast:

Last name	First name	Roles	Guest star
Anderson	Eddie	Rochester	No
Benny	Jack	Jack Benny	No
Day	Dennis	Dennis Day	No
Harris	Phil	Phil Harris	No
Kilbride	Percy	Special delivery boy	No
Livingstone	Mary	Mary Livingstone	No
Wilson	Don	Don Wilson	No

Songs:

Order	Title	Performers	Vocal
1	I Am an American	Phil Harris	No
2	When You're With Me	Dennis Day	Yes
3	Yankee Doodle Dandy - Give My Regards to Broadway - Mary - You're a Grand Old Flag - Over There	Dennis Day	Yes
3	Yankee Doodle Dandy - Give My Regards to Broadway - Mary - You're a Grand Old Flag - Over There	Quartet	Yes
4	Last Call for Love	Phil Harris	No

Notes:

Notable	Opening commercial is about sugar rationing, apologies for grocers who don't have all flavors, tells people to buy only for present needs
Notable	Audience is cheering so loudly that Don has to practically yell the closing announcements

Date: 5/24/1942 **Sponsor:** Jell-O **City:** Camp Callan, CA

Recording Source: Unknown **Problems:** None

First line:
And now ladies and gentlemen, from Camp Callan, California, we bring you a man who, in my opinion, is the greatest comedian in the world, which is also his opinion, Jack Benny!

Summary:
Jack proves that everyone likes him...Mary gives the audience her telephone number...Jack went swimming in La Jolla, lifeguard had to pull him in by the hair, saved just his hair...Jack staying at the La Jolla Auto Court...Dennis' girl got married to make him jealous...Alice Faye had a 7 pound baby girl, Don says that when he was born he weighed 43 pounds...Phil hands out cigars...Jack forces Dennis to take a cigar...Jack announces that the show will be on for Grape Nuts Flakes next season...Jack contemplates his opening line with the new sponsor...Don breaks down in tears during commercial...Andy Devine tells Phil not to get in a rut like Eddie Cantor...Andy's father drinking gasoline, works at Lockheed as a blow torch...Phil named his daughter after Jack, Alice Jacqueline Harris...Mary reads poem about Camp Callan...Rochester calls, having trouble packing Jack's bags...Rochester found a Japanese submarine in Jack's swimsuit

Cast:

Last name	First name	Roles	Guest star
Anderson	Eddie	Rochester	No
Benny	Jack	Jack Benny	No
Day	Dennis	Dennis Day	No
Devine	Andy	Andy Devine	No
Harris	Phil	Phil Harris	No
Livingstone	Mary	Mary Livingstone	No
Wilson	Don	Don Wilson	No

Songs:

Order	Title	Performers	Vocal
1	A Real American	Phil Harris	No
2	Sleepy Lagoon	Dennis Day	Yes
3	Three Little Sisters	Phil Harris	No
4	Unidentified	Phil Harris	No

Notes:

Notable	Opening commercial is inset, you can barely hear the network feed under the announcement
Running gag	Mary's poem

Date: 5/31/1942 **Sponsor:** Jell-O **City:** Hollywood, CA

Recording Source: Unknown **Problems:** None

First line:
And now ladies and gentlemen, on his final appearance for Jell-O, we bring you that delicious comedian with the locked-in bankroll, Jack Benny!

Summary:
Phil practicing making three-cornered pants with his handkerchief...Jack recalls his first sponsors...skit is Cavalcade of Eight Years with Jell-O, featuring highlights...opening theme is Love in Bloom...when Jack first met Rochester...Buck Benny skit...Andy Devine visits in San Francisco...Benny-Allen feud summary, scene when Jack gives Fred Allen a transfusion...motion picture skit, Lost Horizon, scene where Jack meets the High Lama...Dennis and Mrs. Day's first appearance...phone call from Mary's mother...Rochester calls about the disappearance of the gas man...Mr. Billingsley scene...Don invites gang over to meet the little woman, Jack tells him to call her...New Tenant skit from 12/31/41...Jack thanks everyone for their participation

Cast:

Last name	First name	Roles	Guest star
Anderson	Eddie	Rochester	No
Beloin	Ed	Mr. Billingsley	No
Benny	Jack	Jack Benny, Buck Benny, Old Year	No
Davis	Dix	Baby New Year	No
Day	Dennis	Dennis Day	No
Devine	Andy	Andy Devine	No
Felton	Verna	Mrs. Day	No
Harris	Phil	Phil Harris, Frank Carson, Uncle Sam	No
Hearn	Sam	Schlepperman/High Lama	No
Lewis	Elliott	Chang	No
Livingstone	Mary	Mary Livingstone, Daisy Carson, Columbia	No
Nelson	Frank	Doctor	No
Stewart	Blanche	Nurse Miss Stewart	No
Wilson	Don	Don Wilson, horse	No

Songs:

Order	Title	Performers	Vocal
1	Salute to Gardner Field	Phil Harris	No
2	When You Wish Upon a Star	Dennis Day	Yes
3	My Great Great Grandfather - Auld Lang Syne	Phil Harris	No

Notes:

Notable	Opening commercial is inset
Running gag	Mary's mother communication
Skit	Cavalcade of Eight Years with Jell-O

CAST INDEX

12/25/1938, 1/1/1939, 1/15/1939, 1/29/1939, 2/5/1939, 2/12/1939, 2/19/1939, 3/5/1939, 3/12/1939, 4/2/1939, 4/23/1939, 5/14/1939, 5/28/1939, 6/4/1939, 6/18/1939, 6/25/1939, 10/8/1939, 10/15/1939, 10/29/1939, 11/5/1939, 11/12/1939, 11/19/1939, 12/10/1939, 12/24/1939, 1/7/1940, 1/21/1940, 1/28/1940, 2/4/1940, 2/11/1940, 2/18/1940, 2/25/1940, 3/3/1940, 3/10/1940, 3/24/1940, 4/7/1940, 4/14/1940, 4/21/1940, 4/28/1940, 5/5/1940, 5/12/1940, 5/26/1940, 6/2/1940, 10/6/1940, 10/13/1940, 10/20/1940, 10/27/1940, 11/3/1940, 11/10/1940, 11/17/1940, 11/24/1940, 12/1/1940, 12/8/1940, 12/22/1940, 12/29/1940, 1/12/1941, 1/19/1941, 1/26/1941, 2/23/1941, 3/2/1941, 3/16/1941, 3/30/1941, 4/6/1941, 4/13/1941, 4/20/1941, 4/27/1941, 5/4/1941, 5/11/1941, 5/18/1941, 5/25/1941, 6/1/1941, 10/5/1941, 10/12/1941, 10/19/1941, 11/2/1941, 11/9/1941, 11/16/1941, 11/23/1941, 12/7/1941, 12/14/1941, 12/21/1941, 1/4/1942, 1/11/1942, 2/8/1942, 2/15/1942, 2/22/1942, 3/1/1942, 3/8/1942, 3/15/1942, 3/22/1942, 3/29/1942, 4/5/1942, 4/12/1942, 4/19/1942, 4/26/1942, 5/3/1942, 5/10/1942, 5/17/1942, 5/24/1942, 5/31/1942

Cliff Arquette 11/6/1938
Ralph Ashe 7/11/1932, 7/20/1932, 8/10/1932, 8/22/1932, 9/14/1932, 9/21/1932, 9/26/1932, 10/3/1932, 10/26/1932, 11/20/1932, 11/27/1932, 12/1/1932, 12/4/1932, 12/8/1932, 1/5/1933, 1/22/1933, 3/24/1933, 3/31/1933, 5/5/1933, 5/19/1933, 5/26/1933, 6/2/1933, 6/9/1933, 6/16/1933, 10/1/1933, 10/8/1933, 11/12/1933, 1/14/1934, 5/11/1934, 1/27/1935
Charley Bagby 4/10/1938
? Baker 10/5/1941
Benny Baker 7/11/1932, 10/24/1932, 12/29/1932, 3/3/1933, 3/10/1933, 5/19/1933, 5/26/1933, 6/1/1934, 4/14/1935, 4/21/1935, 4/28/1935, 5/5/1935, 6/23/1935, 9/29/1935, 10/6/1935, 12/1/1935, 10/4/1936, 10/4/1936, 1/10/1937
Jerry Baker 5/11/1932
Kenny Baker 11/3/1935, 11/10/1935, 11/17/1935, 11/24/1935, 12/1/1935, 12/6/1935, 12/15/1935, 12/22/1935, 12/29/1935, 1/5/1936, 1/12/1936, 1/19/1936, 1/26/1936, 2/2/1936, 2/9/1936, 2/16/1936, 2/23/1936, 3/1/1936, 3/8/1936, 3/15/1936, 3/22/1936, 3/29/1936, 4/5/1936, 4/12/1936, 4/19/1936, 4/26/1936, 5/3/1936, 5/10/1936, 5/17/1936, 5/24/1936, 5/31/1936, 6/7/1936, 6/14/1936, 6/21/1936, 10/4/1936, 10/11/1936, 10/18/1936, 10/25/1936, 11/1/1936, 11/8/1936, 11/15/1936, 11/22/1936, 11/29/1936, 12/6/1936, 12/13/1936, 12/20/1936, 12/27/1936, 1/3/1937, 1/17/1937, 1/24/1937, 1/31/1937, 2/7/1937, 2/14/1937, 2/21/1937, 2/28/1937, 3/7/1937, 3/21/1937, 3/28/1937, 4/4/1937, 4/11/1937, 4/18/1937, 4/25/1937, 5/2/1937, 5/9/1937, 5/16/1937, 5/23/1937, 5/30/1937, 6/6/1937, 6/13/1937, 6/20/1937, 6/27/1937, 10/3/1937, 10/10/1937, 10/17/1937, 10/24/1937, 10/31/1937, 11/7/1937, 11/14/1937, 11/21/1937, 11/28/1937, 12/5/1937, 12/12/1937, 12/19/1937, 12/26/1937, 1/2/1938, 1/9/1938, 1/16/1938, 1/23/1938, 1/30/1938, 2/6/1938, 2/13/1938, 2/20/1938, 2/27/1938, 3/6/1938, 3/13/1938, 3/20/1938, 4/3/1938, 4/10/1938, 4/17/1938, 4/24/1938, 5/1/1938, 5/8/1938, 5/15/1938, 5/22/1938, 5/29/1938, 6/5/1938, 6/12/1938, 6/19/1938, 10/2/1938, 10/9/1938, 10/16/1938, 10/23/1938, 10/30/1938, 11/6/1938, 11/13/1938, 11/20/1938, 11/27/1938, 12/4/1938, 12/18/1938, 12/25/1938, 1/1/1939, 1/8/1939, 1/15/1939, 1/22/1939, 1/29/1939, 2/5/1939, 2/12/1939, 2/19/1939, 2/26/1939, 3/5/1939, 3/12/1939, 3/19/1939, 3/26/1939, 4/2/1939, 4/9/1939, 4/16/1939, 4/23/1939, 4/30/1939, 5/7/1939, 5/14/1939, 5/21/1939, 5/28/1939, 6/4/1939, 6/11/1939, 6/18/1939, 12/10/1939

Wally Baker.. 5/5/1935,
    5/12/1935, 5/26/1935, 6/9/1935, 11/24/1935, 1/19/1936, 6/6/1937, 4/24/1938,
    2/5/1939
Harry Baldwin 7/20/1932,
    7/25/1932, 8/3/1932, 8/17/1932, 8/22/1932, 9/7/1932, 9/19/1932, 10/17/1932,
    1/5/1933, 10/1/1933, 10/29/1933, 12/31/1933, 1/7/1934, 1/14/1934, 1/21/1934,
    2/4/1934, 2/18/1934, 2/25/1934, 3/4/1934, 3/18/1934, 5/4/1934, 6/22/1934,
    7/6/1934, 7/20/1934, 8/17/1934, 8/24/1934, 8/31/1934, 9/7/1934, 9/28/1934,
    10/28/1934, 11/18/1934, 11/25/1934, 12/2/1934, 1/6/1935, 1/27/1935, 2/17/1935,
    3/17/1935, 4/14/1935, 4/21/1935, 4/28/1935, 6/2/1935, 6/16/1935, 6/30/1935,
    7/14/1935, 10/13/1935, 10/20/1935, 11/3/1935, 11/10/1935, 11/17/1935,
    11/24/1935, 12/1/1935, 12/15/1935, 12/22/1935, 1/19/1936, 1/26/1936, 2/2/1936,
    2/9/1936, 2/16/1936, 2/23/1936, 3/1/1936, 3/8/1936, 3/15/1936, 3/22/1936,
    3/29/1936, 4/26/1936, 5/3/1936, 5/10/1936, 5/17/1936, 5/24/1936, 5/31/1936,
    6/7/1936, 6/14/1936, 6/21/1936, 10/4/1936, 10/11/1936, 10/18/1936, 10/25/1936,
    11/1/1936, 11/8/1936, 11/15/1936, 11/22/1936, 11/29/1936, 12/6/1936,
    12/13/1936, 12/27/1936, 1/3/1937, 1/10/1937, 1/17/1937, 1/24/1937, 1/31/1937,
    2/7/1937, 2/14/1937, 2/21/1937, 2/21/1937, 3/14/1937, 3/21/1937, 3/28/1937,
    4/11/1937, 4/25/1937, 5/2/1937, 5/9/1937, 5/30/1937, 6/6/1937, 6/13/1937,
    6/20/1937, 6/27/1937, 10/3/1937, 10/17/1937, 10/31/1937, 11/14/1937,
    11/28/1937, 12/5/1937, 12/12/1937, 12/19/1937, 12/26/1937, 1/2/1938, 1/9/1938,
    1/16/1938, 1/23/1938, 1/30/1938, 2/6/1938, 2/6/1938, 2/13/1938, 2/27/1938,
    3/13/1938, 3/27/1938, 4/3/1938, 4/10/1938, 4/17/1938, 4/24/1938, 5/1/1938,
    5/15/1938, 5/29/1938, 6/5/1938, 6/12/1938, 6/19/1938, 6/26/1938, 10/2/1938,
    10/9/1938, 10/23/1938, 11/6/1938, 11/20/1938, 12/4/1938, 12/11/1938,
    12/25/1938, 1/1/1939, 1/8/1939, 1/15/1939, 1/22/1939, 1/29/1939, 2/12/1939,
    3/5/1939, 3/26/1939, 4/2/1939, 4/9/1939, 4/16/1939, 4/30/1939, 5/7/1939,
    5/14/1939, 5/28/1939, 6/4/1939, 6/18/1939, 6/25/1939, 10/8/1939, 10/15/1939,
    11/5/1939, 11/19/1939, 12/3/1939, 12/31/1939, 1/7/1940, 1/28/1940, 2/25/1940,
    3/3/1940, 3/10/1940, 3/31/1940, 4/14/1940, 4/21/1940, 5/5/1940, 5/19/1940,
    6/2/1940, 6/16/1940, 10/6/1940, 10/13/1940, 10/20/1940, 10/27/1940,
    11/10/1940, 11/17/1940, 11/24/1940, 12/8/1940, 12/15/1940, 12/29/1940,
    1/5/1941, 1/12/1941, 1/26/1941, 2/23/1941, 3/2/1941, 3/9/1941, 4/20/1941,
    4/27/1941, 5/18/1941, 5/25/1941, 6/1/1941, 10/5/1941, 10/12/1941, 10/26/1941,
    11/16/1941, 11/30/1941, 12/7/1941, 12/14/1941, 12/21/1941, 12/28/1941,
    1/11/1942, 1/25/1942, 2/1/1942, 2/8/1942, 2/22/1942, 3/1/1942, 3/8/1942,
    3/29/1942, 4/19/1942, 5/3/1942
? Balonin 6/27/1932
Brad   Barker7/25/1932,
    8/31/1932, 9/14/1932, 1/1/1933, 4/28/1933, 12/10/1933, 1/28/1934, 3/18/1934,
    9/21/1934
Michael Bartlett 9/29/1935, 10/6/1935, 10/13/1935, 10/20/1935, 10/27/1935
? Barton 11/24/1935
? Beach 2/11/1934
Ed Beloin 5/10/1936,
    5/24/1936, 10/4/1936, 10/18/1936, 10/25/1936, 11/1/1936, 11/29/1936,
    1/24/1937, 1/31/1937, 2/7/1937, 2/14/1937, 5/2/1937, 5/9/1937, 6/6/1937,
    6/13/1937, 6/20/1937, 10/3/1937, 10/17/1937, 10/24/1937, 11/21/1937,
    11/28/1937, 12/12/1937, 12/19/1937, 1/9/1938, 1/16/1938, 2/6/1938, 2/13/1938,
    2/20/1938, 3/6/1938, 3/13/1938, 3/20/1938, 4/3/1938, 4/10/1938, 4/17/1938,
    4/24/1938, 4/24/1938, 5/1/1938, 5/15/1938, 6/5/1938, 6/5/1938, 6/12/1938,
    6/12/1938, 10/2/1938, 10/2/1938, 10/9/1938, 10/16/1938, 10/23/1938,
    11/13/1938, 11/20/1938, 11/27/1938, 12/4/1938, 12/11/1938, 12/11/1938,

12/11/1938, 12/18/1938, 1/1/1939, 1/8/1939, 1/15/1939, 1/22/1939, 1/29/1939, 2/5/1939, 2/12/1939, 2/19/1939, 2/19/1939, 2/26/1939, 3/5/1939, 4/2/1939, 4/9/1939, 4/23/1939, 4/30/1939, 5/7/1939, 5/14/1939, 5/21/1939, 5/28/1939, 6/18/1939, 6/25/1939, 10/22/1939, 12/10/1939, 12/17/1939, 12/24/1939, 12/31/1939, 1/7/1940, 1/14/1940, 1/21/1940, 1/28/1940, 2/4/1940, 2/11/1940, 2/18/1940, 2/25/1940, 3/3/1940, 3/10/1940, 3/17/1940, 3/31/1940, 4/14/1940, 4/21/1940, 5/5/1940, 5/12/1940, 5/19/1940, 5/26/1940, 6/2/1940, 6/16/1940, 10/6/1940, 10/20/1940, 11/3/1940, 11/10/1940, 11/17/1940, 12/1/1940, 12/15/1940, 12/22/1940, 1/5/1941, 1/12/1941, 1/26/1941, 2/9/1941, 2/16/1941, 3/2/1941, 3/23/1941, 3/30/1941, 4/6/1941, 4/13/1941, 4/27/1941, 5/18/1941, 6/1/1941, 10/5/1941, 10/19/1941, 10/26/1941, 11/2/1941, 11/23/1941, 12/14/1941, 12/21/1941, 1/4/1942, 2/8/1942, 2/15/1942, 3/1/1942, 3/22/1942, 3/29/1942, 4/19/1942, 4/26/1942, 5/3/1942, 5/10/1942, 5/31/1942

Bea Benaderet.. 12/12/1937, 12/26/1937, 10/23/1938, 2/5/1939
? Bennett 10/27/1935, 11/10/1935, 11/17/1935
Jack Benny 5/2/1932, 5/4/1932, 5/9/1932, 5/11/1932, 5/16/1932, 5/18/1932, 5/23/1932, 5/25/1932, 5/30/1932, 6/1/1932, 6/6/1932, 6/8/1932, 6/13/1932, 6/15/1932, 6/20/1932, 6/22/1932, 6/27/1932, 6/29/1932, 7/4/1932, 7/6/1932, 7/11/1932, 7/13/1932, 7/18/1932, 7/20/1932, 7/25/1932, 7/27/1932, 8/1/1932, 8/3/1932, 8/8/1932, 8/10/1932, 8/15/1932, 8/17/1932, 8/22/1932, 8/24/1932, 8/29/1932, 8/31/1932, 9/5/1932, 9/7/1932, 9/12/1932, 9/14/1932, 9/19/1932, 9/21/1932, 9/26/1932, 9/28/1932, 10/3/1932, 10/5/1932, 10/10/1932, 10/12/1932, 10/17/1932, 10/19/1932, 10/24/1932, 10/26/1932, 10/30/1932, 11/3/1932, 11/10/1932, 11/17/1932, 11/20/1932, 11/24/1932, 11/27/1932, 12/1/1932, 12/4/1932, 12/8/1932, 12/11/1932, 12/15/1932, 12/18/1932, 12/22/1932, 12/25/1932, 12/29/1932, 1/1/1933, 1/5/1933, 1/8/1933, 1/12/1933, 1/15/1933, 1/19/1933, 1/22/1933, 1/26/1933, 3/10/1933, 3/17/1933, 3/24/1933, 3/31/1933, 4/7/1933, 4/14/1933, 4/21/1933, 4/28/1933, 5/5/1933, 5/12/1933, 5/19/1933, 5/26/1933, 6/2/1933, 6/9/1933, 6/16/1933, 6/23/1933, 10/1/1933, 10/8/1933, 10/22/1933, 10/29/1933, 11/5/1933, 11/12/1933, 11/19/1933, 11/26/1933, 12/3/1933, 12/10/1933, 12/17/1933, 12/24/1933, 12/31/1933, 1/7/1934, 1/14/1934, 1/21/1934, 1/28/1934, 2/4/1934, 2/11/1934, 2/18/1934, 2/25/1934, 3/4/1934, 3/11/1934, 3/18/1934, 3/25/1934, 4/1/1934, 4/6/1934, 4/13/1934, 4/20/1934, 4/27/1934, 5/4/1934, 5/11/1934, 5/18/1934, 5/25/1934, 6/1/1934, 6/8/1934, 6/15/1934, 6/22/1934, 6/29/1934, 7/6/1934, 7/13/1934, 7/20/1934, 7/27/1934, 8/3/1934, 8/10/1934, 8/17/1934, 8/24/1934, 8/31/1934, 9/7/1934, 9/14/1934, 9/21/1934, 10/14/1934, 10/21/1934, 10/28/1934, 11/4/1934, 11/11/1934, 11/18/1934, 11/25/1934, 12/2/1934, 12/9/1934, 12/16/1934, 12/23/1934, 12/30/1934, 1/6/1935, 1/13/1935, 1/20/1935, 1/27/1935, 2/3/1935, 2/10/1935, 2/17/1935, 2/24/1935, 3/3/1935, 3/10/1935, 3/17/1935, 3/24/1935, 3/31/1935, 4/7/1935, 4/14/1935, 4/21/1935, 4/28/1935, 5/5/1935, 5/12/1935, 5/19/1935, 5/26/1935, 6/2/1935, 6/9/1935, 6/16/1935, 6/23/1935, 6/30/1935, 7/7/1935, 7/14/1935, 9/29/1935, 10/6/1935, 10/13/1935, 10/20/1935, 10/27/1935, 11/3/1935, 11/10/1935, 11/17/1935, 11/24/1935, 12/1/1935, 12/6/1935, 12/15/1935, 12/22/1935, 12/29/1935, 1/5/1936, 1/12/1936, 1/19/1936, 1/26/1936, 2/2/1936, 2/9/1936, 2/16/1936, 2/23/1936, 3/1/1936, 3/8/1936, 3/15/1936, 3/22/1936, 3/29/1936, 4/5/1936, 4/12/1936, 4/19/1936, 4/26/1936, 5/3/1936, 5/10/1936, 5/17/1936, 5/24/1936, 5/31/1936, 6/7/1936, 6/14/1936, 6/21/1936, 10/4/1936, 10/11/1936, 10/18/1936, 10/25/1936, 11/1/1936, 11/8/1936, 11/15/1936, 11/22/1936, 11/29/1936, 12/6/1936, 12/13/1936, 12/20/1936, 12/27/1936, 1/3/1937, 1/10/1937, 1/17/1937, 1/24/1937, 1/31/1937, 2/7/1937, 2/14/1937, 2/21/1937, 2/28/1937, 3/7/1937, 3/14/1937, 3/21/1937, 3/28/1937,

4/4/1937, 4/11/1937, 4/18/1937, 4/25/1937, 5/2/1937, 5/9/1937, 5/16/1937, 5/30/1937, 6/6/1937, 6/13/1937, 6/20/1937, 6/27/1937, 10/3/1937, 10/10/1937, 10/17/1937, 10/24/1937, 10/31/1937, 11/7/1937, 11/14/1937, 11/21/1937, 11/28/1937, 12/5/1937, 12/12/1937, 12/19/1937, 12/26/1937, 1/2/1938, 1/9/1938, 1/16/1938, 1/23/1938, 1/30/1938, 2/6/1938, 2/13/1938, 2/20/1938, 2/27/1938, 3/6/1938, 3/13/1938, 3/20/1938, 3/27/1938, 4/3/1938, 4/10/1938, 4/17/1938, 4/24/1938, 5/1/1938, 5/8/1938, 5/15/1938, 5/22/1938, 5/29/1938, 6/5/1938, 6/12/1938, 6/19/1938, 6/26/1938, 10/2/1938, 10/9/1938, 10/16/1938, 10/23/1938, 10/30/1938, 11/6/1938, 11/13/1938, 11/20/1938, 11/27/1938, 12/4/1938, 12/11/1938, 12/18/1938, 12/25/1938, 1/1/1939, 1/8/1939, 1/15/1939, 1/22/1939, 1/29/1939, 2/5/1939, 2/12/1939, 2/19/1939, 2/26/1939, 3/5/1939, 3/12/1939, 3/19/1939, 3/26/1939, 4/2/1939, 4/9/1939, 4/16/1939, 4/23/1939, 4/30/1939, 5/7/1939, 5/14/1939, 5/21/1939, 5/28/1939, 6/4/1939, 6/11/1939, 6/18/1939, 6/25/1939, 10/8/1939, 10/15/1939, 10/22/1939, 10/29/1939, 11/5/1939, 11/12/1939, 11/19/1939, 11/26/1939, 12/3/1939, 12/10/1939, 12/17/1939, 12/24/1939, 12/31/1939, 1/7/1940, 1/14/1940, 1/21/1940, 1/28/1940, 2/4/1940, 2/11/1940, 2/18/1940, 2/25/1940, 3/3/1940, 3/10/1940, 3/17/1940, 3/24/1940, 3/31/1940, 4/7/1940, 4/14/1940, 4/21/1940, 4/28/1940, 5/5/1940, 5/12/1940, 5/19/1940, 5/26/1940, 6/2/1940, 6/9/1940, 6/16/1940, 10/6/1940, 10/13/1940, 10/20/1940, 10/27/1940, 11/3/1940, 11/10/1940, 11/17/1940, 11/24/1940, 12/1/1940, 12/8/1940, 12/15/1940, 12/22/1940, 12/29/1940, 1/5/1941, 1/12/1941, 1/19/1941, 1/26/1941, 2/9/1941, 2/16/1941, 2/23/1941, 3/2/1941, 3/9/1941, 3/16/1941, 3/16/1941, 3/23/1941, 3/30/1941, 4/6/1941, 4/13/1941, 4/20/1941, 4/27/1941, 5/4/1941, 5/11/1941, 5/18/1941, 5/25/1941, 6/1/1941, 10/5/1941, 10/12/1941, 10/19/1941, 10/26/1941, 11/2/1941, 11/9/1941, 11/16/1941, 11/23/1941, 11/30/1941, 12/7/1941, 12/14/1941, 12/21/1941, 12/28/1941, 1/4/1942, 1/11/1942, 1/25/1942, 2/1/1942, 2/8/1942, 2/15/1942, 2/22/1942, 3/1/1942, 3/8/1942, 3/15/1942, 3/22/1942, 3/29/1942, 4/5/1942, 4/12/1942, 4/19/1942, 4/26/1942, 5/3/1942, 5/10/1942, 5/17/1942, 5/24/1942, 5/31/1942

Sadye Benny (see also Mary Livingston, Mary Livingstone).............................. 7/27/1932, 8/3/1932, 8/8/1932, 8/17/1932, 9/5/1932, 9/7/1932, 9/12/1932, 9/14/1932, 9/19/1932, 9/21/1932, 9/26/1932, 9/28/1932, 10/3/1932, 10/5/1932, 10/10/1932

Don Bestor... 4/6/1934, 4/13/1934, 4/20/1934, 4/27/1934, 5/4/1934, 5/11/1934, 5/25/1934, 8/3/1934, 8/10/1934, 8/17/1934, 8/24/1934, 8/31/1934, 9/7/1934, 9/14/1934, 9/21/1934, 9/28/1934, 10/14/1934, 10/21/1934, 10/28/1934, 11/4/1934, 11/11/1934, 11/18/1934, 11/25/1934, 12/2/1934, 12/9/1934, 12/16/1934, 12/23/1934, 12/30/1934, 1/6/1935, 1/13/1935, 1/20/1935, 1/27/1935, 2/3/1935, 2/10/1935, 2/17/1935, 2/24/1935, 3/3/1935, 3/10/1935, 3/17/1935, 3/24/1935, 3/31/1935, 4/7/1935, 4/21/1935, 4/28/1935, 5/5/1935, 5/12/1935, 5/19/1935, 5/26/1935, 6/2/1935, 6/9/1935, 6/16/1935, 6/23/1935, 6/30/1935, 7/7/1935, 7/14/1935

Frank Bingman 4/13/1941, 4/20/1941, 4/27/1941, 5/4/1941, 5/11/1941, 5/18/1941, 5/25/1941

Frank Black... 3/3/1933, 3/10/1933, 3/17/1933, 3/24/1933, 3/31/1933, 4/7/1933, 4/14/1933, 4/21/1933, 4/28/1933, 5/5/1933, 5/12/1933, 5/19/1933, 5/26/1933, 6/2/1933, 6/9/1933, 6/16/1933, 6/23/1933, 10/1/1933, 10/8/1933, 10/22/1933, 10/29/1933, 11/5/1933, 11/12/1933, 11/19/1933, 11/26/1933, 12/3/1933, 12/10/1933, 12/17/1933, 12/24/1933, 12/31/1933, 1/7/1934, 1/14/1934, 1/21/1934, 1/28/1934, 2/4/1934, 2/11/1934, 2/18/1934, 2/25/1934, 3/4/1934, 3/11/1934, 3/18/1934, 3/25/1934, 4/1/1934

Mel Blanc 6/7/1936,
       3/12/1939,   3/19/1939,   10/29/1939,   12/24/1939,   11/17/1940,   3/30/1941,
       12/28/1941
Jesse Block 4/25/1937
Ben Blue 10/25/1936, 11/8/1936, 11/22/1936
? Boardman 3/16/1941
Bobby Borger 5/2/1932,
       5/16/1932, 6/8/1932, 6/29/1932, 9/19/1932, 9/21/1932, 10/26/1932
? Brown 11/21/1937, 12/5/1937
Bob Brown 1/20/1935
John Brown 4/5/1936,
       4/19/1936, 5/17/1936, 5/24/1936, 3/27/1938, 12/4/1938, 12/11/1938, 4/21/1940,
       5/5/1940, 12/22/1940
Arthur Q. Bryan 11/16/1941
? Bunker 6/12/1938
? Burns 10/28/1934
? Campbell 4/23/1939
Charles Cantor 5/24/1936, 12/11/1938, 4/21/1940, 4/28/1940, 5/5/1940, 12/15/1940
? Caryl 7/25/1932
Norman Case 8/3/1934
Joe Cates 10/29/1933, 12/3/1933, 12/24/1933, 12/29/1935, 10/11/1936
Howard Claney 3/3/1933,
       3/10/1933, 3/17/1933, 3/24/1933, 3/31/1933, 4/7/1933, 4/14/1933, 4/21/1933,
       5/5/1933, 5/12/1933, 5/19/1933, 5/26/1933, 6/2/1933, 6/9/1933, 6/16/1933,
       6/23/1933
Cliff Clarke 3/8/1942, 3/29/1942
Leo Cleary 6/4/1939, 12/8/1940, 12/29/1940
Pinto Colvig 11/14/1937, 11/28/1937, 6/5/1938, 10/9/1938
Harry Conn 6/15/1932,
       7/6/1932, 7/13/1932, 7/18/1932, 8/8/1932, 8/10/1932, 8/17/1932, 8/22/1932,
       8/24/1932, 8/31/1932, 9/5/1932, 9/12/1932, 9/14/1932, 9/19/1932, 9/21/1932,
       9/28/1932,   10/3/1932,   10/12/1932,   10/19/1932,   10/30/1932,   11/3/1932,
       11/6/1932,   11/10/1932,   11/13/1932,   11/17/1932,   11/20/1932,   12/11/1932,
       1/15/1933
Mildred Conn 11/10/1932
? Conrad 11/3/1935, 12/29/1940
? Corni 10/19/1941
Doug Coulter 6/13/1932, 7/6/1932, 8/24/1932
Dick Cunliffe 10/30/1932
? Dallas 2/4/1934, 2/11/1934
Dix Davis 10/19/1941,
       10/26/1941, 11/2/1941, 11/9/1941, 11/30/1941, 12/28/1941, 5/31/1942
Dennis Day 10/8/1939,
       10/15/1939,   10/22/1939,   10/29/1939,   11/5/1939,   11/12/1939,   11/19/1939,
       11/26/1939,   12/3/1939,   12/10/1939,   12/17/1939,   12/24/1939,   12/31/1939,
       1/7/1940, 1/14/1940, 1/21/1940, 1/28/1940, 2/4/1940, 2/11/1940, 2/18/1940,
       2/25/1940, 3/3/1940, 3/10/1940, 3/17/1940, 3/24/1940, 3/31/1940, 4/7/1940,
       4/14/1940, 4/21/1940, 4/28/1940, 5/5/1940, 5/12/1940, 5/19/1940, 5/26/1940,
       6/2/1940, 6/9/1940, 6/16/1940, 10/6/1940, 10/13/1940, 10/20/1940, 10/27/1940,
       11/3/1940,   11/10/1940,   11/17/1940,   11/24/1940,   12/1/1940,   12/8/1940,
       12/15/1940, 12/22/1940, 12/29/1940, 1/5/1941, 1/12/1941, 1/19/1941, 1/26/1941,
       2/2/1941, 2/9/1941, 2/16/1941, 2/23/1941, 3/2/1941, 3/9/1941, 3/16/1941,
       3/23/1941, 3/30/1941, 4/6/1941, 4/13/1941, 4/20/1941, 4/27/1941, 5/4/1941,

5/11/1941, 5/18/1941, 5/25/1941, 6/1/1941, 10/5/1941, 10/12/1941, 10/19/1941, 10/26/1941, 11/2/1941, 11/9/1941, 11/16/1941, 11/23/1941, 11/30/1941, 12/7/1941, 12/14/1941, 12/21/1941, 12/28/1941, 1/4/1942, 1/11/1942, 1/18/1942, 1/25/1942, 2/1/1942, 2/8/1942, 2/15/1942, 2/22/1942, 3/1/1942, 3/8/1942, 3/15/1942, 3/22/1942, 3/29/1942, 4/5/1942, 4/12/1942, 4/19/1942, 4/26/1942, 5/3/1942, 5/10/1942, 5/17/1942, 5/24/1942, 5/31/1942

9/21/1932, 9/26/1932, 9/28/1932, 10/3/1932, 10/5/1932, 10/10/1932, 10/12/1932, 10/17/1932, 10/19/1932, 10/24/1932, 10/26/1932

Dick Hotcha Gardner 5/23/1932, 6/13/1932, 6/15/1932, 6/20/1932, 6/22/1932, 6/29/1932, 7/6/1932, 7/18/1932, 7/20/1932, 8/1/1932, 8/3/1932, 8/8/1932, 8/10/1932, 8/15/1932, 8/22/1932, 8/24/1932, 8/29/1932, 9/5/1932, 9/7/1932, 9/12/1932, 9/14/1932, 9/19/1932, 9/21/1932, 9/26/1932, 9/28/1932, 10/3/1932, 10/5/1932, 10/10/1932, 10/12/1932, 10/17/1932, 10/19/1932, 10/24/1932, 10/26/1932

Parker Gibbs 11/10/1932, 11/13/1932, 12/15/1932, 12/18/1932, 12/22/1932, 12/25/1932, 12/29/1932, 1/12/1933, 1/15/1933, 1/19/1933, 1/26/1933

John Gibson 3/28/1937, 5/2/1937, 6/13/1937

? Gilly 1/15/1939

Gwen Gilroy 1/4/1942

? Gordon 9/21/1934

? Granby 1/6/1935

Eddie Green 4/28/1940, 12/15/1940, 10/12/1941, 8/3/1934

Johnny Green 9/29/1935, 10/6/1935, 10/13/1935, 10/20/1935, 10/27/1935, 11/3/1935, 11/10/1935, 11/17/1935, 11/24/1935, 12/1/1935, 12/6/1935, 12/15/1935, 12/22/1935, 12/29/1935, 1/5/1936, 1/12/1936, 1/19/1936, 1/26/1936, 2/2/1936, 2/9/1936, 2/16/1936, 2/23/1936, 3/1/1936, 3/8/1936, 3/15/1936, 3/22/1936, 3/29/1936, 4/5/1936, 4/12/1936, 4/19/1936, 4/26/1936, 5/3/1936, 5/10/1936, 5/17/1936, 5/24/1936, 5/31/1936, 6/7/1936, 6/14/1936, 6/21/1936

Bob Gregory 11/6/1932, 11/13/1932

Jack Gregory 11/6/1932

Jimmy Grier 7/20/1934, 6/8/1934, 6/15/1934, 6/22/1934, 6/29/1934, 7/6/1934, 7/13/1934, 7/27/1934, 4/14/1935

? Hamilton 2/4/1934, 2/18/1934

Phil Harris 10/4/1936, 10/11/1936, 10/11/1936, 10/18/1936, 10/25/1936, 11/1/1936, 11/8/1936, 11/15/1936, 11/22/1936, 11/29/1936, 12/6/1936, 12/13/1936, 12/20/1936, 12/27/1936, 1/3/1937, 1/10/1937, 1/17/1937, 1/24/1937, 1/31/1937, 2/7/1937, 2/14/1937, 2/21/1937, 2/28/1937, 4/4/1937, 4/11/1937, 4/18/1937, 4/25/1937, 5/2/1937, 5/9/1937, 5/16/1937, 5/23/1937, 5/30/1937, 6/6/1937, 6/13/1937, 6/20/1937, 6/27/1937, 10/3/1937, 10/10/1937, 10/17/1937, 10/24/1937, 10/31/1937, 11/7/1937, 11/14/1937, 11/21/1937, 11/28/1937, 12/5/1937, 12/12/1937, 12/19/1937, 12/26/1937, 1/2/1938, 1/9/1938, 1/16/1938, 1/23/1938, 1/30/1938, 2/6/1938, 2/13/1938, 2/20/1938, 2/27/1938, 3/6/1938, 3/13/1938, 3/20/1938, 4/3/1938, 4/10/1938, 4/17/1938, 4/24/1938, 5/1/1938, 5/8/1938, 5/15/1938, 5/22/1938, 5/29/1938, 6/5/1938, 6/12/1938, 6/19/1938, 6/26/1938, 10/2/1938, 10/9/1938, 10/16/1938, 10/23/1938, 10/30/1938, 11/6/1938, 11/13/1938, 11/20/1938, 11/27/1938, 12/4/1938, 12/11/1938, 12/18/1938, 12/25/1938, 1/1/1939, 1/8/1939, 1/15/1939, 1/22/1939, 1/29/1939, 2/5/1939, 2/12/1939, 2/19/1939, 2/26/1939, 3/5/1939, 3/12/1939, 3/19/1939, 3/26/1939, 4/2/1939, 4/9/1939, 4/16/1939, 4/23/1939, 4/30/1939, 5/7/1939, 5/14/1939, 5/21/1939, 5/28/1939, 6/4/1939, 6/11/1939, 6/18/1939, 6/25/1939, 10/8/1939, 10/15/1939, 10/22/1939, 10/29/1939, 11/5/1939, 11/12/1939, 11/19/1939, 11/26/1939, 12/3/1939, 12/10/1939, 12/17/1939, 12/24/1939, 12/31/1939, 1/7/1940, 1/14/1940, 1/21/1940, 1/28/1940, 2/4/1940, 2/11/1940, 2/18/1940, 2/25/1940, 3/3/1940, 3/10/1940, 3/17/1940, 3/24/1940, 3/31/1940, 4/7/1940, 4/14/1940, 4/21/1940, 4/28/1940, 5/5/1940, 5/12/1940, 5/19/1940, 5/26/1940,

6/2/1940, 6/9/1940, 6/16/1940, 10/6/1940, 10/13/1940, 10/20/1940, 10/27/1940, 11/3/1940, 11/10/1940, 11/17/1940, 11/24/1940, 12/1/1940, 12/8/1940, 12/15/1940, 12/22/1940, 12/29/1940, 1/5/1941, 1/12/1941, 1/19/1941, 1/26/1941, 2/2/1941, 2/9/1941, 2/16/1941, 2/23/1941, 3/2/1941, 3/9/1941, 3/16/1941, 3/23/1941, 3/30/1941, 4/6/1941, 4/13/1941, 4/20/1941, 4/27/1941, 5/4/1941, 5/11/1941, 5/18/1941, 5/25/1941, 6/1/1941, 10/5/1941, 10/12/1941, 10/19/1941, 10/26/1941, 11/2/1941, 11/9/1941, 11/16/1941, 11/23/1941, 11/30/1941, 12/7/1941, 12/14/1941, 12/21/1941, 12/28/1941, 1/4/1942, 1/11/1942, 1/25/1942, 2/1/1942, 2/8/1942, 2/15/1942, 2/22/1942, 3/1/1942, 3/8/1942, 3/15/1942, 3/22/1942, 3/29/1942, 4/5/1942, 4/12/1942, 4/19/1942, 4/26/1942, 5/3/1942, 5/10/1942, 5/17/1942, 5/24/1942, 5/31/1942

Alois Havrilla 7/18/1932, 4/28/1933, 10/1/1933, 10/8/1933, 10/22/1933, 10/29/1933, 11/5/1933, 11/12/1933, 11/19/1933, 11/26/1933, 12/3/1933, 12/10/1933, 12/17/1933, 12/24/1933, 12/31/1933, 1/7/1934, 1/14/1934, 1/21/1934, 1/28/1934, 2/4/1934, 2/11/1934, 2/18/1934, 2/25/1934, 3/4/1934, 3/11/1934, 3/18/1934, 3/25/1934, 4/1/1934

Peter Lind Hayes 1/31/1937, 5/22/1938, 1/22/1939, 3/5/1939, 11/12/1939, 3/1/1942, 3/15/1942

Will Hays 6/1/1934

Sam Hearn 6/2/1933, 6/9/1933, 11/5/1933, 11/19/1933, 11/26/1933, 12/3/1933, 12/17/1933, 12/24/1933, 1/7/1934, 1/14/1934, 1/21/1934, 2/4/1934, 2/25/1934, 3/11/1934, 3/25/1934, 4/6/1934, 4/27/1934, 5/11/1934, 5/25/1934, 8/3/1934, 8/10/1934, 8/24/1934, 9/7/1934, 9/28/1934, 10/14/1934, 11/4/1934, 11/11/1934, 11/18/1934, 11/25/1934, 12/2/1934, 12/9/1934, 12/16/1934, 12/23/1934, 12/30/1934, 1/6/1935, 1/13/1935, 1/27/1935, 2/3/1935, 2/10/1935, 2/17/1935, 2/24/1935, 3/10/1935, 3/17/1935, 3/24/1935, 3/31/1935, 4/7/1935, 12/6/1935, 12/15/1935, 12/22/1935, 12/29/1935, 1/5/1936, 1/12/1936, 1/19/1936, 1/26/1936, 2/2/1936, 2/23/1936, 3/29/1936, 4/5/1936, 4/5/1936, 4/5/1936, 4/12/1936, 4/19/1936, 4/26/1936, 5/3/1936, 5/10/1936, 5/17/1936, 5/24/1936, 6/14/1936, 6/21/1936, 3/7/1937, 3/14/1937, 3/21/1937, 10/10/1937, 10/17/1937, 10/24/1937, 10/31/1937, 11/7/1937, 11/21/1937, 11/28/1937, 12/12/1937, 12/26/1937, 1/9/1938, 1/30/1938, 2/20/1938, 3/13/1938, 3/20/1938, 4/3/1938, 4/17/1938, 4/24/1938, 5/15/1938, 4/2/1939, 4/9/1939, 4/30/1939, 5/7/1939, 5/28/1939, 10/27/1940, 1/5/1941, 2/15/1942, 5/31/1942

Charley Herbert 10/19/1932

Grace Herbert 10/19/1932

Milton Herman 8/3/1932

George Hicks 6/27/1932, 8/8/1932, 8/10/1932, 8/17/1932, 8/24/1932, 9/5/1932, 9/7/1932, 9/12/1932, 9/14/1932, 9/19/1932, 9/21/1932, 9/26/1932, 9/28/1932, 10/3/1932, 10/5/1932, 10/10/1932, 10/12/1932, 10/17/1932, 10/19/1932, 10/24/1932, 10/26/1932

Russell Hicks 6/21/1936, 6/13/1937, 4/23/1939, 5/26/1940

John Hiestand 2/11/1940, 2/18/1940

? Higby 10/27/1935

Tommy Horan 1/20/1935

? Huey 12/15/1940, 10/12/1941

Red Ingle 11/3/1932, 11/6/1932, 11/10/1932, 11/13/1932, 12/11/1932, 12/15/1932, 12/18/1932, 12/22/1932, 12/25/1932, 12/29/1932, 1/5/1933, 1/12/1933, 1/15/1933, 1/19/1933, 1/22/1933, 1/26/1933

Charles Irwin 10/11/1936

11/3/1932, 11/6/1932, 11/10/1932, 11/13/1932, 11/20/1932, 12/1/1932, 12/8/1932, 12/11/1932, 12/15/1932, 12/18/1932, 12/22/1932, 12/25/1932, 12/29/1932, 1/1/1933, 1/5/1933, 1/12/1933, 1/15/1933, 1/19/1933, 1/22/1933, 1/26/1933

Dave Marshall 9/28/1932, 10/3/1932, 10/5/1932, 10/10/1932, 10/12/1932, 10/17/1932, 10/19/1932, 10/24/1932

Minnie Martin 6/15/1934, 6/22/1934, 6/29/1934, 7/6/1934, 7/13/1934, 7/20/1934, 7/27/1934

? Mather 10/4/1936, 3/17/1940, 1/4/1942

? Mathews 10/28/1934

Ed Max 11/24/1940, 12/1/1940, 3/2/1941, 5/18/1941, 12/14/1941

John McGowan 5/3/1936

Hugh McIlevey 3/15/1936

? McIntire 4/14/1935, 4/21/1935, 6/2/1935

Harry McNaughton 7/20/1934

James Melton 3/3/1933, 3/10/1933, 3/17/1933, 3/24/1933, 3/31/1933, 4/7/1933, 4/14/1933, 4/21/1933, 4/28/1933, 5/5/1933, 5/12/1933, 5/19/1933, 5/26/1933, 6/2/1933, 6/9/1933, 6/16/1933, 6/23/1933

Mahlon Merrick 1/18/1942

Georges Metaxa 3/15/1936

? Milford 4/23/1939, 5/12/1940

? Miller 5/18/1934, 12/12/1937

? Moore 12/29/1935

Bobby Moore 5/25/1932

? Morrison 3/16/1941

Bill Morrow 10/18/1936, 11/1/1936, 1/17/1937, 1/24/1937, 2/7/1937, 2/14/1937, 5/2/1937, 5/30/1937, 6/6/1937, 6/13/1937, 6/20/1937, 6/27/1937, 1/16/1938, 2/6/1938, 2/20/1938, 3/6/1938, 4/10/1938, 5/1/1938, 6/12/1938, 10/2/1938, 12/4/1938, 12/11/1938, 1/8/1939, 4/30/1939, 1/21/1940, 2/25/1940, 3/3/1940, 3/10/1940, 3/31/1940, 4/14/1940, 4/21/1940, 5/5/1940, 5/12/1940, 5/19/1940, 6/2/1940, 6/16/1940, 10/6/1940, 11/24/1940, 12/15/1940, 1/5/1941, 1/12/1941, 2/23/1941, 3/30/1941, 4/6/1941, 4/13/1941, 5/18/1941, 6/1/1941, 10/5/1941, 12/21/1941, 3/22/1942, 4/26/1942, 5/3/1942

Clarence Muse 1/19/1936, 2/2/1936

Cliff Nazarro 11/1/1936, 1/17/1937, 4/25/1937, 3/6/1938, 3/13/1938, 4/10/1938, 4/10/1938, 4/17/1938, 5/15/1938, 5/29/1938, 6/26/1938, 10/9/1938, 10/23/1938, 11/6/1938, 11/20/1938, 1/8/1939, 2/12/1939, 6/11/1939, 6/18/1939, 12/10/1939, 3/10/1940, 1/19/1941, 2/9/1936

? Nelson 3/28/1937

Frank Nelson 6/1/1934, 6/20/1937, 12/12/1937, 2/6/1938, 5/1/1938, 10/9/1938, 11/13/1938, 11/27/1938, 12/18/1938, 1/15/1939, 1/22/1939, 3/19/1939, 3/26/1939, 5/7/1939, 6/11/1939, 6/18/1939, 11/12/1939, 12/3/1939, 2/18/1940, 2/25/1940, 3/10/1940, 5/12/1940, 5/19/1940, 10/6/1940, 10/27/1940, 11/10/1940, 11/17/1940, 12/1/1940, 12/8/1940, 12/15/1940, 1/19/1941, 3/30/1941, 4/13/1941, 4/20/1941, 5/18/1941, 10/19/1941, 11/16/1941, 12/14/1941, 1/4/1942, 2/1/1942, 2/8/1942, 3/29/1942, 4/12/1942, 4/19/1942, 5/31/1942

? Noa 8/3/1934, 1/27/1935

? Norton 1/5/1941
Junior O'Day 3/21/1937
George Olsen 5/2/1932,
      5/4/1932, 5/9/1932, 5/11/1932, 5/16/1932, 5/18/1932, 5/23/1932, 5/25/1932,
      5/30/1932, 6/1/1932, 6/6/1932, 6/8/1932, 6/13/1932, 6/15/1932, 6/20/1932,
      6/22/1932, 6/27/1932, 6/29/1932, 7/4/1932, 7/6/1932, 7/11/1932, 7/13/1932,
      7/18/1932, 7/20/1932, 7/25/1932, 7/27/1932, 8/1/1932, 8/3/1932, 8/8/1932,
      8/10/1932, 8/15/1932, 8/17/1932, 8/22/1932, 8/24/1932, 8/29/1932, 8/31/1932,
      9/5/1932, 9/7/1932, 9/12/1932, 9/14/1932, 9/19/1932, 9/21/1932, 9/26/1932,
      9/28/1932, 10/3/1932, 10/5/1932, 10/10/1932, 10/12/1932, 10/17/1932,
      10/19/1932, 10/24/1932, 10/26/1932
Frank Parker 10/1/1933,
      10/8/1933, 10/22/1933, 10/29/1933, 11/5/1933, 11/12/1933, 11/19/1933,
      11/26/1933, 12/3/1933, 12/10/1933, 12/17/1933, 12/24/1933, 12/31/1933,
      1/7/1934, 1/14/1934, 1/21/1934, 1/28/1934, 2/4/1934, 2/11/1934, 2/18/1934,
      2/25/1934, 2/25/1934, 3/4/1934, 3/11/1934, 3/18/1934, 3/25/1934, 4/1/1934,
      4/6/1934, 4/13/1934, 4/20/1934, 4/27/1934, 5/4/1934, 5/11/1934, 5/18/1934,
      5/25/1934, 6/8/1934, 6/15/1934, 6/22/1934, 6/29/1934, 7/6/1934, 7/13/1934,
      7/20/1934, 7/27/1934, 8/3/1934, 8/10/1934, 8/17/1934, 8/24/1934, 8/31/1934,
      9/7/1934, 9/14/1934, 9/21/1934, 9/28/1934, 10/14/1934, 10/21/1934, 10/28/1934,
      11/4/1934, 11/11/1934, 11/18/1934, 11/25/1934, 11/25/1934, 12/2/1934,
      12/9/1934, 12/16/1934, 12/23/1934, 12/30/1934, 1/6/1935, 1/13/1935, 1/20/1935,
      1/27/1935, 2/3/1935, 2/10/1935, 2/17/1935, 2/24/1935, 3/3/1935, 3/10/1935,
      3/17/1935, 3/24/1935, 3/31/1935, 4/7/1935, 4/14/1935, 4/21/1935, 4/28/1935,
      5/5/1935, 5/12/1935, 5/19/1935, 5/26/1935, 6/2/1935, 6/9/1935, 6/16/1935,
      6/23/1935, 6/30/1935, 7/14/1935
? Pearson 5/12/1935
? Perez 3/16/1941
Minerva Pious 5/5/1940, 12/22/1940, 10/5/1941
A. Purvis? Pullen 2/11/1940
John Rarig 1/25/1942
Thurl Ravenscroft 1/25/1942
Frank Remley 4/10/1938
Bob Rice 5/2/1932, 5/16/1932, 6/8/1932, 6/29/1932, 7/4/1932, 10/26/1932
Guy Robertson.. 5/10/1936, 5/31/1936
Betty Rome ...4/28/1935, 5/5/1935, 5/12/1935, 5/19/1935, 6/9/1935, 6/23/1935, 7/14/1935
? Ross 2/5/1939
Dorothy Ross 7/13/1932,
      7/18/1932, 7/20/1932, 8/3/1932, 8/10/1932, 8/22/1932, 8/24/1932, 9/14/1932,
      10/10/1932, 6/23/1935
William Royale 11/15/1936, 12/13/1936, 3/28/1937, 1/2/1938, 6/26/1938
Benny Rubin 2/9/1936,
      2/16/1936, 3/8/1936, 11/14/1937, 12/31/1939, 3/17/1940, 6/16/1940, 10/20/1940,
      11/17/1940, 11/17/1940, 1/5/1941, 3/30/1941, 5/4/1941, 12/14/1941, 12/21/1941,
      1/4/1942
Mel Ruick 1/16/1938, 12/18/1938, 12/18/1938
? Saranoff 12/15/1932
? Schlossberg 9/21/1932
Bill Shelley 1/7/1934, 3/29/1936, 5/3/1936
Fred Shields.. 1/19/1936, 2/2/1936
Tom Shirley.. 10/5/1941
Harry Shutan.. 6/8/1934, 6/15/1934
Ethel Shutta 5/2/1932,

5/4/1932, 5/9/1932, 5/11/1932, 5/16/1932, 5/18/1932, 5/23/1932, 5/25/1932, 5/30/1932, 6/1/1932, 6/6/1932, 6/8/1932, 6/13/1932, 6/15/1932, 6/20/1932, 6/22/1932, 6/27/1932, 6/29/1932, 7/4/1932, 7/6/1932, 7/11/1932, 7/13/1932, 7/18/1932, 7/20/1932, 7/25/1932, 7/27/1932, 8/1/1932, 8/3/1932, 8/8/1932, 8/10/1932, 8/15/1932, 8/17/1932, 8/22/1932, 8/24/1932, 8/29/1932, 8/31/1932, 9/5/1932, 9/7/1932, 9/12/1932, 9/14/1932, 9/19/1932, 9/21/1932, 9/26/1932, 9/28/1932, 10/3/1932, 10/5/1932, 10/10/1932, 10/12/1932, 10/17/1932, 10/19/1932, 10/24/1932, 10/26/1932

Jack Shutta 8/22/1932
Sid Silvers 8/10/1932, 11/20/1932, 11/27/1932, 12/1/1932, 12/4/1932, 6/22/1934
? Simmons 9/7/1934
? Slattery 8/3/1934
Paul Small 5/23/1932, 5/25/1932, 6/1/1932, 6/6/1932, 6/8/1932, 6/13/1932, 6/15/1932, 6/20/1932, 6/22/1932, 6/27/1932, 7/4/1932, 7/6/1932, 7/13/1932, 7/18/1932, 7/20/1932, 7/25/1932, 8/1/1932, 8/3/1932, 8/8/1932, 8/10/1932, 8/15/1932, 8/17/1932, 8/22/1932, 8/24/1932, 8/29/1932, 8/31/1932, 9/5/1932, 9/7/1932, 9/12/1932
? Smith 10/30/1932
Max Smith 1/25/1942
Louis Sorin 10/1/1933, 9/7/1934, 12/16/1934
? Sound 2/4/1934
The Sportsmen Quartet 1/18/1942, 1/25/1942, 3/1/1942, 3/29/1942, 2/25/1940, 3/31/1940
Blanche Stewart 6/15/1932, 9/19/1932, 10/12/1932, 12/1/1932, 12/8/1932, 12/15/1932, 1/1/1933, 1/8/1933, 1/12/1933, 1/15/1933, 1/26/1933, 3/10/1933, 3/24/1933, 3/31/1933, 4/7/1933, 4/21/1933, 4/28/1933, 5/26/1933, 6/16/1933, 6/23/1933, 10/1/1933, 10/8/1933, 10/22/1933, 10/29/1933, 11/5/1933, 11/19/1933, 12/10/1933, 12/24/1933, 12/31/1933, 1/7/1934, 1/14/1934, 1/21/1934, 2/4/1934, 2/11/1934, 2/18/1934, 2/25/1934, 3/11/1934, 3/25/1934, 4/1/1934, 4/6/1934, 4/6/1934, 4/13/1934, 4/13/1934, 4/13/1934, 4/20/1934, 4/27/1934, 5/4/1934, 5/11/1934, 5/18/1934, 5/25/1934, 9/28/1934, 10/14/1934, 10/21/1934, 10/21/1934, 10/28/1934, 11/18/1934, 11/25/1934, 12/2/1934, 12/9/1934, 12/23/1934, 12/30/1934, 1/20/1935, 2/10/1935, 2/17/1935, 2/24/1935, 3/3/1935, 3/10/1935, 3/24/1935, 3/31/1935, 4/7/1935, 9/29/1935, 10/6/1935, 10/13/1935, 10/20/1935, 10/27/1935, 11/3/1935, 11/10/1935, 11/17/1935, 11/24/1935, 12/15/1935, 12/22/1935, 12/29/1935, 1/5/1936, 1/12/1936, 1/19/1936, 1/26/1936, 2/2/1936, 2/16/1936, 2/23/1936, 3/1/1936, 3/8/1936, 3/15/1936, 3/22/1936, 3/29/1936, 4/5/1936, 4/5/1936, 4/12/1936, 4/19/1936, 4/26/1936, 5/3/1936, 5/10/1936, 5/17/1936, 5/24/1936, 5/24/1936, 10/4/1936, 10/4/1936, 10/11/1936, 10/18/1936, 10/25/1936, 11/1/1936, 11/8/1936, 11/15/1936, 11/29/1936, 12/6/1936, 12/13/1936, 12/27/1936, 1/3/1937, 1/10/1937, 1/17/1937, 1/31/1937, 2/7/1937, 2/21/1937, 2/28/1937, 3/28/1937, 4/4/1937, 4/25/1937, 5/9/1937, 5/16/1937, 5/30/1937, 6/6/1937, 6/13/1937, 6/20/1937, 10/17/1937, 10/31/1937, 11/7/1937, 11/14/1937, 11/21/1937, 12/12/1937, 12/12/1937, 12/19/1937, 12/26/1937, 1/2/1938, 1/9/1938, 1/16/1938, 1/23/1938, 2/6/1938, 2/6/1938, 2/27/1938, 4/3/1938, 4/10/1938, 4/10/1938, 4/17/1938, 4/24/1938, 5/1/1938, 5/22/1938, 5/29/1938, 5/29/1938, 5/29/1938, 6/5/1938, 6/5/1938, 10/2/1938, 10/9/1938, 10/23/1938, 11/20/1938, 12/18/1938, 1/8/1939, 1/15/1939, 1/22/1939, 1/29/1939, 2/5/1939, 2/12/1939, 2/19/1939, 3/5/1939, 3/19/1939, 3/26/1939, 4/16/1939, 4/23/1939, 4/30/1939, 5/7/1939, 5/14/1939, 5/28/1939, 6/4/1939, 6/11/1939, 6/18/1939, 10/8/1939, 11/5/1939, 11/12/1939, 12/17/1939, 12/31/1939, 1/7/1940, 1/28/1940, 2/4/1940, 2/11/1940, 2/18/1940, 2/25/1940, 3/10/1940, 4/7/1940,

4/14/1940, 5/12/1940, 11/17/1940, 4/13/1941, 11/30/1941, 12/14/1941, 3/22/1942, 3/29/1942, 4/12/1942, 5/10/1942, 5/31/1942, 4/9/1939

10/10/1937, 10/17/1937, 10/24/1937, 10/31/1937, 11/7/1937, 11/14/1937, 11/21/1937, 11/28/1937, 12/5/1937, 12/12/1937, 12/19/1937, 12/26/1937, 1/2/1938, 1/9/1938, 1/16/1938, 1/23/1938, 1/30/1938, 2/6/1938, 2/13/1938, 2/20/1938, 2/27/1938, 3/6/1938, 3/13/1938, 3/20/1938, 4/3/1938, 4/10/1938, 4/17/1938, 4/24/1938, 5/1/1938, 5/8/1938, 5/15/1938, 5/22/1938, 5/29/1938, 6/5/1938, 6/12/1938, 6/19/1938, 6/26/1938, 10/2/1938, 10/9/1938, 10/16/1938, 10/23/1938, 10/30/1938, 11/6/1938, 11/13/1938, 11/20/1938, 11/27/1938, 12/4/1938, 12/11/1938, 12/18/1938, 12/25/1938, 1/1/1939, 1/8/1939, 1/15/1939, 1/22/1939, 1/29/1939, 2/5/1939, 2/12/1939, 2/19/1939, 2/26/1939, 3/5/1939, 3/12/1939, 3/19/1939, 3/26/1939, 4/2/1939, 4/9/1939, 4/16/1939, 4/23/1939, 4/30/1939, 5/7/1939, 5/14/1939, 5/21/1939, 5/28/1939, 6/4/1939, 6/11/1939, 6/18/1939, 6/25/1939, 10/15/1939, 10/22/1939, 10/29/1939, 11/5/1939, 11/12/1939, 11/19/1939, 11/26/1939, 12/3/1939, 12/10/1939, 12/17/1939, 12/24/1939, 12/31/1939, 1/7/1940, 1/14/1940, 1/21/1940, 1/28/1940, 2/4/1940, 2/11/1940, 2/18/1940, 2/25/1940, 3/3/1940, 3/10/1940, 3/17/1940, 3/24/1940, 3/31/1940, 4/7/1940, 4/14/1940, 4/21/1940, 4/28/1940, 5/5/1940, 5/12/1940, 5/19/1940, 5/26/1940, 6/2/1940, 6/9/1940, 6/16/1940, 10/6/1940, 10/13/1940, 10/20/1940, 10/27/1940, 11/3/1940, 11/10/1940, 11/17/1940, 11/24/1940, 12/1/1940, 12/8/1940, 12/15/1940, 12/22/1940, 12/29/1940, 1/5/1941, 1/12/1941, 1/19/1941, 1/26/1941, 2/2/1941, 2/9/1941, 2/16/1941, 2/23/1941, 3/2/1941, 3/9/1941, 3/16/1941, 3/23/1941, 3/30/1941, 4/6/1941, 4/13/1941, 4/20/1941, 4/27/1941, 5/4/1941, 5/11/1941, 5/18/1941, 5/25/1941, 6/1/1941, 10/5/1941, 10/12/1941, 10/19/1941, 10/26/1941, 11/2/1941, 11/9/1941, 11/16/1941, 11/23/1941, 11/30/1941, 12/7/1941, 12/14/1941, 12/21/1941, 12/28/1941, 1/4/1942, 1/11/1942, 1/18/1942, 1/25/1942, 2/1/1942, 2/8/1942, 2/15/1942, 2/22/1942, 3/1/1942, 3/8/1942, 3/15/1942, 3/22/1942, 3/29/1942, 4/5/1942, 4/12/1942, 4/19/1942, 4/26/1942, 5/3/1942, 5/10/1942, 5/17/1942, 5/24/1942, 5/31/1942

CITY INDEX

7/18/1932, 7/20/1932, 7/25/1932, 7/27/1932, 8/1/1932, 8/3/1932, 8/8/1932, 8/10/1932, 8/15/1932, 8/17/1932, 8/22/1932, 8/24/1932, 8/29/1932, 8/31/1932, 9/5/1932, 9/7/1932, 9/12/1932, 9/14/1932, 9/19/1932, 9/21/1932, 9/26/1932, 9/28/1932, 10/3/1932, 10/5/1932, 10/10/1932, 10/12/1932, 10/17/1932, 10/19/1932, 10/24/1932, 10/26/1932, 11/17/1932, 11/20/1932, 11/24/1932, 11/27/1932, 12/1/1932, 12/4/1932, 12/8/1932, 12/11/1932, 12/15/1932, 12/18/1932, 12/22/1932, 12/25/1932, 12/29/1932, 1/1/1933, 1/5/1933, 1/8/1933, 1/12/1933, 1/15/1933, 1/19/1933, 1/22/1933, 1/26/1933, 3/3/1933, 3/10/1933, 3/17/1933, 3/24/1933, 3/31/1933, 4/7/1933, 4/14/1933, 4/21/1933, 4/28/1933, 5/5/1933, 5/12/1933, 5/19/1933, 5/26/1933, 6/2/1933, 6/9/1933, 6/16/1933, 6/23/1933, 10/1/1933, 10/8/1933, 10/22/1933, 10/29/1933, 11/5/1933, 11/12/1933, 11/19/1933, 11/26/1933, 12/3/1933, 12/10/1933, 12/17/1933, 12/24/1933, 12/31/1933, 1/7/1934, 1/14/1934, 1/21/1934, 1/28/1934, 2/4/1934, 2/11/1934, 2/18/1934, 2/25/1934, 3/4/1934, 3/11/1934, 3/18/1934, 3/25/1934, 4/1/1934, 4/6/1934, 4/13/1934, 4/20/1934, 4/27/1934, 5/4/1934, 5/11/1934, 5/18/1934, 5/25/1934, 8/3/1934, 8/10/1934, 8/17/1934, 8/24/1934, 8/31/1934, 9/7/1934, 9/14/1934, 9/21/1934, 9/28/1934, 10/14/1934, 10/21/1934, 10/28/1934, 11/4/1934, 11/11/1934, 11/18/1934, 11/25/1934, 12/2/1934, 12/9/1934, 12/16/1934, 12/23/1934, 12/30/1934, 1/6/1935, 1/13/1935, 1/27/1935, 2/3/1935, 2/10/1935, 2/17/1935, 2/24/1935, 3/10/1935, 3/17/1935, 3/24/1935, 4/7/1935, 2/9/1936, 2/16/1936, 2/23/1936, 3/8/1936, 3/29/1936, 4/5/1936, 4/19/1936, 5/3/1936, 5/17/1936, 5/24/1936, 3/7/1937, 3/14/1937, 3/21/1937, 3/27/1938, 12/4/1938, 12/11/1938, 4/21/1940, 4/28/1940, 5/5/1940, 12/15/1940, 12/22/1940, 10/5/1941, 10/12/1941

Oakland, CA.. 1/28/1940
Palm Springs, CA.. 2/23/1941, 3/2/1941, 3/9/1941
Pittsburgh, PA 3/1/1936
San Diego, CA 6/1/1941, 3/8/1942
San Francisco, CA 12/15/1935, 1/9/1938, 2/22/1942, 4/26/1942
Santa Ana, CA 5/17/1942
Washington, DC 3/15/1936
Waukegan, IL.. 6/25/1939

Zelma O'Neal 3/24/1933
Frank Parker 5/3/1936
The Quiz Kids 4/6/1941, 4/13/1941, 4/20/1941
Ralph Rainger 6/7/1936, 3/6/1938
Basil Rathbone 11/2/1941
Robert Ripley 3/27/1938
Leo Robin 6/7/1936, 3/6/1938
Edward G. Robinson 4/21/1933
Ann Sheridan 5/3/1942
Kate Smith 3/27/1938
August Stackwell 1/11/1942
Barbara Stanwyck 1/7/1940
Ed Sullivan 3/26/1939
Eve Sully 3/22/1936
Mancel Talcott 3/21/1937, 5/8/1938, 6/25/1939, 12/15/1940
Lilyan Tashman 9/12/1932
Robert Taylor 2/13/1938
Peter Van Steeden 4/28/1940
Harry Von Zell 3/27/1938
Orson Welles 3/17/1940
Mort Werner 1/7/1940
Bert Wheeler 9/14/1934, 9/28/1934
Richard Williams 4/6/1941, 4/13/1941, 4/20/1941
Charlie Winninger 6/20/1937
Trudy Wood 5/23/1937

MUSIC – INSTRUMENTAL ARTIST INDEX

(Regularly-scheduled conductors not included)

MUSIC – VOCAL ARTIST INDEX

NOTABLE INDEX

Note: Some notable items have been reworded to increase ease of location and consisttency. Therefore, not all items will exactly match the verbiage listed in the show descriptions.

Notable	Date
Although never discussed on the show, Jack had to return to New York for these shows due to the hearings on his smuggling case. Kenny Baker was also called as a witness during these hearings.	12/4/1938
Andy Devine appearance deleted from script	2/13/1938
At the start of the skit, Jack says "Take it, Mr. Merrick"...may indicate that Mahlon Merrick was conducting orchestra by this time	3/10/1940
Audience is cheering so loudly that Don has to practically yell the closing announcements	5/17/1942
Blue cracks up on every line in the show, but there's no indication to do this in the script	10/25/1936
Carmichael eats the gas man	4/6/1941
Clarence Muse plays a character that is essentially Rochester	2/2/1936
Closing commercial is inset	3/29/1942
Commercial for Montreal-Toronto announcing new Jell-O Chocolate Pudding	11/14/1937
Dennis Day appears but does not sing	2/18/1940
Dennis Day appears but does not sing	3/23/1941
Dennis Day appears but does not sing	2/1/1942
Dennis Day appears but does not sing	5/3/1942
Dennis is not yet announced in the leading credits	10/8/1939
East coast broadcast, Jack mentions getting "a better joke for tonight"	11/20/1938
Ed Beloin and Bill Morrow credited at end of the show, periodically on subsequent shows	12/14/1941
Eddie Anderson now referred to as "Ed" in script	5/23/1937
Eddie Anderson's lines are indicated for "Eddy" in the script	3/28/1937
Eddie Anderson's lines are prompted as both "Eddy" and "Eddie" in the script	6/20/1937
Eddie Anderson's lines now prompted as "Rochester" in the script	10/16/1938
First "Goodnight Joanie"	4/28/1940
First "Jell-O everybody" opening	10/14/1934
First "New Tenant" skit	1/1/1939
First "Now cut that out"	5/19/1940
First "Oh Rohhh-chester..."	11/3/1940
First "Play Ted" call for a music number	11/17/1932
First "Well!" when Jack is being introduced to orchestra members	9/29/1935
First "We're a little late, so goodnight folks"	12/12/1937
First announcement of Dennis Day in opening credits	10/15/1939
First appearance of "Door guy"-type character	12/30/1934
First appearance of Belly Laugh Barton character (but not by name)	10/19/1941
First appearance of Blanche Stewart	6/15/1932
First appearance of Chicken Sisters gag	2/4/1934
First appearance of Dennis Day	10/8/1939
First appearance of Don Bestor	4/6/1934

Notable	Date
First appearance of Don Wilson	4/6/1934
First appearance of Eddie Anderson	3/28/1937
First appearance of Eddie Anderson as Rochester	6/20/1937
First appearance of Harry Conn in speaking role	6/15/1932
First appearance of Kenny Baker	11/3/1935
First appearance of Lena, Kenny's girlfriend	10/4/1936
First appearance of Mary Livingston	7/27/1932
First appearance of Phil Harris	10/4/1936
First appearance of the Sportsmen, possibly	2/25/1940
First apperance of Andy Devine	12/13/1936
First apperance of Shlepperman (as performed by Sam Hearn)	8/3/1934
First association of 39 with Jack's age	4/19/1936
First Beloin-Morrow script	4/5/1936
First Buck Benny skit	11/15/1936
First cheap joke about Jack	7/25/1932
First Christmas shopping show	12/12/1937
First classic Sportsmen Quartet interaction	1/25/1942
First closing in the format of "That, ladies and gentlemen, was the last number on our first program on the second of May."	5/2/1932
First credit of Mary in opening announcement	10/11/1936
First credited appearance of Sportsmen Quartet	1/18/1942
First Dennis Day's "What a perFAWmance!"	12/7/1941
First disclaimer of no endorsement of the product by the War Department	1/11/1942
First drunk joke about Phil	4/3/1938
First encounter with classic Frank Nelson character, sans "yessss"	12/14/1941
First extensive exchange of barbs with Fred Allen	1/10/1937
First glimpse of ultimate Phil Harris character	11/1/1936
First goofy song title	3/19/1939
First guest stars	6/29/1932
First inclusion of Rochester in cast of opening announcement	1/25/1942
First inclusion of Rochester in listing of Jell-O cast in closing announcement	1/18/1942
First joking about Jack's movie career	5/25/1932
First loud "Yipe!" from Jack	12/10/1939
First mention of "That's What I Like About the South"	2/2/1941
First mention of Belly Laugh Barton	2/4/1940
First mention of Charlie Farrell	2/23/1941
First mention of feud between Allen and Benny	7/14/1935
First mention of Frankie Remley and Charlie Bagby by name	4/10/1938
First mention of Gladys Zybysko	10/22/1939
First mention of Jack being from Waukegan	5/11/1932
First mention of Jack's violin playing	5/11/1932
First mention of Joan Benny by name	3/26/1939
First mention of Mrs. Day's first name (Lucretia)	10/29/1939
First mention of polar bear	2/12/1939
First mention of Remley, though not by name	10/24/1937
First mention of Rochester's girl Josephine	4/17/1938
First mention of Ronald Colman being in Jack's neighborhood	10/30/1938

Notable	Date
First mention of the Acme Hotel in New York	11/27/1938
First mention of the Maxwell	10/24/1937
First mention of Wilshire Bowl as Phil's orchestra venue	11/13/1938
First military base broadcast	6/1/1941
First non-studio scenario at soda fountain	5/23/1932
First opening crediting most cast members, "Jack Benny, with Mary Livingston, Phil Harris, Kenny Baker, and yours truly, Don Wilson."	10/2/1938
First permanent California broadcast	5/31/1936
First Phil can't spell/read joke	5/9/1937
First phone call on the show, Jack has Ethel Shutta answer the phone	6/1/1932
First racetrack sequence	2/6/1938
First recorded "Goodnight, Doll" to Mary.	3/27/1938
First recorded "Play Frank" reference	3/4/1934
First recorded Frank Parker and Alois Havrilla appearances	12/10/1933
First recorded occasion of "We're a little late" sign-off	4/18/1937
First recorded remote (I.e., non-studio-based) opening sequence	3/18/1934
First recorded skit show	1/22/1933
First recording of Chevrolet Show	3/31/1933
First recording of Jack playing Kreutzer exercises on the air	2/28/1937
First recording of Mary singing	3/31/1933
First recording where Jack's entrance is played on with "Love in Bloom"	2/9/1936
First show after Fred Allen has Stuart Canin play "The Bee" on his show, considered the start of the feud	1/3/1937
First show after the smuggling case verdict	4/9/1939
First show for Canada Dry	5/2/1932
First show for Chevrolet	3/3/1933
First show for General Tire	4/6/1934
First show for Jell-O	10/14/1934
First show has commercial for Jell-O, second show has close commercial for Jell-O Ice Cream Powder	4/12/1936
First show on radio	5/2/1932
First show where music numbers are reduced from five to four	6/13/1937
First show where plot takes place almost entirely outside the studio	8/22/1932
First show where polar bear is named Carmichael	2/19/1939
First show with closing theme "Rockabye Moon"	5/11/1932
First show with revised Canada Dry cast, via WSDU New Orleans	10/30/1932
First show with theme song "Jolly Good Company"	5/11/1932
First Sister Act gag	8/15/1932
First skit	8/24/1932
First song take-off, "A-Tisket A-Tasket", when Jack asks questions and Madame Zombie answers "no no no no"	11/13/1938
First spelling of Mary Livingstone with an "e"	10/1/1933
First Sunday at 7 show	10/14/1934
First time a fake song title is used at the opening of the show, possibly	12/29/1940
First time an announcer other than Ed Thorgerson (George Hicks) is mentioned	6/27/1932
First time Carmichael speaks	3/12/1939
First time cast asks for words to be defined	7/18/1932

Notable	Date
First time Dennis does dialect	3/17/1940
First time Gladys is given the last name of "Zybysko"	1/14/1940
First time Gladys Zybysko speaks	12/31/1939
First time Jack describes how blue his eyes are ("Alice blue")	4/21/1940
First time Jack plays "Love in Bloom"	1/13/1935
First time Jack plays exercises on violin	8/24/1932
First time Jack plays the violin on the air	6/6/1932
First time Jack says "Goodnight Doll"	3/17/1940
First time Jack's entrance played in with "Love in Bloom"	3/24/1935
First time ostrich is given the name Trudy	12/10/1939
First time Phil calls Jack "Jackson"	1/15/1939
First time Phil says "that was a lu-lu!"	3/24/1940
First time Phil uses "Lu Lu" as a gag	11/19/1939
First time Rochester is given the last name of "Van Jones"	2/27/1938
First time Ronald Colman is presented as Jack's neighbor, in back of Jack's house	12/25/1938
First time the Maxwell is heard	10/31/1937
First time you can distinctly hear Remley's laugh, after jokes about him laughing so much	3/5/1939
First toupee joke	10/4/1936
First train depot scene	10/17/1932
First use of joke about someone giving a tie with sleeves, "she started to knit a sweater and changed her mind'	12/27/1936
First use of Dennis' "Yes please?"	10/15/1939
First use of gag where Jack interrupts conversation to read the cab meter	1/4/1942
First use of the gag where seats closer to the stage are cheaper	11/27/1932
Fortune teller lives at "1002 Dracula Drive", as opposed to Jack's real-life address of 1002 N. Roxbury Drive	11/13/1938
Frank Parker leaves for New York and gang says they'll see him back there, but this is his last performance	6/30/1935
Frank Parker's song is heard	4/6/1934
Frank Parker's song is heard	7/20/1934
Fred Allen is done by Harry Baldwin holding his nose	5/9/1937
Gag about reading a bad review and thinking it's good...originally used with Phil Harris, now with Jack	10/13/1940
Good night, Joanie.	3/2/1941
"Goodnight Joanie" is in the script	10/5/1941
Hand-written addition to end: "And I also want to announce that Mayor Andy Devine has proclaimed next week, June 20th to 25th, as Jello Week in Van Nuys.	6/19/1938
Harry Conn: On-air thanks to Harry Conn and acknowledgement of Ed Beloin and Bill Morrow writing show for past 12 weeks	6/21/1936
ID at end just says "National Broadcasting Company", not red network	11/23/1941
Jack ad libs to Mary "Gee, you're cute tonight"	6/9/1940
Jack and Mary Kelly play lovers and she leaves him for another man, and he finds solace with Mary Livingston; Jack, Kelly, and Livingston had their real lives run similar to this story in the 1920s	1/14/1940
Jack announces that tonight's show is being shortwaved around the	2/22/1942

Notable	Date
world	
Jack calls Ed Beloin "Beloin"	5/19/1940
Jack calls Mary "Mrs. Benny" in the last line of the script	1/26/1933
Jack does not appear	11/13/1932
Jack does not appear	5/23/1937
Jack does not appear	2/2/1941
Jack does not appear	1/18/1942
Jack is calling the piece "Flight of the Bumblebee" when Canin actually played Schubert's "The Bee"	1/10/1937
Jack kisses Ann Sheridan, huge audience reaction	5/3/1942
Jack listed from 8:30 to 9:00 in San Francisco Examiner	10/11/1936
Jack plays "The Bee"	2/28/1937
Jack says "Can you hear that, Doll?" after Dennis' song	3/17/1940
Jack says "We ran over time, so goodnight folks."	10/16/1938
Jack says "You're blushing, Don" and Don ad-libs "That's the strawberry."	6/6/1937
Jack wishes Joan Merry Christmas, calls her "Miss Benny"	12/22/1940
Jack's anniversary is announced as his ninth, but it is really his eighth. Previous years' discussions of Jack's anniversary were correct.	5/5/1940
Kenny Baker is now announced as "Courtesy of Mervyn LeRoy Productions"	10/3/1937
Kenny Baker says "Yes please?"	12/22/1940
Kenny Baker's departure: On previous show, it sounds like Kenny is coming to Waukegan; however, he does not appear. The fact that he was not continuing with the show may have come to light during the intervening week and caused or contributed to this fact.	6/25/1939
Kenny was called as a witness against Jack in his smuggling case…not sure if there's a connection between that and his absence on this show	12/11/1938
Livingston back to no "e"	12/17/1933
Log Cabin Syrup ad substituted for show close	10/13/1940
Longest laugh with Andy's blooper at the end of the program, possibly	12/13/1936
Longest laughs: One of the longest laughs on the Benny show when Mary gets raspberry from bird in the forest	4/24/1938
Marlene DeTruck sequence deleted from previous week's show	5/29/1938
Mary and Ann Sheridan compare notes on Jack, some time thereafter Mary gave a harsh insult to Sheridan when she suspected her of having relations with Jack	5/3/1942
Mary has a call with her mother where both sides are heard	12/29/1935
Mary is listed as "Sadye" in the script	8/3/1932
Mary is now called "Mary" in script, not "Sadye"	8/22/1932
Mary offers to be Jack's secretary	8/17/1932
Mary plays a wife jealous of Ann Sheridan, she later insulted Sheridan in real life for the same reason	12/17/1939
Mary treats Jack very harshly throughout the show	2/18/1940
Mary's first recorded show	1/1/1933
Mary's lines are listed with the name "Mary" and others with "Sadye"	10/17/1932
Mary's name is now consistently spelled "Livingstone" in the scripts	9/29/1935
Maxwell is now a 1923 model	1/28/1940

Notable	Date
Maxwell is said to be a 1920 model	10/8/1939
May Company: On the comment of the May Company, Jack ad libs, "We ought to get something from them pretty soon," referring to practice of mentioned companies sending celebrities free stuff	1/26/1941
Network cuts away from show during Don's closing announcements	2/22/1942
No Mervyn LeRoy mention in the closing announcement; announcement is spotty in subsequent shows	3/20/1938
No script or recording exists for this show	5/9/1932
No script or recording exists for this show	5/18/1932
No script or recording exists for this show	5/30/1932
No script or recording exists for this show	7/27/1932
No show due to speech of President Roosevelt	10/15/1933
Non-standard opening, scenes from each cast member getting ready for the program	10/2/1938
Open commercial maintains that listeners had never been offered a recipe book, but "Jack and Mary's Jell-O Cookbook" is dated 1937	12/15/1940
Opening and closing commercials are inset	2/15/1942
Opening and closing commercials are inset	2/22/1942
Opening and closing commercials are inset	3/1/1942
Opening and closing commercials are inset	3/8/1942
Opening and closing commercials are inset	3/15/1942
Opening and closing commercials are inset	3/22/1942
Opening commercial is about sugar rationing, apologies for grocers who don't have all flavors, tells people to buy only for present needs	5/17/1942
Opening commercial is inset	4/19/1942
Opening commercial is inset	4/26/1942
Opening commercial is inset	5/3/1942
Opening commercial is inset	5/10/1942
Opening commercial is inset	5/31/1942
Opening commercial is inset	4/12/1942
Opening commercial is inset (Don's network announcement can be heard momentarily under open commercial)	4/5/1942
Opening commercial is inset, you can barely hear the network feed under the announcement	5/24/1942
Orchestra leading gag was used as late as 1962 Lawrence Welk appearance on TV show	7/25/1932
Pencil notation on script: "1/18/33 Pd Blanche cash $15.00"	1/12/1933
Performances are very subdued at the start, Mary's continues that way through the show (apparently she has a cold)	1/25/1942
Rochester breaks character for a moment on his blooper	12/22/1940
Rochester was married, owes alimony	5/28/1939
Sahara Desert Canada Dry ad	6/20/1932
Script page says "Musical Program Regular show cancelled on account of Carole Lombard air crash"	1/18/1942
Second appearance of Eddie Anderson, first time he calls Jack "Boss"	5/2/1937
Shlepperman exchange at end of show deleted from script, he announces that he's going to Pittsburgh, Philadelphia, Baltimore, and Washington on personal appearances	5/22/1938
Show cut off in the middle of Jack's closing announcements	4/13/1941

Notable	Date
Show is now announced as on National Broadcasting Company, no "red network" designation	10/10/1937
Show runs long, close cut off	6/2/1940
Show runs long, is cut off by the network	4/26/1942
Someone in the brass section is WAY off on the last note of the final Jell-O call	11/6/1938
Sponsorship is now Jell-O and Jell-O pudding	10/5/1941
Station break-ins during both musical numbers for war announcements	12/7/1941
Structure, and even some gags, reused for later post-"Ladies' Night" show	6/6/1932
Time stamp 10 seconds before 8PM	6/14/1936
Trudy is heard	12/24/1939
Unusual opening, Blue Fairy awakens the cast	10/6/1940
Video clip exists for the first part of this program, but is a different broadcast than the circulating recording	4/12/1942
Wayne Songer solo on "Are You Having Any Fun"	10/22/1939
When Benny Baker and Kenny Baker are on the program, BB is prompted as "Baker" and KB is "Kenny" in the script (KB is usually Baker)	12/1/1935
When Jack interviews Olsen and Shutta, Olsen says he's 42 and Shutta says he's 39	5/4/1932
Writing credit to Bill Morrow and Ed Beloin at the end	1/25/1942
Yosemite show	2/4/1940
Yosemite show	2/11/1940
Yosemite show	2/18/1940
Yosemite show	2/25/1940
Youngest age Jack ever claims: 31	4/18/1937

RUNNING GAG INDEX

SKIT INDEX

SONG INDEX

Notes:
- Compensation has been made here for variations in spelling or punctuation of song titles. So "Can't You Hear Me Calling Caroline" and "Can't Yoh Hear Me Callin' Caroline" are combined into a single entry under one spelling. If you don't see a song exactly as listed in the program song listing, chances are it is very close by under a slightly variant spelling. The show listings have been left intact to reflect the spelling within the script.
- Songs that are in medleys have not been combined with solo performances. Similarly, songs that have alternate numbers in the script (indicated by a slash "/") have been left as separate entries.
- Similar song titles that do not have sufficient evidence to confirm that they are the same song have been left separate (e.g., "Million Dollar Baby" vs. "I Found a Million Dollar Baby").

Any Way the Wind Blows 11/5/1933
Anything Goes 1/6/1935, 4/28/1935, 11/3/1935
Anything That's Part of You 7/6/1934
April in Paris 4/20/1934
April Showers 4/7/1935
Are You Having Any Fun 10/22/1939
Are You Ready 10/26/1941, 11/30/1941
Are You Sure You Love Me 5/19/1933
Arlene 12/24/1933
Army Air Corps/Buckle Down, Buck Private 5/10/1942
As Long As I Live 8/10/1932
As Long As Love Lives On 8/22/1932
Ask Yourself Who Loves You 5/25/1932
Asleep in the Deep 11/1/1936, 3/29/1942
At Last 6/30/1935
At the Baby Parade 12/15/1932
At the Codfish Ball 5/3/1936
At Your Service, Madame 11/10/1935
Au Revoir 8/24/1934, 10/28/1934
Awake in a Dream 3/29/1936
Awake, awake, awake 10/6/1940
Baby 12/15/1932, 12/25/1932
Baby Me 10/15/1939, 12/17/1939
Bad Humor Man 11/10/1940, 12/8/1940
Banking on the Weather 6/13/1932
Be a Good Sport 1/23/1938
Be Honest With Me 1/4/1942
Be Myself 2/27/1938
Be Still My Heart 11/18/1934
Be Young Again 11/2/1941, 11/30/1941
Be Young Again/Thumbs Up 1/4/1942
Beat Me Daddy With a Pickled Beet*/Special #4 .... 5/25/1941
Beat of My Heart 5/25/1934, 6/15/1934
Bee - Plenty of Money and You, The 2/28/1937
Begin the Beguine 12/29/1935, 3/12/1939
Bei Mir Bist Du Schoen 1/9/1938, 2/6/1938
Believe It, Beloved 2/3/1935, 4/7/1935
Believing 5/26/1940
Bells of St. Mary's, The 3/24/1933
Better Think Twice 1/21/1934
Big Boy Blue 4/18/1937
Big City Blues 12/25/1932
Bigger Than the Moon 8/17/1934
Billy 11/5/1939, 1/28/1940
Bixby's Batter jingle 5/5/1940
Black Eyed Susan Brown 1/5/1933, 3/24/1933
Blame It On MyYouth 12/2/1934
Blossoms on Broadway 12/5/1937
Blow Gabriel Blow/Alabama Barbecue 2/21/1937
Blue Bonnet 10/31/1937
Blue Danube 5/23/1932, 6/13/1932
Blue Eyes 11/8/1936
Blue is the Night 6/6/1937

Blue Lou 5/30/1937
Blue Lovebird 6/16/1940
Blue Moon 1/27/1935
Blue Room 1/18/1942
Blue World 2/4/1940
Blueberry Hill 11/10/1940
Bluebirds in the Moonlight 11/19/1939, 3/10/1940
Blues In the Night 2/15/1942
Blues My Naughty Sweetie Gave to Me 1/12/1933
Blues My Naughty Sweetie Taught Me 4/20/1941
Bob White 11/21/1937
Body and Soul 6/27/1937
Bohemia 1/22/1933
Bojangles of Harlem 10/25/1936
Bolt From the Blue, A 12/23/1934
Bon Jour Mamselle 5/19/1935
Boo Hoo 2/7/1937, 4/4/1937
Boy and a Girl Were Dancing, A 12/8/1932
Boy Oh Boy 1/25/1942
Breaking In a New Pair of Shoes 2/23/1936, 4/5/1936
Bright Shines the Moon 5/5/1933, 12/17/1933
Bring Back Those Dear Old Circus Days 6/22/1932
Bring Back Those Minstrel Days 3/29/1942
Broadway Rhythm 9/29/1935, 12/22/1935
Broken Record 2/2/1936
Brown Eyes, Why Are You So Close to My Nose*/Phil Harris Special #3 .... 5/11/1941
Bucking the Wind 10/29/1933
Bugle Call Rag 6/15/1932, 7/25/1932, 10/5/1932, 6/15/1934
Bungalow, a Piccolo, and You, A 6/29/1932
Butterflies in the Rain 5/26/1933
Bye Bye Baby 10/4/1936
Cabin in the Cotton 7/4/1932
Caissons Go Rolling Along 2/22/1942
California Here I Come 5/25/1934
Call Out the Marines 2/1/1942, 3/8/1942
Can't Yo Hear Me Callin' Caroline 11/1/1936, 3/29/1942
Captains of the Clouds 3/1/1942
Careless 1/21/1940
Carioca 1/21/1934, 2/25/1934, 5/4/1934
Carnival Days are Here Again 8/22/1932
Carry Me Back to the Lone Prairie 12/22/1935, 2/9/1936, 2/14/1937, 11/9/1941
Casa Loma Stomp 6/22/1934, 7/27/1934
Casey Jones 3/5/1939
Cause My Baby Says It's So 5/23/1937
Cecilia 6/9/1940
Change Partners and Dance 10/30/1938
Changing of the Guard 4/28/1933
Chapel In the Moonlight 1/17/1937
Charley's Home 6/2/1933
Chatanooga Choo Choo 11/9/1941, 11/23/1941
Cheek to Cheek 11/3/1935, 4/5/1936
Cheerio 12/15/1940
Chicago 1/8/1933

509

Chinatown My Chinatown 11/11/1934, 1/9/1938
Chloe 4/21/1935
Christmas Night in Harlem 6/15/1934
Cinderella Stay In My Arms 10/15/1939
Circus Days 8/1/1932
Ciribiribin 11/19/1939, 4/13/1941
Clarinet Marmalade 1/19/1933
Claudette 1/15/1933
Close to Me 12/6/1936
Clouds 2/24/1935
Clouds Will Soon Roll By, The 6/6/1932
Co si Co sa 2/9/1936
Cocktails for Two 5/4/1934, 7/6/1934
Coffee in the Morning 3/18/1934
College Rhythm 12/30/1934
Colonial From Kentucky 2/25/1934
Come and Sit Beside the Sea 6/27/1932
Come On Home 7/14/1935
Come to Me 12/15/1932
Come West Little Girl Come West 9/26/1932, 5/2/1932
Comin' Down the Chimney 12/12/1937, 12/12/1937
Confidentially 10/2/1938, 6/18/1939
Confucius Say 2/25/1940
Congratulate Me 11/25/1934
Contented 12/18/1932, 4/6/1934, 9/14/1934
Continental, The 10/14/1934
Cop On the Beat 10/17/1932
Coronado Corn*/Special #6 .... 6/1/1941
Could Be/This Can't Be Love 1/15/1939
Crazy People 5/11/1932, 6/15/1932
Cry Baby Cry 4/17/1938, 5/22/1938
Cuban Love Song 5/19/1933
Curly Top 11/29/1936
Dames 8/3/1934
Dancing Feet 2/16/1936, 2/23/1936
Dancing in the Moonlight 3/25/1934
Dancing the Devil Away 3/31/1933
Dardanella 6/6/1937
Dark Eyes 11/19/1933, 12/9/1934
Darktown Strutters' Ball/Alexander's Ragtime Band 3/6/1938
Darling Nellie Gray 3/16/1941
Darn That Dream 2/11/1940
Daughter of Rosie O'Grady, The 10/27/1935
Day Dreams 5/8/1938
Day Dreams Come True At Night 3/17/1940
Day I Let You Get Away, The 1/26/1936
Dear Old Southland 2/21/1937
Deep in a Dream 1/15/1939
Deep In the Heart of Encino*/Harris Spec. #3 .... 3/29/1942
Deep Purple 3/26/1939
Delighted to Meet You 11/7/1937
Diane 12/18/1938
Did an Angel Kiss Me 6/12/1938

Did I Remember 10/11/1936
Did You Ever See a Dream Walking 2/4/1934
Did You Mean It 11/8/1936
Diga-Diga-Doo/I Can't Give You Anything But Love Baby 2/24/1935
Dinah 2/24/1935, 10/27/1935
Dipsy Doodle 12/12/1937, 3/13/1938
Dixie Lee 1/28/1934
Do I Know What I'm Doing? 7/6/1934
Do I Love You 6/22/1934, 7/27/1934, 12/31/1939, 3/24/1940
Do I Love You? Do I? 2/18/1940
Do You Ever Think of Me 1/19/1933, 2/7/1937
Do You Know Why 11/3/1940
Does Your Heart Beat for Me 11/26/1939
Doing the Uptown Lowdown 1/7/1934
Doin' the Prom 3/29/1936
Don't Be That Way 4/17/1938
Don't Cross Your Fingers, Cross Your Heart 10/16/1938
Don't Cry Sweetheart, Don't Cry 1/2/1938
Don't Do It Again 3/4/1934
Don't Give Up the Ship 12/22/1935
Don't Let It Bother You 9/14/1934, 10/28/1934, 12/30/1934
Don't Say a Word, Just Dance 3/8/1936
Don't Sit Under the Apple Tree 4/26/1942, 5/3/1942
Don't Tell a Soul 11/6/1932
Don't Worry About Me 6/18/1939
Donkey Serenade 4/17/1938
Double Trouble 10/6/1935
Down by the Ohio 6/16/1940
Down By the River 1/14/1940
Down in the Alley and Over the Fence 12/3/1939
Dream Valley 11/3/1940
Dream, A 4/7/1933
Dreams in the Night 4/14/1940
Drums in My Heart 5/2/1932, 6/1/1932, 7/25/1932
Dying Zerelda 3/5/1939
Early Bird 3/15/1936
East of the Sun 6/2/1935
Easter Parade 4/5/1942
Easter Parade/Two Cigarettes in the Dark/You Ought to Be in Pictures 10/28/1934
Easy Come, Easy Go 4/20/1934
Easy to Remember 5/5/1935
Eat Drink and Be Merry 6/6/1932, 6/8/1932, 7/13/1932
Echo in the Valley 1/22/1933
Eenie Meenie Miney Mo 11/3/1935, 1/26/1936, 5/10/1936
Eleanor 9/19/1932
Emporia Kansas Stomp*/Phil Harris Tune #2 .... 2/9/1941
Encino Madness*/So and So 12/29/1940
Even Steven 3/30/1941
Every Day 4/28/1935
Every Time I Look At You 2/16/1936
Everything I Have is Yours 1/14/1934
Everything I Love 11/23/1941
Everything I Love - All the Things You Are 12/7/1941, 3/1/1942

Everything is Okey Dokey 10/20/1935
Everything Stops for Tea 4/19/1936
Everything's Going to Be Okay, America 6/20/1932
Everything's in Rhythm With My Heart 1/26/1936, 1/31/1937, 5/29/1938
Exactly Like You/Memories of You/On the Sunny Side of the Street 2/17/1935
Exactly Like You/On the Sunny Side of the Street/Memories of You 6/9/1935
Extra 1/28/1934, 4/13/1934
Eyes of Texas Are Upon You, The - Deep In the Heart of Texas 2/8/1942
F.D.R. Jones 11/6/1938, 12/11/1938
Fair and Warmer 5/11/1934, 6/30/1935
Faithful Forever 11/26/1939
Falling in Love With a Brand New Baby 10/25/1936
Fare Thee Well, Annabelle 5/11/1934, 9/28/1934, 5/5/1935
Farewell to Arms Overture 8/24/1934
Ferry Boat Serenade 10/13/1940, 11/17/1940, 11/24/1940
Fiddle for the Czar 9/26/1932
Fifi 1/16/1938
Fine and Dandy 6/13/1937, 3/12/1939
Fine Romance, A 10/25/1936, 12/27/1936
First Noel, The - Away In a Manger - Hark the Herald Angels Sing 12/21/1941
First Noel, The/Oh Come All Ye Faithful 12/22/1940
Fit as a Fiddle 10/17/1932, 11/13/1932, 11/24/1932, 12/25/1932
Fleet's In, The 4/19/1942
Flirtation Walk 1/6/1935
Flowers for Madame 6/2/1935
Flying Down to Rio 1/14/1934, 3/18/1934
Fooled 2/8/1942
Football Hero 10/1/1933
Footloose and Fancy Free 5/26/1935, 6/2/1935, 12/6/1935
For All We Know 8/24/1934
For My Mother 5/14/1939
For No Rhyme or Reason 10/16/1938, 12/4/1938
For You 3/21/1937
Frasquita Serenade 6/2/1933
Free for All 11/9/1941, 2/8/1942
Frenesi 3/9/1941
From Alpha to Omega 10/23/1938, 6/11/1939
From AM to PM 8/15/1932
From the Top of Your Head 10/20/1935
Frost on the Moon 12/13/1936
Full Moon 4/19/1942
Garden Where the Praties Grow, The 3/15/1942
Gather Lip Rouge While You May 10/8/1933
Gay Ranchero, A 12/7/1941, 1/4/1942
Gee But You're Swell 1/10/1937, 3/21/1937
Gee But You're Swell/I've Got My Love to Keep Me Warm 2/28/1937
Gee It's a Thrill 6/14/1936
German Band 10/12/1932, 10/26/1932
Get Hot Foot 10/1/1933
Get the Moon Out of Your Eyes 10/13/1940
Get Yourself a Broom 5/26/1933
Get Yourself a Cup of Sunshine 7/13/1932, 10/10/1932
Getting Along With Your Gal 5/16/1932

Girl Friend of the Whirling Dervish 11/27/1938
Girl in the Little Green Hat, The 1/5/1933, 1/19/1933
Give a Little Whistle 2/25/1940, 3/31/1940
Give a Little Whistle/Where Was I 3/31/1940
Give Me a Roll on the Drum.. 10/8/1933
Give Me One Hour 6/16/1933, 11/12/1933
Glory of Love... 6/21/1936
Go Fly a Kite 10/8/1939
Go Into Your Dance 3/31/1935
Go South Young Man 11/28/1937, 2/20/1938
Go South Young Man/Joobalai.. 1/15/1939
Going to Heaven on a Mule 3/11/1934
Gold Diggers Song, The 6/16/1933
Good Morning 10/22/1939
Good News medley.. 4/28/1935
Good Night Angel... 4/10/1938
Goodbye Broadway, Hello Figueroa Street*/To a Wild Petunia 3/23/1941
Goodbye Jonah... 10/17/1937
Goodbye Mama 1/25/1942
Goodbye to Summer Love 9/5/1932
Goodnight Kisses.. 10/31/1937
Goodnight Moonlight.. 6/9/1940
Goodnight My Beautiful... 10/8/1939, 1/28/1940
Goodnight My Love... 1/24/1937, 2/7/1937
Goodnight, Sweetheart 6/29/1932, 4/14/1933
Goody Goodbye 11/5/1939, 12/17/1939
Goody Goody 2/23/1936, 4/12/1936
Goona Goo 2/14/1937
Got a Brand-New Suit 11/10/1935
Got a Date With an Angel 5/11/1932
Gotta Go... 5/12/1933, 6/23/1933
Grass is Getting Greener All the Time, The....................................... 3/31/1933, 5/19/1933
Great Big Bunch of You, A... 6/27/1932
Great Day.. 3/15/1936, 5/24/1936
Grounded in Glendale* 1/12/1941
Ha-Cha-Cha... 11/11/1934
Hallelujah 7/13/1934, 4/14/1935, 12/27/1936, 3/27/1938, 6/4/1939
Hallelujah/Love and Learn 3/14/1937
Hallelujah Things Look Rosy Now 4/25/1937
Handwriting on the Wall 1/5/1933
Happy Birthday 2/15/1942
Happy Feet 12/3/1933
Happy in Love 4/12/1942
Happy, Happy Holiday, A... 12/24/1939
Harlem Moon 8/31/1932, 9/12/1932, 10/5/1932
Harris Number #1... 12/22/1940
Harris Spec. #3 .... 1/5/1941
Hats Off, Here Comes a Lady.. 12/1/1932
Have You 1/2/1938
Have You Ever Been in Heaven 11/14/1937
Have You Got Any Castles, Baby... 10/17/1937, 10/31/1937
Have You Met Miss Jones 11/14/1937
Haystraw 3/1/1936

He Ain't Got Rhythm 2/21/1937
He Didn't Say Yes, He Didn't Say No 6/20/1932
He's 1-A in the Army and A-1 In My Heart... 3/8/1942
He's a Son of the South 4/28/1933
He's My Uncle 10/27/1940
Hear the Little German Band 7/6/1932
Heaven Can Wait.. 4/16/1939
Heigh Ho 4/3/1938, 4/24/1938, 1/8/1939
Hell's Bells 12/29/1932, 1/15/1933
Here Come the British.. 9/21/1934
Here Comes the Sandman 6/27/1937
Here is My Heart 6/1/1941
Here it is Monday 12/18/1932
Here Lies Love 11/17/1932, 11/20/1932
Here's Love in Your Eye 10/4/1936, 12/20/1936
Here's My Heart 2/16/1941, 5/18/1941
Here's to Romance 11/24/1935
Hey Diddle Diddle 6/29/1932
Hey Sailor 5/25/1934
Hey Young Fella 4/14/1933
Hi Diddle Dee Dee 3/31/1940
Hi Lee Hi Low... 6/13/1932
Hi Neighbor 10/5/1941, 10/26/1941, 1/25/1942
High on a Windy Hill.. 3/23/1941, 3/30/1941
High Shoes 12/10/1933
High Wide and Handsome 10/3/1937
Hillbilly Medley 5/4/1934
Hindustan/Tiger Rag 5/14/1939
Hit the Deck Medley 11/18/1934
Hoch Caroline 3/17/1933
Hold My Hand 3/25/1934, 4/27/1934
Hold Tight... 2/19/1939, 4/9/1939
Holding My Honey's Hand 8/1/1932
Holy Smoke.. 3/24/1940
Home.. 11/24/1932
Home Town... 1/16/1938
Honey Bunch 5/2/1937
Honey Smile at Me.. 8/15/1932
Honolulu 3/19/1939, 4/23/1939
Hooray for Hollywood.................3/6/1938, 4/24/1938, 6/26/1938, 12/11/1938, 5/14/1939
Hooray for Spinach/Tears From My Inkwell.. 6/11/1939
House is Haunted, The 4/1/1934
How About You 12/28/1941, 2/22/1942
How Can I Ever Be Alone 6/9/1940
How Can I Hold You Close Enough.. 10/20/1935
How Can I Thank You.. 10/9/1938
How Can You Say You Love Me 6/29/1932
How Could You 5/2/1937
How Deep Is the Ocean............................ 10/12/1932, 10/26/1932, 11/10/1932, 1/1/1933
How Do I Know It's Sunday 4/27/1934
How Do I Look 11/5/1933
How Do I Rate With You.. 11/17/1935
How Do You Fall in Love 3/22/1942

How High the Moon 2/18/1940, 5/5/1940
How Many Rhymes Can You Get 12/26/1937
How We All Make Music 5/2/1932
How'd You Like to Love Me 2/27/1938
Hum a Tune 10/5/1932
Humming to Myself 5/4/1932, 6/27/1932
Humoresque 10/29/1933, 7/20/1934
Hustling and Bustling for Baby 3/17/1933
Hut in Old Havana, A 7/13/1934
I Am an American 3/15/1942, 5/17/1942
I Beg Your Pardon Mademoiselle 5/2/1932, 6/8/1932, 6/27/1932, 10/12/1932
I Believe in Miracles 1/27/1935
I Can Dream Can't I 4/3/1938
I Can Pull a Rabbit Out of a Hat 5/10/1936
I Can't Believe It's True 9/5/1932
I Can't Give You Anything But Love Baby 3/10/1933, 5/10/1942
I Can't Lose that Longing for You 5/16/1937
I Can't Say It Too Many Times 11/27/1938
I Can't Understand 6/14/1936
I Cannot Tell You Why 11/10/1932
I Could Use a Dream 1/16/1938
I Cried for You 2/14/1937, 2/5/1939, 5/7/1939
I Do, Do You 5/18/1941
I Don't Know Your Name But You're Beautiful 3/15/1936
I Don't Want to Make History 4/12/1936, 6/7/1936
I Don't Want to Set the World On Fire 10/12/1941, 10/26/1941
I Double Dare You 12/19/1937, 1/30/1938, 3/27/1938
I Dream of Jeannie With the Light Brown Hair 1/29/1939, 11/19/1939
I Fall in Love With You Every Day 5/15/1938, 6/19/1938
I Feel a Song Coming On 10/27/1935, 3/22/1936, 12/20/1936
I Feel Like a Feather In the Breeze 1/12/1936
I Feel Like a Million Dollars 3/18/1934
I Found a Million Dollar Baby 5/2/1932
I Get a Kick Out of You 2/17/1935, 10/20/1935, 12/13/1936, 4/25/1937, 6/20/1937
I Go For That 12/18/1938, 12/25/1938, 4/2/1939
I Got a Brand New Suit 1/19/1936
I Got My Eyes on You 4/28/1940
I Got Rhythm 3/14/1937
I Got to Go To Work Again 3/29/1936
I Guess I'll Have to Change My Plans 8/17/1932
I Guess I'll Have to Change My Plans/Let's Put Out the Lights and Go to Sleep
.... 11/10/1932
I Guess I'll Have to Dream the Rest 11/2/1941
I Hate Myself 3/11/1934
I Hate to Talk About Myself 5/19/1935
I Hear a Rhapsody 1/19/1941
I Hear Bluebirds 4/7/1940, 4/28/1940, 6/2/1940
I Hear You Calling Me 3/17/1933
I Heard You Calling Me 5/31/1936
I Heard You Singing 5/12/1933
I Hit a New High 12/5/1937
I Just Want to Be With You 11/10/1940
I Know a Story 1/5/1933, 1/26/1933

I Know Now 6/13/1937
I Know That You Know 4/14/1935, 11/29/1936, 5/15/1938
I Know Why 11/2/1941
I Know You're Lying 5/4/1932
I Know You're Lying But I Love It 7/11/1932
I Like It That Way 2/11/1934
I Like Mountain Music 3/31/1933
I Long to Belong to You 2/26/1939
I Love a Parade 5/2/1932, 6/6/1932, 9/5/1932, 5/19/1933
I Love to Whistle 3/13/1938
I Love You Lizzicato 10/3/1932
I Love You More and More Every Day 12/14/1941
I Love You So Much 11/5/1933
I Love You, Dear 8/8/1932
I Married an Angel 10/2/1938
I Must Have One Kiss Kiss Kiss 11/26/1939
I Never Had a Chance 6/15/1934, 8/3/1934
I Only Have Eyes for You 8/17/1934
I Played Fiddle for the Czar 9/7/1932
I Poured My Heart Into a Song 10/29/1939
I Promise You 1/1/1939
I Remember You 4/19/1942
I Said No 3/1/1942, 3/15/1942
I Saw Stars 11/4/1934
I See the Moon at Noon 3/16/1941, 5/25/1941
I See Your Face Before Me 3/20/1938
I Told Every Little Star 1/15/1933
I Walk With Music 4/14/1940
I Want to Be Happy 11/19/1933, 5/12/1935
I Want to Go Back To My Little Grass Shack 4/30/1939
I Want to Go Home 7/11/1932
I Want to Learn to Speak Hawaiian 1/5/1936
I Want to Wrap You Up 12/10/1939
I Wanta Ring Bells 10/22/1933
I Was Lucky 2/24/1935
I Wish I Were Twins 6/29/1934, 7/20/1934, 8/10/1934
I Wished On the Moon 6/30/1935, 11/17/1935
I Woke Up Too Soon 1/20/1935
I Won't Dance 4/7/1935
I Wonder Who's Kissing Her Now That I'm Drafted*/Phil Harris Spec. #2 .... 5/4/1941
I'd Better Get Some Shut Eye 2/12/1939
I'd Know You Anywhere 11/17/1940, 12/8/1940
I'd Love to Take Orders from You 10/13/1935
I'd Rather Lead a Band 5/17/1936
I'll Be Faithful 10/22/1933, 12/17/1933
I'll Bet you Tell That to All the Girls 5/24/1936
I'll Follow My Secret Heart 11/25/1934, 4/5/1936
I'll Follow You 11/20/1932
I'll Keep Warm All Winter 11/11/1934
I'll Miss You in the Evening 5/4/1932
I'll Never Be the Same 8/3/1932
I'll Never Have to Dream Again.. 12/4/1932
I'll Never Say Never Again 6/9/1935

I'll Pray For You 3/22/1942, 5/10/1942
I'll See You in Church 2/4/1934
I'll Sing You a Thousand Love Songs 10/18/1936, 11/29/1936
I'll Take You Home Again, Kathleen 2/16/1941
I'm a Hundred Percent for You 1/27/1935
I'm Bubbling Over 3/28/1937, 5/9/1937
I'm Building a Palace for Alice in Dallas*/Phil Harris Special #1 .... 4/27/1941
I'm Building a Sailboat of Dreams 4/9/1939, 4/30/1939
I'm Building Up to an Awful Let Down 12/29/1935
I'm Going Shopping With You 2/3/1935
I'm Going to El Centro with a Banjo on My Knee* 3/2/1941
I'm Going to Round Up My Love 1/5/1941
I'm Gonna Get Some Shut Eye 3/26/1939
I'm Gonna Sit Right Down and Write Myself a Letter 2/9/1936, 4/12/1936, 5/16/1937
I'm Hatin' This Waiting Around 6/6/1937
I'm in a Dancing Mood 12/6/1936
I'm In Love All Over Again 6/23/1935
I'm in Love with a Brand New Baby 12/6/1936
I'm in Love with a Great Big Beauty 1/22/1933
I'm In My Glory 12/12/1937
I'm In the Mood for Love 10/13/1935
I'm Like a Fish Out of Water 12/26/1937
I'm Pins and Needles in Love With You 5/11/1932
I'm Putting All My Eggs in One Basket 3/22/1936
I'm Shootin' High 3/1/1936
I'm Sitting High on a Hilltop 1/5/1936
I'm Sorry Dear 11/22/1936
I'm Sure of Everything But You 11/24/1932
I'm Taking a Fancy to You 6/12/1938
I'm That Way About Broadway 6/15/1932, 8/24/1932
I'm Wishing 4/24/1938, 1/8/1939
I'm Yours For the Asking/Sweet Like You 6/27/1937
I'm Yours for Tonight 8/17/1932
I've Been Working on the Railroad/Oh Susanna 2/26/1939
I've Got a Date With a Dream 10/16/1938
I've Got a Feelin' You're Foolin 9/29/1935, 12/6/1935
I've Got a Heartful of Music 6/5/1938
I've Got a Heavy Date 4/19/1936, 5/10/1936, 6/7/1936
I've Got a Pocketful of Dreams 10/9/1938
I've Got a Right to Sing the Blues 11/27/1932, 12/15/1932
I've Got My Eyes on You 11/12/1939, 2/4/1940, 3/3/1940
I've Got My Fingers Crossed 12/29/1935
I've Got My Love to Keep Me Warm 3/21/1937
I've Got My Love to Keep Me Warm/Gee But You're Swell 2/28/1937
I've Got Rhythm/Fascinating Rhythm/Lady Be Good 12/9/1934
I've Got the Potatoes 5/23/1932, 6/13/1932
I've Got You Under My Skin 1/24/1937
I've Taken a Fancy to You 2/13/1938
I've Told Every Little Star 12/22/1932, 6/12/1938
Ida Sweet as Apple Cider 5/4/1941
If I Had a Million Dollars 11/18/1934, 12/16/1934
If I Loved You More 11/6/1938
If I Should Lose You 1/5/1936

517

If I Were Only Sure of You 6/8/1932
If I Were Sure of You 5/14/1939, 5/21/1939
If It's Good 6/18/1939
If It's Love 1/27/1935
If You Were Mine 12/8/1940
In a Moment of Weakness 3/19/1939
In a Moon Boat 10/13/1940
In a Second Hand Store 5/26/1933
In a Shelter From a Shower 3/4/1934
In an Old Cathedral Garden 4/5/1942
In Dublin's Fair City (aka Cockles and Mussels) 3/16/1941
In My Country That Means Love 2/17/1935
In My Merry Oldsmobile 12/3/1939
In Old Chicago 2/6/1938, 5/22/1938
In Old Vienna 8/15/1932
In the Hills of Old Wyoming 4/12/1936
In the Middle of a Kiss 6/16/1935
International, The 11/24/1935
Irving Berlin medley 4/27/1934
Is I In Love? I Is 6/6/1932, 6/29/1932, 10/24/1932
Isle of Capri 1/20/1935, 2/10/1935
Isle of May, The 2/25/1940
Isn't It a Shame 11/18/1934
Isn't It Romantic 11/3/1932, 11/13/1932
Isn't That Just Like Love 11/17/1940, 12/1/1940
Isn't This a Night for Love 6/16/1933
It All Comes Back to Me Now 1/26/1941, 3/2/1941
It Don't Mean a Thing 12/22/1932, 1/26/1933
It Happened When Your Eyes Met Mine 9/14/1934
It Serves You Right 11/13/1938, 1/8/1939
It Was Only a Summer Night's Dream 10/3/1932
It Was So Beautiful 6/27/1932
It Was Sweet of You 10/28/1934
It's a Blue World 2/11/1940
It's a Hap Hap Happy Day 12/3/1939
It's a Hundred To One 10/15/1939
It's a Whole New Thing 11/19/1939
It's All Yours 2/19/1939, 4/9/1939
It's an Old Southern Custom 4/21/1935
It's Been So Long 4/5/1936
It's De-Lovely 12/13/1936, 3/21/1937, 1/24/1937
It's Easy to Remember 3/24/1935
It's From Hunger 9/14/1932
It's Fun to Be Fooled 10/21/1934
It's Gonna Be You 9/12/1932
It's Got to Be Love 5/17/1936
It's Great to Be Alive 4/21/1933, 6/9/1933
It's No Fun 4/12/1936
It's Raining Sunshine 6/26/1938
It's Sunday Down in Caroline 5/12/1933
It's the Strangest Thing 1/1/1939, 1/29/1939
It's Winter Again 12/4/1932, 12/22/1932
It's You I'm Talking About 5/10/1936

Jamboree 4/18/1937
Jealous 12/28/1941
Jeepers Creepers 11/20/1938, 2/5/1939
Jericho 6/20/1937, 3/26/1939
Jersey Bounce 4/19/1942
Jingle Bells 2/18/1940, 12/22/1940
Joan of Arkansas 2/16/1936
Jockey on the Carrousel 11/17/1935
Johnny Doughboy 5/10/1942
Johnny Doughboy Found a Rose in Ireland 4/26/1942
Johnny Peddler 12/1/1940
Jolly Good Company 5/4/1932
Joobalai 1/29/1939
Joseph, Joseph 4/10/1938
Jump for Joy 11/16/1941, 5/3/1942
June in January 12/23/1934, 1/13/1935
Jungle Love 6/5/1938
Just a Little Home for the Old Folks 12/1/1932, 1/12/1933
Just a Little Love, a Little Kiss 6/8/1934
Just a Rhyme for Love 11/29/1936
Just Another Love Affair 11/10/1932
Just Couldn't Say Goodbye 9/26/1932
Just Knock At My Door 9/21/1932
Just Like Taking Candy From a Baby 10/27/1940
Just One of Those Things 12/1/1935, 12/6/1936, 2/5/1939, 4/16/1939
Kashmiri Song 12/17/1933, 1/10/1937
Keep an Eye on Your Heart 2/2/1941, 2/23/1941, 3/2/1941
Keep Away 6/20/1932, 9/14/1932
Keep Em Smiling 11/30/1941
Keep On Doing What You're Doing 12/31/1933
Keep Young and Beautiful 1/7/1934
Keep Your Fingers Crossed 12/1/1935
Kiddie Kapers 4/14/1933, 1/28/1934
Kiss In the Dark, A 5/25/1934
Kiss Me Goodnight 5/26/1935
Knock at My Door 10/19/1932
Knot Was Tied in Ensenotta, The*/Special #5 .... 5/18/1941
L'Amour Toujours L'Amour 4/21/1933
La Cucaracha 9/28/1934, 12/2/1934
La Cumparsita 1/18/1942
Lady Be Good 7/6/1934, 1/17/1937
Lady is a Tramp, The 1/2/1938
Lady's In Love, The 5/21/1939, 6/25/1939, 6/25/1939
Lamp is Low, The 10/8/1939
Last Call for Love 5/17/1942
Last Night 11/5/1939
Last Night's Gardenias 4/21/1940
Latin Quarter 6/19/1938
Latin Quarter/Life Begins When You're in Love 5/1/1938
Laugh You Son of a Gun 6/15/1934, 7/13/1934
Let Me Whisper 6/19/1938
Let That Be a Lesson to You/You Do Something to Me 2/6/1938
Let Yourself Go 3/8/1936, 5/31/1936

Lovable 6/6/1932
Love and Learn/Hallelujah 3/14/1937
Love Bug Will Bite You If You Don't Watch Out, The 5/16/1937, 6/27/1937
Love for Sale 2/10/1935, 5/5/1935
Love I'd Give My Life for You 12/25/1938
Love in Bloom 9/7/1934,
    1/13/1935, 1/27/1935, 4/7/1935, 5/12/1935, 7/14/1935, 12/15/1935, 1/26/1936,
    3/15/1936, 4/30/1939, 3/10/1940
Love Is 1/26/1941
Love is a Dancing Thing 12/15/1935, 2/9/1936
Love is Just Around the Corner 12/2/1934
Love Is Like a Cigarette 5/24/1936
Love is Love Anywhere 3/25/1934
Love Is On the Air Tonight 10/31/1937
Love Is the Sweetest Thing... 10/8/1933
Love Makes the World Go Round... 11/24/1935
Love Me 10/24/1937
Love Me Forever... 9/29/1935
Love Thy Neighbor... 5/11/1934
Love Walked In 1/23/1938, 5/1/1938
Love You Funny Thing.. 6/6/1932
Lovelight in the Starlight... 5/22/1938
Lovely Lady... 3/22/1936
Lovely Little Lady 4/5/1942
Lovely One.. 4/27/1934, 5/18/1934, 10/17/1937
Lovely to Look At 4/7/1935, 6/2/1935
Lover Come Back to Me 11/12/1933
Low Tide... 12/8/1932
Lucky Little Accident 11/24/1932
Lullaby of Broadway.. 4/28/1935
Lullaby of the Leaves 6/1/1932, 6/13/1932
Lulu's Back in Town 11/17/1935
M-O-T-H-E-R 5/8/1938
Ma He's Making Eyes At Me.. 1/14/1940, 5/5/1940
Ma He's Makin Eyes at Me/Little Girl 4/7/1940
Madeleine 1/18/1942
Madonna Mia 12/29/1935
Magnolias in the Moonlight 11/30/1941
Mah Lindy Lou 4/28/1933
Make Believe 10/25/1936
Make Believe Island.. 6/16/1940
Make Love With a Guitar 3/3/1940
Make Way for Tomorrow.. 5/23/1937
Make With the Kisses 10/29/1939, 12/17/1939
Mama 11/2/1941
Mama Inez 1/17/1937
Mama, that Moon's Here Again 11/28/1937
Man About Town.. 4/30/1939, 6/25/1939
Man and His Dream, A.. 11/12/1939
March of the Musketeers 11/12/1933
March on to Oregon 9/12/1932
March Winds and April Showers... 2/10/1935
Margie 7/6/1932, 10/3/1932

Maria My Own 4/19/1936
Mariella 8/31/1932
Marietta 6/22/1932, 8/1/1932
Marine's Hymn 2/15/1942
Martinique, The 4/14/1935
Masquerade 6/20/1932
Mavis 3/31/1933
May I 5/18/1934
Me and My Buddy Next Door 1/18/1942
Meanest Gal in Town 10/10/1932
Meanest Man in Town 12/18/1932
Meditation 1/14/1940
Meet the People 11/24/1940
Meet the Sun Half Way 5/19/1940
Melancholy Baby 2/28/1937
Melancholy Mood 5/28/1939
Memory Lane 3/5/1939
Memphis in the Morning 12/10/1933
Merry Old Land of Oz 10/8/1939
Merry Widow Waltz 11/12/1933
Mickey Mouse 9/19/1932
Midnight in Paris 12/1/1935, 3/20/1938
Mighty Lak a Rose 12/24/1933, 4/20/1934, 2/13/1938
Mile a Minute 11/10/1935, 2/9/1936
Milenberg Joys 10/30/1932
Milky Way, The 11/10/1935
Million Dollar Baby 9/21/1932
Mimi 4/7/1933
Mimi/Same Old Moon 11/6/1932
Mine 12/10/1933
Miss Liza Jane 10/26/1932
Miss You 2/15/1942, 3/22/1942
Mister and Missus Is the Name 5/12/1935
Moon Got In My Eyes 11/14/1937
Moon of Manakoora 11/28/1937
Moon Over Miami 2/16/1936
Moon Over Tarzana*/Bagby Stomp 1/5/1941
Moon Was Yellow, The 9/28/1934, 11/4/1934
Moonlight and Roses 2/21/1937
Moonlight and Shadows 4/11/1937
Moonlight Brings Me You 5/25/1932
Moonlight Madonna 12/3/1933, 7/13/1934
Moonlight On the River 8/24/1932
Moonlight On the Water 1/28/1934
Moonlight Parade 7/6/1934
Morocco 5/8/1938
Mr. And Mrs. America 3/5/1939, 4/2/1939
Music Box Revue medley 12/16/1934
Music Goes Round and Round, The 1/19/1936, 3/1/1936
Music Makes Me 12/31/1933
Mutiny in the Brass Section 12/20/1936
My Baby's Gone 8/29/1932
My Baby's on Strike 8/31/1934

My Dancing Lady 12/24/1933, 2/18/1934
My Darling 12/8/1932, 1/8/1933, 3/10/1933, 6/2/1933
My Favorite Band 12/18/1932
My Great Great Grandfather - Auld Lang Syne 5/31/1942
My Gypsy Rhapsody 10/1/1933, 12/31/1933
My Hat's On the Side Of My Head 6/29/1934, 8/17/1934
My Heart Belongs to Daddy 3/12/1939
My Heart Stood Still 6/4/1939
My Heart's at Ease 6/20/1932
My Hero 6/16/1935
My Kind of Country 4/7/1940, 4/21/1940
My Little Dreamboat 8/1/1932
My Little Girl 4/21/1940
My Middle Name is Love 7/20/1934
My Mom 5/16/1932
My Oh My 5/26/1933, 6/23/1933, 1/14/1934
My Piano and Me 12/22/1932
My Prayer 12/3/1939
My Reverie 11/27/1938
My River Home 12/1/1932
My Silver Rose 10/10/1932
My Sister and I 5/4/1941
My Sweet 1/19/1936
My Temptation 5/12/1933, 11/5/1933
My Wonderful One, Let's Dance 4/14/1940, 5/12/1940
Mysterious Moe 1/12/1933
Mysterious Mose 3/11/1934, 1/20/1935, 1/10/1937
Nango 12/7/1941
Nasty Man 3/18/1934
Nearness of You, The 10/13/1940
Needle In a Haystack, A 12/16/1934, 3/3/1935
Nellie Bly 1/12/1941
Nelly 7/11/1932
Never In a Million Years 5/23/1937, 6/20/1937
New Deal Rhythm 12/24/1933
New Moon 2/13/1938
New Moon and an Old Serenade 6/4/1939
New Moon Is Over My Shoulder, A 8/31/1934
Nice Work If You Can Get It 1/23/1938
Night After Night 1/21/1940, 3/17/1940
Night and Day 1/8/1933, 3/3/1933, 9/14/1934, 12/23/1934, 12/13/1936
Night Fall 9/19/1932
Night in Manhattan, A 10/18/1936
Night is Beginning, The 1/26/1936
Night is Filled with Music, The 10/9/1938
Night is Young and You're So Beautiful, The 11/1/1936, 12/27/1936, 2/28/1937
Night Shall Be Filled with Music, The 5/25/1932, 6/8/1932
Nightingale Sang in Berkeley Square, A 12/1/1940
Ninon 5/26/1935
No More Blues 3/24/1933
No Other One 10/27/1935
No Regret 5/24/1936
No Strings 10/6/1935

No Wonder 11/20/1938, 1/1/1939
Nobody 5/23/1937
Noon at Midnight 1/12/1936
Not Bad 3/10/1935, 11/24/1935
Not So Long Ago 11/24/1940
Now that I've Learned 10/19/1932
O.K. America 7/18/1932
Object of My Affection, The 12/23/1934
Of Thee I Sing 5/25/1932, 2/11/1934, 6/29/1934, 4/14/1935
Oh Gee Oh Gosh Oh Golly, I'm in Love 5/5/1940
Oh Johnnie 11/12/1939, 12/10/1939
Oh Little Town of Bethlehem - Away in a Manger - Oh Come All Ye Faithful ... 12/25/1938
Oh Little Town of Bethlehem - The First Noel - Away in a Manger 12/24/1939
Oh Moaner 10/30/1932
Oh Molly 5/26/1933
Oh Mona 11/17/1932
Oh Say Can't You See 5/25/1932
Oh What a Thrill 6/6/1932
Oh You Nasty Man 8/10/1934
OK GA 10/1/1933
Okay and Connecticut Yankee medley 11/25/1934
Okay Toots 11/11/1934, 12/2/1934
Ol Man of the Mountain 8/10/1932
Old Drum 3/5/1939
Old King Cole 11/7/1937
Old Kitchen Kettle, The 12/29/1932, 1/5/1933, 1/26/1933
Old Man Harlem 10/29/1933
Old Man Jingle 2/4/1934
Old Man of the Mountain 8/3/1932
Old Man River 3/25/1934
Old Music Box Review medley 5/18/1934
Old Refrain, The 5/5/1933
Old Watermill 4/6/1934
On a Sunday Afternoon 9/29/1935
On My Pony 1/18/1942
On the Isle of Kitchymikoko 5/23/1937
On the Mississippi - I Dream of Jeannie - Waiting for the Robert E. Lee 3/29/1942
On the Road to Pismo Beach* 1/19/1941
On With the Dance 10/17/1937
Once In a Love 10/20/1940
Once In a Love Time 5/11/1941
Once In a While 12/19/1937
Once Upon a Summertime 4/20/1941
Once Upon a Time 4/6/1941
One Alone 5/16/1937
One In a Blue Moon 6/22/1934
One In a Million 7/14/1935, 1/3/1937, 3/7/1937, 4/4/1937
One Little Kiss 12/9/1934
One Look at You 10/27/1940
One Man Band 10/30/1932, 12/4/1932
One Night of Love 10/21/1934, 1/13/1935
One O'Clock Jump 2/5/1939
One on the House 11/23/1941, 3/22/1942

One Rainy Afternoon 5/31/1936
One Song 1/23/1938, 4/24/1938, 1/8/1939
One Two Button Your Shoe 11/22/1936
Only a Rose 11/19/1933
Oo Honey 12/10/1933
Ooh, That Kiss 5/11/1932, 7/27/1934
Ooh Aah 5/30/1937
Ooh You Miser You 8/3/1934, 9/7/1934
Orchids in the Moonlight 4/6/1934, 12/30/1934
Original Music 3/8/1942
Our Love 4/30/1939
Our Love Affair 10/6/1940
Out For No Good 5/19/1935
Out of a Clear Blue Sky 11/25/1934
Out of Sight Out of Mind 12/22/1935
Over My Shoulder 11/4/1934
Over Night 12/5/1937
Over Somebody Else's Shoulders 5/11/1934
Over the Weekend 7/6/1932
Page Miss Glory 10/6/1935
Panama 8/17/1934, 2/24/1935
Panamania 2/28/1937, 4/25/1937
Panhandle Pete 12/11/1932, 1/1/1933
Parade of the Wooden Soldiers 5/26/1935
Paradise 5/2/1932, 6/15/1932
Pardon My Love 3/10/1935
Pennies from Heaven 11/15/1936
Penny Serenade 1/22/1939, 4/16/1939, 5/7/1939
Penthouse for Rent 1/7/1940
Perfidia 12/29/1940, 2/23/1941
Petting In the Park 6/9/1933
Phil Harris Concerto #6 for Oboe and Drum*, The 3/9/1941
Phil the Fluter's Ball 3/17/1940, 1/18/1942
Piccolino, The 12/6/1935, 2/23/1936
Picnic for Two 6/8/1932
Picolo Pete 11/6/1932
Pinch Me 1/7/1940, 1/28/1940
Pink Elephants 9/26/1932, 11/13/1932, 11/27/1932
Play Fiddle Play 10/24/1932
Playing with the Devil 6/2/1933
Playmates 3/31/1940, 5/5/1940
Please 10/30/1932, 12/25/1932
Please/Make Believe 11/17/1932
Please Come Out of Your Dream 2/5/1939
Plenty of Money and You 11/22/1936, 3/7/1937
Ploddin' Along 11/3/1932
Pocketful of Dreams 12/4/1938, 12/11/1938
Poet and Peasant Overture 10/26/1941
Pony Boy 3/18/1934
Poopchen 7/7/1935
Poor Butterfly/La Veeda/Siren Song 11/3/1932
Poor Moon 2/2/1941
Popocataptl 12/21/1941, 2/1/1942

Roses in December 11/7/1937
Roses of Picardy 6/23/1933
Rosita 10/31/1937
Run Rabbit Run 3/10/1940
Saddle Your Blues to a Wild Mustang 3/22/1936
Salute to Gardner Field 5/31/1942
Same Old Moon 11/27/1932
San Diego Serenade* 2/16/1941
San Francisco 1/9/1938, 2/26/1939, 2/22/1942
San Francisco/I Live the Life I Love 1/2/1938
Sapphire 8/31/1934, 1/13/1935
Savage Serenade 3/4/1934
Save the Last Dance for Me 12/17/1933
Say It 4/28/1940, 6/9/1940
Say It Isn't So 9/28/1932, 10/30/1932
Say It With a Kiss 12/4/1938, 1/1/1939
Say the Word and It's Yours 3/1/1936
Say When 1/6/1935
Say, Young Lady 12/29/1932
Says My Heart 6/12/1938, 6/26/1938
Scat Song 6/13/1932, 7/20/1932, 10/24/1932
Second Honeymoon 1/22/1933
Seein' Is Believin' 6/9/1935
Sentimental Gentleman 8/1/1932
Sentimental Gentleman from Georgia 11/3/1932
September in the Rain 5/2/1937, 5/23/1937
September in the Rain/Shades of Hades 6/6/1937
Serenade to a Wealthy Widow 10/28/1934
Seventeen 10/22/1939
Shall We Dance 5/16/1937
Shame on You 10/8/1933
She Didn't Say Yes 5/16/1932
She Shall Have Music 5/3/1936, 6/21/1936
She'll Always Remember - Memories 4/12/1942
She'll Be Comin' Round the Mountain 5/3/1936
She's a Cornfed Indiana Gal 6/8/1932
She's a Latin from Manhattan 3/31/1935, 5/12/1935
She's Tall, She's Tan, She's Terrific 12/19/1937
Shepherd's Serenade 11/16/1941, 1/18/1942
Shine On Your Shoes, A 9/28/1932, 12/8/1932, 7/20/1934, 6/8/1934
Shine on Your Shoes/Louisiana Hayride 3/7/1937
Shooting High 1/12/1936
Shout I am an American 10/6/1940
Shuffle Off to Buffalo 4/7/1933
Siboney 10/11/1936
Silent Love 5/23/1932
Silver on the Sage 5/29/1938
Silver Threads Among the Brass Section*/Phil Harris #3 .... 4/6/1941
Silver Threads Among the Gold 3/25/1934
Simple and Sweet 12/4/1938, 1/8/1939
Since I First Met Thee 1/28/1934
Sing 10/21/1934
Sing (It's Good for You) 12/15/1932

Sing a Little Lowdown Tune... 10/29/1933
Sing a New Song 5/4/1932
Sing Baby Sing 10/4/1936, 12/27/1936, 12/27/1936, 12/27/1936, 12/27/1936
Sing Before Breakfast... 9/29/1935
Sing Me a Song of the Islands 3/15/1942
Sing My Heart 2/12/1939, 5/7/1939
Sing Sing Sing 10/11/1936
Sing to Me... 6/23/1933
Singing in the Rain/April Showers 4/6/1934
Sipping Soda with Suzie 7/4/1932
Sitting By the Fire.. 12/25/1932
Sleep Come On and Take Me 7/18/1932
Sleepy Lagoon 5/24/1942
Slowly But Surely 3/9/1941
Slumming on Park Avenue 2/7/1937, 3/7/1937
Small Hotel.. 5/3/1936
Smiles 2/18/1934
Smoke Gets In Your Eyes...................................... 1/7/1934, 2/25/1934, 10/14/1934
Smooth Sailing... 1/20/1935
Snake Charmer.. 1/30/1938
Snug as a Bug in a Rug 5/28/1939
So Ashamed 9/12/1932
So At Last It's Come to This 11/24/1932
So Close to the Forest 3/17/1935
So Help Me 10/9/1938
So I Married the Girl... 1/1/1933
So Red the Rose.. 4/21/1935
So This is Heaven.. 2/2/1936, 3/29/1936
So To Bed 8/8/1932, 10/17/1932
So You're the One.. 11/10/1940, 12/15/1940
Soft Lights and Sweet Music 8/24/1932, 3/24/1933
Softly As In the Morning Sunrise 10/29/1933
Some Day I'll Find You 12/16/1934
Some Day My Prince Will Come....................... 2/27/1938, 3/6/1938, 4/24/1938, 1/8/1939
Some Day You'll Find Your Bluebird... 3/10/1940
Some of These Days 1/6/1935
Somebody Else Is Taking My Place 5/3/1942
Somebody Else Not Me 3/29/1942
Somebody Loves You... 6/1/1932
Somebody Stole Gabriel's Horn.. 6/9/1933
Somebody Stole My Girl 11/17/1932
Someday I'll Find You 11/26/1933, 6/29/1934
Someday Sweetheart.. 4/12/1942
Someone to Care... 7/6/1932
Someone to Watch Over Me/ S'Wonderful/ Thou Swell medley 5/11/1934
Something Tells Me 4/10/1938, 5/15/1938
Something to Sing About 10/24/1937
Sometimes I'm Happy/Hallelujah.. 6/2/1935
Son of the South 1/8/1933
Song Is You, The 12/17/1933
Song of India.. 7/20/1932, 9/28/1932
Song of Songs 5/26/1933
Song of the Flame.. 11/12/1933

Swing Is Here to Stay 1/2/1938
Swing is Here to Sway 11/21/1937
Swing Low, Sweet Harriet 6/20/1937
Swing Mister Charlie 4/19/1936
Swing the Jinx Away 10/18/1936, 2/14/1937
Swingee Little Thingee 10/22/1933
Swinging Annie Laurie Through the Rye 4/3/1938
Symphony of Love 7/13/1932
Tain't No Use 10/11/1936
Take a Chance Medley 2/25/1934
Take a Lesson from the Lark 8/3/1934
Take a Number from One to Ten 2/17/1935
Take It Easy 12/16/1934
Take Me In Your Arms 12/4/1932
Take the A Train/Be Honest With Me 12/14/1941
Take Your Time 5/10/1936, 6/7/1936
Talking Through My Heart 11/15/1936
Talking to You About Me 7/4/1932, 7/18/1932
Tartar's Darter, The 8/8/1932
Tea for Two 5/18/1934, 1/7/1940
Tears from My Inkwell 4/23/1939
Tell Me That You Love Me 4/14/1935
Tell Me That You Love Me Tonight 10/6/1935
Tell Me Tonight 5/26/1935
Tell Me With Your Kisses 11/20/1938
Ten Hours a Day 9/14/1932
Ten Yards to Go 9/14/1934, 10/21/1934
Tender Child 5/23/1932, 6/1/1932, 8/3/1932
Thank Your Lucky Stars and Stripes 12/14/1941
Thanks a Million 10/27/1935, 3/1/1936
Thanks for Everything 2/12/1939
Thanks for the Memory 2/27/1938, 3/6/1938
Thanksgiving 9/26/1932, 10/17/1932
That Foolish Feeling 4/4/1937, 5/23/1937
That Old Feeling 10/24/1937
That's for Me 10/27/1940
That's How Harlem Was Born 10/29/1933
That's How Rhythm Was Born 4/1/1934
That's How We Make Music 5/16/1932, 7/11/1932, 10/26/1932
That's the Reason 3/24/1935
That's What I Like About the South 2/2/1941
That's What We Do Over Here 4/23/1939
That's You Sweetheart 12/6/1935
There Goes My Heart 4/20/1934
There I Go 12/15/1940
There I Go Dreaming Again 5/11/1932
There Is a New Day Coming 1/19/1933, 5/5/1933, 10/22/1933
There Is a New Moon Over My Shoulder 10/1/1933
There Is a Ring Around My Rainbow 10/8/1933
There Isn't Any Limit to My Love 6/7/1936
There'll Be Some Changes Made 1/5/1941, 2/23/1941, 5/25/1941
There's a Brand New Picture in My Picture Frame 10/23/1938
There's a House in Harlem for Sale 8/24/1934

Turn Off the Moon 4/4/1937
Turn Out the Light 12/11/1932, 12/29/1932
Twelfth Street Rag 1/22/1933
Twenty Four Hours a Day 12/29/1935
Twenty-Four Hours in Georgia 9/28/1934
Twilight Interlude 10/29/1939
Two Cigarettes in the Dark 8/10/1934
Two Dreams Met 11/24/1940
Two Guitars 12/1/1935
Two Hearts in Three-Quarter Time 1/14/1934
Two Hearts That Pass in the Night 4/6/1941
Two Poor People 8/24/1932
Two Sleepy People 10/23/1938
Two Tickets to Georgia 3/31/1933
Umbrella Man 11/13/1938, 1/29/1939
Under the Old Crow's Nest 6/1/1932, 7/18/1932
Under the Spell of the Voodoo Drums 1/3/1937
Underneath the Harlem Moon 1/12/1933
Up Down 8/17/1932
Valencia 9/28/1934, 3/31/1935
Valencia/Barcelona/99 Out of 100 .... 7/20/1934
Varsity Drag 7/13/1934
Veeny Veeny Veeny 11/21/1937
Very Thought of You, The 7/27/1934, 9/21/1934
Vine Street Viggle, The*/Phil Harris #6 .... 4/20/1941
Violetta 5/26/1940
Viva La France 3/25/1934
Vote for Mr. Rhythm 12/6/1936
Wahoo 3/29/1936
Wait Till I Get You In My Dreams 1/19/1933
Wake Up and Sing 3/8/1936
Walking in the Moonlight 10/3/1932
Wanted 4/18/1937
Was It Rain 5/30/1937
Was Wilst Du Haben 12/1/1932
Water Under the Bridge 11/11/1934
Way Down Upon the Los Angeles River*/Phil Harris Special #3 .... 3/30/1941
Way Down Yonder in New Orleans 11/6/1932
Way Down Yonder in Seattle* 2/2/1941
Way You Look Tonight, The 10/4/1936, 1/17/1937
We Did It Before 12/28/1941, 1/11/1942
We Did It Before/Keep Em Flying 4/26/1942
We Go Together 3/2/1941, 4/13/1941
We Saw the Sea 3/8/1936
We Will All Go Ridin' on a Rainbow 8/24/1934
We'll Never Know 2/19/1939
We'll See it Through 12/8/1932, 12/11/1932
We're Alone 10/10/1932
We're Dancing Together Again 8/10/1932
We've Gone a Long Way Together 3/12/1939
Wedding of the Painted Doll 8/29/1932
Weep No More My Baby 12/3/1933
What a Little Moonlight Can Do 6/16/1935

What a Lucky Break 11/20/1932
What a Sweet Sensation 8/22/1932, 10/5/1932
What Do Fellows Do 3/11/1934
What Do You Hear from the Mob in Scotland 6/19/1938
What Goes On Here in My Heart 10/2/1938
What Good Is the Good In Goodbye 5/18/1934, 8/3/1934
What Have We Got to Lose 4/7/1933
What Have You Got That Gets Me? 10/16/1938, 10/30/1938
What This Country Needs is More Love 3/30/1941
What'll We Do 10/12/1941
What's the Matter No Ice Today 10/19/1932
What's the Name of That Song 3/1/1936
What, You Got No Trouble? 7/4/1932
When 6/6/1937
When a Lady Meets a Gentleman Down South 11/1/1936
When Did You Leave Heaven 10/18/1936
When Gabriel Blows His Horn 6/1/1932
When Gimbel Plays the Cymbal 7/4/1932
When Hearts are Young 12/22/1932
When I Grow Too Old to Dream 3/10/1935, 4/28/1935
When I'm With You 10/11/1936
When It's Darkest on the Delta 1/1/1933
When Mother Played the Organ 8/29/1932, 10/12/1932
When My Dreamboat Comes Home 1/10/1937, 2/21/1937
When the Lights Are Soft and Low 5/11/1932
When the Midnight Choo Choo Leaves for Beaumont and Banning* 2/23/1941
When the Morning Rolls Around Again 12/25/1932, 3/17/1933
When the New Moon Shines 8/31/1934
When the Organ Played "Oh Promise Me" 1/9/1938
When the Poppies Bloom Again 3/7/1937
When the Stars Go to Sleep 4/17/1938
When the Sun Kisses the World Goodbye 5/11/1932, 8/31/1932
When the Swallows Come Back to Capistrano 10/6/1940
When We're One 5/16/1932
When You Took My Breath Away 1/19/1936
When You Wish Upon a Star 3/31/1940, 5/31/1942
When You're With Me 5/17/1942
Where Am I 12/15/1935
Where Are You 5/9/1937
Where Do I Go From You 5/19/1940
Where is Love 2/4/1940
Where Is the Rainbow 12/3/1933
Where Was I? 3/3/1940, 4/7/1940, 5/19/1940, 6/2/1940
Where Were You on the Night of June 3rd 2/17/1935
Where's That Rainbow 4/1/1934
Wherever You Are 3/1/1942, 4/5/1942
Whip, The 11/26/1933
Whispering 1/24/1937
Whispers in the Dark 10/10/1937
Whistle While You Work 3/13/1938, 4/24/1938, 1/8/1939
White Cliffs of Dover, The 1/25/1942
White Sails In the Sunsest 6/18/1939
Who 5/16/1932, 10/26/1932, 11/22/1936, 3/21/1937, 12/5/1937, 3/27/1938

Who Are We to Say 4/10/1938
Who Calls.. 12/28/1941
Who Do You Think I Saw Last Night 5/1/1938
Who Don't You Get Lost 6/15/1932
Who Knows.. 11/7/1937, 2/20/1938
Who Loves You.. 1/10/1937
Who Put that Moon in the Sky/Yours for the Asking... 6/27/1937
Who Stole the Jam... 3/20/1938
Who Walks In When I Walk Out 2/4/1934
Who'd Believe 11/6/1932, 11/20/1932
Who's Honey Are You... 3/3/1935
Who's That Knockin' At My Heart 11/29/1936
Who/ Crazy Rhythm medley 10/14/1934
Why 11/17/1935, 1/5/1936, 6/27/1937
Why Can't This Night Go On Forever 1/12/1933, 4/28/1933, 5/4/1934, 9/7/1934
Why Cry, Baby.. 4/27/1941
Why Did You Come Along 6/22/1932
Why Do They Call It Gay Paree 6/9/1935
Wild Rose... 11/24/1935
Will You Remember.. 3/3/1933, 4/18/1937
Willow, Weep for Me 12/11/1932
Wings of America... 1/11/1942
Wise Old Man 4/6/1941
Wise Old Owl 3/9/1941, 5/18/1941
With a Shine On Your Shoes 11/20/1932
With a Song In My Heart.. 11/26/1933, 3/11/1934
With a Twist of the Wrist 6/1/1941
With All My Heart 2/2/1936
With Every Breath I Take 1/6/1935
With the Wind and the Rain In Your Hair.. 1/7/1940, 5/19/1940
With Thee I Swing.. 11/15/1936
Without That Certain Thing 2/11/1934
Wonderful One... 12/18/1932
Woodpecker Song 3/10/1940, 3/17/1940, 4/28/1940
World Is In My Arms, The 10/20/1940
World is Mine, The 12/9/1934
World Is Waiting For the Sunrise, The... 7/11/1932
Would You 6/21/1936
Wyoming, Why Do You Being with W*/Phil Harris #5 .... 4/13/1941
Ya Got Me.. 11/13/1938
Yam, The... 10/23/1938
Yankee Doodle Dandy - Give My Regards to Broadway - Mary - You're a Grand Old Flag
- Over There... 5/17/1942
Yankee Doodle Never Went to Town 12/15/1935
Yeah Man... 5/23/1932, 6/22/1932, 8/29/1932
Yes Sir I Love Your Daughter 6/22/1934
Yes to You 12/9/1934
You 12/3/1933,
        4/6/1934, 4/5/1936, 4/26/1936, 5/31/1936, 11/8/1936, 3/14/1937, 4/11/1937
You Ain't Been Living Right 9/21/1934, 12/2/1934
You Alone 12/17/1933
You and I... 5/25/1941, 10/5/1941
You and the Night and the Music... 3/3/1935

You Are a Heavenly Thing 2/17/1935
You Are My Love 5/23/1937
You Are So Lovely and I Am So Lonely 6/9/1935
You Can Depend on Me 2/9/1941
You Can Make My Life a Bed of Roses 5/25/1932
You Can Tell She Comes from Dixie 12/20/1936
You Can't Brush Me Off 5/26/1940
You Can't Have Everything 10/10/1937, 10/24/1937
You Can't Pull the Wool Over My Eyes 5/31/1936
You Can't Run Away From Love 5/30/1937
You Can't Stop Me from Dreaming 10/24/1937, 11/28/1937
You Can't Tell Love What to Do 7/25/1932
You Catch on Quick 11/3/1940
You Couldn't Be Cuter 5/29/1938, 6/26/1938
You Darling 4/21/1940
You Do Something to Me 2/20/1938
You Do the Darndest Things 11/15/1936, 3/14/1937
You Fit Into the Picture 5/5/1935
You Go Your Way and I'll Go Crazy 12/21/1941
You Got Everything 5/28/1939
You Gotta Give Credit to Love 11/4/1934
You Grow Sweeter As the Years Go By 6/25/1939
You Have Taken My Heart 2/4/1934
You Hit the Spot 12/22/1935, 3/15/1936
You Made a Touchdown In My Heart 2/9/1941
You On My Mind 11/15/1936
You Opened My Eyes 5/19/1935
You Ought to See Sally on Sunday 8/10/1934
You Say the Sweetest Things 12/1/1940
You Should Be Set to Music 1/26/1941, 2/9/1941
You Started Me Dreaming 6/7/1936
You Walked By 11/17/1940, 12/8/1940, 12/29/1940, 1/19/1941, 3/16/1941, 3/23/1941
You'd Better Play Ball with Me 4/26/1936
You'll Get By 10/12/1932
You're a Builder Upper 9/7/1934
You're a Heavenly Thing 3/24/1935, 6/23/1935
You're An Education 2/13/1938
You're an Old Smoothie 3/10/1933, 3/24/1933
You're Devastating 4/20/1934, 11/4/1934
You're Gonna Lose That Gal 4/1/1934
You're Gonna Lose Your Gal 1/21/1934
You're In My Heart 2/18/1934
You're Just About Right for Me 9/7/1932
You're Lonely, I'm Lonely 6/2/1940
You're My Relaxation 4/13/1934
You're My Thrill 12/31/1933
You're Not the Only Oyster in the Stew 11/25/1934
You're Number One on My Love Parade 5/9/1937
You're So Darn Charming 6/30/1935
You're Telling Me 9/5/1932, 9/21/1932, 10/19/1932
You're the Cream in My Coffee 2/4/1934
You're the One 1/26/1941
You're the Top 5/19/1935